Theories and Paradigms of International Business Activity

Theories and Paradigms of International Business Activity

The Selected Essays of John H. Dunning, Volume I

John H. Dunning

Emeritus Esmee Fairbairn Professor of International Investment and Business Studies, University of Reading, UK and Emeritus State of New Jersey Professor of International Business, Rutgers University, USA

Edward Elgar

Cheltenham, UK • Northampton, MA, USA

Published by
Edward Elgar Publishing Limited
Glensanda House
Montpellier Parade
Cheltenham
Glos GL50 1UA
UK

Edward Elgar Publishing, Inc.
136 West Street
Suite 202
Northampton
Massachusetts 01060
USA

A catalogue record for this book is available from the British Library

Library of Congress Cataloging in Publication Data
Dunning, John H.
[Essays. Selections.]
The selected essays of John H. Dunning / John H. Dunning.
p. cm.
Includes bibliographical references and index.
Contents: v. I. Theories and paradigms of international business activity – v. II. Global capitalism, FDI and competitiveness.
1. International business enterprises. 2. Investments, Foreign. 3. International trade. 4. International finance. 5. Globalization–Economic aspects. 6. Competition, International. I. Title.

HD2755.5 .D862 2002 2002024445

ISBN 1 84064 700 0
Printed and bound in Great Britain by MPG Books Ltd, Bodmin, Cornwall

Contents

Acknowledgements vii
Introduction ix

1 The determinants of international production 1

2 Trade, location of economic activity and the multinational enterprise: a search for an eclectic approach 52

3 Trade, location of economic activity and the multinational enterprise: some empirical tests 77

4 Explaining the international direct investment position of countries: towards a dynamic or developmental approach 103

5 The investment development path revisited 138

6 The changing dynamics of international production: an economic and strategic approach 173

7 The eclectic paradigm of international production: a restatement and some possible extensions 199

8 Some historical antecedents to the eclectic paradigm 234

9 Towards an interdisciplinary explanation of international production 259

10 Reappraising the eclectic paradigm in an age of alliance capitalism 282

11 What's wrong – and right – with trade theory? 312

12 Towards a general paradigm of foreign direct and foreign portfolio investment 339

13 Globalization and the theory of MNE activity 381

14 The eclectic paradigm as an envelope for economic and business theories of MNE activity 408

15 The challenge of electronic markets for international business theory 441

16 Relational assets, networks and international business activity 476

Subject index 503
Name index 515

Acknowledgements

My first acknowledgement must be to all those individuals whose writings I have cited in this volume. To each and every one of them, I am grateful for their input into, and influence on my own scholarly thinking.

More especially, I wish to thank a number of my colleagues for their joint authorship of four chapters in this collection of essays. Chapter 8 was jointly written with John Cantwell and Tony Corley of Reading University. Three other chapters were co-authored with three of my former PhD students at Rutgers University – *viz* Rajneesh Narula (Chapter 5), John Dilyard (Chapter 12) and Cliff Wymbs (Chapter 15).

In addition, the Publisher and I wish to thank the following who have kindly given their permission for the use of copyright material:

Elsevier Science Ltd for 'The Eclectic Paradigm as an Envelope for Economic and Business Theories of MNE Activity' (2000), *International Business Review*, **9** (1), 163–90.

Journal of International Business Studies (JIBS) for 'Trade, Location of Economic Activity and the Multinational Enterprise, Some Empirical Tests', *Journal of International Business Studies*, (1980), **11**, Spring/Summer, 9–31; 'The Eclectic Paradigm of International Production: A Restatement and some Possible Extensions', (1988), *Journal of International Business Studies*, **19** (1), 1–31; and 'Reappraising the Eclectic Paradigm in an Age of Alliance Capitalism' (1995), *Journal of International Business Studies*, **26** (3), 461–89.

Oxford University Press for 'The Determinants of International Production' *Oxford Economic Papers*, (1973), **25**, November, 289–325

Palgrave Publishers Ltd for 'Trade, Location of Economic Activity and the Multinational Enterprise: A Search for an Eclectic Approach' in Ohlin, B. Hesselborn, P.O. & Wijkman, P. J. (eds.) *The International Allocation of Economic Activity*, 1997, Macmillan, London, 398–418; and 'Globalization and The Theory of MNE Activity' (1999), Hood, N. & Young, S. (eds.) *The Globalization of Multinational Enterprise Activity*, Macmillan, London, 21–54.

Routledge for 'The Investment Development Path Revisited' (1986), with Rajneesh Narula, in Dunning, J.H. and Narula, R. (eds.), *Foreign Direct Investment and Governments*, Routledge, 1–41.

Taylor and Francis for 'The Challenge of Electronic Markets for International Business Theory' (2001), jointly authored with Cliff Wymbs, *International Journal of the Economics of Business and Economics*, **8**, (2), 273–301: http://www.tandf.co.uk.

United Nations, International Investment for 'Towards a General Paradigm of Foreign Direct and Foreign Portfolio Investment' (1999), jointly authored with John Dilyard, *Transnational Corporations*, **8**, (1), 1–53.

Unwin & Hyman for 'Towards an Interdisciplinary Explanation of International Production' (1998), in Dunning, J.H., *Explaining International Production*, 306–26.

Weltwirtschaftliches Archiv for 'Explaining the International Direct Investment Position of Countries: Towards a Dynamic or Developmental Approach' (1981), *Weltwirtschaftliches Archiv*, **119**, 30–64

An earlier draft of Chapter 6 appeared as chapters 3 and 4 in Dunning, J.H. 1993, *The Globalization of Business*, Routledge, 51–77.

Every effort has been made to trace and contact the copyright holders but if any have been inadvertently overlooked, the publishers will be pleased to make the necessary arrangements at the first opportunity.

Introduction

This volume and volume II of the set consist of some of my more substantial and influential contributions to the study of international business (IB), foreign direct investment (FDI) and global capitalism. The contributions stretch over nearly three decades, although the great majority were written in the 1980s and 1990s.

The first volume deals almost entirely with the evolution of my thinking on the determinants of international production, that is, production financed by FDI and undertaken by multinational enterprises (MNEs). For the most part, the chapters are presented in chronological order.

Chapter 1, after reviewing the state of the art of the subject in 1973, distinguishes between the firm or ownership (O) specific determinants of international production, and the country or location (L) determinants. However, although it acknowledged (pp. 23–36) the need to better understand the modality by which firms exploited (or augmented) their O advantages outside their home countries, it did not identify or evaluate these. This I attempted to do in a paper presented at a Nobel Symposium in Stockholm in 1976. Chapter 2 reproduces this paper, which introduces the concept of the eclectic paradigm (then called theory) of international production; and incorporates an internalization (I) component into the OLI triad of the determinants of MNE activity.

Subsequent to this contribution, in the later 1970s and early 1980s, I attempted to empirically test and refine the eclectic paradigm, and to widen its analytical scope. Chapter 3 presents some evidence on the importance of some of the particular O and I characteristics of firms (drawn largely from industrial organization theory) and the particular L characteristics of countries (drawn largely from location theory), with respect to the industrial distribution of US FDI in several Latin American countries.

In Chapter 4, we examine how the principles of the eclectic paradigm may help us understand and explain the outward and inward direct investment path of countries as they proceed through various stages of development. This application of the paradigm has received extensive attention in the literature;[1] and the paradigm itself has been extended and modified over the last two decades. The current version set out in Chapter 5 was co-authored with Rajneesh Narula in 1996.

Chapters 6 and 7 examine some of the early comments and criticisms directed to the eclectic paradigm in the 1980s, and at the same time attempt to introduce more dynamic and strategic related variables into its main tenets. The 1988 paper (Chapter 7), first published in *The Journal of International Business Studies*, also suggested that the paradigm could be used as a framework for examining the costs and benefits of FDI; and of the act of foreign dis-investment as well as that of investment. Both themes were further taken up in my 1993 volume, *Multinational Enterprises and the Global Economy* (Dunning, 1993).

Chapter 8 reproduces a chapter in a book edited by Peter Hertner and Geoffrey Jones (1986), and jointly authored by John Cantwell and Tony Corley, on the historical antecedents of the eclectic paradigm, or, to put it rather differently, the explanations of how the extra-territorial expansion of firms, from the time of the mercantilistic economists of the eighteenth century onwards, could be reinterpreted in the language of the eclectic paradigm. What, indeed, were the OLI advantages determining trade and foreign-owned production identified by the mainstream economists of their day, such as Adam Smith, J.S. Mill, Alfred Marshall and Joseph Schumpeter? To what extent did they help to explain the growth and maturation of MNE activity?

Towards the end of the 1980s, I (as an economist) was becoming increasingly aware of the necessity to take an interdisciplinary approach to understanding both the determinants and consequences of IB activity. Chapter 9 identifies these, first by examining the variables exogenous to firms, and especially the political and cultural and legal variables; and second those endogenous to firms, especially organizational, financial and marketing variables. Over the course of the last two decades, I believe that mainstream IB scholars have come increasingly to value the contribution of those of other disciplines, notably law, political science, business history and economic geography, to furthering their understanding of the causes and implications of cross-border production and trade.

The 1990s saw the emergence of our contemporary knowledge-based global economy. Later chapters in this volume try to reflect how the specific characteristics of this event and its implications for world trade and investment are affecting our theorizing on the determinants of MNE activity. Chapter 10 introduces the concept of alliance capital into our thinking, and argues that inter-firm coalitions need to be embraced within the framework of the eclectic paradigm, in so far as they affect both the content and significance of the OLI variables, and the interaction between them.

Chapter 11 reviews the implications of the growth of international production for received trade theory; and argues that any paradigm seeking to explain the cross-border transaction of goods and services must embrace both a theory of industrial organization and a theory of the location of economic activity. The matrix set out on p. 315 portrays the evolution of the structure and form of trade in assets and products from inter-industry arm's-length transactions between independent parties to intra-industry intra-firm transactions.

Chapter 12 reproduces a paper jointly written with John Dilyard in 1999. In it an attempt is made to see how far the eclectic paradigm may be used to explain the rapid growth in foreign portfolio investment (FPI) over the past two decades; and in doing so, it introduces the OLE (E = externalization) paradigm. Chapter 13 looks more specifically at the impact of globalization on our theorizing on both the causes and effects of MNEs' activity. This chapter concludes by examining the impact of globalization on the geographical distribution of FDI.

Chapter 14 tries to summarize the state of the art of the eclectic paradigm at the end of the twentieth century, and relates its main contents to other paradigms and theories of IB activity which have been put forward over the past 35 years. A concluding statement of this chapter is perhaps worth reproducing here.

> We believe that recent economic events, and the emergence of new explanations of MNE activity, have added to, rather than subtracted from, the robustness of the paradigm. While accepting that, in spite of its eclecticism, there may be some kinds of foreign owned value-added activities which do not fit comfortably into its construction, we do believe that it continues to meet most of the criteria of a good paradigm; and that it is not yet approaching its own 'creative destruction'.[2]

Chapters 15 and 16 consider two very recent developments in the global economy, and on how the tenets of the eclectic paradigm may require modifications to incorporate these. The first (Chapter 15), written jointly with Cliff Wymbs, is concerned with the (predominantly) technical impact of e-commerce on the content and significance of the OLI variables comprising the paradigm and the interface between them. The second (Chapter 16) looks at the growing importance of the willingness and ability of individuals and corporations to establish and sustain productive intra- and inter-firm relationships as a factor affecting the extent and structure of IB activities. This chapter introduces the concept of relational assets, and argues that the growing significance of these assets is affecting the composition, significance and configuration of the OLI triad of variables.

NOTES

1. See, for example, various contributions in Dunning and Narula (1996), Castro (2000) and Dunning et al. (2001).
2. These words were written before the publication of a special issue of the *International Journal of the Economics of Business* (July 2001), edited by John Cantwell and Rajneesh Narula, which was devoted to the eclectic paradigm. Several articles in this issue suggest further emendations or extensions of the paradigm.

REFERENCES

Cantwell, J. and Narula, R. (2001), 'The eclectic paradigm of international business – A reappraisal', *International Journal of the Economics of Business*, Special Issue **8**(2): 155–327.

Castro, F.S. (2000), *Foreign Direct Investment in the European Periphery*, PhD thesis, University of Leeds, Leeds Business School.
Dunning, J.H. (1993), *Multinational Enterprises and the Global Economy*, Wokingham, Berks: Addison Wesley.
Dunning, J.H. and Narula, R. (1996), *Foreign Direct Investment and Governments*, London and New York: Routledge.
Dunning, J.H., Kim, C. and Lin, J.D. (2001), 'Incorporating trade into the investment development path: a case study of Korea and Taiwan', *Oxford Development Studies*, **29**(2): 145–54.
Hertner, P. and Jones, G. (eds) (1986), *Multinationals: Theory and History*, Aldershot, Hants: Gower.

1. The determinants of international production*

INTRODUCTION

There are few branches of economic analysis which are not directly relevant to an understanding of the origin and growth of multinational enterprises (MNEs). The subject is obviously of interest to those concerned with the resource allocative activities and financial management of firms, and with the theory of industrial organization. Since their operations straddle national boundaries, and involve trade in both goods and factors of production, they come within the scope of international economics; and as vehicles for the transference of new skills and technologies, they are no less pertinent to the theory of economic development. The sharing of the costs and benefits of their activities between the countries in which they operate raises complex and fascinating issues for the welfare economist. The geographical flexibility of their procurement, production, and marketing strategies adds a new dimension to the theories of industrial relations and collective bargaining; while their operations are not only influenced by, but help to fashion, a whole range of monetary and fiscal policies used by national governments to advance economic and social goals.

I make these observations by way of introduction because, in interpreting the various explanations of the origin and growth of international business, one is very conscious of the particular interests of the researcher. This is shown both in the type of questions asked, and the approach and techniques used to answer them. The questions 'why do firms invest overseas?', 'where do firms locate their foreign operations?' and 'what determines the amount and composition of international production?' pose similar, but not identical issues. Each is concerned with the behaviour of firms, but while the first draws on the techniques of micro-investment theory, the second is of interest to the location theorist, and the third needs a knowledge of international trade and industrial organization theory. Moreover, each of the questions may be tackled from a positive or a normative viewpoint; and with sectoral, national, or cosmopolitan interests in mind.

* From *Oxford Economic Papers*, **25** (November 1973): 289–325.

The purpose of this chapter is two-fold: first to survey and critically evaluate the attempts so far made to answer the general question 'why international direct investment and production?' and, second, to suggest some possible lines for further research, illustrating from data recently published about the operations of US affiliates in the UK.

THE ISSUES INVOLVED

What, then, is the subject for explanation? Basically, most writers have been concerned to explain the growth and significance of enterprises which operate and control income-creating activities in more than one country, or, more specifically, the growth and significance of the foreign activities of such companies. It is when one starts to translate this general rubric into operational terms that one runs into difficulties. Precisely at what point does an enterprise become 'multinational'? What does one mean by 'control'? What exactly are income-creating activities?

The MNE has been variously interpreted in the literature (Aharoni, 1971). Definitions range from those which embrace all firms which operate and control income-creating activities in more than one country (Brooke and Remmers, 1970; Dunning, 1971) to those which would include only those enterprises which operate a common management and operational strategy towards their foreign and domestic operations (Perlmutter, 1969; Behrman, 1969). Others introduce more pragmatic constraints, e.g. the number of countries in which a firm operates (Vernon, 1972) or the proportion of total sales, assets, or employment accounted for by their foreign activities (Bruck and Lees, 1966). There is also the totally different approach which interprets multinationalism in terms of the geographical spread of ownership or control of equity capital (or capital employed). While respecting the views of the particularists, I have long favoured a broad rather than a narrow definition of the MNE, partly because all other definitions are bound to be arbitrary, and partly because I do not consider the attributes of the MNE stressed by Perlmutter et al. are necessarily unique to such enterprises; cf., e.g., multi-regional national or international trading enterprises. The distinction between the geographical origin of capital and of the ownership of production facilities is best overcome by placing the appropriate adjective between the words 'multinational' and 'enterprise' (Dunning, 1971).

Second, as regards the question of control, definitions again vary from including affiliates and associated companies of MNEs in which there is any financial stake to those in which there is a 100 per cent equity holding. Here, too, there is no purist definition, simply because there is no such definition of control of decision-taking, either of its amount or its extent. But this much can be said. Since, first, a 51 per cent ownership of equity capital ensures the *power* of control over decision-taking, and, second, an overwhelming proportion of the capital of the affiliates in which MNEs have a stake *is* financially controlled by them,[1] we would not go far wrong by considering all companies with a foreign direct investment stake as MNEs.

Third, the interpretation and measurement of income-creating activities. These include all activities in which there is a capital stake of some kind involved. This immediately distinguishes multinational *producing* enterprises from multinational *trading* enterprises. Again, in practice, the line between setting up one's own sales outlet and using a local distributor may be difficult to draw, but this need not greatly concern us, as the great majority of MNEs are engaged in the production of goods or financial services and most of the current discussion about their origins and effects is to do with these companies, rather than with wholesaling or retailing ventures.

The measurement of the economic activities of MNEs raises no new conceptual problems and, in most cases, the indicator chosen will be determined by the data available and the purpose of the exercise. In general, output measures are preferable to input measures, for the simple reason that the latter are usually expressed in terms of one input, e.g. capital stock, investment flows, employment, etc. Output indices, on the other hand, pose the problem of whether output should be *gross*, i.e. values or sales, or *net*, i.e. sales less purchases from other firms. In fact, most published statistics of international production are of sales rather than net output; these tend to exaggerate the direct economic contribution of MNEs or their affiliates to the gross national products of the countries in which they operate.

This last point raises two others. The first arises when one asks the question 'from whose viewpoint are we measuring income-creating activities?' From the viewpoint of MNEs, their own sales, or net output or profits may be the appropriate index. From the viewpoint of countries in which they operate, the contribution they make to the gross national product may be the chief (economic) consideration; this includes not only their own output but the effect which they have on the net output of other economic agents in the economy. But the value of this contribution depends on the assumptions made about what would have happened in their absence and, in any case, it may be reasonably argued that since it is individual firms that take the decisions about their activities (albeit in response to signals from governments), it is the factors which influence these decisions that are the relevant ones. But in looking at the appropriate policies for governments to pursue towards MNEs, the external effects of their behaviour may be equally important.

The second point is specific to foreign direct investment and arises because the factor inputs of MNEs are sourced from both (*a*) the countries in which they operate and (*b*) other countries. The ratio of (*a*) to (*b*) will determine that part of the value added by a particular affiliate from which the rest of the enterprise benefits. This means that, just as expressing the activity of an affiliate in terms of a single input may underestimate its contribution, so assessing it in terms of gross or net output may overstate its contribution to the enterprise. If, for example, an MNE owns one-half of the equity capital of its affiliate, then the ratio of the sales to its affiliates to the total sales of the enterprise will be twice that of the ratio of the profits earned by the affiliate to that of the enterprise as a whole, assuming that the profit/sales ratios and taxation rates are the same for all the operating units of the enterprise. Once again, it depends on what questions one is seeking to answer, but it is worth emphasizing that identifying and measuring activities of MNEs is not as straightforward as it may appear to be.

In practice, the matter is often settled by the data available and the economist has to cut his coat according to the cloth given him, or obtained by himself! And the research so far done on the growth of the multinational enterprise strongly reflects this constraint. Broadly speaking, economists have obtained their data from three sources. First, from information published, mainly by governments of host and investing countries, on the stock or flow of inward and outward direct investment. Due mainly to different reporting requirements of governments, the form, coverage, and reliability of these data vary enormously between countries, and within a country over time, and they are rarely directly comparable. Valiant attempts have been made by Polk (1971), Behrman (1969), and Rolfe (1969) to construct a world matrix of the value of international direct investment and/or production, but none has been completely successful.[2] As far as *investing* countries are concerned, the most comprehensive data are those published by the US Department of Commerce.[3] These include investment, output, and income data for 1966 and 1970, broken down both by country and industry. UK statistics are confined to a fairly detailed geographical breakdown of the capital stake and investment flows; the industrial breakdown is very broad. There are also quite reasonable data on outward direct investment for Canada, Australia, and latterly Japan. Of the *host* countries, Canada, Australia, the USA, and UK, Sweden, and Belgium, and some of the LDCs, e.g. Argentina, India, Ghana, Nigeria, Malaysia, Korea, the Philippines, Taiwan, and Indonesia provide reasonably good statistics.[4] Major surveys on the extent and pattern of Swedish and German foreign investments are currently being undertaken.

The second form of data is that derived from field work carried out by research institutions or individual research workers in pursuance of a specific project to do with foreign direct investment or the MNE. Most of these projects have taken the form of country or industry case studies,[5] although some have been specifically concerned with the determinants of foreign investment. Again, the quality of the data varies as, in most cases, the investigators have had to rely on the good offices of firms, but for some of the less-well-documented countries, particularly the LDCs, and for a more detailed breakdown of industry statistics, these studies usefully supplement (and sometimes improve upon) the official statistics.

The third source of information is that being gradually amassed in data banks and is based largely on statistics related to individual companies. The first of these was established at Harvard and supplied much of the data for the studies led by Raymond Vernon (1972); more recently, Gilles Bertin has set up a European counterpart at Rennes. In spite of the interpretative difficulties, I believe that these data banks have much to commend them. Already, useful progress has been made by international and government agencies, notably UNCTAD, the OECD, and the EEC, and the US Tariff Commission, by research institutions, e.g. the Foreign Policy Research Institute at Pennsylvania and the Center for Multinational Studies at Washington and by such organizations as the International Chamber of Commerce and Business International. Various international trade union secretariats are also actively gathering material. One feels that the time is rapidly approaching for some rationalization of data collection, partly to avoid unnecessary duplication of research and clerical effort, and partly to reduce the work on individual MNEs, which, after all, are the main providers of information.

I will return to this point later in the paper. But one practical difficulty should be mentioned here. The number of enterprises which make up the great bulk of foreign direct investment is small. The 50 largest MNEs probably account for one-half of the total international direct investment and an even higher percentage of international production in the world; the 50 next largest account for up to another 25 per cent. When one comes to break down these operations geographically and industrially in any meaningful sense one is soon dealing with a handful of companies. The possibility of identification then becomes very real, and this may well impose the ultimate limit to sophisticated econometric work in this field. This point is further underlined when one comes to classify MNEs by the operational strategies they pursue, and/or other variables, e.g. by activity, intra-group exports, size, age, etc.; one is soon down to a few observations in each cell of the matrix, which raises conceptual as well as identification problems.

So much by way of introduction. We now turn to examine the work so far done on identifying the factors influencing the origin and growth of international production. We shall mainly concentrate on the *positive* approaches to the subject and discuss these under six main headings.

1. THE SURVEY APPROACH

One approach to explaining the extent and character of foreign business operations has been to ask the companies themselves to identify the reasons for their behaviour. Usually, this approach has confined itself to analysing the *initial* decision to produce abroad, and, more often than not, the questions have been formulated in the most general terms, e.g. 'what are the main factors which influenced your decision to invest overseas?'; and rarely does any guidance seem to have been given to the respondents as to assumptions underlying the questions asked. Because of this, the surveys have produced a wide range of answers, which reflect as much the respondents' interpretation of the questions as the determinants of the investment decision.

There were several surveys of this kind in the later 1950s and 1960s (Barlow and Wender, 1955; National Industrial Conference Board, 1961; Robinson, 1961; McGraw Hill, 1961; Behrman, 1962; Basi, 1966; Hakam, 1966; Kreinin, 1967; Kolde, 1968; Hogan, 1968), and frequently, too, in broader-based works on foreign direct investment (Safarian, 1966; Brash, 1966; Brooke and Remmers, 1970; Deane, 1970; Daniels, 1971; Andrews, 1972; Forsyth, 1972), questions of this type have been asked. Some of these focused on the goals of foreign direct investment, and others on means of achieving goals, but most did not distinguish between the two. In the main, the results of the surveys were presented as a tabulation of the reasons for moving abroad, or to particular countries listed by the respondents in the sample. In Basi's analysis, a three-point 'importance' scale was used; but mostly the only evaluation was by the times particular determinants were mentioned, the number of which ranged from nine in the Kolde study to 25 in the Robinson study. No attempt was made to classify the results by types of economic activity, or by country, although some of the studies concentrated on particular regions within countries or areas (Johns and Brash (Australia), Forsyth (Scotland), Kreinin (Europe), Hakam (Nigeria)).

It is clear that these studies can, at best, do little more than identify and perhaps rank by importance the sort of factors which businesses take into account in establishing production units abroad. At worst, they can be thoroughly misleading. Quite apart from the confusion between goals (e.g. increased profits or share of market) and factors affecting the achievements of goals (e.g. transport costs, market growth, etc.), the reasons cited by firms were sometimes dependent on each other, e.g. lower costs of production and higher labour productivity; in some cases the reasons cited were quite specific, e.g. the existence of local engineering facilities, or to match a rival's investment; in others, they were very general, e.g. diversification, inflation. Moreover, as we have said, there was little attempt to classify types of foreign operations, and only a casual acquaintance with the literature suggests that the determinants of investment vary so much with the *type* of investment, cf. the reasons for upstream and downstream investment, that any generalizations are not very helpful.

As Table 1.1 illustrates, almost without exception, the studies stress the host government's attitude to inward foreign investment, political stability, and the prospects of market growth as the most important considerations prompting foreign activities; next in order come the fear of losing an existing market, the likelihood of exchange rate fluctuations, limitations imposed on foreign ownership, and barriers to trade.[6] Only a minority of firms appear to have been enticed abroad by lower production costs; neither do savings in movement costs loom large in their calculations. But again, the studies do not tell us the way in which these determinants may vary with geographical or industrial composition of the investment. In summary, they may be criticized, partly because they fail to differentiate between motives and determinants, partly because they do not identify the assumptions underlying the answers given by firms, and partly because no attempt is made to normalize for differences in the characteristics of firms (or countries). Certainly none of them takes us much further in a generalized theory of international production, or helps us to understand the determinants of new investment once the initial locational decision has been made.

More recently, efforts have been made to improve the methodology of the survey approach, both by giving respondents a clearer conception of the type of variables it is sought to identify, and by suggesting ways in which they might be evaluated.

Stobaugh (1969a), for example, makes use of a matrix which identifies two main groups of variables which gauge locational attractions to companies. For example, he relates *product-related* influences, technological and marketing characteristics, life cycle pattern, cost structure, and economies of scale to *country-related* influences, e.g. market size, investment climate, local technology, and distance from major exporting nations. Schöllhammer (1972) adds a third group of influences, viz. *company-related* influences, e.g. size of firm, scope of international operations management strategy.

The same authors and Piper (1971) have also suggested schemes for the evaluation of these variables. Stobaugh (1969), for example, sets out ranges of marks which might be given for each particular environmental variable (attitude to capital repatriation (0–12), extent to which foreign ownership is allowed (0–12), currency stability (4–20), etc.), which are then assigned by firms according to some predefined criteria. The marks are then aggregated and an index of environmental attraction, or investment climate, obtained. Schöllhammer (1972), in a study of 140 American and European MNEs, asked corporate executives involved in making location decisions to rank 78 country-related influences (classified into nine broad categories, e.g. economic, legal, geographical, political, labour, tax, etc., factors) on a scale from 1 (of no importance) to 4 (very important). His findings broadly confirmed those of earlier surveys. The two most important individual location factors were existing market size and anticipated market growth, but of the nine broad groupings, political, supply, and tax considerations outranked the rest.

Such schemes as these have their obvious attractions, but they also have their drawbacks; among the latter are first, that they almost always set the same

Table 1.1 Summary of determinants of foreign direct investment (selected studies) – number of times factors mentioned

	(a) Foreign investment in general					(b) Investment in specific countries			
Name of researcher	Robinson[1]	Behrman	Basi[2]	Kolde	Forsyth[(a)3]	Brash	Deane	Forsyth[(b)3]	Andrews[4]
Date of publication	(1961)	(1962)	(1966)	(1968)	(1972)	(1966)	(1970)	(1972)	(1972)
Number of firms in sample	205	72	214	104	105	100	139	105	80
(a) Marketing factors									
(i) Size of market	} 262	–	141	–	–	–	} 21	–	–
(ii) Market growth		19	158	7	82	89		14	28
(iii) To maintain share of market or match a rival's investment	130	–	126	12	35	–	30	6	–
(iv) To advance exports of parent company	–	1	–	–	2	–	–	1	–
(v) Necessity to maintain close contact with customers	–	7	–	–	5	–	15	9	–
(vi) Dissatisfaction with existing market arrangements	–	3	–	25	–	–	–	–	–
(vii) Export base for neighbouring markets	104	3	–	–	–	30		–	39
Subtotal	496	33	425	44	124	119	66	30	57
(b) Barriers to trade									
(i) Barriers to trade	130	} 14	–	21	28	78	76	–	11
(ii) Preference of local customers for local products	–		–	–	1	24	–	–	–
Subtotal	130	14	–	21	29	102	76	–	11
(c) Cost factors									
(i) To be near source of supply	–	–	–	–	3	–	14	2	–
(ii) Availability of labour	209	–	–*	–	–	–	–	53	–
(iii) Availability of raw materials	–	12	114	–	–	–	7	–	–

(iv) Availability of capital/technology	–	–	78	–	–	–	–	11	} 40
(v) Lower labour costs	79	–	103	–	–	–	–	18	
(vi) Lower other production costs	–	7	–	20	–	11	–	–	
(vii) Lower transport costs	–	–	–	–	–	22	–	18	
(viii) Financial (*et al.*) inducements by governments	50	–	–	–	1	13	–	52	45
(ix) General cost levels more favourable (less inflation)	–	–	134	–	–	–	14	–	–
Subtotal	338	19	429	20	4	46	35	154	85
(d) Investment climate									
(i) General attitude to foreign investment	–[5]	–	145	6	–	–	10	–	–
(ii) Political stability	115	–	159	–	–	–	–	–	–
(iii) Limitation on ownership	20	–	–	–	–	–	–	–	–
(iv) Currency exchange regulations	} 105[6]	–	–	–	–	–	–	–	–
(v) Stability of foreign exchange			151	–	–	–	–	–	–
(vi) Tax structure	–	–	131	4	–	–	–	–	–
(vii) Familiarity with country	–	–	100	–	–	–	–	–	–
Subtotal	240	–	686	10	–	–	10	–	–
(e) General									
(i) Expected higher profits	182	20	144	–	–	–	–	–	–
(ii) Other[7]	252	14	112	5	14	37	39	43	50[8]
Subtotal	434	34	256	5	14	37	39	43	50
Total	1638	97	1796	100	171	304	226	227	203

* Included in lower labour costs.
1 Number of times factors are ranked 1–3 on a 6-point scale.
2 Listed as 'crucially' or 'fairly important' in Basi's 3-point scale.
3 Forsyth[(a)] refers to reasons given by firms on decision to invest outside the USA.
4 Andrews's survey was concerned with identifying reasons for investing in Ireland.
5 Dealt with in a separate part of the survey and regarded as crucially important.
6 Classified as 'financial stability'.
7 Including 192 mentions for availability of infrastructure, power, and banking facilities.
8 Including 40 mentions 'to take advantage of Ireland's entry into the Common Market should that occur'.

standards for all types of investment and in all countries; second, they assume that over the life of the plant, the investment climate will remain unchanged; and third, they assume that individual locational determinants can be separately and independently evaluated.

We conclude: while the survey approach may be helpful in identifying the factors which influence international production, it can do little more than this. In the past, it has not been satisfactory in evaluating particular goals or determinants, and even attempts to use a ranking procedure have been of limited value because of the failure to take account of different types of investment. None of the surveys has so far distinguished between factors affecting the establishment of foreign production units from those influencing increases in international production. Finally, all too frequently they have rarely defined the form of the involvement of companies abroad (when investment is taken as the dependent variable it is not clear whether this means investment-owned or investment-controlled).

2. CAPITAL THEORY

The second approach to the study of 'why international production?' focuses attention on one factor input, viz. capital, or changes in capital, viz. investment, and is essentially an extension of received capital theory. Mainly because of data constraints, almost all the empirical work done in this area has been on the behaviour of US MNEs. In most cases, the US *share* of the capital stock, or investment, of US foreign affiliates is taken as the dependent variable, but occasionally the *total* plant and equipment expenditure of affiliates, i.e. investment in fixed assets, is used.

The traditional theory of international capital movements asserts that such movements arise because of differences in the levels of interest rates between countries. Under these conditions, money capital flows across the exchanges if the margin by which the expected yield exceeds the cost of capital is greater than that of projects at home. Until the mid-1960s, this relationship was thought, by most economists, to explain movements in *portfolio* investment fairly well (Mundell, 1960; Kenen, 1963). Since then, partly as a result of developments in the theories of investment behaviour and portfolio distribution, a new view has emerged which argues that, while the allocation of the *stock* of assets held at home and abroad depends on the level of interest rates and risk evaluations, changes in this allocation, i.e. capital flows, will depend on *changes* in interest rates (Branson, 1970; Floyd, 1969). According to this view, an increase in foreign interest rates will have a two-fold effect. First, it will cause a shift in the stock of portfolios towards foreign assets; this is the so-called *stock-shift* effect, which will vary *inter alia* with the size of the portfolio and the amount of change in the interest differential. Second, there will be a reallocation of portfolios at the margin towards foreign assets – the so-called 'continuing flow' effect. Where the latter component is small, the supply-elasticity of capital with respect to changes in interest rates between countries is likely to be substantial only in the adjustment period. For there to be a permanent redistribution of capital movements between countries their relative interest rates must be constantly changing. This new view is generally supported by the empirical studies of the last few years (Branson and Hill, 1971), although the period of stock adjustment is now being shown to be somewhat longer than was first thought.

It is generally accepted that models of this kind, designed to explain international flows in portfolio investment, can only partially explain the international capital formation of firms or that part of it financed by direct foreign investment. This is mainly because, unlike movements in portfolio capital, which are essentially financial transactions between independent lenders and borrowers, direct investment involves no change in ownership. It does, however, involve the transmission of other factor inputs than money capital, viz. entrepreneurship, technology, and management expertise, and is likely to be as affected by the relative profitability of the use of these resources in different countries as that of money capital (Stubenitsky, 1970). Put another way, the models are inadequate because they assume that the transactors engaged in the activity of international investment have similar behavioural characteristics (Learner and Stern, 1972).

Nevertheless, recent research on the origin of international financial and real capital flows has provided useful new insights which have a direct bearing on the investment behaviour of MNEs (Spitaller, 1971; Stevens, 1972). Harry Johnson (1966), for example, makes the useful distinction between movements in capital which occur in response to interest rate differentials and those which are generated by the expectation of higher profits. At a macro-level, it is this latter type of movement that Borts and Kopecky (1972) argue can best be explained by the same factors which explain economic growth, e.g. increases in population, technological advances, the improvement in the terms of trade between exports and imported capital goods, the savings rate, and the capital coefficient; and that it is not normally necessary to introduce monetary factors to explain why or how capital transfers occur. Monetary variables may affect capital movements but only in so far as an excess demand for liquid assets has an influence on the excess demand for goods.

The alternative approach is more *micro*-oriented and represents the mainstream of thinking on the subject. This is directed to extending the theory of domestic corporate investment to the international activities of firms. There are two main strands to this approach. The least developed is that which looks at the firm's foreign investment decision as an extension of the theory of portfolio distribution. Following attempts by Grubel (1968), Miller and

Whitman (1970), and Levy and Sarnat (1970) to explain the distribution of *portfolio* investment across national boundaries using a stock adjustment model of the Markowitz (1959)/Tobin (1958, 1965) variety, Prachowny (1972) and Stevens (1969a) set out to test whether or not firms allocated their *direct* investment expenditures so as to maximize a utility function positively related to expected returns and negatively related to risk. Their results were inconclusive, particularly when disaggregated data were used. Cohen (1972), on the other hand, has demonstrated that large US corporations with more extensive foreign activities tended to have smaller fluctuations in their profits during the 1960s. Finally Mellors (1973), using a technique first developed by Smith and Schreiner (1969) to explain the domestic diversification of conglomerate firms, has demonstrated that the geographical allocation of direct investment by UK firms, in response to post-tax rates of return, provides some support to the portfolio model.

More extensive have been the attempts to apply various models of domestic capital formation by businesses to explain foreign investment.[7] In particular, two main lines of research may be mentioned. The first is an extension of the neo-classical theory of real investment, and assumes the maximization of the market value of assets to be the goal of firms. Here the most popular model is that developed by Jorgenson (1963), in which investment is viewed as a gradual adjustment of a firm's actual capital stock to its desired level, i.e. $K_t^* = ap_t Q_t/c_t$, where K_t^* = desired level of capital stock (at time t), p_t = product price (at time t), Q_t is expected output, c_t = the rental price of capital (which in turn is a function of the price of capital goods and its rate of change, the cost of capital; the depreciation and tax rates), and 'a' as a constant from the Cobb–Douglas production function measuring the elasticity of output with respect to capital. This is a modified version of the flexible accelerator explanation of investment, which in most tests has out-performed the simple accelerator model, liquidity and cash flow models, and security valuation models (Stevens, 1972).

There have been numerous studies which have examined the determinants of foreign investment over the last five years. Again, it is convenient to classify these into two groups. The first is illustrated by the work of Stevens (1969a, 1972), Moose (1968), Severn (1972), Popkin (1965), Kopits (1972), Richardson (1971, 1972), and Kwack (1973). Each of these strongly supports the standard investment theory by demonstrating that expenditure by US firms on foreign plant and equipment is highly correlated either with the sales of US foreign affiliates or some measure of output for the area of industry in question. Severn, for example, used a two-country model (the USA and the rest of the world) to explain differences both in the specification of domestic and foreign investment functions, and the distribution of corporate funds between home and foreign uses. He concluded that subject to a liquidity constraint, investment was strongly correlated to changes in sales in both cases. He also asserted that MNEs allocated funds without reference to national boundaries and that, eliminating factors common to both foreign and domestic investment, the two were at least partially substitutable and interrelated through the financing mechanism. Popkin, in his study of US manufacturing affiliates (1965), claimed that the relative profit rates and other financial variables were more important than market structure or technological factors in explaining variations in the behaviour of firms. Stevens (1972), using similar data, and an extension of the Modigliani–Miller theorem (1958), derived equations which, *inter alia*, related plant and equipment expenditure and changes in current assets to the present market value of firms, and also financial flows to the same goal and that of exchange loss minimization. He found that all equations explained past data quite well. In his study, Kwack (1973) identified a negative correlation between US interest rates and foreign investment but, like Stevens (1972), concluded that the voluntary restraint programme aimed at improving the US balance of payments was statistically insignificant.

Richardson (1971, 1972) took these discussions a stage further by distinguishing between different types of foreign direct investment. In particular, he argued for the need for a separate theory to explain investment in new ventures, the main goal of which is likely to be market penetration, rather than the profit-maximizing or growth goals of established ventures. He also considered that domestic-type theories were less successful in explaining the investment policies of the affiliates of integrated multinational firms, which were more likely to be geared to a global strategy, than in the case of independent affiliates, where an 'every tub on its own bottom' type of policy was the usual practice. In his contributions, he suggested the kind of modifications necessary to the accepted variables to explain the optimal capital stock of each of these types of foreign investment, although he did not attempt to put these to the test. His, however, is perhaps one of the most rewarding lines of research in that he recognizes that both the motives and determinants of MNEs will vary according to the type of foreign operation, a point to which we shall return later.

Most of the research so far mentioned accepts that there are certain factors affecting foreign capital formation which are specific to such investment, although Herring and Willett (1973) have demonstrated that between 1957 and 1969, US plant and equipment expenditures at home and abroad were significantly correlated. Other studies have attempted to isolate some of these, e.g. Cairncross (1973) and Herring and Willett (1972) control over capital exports, Kopits (1972) and Mellors (1973) the tax variable, Stevens (1969b) and Heckerman (1969) exchange risks, and Horst (1972b) and Jud (1973) tariffs. Much more difficult is to test statistically the significance of non-quantifiable variables such as the investment climate, which, as we have seen (Table 1.1) businessmen consider to be an influence on their investment plans. One way out of this dilemma has been suggested by Miller and Weigel (1972) who argue, on the lines of Aharoni (1966), that decisions about the location of investment should be regarded as a two-stage discriminant process. In the first stage, locations are classified as 'suitable' or 'potentially unsuitable', on fairly basic grounds: size of market, prior investment, barriers to exports, investment climate, etc. In the second stage detailed calculations are made of the expected economic profitability of the locations considered potentially suitable. The fact that the variables included in many models may not hold up well when predicting *all* decisions may be due to the fact that the first stage rejections have already been made, but on non-economic grounds.

The second group of studies on investment behaviour have sought to explain movements in foreign capital formation in particular geographical areas; the writings of Bandera and White (1968), d'Arge (1969), Scaperlanda (1967), Wallis (1968), Scaperlanda and Mauer (1969, 1971, 1972), Schmitz and Bieri (1972), all dealing with US direct investment in Western Europe,[8] are some examples. Most of these, using either time-series or cross-sectional data, relate absolute amounts of investment (or capital stake), or shares of investment (or capital stake) to profit rates, size of markets, growth of markets, tariff rates, and some kind of trend and/or slope-shifting variables; the 1968 Bandera and White study included an international liquidity variable. The cross-sectional studies strongly support the hypothesis that US investment has been directed most to countries with the fastest rate of growth of GNP, with profitability and other variables, including tariffs, being a secondary consideration. On the other hand, there is little evidence that, in itself, the formation of the EEC had a substantial effect on the level or direction of US investment flows, although much depends on the precise specification of the relationships, the level of disaggregation,[9] and the years for which the comparison is made. The time-series data lend support to the cross-sectional data when the capital stake is taken as the dependent variable (Bandera and White, 1968). Again, in both cases, the market variable showed up better than the profit rate.

What conclusions can be drawn from these studies? In my view, none of them can take us far along the way to understanding 'why international production?'. This, I think, is chiefly because their attempts to explain either foreign capital formation or movements in capital across national boundaries evade the more interesting questions to do with international production. The studies take as given the value of variables, which themselves need explaining. Anticipated profits are a good illustration. These are almost always expressed in terms of the profitability *of the foreign affiliates*. But not only may these be a very imperfect indication of the contribution of the affiliate to the investing enterprise (Reddaway, 1968; Vaitsos, 1972) but to explain direct foreign investment in terms of profitability begs the question '*why* that profitability?', the answer to which is bound up *inter alia* with the competitive position of foreign affiliates *vis-à-vis* indigenous firms and exports.

In other words, the questions asked by capital theory do not get to the heart of the matter. The concern of this approach is not to explain foreign investment or capital formation *per se*, but, assuming this to exist, to determine how far its allocation is influenced by profit rates and market growth. This is a perfectly valid and legitimate interest, and when related to the same variable for domestic investment, does point to some interesting differences in the behaviour of firms (Richardson, 1971). But we are little wiser in understanding *why* this is so.

Moreover, all the studies are, to some extent, deficient in their choice of explanatory variables and we have said that investment, particularly investment financed by a particular source, is not necessarily a good index of the activity of firms, as it underestimates the importance of labour-intensive firms. Of the independent variables, the rate of profit earned by affiliates may inadequately express their contribution to the organization of which they are part, particularly where there is a good deal of product or process specialization between affiliates, and intra-group trading at other than arm's-length prices. Moreover, the more vertically or horizontally integrated an MNE becomes, the less significance can be attached to the market size or potential of the country in which production is located. This especially applies to those enterprises which practise a policy of global or regional, horizontal or vertical specialization, e.g. the Philips and IBMs of this world. They are not primarily dependent on markets of the countries in which they operate because their decisions will be influenced by other considerations.

Finally, the data on which the analyses of investment are based are rarely disaggregated by type of economic activity. Because of this, it is impossible to assess the extent to which different types of overseas operations are influenced by different variables. This, in fact, one knows to be the case and the importance of the profit (or sales) of the affiliate as the contribution to the goals of the enterprise may be small. The objective of foreign sales and marketing ventures is primarily to advance the exports of the investing company; even a manufacturing affiliate may spur the exports of related goods from its parent company. (In 1966, US affiliates imported goods worth $6.1 billion from the USA – about 11 per cent of their total foreign sales); similarly an investment in raw materials may be made to safeguard supplies to the rest of the organization, while Reddaway (1968) and Dunning (1970) have observed that the feedback of knowledge resulting from an investment in a technologically advanced country can more than compensate for any low profits earned.

3. THE TRADE APPROACH

The third approach to 'why international production?' is that of international economics, and stems from the dissatisfaction with received theory to explain recent trends in the level and composition of trade. It is worth emphasizing that, in the classical model of static comparative advantage, there is no room for the MNE at all. With completely free movement of goods but immobility of factors of production, and with all firms transacting goods and services in a price-taking situation, there is little incentive for international direct investment (Kindleberger, 1968). But, with production by firms outside their national boundaries now thought to account for 15 per cent of the world's output, these are no longer reasonable assumptions. Standard theory, whether it be of the classical or neo-classical variety, makes no allowance for trade in factor inputs (Baldwin, 1970), largely because the conditions necessary to such trade are assumed not to exist.

The most powerful attempts to incorporate capital movements into trade theory in recent years have come from two directions. First, Mundell (1957), using the Heckscher–Ohlin–Samuelson model, asserted the proposition that trade and capital movements are substitutes for each other and that the equalization of factor–price ratios implies the equalization of commodity–price ratios. Second, there has been the attempt to take account of changes in technology or advances in knowledge in the analysis (Johnson, 1968). In the static model, innovations are ignored altogether as production functions are assumed constant and identical (or nearly identical) throughout the world. Where they are introduced, e.g. in a comparative static situation, their benefits are assumed to be instantaneously and freely transferable. Such an assumption is totally unrealistic in a situation where information is costly to produce, is enterprise specific, and is sold under conditions of imperfect competition, where governments both finance the output of new knowledge and impose barriers on its dissemination, e.g. by the patent system, and, hence, affect the patterns of trade and resource allocation.

These and other market constraints both help fashion the initial location of new products and processes and, at the same time, induce the means by which barriers to the diffusion of the knowledge giving rise to these products and processes may be overcome. Beginning with Posner (1961), a steady stream of writers has attempted to demonstrate how innovations in one country may affect the comparative advantage of countries, and how the trade initially generated might be gradually eliminated by the recognition and imitation of the innovations elsewhere. Various models have sought to explain the process of the transference of production from the innovating country. Of these, the product cycle model (Hufbauer, 1966; Vernon, 1966; Stobaugh, 1968; Wells, 1972a) has, perhaps, come nearest to explicitly recognizing the role of MNEs in this process, although in their writings, Hirsch (1967), Wilkinson (1968), and Quinn (1970) also accept that it may play an important role. Other economists, e.g. Gruber, Mehta, and Vernon (1967) and Keesing (1966), have also observed the relationship between the production of knowledge, international investment and trade, and more recently Baldwin (1970) has called for an explicit incorporation of trade in factor inputs into trade theory.

In explaining how and why international production arises, trade economists have tended to emphasize, first, the conditions under which the foreign markets of a particular country are best exploited through the affiliates of its firms producing in those markets rather than by exports, and second, the possible consequences of this on existing production outlets and trade patterns. The product cycle theory asserts that initially production will be located in the country of innovation, and sold there. Exports follow as new markets are sought, but in due course, depending on relative exchange rates[10] and demand and supply conditions in importing countries, indigenous production may become profitable. Whether or not this output will be supplied by local firms or affiliates of firms of the innovating country will depend on the barriers to entry facing the two groups of firms, and their relative efficiencies. It will also be influenced by the strategy of enterprises towards their foreign operations and the type of market structure(s) in which they are competing. Of the barriers to entry facing indigenous firms, Hufbauer (1966) has stressed the technological gap caused by the lag in the international transfer in technology, while Vernon (1966) places rather more emphasis on market constraints. Both writers, however, see the MNE as an instrument for surmounting these barriers. The final phase of the cycle is where these producers may themselves begin exporting, competing with the product-innovating firms even in their domestic markets.

Both approaches and other neo-technological theories of trade (Hufbauer, 1971) are micro-oriented and differ from received theory in two major respects. First, they are more concerned with the behaviour of firms than of countries; second, as they have so far been presented, they are particular, rather than general, models as they tend to endow innovating firms and countries with special economic characteristics and, in consequence, patterns of production and trade. Vernon himself accepts that the product cycle sequence is less satisfactory in explaining the territorial distribution of production of MNEs which adopt a global strategy towards their operations (Vernon, 1972), while there is some doubt that the process adequately explains the sequence of events when innovations originate from countries with (relatively) low incomes and wage costs and/or small markets (Dunning, 1971). Nevertheless, the models are of especial interest in that they emphasize the role of innovations in forging new trade patterns within an imperfectly competitive environment, conditions which are the seed-bed of growth of the modern MNE.

The value of the trade approach to understanding 'why international production?' is that it reminds us that foreign direct investment is one of various ways of exploiting a foreign market. Though the precise relationship between these alternatives has yet to be analysed in the literature, various case studies of the product cycle (Wells, 1972a) give useful glimpses at which point one means will tend to replace another. It is, of course, here that the overlap with the location theory approach is best seen; it is here, too, where trade theory most needs restructuring to incorporate movements in factor inputs, even if some of these movements are not strictly trade, but the transference of resources between one part of an MNE and another.

One foresees further interest of trade theorists in this area because of the growing impact of the MNE on the flows of goods and services across national boundaries (Robertson, 1971). This will force attention on explaining the behaviour of such companies. Until recently, there have been few data to test systematically any trade-type hypotheses. These are now starting to emerge – for example data recently collected by the US Tariff Commission give sales and exports (including intra-group exports) of US foreign affiliates, classified both by industry and country, although, compared with the quality and detail of trade statistics, the situation is still unsatisfactory. Conceptually, the most helpful lines of approach seem likely to be two-fold: first, the implications of dynamic comparative advantage (Bruno, 1970; Klein, 1973), and particularly those which arise from the incorporation of human capital and productive knowledge into capital (Johnson, 1968); second, an analysis of the way in which trade is influenced by the ways in which markets are exploited (e.g. by investment, exports, licensing, etc.). The explanation of factor endowment and its impact on trade may give some insight into the geographical and industrial composition of international investment. Although these are largely macro-concepts, they should provide a useful insight into reasons behind these forms of international transactions.

So far, we have thought of the MNE as an instrument for exploiting foreign markets. The second aspect of trade theory concerns the question of the distinctive character of the MNE as an owner of resources in different countries compared with national (i.e. indigenous) firms. The implications of this will depend on the type of operations and the strategies adopted by the MNE, but in principle they raise two issues. First, there is likely to be more specialization and integration when such advantages occur than if these operations were conducted by independent firms; second, all intra-group transactions involve the setting of transfer prices, which will affect the *terms* of trade. The determination of such prices will depend on circumstances which, again, may require modifications to the assumptions underlying trade theory.

4. LOCATION THEORY

Like trade theory, location theory has so far had little to contribute to an explanation of the level or composition of international production. This is because location theory has traditionally confined its attention to the territorial allocation of resources, and trade of firms *within* national boundaries; and only Ohlin (1967) and, to a lesser extent, Giersch (1950) and Weber (1958) have attempted to go beyond this point. Yet, removing this geographical constraint, the theory of location would seem central to answering the question 'why international production?'. Assuming the goals of enterprises are unaffected by the countries in which they produce, there is no reason why a US firm, in choosing between a New York or a Paris location for its new plant, will be influenced by different criteria. To be sure, additional factors will affect the choice of a foreign location, e.g. the possibility of exchange fluctuations and differences in corporate tax rates, the risk of expropriation, etc., but, conceptually, there is no difficulty in embracing these in the basic analysis.[11]

Location theory is concerned with both *supply*- and *demand*-oriented variables influencing the spatial distribution of production processes, research and development, and administration of firms; unlike trade theory it is not concerned with the division of labour between countries. Assuming a certain size and distribution of markets, and that each firm is a profit maximizer operating in a price-taking situation, production will be located where costs are lowest (Greenhut, 1952). This, in turn, will depend on the availability and cost of factor inputs, the efficiency with which these are transformed into outputs, and the costs of movement from the point of production to that of marketing. Some of the special features of producing outside national boundaries can be incorporated into this kind of model and an optimal solution found. But others may be more difficult to deal with, e.g. the possibility of exchange rate adjustments or political actions, partly because they cannot easily be quantified and partly because of the inherent uncertainty attached to them.

In contrast to this approach, demand-oriented theories assume production costs to be independent of location and assert that the distribution of markets and the location of competitors will govern the siting of production units (Lösch, 1954). The theories of spatial interdependence are essentially an extension of the principles of monopolistic competition and oligopoly. Each location guarantees an element of spatial monopoly, the extent of which will depend on the character of the market, the locational strategy and efficiency of competitors, and movement costs. It will also be affected by the character of production, for example whether or not a firm is operating under economies of scale, as this will influence both the extent to which firms tend to cluster or disperse and the number of firms involved.

It is now generally accepted that any comprehensive theory of location must incorporate both cost and market factors, and that in an imperfectly competitive situation, the maximum profit location will not necessarily be the one where costs are minimized (Greenhut, 1952). (An analogy is with output and price determination of a firm producing under conditions of oligopoly where it can affect its profits by the size of the market it chooses to exploit as well as its cost conditions.)

Again, evaluating these factors as they affect the location of international production, the picture is more complex but not significantly changed. Looked at from the viewpoint of supplying any given market, the question can be discussed in two parts. One is to explain the spatial distribution of production units irrespective of ownership; the other is to explain the ownership of these units. Assume, for example, a certain size of market for a particular product in the UK, and that there are two nationalities of firms – UK and US – which could supply that market, then what determines (*a*) the extent to which the market is supplied from production units located in the UK or the USA, irrespective of ownership, and (*b*) given the location of production, whether the nationality of ownership of these units is UK or US?

The answer to these questions, to my mind, provides one of the keys to the unique character of the MNE and lies at the core of the industrial structure approach to 'why international production?'. For, rephrased, the question asks 'why is a market of a particular country served by the affiliates of foreign-owned firms producing in that country rather than by indigenous firms?'

Location theory tackles this question from the viewpoint of individual firms; like capital and trade theory, however, it takes as data the information on costs and market size and structure. And, as we have suggested, given this data, it can not only explain actual location patterns, but can also indicate optimal patterns, subject to the uncertainties surrounding particular markets and future events. From the *supply* side, an MNE is faced with the same type of cost decisions as a national enterprise; but its purchasing and marketing options may be wider, and the evaluation of foreign investment climates may be a complicated business (Stobaugh, 1969). From the *demand* side, one observes the structure of competition, and hence markets served, may be somewhat different. The Vernon thesis argues that the production of many new products and processes, first discovered in one country, is later transferred to another by a variety of means, one of which is through affiliates of the innovating firms. This assumes that the innovating firms both create new markets and supply these markets initially from a domestic and then from a foreign location, and, in so doing, they may induce a certain response from other firms and create a market structure which may influence future locational decisions. Here a distinction between *leading* and *following* firms is necessary (Kindleberger, 1969), as the market size and structure are both dynamic concepts.

In a price-taking competitive situation, all profit-maximizing firms will aim to produce an output at which marginal cost equals price. To do this, they may require to produce in one or more locations, depending on the relationships between production costs as output increases and transport costs as distance increases. There are no leaders or followers. In an imperfect market, the firm can influence the character of its market, and hence its optimal location. As far as producing overseas is concerned, the firm may do so to gain an advantage over existing producers, or forestall new competition, or to protect its market share even though the rate of return on *new* investment may be very small. In other words, the choice between exports and foreign production will not be taken on purely cost criteria; consideration will also be given to the effects of local production on the market structure in which the investing firm competes and its ability to sell in an imperfectly competitive situation. In stressing this factor, location theory is useful, though both the ability and desire of the MNE to gain a foothold in a market may be influenced by the fact that it *is* an MNE, and explaining the implications of this falls outside the scope of the theory.

Empirical studies on location relevant to MNEs have so far fallen into three main groups. First, there are those which have sought to evaluate the importance of specific factors affecting the location of either foreign investment or production of MNEs. These include Balassa (1967), Horst (1972a and b), Jud (1973), NICE (1961) (costs), Kreinin (1967b) (anti-trust legislation in investing countries), Krause (1972) (economic integration in host countries), Stobaugh (1969) (investment climate), Scaperlanda and Mauer (1969) and Schöllhammer (1972) (size of markets), Caves and Reuber (1971) and Morley (1966) (market growth), McAleese (1972) and Falise and Lepas (1970) (investment incentives), Vernon (1972) (threat of competitive firms), and (Dunning 1973a) I tried to examine some of the principles underlying Britain's entry into the EEC on the location of international firms in the enlarged Community. It is difficult to generalize from these studies; such econometric work as has been done seems to point to the size and growth of market as the single most important demand variable influencing foreign investment (Parry and Ahlburg, 1973).

The second group of studies has adopted a sectoral approach and looked at factors influencing the location of foreign enterprises in particular countries, e.g. Stonehill (1965), Brash (1966) (Australia), Daniels (1972) (United States), Deane (1970) (New Zealand), Forsyth (1972) (Scotland), Safarian (1966) (Canada), Schreiber (1970) (Taiwan), or industries, e.g. Branson (1970) (motor vehicles), Harman (1971) (computers), Hufbauer (1966) (synthetic materials), Stobaugh (1973) (petro-chemicals), Tilton (1973) (semi-conductors) and Wortzel (1973) (pharmaceuticals), though most of these, as we have seen, have tended to be an extension of the survey approach. A third group of economists has been interested in location of industry as a feature of international competitiveness (Hirsch, 1967,1973; Clark, Wilson, and Bradley, 1969; Dunning,

1971,1973a) and, in so doing, have given some attention to the way in which location is influenced by the ownership of firms.

Of the more recent attempts to incorporate the activities of MNEs into the general framework of location theory, those of Hymer (1970, 1972b), Murray (1973), and Vernon (1973) deserve special mention. Vernon argues that the determinants of locational strategy of MNEs will vary according to the stage of the product cycle which they are in. In both the initial stage of innovative oligopoly and in the final stage of mature oligopoly, their behaviour accords most closely with the interdependence model. In the intermediary phases where oligopoly exists with some degree of price competition, cost considerations are likely to be more important. As, however, MNEs tend to be concentrated in oligopolistic industries and are an important influence on the form of the product cycle, Vernon claims that location theorists should place rather more stress on the interdependence model.

A rather different approach is taken by Hymer and Murray, who perceive that, parallel to the increasing concentration of firms within industry, there is a trend towards the increasing spatial hierarchy of economic activity. MNEs are accelerating this trend: on the one hand routine manufacturing or marketing activities are being dispersed according largely to cost criteria (e.g. why do US firms choose to produce transistor radios and cameras in Taiwan (rather than, e.g., Mexico) for export back to the USA?); on the other, certain activities, e.g. top level administration, policy formulation, decision-taking and risk-hedging operations, and the specialized inputs which serve these, e.g. technical and financial information, management expertise, skilled labour, etc., are being increasingly centralized. The spatial interdependence arising from these trends, and particularly the agglomeration of the higher-order functions, has important implications both for the distribution of income earned by MNEs (and their affiliates), and of economic power between nations.

Standard location theory is generally concerned with these issues but tends to confine itself to explaining the location of plants of single-product, national firms. Moreover, within its analysis, many of the unique qualities associated with the MNE, e.g. its ability to shift inputs, such as human capital information and knowledge, across national boundaries at low or zero costs, are not brought out. Product acceptability is also assumed to be independent of the location of supply. Because, too, received theory treats the distribution of resources as fixed, it cannot incorporate the situation, often common to MNEs in the resource-based industries, in which firms can themselves affect this distribution, e.g. by their pricing policies and/or exploitation policies. This is particularly true of operations of MNEs in the less developed countries. For these reasons, location theory can give only a partial answer to the question ‘why international production?’.

5. INDUSTRIAL ORGANIZATION AND MARKET STRUCTURE

(a) Concepts and Analysis

The approaches to 'why international production?' so far discussed have been concerned with identifying and evaluating the variables which influence firms in the location of their foreign investment and/or productive activities. The type of answers to the question 'why international production?' they tend to elicit are 'because the prospects for profits or growth are promising' or, focusing more on determinants than goals, 'because foreign labour costs are lower' or 'because there are barriers to exports, etc.' or 'because only by so doing can we protect our competitive position'. The following paragraphs attempt to get beyond these indicative variables, and instead of asking 'what causes firms to produce abroad?' – which, in general, can be answered within the existing framework of capital, location, or trade theory – ask 'under what conditions will particular markets be supplied by the foreign affiliates producing in that market rather than by indigenous firms or imports?'.

In answering this latter type of question it seems to me a complementary approach, viz. that of industrial organization theory, is needed. This not only recognizes that international direct investment involves the transmission of a package of capital, knowledge, and entrepreneurship across national boundaries, but that the ownership and control of the organizing unit of this package, i.e. the foreign affiliate, is domiciled in a different country (or countries). This immediately suggests distinctiveness on the part of these affiliates *vis-à-vis* indigenous companies.

To simplify our analysis, assume there are only two countries (A and B) in the world and that we wish to identify both the *location* and *ownership* of firms manufacturing one particular product – say a drug. Assume, too, that there are three ways the market in each country may be supplied, viz. by the production of indigenous firms, by imports from firms with production units in the other country, and by the production of affiliates of these firms located in the local market. What will determine the extent to which Country A's firms will supply Country B's market from production units located and owned by them in Country B or the extent to which Country B's firms will supply Country A's market by plants located and owned in Country A?

The way in which the question is phrased suggests that there are two primary determinants of the amount of international production. The first is the extent of the market in each country and the second is the competitiveness of foreign affiliates *vis-à-vis* indigenous and non-resident firms. To simplify matters still further, suppose both the size of the market and the price of the drug are fixed and identical in both countries. We are left, then, with deciding how the market is shared between the three groups of firms.

Take, first, some extreme situations. Suppose transport costs (or other barriers to trade) between Country A and Country B are such that it pays neither country to export to the other. This means that each market will be supplied from local production units. How will the production be shared between indigenous firms and the affiliates of foreign firms? If it is a question of costs, what will determine whether these favour one group of firms or the other?

Again, take an extreme case. Assume that the production of the drug requires knowledge of a formula which is the sole property of firms in Country A. In the absence of licensing or similar arrangements, Country A's firms will supply the market in both Country A and Country B until indigenous producers in Country B are both willing and able to innovate and produce a substitute product. If they do not, then the market will continue to be supplied by Country A's firms.

In this particular example, international production (by Country A's firms in Country B) arises because of two absolute barriers: (*a*) the export of goods from Country A to B, and (*b*) the inability of indigenous firms in Country B to produce a competitive product.

Now examine the opposite extreme. Suppose transport costs are zero and that there are no barriers to production facing firms in either country. Since knowledge is freely and instantaneously transferable, production functions will be the same in both countries. In this situation, input prices will determine relative costs. Suppose these strongly favour Country B. Then in a perfectly competitive situation, it could well be that all production will be concentrated in Country B and that Country B's firms will supply Country A's market through exports. Since production is zero in Country A, it is unlikely there will be any firms in Country A who would wish to invest in Country B, because of the additional risks and costs of operating in a different political and economic environment at a distance from its decision-taking centre (Kindleberger, 1969). It is still possible for firms in Country A to invest in Country B's firms, but the investment would be a portfolio kind.

In between these two extreme cases, there is a host of intermediary situations, each of which will reflect a combination of the ease or difficulty of supplying a particular market with a product (or group of products) from alternative locations, and the ease or difficulty with which firms of different ownership can supply the product (or group of products) from the same location.

Most of the research on international direct investment has been concerned with explaining the second characteristic in terms of monopolistic competitive theory (i.e. firms of different nationality but producing in the same location). They are succinctly summarized by Kindleberger (1969), Caves (1971), and Gray (1972). Expressed in terms of net advantages MNEs or their affiliates possess over indigenous firms, the former are usually considered under four headings:

(i) an easier or cheaper access to knowledge and information;
(ii) an easier or cheaper access to factor inputs;
(iii) a better access to markets or to the saleable characteristics of products e.g. brand names;
(iv) economies of scale and vertical integration.

It will be observed, however, that some of these advantages may be enjoyed by all branch plants, irrespective of the nationality of the investing firm, and are to do with the internal and/or external economies of size (Coase, 1937; Penrose, 1958). Others arise because the affiliate is part of a *foreign* company and a third group because the affiliate is part of an integrated multinational complex of operations.

These advantages, according to the Gray Report on *Foreign Direct Investment in Canada*, confer on the MNE (or its affiliates) an element of distinctiveness which gives them an edge over their competitors (or potential competitors) in *similar locations*. Essentially, they are enterprise-specific, i.e. they are not transferable between firms, and are a function of their character and ownership. The report perceives that some firms and countries tend to possess the type of qualities which spawn distinctive advantages more than others. These include firms in research-intensive industries and those producing differentiated products, while countries with large markets, a competitive environment, a rapid rate of technological innovation, etc., also tend to be more distinctive. Yet small countries may possess distinctive advantages in particular industries or spawn firms with distinctive advantages *within* industries, which explains why trade and investment can be multilateral.

Other economists have also probed into the unique characteristics of MNEs. Johnson (1968), for example, has stressed the importance of the role played by enterprise-specific knowledge; Caves (1971, 1973) adds to this product differentiation; equally important may be the advantages of multinationalism in terms of economies external to the particular production unit but internal to the MNE, particularly in *industries* which are research intensive and afford greatest scope for integration, and in firms which are globally integrated in their operations, including those arising from integration. H. Peter Gray (1972) elaborates on this point, and distinguishes between 'aggressive' and 'defensive' motives for investing abroad. The former seek to increase the economic rent of the investing firm largely by the means just described, and/or by obtaining a higher rate of return on capital than is available domestically. Defensive investments are those which are made to protect some level of profit (or growth rate) attained earlier (Gray, p. 77). These include investments undertaken to preserve a foreign market previously served by exports, and to acquire a safe source of raw materials. Finally, some of the younger economists, e.g. Wolfe (1971), Horst (1972b,1973), Parry (1973), Knickerbocker (1973), extending the earlier work of Edith Penrose (1958, 1968), are interesting themselves in the factors influencing the growth of the multinational firm, the form it takes, and the importance of market structure in influencing both.

Rather less attention has been paid to the way in which firms exploit their distinctive advantages. Where production remains in the hands of the firm with the advantages, this comes back to a question of location theory; but, in some cases, it may be preferable to sub-contract or to license foreign producers, or to engage in some other scheme to maximize the economic rent on distinctiveness (Hymer, 1972b). Though the literature (Kolde *et al.*, 1968) is full of examples of the conditions under which licensing is likely to be preferred to direct investment as a means of exploiting foreign markets, there has been little systematic attempt to formalize these into the theory of marketing.

(b) The Aliber Thesis

Before considering some empirical work on the industrial structure approach, I would like to refer briefly to the currency area approach to international production, which is reflected chiefly in the writings of Aliber (1970,1972). I can deal with it briefly not because I do not think it important, but because I think it can be accommodated into the conceptual scheme of the industrial structure approach: it is also of direct relevance to capital theory.

Of all approaches, Aliber is the one which recognizes some of the specific aspects of foreign investment which are absent from domestic investment. Of these, investment in a different currency area is the most obvious. As I understand it, Aliber is not concerned with explaining investment in the *same* currency area, e.g. UK investment in Australia, but only where the assets are in different currencies. Since the value of any one currency fluctuates over time it immediately follows that in addition to the variables which influence the worthwhileness of an investment in the local currency, its value in relation to other currencies has to be considered. A rate of return of 10 per cent with a currency that devalues by 5 per cent is worth 5 per cent less the depreciated value of the assets in other currencies. When they invest, firms will then capitalize their income streams taking account of these uncertainties. They will also affect the worthwhileness of trade relative to investment (though observe that a devaluing currency will also affect the worthwhileness of trade), but fundamentally, the relationship with their competitors. In other words, the Aliber approach adds to the theory of industrial organization, but I do not think it supplants it.[12]

Surveys have revealed that the value and expected variability of the exchange rate are taken account of by firms in deciding the location of their investment;

neither is there any doubt that short-term movements of resources are strongly influenced by monetary considerations. International companies have been seen to be both at an advantage and a disadvantage in this respect (Manser, 1973).

(c) Recent Empirical Work

As yet there have been few attempts to test systematically the type of hypothesis which the above approach suggests. There has been a good deal of descriptive analysis and casual empiricism, mainly contained in case studies of countries and industries, and some hints from related studies on technology (Gruber, Mehta, and Vernon, 1907; Mansfield, 1973). Primarily, the lack of progress is due to data deficiencies, but also the subject has generally lacked appeal to economists interested in market structure and location theory. However, recent contributions by Parry (1973) on the determinants of foreign investment in Australian industry, and by Horst (1972a) in which he produces a model to explain the ways in which US firms exploit their Canadian and European markets – viz. by exports or direct investment – provide useful starting-points.

Perhaps the most rewarding attempt to pinpoint the special characteristics of MNEs has been that of James Vaupel (1971) in an examination of the 491 largest US companies.[13] Vaupel classifies these companies into three groups, viz. national enterprises (NEs) – i.e. those which manufacture only in the USA; transnational enterprises (TNEs) – i.e. those which manufacture in at least one foreign country but in fewer than six; and multinational enterprises (MNEs) – i.e. those which manufacture in at least six foreign countries. For the year 1964, there were 125 NEs, 194 TNEs, and 172 MNEs. He found that MNEs had certain distinctive characteristics; for example, they funded 2.4 per cent of their sales on research and development (compared with 1.6 per cent for TNEs and 0.6 per cent for NEs); they spent 2.5 per cent on advertising (compared with 1.9 per cent for TNEs and 1.7 for NEs); they earned net profits of 8.9 per cent on invested capital for the period 1960/64 (compared with 7.3 per cent for TNEs and 6.7 per cent for NEs); their average sales were $460m. (compared with $200m. for TNEs and $160m. for NEs); they were more diversified in their product structure;[14] they recorded a higher export/sales ratio (6.4 per cent, cf. 5.5 per cent) and they paid higher annual wages in the USA ($6841 cf. $6774).

From the angle of recipient countries, a number of studies have examined the comparative behaviour of foreign affiliates and indigenous domestic firms in Denmark, Holland, and Israel and found that the former were larger, more capital- and skill-intensive and exported a higher proportion of their total output. By contrast, Cohen's study of foreign and local firms in South Korea, Taiwan, and Singapore (Cohen, 1973) showed that while the foreign affiliates exported more, they also imported more, and had a lower net output per head. Other studies of foreign affiliates in developing countries reveal there is no clear pattern to their capital/labour ratios (*vis-à-vis* indigenous firms) (Strassman, 1968; Pack, 1972; Wells, 1972b) or to their record as wage payers (Katz, 1972). In our own most recent research on US investment in the UK (Dunning, 1976), we attempted to analyse and explain the industrial distribution of the 500 largest US manufacturing affiliates. Tables 1.2 and 1.3 present details of the distribution of sales of US affiliates in 40 sectors of UK industry in 1970/71, their concentration coefficients, and certain supply and marketing characteristics of the industries in question. The concentration coefficient is derived by calculating the percentage of sales of all US affiliates accounted for by a particular industry divided by the percentage of sales of all UK firms accounted for by that industry. A concentration coefficient of more than one shows that US affiliates are rather more concentrated in that industry than for all industry; a concentration coefficient of less than one suggests the reverse:

The five supply features examined in Table 1.2 are:

1. total net capital expenditure per employee (an average of 1963 and 1970 figures), as an index of the use made of non-human capital, i.e. plant and equipment, etc.;
2. the proportion of non-operative to all workers in 1970 as an index of the use made of human skills;
3. the value of research and development expenditure (annual average 1967/69 as a percentage of sales (1968) as an index of technological intensity;
4. the labour productivity of the largest 10 per cent of establishments of 1963 divided by the labour productivity of the other 90 per cent as an index of the extent to which large firms enjoy economies of scale;
5. the proportion of advertising costs to total sales in 1963 as an index of product differentiation.

The three marketing features examined in Table 1.3 are:

1. the growth of output between 1968 and 1970 divided by the growth in GNP as an index of the expenditure elasticity of demand;
2. the export/import ratio in 1967 as an index of the comparative trading advantage of the UK; and
3. the output of the five largest firms in an industry as a proportion of the total output of that industry in 1963, which illustrates the type of market structure in which US affiliates operate.

Tables 1.4 and 1.5 summarize the data contained in these tables. Table 1.4 compares the industrial distribution of US affiliates with that of UK firms as a whole. The value of each characteristic presented in Tables 1.2 and 1.3 is

Table 1.2 Supply characteristics of industrial distribution of US affiliates

	% of total sales of US affiliates[1]	US sales concentration coefficient[2]	1 £	2 %	3 %	4 %	5 %
Food, drink, and tobacco	16.9	0.90	234.8	21.5	0.24	1.12	2.12
Food	8.5	0.77	196.3	19.9	nas	1.00	2.40
Drink	0.3	0.07	396.8	28.6	nas	1.29	2.07
Tobacco	8.1	2.38	249.2	22.5	nas	0.92	1.53
Chemicals	18.6	1.69	666.1	38.7	1.98	1.22	2.52
Mineral oil refining	6.8	3.09	2313.9	32.0	1.37	1.03	1.03
General chemicals (including dyestuffs and pigments)	1.9	0.58	1084.4	38.2	nas	1.02	0.79
Pharmaceutical chemicals and preparations	2.7	3.00	445.5	43.9	} 3.54	1.24	7.96
Toilet preparations	0.6	2.00	172.5	40.6		1.02	16.39
Soap and detergents	1.5	2.50	377.8	45.1	nas	1.10	6.65
Synthetic resins and plastics	2.9	2.64	789.1	37.4	2.73	1.03	1.14
Other chemicals	2.2	0.88	226.5	36.9	nas	0.99	1.37
Metal manufacture	4.3	0.46	300.5	23.5	0.25	1.10	0.17
Non-electrical engineering	16.0	1.57	128.4	31.9	1.33	nas	0.63
Agricultural machinery	0.7	3.50	174.3	42.9	1.14	1.12	nas
Machine tools	1.0	1.43	104.9	31.2	0.57	1.02	nas
Pumps, valves, compressors	0.7	0.88	153.6[3]	35.5	na	1.00	nas
Construction and earth-moving equipment	2.9	4.83	218.8	35.1	} 0.67	0.77	nas
Medical handling equipment	0.5	0.71	88.5	34.5		1.08	nas
Office machinery	2.1	7.00	149.4	32.9	nas	0.98	nas

Table 1.2 *continued*

	% of total sales of US affiliates[1]	US sales concentration coefficient[2]	1 £	2 %	3 %	4 %	5 %
Non-electrical engineering *continued*							
Other machinery	3.7	1.19	137.4[3]	32.9	nas	1.01	nas
Industrial (including process) plant and steel work	3.0	1.58	82.2	34.6	1.05	1.14	nas
Other non-electrical engineering	1.0	0.59	170.2	25.2	nas	1.00	nas
Instrument engineering	4.8	3.43	105.3	36.1	3.03	nas	1.70
Photographic and document copying equipment	1.5	7.50	169.2	38.9	nas		nas
Scientific and industrial instruments and systems	3.2	3.56	116.2	41.0	nas	1.10	nas
Other instrument engineering	0.1	0.33	180.5	21.1	nas	0.92	nas
Electrical engineering	8.5	1.09	117.3	33.0	5.23	nas	1.48
Electrical machinery	–	0.02	71.2	34.9	2.81	0.94	0.75
Electronic computers	2.1	5.25	381.6[3]	50.9	} 13.3 (both rows)	nas	} 1.12 (both rows)
Other electronic apparatus (inc. telecommunications equipment	4.2	1.35	136.6[3]	35.4		1.00	
Domestic electrical appliances	1.5	2.14	113.2	30.6	0.93	0.99	5.07
Other electrical goods	0.7	0.30	150.0	25.2	1.16	1.15	1.27
Vehicles	21.3	2.09	188.2	29.6	na	1.16	0.48
Motor vehicle manufacturing	21.2	2.90	249.1	22.5	1.58	1.28	0.53
Other products	0.1	0.03	98.9	40.9	nas	1.00	0.35
Metal goods not elsewhere specified	1.8	0.32	132.4	23.1	0.31	1.09	0.64

Textiles and clothing	1.5	0.17	113.0	15.5	0.32	1.20	0.69
Man-made fibres	0.9	1.13	597.4	23.1	nas	1.16	1.47
Other products	0.6	0.08	92.5	15.2	nas	1.06	0.63
Bricks, pottery, glass, cement, etc.	1.1	0.39	243.6	21.9	0.85	1.07	0.71
Abrasives	0.4	4.00	191.0	35.2	nas	1.17	0.91
Other goods	0.7	0.26	245.2	21.4	nas	1.08	0.57
Paper, printing and publishing	1.5	0.25	173.0	29.8	0.23	1.29	1.02
Paper and board	1.1	0.35	251.2	23.0	nas	1.25	0.63
Printing and publishing	0.5	0.15	120.9	34.4	nas	1.32	1.36
Other manufacturing industries	3.7	0.47	120.2	21.9	0.53	1.16	1.10
Rubber	2.4	1.71	211.6	25.9	1.00	1.20	1.27
Other products	1.3	0.20	106.3	21.2	0.35	1.13	1.05
Total manufacturing	100%	–	191.0	26.2	1.08[4]	1.20	1.18

[1] From EAG survey.
[2] Reference in text.
[3] 1970 only.
[4] Excludes aerospace.

Measures:
1. Total net capital expenditure per employee (£); 1963 and 1970 average. Sources: *Census of Production 1963*, and *Provisional Results of Census of Production 1970*.
2. Proportion of non-operatives (administrative, technical, and clerical employees) to all workers, 1970 (%). Source: *Provisional Results of Census of Production 1970*.
3. R & D expenditure as a % of sales 1967/69. Source: *Annual Abstract of Statistics: Census of Production*.
4. The labour productivity of the largest 10 per cent of establishments in 1963 divided by the labour productivity of the other 90 per cent as an index of the economies of large scale production. Source: *Census of Production 1963*.
5. The proportion of advertising costs to total sales in 1963 as an index of product differentiation. Source: *Census of Production 1963*.

na = not available, nas = not available separately.

Table 1.3 Marketing characteristics of industrial distribution of US affiliates

	% of total sales of US affiliates	US sales concentration coefficient	1	2	3
Food, drink and tobacco	16.9	0.90	0.95	0.27	85.72
Food	8.5	0.77	1.02	0.12	80.25
Drink	0.3	0.07	1.00	1.89	69.25
Tobacco	8.1	2.38	0.75	0.26	99.52
Chemicals	18.6	1.69	1.03	0.86	77.82
Mineral oil refining	6.8	3.09	1.25	0.34	99.55
General chemicals (including dyestuffs and pigments)	1.9	0.58	0.86	1.19	71.38
Pharmaceutical chemicals and preparations	2.7	3.00	1.38	} 6.08	29.20
Toilet preparations	0.6	2.00	1.52		46.72
Soap and detergents	1.5	2.50	1.02	nas	83.34
Synthetic resins and plastics	2.9	2.64	1.71	1.34	72.61
Other chemicals	2.2	0.88	0.85	0.55	62.58
Metal manufacture	4.3	0.46	0.88	0.81	69.89
Non-electrical engineering	16.0	1.57	1.09	2.01	55.77
Agricultural machinery	0.7	3.50	0.94	2.02	45.90
Machine tools	1.0	1.43	1.20	0.80	25.00
Pumps, valves, compressors	0.7	0.88	nas	nas	22.00
Construction and earth-moving equipment	2.9	4.83	1.81	2.22	57.69
Mechanical handling equipment	0.5	0.71	1.61	1.52	48.87
Office machinery	2.1	7.00	1.49	1.52	na

Table 1.3 continued

Other machinery	3.7	1.19	nas	2.33	56.59
Industrial (including process) plant and steel work	3.0	1.58	nas	3.55	50.99
Other non-electrical engineering	1.0	0.59	nas	2.39	78.03
Instrument engineering	4.8	3.43	1.60	1.07	57.34
Photographic and document copying equipment	1.5	7.50	nas	nas	49.17
Scientific and industrial instruments and systems	3.2	3.56	nas	nas	
Other instrument engineering	0.1	0.33	nas	nas	80.81
Electrical engineering	8.5	1.09	1.33	1.55	71.84
Electrical machinery	–	0.02	0.57	3.72	55.20
Electronic computers	2.1	5.25	1.82	1.04	81.90[1]
Other electronic apparatus (inc. telecommunications equipment)	4.2	1.35			77.31
Domestic electrical appliances	1.5	2.14	1.39	1.77	88.26
Other electrical goods	0.7	0.30	1.37	2.35	73.19
Vehicles	21.3	2.09	0.99	3.93	89.60
Motor vehicle manufacturing	21.2	2.90	1.18	7.42	88.52
Other products	0.1	0.03	0.72	1.70	95.23
Metal goods not elsewhere specified	1.8	0.32	1.08	1.21	66.02
Textiles and clothing	1.5	0.17	0.71	0.84	50.47
Man-made fibres	0.9	1.13	1.51	2.03	100.00
Other products	0.6	0.08	0.67	0.80	38.40
Bricks, pottery, glass, cement, etc.	1.1	0.39	1.04	2.13	69.20
Abrasives	0.4	4.00	1.17	1.49	65.53
Other goods	0.7	0.26	1.04	2.33	70.42

Table 1.3 continued

Paper, printing and publishing	1.6	0.25	1.10	0.34	54.55
Paper and board	1.1	0.35	1.11	0.18	55.98
Printing and publishing	0.5	0.15	1.09	1.79	33.90
Other manufacturing industries	3.7	0.47	1.00	0.56	65.45
Rubber	2.4	1.71	1.10	2.79	89.61
Other products	1.3	0.20	0.98	0.46	50.89
Total manufacturing	100.0	–	0.99	0.99	–

[1] Four firm ratio for 1968.

Measures:
1. The growth of output between 1958 and 1970 divided by the growth of GNP, as an index of the expenditure elasticity of demand. Sources: *Censuses of Production; National Income and Expenditure*.
2. Export/import ratio in 1967 as an index of the comparative trading advantage of the UK. Source: Special tabulations prepared by DTI.
3. Five firm concentration ratios in 1963, which illustrate the type of market structure in which US firms operate. Source: *Census of Production 1963*.

weighted by the distribution of, first, UK firms, and second, US affiliates, and then averaged to give the figure set out in Table 1.4.

The conclusions of this exercise are self-evident. US affiliates tend to be more concentrated in faster-growing and export-oriented industries. They are also attracted to the technologically advanced industries, and to those where both capital and advertising expenditure is slightly above average: these are also the industries in which the barriers to entry facing indigenous firms are likely to be higher than those facing US affiliates. There is, however, no evidence to suggest that their share of industries which benefit from the economies of scale is greater than that of UK companies, and their market structure is only slightly more oligopolistic.

Table 1.5 classifies these same characteristics by four groups of US affiliates. Group 1 consists of the ten affiliates with the highest concentration ratios (from 7.50 to 2.90); Group 2 of the 11 affiliates with the next highest concentration ratios (from 2.38 to 1.19); and Groups 3 and 4 of the 18 firms with concentration ratios of below 1. The results of this exercise confirm the general pattern already stated.

What, next, of an explanation for the structure of US participation in UK industry? Two propositions might be tested. First, that US firms will produce

Table 1.4 Summary of characteristics of all UK firms and US affiliates

	Average figures	
	UK firms	US affiliates
Supply characteristics		
1. Net capital expenditure per employee	£191.0	£221.2[1]
2. Non operatives/total workers	26.2%	30.3%[1]
3. R & D expenditure as a % of sales	1.08	1.60[1]
4. Economies of scale	1.09[2]	1.09[2]
5. Advertising expenditure as a % of sales	1.18	1.33[1]
Marketing characteristics		
1. Output growth/GNP growth	1.02[2]	1.14[2]
2. Exports/imports ratio	1.23[2]	1.66[2]
3. Concentration ratio	70.9[2]	74.7[2]

[1] Values of characteristics from Table 1.2 weighted by distribution of US sales/employment.
[2] Values of characteristics from Tables 1.2 and 1.3 weighted by distribution of UK and US sales respectively.

Source: Tables 1.2 and 1.3.

Table 1.5 Classification of supply and marketing characteristics of US affiliates by concentration coefficient

	Supply characteristics[1]					Marketing characteristics[2]		
	1	2	3	4	5	1	2	3
	£	%	%					
Group 1 (10 industries)								
US sales concentration coefficient 7.50 to 2.90	440.9	37.5		1.09[4]	2.42[5]	1.35[4]	2.30[7]	54.41[4]
Group 2 (11 industries)			2.75[3] (Groups 1 and 2)					
US sales concentration coefficient 2.64 to 1.13	270.0	32.7		1.05	4.27[4]	1.28[4]	1.90[4]	71.81
Group 3 (9 industries)								
US sales concentration coefficient 0.88 to 0.33	294.4	28.6		1.04	1.07[5]	1.06[6]	0.97[7]	63.30
Group 4 (9 industries)			0.71[4] (Groups 3 and 4)					
US sales concentration coefficient 0.32 to 0.02	157.1	27.2		1.12	0.96	0.95[4]	1.80	61.37

1 For definitions of supply characteristics see Table 1.2.
2 For definitions of marketing characteristics see Table 1.3.
3 11 industries only.
4 8 industries only.
5 5 industries only.
6 6 industries only.
7 7 industries only.

Source: Tables 1.2 and 1.3.

most in the UK in those industries where both the growth and/or profit potential is favourable relative to that of exploiting foreign markets by other means, e.g. exports. The second is that US firms will invest in those industries where the comparative advantage of the US firms is greatest *vis-à-vis* that of UK firms.

While data limitations preclude any systematic testing of these hypotheses, certain pointers may be obtained by looking again at some of the statistics contained in Tables 1.1, 1.2, and 1.3 and also some additional figures set out in Tables 1.6 and 1.7.

Index (1) in Tables 1.6 and 1.7 for example, expresses the sales of US affiliates in the UK as a ratio of UK imports from the USA. This shows very clearly that this ratio is highest in those sectors where the U.S. concentration coefficient is the highest. Index (2) presents details of the UK nominal tariff on the imports of various goods; there appears to be no obvious relationship between the size of the tariff and either the US concentration coefficient or the previous index. (An exercise by Horst, 1972, which used estimates of effective rates of protection came to broadly similar conclusions.) Index (3) gives details of the total productivity of US affiliates and suggests that the affiliates do tend to concentrate where this is highest, and the remaining three indices ((4) to (6)) present data which are intended to be surrogates for barriers to entry into particular industries. Here, the proposition is that these are likely to be the greatest in those industries where the content of productive knowledge is important, or where the costs of entry are high, or where product differentiation is most marked. The data in Table 1.4, which summarize our conclusions, lend some corroboration to this hypothesis.

The data analysed hint of some *raison d'être* to the structure of US participation in UK industry, but it does little more than this. There are various reasons for this, but perhaps the main ones are (i) that the industrial classification is not fine enough for us to be able to say much about the relationship between investment and exports as a means of exploiting a market, (ii) other locational variables, noticeably transport and labour costs, are ignored, and (iii) sales are not always a good guide to the value added by the firms.

The first problem is particularly acute where firms are multi-product and investment and exports may complement as well as substitute for each other. This suggests that international production only recognizes products produced by the investing company in local markets; moreover, parts and components might be required. The evidence on the relationship between exports and foreign investment at a macro-level is inconclusive (Hufbauer and Adler, 1968; Reddaway, 1968), however much at a micro-level clearly they may substitute for each other.

Such relationships become rather more complex when the activities of MNEs become *industrially* and *regionally* integrated. Taking the latter point first, a

Table 1.6 Indices of comparative advantage of US affiliates in UK

	% of total sales of US affiliates	US sales concentration coefficient	1	2 %	3	4 £	5 %	6 %
Food, drink, and tobacco	16.9	0.90	39.6	na	1.38	234.8	0.24	2.12
Food	8.5	0.77	21.6	na	1.38	196.2	nas	2.40
Drink	0.3	0.07	28.8	na	0.93	396.8	nas	2.07
Tobacco	8.1	2.38	342.4	na	1.41	249.2	nas	1.53
Chemicals	18.6	1.69	9.4	15.6	1.34	666.1	1.98	2.52
Mineral oil refining	6.8	3.09	44.4	na	na	2313.9	1.37	1.03
General chemicals (including dyestuffs and pigments)	1.9	0.58	2.4	18.5	1.61	1084.4	nas	0.79
Pharmaceutical chemicals and preparations	2.7	3.00	28.5	15.3	1.39	445.5	3.54	7.96
Toilet preparations	0.6	2.00	23.2	17.3	1.46	172.5		16.38
Soap and detergents	1.5	2.50		12.2	1.61	377.8	nas	6.65
Synthetic resins and plastics	2.9	2.64	5.7	17.7	1.39	789.1	2.73	1.14
Other chemicals	2.2	0.88	6.1	12.7	1.74	226.5	nas	1.37
Metal manufacture	4.3	0.46	3.0	10.4	1.06	300.5	0.25	0.17
Non-electrical engineering	16.0	1.57	3.8	16.0	1.24	128.4	1.33	0.63
Agricultural machinery	0.7	3.50	12.9	14.0	0.74	174.3	1.14	nas
Machine tools	1.0	1.43	5.4	16.8	1.18	104.9	0.57	nas
Pumps, valves, compressors	0.7	0.88	3.1	16.2	1.54	153.6	na	nas
Construction and earth-moving equipment	2.9	4.83	7.4	15.5	1.55	218.8	0.67	nas
Mechanical handling equipment	0.5	0.71	4.3	15.5	1.05	88.5		nas
Office machinery	2.1	7.00	2.2[1]	15.4	1.35	149.4	nas	nas
Other machinery	3.7	1.19	nas	14.7	1.21	137.4	nas	nas
Industrial (including process) plant and steel work	3.0	1.58	nas	17.5	1.10	82.2	1.05	nas
Other non-electrical engineering	1.0	0.59	nas	18.0	1.20	170.2	nas	nas
Instrument engineering	4.8	3.43	6.2	27.5	1.33	105.3	3.03	1.70
Photographic and document copying equipment	1.5	7.50	nas	22.9	1.86	169.2	nas	nas
Scientific and industrial instruments and systems	3.2	3.56	nas	32.0	1.18	116.2	nas	nas
Other instrument engineering	0.1	0.33	nas	27.5	1.20	180.5	nas	nas

Electrical engineering	8.5	1.09	3.3	17.2	1.48	117.3	5.23	1.48
Electrical machinery	–	0.02	nas	18.9	1.80	71.2	2.81	0.75
Electronic computers	2.1	5.25	–	na	2.35	381.5	13.3	1.12
Other electronic apparatus (inc. telecommunications equipment)	4.2	1.35	nas	20.1	1.19	136.6		
Domestic electrical appliances	1.5	2.14	59.9	14.5	1.36	113.2	0.93	5.07
Other electrical goods	0.7	0.30	nas	16.9	1.53	150.0	1.16	1.27
Vehicles	21.3	2.09	15.2	19.3	1.12	185.2	na	0.48
Motor vehicles manufacturing	21.2	2.90	97.6	21.1	1.12	249.1	1.58	0.53
Other products	0.1	0.03	0.1	18.8	1.04	98.9	nas	0.35
Metal goods not elsewhere specified	1.8	0.32	5.3	18.0	1.26	132.4	0.31	0.64
Textiles and clothing	1.5	0.17	4.0	18.5	1.63	113.0	0.32	0.69
Man-made fibres	0.9	1.13	nas	16.0	1.63	597.4	nas	1.47
Other products	0.6	0.08	nas	20.9	1.62	92.5	nas	0.63
Bricks, pottery, glass, cement, etc.	1.1	0.39	6.5	18.0	1.23	243.6	0.85	0.71
Abrasives	0.4	4.00	nas	18.5	1.31	191.0	nas	0.91
Other goods	0.7	0.26	nas	17.5	1.19	245.2	nas	0.57
Paper, printing, and publishing	1.6	0.25	2.7	na	1.10	173.0	0.23	1.02
Paper and board	1.1	0.35	3.0	17.2	1.10	251.2	nas	0.63
Printing and publishing	0.5	0.15	2.2	na	1.11	120.9	nas	1.36
Other manufacturing industries	3.7	0.47	9.7	20.7	1.41	120.2	0.53	1.10
Rubber	2.4	1.71	18.4	23.0	1.34	211.6	1.00	1.27
Other products	1.3	0.20	5.2	18.5	1.56	106.3	0.35	1.05
	100.0	–	6.9	–	1.26	191.0	1.08	1.18

[1] Electronic computers including office machinery.

Indices:

1. Sales of US affiliates in UK divided by imports into UK from USA. *Sources*: EAG Survey (sales); OECD, Commodity Trade Statistics (imports)
2. Nominal tariff (unweighted average for components of group) derived from S.S. Hen and H.H. Liesner, *Britain and the Common Market*, Cambridge University Press, 1971.
3. Total productivity of US affiliates.
4. As measure 1, Table 1.2.
5. As measure 3, Table 1.2.
6. As measure 5, Table 1.2.

na = not available. nas = not available separately.

company may replace exports to half a dozen European countries by setting up a plant in one of these and supplying the entire market from there. In this case, the production implications for the country in which the plant is located will be much greater than the replacement of imports might suggest, while, in other countries, European imports will replace US imports.

As to *industrial* integration, this will take the pattern mentioned earlier of *horizontal* or *vertical* specialization of products or processes. In our earlier example, if the firm owned by Country A manufactured two drugs it might decide to concentrate the production of one in Country A and supply both countries from that plant, and concentrate the production of the other in Country B and supply both markets from there. Or it may engage in first-stage production in a plant in Country A, export the semi-processed good to Country B, have it made up there and then sold in both countries. In this case there is intra-group trading as well as two-way investment. Seeking to explain the determinants of international production then becomes extremely complex, although basically it is an exercise in the theory of the growth of the firm (Penrose, 1958; Horst, 1973), and, as we have said, the fact that an affiliate of a foreign firm may possess net advantage over local producers may lie in the nature of branch plant economies, and enterprise-specific integration. An indigenous competitive firm, for example, might have to engage in setting-up costs already incurred elsewhere in the firm's organization.

The desire to achieve the economies of industrial or regional integration is, of course, less an explanation of the *initial* decision of an enterprise to set up a foreign production unit as a strategy that an established company might pursue. Many American firms already operating in different parts of Western Europe are now rationalizing their production programmes in such a way that is likely to have important locational repercussions, and will almost certainly increase the volume of intra-group trade between the individual European affiliates. But again, here, no new principles of growth are involved.

(d) Lines for Further Research

One conclusion which follows from the previous paragraphs is that the question 'why international production?' is now less interesting than 'why the present rate of growth in international production?' or 'why the particular geographical or industrial pattern of international production?' and that future research should be focused on the dynamics of multinational enterprises and comparative studies. On the first point, various explanations might be adduced both of the increasing role of such institutions in the world economy and their changing character. One of these is simply that they tend to be concentrated in the new industries, which are growing faster than the average in the world economy. The second is that MNEs seem to be more profitable and grow faster than indigenous firms (Dunning and Pearce, 1971), which enables them to acquire the necessary resources for additional growth. The third is that as the firms increase in size and become more established, the chances of competitors breaking into the market are less. The fourth is that as they grow, the companies often enhance their competitive advantages, sometimes by tightening up on control of market, sometimes increasing integration and so on.

Table 1.7 Classification of comparative advantage characteristics of US affiliates by sales concentration coefficient

	1	2 %	3	4 £	5 %	6 %
Group 1 (10 industries)						
US concentration coefficient 7.5 to 2.90	28.5[1]	19.3[5]	1.43[5]	440.9	2.75[6] (Groups 1–2)	2.42[7]
Group 2 (11 industries)						
US concentration coefficient 2.64 to 1.13	19.3[2]	16.9	1.49	270.0		4.27[3]
Group 3 (9 industries)						
US concentration coefficient 0.88 to 0.33	6.3[3]	17.0[3]	1.32	294.4	0.71[3] (Groups 3–4)	1.07[7]
Group 4 (9 industries)						
US concentration coefficient 0.30 to 0.02	7.6[4]	18.5[1]	1.34	157.1		0.96

1 Seven industries only.
2 Excludes tobacco: six industries only.
3 Eight industries only.
4 Six industries only.
5 Eight industries only.
6 Eleven industries only.
7 Five industries only.

Source: Table 1.6.

All of these are symptomatic of broad trends in industrial structure. One of these is the general increase in industrial concentration within particular countries although not for the world as a whole. The proportion of motor cars, petrol, rubber tyres, pharmaceuticals, etc., produced by (say) the five largest companies in the world has fallen in recent years – largely due to the resurgence in Japanese and European competition (Rowthorn, 1969). There is nothing inevitable about this trend of growth of MNEs. Anything which reduces the barriers to competition on which these companies thrive may reduce their share of output. The end of a patent could mean that a foreign affiliate is no longer protected from indigenous firms, and loses its competitive edge; this has happened in the UK pharmaceutical industry (Cooper and Culyer, 1973). Or a new product might replace an old one which can be more easily produced by competitive companies; the decline of the share of US affiliates in the foundation garment industry is an illustration here. There is a substantial learning process associated with competition engendered by international companies; the declining share of the main US affiliate in the razor blade industry is a case in point, though, as often as not, competition comes from other international companies.

The second line of research which needs pursuing is a more systematic analysis of the distinctiveness of MNEs and alternative forms of market penetration, by country and industry.[15] Why is it, for example, that although the UK and USA account for 35 per cent of world exports, they are responsible for 70 per cent of the world's investment income in 1968? Why is the broad industrial pattern of the Japanese MNEs different from that of their US and European counterparts? (United Nations, 1971). Why do the sales of foreign affiliates/export ratios of countries differ enormously, being, for example, high for the USA, Switzerland, Sweden, and Holland and low in Japan, France, and Italy?; and of industries within countries, e.g. cf. motor vehicles and computers with industrial instruments and cotton textiles? Various possible explanations come to mind. One is to do with the structure of a country's comparative advantage. Where this is in goods which can be easily tradable or can be easily assimilated abroad, the percentage might be less. Another may have to do with structure of markets; dispersed markets may make foreign production uneconomical while more concentrated markets would not do so. A third is to do with the different organizational patterns of MNEs of different nationality (Stopford, 1973; Franko, 1972); and a fourth with the attitudes and policies of both exporting countries to exports relative to outward investment, and importing countries to imports relative to inward investment. This, in turn, will be related to balance of payments questions. If the dollar is in short supply but the yen is plentiful, then under a fixed exchange rate, tariffs might be placed on dollar goods which might encourage defensive investment, while Japanese firms can export freely. Methods of restricting capital outflows also vary between countries (Cairncross, 1973).

A fourth reason concerns economic conditions in investing or exporting countries. Firms do not usually look overseas for markets if ones nearer home can be satisfied. And generally they prefer exports to foreign production. The more profitable the opportunities for growth at home, the less foreign markets will be vigorously pursued. I believe the lack of German and Japanese foreign investment for a long time since the Second World War can be largely explained in terms of the rapid internal growth of the two economies, and the fact that the undervaluation of their currencies favoured the exploitation of foreign markets by exports rather than by outward direct investment. Now these conditions no longer hold, there are signs that both countries are becoming important foreign investors. But the extent to which firms face demand pressures in domestic or foreign markets which can be met without production overseas will influence their levels of foreign activities.

Lastly, government policy is vitally important. This may be exerted in various ways, both by direct controls (Herring and Willett, 1972) and affecting the value of the variables which influence decision-taking by firms to invest overseas. This is very relevant to the question 'how much international production?' but can also influence 'why international production?'. There are many obvious examples of government affecting the behaviour of international companies and it seems likely that the role will become even more important in the future.

NOTES

1. For example, according to the US Department of Commerce, in 1966, 95 per cent of the earnings and 93 per cent of the net capital flows of US foreign affiliates were accounted for by affiliates in which there was a 51 per cent or more US equity stake. Similarly, in 1965, 91 per cent of all UK direct investment, outside oil, banking, and insurance, was 51 per cent or more UK financed.
2. The work of Judd Polk deserves mention in this context. He defines (US) production abroad as 'production in which U.S. management and financing work together with foreign factors of production' (Polk, 1971, p. 9); or, even more succinctly, 'product emanating from foreign investment' or the 'product profits of an investment activity abroad'. His estimate of the value of this component of world production in 1969 was $450 million, or 15 per cent of gross world product, and that since 1950 this has been increasing at a steady rate of 10 per cent per year (Polk, 1971, pp. 5 and 8).
3. Usually in the *Survey of Current Business* or in special supplements to this periodical.
4. For a comprehensive analysis of foreign direct investment in Asia and the Far East see United Nations (1971).
5. See particularly those mentioned in Table 1.1, pp. 8–9, May and Arena (1971), FIEL (1971), and United Nations (1971).
6. For an interesting examination of the reasons for establishing foreign manufacturing plants by US firms prior to 1900, see Vernon (1972) (Table 3.5. pp. 72–3) and Wilkins (1970).
7. For a survey of some of the recent literature, see Stevens (1973).
8. For an analysis of the determinants of foreign direct investment in the US see Daniels (1972).
9. Compare the significance of the tariff variable with that suggested by individual industry studies.
10. Where, for example, the exchange rate of the exporting country is overvalued, outward investment will be favoured relative to exports; where the exchange rate of the importing country is overvalued, inward investment will be favoured relative to imports. Some commentators have argued that the rapid increase in the level of US foreign investment in the 1960s largely reflected the overvaluation of the dollar.
11. Location theory also links with the theory of the growth of the firm. Firms expand either by selling more of the same product to existing markets, or by diversifying their products, processes, or markets. The territorial spread of production across national boundaries partly arises from a similar diversification of markets; but it may also be linked to the new oppor-

tunities for spatial specialization arising from the diversified product or process (or even functional) structure of firms.

12. Important to these discussions is *the numéraire* in which the MNE keeps its accounts. Moreover, one needs to distinguish between the change in parities due to shifts in the terms of trade needed for balanced payments, and those due to differential rates of inflation. I am indebted to H. Peter Gray for reminding me of this distinction.
13. As listed by *Fortune*.
14. The measure chosen here was the number of 2, 3, and 5 digit industries in which they operated: the results were MNEs 5, 10, and 22; TNEs 4, 7, and 16; and NEs 2, 3, and 8.
15. The work now being undertaken by Raymond Vernon and his colleagues on European and Japanese MNEs should prove particularly illuminating in this respect. See also Hellman (1970).

REFERENCES

Aharoni, Y. (1966), *The Foreign Investment Decision*, Harvard University Press.

Aharoni, Y. (1971), 'The definition of a multinational corporation', *Quarterly Review of Economics and Business*, Autumn.

Aliber, R.Z. (1970), 'A theory of direct investment', in C.P. Kindleberger (ed.), *The International Corporation*, MIT Press.

Aliber, R.Z. (1971), 'The multinational enterprise in a multiple currency world', in J.H. Dunning (ed.), *The Multinational Enterprise*, London, Allen and Unwin.

Andrews, M. (1972), *American Investment in Irish Industry*, Senior Honours thesis, Harvard University.

Balassa, B. (1967), *Trade Liberalisation Among Industrial Countries*, McGraw-Hill.

Baldwin, R. (1970), 'International trade in inputs and outputs', *American Economic Review*, vol. 60.

Bandera, V.N., and White, J.J. (1968), 'US direct investment and domestic markets in Europe', *Economica International*, vol. 21.

Barlow, E.R. and Wender, I.T. (1955), *Foreign Investment and Taxation*, Prentice Hall.

Basi, R.S. (1966), *Determinants of US Direct Investment in Foreign Countries*, Kent University Press.

Behrman, J. (1962), 'Foreign associates and their financing', in R. Mikesell (ed.), *US Private and Government Investment Abroad*, Oregon University Press.

Behrman, J. (1969), *Some Patterns in the Rise of the Multinational Enterprise*, University of Carolina research paper.

Borts, G.H. and Kopecky, K.J. (1972), 'Capital movements and economic growth in developed countries', in F. Machlup, W. Salant and L. Tarshis (eds), *International Mobility and Movement of Capital*, National Bureau of Economic Research.

Branson, W.H. (1970), 'Monetary policy and the new view of international capital movements', *Brookings Papers on Economic Activity*, No. 2.

Branson, W.H. and Hill, R. D. (1971), *Capital Movements in the OECD Area: an Economic Analysis*, OECD.

Brash, D. (1966), *American Investment in Australian Industry*, Australian National University Press.

Brooke, M.Z. and Remmers, H.L. (1970), *The Strategy of Multinational Enterprise*, Longmans.

Bruck, N.A. and Lees, F.A. (1966), 'Foreign content of US corporate activities', *Financial Analysts Journal*, vol. 22, Sept/Oct.

Bruno, M. (1970), 'Development policy and dynamic comparative advantage', in R. Vernon (ed.), *The Technology Factor in International Trade*, Columbia University Press.

Cairncross, A.K. (1973), *Control over International Capital Movements*, The Brookings Institution.

Caves, R. (1971), 'International corporations: the industrial economics of foreign investment', *Economica*, vol. 38.

Caves, R. (forthcoming), 'The multinational enterprise and industrial structure', in J.H. Dunning (ed.), *Economic Analysis and the Multinational Enterprise*, London, Allen and Unwin.

Caves, R, and Reuber, G.L. (1971), *Capital Transfers & Economic Policy, Canada, 1957/62*, Harvard University Press.

Clark, C., Wilson, F. and Bradley, J. (1969), 'Industrial location and economic potential in Western Europe', *Regional Studies*, vol. 3.

Coase, R.H. (1937), 'The nature of the firm', *Economica*, n.s. vol. 4.

Cohen, Benjamin I. (1972), 'Foreign investment by US corporations as a way of reducing risk', Economic Growth Centre Discussion Paper No. 151, Yale University.

Cohen, Benjamin I. (1973), 'The role of the multinational in the exports of manufactures from developing countries', Economic Growth Centre Discussion Paper No. 177, Yale University.

Cooper, M. and Culyer, A. (1973), *The Pharmaceutical Industry*, EAG/Dun and Bradstreet Industry Profile No. 2.

Daniels, J.D. (1972), *Recent Foreign Direct Manufacturing Investment in the United States*, Praeger.

d'Arge, R. (1969), 'Notes on customs unions and foreign direct investment', *Economic Journal*, vol. 74.

Deane, R.S. (1970), *Foreign Investment in New Zealand manufacturing*, Sweet and Maxwell.

Dunning, J.H. (1970), *Studies in international investment*, London, Allen and Unwin, Chapters 3 and 5.

Dunning, J.H. (1971), *The Multinational Enterprise*, London, Allen and Unwin.

Dunning, J.H. (1972), *The Location of International Firms in an Enlarged EEC*, Manchester Statistical Society.

Dunning, J.H. (1973), *United States Industry in Britain*, an EAG Business Research Study, Financial Times.

Dunning, J.H. and Pearce, R.D. (1971), 'The world's largest companies: a statistical profile', *Business Ratios*, vol. 3.

Falise, M. and Lepas, A. (1970), 'Les Motivations de localisation des investissements internationaux dans l'Europe du Nord-Ouest', *Revue Economique*, No. 1.

Floyd, J.E. (1969), 'International capital movements and monetary equilibrium', *American Economic Review*, vol. 59.

Forsyth, D.J.C. (1972), *US Investment in Scotland*, Praeger Special Studies in International Economics and Development.

Franko, L.G. (1972), *Organisational Change in European Enterprise*, Centre for Education and International Management.

Fundación do Investigacionos Económicas Latin American (FIEL) (1971), 'Las inversiones extranjeras en la Argentina'.

Goldberg, M.A. (1972), 'The determinants of US direct investment in the EEC: comment', *American Economic Review*, vol. 62.

Giersch, H. (1950), Economic union between nations and the location of industries', *Review of Economic Studies*, vol. xvii(2).
Gray, H.P. (1972), *The Economics of Business Investment Abroad*, Macmillan.
Greenhut, M. (1952), 'The size and shape of the market area of the firm', *Southern Economic Journal*, July.
Grubel, H. (1968), 'Internationally diversified portfolios: welfare gains and capital flows', *American Economic Review*, vol. 58.
Gruber, W., Mehta, D. and Vernon, R. (1967), 'The research and development factor in investment of US industries', *Journal of Political Economy*, vol. 76.
Hakam, A.N. (1966), 'The motivation to invest and the locational pattern of foreign private industrial investments in Nigeria', *Nigerian Journal of Economic and Social Studies*, vol. 8, Mar.
Harman, A.J. (1971), *The international computer industry: innovation and comparative advantage*, Harvard University Press.
Heckerman, D.G. (1969), *The Exchange Risks of Foreign Operations*, Graduate School of Chicago (mimeo).
Hellman, R. (1970), *The Challenge to US Dominance of the International Corporation*, Dunellen.
Herring, R. and Willett, T.D. (1972), 'The capital control program and US investment activity abroad', *Southern Economic Journal*, July.
Herring, R. and Willett, T.D. (1973), 'The relationship between US direct investment at home and abroad', *Rivista Internazionale di Scienze Economiche e Commerciali*, Anno XX.
Hirsch, S. (1967), *Location of Industry and International Competitiveness*, Oxford University Press.
Hirsch, S. (1973), 'Multinational corporations: how different are they?' in G. Bertin (ed.), *The Growth of the Large Multinational Enterprise*, Rennes.
Hogan, W. (1968), *Foreign Investments and Capital Inflows*, The English, Scottish & Australian Bank Ltd., Research Lecture.
Horst, T. (1972a), 'The industrial composition of US exports and subsidiary sales to the Canadian market', *American Economic Review*, vol. 62.
Horst, T. (1972b), 'Firm and industry determinants of the decision to invest abroad: an empirical study', *Review of Economics and Statistics*, vol. 14.
Horst, T. (1974), 'The multinational enterprise and the theory of the firm', in J.H. Dunning (ed.), *Economic Analysis and the Multinational Enterprise*, London, Allen and Unwin.
Hufbauer, G.C. (1966), *Synthetic Materials and the Theory of International Trade*, Duckworth.
Hufbauer, G.C. and Adler, M. (1968), *Overseas Manufacturing Investment and the Balance of Payments*, US Treasury Department.
Hufbauer, G.C. and Adler, M. (1971), 'The impact of national characteristics and technology on the commodity composition of trade in manufactured goods', in R. Vernon (ed.), *The Technology Factor in International Trade*, Columbia University Press.
Hymer, S. (1960), 'The International Operations of National Firms: a Study in Direct Investment'. Unpublished doctoral dissertation, MIT.
Hymer, S. (1970), 'The multinational corporation find the law of uneven development', in J.N. Bhagwati (ed.), *Economics and the World Order*, World Law Fund.
Hymer, S. (1972a), 'The internationalization of capital', *Journal of Economic Issues*, Mar.

Hymer, S. (1972b), 'United States investment abroad', in Peter Drysdale (ed.), 'Direct foreign investment in Asia and the Pacific', *Australian National Pacific*.

Johns, B.L. (1967), 'Private overseas investment in Australia: profitability and motivation', *Economic Record*, vol. 43.

Johnson, H.G. (1966), 'International capital movements and economic policy', in *Essays in Honour of Marco Fanno*, Padova, Italy.

Johnson, H.G. (1968), *Comparative Cost and Commercial Policy for a Developing World Economy*, The Wicksell Lectures.

Johnson, H.G. (1970), 'The efficiency and welfare implications of the international corporation', in C.P. Kindleberger (ed.), *The International Corporation*, MIT Press.

Jorgenson, D.U. (1963), 'Capital theory and investment behaviour', *American Economic Review*, vol. 53.

Jorgenson, D.U. and Siebert, C.D. (1968), 'A comparison of alternative theories of corporate investment behaviour', *American Economic Review*, vol. 58.

Jud, C.D. (1973), 'An empirical study of the industrial composition of US exports and foreign subsidiary sales', paper read to South Western Economic Association, March.

Katz, J. (1972), 'Importacion de tecnologia, aprendizaje local e industrializacion dependiante', *Buenos Aires Instituto Di Tella*.

Keesing, D. (1966), 'Labour skills and comparative advantage', *American Economic Review*, vol. 56.

Kenen, P.B. (1963), 'Short term capital movements and the US balance of payments' in *The United States Balance of Payments*. Hearings before the Joint Economic Committee, 88 Congress, First Session.

Kindleberger, C. (1969), *American Business Abroad*, Yale University Press.

Klein, R.W. (forthcoming), 'A dynamic theory of comparative advantage', unpublished manuscript in *American Economic Review*.

Knickerbocker, F.T. (1973), *Oligopolistic Reaction and the Multinational Enterprise*, Harvard University Press.

Kolde, E. (1968), *International Business Enterprise*, Prentice Hall.

Kopits, G. (1972), 'Dividend remittance behaviour within the international firm: a cross country analysis', *Review of Economics and Statistics*, Aug.

Krause, L.R. (1972), *European Economic Integration and the US*, Washington.

Kreinin, M.E. (1965), 'Freedom of trade and capital movement: some empirical evidence', *Economic Journal*, vol. 75.

Kreinin, M.E. (1967), 'Trade arrangements among industrial countries: effects on the United States', in B. Balassa (ed.), *Studies in Trade Liberalisation*, Johns Hopkins Press.

Kreinin, M. (1967), *Alternative Commercial Policies: Their Effect on the American Economy*, Michigan State University Press.

Kwack, S.Y. (forthcoming), 'A model of US direct investment abroad. A new classical approach', *Western Economic Journal*.

Learner, E.E. and Stern, R.M. (1972), 'Problems in the theory and empirical estimation of international capital movements', in F. Machlup, W. Salant, and L. Tarshis (eds), *International Mobility and Movement of Capital*, National Bureau of Economic Research.

Leftwich, R.B. (1973), 'Foreign direct investments in the United States', *Survey of Current Business*, Feb.

Levy, H. and Sarnat, M. (1970), 'International diversification of investment portfolios', *American Economic Review*, vol. 60.

Lintner, J. (1965), 'The valuation of risk assets and the selection of risky investments in stock portfolios and capital budgets', *Review of Economics and Statistics*, vol. 47.
Lösch, A. (1954), *The Economics of Location*, New Haven, Yale University Press.
McAleese, D. (1972), 'Capital Inflows and Direct Foreign Investment in Ireland 1947–1970' (unpublished paper).
McGraw Hill Economics Department (1961), *Overseas Operations of US Industrial Companies 1960–1961*, McGraw Hill.
Manser, W. (1973), *The Financial Role of Multinational Enterprises*, International Chamber of Commerce.
Mansfield, E. forthcoming, 'The multinational enterprise and technological change', in J.H. Dunning (ed.), *Economic Analysis and the Multinational Enterprise*, London, Allen and Unwin.
Markowitz, H. (1959), *Portfolio selection. Efficient Diversification of Investment*, Wiley.
May, H.K. and Arena, J.A.F. (1971), *Impact of Foreign Investment in Mexico*, National Chamber Foundation and Council of the Americas.
Mellors, J. (1973), *International Tax Differentials and the Location of Overseas Direct Investment: a Pilot Study*, University of Reading Research Papers in International Investment and Business, No. 4.
Miller, R.R. and Weigel, D.R. (1972), 'The motivation for foreign direct investment', *Journal of International Business Studies*, vol. 3, Fall.
Miller, N.C. and Whitman, M.V.N. (1970), 'A mean variance analysis of US long term portfolio foreign investment', *Quarterly Journal of Economics*, vol. 84.
Modigliani, F. and Miller, M. (1958), 'The cost of capital, corporation finance and the theory of investment', *American Economic Review*, vol. 48, June.
Moose, J. (1968), 'US direct investment abroad in manufacturing and petroleum: a recursive model', unpublished doctoral thesis, Harvard.
Morley, S. (1966), 'American Corporate Investment Abroad Since 1919', unpublished doctoral dissertation, University of California (Berkeley).
Mundell, R.A. (1957), 'International trade and factor mobility', *American Economic Review*, vol. 47.
Mundell, R.A. (1960), 'The monetary dynamics of international adjustment under fixed and flexible exchange rates', *Quarterly Journal of Economics*, vol. 74, May.
Murray, R. (1973), 'Underdevelopment, international firms and the international division of labour', in *Towards a New World Economy*, Rotterdam University Press.
National Industrial Conference Board (1961), *Costs and Competition: American Experience Abroad*, NICB.
Ohlin, B. (1967), *Inter-regional and International Trade* (revised edition), Harvard University Press.
Pack, H. (1972), *Employment in Kenyan Manufacturing: Some Microeconomic Evidence* (mimeo).
Parker, J. (1973), 'The Diffusion of Technology and the Multinational Enterprise' (unpublished University of Exeter Ph.D. thesis).
Parry, T. (1972), 'Technology and Performance of the Foreign Subsidiary in Australia' (paper presented to New Zealand Association for the Advancement of Science, Aug).
Parry, T. and Ahlburg, D.A. (1973), *Determinants of US Direct Investment in Australian Manufacturing Industry*. University of Reading Research Paper in International Investment and Business, No. 2.
Penrose, E.T. (1958), *The Theory of the Growth of the Firm*, Basil Blackwell.
Penrose, E.T. (1968), *The Large International Firm in Developing Countries*, London, Allen and Unwin.

Perlmutter, H. (1969), 'The tortuous evolution of the multinational company', *Columbia Journal of World Business*, Jan/Feb.

Piper, J.R. (1971), 'How US firms evaluate foreign investment opportunities', Michigan State University *Business Topics*, Summer.

Polk, J. (1968), 'The new world economy', *Columbia Journal of World Business*, Jan./Feb.

Polk, J. (1971), 'World Companies and the New World Economy' (unpublished paper prepared for discussion group at Council for Foreign Relations, New York).

Polk, J., Meister, I.W. and Veit, L.A. (1966), *US Production Abroad and the Balance of Payments*, NICB.

Popkin, J. (1965), 'Interfirm Differences in Direct Investment Behaviour of US Manufacturers', unpublished doctoral dissertation, University of Pennsylvania.

Posner, M.V. (1961), International trade and technical change, *Oxford Economic Papers*, vol. 13.

Prachowny, M.J. (1972), 'Direct investment and the balance of payments of the US: a portfolio approach', in F. Machlup, W. Salant, and L. Tarshis (eds.) *International Mobility and Movement of Capital*. National Bureau of Economic Research.

Quinn, D. (1970), 'Scientific and technical strategy at the national and major enterprise level', paper for UNESCO symposium on *The Role of Science and Technology in Economic Development*, Paris.

Reddaway, N.B., Potter, S.T. and Taylor, C.T. (1967 and 1968), *The Effects of UK Direct Investment Overseas*, Cambridge University Press.

Richardson, J. D. (1971), 'Theoretical consideration in the analysis of foreign direct investment', *Western Economic Journal*, Mar.

Richardson, J. D. (1972), 'On going abroad, the firms initial foreign investment decision', *Quarterly Journal of Economics and Business*, vol. 11.

Robertson, D. (1971), 'The multinational enterprise: trade flows and trade policy', in J.H. Dunning (ed.), *The Multinational Enterprise*, Allen and Unwin.

Robinson, H.J. (1961), *The Motivation and Flow of Private Foreign Investment*, Stanford Research Institute, California.

Rolfe, S. (1969), *The International Corporation*, International Chamber of Commerce.

Rowthorn, R. (1969), *International Big Business, 1957–1967*, Cambridge University Press.

Safarian, A.E. (1966), *Foreign Ownership in Canadian Industry*, McGraw Hill.

Scaperlanda, A.E. (1967), 'The EEC and US foreign investment: some empirical evidence', *Economic Journal*, vol. 77.

Scaperlanda, A.E. and Mauer, L.J. (1969), 'The determinants of US direct investment in the EEC', *American Economic Review*, vol. 59.

Scaperlanda, A.E. and Mauer, L.J. (1971), 'Errata: the determinants of US direct investment in the EEC', *American Economic Review*, vol. 61.

Scaperlanda, A.E. and Mauer, L.J. (1972), 'The determinants of US direct investment in the EEC. Reply to comments by M. A. Goldberg', *American Economic Review*, vol. 62.

Schmitz, A. and Bieri, J. (1972), 'EEC tariff and US direct investment', *European Economic Review*, vol. 3.

Schöllhammer, H. (1972), *Locational Strategies of Multinational Corporations* (mimeo).

Schreiber, J. (1970), *US Corporate Investment in Taiwan*, Harvard University Press.

Severn, A.K. (1972), 'Investment and financial behaviour of American investors in manufacturing industry', in F. Machlup, W. Salant and L. Tarshis (eds.), *International Mobility and Movement of Capital*, National Bureau of Economic Research.

Sharpe, W.F. (1964), 'Capital asset prices: a theory of market equilibrium under conditions of risk', *Journal of Finance*, vol. 19.

Smith, K.V. and Schreiner, J.C. (1969), 'A portfolio analysis of conglomerate diversification', *Journal of Finance*, vol. 24.

Spitaller, E. (1971), 'A survey of recent quantitative studies of long term capital movements', *IMF Staff Papers*, Mar.

Stevens, G.V.G. (1969a), 'Fixed investment expenditure of foreign manufacturing affiliates of US firms: theoretical models and empirical evidence, *Yale Economic Essays*, vol. 9, Spring.

Stevens, G.V.G. (1969b), *Risk and Return on Selection of Foreign Investments* (mimeo).

Stevens, G.V.G. (1972), 'Capital mobility and the international firm', in F. Machlup, W. Salant and and L. Tarshis (eds.), *International Mobility and Movement of Capital*, National Bureau of Economic Research.

Stevens, G.V.G. (1974), 'The multinational enterprise and the determinants of investment' in J.H. Dunning (ed.), *Economic Analysis and the Multinational Enterprise*, London, Allen and Unwin, pp. 47–88.

Stobaugh, R.B. (1968), 'Where in the world should we put that plant?', *Harvard Business Review*, Jan/Feb.

Stobaugh, R.B. (1969), 'How to analyse foreign investment climates', *Harvard Business Review*, Sept/Oct.

Stobaugh, R.B. (1973), *The Multinational Enterprise and the Petrochemical Industry*,, New York, Basic Books.

Stonehill, A.I. (1965), *Foreign Ownership in Norwegian Enterprise*, Oslo, Central Bureau of Statistics.

Stonehill, A.I. and Nathanson, L. (1970), 'Capital budgeting and the multinational corporation', in A.I. Stonehill (ed.), *Readings in International Financial Management*, Good Year Publishing Co.

Stopford, J.M. (1973), *Organising the Multinational Firm: Can the Americans Learn from the Europeans*? (mimeo).

Strassman, W. Paul. (1968), *Technological Change and Economic Development*, Cornell University Press.

Stubenitsky, F. (1970), *American Direct Investment in the Netherlands Industry*, Rotterdam University Press.

Tilton, J.E. (1973), *International Diffusion of Technology: the Case of Semiconductors*, The Brookings Institution.

Tobin, J. (1968), 'Liquidity preferences as behaviour towards risk', *Review of Economic Studies*, vol. 26.

Tobin, J. (1965), 'The theory of portfolio selection', in F. Hahn and F.P.R. Brechling (eds), *The Theory of Interest Rates*, Macmillan.

United Nations (1971), *Economic Survey of Asia and the Far East*, Bangkok.

US Department of Commerce (1972), *US Direct Investments Abroad 1966*, Part II: Investment position, financial and operating data, Group 2 Manufacturing industries.

Vaitsos, C. (1972), 'Intercountry Income Distribution and Transnational Corporations' (unpublished).

Vaupel, J.W. (1971), 'Characteristics and Motivations of the US Corporations which manufacture Abroad', paper presented to meeting of participating members of the Atlantic Institute, Paris, June.

Vernon, R. (1966), 'International investment and international trade in the product cycle', *Quarterly Journal of Economics*, vol. 80.

Vernon, R. (1972), *Sovereignty at Bay*, Basic Books.

Vernon, R. (1974), 'The multinational enterprise and the location of economic activity' in J.H. Dunning (ed.), *Economic Analysis and the Multinational Enterprise*, London, Allen and Unwin, pp. 89–114.

Wallis, K.F. (1968), 'Notes on Scaperlanda's article', *Economic Journal*, vol. 73.

Weber, A. (1958), 'Location theory and trade policy', *International Economic Papers*.

Wells, L.T. (1972a), *The Product Life Cycle and International Trade*, Harvard University Press.

Wells, L.T. (1972b), *Economic Man and Engineering Man: Choice of Technology in a Low Wage Country* (mimeo).

Wilkins, M. (1970), *Emergence of Multinational Enterprise*, Harvard University. Press.

Wilkinson, B. (1968), *Canada's International Trade: an Analysis of Recent Trends and Patterns*, Montreal, Private Planning Association of Canada.

Wolfe, B. (1971), 'Internationalisation of US Manufacturing Firms: a Type of Diversification' (unpublished doctoral thesis, Yale).

Wortzel, W.H. (1973), *The Multinational Enterprise and the Pharmaceutical Industry*, New York, Basic Books.

2. Trade, location of economic activity and the multinational enterprise: a search for an eclectic approach*

I

The main task of this chapter is to discuss ways in which production financed by foreign direct investment, that is, undertaken by MNEs, has affected our thinking about the international allocation of resources and the exchange of goods and services between countries. The analysis takes as its starting-point the growing convergence between the theories of international trade and production, and argues the case for an integrated approach to international economic involvement, based both on the location-specific advantages of countries and the ownership-specific advantages of enterprises. In pursuing this approach, the chapter sets out a systemic explanation of the foreign activities of enterprises in terms of their ability to internalize markets to their advantage. It concludes with a brief examination of some of the effects which the MNE is allegedly having on the spatial allocation of resources, and on the patterns of trade between countries.

I begin by looking at the received doctrine on international economic involvement. Until around 1950 this mainly consisted of a well-developed formal theory of international trade and a complementary but less well-developed theory of capital movements. With the notable exceptions of John Williams (1929)[1] and Bertil Ohlin (1933), international economists of the interwar years were less concerned with explanations of the composition of goods and factors actually traded across boundaries (and implicitly, at least, of the spatial distribution of economic activity) as with theorizing on what would occur if, in the real world, certain conditions were present. The Heckscher–Ohlin model, for example, asserted that, provided certain conditions were met, countries would specialize in the production of goods which required relatively large inputs of resources with which they were comparatively well endowed, and would export these in exchange for others which required relatively large inputs of factors

* From B. Ohlin, P.O. Hesselborn and P.J. Wijkman (eds), *The International Allocation of Economic Activity*, London: Macmillan, 1977, pp. 398–418. This chapter was reproduced with minor changes to the text and references in Dunning, J.H. (1981), *International Production and the Multinational Enterprise*, London, Allen and Unwin, pp. 21–45.

with which they were comparatively poorly endowed. The conditions included that countries had two homogeneous inputs, labour and capital, both of which were locationally immobile (i.e. they were to be *used* where they were *located*); inputs were converted into outputs by the most efficient (and internationally identical) production functions; all enterprises were price-takers, operating under conditions of atomistic competition; there were no barriers to trade and no transaction costs; and international tastes were similar.

The Heckscher–Ohlin model has been criticized in the literature on various grounds, including the unreality or inapplicability of its assumptions. Here, I would underline some of the implications of three of these assumptions: factor immobility, the identity of production functions and atomistic competition. These are, first, that all markets operate efficiently; second, there are no external economies of production or marketing; and third, information is costless and there are no barriers to trade or competition. In such a situation international trade is the only possible form of international involvement; production by one country's enterprises for a foreign market must be undertaken within the exporting country; and all enterprises have equal access to location-specific endowments.

One of the deductions of the Heckscher–Ohlin theory is that trade will equalize factor prices. Replacing the assumption of factor immobility with that of the immobility of goods, it may be shown that movements of factors also respond to differential resource endowments. This was the conclusion of the early writings of Nurkse (1933), Ohlin (1933) and Iversen (1935), which explained international (portfolio) capital movements in terms of relative factor prices, or differential interest rates. For many years trade and capital theory paralleled each other, it being accepted that, in practice, trade in goods was at least a partial substitute for trade in factors. Eventually, the two were formally integrated into the factor price equalization theorem by Samuelson (1948) and Mundell (1957).

In the late 1950s there was a striking shift of direction in the interests of international economists brought on, *inter alia*, by the tremendous post-war changes in the form and pattern of trade and capital exports. Building on the empirical work of MacDougall (1951) and Leontief (1953, 1956), and taking advantage of much improved statistical data, the 1960s saw the first real attempts to explain trade patterns as they were, rather than as they might be; contemporaneously, the emergence of international production as a major form of non-trade involvement was demanding an explanation.

Over the past 20 years the positive theory of international economic involvement has 'taken off'. For most of the period it comprised two quite separate strands. The first concerned explanations of trade flows. Here, contributions were mainly centred on introducing more realism into the Heckscher–Samuelson–Ohlin doctrine. Basically, there were two main approaches. The first was that of the neofactor theories, which extended the two-factor Heckscher–Samuelson–Ohlin model to embrace other location-specific endowments (notably natural resources) and differences in the *quality* of inputs, especially labour. The second group of theories was more path-breaking, as it cut at the heart of the Heckscher–Samuelson–Ohlin model by allowing for the possibility of differences in the production function of enterprises and of imperfect markets. These theories, which included the neotechnology and scale economy models, were different in kind to the neofactor theories because they introduced new explanatory variables which focused not on the specific resource endowments of countries but on the exclusive possession of certain assets by enterprises. Sometimes, in addition to, but more often as a substitute for, orthodox theories, these new hypotheses of trade flows have been exposed to various degrees of testing. Yet as Hufbauer (1970) has shown, the predictive power of the neofactor and the neotechnology theories is scarcely better than that of the crude factor proportions theory. In his own words, 'No one theory monopolizes the explanation of manufacturing trade'.

The second strand of research in the 1960s centred on explaining the growth and composition of foreign direct investment, or of production financed by such investment. At first causes were sought either from orthodox location theory (witness the plethora of microeconomic field studies and more macro-oriented econometric studies) or from neoclassical investment doctrine; but for various reasons, discussed elsewhere (Dunning, 1973a), neither approach proved very helpful. More rewarding were the attempts to identify the distinctive features of foreign *direct* investment in terms of ownership advantages of foreign firms. Though the gist of this idea was contained in the writings of Southard (1931) and Dunning (1958), it was left to Stephen Hymer in his seminal PhD thesis (Hymer, 1960) to explore it in depth. Out of this approach, later refined and extended by Caves (1971, 1974a, 1974b), several hypotheses, focusing on particular kinds of ownership advantages of MNEs, were put forward: for example, access to superior technology (Johnson, 1970), better capabilities for product differentiation (Caves, 1971), under-utilization of entrepreneurial and managerial capacity (McManus, 1972; Wolf, 1977), etc., while a more behavioural perspective was taken by Vernon and his colleagues, notably Knickerbocker (1973), who chose to emphasize the role played by defensive oligopolistic strategy. These theories, too, have been subject to some testing,[2] but again it seems clear that no single hypothesis offers a satisfactory explanation of non-trade involvement.

Though these new theories of trade and production originated quite independently of each other, by the early 1970s it was clear they were converging on, and even overlapping, each other. Though expressed differently, the same variables were being increasingly used to explain both trade and non-trade involvement. Comparable to the technological gap theory of trade was the knowledge theory of direct investment; analogous to monopolistic competitive theories of trade were theories of direct investment focused on product differentiation and multi-plant economies. Yet, with the exception of Vernon's early integration of trade and investment as different stages of the product cycle (Vernon, 1966), which took as its starting-point the innovative advantages of *enterprises* in a particular country, and the later discovery of Horst (1972) that the same variable – *size* of firm – which best explained foreign investment also explained investment plus trade, no attempt was made to integrate the two forms of involvement into a single theory, although the need for this had been discerned by Baldwin (1970) and others. Nor, indeed, was there any explicit recognition that, because the decisions to trade or engage in foreign production are often alternative options to the same firm, any explanation of one must, of necessity, take account of the other.

The last decade has seen the first, albeit faltering, attempts to do just this. In a paper published in 1973, this author suggested that only by considering trade and foreign production as alternative forms of international involvement in terms of ownership and location endowments could the economic implications of the UK joining the EEC be properly evaluated (Dunning, 1972). Seev Hirsch (1976) formalized these concepts into a model that specifies, very clearly, the conditions under which foreign markets will be serviced by alternative routes. Tom Parry (1975) applied these concepts to a study of the pharmaceutical industry; his contribution is especially noteworthy as he included licensing as a third form of economic involvement. Buckley and Dunning (1976) examined comparative US and UK trade and non-trade in these terms. Birgitta Swedenborg (1979) uses a similar approach in her analysis of the international operations of Swedish firms. In the belief that this is a helpful route towards an eclectic theory of international economic involvement, I now explore it in more detail.

II

Exactly what is to be explained? Here an important point of taxonomy arises. A country's economic involvement outside its national boundaries may be perceived in two ways. First, it may mean the extent to which its own resources, that is, those located within its boundaries, are used by economic agents (irrespective of their nationality) to produce goods or services for sale outside its boundaries; or the extent to which it imports either resources or the products of resources located in other countries. This is the interpretation of orthodox international economics; *inter alia* it implies arm's-length trade in inputs and outputs. But secondly, a country's involvement may mean the extent to which its own economic agents[3] service foreign markets with goods and services, irrespective of where the resources needed to do this are located or used, and the extent to which its own economic agents are supplied goods by foreign owned firms, irrespective of where the production is undertaken. Here, a country's economic space is perceived more in terms of the markets exploited by its institutions than of its geographical boundaries.

Like the distinction between gross national product and gross domestic product,[4] which of the two interpretations is the more appropriate depends on the purpose for which it is being used. But for an evaluation of the contribution of a country's international economic involvement to the economic welfare of its citizens, the second has much to commend it, particularly where inward or outward investment account for a substantial proportion of its net capital formation.

Economic involvement by one country's enterprises in another may be for purposes of supplying both foreign and home markets. Production for a particular foreign market may be wholly or partly located in the home country, in the foreign market, in a third country or in a combination of the three. Similarly, production for the home market may be serviced from a domestic or a foreign location.

The capability of a home country's enterprises to supply either a foreign or domestic market from a foreign production base depends on their possessing certain resource endowments not available to, or not utilized by, another country's enterprises. We use resource endowments in the Fisherian sense (Johnson, 1968) to mean assets capable of generating a future income stream; they include not only tangible assets, such as natural resources, manpower and capital, but intangible assets, such as knowledge, organizational and entrepreneural skills, and access to markets. Such endowments could be purely location specific to the home country, in other words they have to be used where they are located[5] but are available to all firms, or they could be ownership specific, that is, internal to the enterprise of the home country, but capable of being used with other resources in the home country or elsewhere.[6] In most cases, both location and ownership endowments affect competitiveness.

For some kinds of trade it is sufficient for the exporting country to have a location-endowment advantage over the importing country, that is, it is not *necessary* for the exporting firms to have ownership-endowment advantage over indigenous enterprises in the importing country. Much of the trade between industrialized and non-industrialized countries (which is of the Ricardian or H/O type) is of this kind. Other trade, such as that which mainly takes place between developed industrialized countries, is of high skill intensive or sophisticated consumer goods products, and is based more on the ownership advantages of the exporting firms;[7] but, observe, this presupposes that it is better to use these advantages in combination with location-specific endowments in the exporting rather than in the importing (or in a third) country. Where, however, these latter endowments favour the importing (or a third) country, foreign production will replace trade. Foreign production then implies that location-specific endowments favour a foreign country, but ownership endowments favour the home country's firms, these latter being sufficient to overcome the costs of producing in a foreign environment (Hirsch, 1976). (Again we assume that transfer costs can be considered as a negative endowment of countries other than the country of marketing.)

From this it follows that any theory that purports to explain the determinants of any one form of international economic involvement is unlikely to explain the whole; nor, where that form is one of a number of possible alternatives, will it be adequately explained unless the forces explaining these alternatives are also taken into account. One should not be surprised, then, if trade theories of the neofactor brand, based on location-specific endowments, will not normally be able to explain trade in goods based on ownership-specific endowments. But neither should one be disquieted if the neotechnology and monopolistic competitive theories of trade, based on ownership-specific endowments, are also inadequate where the *use* of such advantages is better exploited in conjunction with location-specific endowments of foreign countries.

It may be reasonably argued, however, that this latter criticism would be better directed against the way in which data on international transactions are collected and presented, and the way in which the exported ownership advantages are priced. First, trade statistics usually give details of the *gross output* of goods exported. But where exports contain a high import content, their total value may tell us little about the use made of indigenous endowments. This deficiency can only be overcome by recording exports on a domestic value-added basis. Second, trade statistics either ignore, or classify completely separately, intermediary goods, such as technology, management and organization, which are exported in their own right. If these could be given a commodity classification, and their value added to the export of final products, then the ownership advantages of exporting enterprises would be better captured. Third, where trade takes place within the same enterprises the recorded prices may bear little resemblance to arm's-length prices, and so to the value of factor inputs used. If these problems could be overcome, a combination of the neofactor, neotechnology and monopolistic competitive theories of trade would probably explain trade patterns very well.

III

So far the multinational enterprise has not been explicitly introduced into the discussion. MNEs are companies which undertake productive activities outside the country in which they are incorporated. They are, by definition, also companies which are internationally involved. The extent to which they engage in foreign production will depend on their comparative ownership advantages *vis-à-vis* host country firms, and the comparative location endowments of home and foreign countries.

Unlike location-specific endowments, which are *external* to the enterprises that use them, ownership-specific endowments are *internal* to particular enterprises. They consist of tangible and intangible resources, including technology, which itself dictates the efficiency of resource usage. Unlike location endowments, many ownership endowments take on the quality of public goods, that is, their marginal usage cost is zero or minimal (hence, wherever a marginal revenue can be earned, but is not earned, they are under-utilised); and although their *origin* may be partly determined by the industry or country characteristics of enterprises, they can be used anywhere.

What, then, determines the ownership advantages which one country's enterprises possess over those of another? For our purposes, we distinguish between three kinds of advantage. The first comprises those which any firms may have over another producing in the same location. Here, Bain's (1956) classic work on the barriers to new competition provides the basic answer. Such benefits may lie in the access to markets or raw materials not available to competitors; or in size (which may both generate scale economies and inhibit effective competition); or in an exclusive possession of intangible assets, for example, patents, trademarks, management skills, etc., which enable it to reach a higher level of technical or price efficiency and/or achieve more market power. These advantages, then, stem from *size*, *monopoly power*, and better *resource capability and usage*.

The second type of advantage is that which a branch plant of a national enterprise may have over a *de novo* enterprise (or over an existing enterprise breaking into a new product area), again producing in the same location. This arises because, while the branch plant may benefit from many of the endowments of the parent company, for example, access to cheaper inputs, knowledge of markets, centralized accounting procedures, administrative experience, R&D, etc., at zero or low marginal cost, the *de novo* firm will normally have to bear their full cost. The greater the non-production overheads of the enterprise, the more pronounced this advantage is likely to be.

The third type of advantage is that which arises specifically from the multinationality of a company, and is an extension of the other two. The larger the number and the greater the differences between economic environments in which an enterprise operates, the better placed it is to take advantage of different factor endowments and market situations. I shall return to this point later in the chapter.

Most of these benefits, both individually and collectively, have been used by economists to explain the participation of affiliates of MNEs in the output of industries in host countries. However, while recognizing they are interrelated, there have been few explicit attempts to explain either the basis of the interrelationship or why the more marketable of the advantages are not sold directly to *other* firms. In consequence, not only has one of the fundamental attributes of MNEs been largely overlooked, but so also has the basis for much of the concern about the present international economic order. The substance of our thesis is not, in itself, new; it is more a reinterpretation and extension of an idea first formulated by Coase in 1937, and more recently resurrected in the literature by Arrow (1969, 1975), Williamson (1971, 1975, 1979), Alchian and Demsetz (1972), Furbotn and Pejovich (1972), McManus (1972), Baumann (1975), Brown (1976), Magee (1977a, b) and, perhaps most systematically of all, by Buckley and Casson (1976).[8]

The thesis is that the international competitiveness of a country's products is attributable not only to the possession of superior resources and, in some cases, the necessity of its enterprises, but also to the desire and ability of those enterprises to internalize the advantages resulting from this possession; *and* that servicing a foreign market through foreign production confers unique benefits of this kind. Where, for example, enterprises choose to replace, or not to use, the mechanism of the market, but instead allocate resources by their own control procedures, not only do they gain but, depending on the reason for internalization, others (notably their customers and suppliers prior to *vertical* integration, and their competitors prior to *horizontal* integration) may lose. Internalization is thus a powerful motive for takeovers or mergers, and a valuable tool in the strategy of oligopolists.

It has long been recognized that such gains may follow from vertical integration and, to a lesser extent, from horizontal integration of a firm's activities; and much of current antitrust legislation is designed to prevent or minimise abuses arising as a result. But much less attention has been paid to the type of internalizing practised by conglomerates, or that which reflects in the internal extension of a company's activities, or that associated with the internalization of resources, products or markets over geographical space.

Consider, for example, the areas in which the participation of MNEs, irrespective of their country of origin, is most pronounced in host countries. These include export-oriented primary goods sectors requiring large amounts of capital, for example, aluminium, oil, copper and/or those faced with substantial barriers to foreign marketing and distribution, for example, bananas, pineapples, coffee, etc.; technologically advanced manufacturing industries or those supplying branded consumer products with a high income elasticity of demand and subject to the economies of large-scale production; capital or skill intensive service industries, such as insurance, banking and large-scale construction; and activities in which the spatial integration of inputs, products or markets is essential to efficiency, for example, airlines, hotels, etc. All of these not only require endowments in which MNEs have a comparative advantage, and which are difficult to acquire by *de novo* entrants, but, more pertinent to our argument, they are all sectors in which there is a pronounced propensity of firms to internalize activities, particularly across national boundaries.

What, then, are these incentives of firms to internalize activities? Basically they are to avoid the disadvantages or capitalize on the advantages of imperfections or disequilibria in external mechanisms of resource allocation.[9] These mechanisms are mostly of two kinds – the price system and public authority fiat. Where markets are perfectly competitive, the co-ordinating of interdependent activities cannot be improved upon; once imperfections arise or can be exploited through internalization, this becomes a possibility.

Market imperfections may be both structural and cognitive. Uncertainty over future market conditions in the absence of competitive future markets, or about government policies, is another kind of imperfection. *Structural imperfections* arise where there are barriers to competition and economic rents are earned; where transaction costs are high; or where the economies of interdependent activities cannot be fully captured. *Cognitive imperfections* arise wherever information about the product or service being marketed is not readily available, or is costly to acquire. The cost of *uncertainty* may be gauged by the risk premium required to discount it, which may differ quite significantly between firms. From the buyer's viewpoint, market imperfections to avoid include uncertainty over the availability and price of essential supplies, and lack of control over their delivery timing and quality. From the seller's viewpoint, the propensity to internalize will be greatest where the market does not permit price discrimination; where the costs of enforcing property rights and controlling information flows are high; where the output produced is of more value to the seller than the buyer is willing to pay (again, possibly because of ignorance on the part of the buyer),[10] or, in the case of selling outlets, where the seller, to protect his reputation, wishes to ensure a certain quality of service, including after-sales maintenance. For both groups of firms, and for those considering horizontal integration, the possession of underutilized resources, particularly entrepreneurial and organisational capacity, which may be used at low marginal cost to produce products complementary to those currently being supplied, also fosters internalization.

At the same time, to benefit from some of these advantages an enterprise must be of sufficient size. This prompts firms to engage in product diversification or integration, which, in turn, increases their opportunities to profit from other internalizing practices such as cross-subsidisation of costs, predatory pricing, etc. One suspects that many of the advantages of conglomerate mergers are of this kind; and it cannot be a coincidence that, in recent years, takeovers and mergers have been concentrated in areas in which advantages of internalization are most pronounced.[11]

Public intervention in the allocation of resources may also encourage enterprises to internalize activities. Many policy instruments of governments, however justified in the pursuance of macroeconomic (and other) goals, may create distortions in the allocation of resources which enterprises may seek to exploit or protect themselves against. Some of these provoke reactions from all enterprises; others from only those which operate across national boundaries.

Here the analysis will be confined to two kinds of government intervention especially relevant to the behaviour of MNEs. The first concerns the production and marketing of public goods, which are not only characterized by their zero marginal cost, but by the fact that their value to the owner may hinge on the extent to which others also possess them. Under these circumstances, an orthodox perfect market is impossible, unless the purchaser relies on the seller to withhold the sale of a good to other buyers, or not to price it lower.

Some commodities and services produced by private enterprises also have the characteristics of public goods. The major example is technology – an intermediary good which embraces all kinds of knowledge embodied in both human and non-human capital (Johnson, 1970). The significance of technology in the modern world economy needs no elaboration: it is the main engine of development, a leading determinant of both absolute and relative living standards, and a controlling factor in the spatial allocation of resources. Its phenomenal growth since the Second World War, especially in the field of information and communications technology, has undoubtedly facilitated the internationalization of firms, just as the railroad, telegraph and telephone helped the creation of national enterprises a century ago.[12]

It is my contention that the need both to generate innovations and ideas and to retain exclusive right to their use has been one of the main inducements for enterprises to internalize their activities in the last two decades. Governments have encouraged this by extensively subsidising R&D, continuing to endorse the patent system and by recognizing that, in some industries, if the benefits of technological advances are to be fully exploited, not only may it be necessary to restrict the number of producers, but that enterprises should be free to internalize their knowledge-producing with their knowledge-consuming activities. Even without the intervention of governments, technology possesses many of the attributes for internalizing (or not externalizing) markets. At the time of its production, it is the sole possession of the innovator, who naturally wishes to exploit it most profitably; it is costly and takes time to produce but there is no future market in it; it is often difficult for a potential buyer to value as its usefulness can only be determined after it has been purchased. Yet often, for its efficient exploitation, it needs complementary or back-up resources. These qualities apply particularly to the kind of knowledge which *cannot* be patented, for example, financial systems, organizational skills, marketing expertise, management experience and so on.

The second example of government intervention is particularly relevant to the operations of MNEs. It both encourages such enterprises to internalize existing activities and to engage in new activities which offer the possibility of internalising gains. It arises because of different economic policies of national governments which often lead to distortions in the international allocation of resources. Assume, for example, that an MNE wishes to maximize its post-tax profits and that corporate tax rates differ between countries. One way it can reduce its total tax burden is to capitalize on its intra-group transactions by manipulating its transfer prices so as to record the highest profits in the lowest tax areas. Other things being equal, the more internal transactions the company engages in the greater its opportunities for doing this – hence, in the case of MNEs, the added impetus to engage in a global strategy and to practise product or process specialization within its organisation.

The MNE has other reasons for internalizing its operations across boundaries (Rugman, 1980). These include the desire to minimize the risk and/or costs of fluctuating exchange rates; to cushion the adverse effects of government legislation or policy, for example, in respect to dividend remittances; to be able to take advantage of differential interest rates and 'leads' and 'lags' in intra-group payments; and to adjust the distribution of its short-term assets between different currency areas. Some of these benefits of internalization are now being eroded by government surveillance over transfer pricing and by the tendency for contractual arrangements between foreign and indigenous firms to replace equity investments of the former.

How far MNEs actually *do* manipulate intra-group prices to transfer income across national boundaries is still a matter for empirical research; so far the evidence collected is partial and impressionistic. Suffice to say there are many reasons why an MNE may wish to take advantage of such opportunities (Lall, 1973), and that however vigilant the tax authorities may be in some areas, for example, the pricing of intangible assets, the difficulty of (1) estimating the extent to which a transfer of goods or services has taken place, and (2) assigning a value to them, is a very real one.

It has been illustrated, at some length, why firms, and MNEs in particular, gain from internalizing their activities, especially in respect of the production and marketing of technology. Another sector in which MNEs are particularly active is the capital-intensive, resource-based industries. Here, all the traditional reasons for vertical integration hold good, in addition to those which result from multinationality *per se*; the classic example is the oil industry. They imply, for the most part, a vertical division of activity of firms, though the operations may be horizontal as well, where similar products are produced. Here, too, the impetus to internalize transactions (as opposed to engaging in contractual arrangements) in the case of international vertical integration is likely to be greater than in the case of domestic vertical integration.

It must not be forgotten, however, that there are costs as well as benefits to internalizing economic activities; for an examination of these see Coase (1937) and Buckley and Casson (1976). As markets become less imperfect the net gains of internalization are reduced. The move towards externalizing the marketing of many raw materials, partly stimulated by the actions of governments, testifies to this. In his study of UK direct investment overseas, Reddaway (1968) found that only 4 per cent of the output of UK plantation and mining affiliates, originally set up to supply the investing firms, was now directly imported by them.

It can be concluded, therefore, that the ownership advantages of firms stem from their exclusive possession and use of certain kinds of assets. Very often, enterprises acquire these rights by internalizing those previously distributed by the market or public fiat, or by not externalizing those which they originate themselves. This will only be profitable in imperfect market conditions, and where it is thought the co-ordinating and synergizing properties of the firm to allocate resources are superior to those of markets or public fiat. It is possible to identify the source of such imperfections, both within countries and internationally, and to point to the types of activities which offer the greatest gains from internalization. Of these, the production and marketing of intangible assets and of essential location-specific resources are the two most important. Both happen to be areas in which MNEs are particularly involved; the fact that the ownership advantages are exploited by foreign production is partly explained by location-specific endowments of the foreign country, and partly by certain ownership advantages which accrue only when a firm produces outside its national boundaries.[13]

IV

What is the link between the above discussion and other explanations of international involvement? Simply this. The neotechnology theories of trade and the knowledge theories of direct investment both emphasise the possession of superior technology as an explanation of both trade and production. The monopolistic competitive theories concentrate on some aspect of arm's-length imperfect competition as the explanation for trade and investment.

It is my contention that the two approaches should be treated as complementary aspects of an eclectic theory of international involvement, which should embrace not only the product but also the factor and intermediary goods markets, and should acknowledge that the ownership advantages arise not only from the exclusive possession of certain assets, but from the ability of firms to internalize these assets to protect themselves against the failure of markets (including the consequences of this failure for competitors' behaviour) and government fiat over the rest of their activities. Because it relates to the way in which the enterprise co-ordinates its activities, this approach may be called a *systemic* theory of ownership advantages, applied to both trade and international production.[14] In favouring such an approach admittedly I may be in danger of being accused of eclectic taxonomy. I also acknowledge the interdependence between technology, imperfect competition and the internalization process, and that it is not always easy to separate cause and effect.

But in the search for a composite measure of ownership advantage a systemic approach has something to commend it. Empirically, there can be little doubt of the increase in the vertical and horizontal integration of firms and of market and product diversification, which has enabled firms to benefit from the internalization of their activities. This is demonstrated both by the increase in the concentration of enterprises in industrial economies in the postwar period and by the growing importance of the pre- and post-production activities of firms. Other data suggest that about one-half of all exports of MNEs are intra-group in character.

More generally, the eclectic model can be perceived as a general theory of international production in so far as it provides an analytical framework for explaining all forms of such production. This, however, is not to assert that particular forms of international production are to be explained by the *same* ownership, location or internalization characteristics. This is clearly not the case, and it is readily accepted that different types of international production may call for quite different explanations. But our contention is that these should be regarded as complementary, rather than alternative, interpretations of MNE activity and of the eclectic paradigm. For this reason, I have no difficulty in reconciling seemingly competing theories within this paradigm, as, more often than not, they are seeking to explain different things.

What, then, is the positive value of the eclectic theory of international production? The theory suggests that, given the distribution of location-specific endowments, enterprises which have the greatest opportunities for and derive the most from, internalizing activities will be the most competitive in foreign markets.[15] *Inter alia* these advantages will differ according to industry, country and enterprise characteristics Hence, the ownership advantages of Japanese iron and steel firms over South Korean iron and steel firms will be very different from those of UK tobacco firms over Brazilian tobacco firms or US computer firms over French computer firms. Enterprises will engage in the type of internalization most suited to the factor combinations, market situations and government policies with which they are faced. For example, the systemic theory would suggest not only that research intensive industries would tend to be more multinational than other industries, but that internalization to secure foreign based raw materials would be greater for enterprises from economies which have few indigenous materials than those which are self-sufficient; that the most efficient MNEs will exploit the most profitable foreign markets – compare, for example, the US and UK choice of investment outlets (Stopford,

1976), that the participation of foreign affiliates is likely to be greatest in those sectors of host countries where there are substantial economies of *enterprise* size. This theory is consistent with Horst's conclusion (1972) that most of the explanatory variables of foreign direct investment can be captured in the size of enterprise; indeed, one would normally expect size and the propensity to internalize to be very closely correlated, and MNEs to be better equipped to spread risks than national multiproduct firms

What does the eclectic theory predict that the other theories of international production do not? Taking the theories as a group, probably very little, except in so far as the independent variables fail to capture the advantages of internalization. Indeed, it could be argued that this theory is less an alternative theory of ownership advantages of enterprises than one which pinpoints the essential and common characteristics of each of the traditional explanations There is, however, one difference of substance. The eclectic approach would argue that it is not the possession of technology *per se* which gives an enterprise selling goods embodying that technology to foreign markets (irrespective of where they are produced) an edge over its competitors, but the advantage of internalizing that technology, rather than selling it to a foreign producer for the production of those goods. It is not the orthodox type of monopoly advantages which give the enterprise an edge over its rivals – actual or potential – but the advantages which accrue through internalization, for example, transfer price manipulation, security of supplies and markets, and control over use of intermediate goods. It is not surplus entrepreneurial resources *per se* which lead to foreign direct investment, but the ability of enterprises to combine these resources with others to take advantage of the economies of production of joint products.

In other words, without the incentive to internalize the production and/or sale of technology, foreign investment in technology-based industries would give way to licensing agreements and/or to the outright sale of knowledge on a contractual basis. Without the incentive to internalize market imperfections there would be much less reason to engage in vertical or horizontal integration, and again transactions would take place between independent firms. This, it could be argued, is the distinctiveness of this approach.

V

So far the discussion has concentrated on the ownership endowments of its enterprises as an explanation of a country's international competitiveness, whatever the form of the involvement. It has been argued that, although the advantages are enterprise specific, the fact that these may differ according to nationality of enterprise suggests that such advantages, though endogenous to the individual firms at that time, are not independent of their industrial structure, or of the general economic and institutional environment of which they are part. For example, US government science and education policy may be a key variable in explaining the technological lead of US firms in many industries, while, as Vernon (1974) has pointed out, innovations respond to factor endowment and market needs, which also influence the likely advantages of internalizing those innovations. The institutional arrangements by which innovations are rewarded are no less relevant.

But these country or industry variables affecting ownership advantages are not the same as the location-specific endowments referred to earlier. With this interpretation, these comprise three components, the resources which can only be *used* by enterprises in the locations in which they are sited, unavoidable or non-transferable costs such as taxes, government constraints on dividend remission, etc., and the costs of shipping products from the country of production to the country of marketing.

Each of these elements has received extensive attention in the literature of location theory, which usually assumes ownership endowments as the same between firms, and seeks to explain *where* they are exploited. Our concern here is a different one. Put in question form it is: given the ownership endowments, is the location of production by MNEs likely to be different from that of non-MNEs? The systemic theory suggests that it is, and for three reasons. First, there may be particular internalizing economies resulting from the friction of geographical space. Second, the location-specific endowments, which offer the greatest potential for internalization, are not distributed evenly between countries.[16] Third, where there are differences in the market imperfections or government policies of countries, then MNEs might be influenced by the extent to which they take advantage of these imperfections by internalizing their operations.

In elaboration of these points, four observations can be made. First, various studies have underlined the advantages of co-ordinating R&D activities of MNEs (Ronstadt, 1977; Fischer and Behrman, 1979; Lall, 1979) and centralizing them in or near the markets which stimulate such activities (Michalet, 1973; Creamer, 1976). In the case of US-based MNEs, this suggests, that for most kinds of R&D, both ownership and location endowments work in favour of a home R&D base.[17] In the case of MNEs from smaller home markets this tendency may not be so pronounced. By contrast, because the advantages of internalization are generally much less, it may be profitable to spatially disperse some kinds of manufacturing activities, especially where the production processes involved have become standardized (Vernon, 1974).

Second, an MNE which produces in different market environments may well seek to co-ordinate its activities differently The degree of uncertainty over local consumer tastes, future market conditions and government policy certainly varies between countries. For example, the less imperfect is the market for technology, the less likely is an enterprise to market technology-based products itself. Compare, for example, the role of foreign pharmaceutical companies in Italy, which does not recognize patent protection on drugs, with that of such companies in almost any other European country. By contrast, in some developing countries, MNEs may be reluctant to license local firms because they feel that the complementary technology is insufficient to ensure the quality control they need.[18]

Third, and perhaps most important, is the advantage that a diversified earnings base provides for an MNE to exploit differential imperfections in national or international markets and/or currency areas (Aliber, 1970), *inter alia*, through transfer-price manipulation, the use of leads and lags in intra-group transactions; the acquisition and monitoring of information; and the extension of benefits enjoyed by multi-plant national firms at an international level. These are some of the (potential) advantages of internalization afforded by international production, compared with international trade.

Fourth, there is the drive towards international production as part of oligopolistic behaviour (Knickerbocker, 1973; Flowers, 1976; Graham, 1978). This is really a territorial extension of domestic strategy, and does not pose any new conceptual problems (but see Vernon, 1974). Again, however, in so far as a company perceives its foreign interests to be part of a global strategy, rather than as an independent entity, the internalizing advantages may be crucial to the locational decision of both leaders and followers.

VI

In the light of the above analysis, what might one expect the impact of the MNE to be on location of production, the international diffusion or transfer of technology and trade patterns?

There are many different views about the effect of MNEs on the international distribution of resources. Partly, these reflect differences in the perspective one takes, for example, that of a particular country or region, or that of all countries, or of the goals one is seeking to promote. We shall confine ourselves to economic issues seen in a global context from two main viewpoints. The first is that MNEs promote a more efficient distribution of resources since, by internalizing imperfect markets, they are able to overcome distortions in the economic system such as barriers to the transfer of technology, import controls and inappropriately valued exchange rates. Moreover, in a world of uncertainty and information imperfections, their more efficient scanning and monitoring processes, and their flexibility to respond better to market signals, is a useful competitive stimulus. In short, this view extols the MNE as an integrating force in the world economy, surmounting national barriers, circumventing high transaction costs and improving the allocating of resources.

The second view asserts that, far from overcoming market imperfections, the MNEs are themselves a major distorting force in resource allocation; this is partly because they operate mostly in oligopolistic markets and partly because of their ability to bypass market mechanisms and/or government regulations (Hymer, 1970). As a result, it is argued, they engage in restrictive practices, raise barriers to entry and, by their internalization and centralization of decision taking, adversely affect the efficiency of resource allocation between countries. Far from promoting competition, the co-ordination of activities by entrepreneurs freezes existing production patterns, encourages agglomeration and makes it more difficult for countries to exploit their dynamic comparative advantages. Since MNEs *do* exert monopoly power, it is legitimate (on the lines of the optimum tariff argument) for home or host countries to impose restrictions on their activities.

The truth, in so far as it is possible to generalize, is obviously somewhere between these two extremes, with the balance steering one way or another according to (1) the efficiency of the resource allocative mechanism prior to the entrance of the MNEs and (2) the market conditions under which MNEs compete – which will vary *inter alia* according to industry and country.

But there are certain effects of MNEs, however they may be interpreted, which do seem to have been reasonably well established in the literature, and we will now touch on three of these.

1. In some instances, MNEs have been an integrating force and have taken advantage of existing factor endowments, thus promoting the more efficient use of resources. The best example is where mobile resources of capital and technology are transferred from a capital- and technology-rich country and combined with immobile resources of labour and/or materials in labour- and materials-rich countries, thereby helping these countries to exploit their dynamic comparative advantage. Other examples include what is currently happening in Europe as a result of the EEC, namely, that the MNEs are rationalising their activities to take advantage of the economies of specialization. This is a slow process but no different, in principle, to the behaviour of multiregional (national) enterprises in the USA, which may well be one of the explanations of the greater specialization in the US than within the EEC, as demonstrated by Hufbauer and Chilas (1974).
2. There is some evidence of a spatial specialization of the activities of MNEs and, in particular, the centralization of R&D activities in the home country. Something over 90 percent of the R&D activities of Swedish and US MNEs is undertaken in their home countries, and the proportion is probably not very different for most of the other leading investors. Hymer suggests that

MNEs are encouraging the specialization of activities, not for technological as much as organizational or strategic reasons, most of which enhance the incentive to internalize R&D in the home country. But it does not necessarily follow that, without MNEs, the distribution of innovative activities would have been any the less centralized. R&D among Japanese and European enterprises has certainly been stimulated by the competition from US MNEs. The impact on the UK pharmaceutical and semiconductor industries are classic examples (Tilton, 1971; Lake, 1976). In the LDCs, because of the lack of indigenous competitors, the Hymer hypothesis probably holds more weight, though even here there are examples of MNEs setting up specialized R&D facilities (Behrman and Fischer, 1980).[19]

3. In any analysis of the impact of MNEs on trade and location it is useful to distinguish between the different motives for foreign direct investment. Kojima (1978), for example, has distinguished between trade-oriented and anti-trade-oriented activities of MNEs. He suggests that current Swedish and Japanese investments are mainly made in areas in which the home countries are losing a comparative advantage and host countries are gaining it. These have been of two kinds: one to exploit natural resources not available indigenously, and the other to switch labour-intensive activities from high labour cost to low labour cost locations. On the other hand, Kojima asserts that many foreign investments by US firms have been made to protect an oligopolistic position in world markets and in response to trade barriers, and have transferred activities from which they have a comparative advantage to where they have a disadvantage. Such investments, he claims, are anti-trade oriented and run against the principles of comparative advantage. Kojima cites here the extensive US foreign investments in the capital and technologically intensive industries.

The border between transferring a comparative advantage and creating a new one is a narrow one, and the Kojima distinction between trade-generating and trade-destroying investments is not altogether convincing. Moreover, his approach tends to be a static one and is couched in terms of first-best solutions. It also fails to consider vertical specialisation *within* industrial sectors. Assuming technology (as an intermediate good) can be sold for a competitive price between independent parties, one might reasonably expect non-skilled labour-intensive operations of high-technology industries to be transplanted to those areas which possess such labour in abundance, and countries with an abundance of materials to utilise such materials with technology developed by nations which have a limited amount of materials. The Japanese and US patterns may be complementary to each other; their ownership and locational advantages may reflect country-specific characteristics.[20] Evidence collected about the trading patterns of US MNEs (Lipsey and Weiss, 1973) supports this view. The imports of US MNEs tend to be more capital intensive than those of other US firms, mainly because of the ability of MNEs to export capital and technology to undertake the labour-intensive production processes of a capital-intensive product in low labour cost areas.

From a normative viewpoint, the point of greater interest is the extent to which technology transfer through the co-ordination of the firm is preferable to that of the market, but, on this subject, there has been only limited research (Arrow, 1969; Williamson, 1979; Teece, 1979). Yet this, as has been suggested, is a crucial issue, which both helps explain the growth of the MNEs (relative to non-MNEs) and their effect on the spatial distribution of economic activity. Assuming perfectly competitive markets are not generally feasible (nor, from viewpoints other than economic efficiency, necessarily desirable), under what circumstances is it preferable for the resource allocative process to be decided upon by markets or governments, however imperfect they may be, and under what circumstances by the internal governance of MNEs? For there is no *a priori* reason to suppose one form of resource allocation is preferable to the other. In remedying the imperfections and alleged distorting behaviour of MNEs, should not as much attention be given to removing some of the distortions of the environment in which they operate, so that they have less incentive to internalize their activities? To give a recent example, the replacement of fixed by flexible rates has decisively reduced the impetus for MNEs to engage in speculative or protective currency movements across boundaries. The candidate most in need of attention at the moment is technology. It is here that the present system of rewards and penalties leaves so much to be desired (Johnson, 1970) and it is here that both the incentive to internalize by MNEs *and* the potential for distorting behaviour on their part in exploiting the benefits of that internalization arise.

In the last resort, however, we must acknowledge that it is not efficiency, and certainly not efficiency viewed from a global standpoint, that is the standard by which the relative merits of internalization of MNEs and imperfect markets of allocating resources is likely to be assessed. It is the effects of such patterns of resource allocation on the distribution of income between or within nations; on the relative economic powers of countries or of different groups of asset owners; on the sovereignty of one country to manage its own affairs. It is these matters which are at the centre of the arena of public debate at the moment; and it is on such criteria as these that the actions of MNEs are judged.

Some countries facing the choice offered above have clearly preferred to buy their resources in imperfect markets than through MNEs (Japan is the obvious example), while many LDCs are increasingly seeking to depackage the package of resources provided by MNEs in the belief that they can externalize the internal economies. Within the advanced countries the non-market route is generally accepted. But here, too, there are murmurings of concern, articulated not only in such polemics as *The Global Reach* (Barnet and Muller, 1974) but in research studies done at the Brookings Institution (Bergsten, Horst and Moran, 1978) and by Peggy Musgrave (1975) on the effect of the (internalizing) advantages of international production on the domestic economic power of US corporations.

This particular area of the debate on the role of MNEs in trade and the transfer of technology and the location of production is still in its infancy. It is an area hazardous and not altogether attractive for the academic economist; the issues are controversial; the concepts are elusive; the data are not easily subject to quantitative manipulation and appraisal; and the standard of debate is often low. But, intellectually, it presents a great challenge, offering much scope for the collaboration not only of economists of different specialities and persuasions, but between economists and researchers from other disciplines. For these reasons alone, it deserves to attract our ablest minds.

NOTES

1. The following observation by Williams (1929) about industries which had expanded beyond their political frontiers is of especial interest to our discussion.

   > They represent in some cases the projection by one country into others of its capital, technique, special knowledge along the lines of an industry and its market, as against the obvious alternative of home employment in other lines. They represent, in other cases, an international assembling of capital and management for world enterprises ramifying into many countries. They suggest very strikingly an organic inter-connection of international trade, movement of productive factors, transport and market organisation.

2. For further details see Chapter 3 of this volume.
3. Mainly enterprises: by a country's enterprises is meant those whose head offices are legally incorporated in that country.
4. Gross domestic product = incomes earned from domestic resources; gross national product = gross national product + income earned from assets abroad less income paid to foreigners on domestic assets.
5. Proximity to the point of sale may be treated as a location-specific endowment for these purposes; distance (implying transport and other transfer costs) is thus considered as a negative endowment.
6. See Lall (1980) for a discussion on the extent to which ownership-specific advantages are mobile, that is, transferable across national boundaries.
7. For an elaboration of the complementarity between the neofactor and neotechnology theories of trade, see Hirsch (1974).
8. One of the most recent and stimulating contributions on these lines is contained in Swedenborg (1979). For a general reappraisal on the literature on internalization see Rugman (1980), Calvet (1980) and Teece (1981).
9. To avoid being subject to imperfections of markets when they are the weaker party to an exchange but to capitalize on imperfections when they are the stronger party.
10. Such as particularly applies in the case of transactions involving non-standard technology or information, and which are infrequent and conducted under uncertainty.

11. For a recent study of the applicability of the eclectic theory and the markets and hierarchies paradigm to the acquisition activity of foreign firms in Canada and that of domestic firms in the USA see Calvet (1980).
12. The transition from regional to national railroads in the nineteenth and early twentieth centuries was paralleled by the transition from national to multinational airlines after the Second World War.
13. We have not the space to deal with the role of internalization in prompting other forms of foreign direct investment; in some cases, the co-ordinating advantages of the firm clearly transcend those of the market for technological reasons, such as airlines; in others it is more to do with controlling information among interdependent activities, such as advertising and tourism; or as a form of oligopolistic strategy. In many cases, an investment based on technological innovation has managed to create its own barriers to entry through economies of size.
14. Licensing and other forms of contractual arrangements of intermediate products.
15. The points made in this paragraph are extended and set out in a rather different way in Table 3.1 and Table 4.2 of Dunning 1981.
16. This point is elaborated in Chapter 4 of Dunning 1981.
17. Lall (1979) suggests that in cases where major technological efforts on products and processes are not crucially linked to each other, international experience and cost advantages tend to promote greater reliance on foreign R&D. By contrast, in those sectors where innovation centres around product development and testing it is much more difficult to separate any major part of R&D activity from the main markets and centre of decision taking. Michalet (1973), on the other hand, distinguishes between a specialized and imitative R&D strategy of MNEs, while Ronstadt (1977) adopts a more functional approach arguing that different types of R&D have different location needs. In a study of the overseas R&D activities of 55 US-based MNEs, Mansfield, Teece and Romeo (1979) found that such activities were increasing relative to those in the USA and were concentrated on product and process improvements and modifications rather than the discovery of new products and processes. The authors argued that one important reason – at least in the 1960s and early 1970s – for foreign R&D activities was that the cost of R&D inputs was considerably lower in Japan, Europe and Canada than in the USA.
18. See Chapter 5 of Dunning 1981.
19. Mainly in material processing or product adaptation to meet specialized local needs. Behrman and Fischer (1980) note that US enterprises have some R&D facilities in Hong Kong, Argentina, Colombia, Egypt, the Philippines and Taiwan, whereas Argentina, Hong Kong and Singapore are among developing countries attracting such activities by European MNEs.
20. This point is further explored in Chapter 4 of Dunning 1981. Here it is worth pointing out that vertical foreign direct investment often precedes horizontal foreign direct investment (as it did in the UK and USA) and that the pattern of new Japanese investment in the late 1970s resembles much more that traditional US kind than it did in the 1960s.

REFERENCES

Alchian, A. and Demsetz, H. (1972), 'Production, information costs and economic organisation', *American Economic Review*, Vol. 62 (December).

Aliber, R. (1970), 'A theory of foreign direct investment', in C.P. Kindleberger (ed.), *The International Corporation* (Cambridge, MA: MIT Press).

Arrow, K.J. (1969), 'The organisation of economic activity: issues pertinent to the choice of market and non market considerations', in Joint Economic Committee, *The Analysis and Evaluation of Public Expenditures: the PPB System*, (Washington, DC: US Government Printing Office).

Arrow, K.J. (1975), 'Vertical integration and communication', *Bell Journal of Economics*, Vol. 5, no. 1 (Spring).

Bain, J.S. (1956), *Barriers to New Competition*, (Cambridge, MA: Harvard University Press).

Baldwin, R.E. (1970), 'International trade in inputs and outputs', *American Economic Review*, Vol. 60 (May).

Barnet, R.J. and Muller, R.E. (1974), *The Global Reach*, (New York: Simon and Schuster).

Baumann, H. (1975), 'Merger theory, property rights and the pattern of US direct investment in Canada', *Weltwirtschaftliches Archiv*, Vol. III, no. 4.

Bergsten, E.F., Horst, T. and Moran, T.E. (1978), *American Multinationals and American Interests*, (Washington, DC: Brookings Institution).

Behrman, J.N. and Fischer, W.A. (1980), *Overseas R and D Activities of Transnational Corporations*, (Cambridge, MA: Oelgeschlager, Gunn and Hain).

Brown, W.B. (1976), 'Islands of conscious power: MNCs in the theory of the firm', *MSU Business Topics* (Summer).

Buckley, P.J. and Dunning, J.H. (1976), 'The industrial structure of US direct investment in the UK', *Journal of International Business Studies*, Vol. 7 (Summer).

Buckley, P.J. and Casson, M. (1976), *The Future of the Multinational Enterprise* (London: Macmillan).

Calvet, A.L. (1980), 'Markets and hierarchies: towards a theory of international business', PhD thesis, Sloane School of Management, Cambridge, MA.

Caves, R.E. (1971), 'Industrial corporations: the industrial economics of foreign investment', *Economica*, Vol. 38 (February).

Caves, R.E. (1974a), 'Causes of direct investment: foreign firms' shares in Canadian and United Kingdom manufacturing industries', *Review of Economics and Statistics*, Vol. 56 (August).

Caves, R.E. (1974b), 'Industrial organisation', in J.H. Dunning (ed.), *Economic Analysis and the Multinational Enterprise*, (London: Allen & Unwin).

Coase, R. H. (1937), 'The nature of the firm', *Economica*, Vol. 4 (November).

Creamer, D. (1976), *Overseas Research and Development by US Multinationals 1966–75*, (New York: The Conference Board).

Davidson, W.H. and McFetridge, D.G. (1980), *International Technology Transactions and the Theory of the Firm* (mimeo).

Dunning, J.H. (1958), *American Investment in British Manufacturing Industry*, (London: Allen & Unwin).

Dunning, J.H. (1972), 'The location of international firms in an enlarged EEC: an exploratory paper', Manchester Statistical Society.

Dunning, J.H. (1981), 'International Production and the Multinational Enterprise, London, Boston and Sydney: George Allen and Unwin.

Fischer, W.A. and Behrman, J.N. (1979), "The co-ordination of foreign R and D activities by transnational corporations', *Journal of International Business Studies*, Vol. 10 (Winter).

Flowers, E.B. (1976), 'Oligopolistic reaction in European and Canadian direct investment in the US', *Journal of International Business Studies*, Vol. 7 (Fall/Winter).

Furubotn, E.G. and Pejovich, S. (1972), 'Property rights and economic theory: a survey of recent literature', *Journal of Economic Issues*, Vol. 6 (December).

Graham, E.M. (1978), 'Transatlantic investment by multinational firms: a rivalistic phenomenon', *Journal of Post Keynesian Economics*, Vol. 1 (Fall).

Hirsch, S. (1974), 'Capital and technology confronting the neo-factor proportions and neo-technology accounts of international trade', *Weltwirtschaftliches Archiv*, Vol. 110, No. 4.

Hirsch, S. (1976), 'An international trade and investment theory of the firm', *Oxford Economic Papers*, Vol. 28 (July).
Horst, T. (1972), 'Firm and industry determinants of the decision to invest abroad: an empirical study', *Review of Economics and Statistics*, Vol. 54 (August).
Hufbauer, G.C. (1970), 'The impact of national characteristics and technology on the commodity composition of trade in manufactured goods', in R. Vernon (ed.), *The Technology Factor in International Trade*, (New York: Columbia University Press).
Hufbauer, G.C. and Chilas, J.G. (1974), 'Specialisation by industrial countries: extent and consequences', in H. Giersch (ed.), *The International Division of Labour: Problems and Perspectives*, (Tübingen: Mohr).
Hymer, S. (1960), 'The international operations of national firms: a study of direct investment', unpublished doctoral thesis, MIT.
Hymer, S. (1970), The multinational corporation and the law of uneven development', in J. Bhagwati (ed.), *Economics and World Order*, (New York: World Law Fund).
Iversen, C. (1935), *Aspects of International Capital Movements*, (London and Copenhagen: Levin and Munksgaard).
Johnson, H. (1968), *Comparative Cost and Commercial Policy Theory for a Developing World Economy*, (Stockholm: Almqvist and Wiksell).
Johnson, H. (1970), 'The efficiency and welfare implications of the international corporation', in C. P. Kindleberger (ed.), *The International Corporation*, (Cambridge, MA: MIT Press).
Knickerbocker, F.T. (1973), *Oligopolistic Reaction and the Multinational Enterprise* (Cambridge, MA: Harvard University Press).
Kojima, K. (1978), *Direct Foreign Investment*, (London: Croom Helm).
Lake, A. (1976), *Transnational Activity and Market Entry in the Semiconductor Industry* and *Foreign Competition and the UK Pharmceutical Industry*, (National Bureau of Economic Research: New York, Working Papers Nos 126 and 155).
Lall, S. (1973), 'Transfer pricing by multinational manufacturing firms', *Oxford Bulletin of Economics and Statistics*, Vol. 35 (August)
Lall, S (1979), 'The international allocation of research activity by US multinationals', *Oxford Bulletin of Economics and Statistics*, Vol. 41 (November).
Lall, S (1980), 'Monopolistic advantages and foreign involvement by US manufacturing industry', *Oxford Economic Papers*, Vol. 32 (March).
Leontief, W (1953), 'Domestic production and foreign trade, the American capital position re-examined', *Proceedings of the American Philosophical Society*, Vol. 97.
Leontief, W (1956), 'Factor proportions and the structure of American trade, further theoretical and empirical analysis', *Review of Economics and Statistics*, Vol. 38.
Lipsey, R.E. and Weiss, M.Y. (1973), 'Multinational firms and the factor intensity of trade', National Bureau of Economic Research Working Paper 8.
MacDougall, G.D.A. (1951), 'British and American exports. A study suggested by the theory of comparative, Part I', *Economic Journal*, Vol. 61.
MacDougall, G.D.A. (1952), 'British and American exports. A study suggested by the theory of comparative costs, Part II', *Economic Journal*, Vol. 62.
McManus, J.C. (1972), 'The theory of the multinational firm', in G Pacquet (ed.), *The Multinational Firm and the Nation State*, (Toronto: Collier-Macmillan).
Magee, S.P. (1977a), 'Multinational corporations, the industry technology cycle and development', *Journal of World Trade Law*, Vol. XI (July/August).
Magee, S.P. (1977b), 'Technology and the appropriability theory of the multinational corporation', in J Bhagwati (ed.), *The New International Economic Order*, (Cambridge, MA: MIT Press).

Mansfield, E., Teece, D. and Romeo, A. (1979), 'Overseas research and development by US based firms, *Economica*, Vol. 46 (May).
Michalet, C. (1973), 'Multinational enterprises and the transfer of technology', unpublished paper for OECD, DAS/SPR/73.64.
Muller, R. (1975), 'Global corporations and national stabilisation policy: the need for social planning', *Journal of Economic Issues*, Vol. 9 (June).
Mundell, R.A. (1957), 'International trade and factor mobility', *American Economic Review*, Vol. 47 (June).
Musgrave, P.B. (1975), *Direct Investment Abroad and the Multinationals: Effects on the US Economy*. Prepared for the use of the Sub-Committee on Multinational Corporations of the Committee on Foreign Relations, US Senate, August, (Washington, DC: US Government Printing Office).
Nurkse, R. (1933), 'Causes and effects of capital movements', reprinted in J.H. Dunning, *International Investment*, (Harmondsworth: Penguin Readings, 1972).
Ohlin, B. (1933), *Interregional and International Trade*, (Cambridge, MA: Harvard University Press), rev. edn. 1967.
Orr, D. (1973), 'Foreign control and foreign penetration in Canadian manufacturing industries', unpublished manuscript.
Owen, R.F. (1979), *Inter-Industry Determinants of Foreign Direct Investment. A Perspective Emphasising the Canadian Experience*, Working Papers in International Economics, Princeton University (May).
Parry, T.G. (1975), 'The international location of production studies in the trade and non-trade servicing of international markets by multinational manufacturing enterprise', PhD Thesis, University of London.
Parry, T.G. (1980), *The Multinational Enterprise: International Investment and Host Country Impacts* (Greenwich, CT: JAI Press).
Reddaway, N.B., Potter, S.T. and Taylor, C.T. (1968), *The Effects of UK Direct Investment Overseas*, (Cambridge: Cambridge University Press).
Ronstadt, R. (1977), *Research and Development Abroad by US Multinationals*, (New York: Praeger).
Rugman, A.M. (1980), 'Internalisation as a general theory of foreign direct investment. A reappraisal of the literature', *Weltwirtschaftliches Archiv*, Vol. 116, no. 2.
Samuelson, P. (1948), 'International trade and equalisation of factor prices', *Economic Journal*, Vol. 58 (June).
Southard, F.A. (1931), *American Industry in Europe*, (Boston MA: Houghton Mifflin).
Stopford, J. (1976), 'Changing perspectives on investment of British manufacturing multinationals', *Journal of International Business Studies*, Vol. 7 (Fall/Winter).
Swedenborg, B. (1979), *The Multinational Operations of Swedish Firms: An Analysis of Determinants of Effects*, (Stockholm: Almqvist and Wiksell).
Teece, D.J. (1979), *Technology transfer and R&D Activities of Multinational Firms: Some Theory and Evidence* (mimeo), Stanford University (November).
Teece, D.J. (1981), 'The multinational enterprise: market failure and market power considerations', *Share Management Review*, Vol. 22, no. 3.
Tilton, J.E. (1971), *International Diffusion of Technology: The Case of Semi-conductors*, (Washington, DC: The Brookings Institution).
Vernon, R. (1966), 'International investment and international trade in the product cycle', *Quarterly Journal of Economics*, Vol. 80 (May).
Vernon, R. (1974), The location of economic activity', in J.H. Dunning (ed.), *Economic Analysis and the Multinational Enterprise*, (London: Allen & Unwin), pp. 89–114.

Williams, J.H. (1929), 'The theory of international trade reconsidered', *Economic Journal*, Vol. 39 (June).
Williamson, O.E. (1971), 'The vertical integration of production market failure considerations', *American Economic Review*, Vol. 61 (May)
Williamson, O.E. (1975), *Markets and Hierarchies: Analysis and Antitrust Implications* (New York: The Free Press).
Williamson, O.E. (1979), 'Transaction-cost economics: the governance of contractual relations', *Journal of Law and Economics*, Vol. 22 (October).
Wolf, B.M. (1977), 'Industrial diversification and internationalisation: some empirical evidence', *Journal of Industrial Economics*, Vol. 26 (December).

3. Trade, location of economic activity and the multinational enterprise: some empirical tests*

I

There is now a consensus of opinion that the propensity of an enterprise to engage in international production, that is, production financed by foreign direct investment, rests on three main determinants: first, the extent to which it possesses (or can acquire, on more favourable terms) assets[1] which its competitors (or potential competitors) do not possess; second, on how far it is possible, and in its best interests, to lease these assets to other firms, or make use of them itself; and third, on whether it is more profitable to exploit these assets in conjunction with the indigenous resources of foreign countries or with those of the home country. The more the ownership-specific advantages possessed by an enterprise, the greater the inducement to internalise them, and the wider the attractions of a foreign rather than a home country production base, the greater the likelihood that an enterprise will engage in international direct investment.

A national firm supplying its own market has various avenues for growth. It can diversify horizontally or laterally into new product lines, or vertically (i.e. upstream or downstream) into new activities, including the production of knowledge; it can acquire existing enterprises; or it can exploit foreign markets. When it makes good economic sense to choose the last route (which may also embrace one or more of the others), the enterprise becomes an international enterprise. However, for it to be able to produce alongside indigenous firms domiciled in these markets, it must possess additional ownership advantages sufficient to outweigh the costs of servicing an unfamiliar and/or distant environment (Hirsch, 1976).

An enterprise is an integrated and co-ordinated unit of decision taking, the function of which is to transform, by the process of production, valuable inputs into more valuable outputs. The boundaries of an enterprise extend to where it no longer has control over the use of such inputs, or the assets from which they

* From *Journal of International Business Studies*, **11**(1) (Spring/Summer 1980), 9–31.

are derived.[2] In the present context, it is helpful to distinguish between two kinds of assets. The first are those which are available, on the same terms, to all firms whatever their size or nationality, but which are specific in their origin to particular locations, and have to be used in those locations. These include not only Ricardian type assets, viz. natural resources, most kinds of labour and proximity to markets,[3] but also the social, legal and commercial environment in which the endowments are used, market structure, and government legislation and policies. In classical and neoclassical trade theories, differences in the possession of these endowments between countries entirely explain the willingness and the ability of enterprises to become international;[4] but since all firms, whatever their nationality of ownership, are assumed to have full and free access to them there are no advantages to be gained from foreign production.

The second type of asset is that which an enterprise may create for itself (e.g. certain types of knowledge, organisation and human skills) or can purchase from other institutions, but which, in so doing, it acquires some proprietary right of use. Such ownership-specific assets may take the form of a legally protected right, or of a commercial monopoly, or they may arise from the size diversity or technical characteristics of firms, for example, economies of joint production and/or marketing and surplus entrepreneurial capacity (Kojima, 1978).

The essential feature about this second type of asset is that although its *origin* may be linked to location-specific endowments, its *use* may not be so confined. This can be explained as follows. The ability of enterprises to acquire ownership endowments is clearly not unrelated to the endowments specific to the countries in which they operate, and particularly their country of origin. Otherwise, there would be no reason why the structure of foreign production of firms of different nationalities should be different. But, in fact, as another contribution of Dunning has shown, it is so, and substantially so (Dunning, 1979). Such differences as these can only be explained by an examination of the characteristics of the countries in which the MNEs operate, and especially those of the home country, which normally give rise to the ownership advantages in the first place. Raymond Vernon's product cycle theory was among the first to use this approach from the viewpoint of the activities of US MNEs (Vernon, 1966). More recently Birgitta Swedenborg (1979) has extended and applied it to a study of Swedish, US and UK direct foreign investment. It is also implicit in Aliber's thesis (Aliber, 1970) that differences in the capitalisation rates for firms of different nationality explain much of foreign direct investment, because while these rates may be largely determined by country-specific factors, they create an asset which only firms of a particular nationality are able to exploit.[5]

There is one final strand to the eclectic theory of international production. The possession of ownership advantages determines *which* firms will supply a particular foreign market, whereas the pattern of location endowments explains whether the firm will supply that market by exports (trade), or by local production (non-trade). But why does a firm choose to use the ownership advantages itself to exploit a foreign market – whatever route it chooses – rather than sell or lease these advantages to a firm located in that market to exploit? The answer – as set out at some length in Chapter 2 of this volume[6] – is that it does so wherever it is in the firm's interests to internalise the use of its ownership-specific endowments rather than lease or sell these to other firms or where by the act of internalising an external contractual relationship, for example, by a takeover, a firm is able to use these assets better than can the acquired firm.

The matrix set out in Table 3.1 attempts to relate, in an encapsulated form, the main types of activities in which MNEs tend to be involved to the three main determinants of the extent and form of international involvement. Such a table may be used as a starting-point for an examination of the industrial and geographical distribution of foreign direct investment. It will be noted that, as part of the explanation of ownership advantages, the possession of country endowments is also introduced, as these will influence the geographical origin of such investment.

II

Broadly speaking, there have been five approaches to testing the theory of international production. The first has attempted to explain the causes of direct foreign investment by examining its industrial composition from the viewpoint of individual home countries (almost exclusively the USA) and host countries (notably Canada, the UK and Australia). A common thread running through all these studies[7] is that they have sought to explain the pattern of foreign direct investment in terms of ownership advantages of MNEs. The second approach has been to look at the form of international economic involvement, and to identify the determinants of whether foreign markets are exploited by trade or non-trade routes.[8] The third has combined the two approaches by examining both the level and composition of international involvement, in terms of ownership and locational characteristics.[9] The fourth approach has been to extend the first three to incorporate the internalisation thesis,[10] and the fifth has been to relate the ownership endowments of firms to those of home countries (Vernon, 1966; Swedenborg, 1979; Lall, 1980). The empirical contribution of this chapter is primarily of the third kind but with the issues of the fourth very much in mind.

From both a technical and motivational standpoint these strands of research have much in common. Each uses, with varying degrees of sophistication, multiple regression analysis to test explanations about the relationship between

Table 3.1 Types of international production: some determining factors

Types of international production	Ownership advantages (the 'why' of MNC activity)	Location advantages (the 'where' of production)	Internalisation advantages (the 'how' of involvement)	Illustration of types of activity which favour MNEs
1. Resource based	Capital, technology, access to markets	Possession of resources	To ensure stability of oil supply at right price. Control of markets	Oil, copper, tin, zinc, bauxite, bananas, pineapples, cocoa, tea
2. Import substituting manufacturing	Capital, technology, management and organisational skills; surplus R&D and other capacity, economies of scale. Trade marks.	Material and labour costs, markets, government policy (e.g. with respect to barrier to imports, investment incentives, etc.)	Wish to exploit technology advantages, high transaction or information costs, buyer uncertainty, etc.	Computers, pharmaceuticals, motor vehicles, cigarettes
3. Rationalised specialisation (a) of products (b) of processes	As above, but also access to markets	(a) Economies of product specialisation and concentration (b) Low labour costs, incentives to local production by host governments	(a) As type 2 plus gains from interdependent activities (b) The economies of vertical integration	(a) Motor vehicles, electrical appliances, agricultural machinery (b) Consumer electronics, textiles and clothing, cameras, etc.
4. Trade and distribution	Products to distribute	Local markets. Need to be near customers. After-sales servicing, etc.	Need to ensure sales outlets and to protect company's name	A variety of goods, particularly those requiring close consumer contact
5. Ancillary services	Access to markets (in the case of other foreign investors)	Markets	Broadly as for types 2 and 4	Insurance, banking and consultancy services
6. Miscellaneous	Variety – but include geographical diversification (e.g. airlines and hotels)	Markets	Various (see above)	Various kinds (a) Portfolio investment in properties (b) Where spatial linkages essential, e.g. airlines and hotels

various measures of international involvement and a variety of explanatory variables. Each, too, is beset by the same kind of methodological and statistical problems, notably the establishment of operationally testable hypotheses, data limitations and multicollinearity between the individual variables. From a motivational standpoint, with one exception (Knickerbocker, 1973), all the studies assume either that enterprises are profit maximisers or that their behaviour is not inconsistent with that which might be expected from a profit maximising firm.

Turning now to an empirical testing of the two hypotheses implicit in the eclectic theory of international production, we concentrate on only two forms of international economic involvement, viz. exports and production, which are assumed to be alternative to each other in servicing foreign markets.[11]

The data used are those covering the foreign activities of US MNEs in manufacturing industry as published by the US Tariff Commission (1973). In particular, interest is centred on the involvement of US firms in seven countries and in 14 manufacturing industries. The Commission published data for two years, 1966 and 1970, but we shall confine ourselves to an analysis of the 1970 data as set out in Table 3.2. The two basic hypotheses to be tested are:

H1 The competitive advantage of a country's enterprises in servicing foreign markets is determined both by the ownership advantages of these enterprises, relative to those of enterprises of other nationalities, and the location advantages of the countries in which they produce, relative to those of other countries.

H2 The *form* of the involvement, or participation, will essentially depend on the relative attractiveness and/or production of the endowments of the home and host countries.[12]

It is also contended that the gains to be derived from internalising activities, which would otherwise be allocated by markets or government fiat, make up an important part of ownership advantages and, in some cases, of location advantages as well.

Concerning H1, the dependent variable is taken to be the share of the output of a particular industry (*IS*) in a particular country supplied by exports (*X*) plus local production (*AS*) of US-owned firms,[13] that is, *AS* + *X*/*IS*. These components can, of course, be considered separately, but in this hypothesis, we wish to exclude location-specific variables influencing the form of involvement. This dependent variable is noted as DV1.

The two components of international involvement may be considered separately. The share of the affiliates' sales of total output in the host country (*AS*/*IS*) is noted as DV2 and the share of exports from the USA of that output

Table 3.2 US affiliate sales, US exports and total industry sales in seven countries, 1970 ($b)

	Canada			United Kingdom			France			West Germany			Belgium-Luxembourg			Mexico			Brazil			Total		
	AS	*X*	*IS*	*AS*	*X*	*75*	*AS*	*X*	*IS*	*AS*	*X*	*IS*	*AS*	*X*	*IS*	*AS*	*X*	*IS*	*AS*	*X*	*IS*	*AS*	*X*	*IS*
1 Food product	2220	98	8532	1054	56	10294	473	7	17137	634	33	15583	121	9	2415	487	16	5773	107	8	3947	5096	227	63681
2 Paper and allied products	1503	118	3840	141	118	2763	183	61	2161	69	103	3474	96	27	496	121	52	525	65	9	504	2180	488	13763
3 Chemicals and allied products	2124	554	2490	1918	226	9356	971	107	8190	963	215	13888	654	220	1357	764	171	3888	623	146	3325	8017	1639	42494
4 Rubber products	613	146	628	373	22	1185	119	24	1854	211	36	1972	79	13	96	108	19	267	175	9	363	1678	269	6365
5 Primary and fabricated metals	1964	631	6877	804	237	7905	208	167	10750	1821	228	25280	252	81	3989	749	95	1981	262	83	2209	6060	1522	58991
6 Non-electric machinery	2222	1837	2778	2496	578	11862	1439	395	10581	1742	508	16529	429	221	1059	208	367	330	304	247	895	8840	4153	44034
7 Electrical machinery	1822	603	2213	1607	221	8961	514	136	6059	876	237	13888	425	52	993	478	195	919	246	49	1014	5968	1493	34047
8 Transportation equipment	5600	2430	6222	3430	211	12645	936	180	12086	3250	261	12843	275	139	1523	567	239	1261	1171	88	1792	15229	3548	48372
9 Textiles and apparel	532	168	3281	77	46	10275	21	13	8220	100	29	10470	207	54	2002	66	41	1969	124	10	2405	1127	361	38622
10 Lumber, wood and furniture	1322	91	2632	35	22	2763	15	4	3135	33	25	4475	0	2	478	5	16	316	5	1	705	1415	161	14504
11 Printing and publishing	176	153	1516	125	29	5003	51	4	4320	35	6	2589	5	2	390	6	9	396	4	4	429	401	207	14643
12 Stone, clay and glass	406	140	1260	242	14	3818	252	13	2897	239	20	6043	45	7	727	191	19	725	76	5	821	1451	218	16291
13 Instruments	563	219	626	739	101	1321	399	48	1976	406	90	1608	15	21	33	76	42	–[a]	91	26	–[a]	2289	547	5564
14 Other manufacturing	567	135	1916	3205	53	10541	35	36	3122	409	63	7282	5	44	1093	411	38	645	128	9	630	4760	378	25229
Total	21636	7323	44811	16246	1934	98692	5616	1195	92488	10788	1854	135924	2603	892	16651	4236	1319	18995	3381	694	19039	64511	15211	426600

[a] not available.

Source: US Tariff Commission (1973).

(*X*/*IS*) as DV3; DV2 and DV3 can be similarly derived to obtain comparative advantage indices.

Concerning H2, the dependent variable (DV4) is defined as $X/IS \div AS/IS$ (or simply *X*/*AS*); in other words, it is the ratio between exploiting a particular market by exports from the USA relative to local production by US affiliates in the country of marketing. The higher this ratio, the more the USA is favoured as a location for production, relative to the country in which the goods are being sold (or being exported from). It should be emphasised that, for the purposes of this exercise, it is assumed that the market can only be supplied from these two locations.

III

We now turn to a statistical testing of the two main hypotheses.

(a) The Dependent Variables: Hypothesis 1 – The International Competitive Hypothesis

The overall involvement index reflects both location- and ownership-specific advantages. The explanation of the foreign production ratio lies in identifying and measuring ownership advantages (as the location of production is assumed to be the same for all firms), and that of the export ratio in identifying both location and ownership advantages. In examining the export ratio, one naturally turns to trade type theories for guidance. Here, as we have seen, the neofactor and neotechnology theories suggest that trade is related both to resource endowments and factor costs, and to certain ownership variables, notably technology and scale economies. But no attempt, to my knowledge, has been made to explain shares of a particular industry's sales accounted for by foreign imports.[14] In discussing the determinants of foreign production, one should be solely concerned with ownership advantages. Yet the fact that trade and production are often related to each other suggests that these advantages may also be associated with location-specific endowments.[15] Explanations of foreign production that ignore the latter specific advantages are thus likely to be inadequate.

The share of a particular industry's output supplied by foreign affiliates is determined by the competitive advantages of the affiliates and the relative attractions of the host country as a production base. It is likely to be greatest where the barriers to entry facing indigenous producers *and* exports from the home (and other countries) are highest. Trade is similarly determined, except that it will flourish where barriers to exports are low and where barriers to entry to all producers in the host country are high. International involvement is determined simply by the competitive advantage of the investing and exporting firms *vis-à-vis* indigenous and other foreign companies.

In symbolic terms:

DV1 $$AS + X/IS = f(C)$$

where C is the international competitive advantage

DV2 $$AS/IS = f(C, X/AS)$$

and

DV3 $$X/IS = f(C, X/AS)$$

(b) The Dependent Variables: Hypothesis 2 – The Location Hypothesis

This is simple and straightforward. To produce a particular good, an enterprise will choose that location which best advances its overall goals. The interface between received location theory and the MNE is a relatively unexplored territory, but a good start has been made by Vernon (1974). In principle, there is no reason to suppose a national multi-location firm would behave very differently if its activities were in a different country. New variables, for example, exchange risks, differences in taxation rates, and policies of host governments towards inward direct investment, may need to be incorporated, but this can be done without too much difficulty.

The location hypothesis is solely concerned with country-specific variables affecting (1) the size and character of markets[16] and (2) production and transfer costs, though, as we have seen, these may have a special impact on MNEs because of their ability to internalise the costs and benefits of some of the differences that exist between countries.

DV4 $$X/AS = f(L)$$

where L is the locational advantage of the home country.

(c) The Independent Variables: Hypothesis 1

How does one assess the competitive advantage of firms of one nationality over those of another – both in particular industries and countries? This essentially reduces to a question of (1) allocative, technical and scale efficiency, (2) product range and quality, and (3) market power. Since we are concerned with inter-industry comparisons, allocative efficiency, that is, of resources between industries, may be discounted. However, goals may differ between firms, as may the competence of firms to achieve these goals. For example, the greater the innovative ability of an enterprise, the greater its resourcefulness, and the more talented its managerial and labour force, the higher its market share is likely to be. Similarly, the advantages of size, of being part of a larger organisation and of being able to internalise external economies will affect a firm's competitive strength, independently of the location of its activities.

Some of these variables, of course, reflect industry- or country-specific characteristics of firms. Governments, for example, can and do influence the extent to which there is an adequate labour force to draw upon, the promotion of new technologies, the role of advertising in fostering product differentiation, and so on. These factors are acknowledged and have been considered explicitly elsewhere (Dunning, 1979).

It may be helpful to break H1 down into two sub-hypotheses. The first is:

$H1_a$ Given the export participation ratio (*X/IS*), the foreign production participation ratio (*AS/IS*) will be highest in those industries where the comparative advantage of foreign (meaning US here) firms is greatest *vis-à-vis* indigenous firms.

In principle, many of these advantages may be captured in a catch-all measure, viz. the comparative productivity of US firms and host country firms or some proxy for integration, for example, percentage of net to gross output. The comparative advantage of US firms is presumably highest where their relative productivity and/or value-added ratio is highest and, therefore, in those cases, the affiliate penetration ratio should be highest. In practice, difficulties in measuring productivity and identifying internalising economies makes both measures of doubtful applicability.

$H1_b$ Given the production participation ratio (*AS/IS*), the export penetration participation ratio (*X/IS*) will be highest in those industries where the national resource endowments of the USA are greatest in comparison to those of other countries, and where barriers to trade are minimal.

The contribution of trade theory to these determinants of location-specific advantages has been examined in terms of comparative cost advantages. Location theory approaches export success more in terms of differences in absolute production costs and the costs of traversing space. Artificial barriers to trade include those imposed by governments or imperfect markets. An incentive to export may also result from the inability of a host country's firms to effectively compete, due to the absence of a market sufficiently large to yield economies of scale in production.

(d) The Independent Variables: Hypothesis 2

Like $H1_b$, the second hypothesis appears to be best explained by the theories of trade and location. Among the relative costs that play an important part in determining the location choice are those of labour and material inputs. The former is particularly critical in this study as it is limited to manufacturing industries where horizontal direct investment is the rule. This is in contrast to the situation in resource industries, where vertical direct investment plays a much greater role. By the same token, labour productivity and its growth will be important elements in determining the real value of labour.

Production costs may also be closely related to the scale of plant which can be built. Market size will therefore be relevant. So also will rates of growth of the markets involved, as these will determine the extent to which economies of scale may be exploited in the future.

(e) The Choice of Independent Variables for this Exercise

Table 3.3 lists some of the variables which might be considered as proxies for ownership- and location-specific advantages. Also identified, with an asterisk, are those which might also be used as indices of internalisation advantages.[17] Some of these are very similar to each other, but not all can be used for this particular exercise, partly because we are concerned with explaining patterns of involvement by *industries* rather than by *firms*, and partly because of data constraints.

It will also be noted that for some variables listed, data are required for host countries; in others, for the home country, or for both host and home countries. Where only the home country is involved, then location advantages become irrelevant and one cannot use the data to determine both industry and country participation ratios. But the main constraint has been the paucity of good data about *host* countries, which seriously inhibits testing both hypotheses for the seven countries considered separately. An exercise has also been conducted omitting the two LDCs, partly because there is less confidence in the data for these two countries, and partly in order to use a tariff variable, data for which were not available for Mexico and Brazil.

Ultimately, the independent variables were chosen and then used to test both hypotheses. Data on each relate to 1970, or nearest year, except where otherwise stated. The data for these variables were mainly extracted from the US Tariff Commission Study, except for those on imports, which were obtained from the OECD Commodity Trade Statistics Series C and tariffs and from a Political and Economic Planning publication (1962).

A schematisation of variables follows:

For the seven-country exercise

1. Ownership-specific variables
   (a) SER – skilled employment ratio, viz. the ratio of salaried employees to production employees for all firms in the host countries;
   (b) AHC – average hourly compensation of all employees in the host countries (1a and 1b are both measures of human capital intensity);
   (c) RSM – relative sales per man (an efficiency index), viz. the sales per man year of firms in the USA divided by sales per man year of firms (including the affiliates of US firms) in the host countries;
   (d) GRSPM – growth in sales per man of all firms (in the host country), 1966/70.

   The predicted sign for each of these variables for each of the hypotheses is positive, but their significance is likely to be greater for H1 than H2. US firms will invest in those industries and countries in which they have the greatest technological advantage and where their productivity *vis-à-vis* local firms is the highest.
2. Location-specific variables
   (a) XMR – the export/import ratio, measured by the ratio of value of exports to value of imports of *host* countries (as a measure of a country's ability to produce particular products);
   (b) RMS – relative market size, viz. value of industry sales in the USA divided by value of industry sales in the host countries;
   (c) RW – relative wages, viz. average hourly compensation (in particular industries) in the USA divided by average hourly compensation in the host countries for all employees (an often quoted cost determinant of foreign production);
   (d) RES – relative export shares of USA and host countries – another measure of country performance;
   (e) CMG – comparative market growth of USA (domestic industry local sales plus imports) and host countries, 1966/70.

   The predicted signs of these variables vary. In the case of RES it is positive, but in the case of XMR, RMS and CMG it is negative. It might also be expected that these variables would be most often used to support hypothesis H2.
3. General performance indicators
   (a) AVNIS – the average ratio of net income to sales of all firms in different industries and countries for 1966 and 1970;
   (b) MG – market growth (domestic industry local sales plus imports) in host countries, 1966/70.

   The predicted sign of AVNIS is negative for H1 but positive for H2, that for MG is positive for all hypotheses.

Table 3.3 Identifying the main ownership and location advantages[a]

Determinants	By industry and/or country
Ownership advantages: specific determinants	
1 *Access to productive knowledge*	
(a) Skilled (professional and technical)/unskilled labour ratio*	Home cf. host firms
(b) R&D as percentage of sales*	Home cf. host firms
2 *Economics of the firm*	
(a) Size of enterprise*	Home firms
(b) Relative size of enterprises	(Average) Home cf. host firms
(c) Number of non-production to all workers* *or* wage bill of non-production to all workers *or* non-production[b] costs/total costs* (gross output) *or* R&D plus advertising costs to total costs (or sales)*	Home firms
(d) Capital/labour ratio	Home firms
3 *Opportunities for investment*	
(a) Size of local market	(Industry) sales of host firms
(b) Size of local market plus exports	(Industry) sales of host firms
4 *Diversification indices*[c]	
(a) Average number of countries MNEs operate in* or	Home firms
(b) % of foreign/total production of home firms*	Home firms
(c) % of intra-group exports to total exports of MNEs*	Home firms
(d) Number of product groups in which parent companies produce *or* % of output of main product group to all output*	Home firms
(e) % of shipments from multi-plant enterprises to total shipments (in home country)*	Home firms
5 *Market concentration*	
(a) Percentage of output of industry accounted for by *x* largest firms	Home firms
6 *Efficiency*	
(a) Wage costs (per man hour) of production workers	Foreign affiliates as % of home firms
7 *Resource availability*	
(a) % of main material(s) imported*	Either import/export ratio of home firms *or* % imports to total consumption
(b) % of main material(s) used in production process	% of main material costs to gross output
8 *Product differentiation* Advertising/sales ratio	Home firms
9 *Oligopolistic behaviour* Entry Concentration Index Knickerbocker PhD thesis	Home firms in host countries

Table 3.3 continued

Determinants	By industry and/or country
Ownership advantages: general determinants	
1 *Productivity*	
Net output or sales per man	1 Home firms cf. host firms 2 Foreign affiliates cf. host firms
2 *Profitability*	
Profits/assets or sales	1 Home firms cf. host firms 2 Foreign affiliates cf. host firms
3 *Growth*	
Increase in sales	1 Home firms cf. host firms 2 Foreign affiliates cf. host firms
Location advantages: specific determinants	
1 *Production costs*	
(a) Wages per man hour	Home firms cf. host firms
(b) Energy costs (e.g. electricity or oil)	Home firms cf. host firms
(c) Material costs (cost of major inputs; or commodity price indices for main materials) *or* some index of resource availability	Home firms cf. host firms
(d) Tax rates (including, where possible, tax allowances)*	Home firms cf. host firms
(e) Average number of countries MNEs operating in	Home firms only
2 *Transfer costs*	
(a) Transport costs	Home–host country
(b) Tariffs	Host country
(c) Non-tariff barriers	Host country
3 *General*	
(a) Political risks	Host country
Location advantages: general determinants	
1 *Productivity*	
(a) Production costs per man *or* (b) Net output or sales per man	Host firms cf. foreign affiliates
2 *Profitability*	
Profits/assets or sales	Host firms cf. foreign affiliates
3 *Growth*	
Increase in sales	Host firms cf. foreign affiliates

[a] Internalising advantages marked with an asterisk.
[b] Non-production = pre- + post-direct production costs.
[c] (a)–(d) specific to MNEs; (e) general to multi-plant enterprises.

The five advanced countries
As above, but with an additional location-specific variable.

(f) TR – average tariffs measured on a country and industry basis. The predicted sign of this variable is negative for DV4.

Such a large number of independent variables invites problems associated with multicollinearity. These problems were compounded when the two different groups of independent variables were tested against the 'wrong' dependent variables as well, in order to determine if the general hypotheses were too restrictive. It was therefore decided to correlate separately each of the independent variables to the dependent variables (DV1–4) to determine which ones appeared worthy of further statistical investigation. Only those that approached significance at a 95 per cent level were incorporated into multivariate form.

The large number of equations tested, given four dependent variables and 12 independent variables, also sharply increased the possibility of chance significance. Because of this, any value below the 99 per cent significance should be treated with caution.

IV

(a) Statistical Results – Case A: The Seven Countries

These countries vary quite considerably in income levels, economic structure, political ideologies, culture and proximity to the USA and the extent to which they themselves spawn MNEs which compete in international markets with US-based MNEs. It would not be surprising to find that different factors explain the absolute and relative success of US exports and affiliate production in these countries when tested individually; here, however, we are concerned with factors which explain export and affiliate success in the seven countries *as a group*, and which can, perhaps, be regarded as 'worldwide' determinants of such success.

H1(DV1–3). Table 3.4 summarises the more significant results of the regression analyses. The explanatory variables presented were extracted from the bivariate analysis and a series of multivariate equations constructed from them. For each of the variants of H1, most of the variation in the share of US firms in the output of countries can be put down to two or three variables, with the best results coming from the overall international competitiveness index (DV1). Since we are dealing with 98 observations, the explanatory power of the three variants

Table 3.4 Determinant of participation ratios of US MNEs in seven countries, 1970

	Constant	AVNIS	RMS	SER	AHC	RW	RES	CGS	R(R^2)
	(1) DV1 (*AS* + *X*/*IS*)								
1.1	0.060		–0.991 (4.058)**	1.133 (4.993)**					0.546 (0.298)
1.2	–0.068		–1.137 (4.831)**	1.007 (4.613)**			0.375 (3.422)**		0.613 (0.376)
1.3	–0.051		–1.219 (4.759)**	0.910 (3.652)**	0.027 (0.815)		0.279 (1.728)		0.617 (0.380)
1.4	0.002	–0.002 (2.474)**	–1.155 (4.635)**	0.732 (2.987)**	0.161 (2.603)*	–0.777 (2.615)*	0.494 (2.880)*		0.673 (0.452)
1.5	–0.028	–0.002 (2.365)*	–1.136 (4.519)**	0.809 (2.994)**	0.131 (1.735)	–0.648 (1.840)	0.480 (2.765)**	0.0065 (0.683)	0.675 (0.455)
	(2) DV2 (*AS*/*IS*)								
2.1	0.018		–0.580 (3.459)	0.497 (3.192)**					0.430 (0.185)
2.2	0.0026		–0.693 (3.829)**	0.374 (2.164)*	0.026 (1.585)				0.454 (0.206)
2.3	0.016	–0.0009 (1.151)	–0.717 (3.942)**	0.388 (2.129)*	0.025 (1.522)				0.466 (0.217)
2.4	0.028	–0.0010 (1.260)	–0.669 (3.545)**	0.295 (1.597)	0.084 (1.801)	–0.322 (1.438)	0.072 (0.599)		0.485 (0.235)
	(3) DV3 (*X*/*IS*)								
3.1	0.078		–1.571 (4.372)**	1.631 (4.883)**					0.553 (0.306)
3.2	–0.079		–1.750 (4.957)**	1.476 (4.510)**			0.459 (2.792)**		0.599 (0.359)
3.3	0.022		–1.987 (5.265)**	1.177 (3.260)**	0.095 (2.803)**				0.599 (0.359)
3.4	0.030	–0.0038 (2.271)*	–1.824 (4.856)**	1.027 (2.780)**	0.245 (2.627)*	– 1.098 (2.454)*	0.566 (2.190)*		0.657 (0.432)

* Significant at the 95 per cent level.
** Significant at the 99 per cent level.

of the hypothesis is encouraging. All the signs (apart from that of RW) are consistent and in the right direction.

The equations reveal that the main advantage of US firms is revealed in one location-specific variable, viz. relative market size (RMS), and one ownership-specific variable, viz. the skilled employment ratio (SER). It has also been suggested (see Table 3.4) that this latter ratio may be used as a proxy for internalising advantages. Both are consistently significant at the 'double asterisk', that is, 99 per cent level for each of the dependent variables. The other ownership variables, which are significant at this level for DV1 and DV3, are the productivity index, viz. relative sales per man (RSM), and average hourly compensation (AHC). Two location variables, viz. wage differentials (RW) and net income per sales (AVNIS), are also significant for the same two dependent variables, but only at the 95 per cent level. For DV2, no variables, other than RMS and SER, were significant, although average hourly compensation (AHC) came closest. This last variable appears to be collinear with SER; this is not unexpected, as higher salaries are usually obtained by more highly skilled non-production employees.

These same relationships were also run using the 1966 data and much the same results obtained, with the exception that the 1966 profit variable (net income to sales AVNIS) is never quite significant.

Table 3.5 Determinants of export/local production ratios of US MNEs in seven countries, 1970

	Constant	XMR	AVNIS	RMS	RSM	GRSPM	R(R^2)
	(4) *DV4(X/AS)*						
4.1	0.308	–0.101	0.043				0.601
		(3.301)**	(7.256)**				(0.362)
4.2	0.042	–0.101	0.043			0.0085	0.622
		(3.363)**	(7.277)**			(1.942)	(0.386)
4.3	0.103	–0.099	0.042	–0.561		0.0084	0.624
		(3.210)**	(7.007)**	(0.600)		(1.896)	(0.389)
4.4	0.100	–0.100	0.042		–0.0000048	0.0090	0.623
		(3.287)**	(7.101)**		(0.441)	(1.983)	(0.388)

** Significant at 99 per cent level.

H2(DV4). The results obtained from this hypothesis set out in Table 3.5 are quite different from those of H1. Two variables, viz. the export/import ratio (XMR) and net income to sales (AVNIS), are consistently significant at the 99 per cent level, and explain nearly 60 per cent of the variation in the location ratio. Growth of relative sales per man (GRSPM) comes very close but is never quite significant. The results for 1966 were virtually the same as for 1970.

(b) Statistical Results – Case B: The Five Advanced Countries

Quite early in the study, it was decided to run the data with Mexico and Brazil excluded. Although to a certain extent, each country exercises its own unique set of influences on the involvement of foreign firms, there is something to be said for separating Mexico and Brazil from the five other countries. Historically, LDCs have produced relatively more raw materials and semi-finished manufactures and less of finished products for world markets than the developed countries. And, as we have seen, investment in resource-based industries is often based on very different considerations than investment in manufacturing. Mexico and Brazil, in spite of recent rates of rapid industrial growth, are still sufficiently different in their stages of development to justify separate treatment.

H1(DV1–3). The results are presented in Table 3.6. In all equations one ownership variable, viz. the skilled employment ratio (SER), and two location variables, viz. relative market shares (RMS) and average hourly compensation (AHC), are consistently significant at the 99 per cent level. These three variables clearly have some influence on both US trade and affiliate success in each of the five countries. Relative export shares (RES) and relative wages (RW) appear significant at the 95 per cent (and in one case at the 99 per cent) level in some of the equations of DV2 and DV3, but only where there are few independent variables regressed together. This suggests that these latter two location variables exert some influence on the competitiveness of US trade but not on that of foreign production.

The tariff variable (T) appears to be a significant explanation of the overall involvement of US firms in the five countries. In combination with the three universally successful variables above (RMS, SER and AHC) it yielded an R^2 of 0.577 which is quite satisfactory.

The data for 1966 suggest much the same results, with the exception that, in some combinations, involving four or less independent variables, RS and RW also become significant as an explanation of DV1. This rather weakens the argument, based on the 1970 data, that these two have an influence on trade, but not on foreign production. But probably they are only marginally significant in all three cases. For both years, 1966 and 1970, when the number of independent variables is increased, these two variables become less significant, which suggests that the added variables capture the significant influences duplicated in RS and RW. There appears, for example, to be a fair amount of collinearity between RW and AHC and between RS and SPM. For 1970, the correlation coefficients (at the seven-country level) between these variables are 0.944 and 0.705, respectively.

As may be seen in Table 3.7, quite different variables explain most of the form of penetration than those which explain H1. The profitability ratio

Table 3.6 Determinants of participation ratios of US MNEs in five advanced countries, 1970

	Constant	AVNIS	RMS	SER	AHC	RW	RES	SPM	T	R(R^2)
	(1) DV1 (*AS + X/IS*)									
1.1	0.058		–0.990	1.162						0.587
			(3.323)**	(4.445)**						(0.343)
1.2	0.0956	–0.0028	1.084	1.137						0.614
		(1.884)	(3.653)**	(4.425)**						(0.377)
1.3	–0.014	–0.0026	–1.015	1.289					0.010	0.653
		(1.791)	(3.522)**	(2.373)*					(2.373)*	(0.427)
1.4	0.470	–0.0019	–0.9234	0.872	0.152				0.014	0.755
		(1.482)	(3.660)**	(3.608)**	(4.609)**				(3.486)	(0.570)
1.5	–0.436	–0.0022	–0.912	0.891	0.173	–0.318	0.202		0.013	0.760
		(1.688)	(3.576)**	(3.409)**	(2.844)**	(0.942)	(0.943)		(3.330)**	(0.577)
	(2) DV2 (*AS/IS*)									
2.1	0.0125		–0.540	0.506						0.566
			(3.595)**	(3.841)**						(0.321)
2.2	–0.096		–0.522	0.334	0.056					0.634
			(3.675)**	(2.438)*	(3.007)**					(0.403)
2.3	–0.055	–0.0010	–0.539	0.339	0.077	–0.274	0.148			0.657
		(1.346)	(3.727)**	(2.291)*	(2.254)*	(1.426)	(1.225)			(0.432)
2.4	–0.051	–0.0012	–0.545	0.391	0.099	–0.390	0.283	–0.0000043		0.681
		(1.609)	(3.845)**	(2.648)*	(2.787)**	(1.969)	(2.059)	(1.900)		(0.464)
	(3) DV3 (*X/IS*)									
3.1	0.070		–1.530	1.669						0.617
			(3.771)	(4.686)**						(0.381)
3.2	0.307		–1.467	1.071	0.194					0.710
			(4.007)**	(3.031)**	(4.051)**					(0.504)
3.3	–0.314		–1.466	1.464		0.695				0.677
			(3.830)**	(4.282)**		(3.079)*				(0.459)
3.4	–0.250	–0.0030	–1.570	1.070	0.185					0.723
		(1.616)	(4.275)**	(3.064)**	(3.903)**					(0.523)
3.5	–0.206	–0.0037	–1.536	1.137	0.221	–0.627	0.438			0.735
		(1.938)	(4.072)**	(3.016)**	(2.532)*	(1.280)	(1.422)			(0.540)

* Significant at 99 per cent level.
** Significant at 95 per cent level.

Table 3.7 Determinants of export/local production ratios of US MNEs in five advanced countries, 1970

	Constant	AVNIS	AHC	RW	RSM	RES	CMG	GRSPM	MG	T	R(R^2)
	(4) DV4 *X/AS*)										
4.1	–0.251	0.050						0.012			0.717
		(7.953)**						(2.206)*			(0.515)
4.2	–0.130	0.050						0.025	–1.309		0.736
		(7.857)**						(2.942)**	(1.967)		(0.542)
4.3	1.777	0.050			–0.000045		–3.517	0.013			0.755
		(8.119)**			(2.510)*		(2.845)**	(2.515)**			(0.570)
4.4	0.508	0.044		–2.548		1.803		0.024	–1.240		0.766
		(7.150)**		(2.657)*		(2.174)*		(2.914)**	(1.928)		(0.587)
4.5	1.492	0.046		–1.509	–0.000043	1.647	–2.534	0.012			0.767
		(7.325)**		(1.289)	(1.906)	(1.645)	(1.694)	(2.316)*			(0.588)
4.6	1.277	0.045		–1.760	–0.000030	1.605	–1.848	0.021	–0.864		0.773
		(7.159)**		(1.486)	(1.212)	(1.608)	(1.159)	(2.361)*	(1.210)		(0.598)
4.7	1.603	0.045	0.249	–2.516	–0.000045	1.672	–2.598	0.022	–1.004		0.776
		(7.086)**	(0.859)	(1.703)	(1.483)	(1.666)	(1.427)	(2.436)*	(1.367)		(0.602)
4.8	1.521	0.045	0.307	–2.430	–0.000050	1.483	–3.002	0.023	–0.964	0.012	0.778
		(7.082)**	(1.008)	(1.630)	(1.600)	(1.415)	(1.555)	(2.499)*	(1.303)	(0.656)	(0.605)

* Significant at the 95 per cent level.
** Significant at the 99 per cent level.

(AVNIS) and the growth in sales per man (GRSPM) are consistently significant, the former at extremely high levels of significance and the latter at either 99 per cent or 95 per cent levels of significance. These two alone explain more than half the variance in the location ratio. Other variables which are occasionally significant are three location-specific variables: relative export shares (RES), relative wage costs (RW) and comparative market growth (CMG). They are only significant in small groups, however, which suggests an overlap between many of these variables. Equation 4 of DV4 is a good example where relative wage costs (RW) and relative export shares (RES) are both significant at a 95 per cent level and where the R^2 is 0.587.

The data for 1966 yield similar results with country or industry (rather than ownership) differences in profitability (AVNIS) and growth in sales per man (GRSPM) (an ownership variable) being rather more significant. But in this case (market share) MG becomes marginally significant in combination with GRSPM. None of the labour cost and productivity variables is significant.

Comparing Case A and Case B

Excluding Mexico and Brazil, the seven-country analysis produced some noticeable differences in the results of the statistical analysis. This section deals with a few of these and speculates on the reasons for them.

First the general level of the R^2s rises quite noticeably. This suggests that the independent variables used were more relevant in explaining export and affiliate success in the more homogeneous advanced countries than in Mexico and Brazil. Running the regressions excluding Canada suggests even higher R^2s could have been obtained.[18]

Second, considering the data for 1966 as well as 1970, differences in wage costs (RW) and export shares (RS) tend to be more significant in explaining H1(DV2) in the seven-country than in the five-country case. Perhaps these variables are too similar over different industries in the industrialised countries, and, not until the widely different figures for Mexico and Brazil are included, is their influence clearly indicated.

Third, AHC differences are significant in the compensation of the five-country but not in the seven-country case for H2(DV4). This result is difficult to interpret. It may be due to less reliable figures on hourly compensation in Mexico and Brazil than in the other countries, or to a vastly different labour force structure which influences the extent to which local firms can compete successfully against imports in different ways.

Fourth, in the case of H1(DV1), there are virtually no differences between Cases A and B. There is one major difference between the two cases involving DV4, viz. the export/import ratio (XMR) is significant with the larger group but not with the smaller. This may be interpreted to mean that the export potential of an industry may be more important in a less developed economy in determining the form of penetration. The negative sign implies that US firms in those industries will tend to establish affiliates rather than export to the less developed countries, and perhaps even export some portion of their output. This is consistent with both the product cycle model's last stage and the growth of export-platform investments in some developing countries, including Mexico.

APPENDIX 3.1 NOTE ON METHODOLOGY

The statistical analysis was restricted to common linear regression analysis and was carried out by Guy Landry at the University of Reading Computing Centre. Initially, single variable regressions with each of the independent variables and for each dependent variable were run. The purpose was to choose potentially useful explanatory variables from the number available. As a result of this a few variables were dropped because they either indicated no explanatory value or appeared less useful than very similar variables which were retained.

The next step involved multiple regressions. As explained in the body of this chapter, the independent variables were divided into three categories:

1. the *ownership*-specific variables: SER, AHC, RSM, and GRSPM. These are variables suggested by industrial organisation theory.
2. the *country*-specific variables XMR, RMS, RW, RES, and CMG. These are mostly suggested by trade and location theory.
3. the general performance indicators AVNIS and MG.

For each of the dependent variables, various combinations of the independent variables in each category were subjected to regression analysis. The most significant results are those shown in the tables. The purpose of this step was to determine which independent variables in each category best explained the dependent variables. Next, these same variables were analysed, but with the categories grouped in different combinations. Once again the tables reveal the results. These particular equations should reveal the explanatory power of various combinations of the independent variables chosen from two or all of three categories.

The values in parentheses are the *t*-values: those marked by a single asterisk are significant at the 95 per cent level, while those marked by two asterisks are significant at the 99 per cent level.

The last column of each table gives the values of the coefficient of determination.

APPENDIX 3.2 LIST OF INDUSTRIES (AND CONCORDANCE)

		BEA Code	SIC Code	SITC Code		
1	Food products	410	20	013	047	062
				023	048	092
				024	053	099
				032	055	111
				046	061	112
2	Paper and allied products	420	26	64		
				251		
3	Chemical and allied products	430	28	5		
4	Rubber	440	30	231.2		
				62		
				893		
5	Primary and fabricated metals	450	33	67		
				68		
				69		
				812.3		
6	Non-electrical machinery	460	35	71		
7	Electrical machinery	470	36	72		
8	Transportation equipment	480	37	73		
9	Textiles and apparel	491	22	65		
			23	84		
				266		
10	Lumber, wood and furniture	492	24	63		
			25	243		
				82		
11	Printing and publishing	493	27	892		
12	Stone, clay, and glass products	495	32	66		
				–667		
13	Instruments	496	38	86		
				–863		
14	Ordnance, leather, tobacco,	494	19	122	891	
	and other manufacturing	497	21	61	894	
		498	31	667	895	
		499	39	81	897	
				–812.3	899	
				83	951.0	
				85		

APPENDIX 3.3 STATISTICAL SOURCES

Dependent Variables

The dependent variables of the analysis are described in the text and are all ratios based on the following four variables.

1 *AS* – Affiliate Sales: foreign sales of all affiliates of US MNEs, by industry and by country. From US Tariff Commission (USTC) (1973), p. 372.
2 *X* – Exports: exports from USA, by countries receiving and by industry. From USTC Study, p. 384.
3 *ASX* (or *AS* + *X*) – Affiliate Sales plus Exports: the sum of the above two.
4 *IS* – Industry Sales: sales (production) by all firms, by industry and by country. From USTC Study, pp. 693–706.

Independent Variables

A. By industry, for all seven selected countries.
1 SER – Skilled Employment Ratio: the ratio of salaried employment to total (salaried plus production) employment for all firms. Derived from USTC Study, pp. 693–706.
2 AHC – Average Hourly Compensation: estimate average hourly compensation of all employees. From pp. 724–5 of USTC Study.
3 AVNIS – Net Income to Sales: the ratio of net income (after foreign income tax) to sales of affiliates of US MNEs. Derived from USTC Study, pp. 446–52. Unlike the case of most of the other variables where the data is for 1970, this refers to an average of 1966 and 1970.
4 XMR – Export–Import Ratio: the ratio of exports to imports. Derived from USTC Study, p. 377 (for exports) and OECD, Series C, Commodity Trade (for imports).
5 RES – Relative Export Share: a Balassa-type measure of export performance, based on data from USTC Study, p. 377.
6 RSM – Relative Sales per Man: estimated sales per man in the host country/estimated sales per man in the USA, for all employees. Derived from USTC Study, pp. 748–9.
7 RW – Relative Wages: estimated average hourly compensation in the host country/estimated average hourly compensation in the USA, for all employees. Derived from USTC Study, pp. 724–5.
8 GRSPM – Growth in Sales Per Man, 1966–1970. Based on USTC Study, pp. 748–9.
9 RMS – Relative Market Size: industry sales in the host country/industry sales in the USA. Based on USTC Study, pp. 691–706.

10 CMG – Comparative Market Growth, 1966–1970. Market growth in the host country/market growth in the USA. The market is here defined as industry sales plus imports. Based on USTC Study, pp. 691–706 (for industry sales) and OECD, Series C, Commodity Trade (for imports).

11 MG – Market Growth rate, 1966–1970. The market is here defined as industry sales plus imports. Based on USTC Study, pp. 693–706 (for industry sales) and OECD, Series C, Commodity Trade (for imports).

B. By industry, for the industrialised five countries.

1 TR – Tariffs: average tariff rates in effect, 1958. Based on Political and Economic Planning (1962).

NOTES

1. Throughout this chapter, 'assets', 'endowments' and 'resources' are used interchangeably, and in the Fisherian sense, to mean 'anything capable of generating a future income stream'.
2. Thus a firm of one nationality may *own* assets but sell the right of their *use* to firms of another nationality, for example, by engaging in portfolio investment or international licensing; where it owns them, but uses them itself in another country, then it engages in foreign direct investment, that is, it becomes an MNE.
3. In this chapter, distance from foreign markets is treated as a negative location-specific endowment.
4. Moreover, since perfect competition and identical production functions between firms were two of the assumptions underlying the theories, they were not interested in explaining the international activities of firms – only of countries.
5. That is, an advantage which is country specific *in origin* becomes an ownership-specific advantage *in use*.
6. For a succinct review of the literature on the theory of internalisation, see Rugman (1980).
7. Among these one might mention particularly those of Vaupel (1971) and Horst (1972a, b, 1975) (in this latter paper the author explicitly acknowledges the importance of internalising advantages). The study of Wolf (1977) is also particularly pertinent to explaining why firms choose to engage in foreign direct investment rather than other forms of growth. Writers doing research on host country data include Orr (1973), Baumann (1975), Caves (1974), Buckley and Dunning (1976), Lall (1979), Owen (1979), Parry (1980) and Papandreou (1980).
8. See here particularly the work of Hirsch (1976), Buckley and Pearce (1979), Hawkins and Webbinek (1976), Parry (1975, 1976), Buckley and Davies (1979) and Buckley and Casson (1981). The question of the extent to which trade and foreign investment substitute for each other has been very well explored by Lipsey and Weiss (1973, 1976a, b), Cornell (1973) and Horst (1974).
9. There has been only limited empirical testing of this approach. The Hirsch contribution (Hirsch, 1976) is again very relevant. See also Dunning and Buckley (1977).
10. Here the work of Buckley and Casson (1976) is especially relevant.
11. The complications of this assumption will be dealt with later in this chapter. See also Horst (1974).
12. We extract from the possibility that firms might supply foreign markets from third locations.
13. Consumption figures would have been more appropriate but these were not available.
14. But see Dunning and Buckley (1977).
15. In other words, some ownership advantages are not independent of the location of production.
16. Which *inter alia* may be affected by competitors' behaviour.
17. For a different approach to the measurement of these advantages see Buckley and Casson (1976).
18. This was not actually done because to do so would have substantially reduced the degrees of freedom.

REFERENCES

Aliber, R.Z. (1970), 'A theory of foreign direct investment', in C.P. Kindleberger (ed.), *The International Corporation*, (Cambridge, MA: MIT Press).

Baumann, H. (1975), 'Merger theory, property rights and the pattern of US direct investment in Canada', *Weltwirtschaftliches Archiv*, Vol. III, no. 4.

Buckley, P.J. and Casson, M.C. (1976), *The Future of the Multinational Enterprise*, (London: Macmillan).

Buckley, P.J. and Casson, M.C. (1981), 'The optimal timing of a foreign direct investment', *Economic Journal*, Vol. 91 (March).

Buckley, P.J. and Davies, H. (1979), *The Place of Licensing in the Theory and Practice of Foreign Operations*, University of Reading Discussion Papers in International Investment and Business Studies No. 47.

Buckley, P.J. and Dunning, J.H. (1976), "The industrial structure of US direct investment in the UK', *Journal of International Business Studies*, Vol. 7, (Summer).

Buckley, P.J. and Pearce, R.D. (1979), 'Overseas production and exporting by the world's largest enterprises', *Journal of International Business Studies*, Vol. 10 (Spring).

Caves, R.E. (1974), 'The causes of direct investment: foreign firms' shares in Canadian and UK manufacturing industries', *Review of Economics and Statistics*, Vol. 56 (August).

Cornell, R. (1973), 'Trade of multinational firms and nation's comparative advantage', paper presented to a Conference on Multinational Corporations and Governments, UCLA, November 1973.

Dunning, J.H. (1979), 'Explaining changing patterns of international production: in defense of the eletic theory', *Oxford Bulletin of Economics and Statistics*, Vol. 41 (94), 269–95.

Dunning, J.H. and Buckley, P.J. (1977), 'International production and alternative models of trade', *Manchester School of Economic and Social Studies*, Vol. 45 (December).

Hawkins, R. and Webbinek, E.S. (1976), Theories of direct foreign investment: a survey of empirical evidence', unpublished manuscript.

Hirsch, S. (1976), 'An international trade and investment theory of the firm', *Oxford Economic Papers*, Vol. 28 (July).

Horst, T. (1972a), 'Firm and industry determinants of the decision to invest abroad: an empirical study', *Review of Economics and Statistics*, Vol. 54 (August).

Horst, T. (1972b), 'The industrial composition of US exports and subsidiary sales to the Canadian market', *American Economic Review*, Vol. 62 (March).

Horst, T. (1974), *American Exports and Foreign Direct Investments*, Harvard Institute of Economic Research Discussion Paper No. 362 (May).

Horst, T. (1975), 'American investments abroad: and domestic market power', unpublished paper (for Brookings Institution, Washington, DC).

Kojima, K. (1978), *Direct Foreign Investment*, (London: Croom Helm).

Knickerbocker, F.T. (1973), *Oligopolistic Reaction and the Multinational Enterprise* (Cambridge, MA: Harvard University Press).

Lall, S. (1979), 'Multinationals and market structure in an open developing economy. The case of Malaysia', *Weltwirtschaftliches Archiv*, Vol. 114 (2).

Lall, S. (1980), 'Monopolistic advantages and foreign involvement by US manufacturing industry', *Oxford Economic Papers*, Vol. 32 (March).

Lipsey, R.E. and Weiss, M.Y. (1973), *Multinational Firms and the Factor Intensity of Trade*, National Bureau of Economic Research, New York, Working Paper No. 8.

Lipsey, R.E. and Weiss, M.Y. (1976a), *Exports and Foreign Investment in the Pharmaceutical Industry*, National Bureau of Economic Research, New York, Working Paper No. 87 (revised).

Lipsey, R.E. and Weiss, M.Y. (1976b), *Exports and Foreign Investment in Manufacturing Industries*, National Bureau of Economic Research, New York, Working Paper No. 13 (revised).

Orr, D. (1973), 'Foreign control and foreign penetration in Canadian manufacturing industries', unpublished manuscript.

Owen, R.F. (1979), *Inter-industry Determinants of Foreign Direct Investment: A Perspective Emphasising the Canadian Experience*, Working Papers in International Economics, Princeton University (May).

Papandreou, V.A. (1980), 'Multinational enterprises, market industrial structure and trade, balance in less developed countries: the case of Greece', University of Reading PhD thesis.

Parry, T.G. (1975), 'Trade and non trade performance of US manufacturing industry: "revealed" comparative advantage', *Manchester School of Economics and Social Studies*, Vol. 43 (June).

Parry, T.G. (1976), *Methods of Servicing Overseas Markets: The UK Owned Pharmaceutical Study*, University of Reading Discussion Paper (Series 2) No. 27.

Parry, T.G. (1980), *The Multinational Enterprise: International Investment and Host Country Impacts*, (Greenwich, CT: JAI Press).

Political and Economic Planning (1962), *Atlantic Tariffs and Trade*, (London: Allen & Unwin).

Rugman, A. (1980), 'Internalisation as a general theory of foreign direct investment', *Weltwirtschaftliches Archiv*, Vol. 116 (June).

Swedenborg, B. (1979), *The Multinational Operations of Swedish Firms: An Analysis of Determinants and Effects*, (Stockholm: Almqvist and Wiksell International).

US Tariff Commission (1973), *Implications of Multinational Firms for World Trade and Investment and for US Trade and Labor*, (Washington, DC: US Government Printing Office).

Vaupel, J.W. (1971), 'Characteristics and motivations of the US corporations which invest abroad', unpublished manuscript.

Vernon, R. (1966), 'International investment and international trade in the product cycle', *Quarterly Journal of Economics*, Vol. 80 (May).

Vernon, R. (1974), The location of economic activity', in J.H. Dunning (ed.), *Economic Analysis and the Multinational Enterprise* (London: Allen & Unwin).

Wolf, B. (1977), 'Industrial diversification and internationalisation: some empirical evidence', *Journal of Industrial Economics*, Vol. 26 (December).

4. Explaining the international direct investment position of countries: towards a dynamic or developmental approach*

I

This chapter explores the proposition that a country's international direct investment position, and changes in that position, may be usefully explained by the eclectic theory of international production. Using data on the direct investment flows (or changes in the direct capital stock) of some sixty-seven countries over the period 1967–78, it also suggests that there is a systematic relationship between the determinants of those flows and the stage and structure of a country's economic development.

II

A country's net international direct investment position is the sum of the direct investment by its own enterprises[1] outside its national boundaries minus the direct investment of foreign owned enterprises within its boundaries.[2]

The eclectic theory suggests that this position, whether one is concerned with the stock of accumulated investment, that is, the direct capital stock, on changes in the stock over time, is determined by three sets of factors. The first is the extent to which its own enterprises possess, or can gain access to, assets or rights which foreign enterprises do not possess or to which they cannot gain access, at least on such favourable terms. Such assets are called ownership-specific advantages[3] in so far as they are assumed to be exclusive to the enterprise that owns them, and at least some of them are likely to be transferable (i.e. mobile) across national boundaries (Lall, 1980). The second is whether the enterprises possessing the assets perceive it to be in their best interests to internalise their use or sell this right (but not the assets themselves[4]) to enter-

* From *Weltwirtschaftliches Archiv*, **117** (1981), 30–64.

prises located in other countries; such internalising advantages reflect the perceived efficiency of multinational hierarchies, compared with market mechanisms, as asset administrators and allocators.[5] The third factor determining international production is the extent to which enterprises find it profitable to locate any part of their production facilities outside their home countries; this will depend on the attractions of location-specific endowments, that is, those which are not transferable or mobile across national boundaries and offered by the home, as compared with a foreign, country.

The generalised predictions of the eclectic theory are straightforward. At any given moment of time, the more a country's enterprises possess ownership-specific advantages, relative to enterprises of other nationalities, the greater the incentive they have to internalise rather than externalise their use; and the more they find it in their interest to exploit them from a foreign location, the more they (and the country as a whole) are likely to engage in international production.[6] By the same token, a country is likely to attract investment by foreign enterprises when the reverse conditions apply. Similarly the theory can be expressed in a dynamic context:[7] changes in the outward or inward investment position of a particular country can be explained in terms of changes in the ownership and internalisation advantages of its enterprises, relative to those of other nationalities, and/or changes in its location-specific endowments, relative to those of other countries, as perceived by its own and foreign enterprises.

A good deal of work has been done on identifying the origin and nature of these ownership–location–internalisation (OLI) advantages, and the conditions under which they are most likely to exist. These were first identified in Dunning (1979), and later refined and modified in Dunning (1993). They are reproduced as Appendix 1 of this chapter. The O-specific advantages are derived from the theories of industrial organisation and the resource-based theory of the firm; the L-specific advantages from the theory of location and the I-specific advantages from the theory of the firm.

This approach to the theory of international production has been called eclectic for three main reasons. First, it draws on each of the three main lines of explanation which have emerged over the past twenty or so years;[8] second, it is relevant to all types of foreign direct investment; third, and perhaps of most interest, it embraces the three main vehicles of foreign involvement by enterprises, viz. direct investment, exports and contractual resource transfers, e.g. licensing, technical assistance, management and franchising agreements, and suggests which route of exploitation is likely to be preferred. In the case of each modality, the possession of ownership advantages is a necessary prerequisite for foreign involvement.[9] But the presence of internalisation advantages suggests that enterprises will exploit these advantages by way of exports or foreign direct investment rather than by contractual resource exchanges, whereas the equity investment route, rather than exports, will be

Table 4.1 Alternative routes of servicing markets

	Advantages	Ownership	Internalisation	(Foreign) Location
Route of servicing market	Foreign direct investment	Yes	Yes	Yes
	Exports	Yes	Yes	No
	Contractual resource transfers	Yes	No	No

chosen where locational advantages favour a foreign rather than a domestic production base. The matrix in Table 4.1 summarises the conditions underlying these choices.

Although the three strands in the explanation of international production interact with each other, conceptually there is something to be said for considering them separately. Certainly the location and mode of foreign involvement are two quite independent decisions which a firm has to take, while, by itself, no one strand is both a necessary and a sufficient condition to explain international production. Take, for example, the distinction between ownership and internalisation advantages. Ownership advantages may be internally generated (e.g. through product diversification or innovations) or acquired by enterprises. If acquired, for example, by way of a purchase (be it domestic or foreign) of another enterprise, the presumption is that this act will add to the acquiring firm's ownership advantages *vis-à-vis* those of its competitors (including the acquired firm).[10]

It is convenient to distinguish between two kinds of ownership advantages. The first is that which may generate income whether its use is externalised or internalised; most patents and trademarks, and some management marketing, financial and organisational assets fall into this category. The second is that which can only be realised if it is internalised within the firm, that is, not saleable to other firms. This includes the genuine joint economies of hierarchical activities, for example, product and process integration, the spreading of managerial and technological capacity, the reduction in transaction costs and the gains arising from asset, product or market diversification. Quite a lot of international backward and forward integration is designed to capture the benefits of internalisation as well as to secure exclusive access to inputs and markets.

There is some reason for supposing that the greater the diversification practised by an MNE, the higher the proportion of ownership advantages attributable to internalisation gains (or more correctly the capitalisation of such gains[11]) is likely to be. To this extent, the internalisation paradigm may be more helpful in explaining degrees of multinationality than discrete acts of foreign direct investment.[12] But, except where foreign investment is undertaken to acquire ownership advantages which can only be reaped if they are exploited within the acquiring firm, the two kinds of advantages are quite distinct and should be analysed separately from each other.

In seeking to test the eclectic theory of international production, economists have found it useful to distinguish three structural determinants, viz. those which are specific to particular *countries*, to particular *types of activities* (or industries) and to particular *firms* or *enterprises*. In other words, the propensity of enterprises of a particular nationality to engage in foreign production will vary according to the economic and other characteristics of their home countries and the country(ies) in which they propose to invest, the range and type of products (including intermediate products) they intend to produce, and their underlying management and organisational strategies (which *inter alia* may be affected by their size and attitude to risk diversification). Again, as is illustrated in Table 4.2, these characteristics can be readily identified.

Combining the data in Table 4.2 and that of Appendix 4.2 (pp. 134–136) gives the framework of the eclectic theory that explains each of the main types of foreign direct investment. As can be seen, it is a very general theory. Up to now, most empirical tests of it have been directed to explaining either the industrial composition of a particular country's outward or inward direct investment (or capital stake)[13] or the determinants of the location of that investment.[14] Much less work has so far been done on explaining the country-specific characteristics of the geographical origin of inward direct investment, and none, to my knowledge, on the determinants of the balance between such investment flows. Apart from the product cycle literature, the dynamics of foreign direct investment have been largely ignored while, viewed from a global standpoint, scant attention has been paid to the interaction between the international investment position of a country and its stage and character of economic development.

This chapter should be taken as a starting point in correcting some of these lacunae. I have taken as the variables to be explained the average annual outward, inward and net outward direct investment flows of countries (including reinvested profits and intra-company transfers[15]) for the period 1967–75.[16] Data on the *flow* rather than on the *stock* of foreign direct investment were used because the main source, the IMF *Balance of Payments Yearbook*, provides statistics on both inward and outward investment flows, while the main sources of comparative stock data, viz. the OECD and UN Centre on Transnational Corporations, do not. Information is available for 67 countries over this period, although in the case of a number of countries it had to be supplemented by data from other sources, especially where IMF statistics did not take account of reinvested profits.

Table 4.2 Some illustrations of how OLI characteristics may vary according to structural variables

OLI characteristics	Structural variables Country Home – Host	 Industry	 Firm
Ownership	Factor endowments (e.g. resources and skilled labour), market size and character. Government policy towards innovation, protection of proprietary rights, competition and industrial structure. Government controls on inward direct investment.	Degree of product or process technological intensity. Nature of innovation. Extent of product differentiation. Production economics (e.g. if there are economies of scale). Importance of favoured access to inputs and/or markets.	Size, extent of production process or market diversification. Extent to which enterprise is innovative or marketing-oriented or values security and/or stability, e.g. in sources of inputs, markets, etc. Extent to which there are economies of joint production.
Internalisation	Government intervention and extent to which policies encourage MNEs to internalise transactions, e.g. transfer pricing. Government policy towards mergers. Differences in market structures between countries e.g. with respect to transaction costs, enforcement of contracts, buyer uncertainty, etc. Adequacy of technological, educational, communications, etc., infrastructure in host countries and ability to absorb contractual resource transfers.	Extent to which vertical or horizontal integration is possible/desirable, e.g. need to control sourcing of inputs or markets. Extent to which internalising advantages can be captured in contractual agreements (cf. early and later stages of product cycle). Use made of ownership advantages. Cf. IBM with Unilever type operation. Extent to which local firms have complementary advantages to those of foreign firms. Extent to which opportunities for output specialisation and international division of labour exist.	Organisational and control procedures of enterprise. Attitudes to growth and diversification (e.g. the boundaries of a firm's activities). Attitudes towards sub-contracting – contractual ventures, e.g. licensing, franchising, technical assistance agreements, etc. Extent to which control procedures can be built into contractual agreements. Type of transactions undertaken, e.g. the degree of uncertainty or idiosyncrasy attached to technology transfers. The frequency with which transactions occur.
Location	Physical and psychic distance between countries. Government intervention (tariffs, quotas, taxes, assistance to foreign investors or to own MNEs, e.g. Japanese government's financial aid to Japanese firms investing in South East Asian labour-intensive industries).	Origin and distribution of immobile resources. Transport costs of intermediate and final good products. Industry-specific tariff and non-tariff barriers. Nature of competition between firms in industry. Can functions of activities of industry be split? Significance of 'sensitive' locational variables, e.g. tax incentives, % energy and labour costs.	Management strategy towards foreign involvement. Age and experience of foreign involvement (position of enterprise in product cycle, etc.). Psychic distance variables (culture, language, legal and commercial framework). Attitudes towards centralisation of certain functions, e.g. R&D, regional office and market allocation, etc. Geographical structure of asset portfolio and attitude to risk diversification.

III

As an initial proposition (and it is not difficult to find reasons to support this)[17] let us suppose that a country's international investment position is related to the value of its gross national product (GNP) – both variables being normalised by size of population. Table 4.3 sets out a frequency distribution between gross outward (GOI), gross inward (GII) and net outward investment flows (NOI) averaged for the period 1967–75,[18] and the GNP per capita in 1971 for 67 countries.[19] Illustrated diagrammatically (see Figure 4.1) these data suggest that, after a 'threshold' GNP per capita has been reached, further increases are associated with rising GOI and GII, but that the shape of the NOI curve takes a U-, or J-shaped, form. It would also appear that countries may be classified into four main groups corresponding to four stages of development.

Table 4.3 Direct investment flows per capita 1967–75 and GNP per capita 1971 for 67 countries

GNP per capita (1971)	Investment (annual average) ($)						
	Weighted average[a] 1967–75			Unweighted average[b] 1967–75			
	Outward	Inward	Net outward	Outward	Inward	Net outward 1967–75	1976–78
1 $4000 and over	33.0	16.3	16.7	24.8	30.3	–5.5	7.9
2 $2500 to $3999	20.0	15.7	4.3	20.8	31.4	–10.6	–7.6
3 $1000 to $2499	3.2	12.9	–9.7	1.2	39.6	–37.4	–32.6
4 $500 to $999	0.4	8.6	–8.2	0.4	21.8	–21.4	–14.4
5 $400 to $499	0.2	7.4	–7.2	0.2	9.0	–8.8	–7.1
6 $300 to $399	0.2	3.2	–3.0	0.1	3.7	–3.6	–3.2
7 $125 to $299	0	3.1	–3.1	0	1.9	–1.9	–2.9
8 Less than $125	0	0.5	–0.5	0	1.3	–1.3	–1.6

[a] Weighted average – obtained by summing outward/inward/net outward investment flows for the *x* countries in the group and dividing by the population of the *x* countries. This gives a country with a large population a dominating influence on the result for an income group, for example, the USA in the over $4000 group. (GNP per capita data from UN *Statistical Year Book*.)

[b] Unweighted average – obtained by (1) calculating outward/inward/net outward flow per capita separately for each of the *x* countries in an income group; (2) summing these separate results; (3) dividing by *x*.

Source: IMF with adjustments, in some cases, by author to allow for reinvested profits and/or expropriation of foreign investments over period 1967–75.

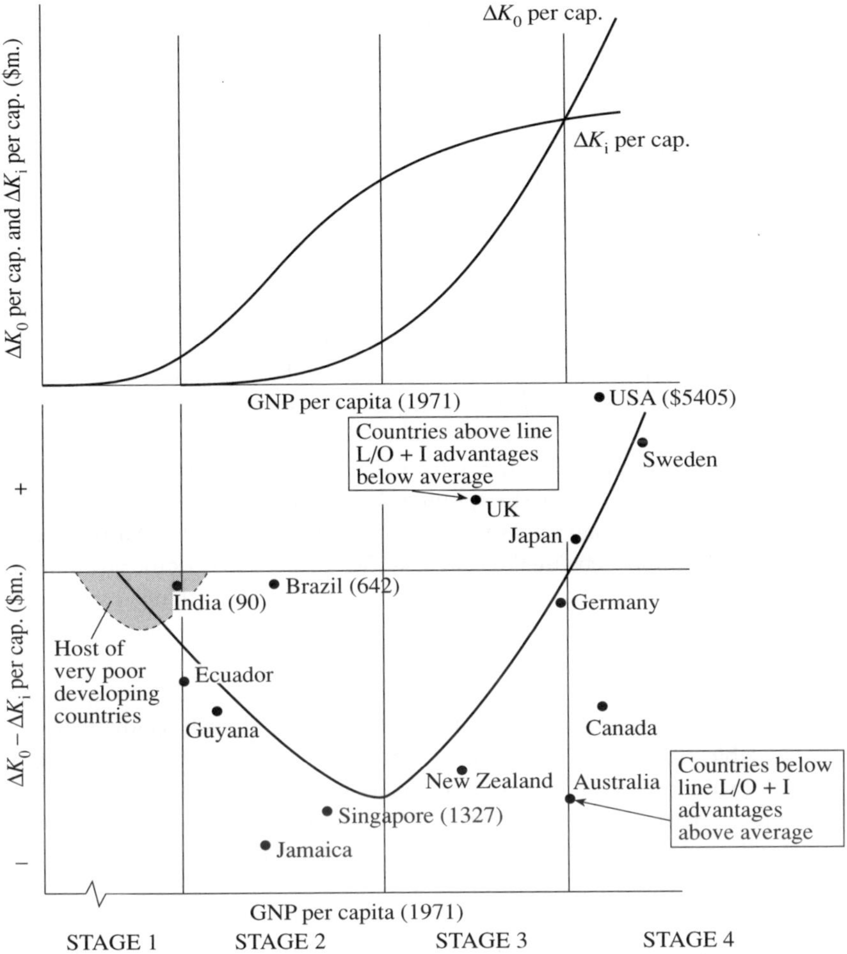

Note: Not to scale.

Figure 4.1 Illustration of relationship between Direct Investment Flows and Income levels (Investment 1967–75 annual average).

The first group of countries consists of those in which there is little inward and, apart from India, no outward direct investment, and a small negative NOI; it includes 25 of the poorest developing countries with a GNP per capita of $400 or less. The second group is made up of those in which inward direct investment is rising but outward direct investment remains very small, that is, where NOI is negative but is becoming larger; there are 25 countries at this stage of development with a GNP per capita ranging between $400 and (about)

$1500. The third group of countries consists of those in which NOI is still negative but is becoming smaller; this may occur either because, with a constant outward investment, inward investment is falling, or because outward investment is rising faster than inward investment. Some 11 countries with GNPs per head ranging from $2000 to $4750 fall into this category. The fourth stage is where NOI per capita is positive and rising; this suggests that either the level of inward investment has fallen below that of outward investment or that outward investment is rising faster than inward investment. Only six countries, with GNPs per head ranging from $2600 to $5600,[20] fall within this category.[21] They are all developed countries and are dominated by the USA, which has far and away the largest NOI per capita.

This kind of investment development cycle can be explained by use of the eclectic theory just described in a way that is summarised in Table 4.4. In Stage 1 there is no GOI either because the country's own enterprises are generating no ownership-specific advantages to make this possible or because what advantages there are, are best exploited through other routes, viz. minority direct investment,[22] contractual resource flows and/or exports. But neither is there any GII, simply because there are insufficient location-specific advantages offered by the host country to warrant the setting up of affiliates by foreign firms. This may be because domestic markets are not large enough or because of an undeveloped, or inappropriate, commercial and legal framework, inadequate transport and communication facilities, and the lack of an educated workforce, which inhibits the profitable exploitation of such endowments as are available. There may be a limited amount of arm's-length capital and/or technology imports, but these are more likely to take the form of aid for infrastructure, from foreign governments or international agencies, while consumer goods will tend to be imported from foreign firms rather than produced locally by them.

In Stage 2, inward direct investment begins to become commercially viable as domestic markets increase and the variable costs of servicing those markets are reduced (Buckley and Casson, 1981). At this point, it is helpful to distinguish between the main forms of foreign direct investment. Import-substituting manufacturing investment, aimed at replacing or supplementing consumer and capital good imports (and often stimulated by host governments imposing barriers to imports), will be initially attracted to well-populated, developing industrialising countries, for example, Brazil, India, Malaysia, etc. (Lecraw, 1977; Wells, 1977). On the other hand, investment to exploit national resources, for example, petroleum, raw materials and foodstuffs, mainly for export markets, is likely to wait upon the provision of adequate transport and communications facilities; while rationalised investment designed to take advantage of cheap and productive unskilled or semi-skilled labour will flow as soon as a well-motivated and educated labour force (at secondary school level) is

Table 4.4 Inward and outward direct investment and stages of economic development

	Inward investment		Outward investment	
Stage 1	Of	Substantial	Od	Virtually none
	I	Substantial	I	Not applicable
	Ld	Few	Lf	Not applicable
Stage 2	Of	Substantial	Od	Few
	I	Probably declining	I	Few and specialised
	Ld	Increasing	Lf	Beginning to emerge
Stage 3	Of	Declining/more specialised	Od	Increasing
	I	Probably increasing	I	Still limited
	Ld	Declining	Lf	Increasing
Stage 4	Of	Declining and/or more specialised	Of	Increasing
	I	Substantial	I	Increasing
	Ld	Declining	Lf	Increasing

Key to symbols:
O = ownership advantages f = foreign
L = location advantages d = domestic
I = internalisation advantages

available. However, it seems generally agreed that an essential locational characteristic for all kinds of GII is a congenial investment climate and an adequate legal and commercial framework (Root and Ahmed, 1978). At this stage, most transfers of resources are likely to be internalised within the transferring firm – except where host governments insist otherwise. This may be to overcome or reduce supply instabilities, or because of the lack of local, technological, managerial, organisational and marketing capacity.[23] Also, since information, commodity and capital markets (including futures markets) are extremely imperfect, if they exist at all, transaction and negotiating costs associated with contractual relationships are likely to be very high indeed. As in Stage 1, outward direct investment remains small, simply because indigenous enterprises have not yet generated sufficient ownership advantages of their own to overcome the initial barriers of foreign production. However, even at this stage there may be some foreign direct investment in neighbouring territories, for example, within Africa and Latin America, or that designed to acquire foreign technology or buy an entry into foreign markets; and also some exporting of the kind which may eventually lead to import-substituting investment.

Stage 3 is a particularly interesting one, as net inward investment per capita now starts to fall. This could be because, as they move through the technology cycle (Magee, 1977), the original ownership advantages of foreign investors become eroded;[24] or because indigenous firms, stimulated *inter alia* by larger markets, the presence of foreign affiliates and/or assisted by host governments, improve their competitive capacity; or because outward investment is now rising as indigenous firms develop their own comparative ownership advantages, which they find it best to exploit through foreign direct investment.[25] This stage may mark the beginning of a country's international direct investment specialisation, in which it seeks to attract inward direct investment in those sectors in which its comparative location advantages are strongest, but the comparative ownership advantages of its enterprises are weakest, while it urges its own enterprises to invest abroad in those sectors where their comparative ownership advantages are strongest but their comparative location advantages are weakest.

Again, much will depend on both host government policies and the characteristics of the direct investment. This is the stage of development in which host governments are likely to encourage a fuller integration of foreign affiliates into their economies; for example, subsidiaries in mineral exploitation will be pressed to undertake more of their secondary process in locally while those in import-substituting or export-platform activities will be persuaded to establish linkages with local enterprises. Moreover, as indigenous firms become more competitive, one would expect the ownership advantages of foreign firms m the mature or standard technology sectors to be whittled away.[26] On the other hand, these advantages may be replaced by others as new activities, in which MNEs have even more pronounced ownership advantages, develop. And since it is in the technologically more advanced sectors that MNEs are most prone to internalise their activities,[27] and, indeed, to gain ownership advantages through internahsation,[28] any tendency towards more licensing and other forms of contractual resource transfer in the sectors originally invested in by MNEs will be more than counteracted.[29]

In Stage 4, a country is a net outward investor, that is, its investment flows abroad exceed those of foreign owned firms in its own country. This reflects strong ownership advantages of its firms and/or an increasing propensity to exploit these advantages internally from a foreign rather than a domestic location. The tendency towards more internalisation is again related to the growing size and geographical diversification of home country MNEs, and to take advantage of regional or global product and process specialisation.[30] At the same time companies, especially from the industrialised economies, are increasingly being induced to exploit their ownership advantages from a foreign location, partly because of rising domestic labour costs and lower rates of productivity growth (often associated with high levels of economic development), partly by the pressure to obtain additional resources (including some types of labour) to help sustain their international competitive position in world markets, and partly to overcome increasing barriers to trade in the kind of goods exported by these countries. Again, depending on the amount of specialisation, GOI may be associated with substantial or little GII. For example, the (second) point of zero NOI could mean that the country engages in no inward or outward investment, that is, is self-sufficient in its investment, or that it has a sizeable outward investment which is balanced by an equally sizeable inward investment.

The interpretation of the investment–development cycle just outlined is based on cross-sectional country data. It suggests that a country's international investment position is related to its level of development as measured by its GNP per capita.[31] However, a proper test of this proposition would require an examination of time series data for individual countries over quite a long period. Unfortunately, except in the case of a few developed countries, data are not available to do this, but casual empiricism does lend some support to the idea of an investment–development cycle. Certainly the USA fits neatly into this pattern, as do most continental European countries and Japan; of the developing countries there are some, for example, Nigeria, Indonesia and Kenya, which over the last 15 years have emerged from the first to second stage; while others, including some of the newly industrialised developing countries (NICs), for example, Hong Kong, Singapore, South Korea, Brazil and Mexico, appear to be moving quickly from the second to the third stage.

IV

The previous paragraphs have suggested that the relationship between a country's international direct position and its GNP per capita may be explained in terms of the extent to which its enterprises, relative to those of other nationalities, possess ownership-specific advantages, which are best exploited within these enterprises, and the locational attractions of that country, relative to others, as a site for productive activities. At the same time, a more detailed inspection of the data reveals that there are considerable variations between the outward and inward investment position of countries at a particular stage of development. It will be argued that these differences may also be explained by reference to the eclectic theory of international production.

Again, let us consider Figure 4.1. On this diagram, we illustrate the kind of relationship between NOI and GNP suggested by Table 4.3. But the diagram also shows that the variations around this line at any particular GNP (or ranges of GNPs) per capita (we have shown four stages on the diagram) are as great or are greater than the variations between levels of development. For example, the UK and New Zealand had about the same GNP per capita in 1971; but the former was a substantial net outward investor while the latter was a substantial net inward investor. On the other hand, Australia, with a GNP per capita of

$4099, had an identical (negative) NOI per capita, as did Jamaica with a GNP per capita of $890. Why too, at similar income levels, is Korea already becoming a sizeable outward investor, while Paraguay or Jordan are not?

The first and most obvious explanation for these deviations is that they reflect differences in the economic structure of countries. The distinction used by most development economists,[32] which parallels fairly closely the main types of foreign direct investment, is between mainly industrialising or industrialised countries and resource-rich countries. Table 4.5 and Figure 4.2 trace out two possible investment–development paths (around the average development path illustrated in Figure 4.1). The data show that industrialising or industrialised countries[33] record consistently higher GOIs and NOIs per capita but lower GIIs per capita at any given income level than do the resource-rich countries, and that for the higher income groups the differences are very marked indeed.

Table 4.5 Direct investment flows per capita and GNP per capita 1967–75 by economic structure of countries

GNP per capita (1971) ($ m.)		Investment (ΔK_o or ΔK_i) per capita (annual average) ($) (1) Industrialised/ industrialising countries			(2) Resource-rich countries		
		Outward	Inward	Net	Outward	Inward	Net
1 $4000 and over		32.1	14.9	17.2	17.5	45.7	–28.2
2 $2500 to $3999		25.8	29.6	–3.8	8.4	34.7	–26.3
3 $1000 to $2499	(a)[a]	2.3	11.5	–9.2	neg	69.4	–69.4
	(b)[b]	1.0	43.9	–42.9			
4 $500 to $999		0.1	16.0	–15.9	0.4	26.2	–25.8
5 $400 to $499		neg	5.5	–5.5	0.1	10.2	–10.1
6 $300 to $399		0.1	2.5	–2.4	neg	6.7	–6.7
7 $125 to $299		neg	1.1	–1.1	neg	3.4	–3.4
8 Less than $125		neg	1.1	–1.1	neg	1.7	–1.7

[a] 3(a) Comprising countries mainly producing manufactured goods for domestic markets.
[b] 3(b) Comprising countries mainly producing manufactured goods for export markets, for example, Hong Kong, Singapore and Taiwan.

Source: As for Table 4.3.

How then are such differences to be explained? The eclectic theory suggests that countries with NOIs above the average possess characteristics such as to generate *above* average ownership advantages for their enterprises, and/or *above* average incentives to internalise these advantages, coupled with below average location advantages.[34] In such circumstances foreign MNEs are either less able or less willing to invest in those countries, while domestic companies prefer to

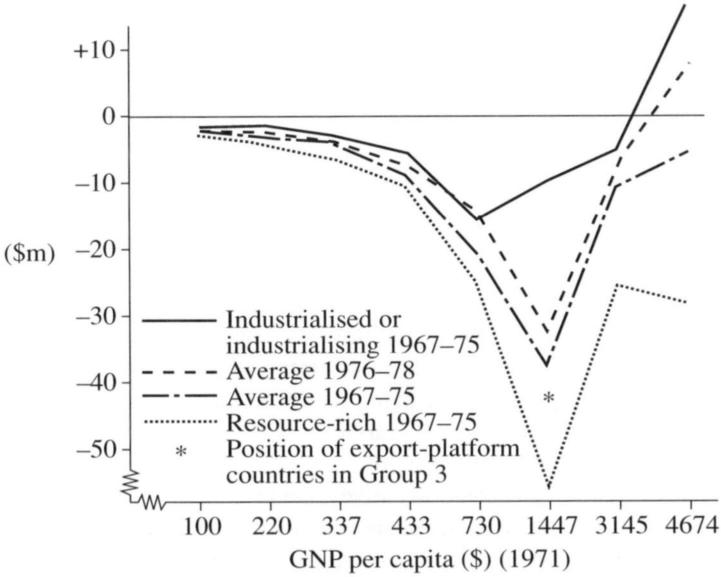

Note: Not to scale.

Figure 4.2 Net outward direct investment flows per capita 1967–78

exploit their growing competitive and/or internalisation advantages from a foreign rather than a domestic production base. By contrast, the features of countries which record NOIs below the average are such as to generate *below* average ownership advantages for their enterprises, and/or below average incentives for them to internalise these advantages, coupled with above average location-specific advantages, such as to encourage inward and discourage outward investment.

Of course, it is not quite as straightforward as this. The NOI line represents the difference between GOI and GII. Therefore, it follows that deviations around this line may be due to deviations around an average GOI and/or GII.[35] In turn, such deviations may reflect the extent to which a country participates in the international division of labour of activities by MNEs. As has already been suggested, a zero NOI in Stage 3 could mean that a country neither imports nor exports direct capital; or that it does a great deal of both but there is an exact balance between the two. In the latter case, countries would tend to exploit the ownership advantages of their own MNEs in economic sectors in which they had a competitive edge *vis-à-vis* foreign firms, and import those (via foreign based MNEs) in those sectors in which their own companies were comparatively disadvantaged.

While it is possible to identify the OLI advantages which might determine the NOI of countries, because of differences in economic structure, and hence in the type of outward and inward investment of countries, it is exceedingly difficult to present a generalised test of the eclectic theory in the sense of pinpointing the particular OLI advantages and/or the balance between them, which might explain all forms of international production in and by all countries.

This is mainly because different kinds of foreign investment tend to be associated with different OLI characteristics.[36] Take for example location-specific advantages. Here, most empirical research suggests that while import-substituting manufacturing investment is determined by such factors as the size and structure of the local market, host government policy towards imports, transport costs, and the strategy of enterprises in exploiting their ownership-specific advantages, investment in primary products and rationalised manufacturing is more governed by such variables as the availability and cost of natural resources, the extent and quality of the local technological and communications infrastructure, taxes and incentives, the proximity of the leading export markets and the extent to which trade (including trade in intermediary products) is free between home and host countries, and between host countries in which foreign affiliates of MNEs are located.[37]

Similarly, while each type of international production implies the presence of some ownership-specific advantages on the part of the investing firms, these differ in both kind and extent. In the case of import-substituting manufacturing investment (which normally replicates part or all of the range of products produced by the affiliate's parent company), technology, trade marks, management and organisational and marketing skills make up the ownership advantages. With vertically or horizontally integrated investments there are additional ownership advantages, which arise uniquely from internalisation economies (notably those of joint production) which cannot be transferred to other firms; in addition, access to markets, the economies of large-scale production and the ability of MNEs to better exploit differences in factor endowments and markets are likely to be more important than in the case of import-substituting investments.

Finally, the propensity of enterprises to internalise the use of their intangible assets will also differ according to type of investment, partly for the reasons just mentioned, and partly because, where the option between internalising and externalising advantages does exist, the net benefit of each route may differ considerably according to the nature of the advantage and the extent to which the market is capable of providing the advantaged firm an economic rent at least equal to what it may earn by internalising the transaction.

Using this kind of approach, then, it is possible to suggest a number of propositions about the causes of deviation of countries above or below the NOI line. From the viewpoint, first, of GII, one might hypothesise that countries with the same GNP per capita, which are (1) rich in natural and/ or human resources, (2) have a large home market, (3) offer a congenial environment to inward investment, (4) have a well-developed infrastructure, and an acceptable legal and/or commercial framework, and yet (5) whose indigenous firms are not able (or do not choose) to generate the kind of ownership advantages to enable them to successfully compete with foreign enterprises, will be those that will record an above average inward investment; whereas those that do not share these characteristics, where competition from indigenous firms is strong, or where host governments control inward direct investment, will record a below average inward investment.

From the viewpoint of GOI one would expect countries to engage in above average outward investment, where their firms generate strong ownership advantages but where it is profitable (or less risky) for them to utilise these advantages in foreign countries. One might then predict that countries which, at a given GNP per capita, were mainly industrialised, yet whose internal markets offered only limited opportunities for domestic growth, whose indigenous and location-specific resources were costly or inefficient, whose general economic and political climate of all kinds of investment was unfavourable and whose governments assisted their less competitive industries to invest in more congenial environments,[38] would generate above average outward investment; while those whose prosperity rested more on immobile resource endowments (e.g. minerals, raw materials and foodstuffs) would generate less than average outward investment.

What does the above analysis imply for the investment–development cycle? There are two ways in which one might take the deviations in NOI per capita at any given income level into account. The first is to classify countries according to the different kinds of investment they tend to attract or generate, and then to relate this variable to GNP; the second is to replace GNP as an explanatory variable by a variable, or set of variables, which reflects the OLI characteristics that might determine NOI, and relate these to NOI per capita.

Analytically, the second is the more attractive of the two alternatives as variations in GNP can themselves be interpreted in terms of differences in the ability of countries to generate the kind of characteristics embraced by the eclectic theory. Pragmatically, the first has some merit as, by distinguishing between different types of investment, one is automatically distinguishing between different types of OLI advantages *at a given stage* of economic development. What remains then is the relationship NOI and the kind of NOI characteristics which are proxied by levels of GNP.[39]

This chapter adopts a two-stage approach. First, some descriptive data are presented on the relationship between selected OLI characteristics and groups of countries classified both by GNP and economic structure (as set out in Table 4.3). Then for the more formal statistical testing, the 67 countries are regrouped by cluster analysis, and, for each cluster, multiple regression analysis is used to identify the more significant OLI variables explaining the investment flows of the constituent countries.

V

Since this approach is macro-oriented, the search for operationally testable OLI variables concentrates on those that are likely to be of the broadest applicability.[40] A reading of the literature, and particularly an article written by Root and Ahmed in 1978, which used multiple discriminant analysis to identify the most important location-specific variables influencing foreign direct manufacturing investment in developing countries, and work by industrial organisation economists in pinpointing the main ownership-specific variables, suggests that there is now a reasonable consensus of opinion about the more significant explanatory variables that should be incorporated in any general cross-sectional country model of international production. It is when one comes to pinpointing operationally testable proxies for internalisation advantages that one runs into difficulties. This is partly because some of these advantages are themselves embodied in ownership advantages, but mostly because the various forms of market failure and/or administrative fiat are extremely difficult to quantify, particularly at a country level. Because of this, a kind of revealed advantage approach[40] has been adopted and variables chosen that seem likely to be associated with internalisation. Three possible proxies will be examined: (1) the ratio of imports plus exports to total sales of foreign affiliates (arguing that the more an affiliate engaged in trade, the more likely it is to gain from the kind of advantages associated with the international division of labour); (2) the ratio of (internalised) intra-group to all imports and exports of MNE affiliates; and (3) the percentage of all foreign earnings derived from transfers of technology derived from non-affiliated companies (in the form of royalties and fees). Data limitations force us to confine ourselves to a modified version of (1) and (3) using US and UK data. As far as (2) is concerned, there are some regional and country data in respect of US MNEs which help corroborate the other two sets of data.

The OLI variables chosen for consideration are set out at the end of Table 4.6. These comprise two ownership variables, two internalisation variables and six location variables. Also included are two structural variables, viz. size of population and share of primary products plus tourism receipts of total trade.

It should be noted that while the eclectic theory would generally predict a positive relationship between location advantages and inward investment and a negative relationship between location advantages and outward investment; and a positive relationship between ownership advantages and outward investment and a negative relationship between ownership advantages and inward investment,[41] it is the *balance* between O, L and I advantages that will affect the propensity of a country to be a net inward or net outward investor. As has already been suggested, a zero NOI could either mean sizeable O and I advantages are evenly balanced by sizeable L advantages or that the country has very few advantages of any kind.

The data on the OLI variables are presented in Table 4.6. Taking first GOI, this appears to be strongly associated with O(1) and O(2), with any substantial amounts of outward investment being restricted to countries whose most educated and trained workers account for 10 per cent or more of the population and whose R&D expenditure is normally 1.6 per cent or more.[42] In the case of the location variables, the picture is mixed. For any given L(1), there is some suggestion that outward investment per capita is greater in industrialised than resource-rich countries, but, other than this, for Groups 1–3 the value of L(1) remains about the same, while thereafter it is positively associated with outward investment. It seems that there is a generally positive association between average earnings (L(2a)) and outward investment; but a generally negative association between growth in industrial output and such flows, at least for countries comprising Groups 1–4. For most of the other locational variables, the association is in the reverse direction to what one might expect, but it is believed this primarily reflects their 'pull' on inward investment rather than their 'push' to outward investment.[43] L(5), the taxation variable, suggests the right relationship, viz. that higher taxation is associated with more outward investment but below Group 4 countries, although the tax incidence continues to fall (at least until Group 6), there is no effect on outward investment (one exception is India). There is some reason to suppose that above average outward investment is associated with (an average of) the two indices of internalisation used, but the relationship is not as clear as one would like. Finally, there seems no obvious relationship between population size and the propensity to engage in outward investment; looking at individual data, of the 12 countries with an average outward investment of more than $10 per capita, five had populations of more than 50 million, and five of less than 22 million.

As far as GII is concerned, the influence of the L(1) variable seems pretty convincing, both between groups of countries and between industrialised or industrialising and resource-rich countries. For the rest, it is useful to distinguish between the first five and last three groups of countries. It seems for there to be any sizeable inward investment (per capita) certain locational advantages must be present. These include a BERI index of at least 50.0 and a combined educational/urbanisation infrastructure ratio of at least 30.0. The only countries which do not meet these minimum requirements are very large industrialised countries, for example, India and Indonesia, and one resource-(oil-)rich country, viz. Nigeria. And as the penultimate column of Table 4.6 suggests, along with

Table 4.6 *Net outward direct investment and indicators of OLI-specific advantages and economic structure 1967–75; countries grouped by GNP per capita*

Countries (GNP per capita)	Investment per capita[a] Outward	Inward	Net	O(1) (%)	O(2) (%)	L(1) ($m.)	L(2a) ($)	L(2b) ($)	L(3) (%)	L(4) (%)	L(5) (%)	I(1) (%)	I(2) (%)	L(1)/ O(1)	S(1) mln.	S(2) (%)
				(averages for countries in each group)												
(a) *Developed countries*																
Group 1: $4000 and over																
I	32.1	14.9	17.2	18.4	2.1	111.5	2.80	3.8	75.7	72.2	34.5	40.9	23.0	0.48	92.1	15.8
R	17.5	45.7	–28.2	15.7	1.2	382.7	2.78	4.4	74.7	70.6	34.4	26.7	18.4	1.66	13.1	36.9
A	24.8	30.3	–5.5	17.0	1.7	221.5	2.79	4.9	75.2	71.4	34.3	33.8	20.7	1.07	52.6	26.4
Group 2: $2500–$3999																
I	25.8	29.6	–3.8	13.8	2.1	112.8	1.77	5.1	71.4	71.8	32.5	39.3	34.2	0.58	45.4	17.9
R	8.4	34.7	26.3	13.9	0.9	355.8	1.77	4.2	72.8	69.5	36.3	37.9	17.0	1.74	6.9	37.8
A	20.8	31.4	–10.6	13.8	1.6	220.8	1.77	4.7	74.4	66.7	34.2	38.7	25.8	1.24	45.4	25.4
(b) *Developing countries*[b]																
Group 3: $1000–$2499																
I	2.3	11.5	–9.2	10.5	1.3	113.6	1.00	6.4	52.0	59.4	25.0	35.8	14.2	0.63	28.8	36.6
E	1.0	43.9	–42.9	8.3	0.4	98.7	0.30	11.2	70.7	57.2	15.5	43.9	nsa	0.77	7.2	8.5
R	neg	69.4	–69.4	8.5	0.3	384.8	0.75	nsa	54.0	36.0	22.8		30.9	3.26	4.0	66.5
A	1.2	38.6	–37.4	9.3	0.6	190.8	0.69	7.2	57.7	51.8	21.5	38.0	22.5	1.40	14.9	40.1
Group 4: $500–$999																
I	0.1	16.0	–15.9	9.5	0.4	66.0	0.68	8.7	nsa	34.7	22.1	nsa	12.9	0.64	39.8	47.8
R	0.4	26.2	–25.8	8.9	0.2	173.8	0.60	7.6	nsa	38.7	11.1	nsa	50.6	1.33	1.5	102.9
A	0.2	21.6	–21.4	9.1	0.3	126.1	0.63	8.1	55.3	36.4	16.4	30.9	28.0	0.95	18.5	78.4
Group 5: $400–$499																
I	neg	5.5	–5.5	6.3	0.3	43.8	0.50	8.0	nsa	32.0	23.1			0.50	9.6	55.3
R	0.1	10.2	–10.1	5.0	0.7	91.0	0.44	7.1	nsa	25.4	17.6			1.13	5.9	65.5
A	0.1	8.9	–8.8	5.4	0.6	77.5	0.47	7.7	47.6	27.3	21.5			0.95	6.9	62.8
Group 6: $300–$399												31.3[d]	9.3[b]			
I[c]	0.1	2.5	–2.4	4.4	0.5	18.0	0.34	10.3	nsa	34.7	15.0			0.49	12.4	55.5
R	neg	6.7	–6.7	5.4	0.3	68.1	0.32	17.9	nsa	24.8	18.3			0.61	4.2	53.1
A	0.1	3.7	–3.6	4.7	0.4	37.4	0.33	9.6	50.7	31.9	16.1			0.54	10.1	54.4

Group 7: ($125–$299)																
I	neg	1.1	−1.1	4.1	0.6	27.2	0.33	8.1	46.4	18.6	nsa			0.64	13.8	63.5
R	neg	3.4	−3.4	2.9	0.6	31.0	0.29	5.5	42.5	18.7	nsa			0.77	23.1	53.9
A	neg	1.9	−1.9	3.7	0.6	28.6	0.31	6.4	45.1	8.6	21.1	29.0[e]	34.8[e]	0.68	16.9	60.3
Group 8: Under $125																
I	neg	1.1	−1.1	2.9	0.3	6.5	0.16	7.8	38.1	13.7	nsa			0.19	130.5	57.1
R	neg	1.7	−1.7	1.2	0.3	10.6	0.18	9.9	nk	6.1	nsa			0.57	3.8	61.5
A	neg	1.3	−1.3	2.4	0.3	8.1	0.17	8.6	38.1	11.1	24.3			0.38	79.7	59.3

[a] Annual average.
[b] Includes two developed countries, viz. Spain and Italy.
[c] Includes one export-platform country, viz. Korea.
[d] Average for Groups 5 and 6.
[e] Average for Groups 7 and 8.
I = Industrialised or industrialising; R = Resource-rich; E = Export-platform; A = Average (see Table 4.3).
nsa = not separately available; nk = not known.

Key to headings of Table 4.6 and sources

O(1) Stock of human capital, measured by percentage of professional, technical, administrative and managerial workers to total workforce in 1973 or nearest year (*ILO Yearbook of Labour Statistics*).
O(2) Expenditure on research and development (R&D) as percentage of GNP in 1973 or nearest year (UNESCO *Statistical Yearbook*).
L(1) Natural resource endowments, measured by exports of primary products plus tourism receipts, per capita in 1973 or nearest year (UN *Statistical Year Book* and IMF *Balance of Payments Yearbook*).
L(2)(a) Average earnings per hour in manufacturing industry in 1971 (*Business International*, 7 and 14 December, 1973).
L(2)(b) Growth of manufacturing (or industrial) output; average growth 1960–77 (World Bank: *World Development Report* 1979).
L(3) BERI Environmental Risk Index; average 1972–76 (100.0 represents a no risk situation) (BERI – unpublished data).
L(4) Infrastructure index; average of two percentages: (1) percentage of urban to total population (average 1960 and 1975) and (b) percentage of secondary school children in appropriate age group (average 1960 and 1975) (World Bank: *World Development Report*, 1978).
L(5) Tax burden; average of two percentages: (a) (realised) corporate income tax rates, 1968 (Kopits, IMF *Staff Papers*, November 1976) and (b) percentage of all taxes to GNP, 1969–71 (Tail, Grätzand, Eichengreen, IMF *Staff Papers*, March 1979; OECD *Revenue Statistics of OECD Member Countries 1965–1975*).
I(1) Internalisation(1); royalties, management and other fees received by UK enterprises from foreign unaffiliated firms as percentage of fees received by UK enterprises from foreign affiliated and unaffiliated firms, 1974 (UK *Business Monitor* M4, 1977 edition).
I(2) Internalisation(2); the percentage of exports of US foreign affiliates in manufacturing industry, 1974 (US *Survey of Current Business*, May 1976).
S(1) Population (UN *Statistical Year Book*).
S(2) The exports of primary products plus tourism receipts as percentage of total visible exports in 1973 (UN *Statistical Year Book* and IMF *Balance of Payments Yearbook*).
S(3) See Table 4.7. GNP per capita.

$\frac{L(1)}{O(1)}$ L(1) ÷ O(1), each set of data being normalised by the highest value in the series.

GNP per capita, the size of population seems to be as important a factor influencing inward investment in industrialised countries as the availability of natural resources is in influencing such investment into resource-rich countries.

It has been said that the NOI ratio should reflect the *balance* of OLI advantages, rather than the *extent* of them. In general, as set out in Table 4.6 we have the kind of OLI relationships which are consistent with the U- or J-shaped investment development pattern. For industrialised countries in Groups 1 and 2, a *positive* NOI is generally associated with strong locational advantages pulling investment in, which are outweighed by stronger locational disadvantages and/or ownership and internalisation advantages pushing investment out. For resource-rich Groups 1 and 2 countries and for industrialised Group 3 countries, this relationship is reversed; fairly strong ownership plus internalisation advantages of domestic enterprises are offset by strong locational advantages which encourage them and foreign based companies to exploit indigenous endowments. Beyond this point, as income levels fall, OLI advantages lessen, but with ownership advantages falling faster than locational advantages until, at an income level of around $400 per capita, in all except highly populated countries, locational advantages are below the threshold necessary to attract any inward investment. Here, minimal O and L advantages are balanced as finely as they are when countries move from Stage 3 to Stage 4 in the development cycle.

There is no single variable which may be used as a proxy for the balance of OLI variables – if for no other reason than the values of these variables are differently denominated. However, as a very rough approximation of such a balance (and no more than this), for each country O(1) and L(1) data were recalculated as index numbers, expressing the highest O(1) and L(1) values as 100; the adjusted L(1) was then divided by the adjusted O(1) figure, and the ratio correlated with the NOI ratio. For the 67 countries the rank correlation coefficient worked out at –0.62; when five countries, which appeared markedly out of line with the rest, were removed the coefficient improved very considerably to –0.77.

VI

We now turn to the more formal statistical testing of the relationship between direct investment flows, OLI characteristics and selected structural variables.[44] Taking GOI, GII and NOI as the dependent variables, we first sought, by use of multiple regression analysis, to identify which of the OLI variables listed on p. 121 best explained the direct investment flows of countries. We did this by means of a stepwise inclusion of variables in the computation of ordinary least square coefficients using a double criterion: a significance level of at least 10 per cent for the coefficient and a correlation tolerance of 70 per cent with the other independent variables. A selection of those variables with the best explanatory power is set out in Table 4.7.

The results are disappointing in two respects. First, the sign of the coefficient of the human capital variable O(1) in equation (2) is unexpected, and second, a plot of residual against predicted values indicated a probable presence of heteroscedasticity for more than half the regression equations. This led us to believe that the specification of the equations needed refining. However, we suspected that it was the differences in economic structures among countries that weakened the explanatory power of the variables rather than the choice of variables themselves. This being so, we first distinguished between industrialised or industrialising countries and resource-rich countries. However, the same problems that we faced earlier continued to affect the results, so we turned to a second option which was to perform an automatic classification of the countries by means of cluster analysis.

To do this, the technique of correspondence analysis[45] was used. This is a type of factoring, analogous to the principal component method of factoring, but designed to permit the comparison of variables and objects in the same factorial space.[46] In this instance, the variables were the OLI characteristics, the investment flows and the structural variables, and the objects the 67 countries. The results showed that, as expected, the factors explaining the largest amount of variance were those representing GNP per capita and NOI per capita. Looking at the factorial space they depicted, and eliminating those variables and countries with correlation coefficients of less than 10 per cent with both factorial axes, we were able to identify three distinct clusters of countries and associated variables which exhibited homogeneous characteristics within each cluster.

To further check this procedure, a discriminant analysis was performed on those remaining countries and variables before applying the regression methodology to the clusters formed. In Table 4.8 the results show that the clusters are indeed natural and distinct.

The countries in each cluster were closely allied to the development stages (rather than to economic structure) described earlier in this chapter. The first group of 16 countries broadly comprised those in which there was some outward investment (GOI); these include most of the developed and a few developing countries. The second group comprised 15 countries which had a considerable inward investment (GII), but little or no GOI, that is, they were all associated with a substantially negative NOI. The third group was made up of 20 very poor developing countries, which attracted only a small amount of inward investment.

Table 4.7 Relationship between investment flows. OLI variables and economic structure of countries

	Dependent variable GOI	GII	NOI	Constant	Independent variables L(1)/O(1)	S(2) ECSTR	S(3) GNP	O(1)	O(2)	L(1)	$\bar{R}^2$	F	DW	N[c]	H
(1)	•			–6.349					17.784 (5.97)***[b]		0.52	35.7***	1.9**	33	*[d]
(2)		•		–0.108				0.290 (0.43)		0.103 (4.16)***	0.44	13.5***	2.4**	33	*
(3)			•	–7.661					11.874 (2.28)**	–0.081 (3.45)***	0.29	7.4***	2.3**	33	
(4)	•			–2.716			–0.006 (8.67)***				0.53	75.2***	2.1**	67	*
(5)		•		8.707			–0.007 (3.56)***				0.15	12.7***	1.4	67	*
(6)		•		5.350	27.7981 (9.31)***	–0.246 (3.56)***					0.57	44.2***	1.8*	67	*
(7)			•	8.725	–23.550 (7.44)***						0.45	55.4***	1.8**	67	
(8)	•			–3.545			–0.007 (6.41)***				0.49	41.2***	2.1**	43	*
(9)			•	–5.066			–0.006 (3.10)***			–0.108 (4.83)***	0.34	11.9***	2.2**	43	

** significant at the 5 per cent level.
*** significant at the 1 per cent level.
[a] The broken-line box indicates the variables that were given to the stepwise procedure. A missing coefficient means that the variable did not meet the criterion. The OLI variables, as well as the structural variables, not represented on this table did not meet the criterion.
[b] The number in parentheses represents the *t*-statistic value.
[c] Number of observations.
[d] The star under H indicates the probable presence of heteroscedastic disturbances.

Table 4.8 Classification of clusters tested by discriminant analysis

Actual cluster	No. of cases	Predicted cluster membership 1	2	3
Cluster 1	16	16	0	0
		100.0%	0.0%	0.0%
Cluster 2	15	0	14	1
		0.0%	93.3%	6.7%
Cluster 3	20	0	1	19
		0.0%	5.0%	95.0%

Percentage of cases correctly classified: 96.08 per cent
F-test = 2.94***[a]
t-test = 9.31***[b]

*** significant at the 1 per cent level.
[a] The *F*-statistic tests the discriminating power of the variables. Here we reject the hypothesis that the clusters' individual centres are positioned with the over-all centre.
[b] This *t*-statistic was used by Mosteller and Bush (1954) to test the hypothesis that the classification obtained from experiment was not better than a chance classification. Here we reject this hypothesis with a high degree of confidence.

This analysis of clustering also identified distinct sets of O, L and I variables within each country cluster, and these variables were used to perform the regression methodology used earlier. The results are set out in Table 4.9.[47] Here it can be quite clearly seen that while the O(1) advantage dominates the explanation for GOI, the balance of O(1) and L(1) advantages dominates the explanation for NOI of group 1 countries; L advantages, in particular the availability of natural resources, L(1), and degree of urbanisation, L(4a), affect GII and NOI of group 2 countries; while in group 3 countries only L(1) is at all significant. However, it may be noted, as far as this last group of countries is concerned, that the urbanisation index L(4a), which is highly significant as an explanation of GII in group 2 countries, is not a significant variable. This is because (as was suggested on p. 119) it is only after the index has risen above 30.0 per cent that foreign companies seriously consider investing in the country.

VII

For the rest of this chapter, I would like to return briefly to some more analytical issues. It was argued earlier that to understand the relationship between a country's international investment position and its economic development not

Table 4.9 Relationship between GII, GOI and NOI and selected O and L variables classified by three groups of countries

Dependent variables				Independent variables[a]										
Countries	GOI	GII	NOI	Constant	L(1)/O(1)	O(1)	L(1)	L(2b)	(L4a)	L(5)	$\bar{R}^2$	F	DW	No. of observations
Cluster 1														
(1)	•			44.559		2.653				–1.507	0.37	5.41**	2.6**	16
						(2.55)**[b]				(2.20)**				
(2)			•	12.401	–19.772						0.23	5.62**	2.1**	16
					(2.37)**									
Cluster 2														
(3)		•		2.941			0.138	–2.030	0.336		0.78	18.03***	1.9**	15
							(5.53)***	(2.33)**	(3.09)***					
(4)			•	–0.149			–0.147				0.63	24.82***	1.6**	15
							(4.98)***							
Cluster 3														
(5)		•		0.813			0.054				0.16	4.66**	1.4**	20
							(2.16)**							
(6)			•	–0.786			–0.055				0.17	4.77**	1.5**	20
							(2.18)**							

** significant at the 5 per cent level.
*** significant at the 1 per cent level.

a The OLI variables, as well as the structural variables not represented here, did not meet the criterion.
b The number in parentheses represents the *t*-statistic value.

only requires a time series rather than a cross-sectional approach, but that development should be viewed in a relative rather than an absolute economic context.

As to the former point, there has been little use of the eclectic model to explain changes in a country's international direct investment position. But the data set out in Table 4.10 do seem to corroborate the idea of an investment–development cycle of countries. As far as the newly emerging foreign investors from developing countries are concerned, each of the five countries, for which IMF data are available, exhibits a clear trend towards a higher outward/inward investment ratio. Separate data on inward and outward investment suggest that this is primarily because outward investment has risen rather than because inward investment has fallen. *Inter alia*, this is shown by the fact that outward plus inward investment per capita has been rising. This, in turn, implies that it has been the rising *ownership* rather than falling *location* advantages of these countries which have been responsible for the changing ratio. The identification and evaluation of these advantages, which are linked to the structure of industry and the strategy of firms, both of which (particularly the former) are affected by the resource endowments of the country, government policy and market size, is a matter for further research.

On the latter point, it is clear that since the NOI for all countries taken together must be zero (i.e. the positive NOI of some countries must equal the negative NOI of others) not all countries will be able to reach the final stage of the investment–development cycle.[48] The eclectic theory predicts neither whether countries will move from Stage 1 through to Stage 4, nor what might subsequently happen to countries currently with the highest income levels.[49] What it does suggest, however, is that, if and when countries advance their relative economic status, the consequential changes in their OLI characteristics will affect their NOI position.[50] The implication of this is that, over time, as average living standards in the world rise, the curve depicted in Figure 4.1 will shift towards the right. Alternatively, normalising each country's GNP per capita by a world average, while the shape of the curve may remain more or less the same, the position of individual countries, on or around the curve, may shift to the left or right. Finally it is interesting to speculate on the nature of the curve in relation to the vertical axis (which reflects the amount and dispersion of GOI and GII). What happens when more countries become outward investors? What if there is a convergence in ownership- and location-specific advantages? What if investment flows follow the pattern of trade flows, and the proportion of intra-industry investment rises? Will the curve then become shallower, that is, more 'saucer' shape than that revealed by the 1967–75 data? These are all fascinating issues, worthy of scholarly investigation.

Table 4.10 *Inward and outward direct investment flows for selected countries: mid-1960s–1978*

Countries	Annual average ($m.) (a) Inward	(b) Outward	(b)/(a) %
Brazil			
1978	1606	102	6.4
1975–77	1555	135	8.7
1972–74	1100	45	4.1
1969–71	403	10	2.5
1966–69	161	0	0
South Korea			
1978	71	24	33.8
1975–77	91	13	14.3
1972–74	84	9	10.7
1969–71	50	2	3.3
1966–68	11	0	0
Singapore			
1978	337	24	7.1
1975–77	453	7	1.5
1972–74	333	3	0.9
1969–71	82	1	1.2
1967–68	30	0	0
Columbia			
1978	60	12	20.0
1975–77	37	11	29.8
1972–74	24	3	12.5
1969–71	47	4	8.5
1967–68	46	2	4.3
Malaysia			
1978	476	22	4.6
1975–77	318	9	2.8
1972–74	241	5	2.1
1969–71	91	2	2.2
1967–68	37	0	0
Germany			
1978	1320	2880	218.2
1975–77	1193	2050	171.8
1972–74	1867	1473	78.9
1969–71	745	878	117.9
1967–68	691	415	60.0
Japan			
1978	n.k.	1870	–
1975–77	103	1520	1475.7
1972–74	97	1273	1312.4
1969–71	125	307	407.2
1967–68	61	172	282.0
1964–66	52	79	153.2

Source: IMF, *Balance of Payments Yearbook*.

VIII

Let us briefly recapitulate the main thesis of this chapter.

1. A country's propensity to engage in foreign direct investment and/or be invested in by foreign enterprises rests upon:
   (a) the extent to which its enterprises (relative to enterprises of other nationalities) possess net ownership advantages;
   (b) whether it pays these enterprises to internalise these advantages or leave them (through the market) to other enterprises to exploit;[51]
   (c) whether it is profitable for enterprises to locate their production units in the home country or a foreign country.
2. It is possible to identify the nature of these advantages by reference to:
   (a) industrial organisation theory,
   (b) location theory,
   (c) the theory of the firm.
3. The extent to which one country's enterprises possess the capacity and willingness to produce abroad will, *inter alia*, depend on:
   (a) country,
   (b) industry,
   (c) enterprise-specific factors.

   These factors, particularly (a) and (b), are clearly interlinked, but given (a) and (b), the advantages described above will differ between enterprises; given (a) and (c), they will differ between industries; given (b) and (c) they will differ between countries.
4. Countries vary in their propensity to engage in foreign direct investment or be invested in, because of their different:
   (a) level and structure of resource endowments,
   (b) size and character of markets,
   (c) government policies (e.g. towards foreign direct investment, innovation, industrial concentration, etc.).

   These differences will reflect themselves in the extent and kind of *ownership* and *internalisation* advantages which firms of different nationalities possess, *location* advantages which different countries possess and *inter alia* the industrial spread of their outward and inward direct investment and capital stake.
5. There is some evidence to suggest that the forces determining the level of inward and outward direct investment and the balance between the two are linked to a country's stage of development, and that it is reasonable to think of a four-stage investment development process or cycle, in which, after the first stage of little inward or outward investment, inward investment rises. This is eventually followed by a third stage, when outward

investment begins to rise and/or inward investment falls, but NOI is still negative, and finally NOI becomes positive. The developing countries now emerging as outward investors are entering into the third stage.

6. At any particular stage of development, countries may differ from each other in their international investment involvement and structures. The deviations from the 'average' NOI can be explained by different country-specific characteristics, reflected in the possession of ownership, location and internalisation advantages set out above. The significant difference between the investment paths of industrialising and resource-rich countries bear this point out.
7. The eclectic theory may also be used to explain changes in the outward/inward investment (or capital stake) ratio of a particular country over time, either in the short or medium term or in the long run. In the case of one industrialised country, the UK, a rising outward/inward direct capital stake in manufacturing industry between 1960 and 1976 reflected both rising ownership advantages on the part of UK firms and falling location advantages on the part of the UK as a site for production. One suspects that in the more recent past, for example, since around 1975, the falling outward/inward investment stake of the USA has reflected the opposite combination of forces. In the case of the five developing countries chosen for illustration, the rising outward/inward investment primarily reflects the rising ownership advantages of their own enterprises *vis-à-vis* those of other countries. Here, it should be noted that ownership-specific advantages, for example, size of firm, may also account for part of these advantages as may the geographical distribution of the investment.[52]
8. Any attempt to forecast the future of NOI by *developing* countries must then rest on the answer to the following question – to what extent do the specific endowment, market and environmental characteristics of developing countries, taken either as a group or individually, generate ownership advantages for its enterprises *relative* to those generated by developing countries which are best exploited by foreign direct investment rather than by exports or contractual resource transfers? Anything which generates such advantages which favour the particular characterisation of developing countries will aid their foreign investment; anything which does not favour these characteristics will inhibit it.
9. The future of NOI of *developed* countries will rest more on their *relative* economic status, which is both reflected in and determined by the balance of their OLI advantages. Much depends, on the one hand, on their ability to create and sustain technological and human capital advantages (which become exploited by their firms) and, on the other, the character of the comparative advantage of their immobile resource endowments.

10. The empirical part of the chapter has confined itself to an examination of inward and outward investment flows. A complete explanatory model of the kind described would need data on exports and imports and on contractual resource flows since investment flows reflect both the ownership advantages of firms and the way in which these are exploited. A change in either or both may affect the timing and nature of both the investment–development cycle described in this chapter and the position of a particular country at a point in the cycle.

NOTES

1. Strictly speaking that of all economic agents, that is, enterprises, individuals and governments.
2. We shall eschew the difficult problem of defining the boundaries between a portfolio and direct investment by taking the IMF definition that a direct investment implies some control of decision taking in the 'invested in' enterprise by the 'investing enterprise'.
3. Sometimes called firm-specific advantages; the reason for our preferred nomenclature will be clear as the argument progresses.
4. This distinction is important; once the assets are sold, then the enterprise disposes of its ownership advantages altogether.
5. For example, in terms of maximising the NPV of the expected income flows from the assets.
6. Strictly speaking, the decision as to whether or not to engage in (or increase) international production should be kept separate from that of whether or not to engage in (or increase) foreign direct investment. But for the purposes of this paper, we are not concerned with the finance of international production. We use investment data as a proxy for international production data as the latter are not available on a country-by-country basis.
7. See Section III.
8. That is, those based respectively on industrial organisation, location and market failure theory. For further details see Rugman (1980).
9. Even when an enterprise is acquiring another for defensive reasons (e.g. as is the case for some Japanese foreign investment), the presumption is that the acquiring firm has some ownership advantages which it wants to protect; hence it is willing to offer a price that will encourage the acquired firm to sell. In some cases, the home government may assist its own firms in this kind of investment (Ozawa, 1979).
10. That is, that the NPV of the asset acquired is perceived to be greater by the acquiring than by the acquired firm.
11. See an interesting chapter in Kojima (1978) in which a distinction is made between genuine economies of scale (arising from internalisation) and pseudo-economies. These latter simply benefit the internalising firm (in the form of additional economic rent) and essentially originate because of the enhanced monopoly power which the firm gains from them. The former consist of the kind of economies of scale which may exist under competitive conditions and which advance efficiency.
12. In a recent paper, Rugman (1980) argues that 'existing theories of foreign direct investment are basically subsets of the general theory of internalisation'. The present author prefers to think of the eclectic theory as the paradigm, with internalisation being a subset of this general theory.
13. See Chapter 3 of this volume.
14. See especially Root and Ahmed (1978).
15. Obviously, for a variety of reasons to do with both the valuation and interpretation of direct investment, these data should be regarded as approximate rather than precise values.

16. I have excluded most developing countries, which have been involved in substantial expropriation or nationalisation programmes over the period 1967–75, and also all tax haven countries.
17. See, for example, Chenery (1977), Bornschier (1978, 1979) and UN (1978).
18. We have chosen to express our data in terms of average investment flows; it would have been possible, and produced exactly the same inter-country patterns, to have taken the aggregate investment flows over the period in question, which, in most cases, is long enough for the flow to be a reasonably good proxy of the stock of investment at the end of the period.
19. A list of these is set out in Appendix 4.1.
20. Note that the income ranges covered by countries whose investment behaviour is classified in groups 3 and 4 overlap. This suggests that, especially in these later stages, investment behaviour cannot be fully explained by GNP per capita. As we shall see, the eclectic theory aspires to explain these exceptional cases as well as the more normal cases.
21. In the period 1976–78, this number had increased to nine.
22. This indeed is the main form of involvement of Third World MNEs, as in most cases they have neither the financial capital nor the complete package of ownership advantages for them to 'go it alone' in their foreign ventures.
23. Reasons not dissimilar to those explaining why, in the early stages of the product cycle, firms prefer to locate their production units near their centres of innovation. Later, as the scale and efficiency of production increases, it may become profitable to locate it elsewhere (Vernon, 1974).
24. An obvious example being the expiry of a patent.
25. Especially if they perceive that supplying foreign markets from a foreign location is likely to involve them in less risk than supplying them from a domestic location. It does not seem unreasonable to suppose that *ceteris paribus* the more risky a particular country is thought to be as a location for inward investment, the more likely its own firms will be prompted to exploit foreign markets from a foreign production base.
26. This, of course, may lead to divestment, or partial divestment, by such firms. According to Wilson (1978), the propensity to disinvest is greatest in those industries producing mature, homogeneous products under near competitive conditions, and least in those industries supplying high technology and/or differentiated products. Location-specific factors – notably government attitudes towards foreign direct investment – are also frequently cited by business men as reasons for divestment.
27. Dunning and Pearce (1981) have shown that in 1977, whereas only 5.9 per cent of the exports of the parent companies of the leading MNEs in low research intensity industries were internalised, the proportions for medium and high research intensity industries were 36.9 per cent and 50.0 per cent respectively.
28. That is, advantages of a non-transferable kind, for example, economies of joint production, of product, process market or financial integration, etc.
29. In addition, there is some evidence to suggest that the more multinational an enterprise is the more likely it is to internalise resource transfers (Dunning and Pearce, 1981).
30. The Dunning and Pearce study shows that internal exports from parent companies of MNEs whose foreign production/worldwide production ratio exceeds 1:8 averaged 48 per cent in 1977; those whose ratio was less than 1:8 averaged 6 per cent.
31. Both absolute and relative to that of other countries. This normalisation would help to explain how a country's net outward investment ratio may decrease as its GNP per capita increases, if the GNP of its major competitors was increasing at a faster rate.
32. See, for example, Chenery and Taylor (1968) and Chenery (1977,1979).
33. Apart from Italy and Spain the industrialised countries were all classified in Groups 1 and 2. All industrialising countries were classified in Groups 3 to 8.
34. It is important to distinguish between location advantages which help generate ownership-specific advantages (i.e. a favourable climate to innovation and the accumulation of knowledge and financial capital) and those which affect the economics of production and marketing.
35. By the same token, a country with an average NOI could be deviating from the norm in both its outward and inward investment, but the two deviations cancel themselves out.
36. See chapter 3 of this volume (p. 80).

37. This applies equally to vertically integrated investment, for example, as shown by the impact of export processing zones, and to horizontal investments, for example, the impact of the EEC on the rationalisation of investments by companies like Ford, Philips and Honeywell within this free trade area.
38. As in the case of some Japanese investments. See Ozawa (1979).
39. A mixture of the two approaches is possible, by distinguishing between the main types of investment and then relating the NOIs to OLI characteristics.
40. Another alternative is to evaluate the advantages of internalisation by studying the kinds of situations (e.g. industries and firms) in which fdi is likely to yield the best results (e.g. in terms of maximising net present value (NPV)) *vis-à-vis* the market (e.g. the licensing route). See, for example, Giddy and Rugman (1979).
41. Internalisation advantages make for both outward and inward investment, depending on whether it is the domestic or foreign MNEs which possess the ownership advantages, and also the extent to which market failure is more pronounced in the home or in the host country.
42. Canada is one exception. With an R&D, as a percentage of GNP, of 1 per cent in 1971, it had the fifth largest outward investment per capita over the 1967–75 period.
43. Also that some variables may 'push' and 'pull' at the same time. For example high earnings per head may reflect high costs (a 'push' factor), but also high spending power (a 'pull' factor).
44. I am most grateful to Mr D. Depelteau of the Ecole des Hautes Etudes Commerciales, University of Montreal, for his most valuable computing assistance, and for introducing me to the concept of correspondence analysis. A fuller version of the results presented in this chapter is published as *Explaining the International Investment Position of Countries: A Statistical Analysis* in Ecole des Hautes Etudes Commerciales (University of Montreal), Les Cahiers du CETAI (Research Paper Series, October 1981).
45. For details of this technique see M.O. Hill, 'Correspondence analysis: a neglected multivariate method', *Applied Statistics*, **23** (3) (1974).
46. Two elements distinguish correspondence analysis from other measures of variance. First is its treatment of distance. Whereas conventional analyses of variance (i.e. regression and other factoring methods) use the deviation to the mean as a measure of distance, correspondence analysis uses a chi-square measure of distance to depict the position of both the objects and the variable with respect to the global centre of gravity of the data. Second is the coding of the data into binary form; this procedure amounts to breaking down a variable into subvariables and then assigning a value to one of them – to indicate its belonging to the original observation – and to the rest the value of 0.
47. At this stage, we are confident we have homoscedastic, normally distributed disturbances. There is however one wrong sign, that of the coefficient of the rate of increase in industrial output, L(2b), in equation (3). It can be explained by the presence of three particular countries, viz. Hong Kong, Barbados and Jamaica, in the sample, whose large inward investment biased the covariance between the two variables. Removing these three countries from the sample results in a *positive* correlation between GII and L(2b) of 0.60.
48. Any more than all firms reach the final stage of the product cycle.
49. The extent to which fdi itself influences patterns of economic development is a subject for further research.
50. Again this chapter has not explored the mechanism of such changes, for example, how far is a rising (declining) advantage brought about by a devaluation (revaluation) of the exchange rate.
51. Foreign firms in the case of outward resource flows; domestic firms in the case of inward resource flows.
52. For example, due to such factors as geographical and/or psychic distance, cultural, political and economic ties, etc. Note that the geographical distribution of foreign investment of LDCs is very different from that of most developed countries. This reflects *inter alia* that the ownership/internalisation advantage of one country's enterprises over those of another may vary considerably according to the destination of the investment. See also Stopford's explanation of the geographical composition of UK direct investment (Stopford, 1976).

APPENDIX 4.1 LIST OF COUNTRIES INCLUDED IN SAMPLE

Group 1 Sweden, USA, Canada, Denmark, Australia, Germany.
Group 2 Norway, France, Belgium and Luxembourg, Netherlands, Finland, Austria, UK, Japan, New Zealand.
Group 3 Israel, Italy, Spain, Gabon, Trinidad and Tobago, Venezuela, Taiwan, Singapore, Hong Kong, Argentina.
Group 4 Jamaica, Panama, Barbados, Costa Rica, Brazil, Malaysia, Nicaragua, Malta, Mexico.
Group 5 Dominican Republic, Ivory Coast, Algeria, Tunisia, Guyana, Peru, Guatemala.
Group 6 Columbia, Ecuador, Paraguay, El Salvador, Honduras, Jordan, South Korea.
Group 7 Ghana, Morocco, Senegal, Bolivia, Nigeria, Sierra Leone, Uganda, Philippines, Kenya.
Group 8 Haiti, Indonesia, Zaïre, Niger, Benin, Malawi, Chad, Ethiopia, Pakistan, India.

APPENDIX 4.2

The eclectic paradigm of international production.*

1. *Ownership-specific advantages* of an enterprise of one nationality (or affiliates of same) over those of another.

(a) Property right and/or intangible asset advantages (Oa): the resource (asset) structure of the firm. Product innovations, production management, organizational and marketing systems, innovatory capacity, organization of work, non-codifiable knowledge; 'bank' of human capital experience: marketing, finance, know-how, etc. Ability to reduce costs of intra and/or inter-firm transactions.

(b) Advantages of common governance, that is, of organizing Oa with complementary assets (Ot).

   (i) Those that branch plants of established enterprises may enjoy over *de novo* firms. Those resulting mainly from size, product diversity and learning experiences of enterprise (e.g. economies of scope and specialization). Exclusive or favoured access to inputs (e.g. labour, natural resources, finance, information). Ability to obtain inputs on favoured terms (e.g. as a result of size or monopsonistic influence). Ability of parent company to conclude productive and cooperative inter-firm relationships; for example, as between Japanese auto assemblers and their suppliers. Exclusive or favoured access to product markets. Access to resources of parent company at marginal cost. Synergistic economies (not only in production, but in purchasing, marketing, finance, etc, arrangements).

(ii) Which specifically arise because of multinationality. Multinationality enhances operational flexibility by offering wider opportunities for arbitraging, production shifting and global sourcing of inputs. More favoured access to and/or better knowledge about international markets (e.g. for information, finance, labour, etc). Ability to take advantage of geographic differences in factor endowments, government intervention, markets, etc. Ability to diversify or reduce risks (e.g. in different currency areas and creation of options and/or political and cultural scenarios). Ability to learn from societal differences in organizational and managerial processes and systems, Balancing economics of integration need to respond to differences in country-specific resources and consumer demands.

2. *Internalisation incentive advantages* (i.e. to circumvent or exploit market failure).
   To avoid search and negotiating costs.
   To avoid costs of moral hazard and adverse selection, and to protect reputation of internalizing firm.
   To avoid cost of broken contracts and ensuing litigation.
   Buyer uncertainty (about nature and value of inputs, for example, technology, being sold).
   When market does not permit price discrimination.
   Need of seller to protect quality of intermediate or final products.
   To capture economics of interdependent activities (see (b) above).
   To compensate for absence of future markets.
   To avoid or exploit government intervention (quotas, tariffs, price controls, tax differences, etc).
   To control supplies and conditions of sale or inputs (including technology).
   To control market outlets (including those which might be used by competitors).
   To be able to engage in practices, such as cross-subsidization, predatory pricing, leads and lags, transfer pricing as a competitive (or anti-competitive) strategy.

3. *Location-specific variables* (these may favour home or host countries).
   Spatial distribution of natural and created resource endowments and markets.
   Input prices, quality and productivity (e.g, labour, energy, materials, components, semifinished goods.

International transport and communication costs.
International incentives and disincentives (including performance requirements, etc.).
Artificial barriers (e.g. import controls) to trade in goods and services.
Societal and infrastructure provisions (commercial, legal, educational, transport and communication).
Cross-country ideological, language, cultural, business, political differences.
Economies of centralization of R&D production and marketing.
Economic system and strategies of government: the institutional framework for resource allocation.

---

* *Source*: first published in Dunning (1979) and modified in Dunning (1993).

REFERENCES

Bornschier, V. (1978), *Multinational Corporations in the World Economy and National Development*, Zürich, Sociologisches Institut der Universität No. 32.

Buckley, P.J. and Casson, M. (1981), 'The optimal timing of a foreign direct investment', *Economic Journal*, vol. 91 (March), no. 48.

Chenery, H.B. and Taylor, L. (1968), 'Development patterns among countries and over time', *Review of Economics and Statistics*, vol. 50 (November).

Chenery, H.B. (1977), 'Transnational growth and world industrialisation', in B. Ohlin, P.O. Hesselborn and P.J. Wisjkman (eds), *The International Allocation of Economic Activity*, (London: Macmillan).

Chenery, H.B. (1979), *Structural Change and Development Policy*, (Washington, DC: The World Bank).

Dunning, J.H. (1979), 'Explaining changing patterns of international production: In defence of the eclectic theory', *Oxford Bulletin of Economics and Statistics*, vol. 41, no. 2, 269–95.

Dunning, J.H. (1993), *Multinational Enterprises and the Global Economy*, (Wokingham, Berkshire: Addison Wesley).

Dunning, J.H. and Pearce, R.D. (1981), *The World's Largest Industrial Enterprises*, (Farnborough: Gower).

Giddy, I.H. and Rugman, A.M. (1979), *A Model of Trade, Foreign Direct investment and Licensing*, Graduate School of Business, Columbia University, Research Working Paper No. 274A.

Kojima, J. (1978), 'Giant multinational corporations: merits and defects', *Hitotsubashi, Journal of Economics*, vol. 18, no. 2.

Lall, S. (1980), 'Monopolistic advantages and foreign involvement by US manufacturing industry', *Oxford Economic Papers*, vol. 32 (March).

Lecraw, D. (1977), 'Direct investment by firms from less developed countries', *Oxford Economic Papers*, vol. 29 (August).

Magee, S.P. (1977), 'Multinational corporations, the industry technology cycle and development', *Journal of World Trade Law*, vol. XI (July/August).

Mosteller, F. and Bush, R.R. (1954), 'Selective quantitative techniques', in G. Lindsay (ed.), *Handbook of Social Psychology*, vol. 1 (Reading, MA: Addison-Wesley).

Ozawa, T. (1979), 'International investment and industrial structure: new theoretical implications from the Japanese experience', *Oxford Economic Papers*, vol. 31 (March).

Root, F. and Ahmed, A.A. (1978), "The influence of policy instruments on manufacturing direct investment in developing countries', *Journal of International Business Studies*, vol. 9 (Winter).

Rugman, A.M. (1980), 'Internalisation: the general theory of foreign direct investment', *Weltwirtschaftliches Archiv*, vol. 116, no. 2.

Stopford, J.M. (1976), 'Changing perspectives on investment by British manufacturing multinationals', *Journal of International Business Studies*, vol. 7 (Fall/Winter).

UN (1978), *Transnational Corporations in World Development: A Re-examination*, (New York: UN Economic and Social Council), E.78 II A5.

Vernon, R. (1974), 'The location of economic activity', in J.H. Dunning (ed.), *Economic Analysis and the Multinational Enterprise*, (London: Allen & Unwin).

Wells, L.T. (1977), 'The internationalisation of firms from the developing countries', in T. Agmon and C.P. Kindleberger (eds), *Multinationals from Small Countries*, (Cambridge, MA: MIT Press).

Wilson, B.D. (1978), *Foreign Disinvestments: Friend or Foe*, Graduate School of Business Administration, University of Virginia, Working Paper DSWP-78–08.

5. The investment development path revisited*

INTRODUCTION

This chapter considers the interaction between inward and outward direct investment, the role of governments, and the upgrading and restructuring of the indigenous assets of countries, from a dynamic or developmental perspective. It particularly examines the impact of some changes now occurring in the global economy on the nature and course of economic development and restructuring, and on the role which both governments and MNEs can play in influencing that development and restructuring.

SOME THEORETICAL ISSUES

The Nature of the Investment Development Path

The notion that the outward and inward direct investment position of a country is systematically related to its economic development, relative to the rest of the world, was first put forward by the present writer in 1979, at a conference on 'Multinational Enterprises from Developing Countries' which took place at the East West Center at Honolulu.[1]

Since then the concept of the investment development path (IDP)[2] has been revised and extended in several papers and books (Dunning, 1981, 1986, 1988a, 1993; Narula 1993, 1996; Dunning and Narula, 1994). The following paragraphs summarize the state of thinking on the nature and characteristics of the IDP.

The IDP suggests that countries tend to go through five main stages of development and that these stages can be usefully classified according to the propensity of those countries to be outward and/or inward direct investors. In turn, this propensity will rest on the extent and pattern of the competitive or ownership-specific (O) advantages of the indigenous firms of the countries concerned, relative to those of firms of other countries; the competitiveness of

* Written with R. Narula. From J.H. Dunning and R. Narula (eds), *Foreign Direct Investment and Governments*, London and New York: Routledge, 1996, pp. 1–41.

the location-bound resources and capabilities of that country, relative to those of other countries (the L-specific advantages of that country); and the extent to which indigenous and foreign firms choose to utilize their O-specific advantages jointly with the location-bound endowments of home or foreign countries through internalizing the cross-border market for these advantages,[3] rather than by some other organizational route (i.e. their perceived I advantages).

A diagrammatic representation of the IDP, which relates the net outward investment (NOI) position of countries (i.e. the gross outward direct investment stock less the gross inward direct investment stock) – as a continuous line – is presented in Figure 5.1. We shall briefly summarize the main features of these stages, but pay particular attention to Stage 5, which we did not consider in our earlier writings.

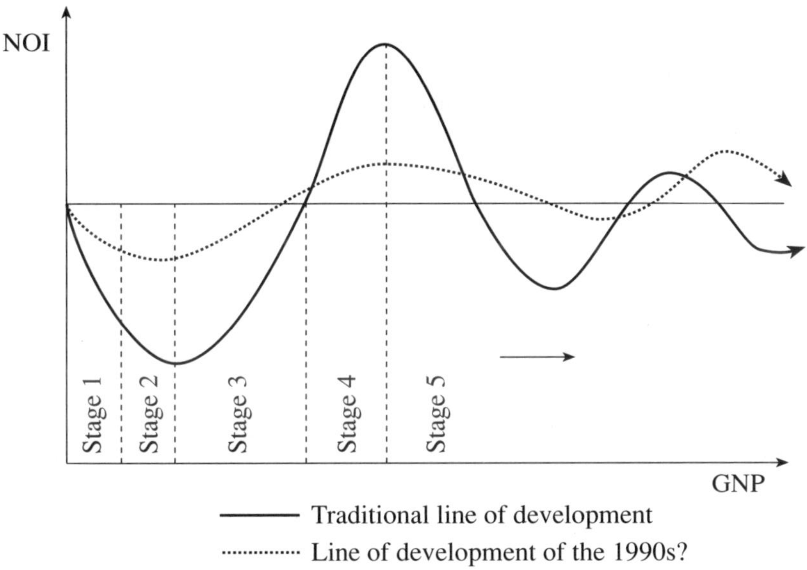

Note: Not drawn to scale – for illustrative purposes only.

Figure 5.1 The pattern of the investment development path

Stage 1

During the first stage of the IDP, the L-specific advantages of a country are presumed to be insufficient to attract inward direct investment, with the exception of those arising from its possession of *natural* assets. Its deficiency in location-bound *created* assets[4] may reflect limited domestic markets – demand levels are minimal because of the low per capita income – inappropriate economic systems or government policies; inadequate infrastructure such as transportation and communication facilities; and, perhaps most important of all, a poorly educated, trained or motivated labour force. At this stage of the IDP, there is likely to be very little outward direct investment. *Ceteris paribus*, foreign firms will prefer to export to and import from this market, or conclude co-operative non-equity arrangements with indigenous firms. This is because the O-specific advantages of domestic firms are few and far between, as there is little or no indigenous technology accumulation and hence few created assets. Those that exist will be in labour-intensive manufacturing and the primary product sector (such as mining and agriculture), and may be government influenced through infant industry protection such as import controls.

Government intervention during Stage 1 will normally take two forms. First it may be the main means of providing basic infrastructure, and the upgrading of human capital via education and training. Governments will attempt to reduce some of the endemic market failure holding back development. Second, they engage in a variety of economic and social policies, which, for good or bad, will affect the structure of markets. Import protection, domestic content policies and export subsidies are examples of such intervention at this stage of development. At this stage, however, there is likely to be only limited government involvement in the upgrading of the country's created assets, for example innovatory capacity.

Stage 2

In Stage 2, inward direct investment starts to rise, while outward investment remains low or negligible. Domestic markets may have grown either in size or in purchasing power, making some local production by foreign firms a viable proposition. Initially this is likely to take the form of import-substituting manufacturing investment – based upon their possession of intangible assets, for example technology, trademarks, managerial skills, etc. Frequently such inbound FDI is stimulated by host governments imposing tariff and non-tariff barriers. In the case of export-oriented industries (at this stage of development, such inward direct investment will still largely be in natural-resource-intensive sectors with some forward vertical integration into labour-intensive low technology and light manufactures) the extent to which the host country is able to offer the necessary infrastructure (transportation, communications facilities and supplies of skilled and unskilled labour) will be a decisive factor. In short, a country must possess some desirable L characteristics to attract inward direct investment, although the extent to which these can be effectively exploited will depend on that country's development strategy and the extent to which it prefers to develop the technological capabilities of its domestic firms.

The O advantages of domestic firms will have increased from the previous stage, wherever national government policies have generated a virtuous circle of created asset accumulation. These O advantages will exist owing to the development of support industries clustered around primary industries, and production will move towards semi-skilled and moderately knowledge-intensive consumer goods. Outward direct investment emerges at this stage. This may be either of a market-seeking or trade-related type in adjacent territories, or of a strategic asset-seeking type in developed countries. The former will be characteristically undertaken in countries that are either further back in their IDP than the home country, or, when the acquisition of created assets is the prime motive, these are likely to be directed towards countries further along the path.

The extent to which outward direct investment is undertaken will be influenced by the home country government-induced 'push' factors such as subsidies for exports, and technology development or acquisition (which influence the I advantages of domestic firms), as well as the changing (non-government-induced) L advantages such as relative production costs. However, the rate of outward direct investment growth is likely to be insufficient to offset the rising rate of growth of inward direct investment. As a consequence, during the second stage of development, countries will increase their net inward investment (i.e. their NOI position will worsen), although towards the latter part of the second stage, the growth rates of outward direct investment and inward direct investment will begin to converge.

Stage 3

Countries in Stage 3 are marked by a gradual decrease in the rate of growth of inward direct investment, and an increase in the rate of growth of outward direct investment that results in increasing NOI. The technological capabilities of the country are increasingly geared towards the production of standardized goods. With rising incomes, consumers begin to demand higher-quality goods, fuelled in part by the growing competitiveness among the supplying firms. The comparative advantage of labour-intensive activities will deteriorate, domestic wages will rise, and outward direct investment will be directed more to countries at lower stages in their IDP. The original O advantages of foreign firms also begin to be eroded, as domestic firms acquire their own competitive advantages and compete with them in the same sectors.

The initial O advantages of foreign firms will also begin to change, as the domestic firms compete directly with them in these sectors. This is supported by the growing stock of created assets of the host country due to increased expenditure on education, vocational training and innovatory activities. These will be replaced by new technological, managerial or marketing innovations in order to compete with domestic firms. These O advantages are likely to be based on the possession of intangible knowledge, and the public-good nature of such assets will mean that foreign firms will increasingly prefer to exploit them through cross-border hierarchies. Growing L advantages such as an enlarged market and improved domestic innovatory capacity will make for economies of scale, and, with rising wage costs, will encourage more technology-intensive manufacturing as well as higher value added locally. The motives of inward direct investment will shift towards efficiency-seeking production and away from import-substituting production. In industries where domestic firms have a competitive advantage, there may be some inward direct investment directed towards strategic asset-acquiring activities.

Domestic firms' O advantages will have changed too, and will be based less on government-induced action. Partly owing to the increase in their multinationality, the character of the O advantages of foreign firms will increasingly reflect their ability to manage and co-ordinate geographically dispersed assets. At this stage of development, their O advantages based on possession of proprietary assets will be similar to those of firms from developed countries in all except the most technology-intensive sectors. There will be increased outward direct investment directed to Stage 1 and 2 countries, both as market-seeking investment and as export platforms, as prior domestic L advantages in resource-intensive production are eroded. Outward direct investment will also occur in Stage 3 and 4 countries, partly as a market-seeking strategy, but also to acquire strategic assets to protect or upgrade the O advantages of the investing firms.

The role of government-induced O advantages is likely to be less significant in Stage 3, as those of FDI-induced O advantages take on more importance. Although the significance of location-bound created assets will rise relative to those of natural assets, government policies will continue to be directed to reducing structural market imperfections in resource-intensive industries. Thus governments may attempt to attract inward direct investment in those sectors in which the comparative O advantages of enterprises are the weakest, but the comparative advantages of location-bound assets are the strongest. At the same time, they might seek to encourage their country's own enterprises to invest abroad in those sectors in which the O advantages are the strongest, and the comparative L advantages are the weakest. Structural adjustment will be required if the country is to move to the next stage of development, with declining industries (such as labour-intensive ones) undertaking direct investment abroad.

Stage 4

Stage 4 is reached when a country's outward direct investment stock exceeds or equals the inward investment stock from foreign-owned firms, and the rate of growth of outward FDI is still rising faster than that of inward FDI. At this stage, domestic firms can not only compete effectively with foreign-owned firms in domestic sectors in which the home country has developed a competitive advantage, but they can also penetrate foreign markets. Production processes and products will be state of the art, using capital-intensive production techniques as the cost of capital will be lower than that of labour. In other words, the L advantages will be based almost completely on created assets. Inward direct investment into Stage 4 countries is increasingly sequential and directed towards rationalized and asset-seeking investment by firms from other Stage 4 countries. The O-specific advantages of these firms tend to be more 'transaction' than 'asset' related, and to be derived from their multinationality *per se*. Some inward direct investment will originate from countries at lower stages of development, and is likely to be of a market-seeking, trade-related and asset-seeking nature.

Outward direct investment will continue to grow, as firms seek to maintain their competitive advantage by moving operations which are losing their competitiveness to offshore locations (in countries at lower stages), as well as responding to trade barriers installed by both countries at Stage 4, as well as countries at lower stages. Firms will have an increasing propensity to internalize the market for their O advantages by engaging in FDI rather than exports. Since the O advantages of countries at this stage are broadly similar, intra-industry production will become relatively more important, and generally follows prior growth in intraindustry trade. However, both intraindustry trade and production will tend to be increasingly conducted *within* multinational enterprises (MNEs).

The role of government is also likely to change in Stage 4. While continuing its supervisory and regulatory function, to reduce market imperfections and maintain competition, it will give more attention to the structural adjustment of its location-bound assets and technological capabilities, for example by fostering asset upgrading in infant industries (i.e. promoting a virtuous circle) and phasing out declining industries (i.e. promoting a vicious circle). Put another way, the role of government is now moving towards reducing transaction costs of economic activity and enabling markets to operate efficiently. At this stage too, because of the increasing competition between countries with similar structures of resources and capabilities, governments begin taking a more strategic posture in their policy formation. Direct intervention is likely to be replaced by measures designed to aid the upgrading of domestic resources and capabilities, and to curb the market-distorting behaviour of private economic agents.

Stage 5

As illustrated in Figure 5.1, in Stage 5, the NOI position of a country first falls and later fluctuates around the zero level. At the same time, both inward and outward FDI are likely to continue to increase. This is the scenario which advanced industrial nations are now approaching as the century draws to a close, and it possesses two key features. First, there is an increasing propensity for cross-border transactions to be conducted not through the market but internalized by and within MNEs. Second, as countries converge in the structure of their location-bound assets, their international direct investment positions are likely to become more evenly balanced. It has been suggested in Dunning, 1993, that these phenomena represent a natural and predictable progress of the internationalization of firms and economies. Thus the nature and scope of activity gradually shifts from arm's-length trade between nations producing very different goods and services (Hecksher–Ohlin trade) to trade within hierarchies (or co-operative ventures) between countries producing very similar products.

Unlike previous stages, Stage 5 of the IDP represents a situation in which no single country has an absolute hegemony of created assets. Moreover, the O advantages of MNEs will be less dependent on their country's natural resources but more on their ability to acquire assets and on the ability of firms to organize their advantages efficiently and to exploit the gains of cross-border common governance. Another feature of Stage 5 is that as firms become globalized their nationalities become blurred. As MNEs bridge geographical and political divides and practise a policy of transnational integration, they no longer operate principally with the interests of their home nation in mind, as they trade, source and manufacture in various locations, exploiting created and natural assets wherever it is in their best interests to do so. Increasingly, MNEs, through their arbitraging functions, come to behave like mini-markets. However, the ownership and territorial boundaries of firms become obscured[5] as they engage in an increasingly complex web of transborder co-operative agreements.[6]

The tendency for income levels to converge among the Triad countries has been noted, among others, by Abramovitz (1986), Baumol (1986), Dowrick and Gemmell (1991) and Alam (1992). Indeed, during the 1970s and 1980s, Japan, the EC and EFTA countries have experienced a 'catching up' in their productivity and growth relative to the United States (the 'lead' country), while a range of the newly industrializing countries began to move from Stage 2 to Stage 3 in their IDP.

As a result of these developments, the economic structures of many industrial economies have become increasingly similar. Countries which were once the lead countries in Stage 4 now find themselves joined by others. This tends to reduce their NOI position and pushes them into Stage 5 of the IDP. At the same time, there has also been a 'catching-up' effect among MNEs since the 1970s. Firms that have had relatively low levels of international operations have been internationalizing at faster rates than their more geographically diversified counterparts. These two effects are not unrelated: firms have had to compensate for slowing economic growth in their home country by seeking new markets overseas. Given the similarity in income levels, the factors of production are broadly similar, and, as Cantwell and Randaccio (1990) have shown, firms that are trying to catch up seek to imitate competitors and develop similar O advantages as their competitors in the same industry, *but not necessarily in the same country.*

To take this argument a step further, as income levels, economic structures and patterns of international production among the Triad countries converge, the relative attractions of a particular location will depend less on the availability, quality and price of their natural assets and more on those of their created assets. It has been noted elsewhere that the prosperity of modern industrial economies is increasingly dependent on their capacity to upgrade continually, or make better use of their technological capacity and human resources (Cantwell and Dunning, 1991). Since many of these advantages are transferable across national boundaries, it may be predicted that, in the long run, this should lead to a more balanced international investment position, and to an increasing convergence of created asset L advantages.

However, the ability of a country to upgrade its technological and human capabilities is a function of its own location-bound endowments and, in particular, of its natural assets, the characteristics of its markets and the macro-organizational strategies of its government. We believe the role of government in affecting dynamic economic restructuring cannot be overstated. In a myriad of ways, governments can promote new trajectories of economic growth which some countries are better able to cope with than others. This has been amply illustrated by the evolution of Japan's economy compared with that of the United States, especially in the 1980s.

In terms of their gross inward and outward direct investment positions, Stage 5 countries, after an initial burst of new inward direct investment (e.g. as occurred in the United States in the 1980s), may be expected to settle down to a fluctuating equilibrium around a roughly equal amount of inward and outward investment. Inward investment will be of two kinds. The first will come from countries at lower stages of the IDP and will be essentially of the market-seeking and knowledge-seeking type. The second will be from Stage 4 (or Stage 5) countries whose firms will continue to indulge in rationalized investment among themselves, as well as making outward direct investments in less developed countries, especially in the natural-resource-intensive sectors. In other words, truly rationalized or efficiency-seeking MNE activity will occur as plant and product specialization is encouraged in sectors where economies of scale and scope are important.

As the world economy begins to resemble a global village, strategic asset-seeking investments may also be expected to rise, and this, too, will lead to increasing convergence among countries as firms seek to improve their O advantages by cross-border mergers and acquisitions (M&As) or strategic alliances. Therefore, in the shorter time frame, inward and outward investment will fluctuate depending on relative innovatory and organizational strength of the participating countries. However as Cantwell has noted,

> The sectoral pattern of innovative activity gradually changes as new industries develop and new technical linkages are forged between sectors. Yet this is a slow process which in general only slightly disturbed the pattern of technological advantages held by firms of the major industrialized countries in the 20 years between the early 1960s and the early 1980s. (Cantwell, 1989, p. 45)

Thus, *pro tem*, at least, it is possible for one country to be a net outward investor compared with another. But over time, according to the extent and speed at which created assets are transferable, the investment gap will again close, leading to a fluctuating investment position around an equilibrium level. It is within this context that the fifth stage will emerge.

In other words, an equilibrium of sorts will be perpetuated, but it will not be a stable equilibrium as the relative comparative and competitive advantages of countries and firms are likely to be continually shifting. Hence, along with these fluctuations in relative comparative advantages, when combined with external and internal changes in the domestic economy, gradually the number of countries at Stage 5 will fluctuate.

The acquisition, diffusion and transfer of O advantages will be influenced by the cumulative causation in trade, production and technology, and whether the industry or sector in each of the countries at Stage 5 experiences a 'vicious' or a 'virtuous' circle (Dunning, 1988b; Cantwell, 1989). In the former case, it may serve to increase technological divergences between countries; in the latter, it may strengthen the technological linkages between them.

In summary, Stage 5 is marked by a gradual convergence of industrial structures among countries and a change in the character of international transactions. MNE activity, in particular, will be directed to efficiency-seeking investment with greater emphasis on cross-border alliances, mergers and acquisitions, and the governance and equity position of MNEs will become increasingly pluralistic. The success of countries in accumulating technology, as well as inducing continued economic growth, will depend increasingly on the ability of their firms to co-ordinate their resources and capabilities at a regional and global level. The economic convergence of industrialized countries on one hand, and high rate of intra-Triad FDI growth on the other, may be expected to foster regional and/or global integration as well as lessening the role of natural assets as a country-specific determinant of FDI. In Stage 5, governments will increasingly assume the role of strategic oligopolists, taking into account the behaviour of other governments in the formation and execution of their own macro-organizational strategies. In this stage, too, governments are likely to play a more pro-active role in the fostering of efficient markets, and co-operating with business enterprises to reduce structural adjustment and other transaction costs.

To conclude: beyond a certain point in the IDP, the absolute size of GNP is no longer a reliable guide to a country's competitiveness; neither, indeed, is its

NOI position. This is for two reasons. First, the competitiveness of a country is better measured by the rate and character of growth of GNP *vis-à-vis* that of its major competitors. Second, as the motivation of FDI has evolved away from being primarily geared to the exploitation of existing O advantages to the acquisition of new O advantages, countries which offer the appropriate location-bound resources for the creation of such advantages may increase their attractiveness to inbound FDI. Investments made to acquire or exploit indigenous competitive advantage, far from representing a weakness of the recipient country, could represent a strength. Certainly, recent evidence seems to suggest that, in the Triad at least, inbound and outbound FDI are increasingly complementary to each other, especially at a sectoral level (UNCTAD, 1993).

Most of the empirical testing of the basic proposition of the IDP, namely that there is a systematic relationship between a country's inward and outward investment and its GNP per capita, has used cross-sectional data, and is generally supportive of the proposition.[7] However, new cross-sectional and time series data – some of which are set out in Dunning and Narula (1996) – seem to be pointing to two things. The first is that the shape and position of the IDP probably varies much more between individual countries than it was originally thought. In particular, the economic structure of countries, and the development strategies and macro-organizational policies of governments, appear to be critical in influencing both the role of MNEs in a country's economy at a given moment of time, and how inward and outward direct investment may help fashion the growth and structure of the economy over time (Dunning, 1993). The second is that the underlying nature of the IDP for all countries appears to be undergoing some change, owing to a series of events in the global economy, which leads us to revise some of our hypotheses about its trajectory. This issue is taken up in greater detail later in this chapter.

Country-specific Factors and the IDP

As in previous contributions (e.g. Dunning, 1986, 1993) we have written extensively about the interaction between inbound and outbound FDI and the level, composition and growth of the GNP of countries, we will need to add comparatively little at this point about country-specific factors. It may, however, be appropriate to remind ourselves that the IDP was first put forward to illustrate the relevance of the eclectic paradigm of international production in explaining the NOI position of countries. It follows, then, that any predictions about the IDP must rest on the contents of the paradigm itself.

Now, as stated earlier, the paradigm avers that a country will attract inbound FDI when (i) foreign firms possess certain O-specific advantages over and above those of indigenous firms; (ii) its L-bound resources and capabilities favour the deployment of these competitive advantages, relative to those offered by other countries; and (iii) foreign firms perceive that it is to their benefit to internalize the intermediate product markets for these advantages, rather than selling them via the external market, or by a co-operative arrangement, to domestic firms in the host country. Similarly the paradigm hypothesizes that the propensity of a country to be an outward direct investor will rest on the strength and character of the O advantages of its indigenous firms, and the extent to which these might best be exploited by adding value to them in a foreign location, and organized through an MNE hierarchy rather than through a non-equity relationship with a foreign firm.

The eclectic paradigm further suggests some of the ways in which, over time, inbound and outbound investment may affect the trajectory of a country's development path. This it might do by its impact both on the composition and productivity of domestic economic activity, and the ease or difficulty with which a country is able to restructure its resources and capabilities to meet the needs of endogenous and exogenous change. The critical role played by inbound FDI in the upgrading of Singaporean indigenous endowments, and that of outbound FDI in the dynamic restructuring of Japan's post-war development, are two cases in point, although other examples show that FDI does not always have such salutary effects on economic welfare.[8]

Over the past 30 years, there have been a large number of studies on the impact of both outbound and inbound MNE activity on the development and economic restructuring of the countries in which they operate. The overwhelming consensus of these studies is that, for good or bad, this is critically dependent on three main variables, namely (i) the type of FDI undertaken, (ii) the structure of the indigenous resources and capabilities of the countries concerned, and (iii) the macro-economic and organizational policies pursued by governments.[9] We would then expect the shape and position of the IDP of countries – which traces the interaction between inbound and outbound FDI and advances in the prosperity of those countries – to be determined by the same variables.

We have suggested that one of the characteristics of economic development identified by several writers (e.g. Porter, 1990; Ozawa, 1992; Narula, 1996; Dunning and Narula, 1994) is that, as development proceeds, the significance of indigenous assets relative to *natural* assets as a locational attraction to inbound FDI increases. Ozawa (1992), in describing the post-war development of Japan, identifies four distinct stages, namely those of labour-intensive manufacturing, scale-economies-based production of heavy and chemical industries, assembly-based mass production of consumer durables, and mechatronics-based flexible manufacturing. For his part, Porter (1990) writes about the nature of competitive advantages of a country according to whether they are factor driven, investment driven, innovation driven or wealth driven. While the prosperity of most poor countries is largely resource driven, that of the richest is largely innovation or wealth driven. Naturally, the precise balance of a country's natural and created assets will vary depending on the extent to which it is endowed with the former (cf. Canada with Japan, and Kuwait with Singapore) but as Ohmae (1987) has powerfully shown, even the value of natural resources such as minerals and agricultural products can be dramatically increased by secondary processing and astute marketing, both of which require the input of created assets.

In view of the fact that an increasing number of countries are now at the innovation stage of their IDP – indeed, as we shall suggest later, innovation-led production is changing the trajectory of global economic development – it is not surprising that both outward and inward FDI are being increasingly evaluated by national governments in terms of their perceived contribution to technological capacity and human resource development (Dunning, 1994). Governments, too, are becoming aware that, if their FDI is properly to achieve their objectives, they need to provide the location-bound resources and capabilities essential for the efficient creation and deployment of the O-specific advantages of both foreign investors and their own MNEs. An appropriate combination of the competitive advantages of firms and countries is likely to make for a *virtuous* cycle of upgrading economic development, with each advantage fostering the other. An inappropriate combination of such advantages – or the lack of one or both – is likely to lead to a vicious cycle to the detriment of economic development.

Structural Changes and the IDP

Let us now turn to the main focus of the first part of this chapter, which is to consider the ways in which recent technological and organizational changes, as they have impinged upon the governance of both firms and national economies, have affected our thinking about the shape and character of the IDP.

Some shifts in the rationale for FDI

Most of the received literature on MNE-related activity tends to assume that firms engage in FDI in order best to exploit, or organize more efficiently, their existing competitive advantages. Sometimes, these resources and capabilities are combined with foreign location-bound assets to supply domestic or adjacent markets, and sometimes to service more distant markets. In some instances, too, inbound FDI may be used to restructure the existing portfolio of foreign value-added activities by MNEs. Such sequential investment is best thought of as efficiency-seeking transborder activity, as contrasted with market- or resource-seeking transborder activity.

In the last decade or more, however, MNE activity has been increasingly motivated by the desire to acquire new competitive advantages, or protect existing advantages. Such strategic asset-acquiring FDI has been particularly pronounced within the Triad of advanced industrial countries, and is most dramatically shown by the spate of cross-border mergers and acquisitions (M&As) which have occurred since the mid- and late 1980s.[10] Essentially, such M&As have been (and still are) undertaken by firms for five main reasons: (i) the rising costs of innovation and of entry into unfamiliar markets, (ii) competitive pressures for firms to be more cost effective, (iii) the growing need to tap into complementary technologies and to capture the economies of scale and scope expected from the merger or acquisition, (iv) a desire to protect or advance their global markets, *vis-à-vis* oligopolistic competitors, and (v) the need to encapsulate the time of the innovating or market entry process.

Such strategic asset-acquiring FDI implies that firms may engage in outward FDI from a position of weakness, and that countries may attract inbound FDI because their resources and capabilities offer competitive advantages to foreign MNEs. Thus, part of the contemporary outbound MNE activity directed to the United States is designed to gain access to the technological capabilities of US firms, and their privileged access to US or adjacent (e.g. NAFTA) markets. Such FDI is likely to be determined by a different configuration of O and L advantages than those facing traditional market- or resource-seeking MNEs.

The effect of strategic asset-seeking investment on the IDP is that it is likely to increase the level of outward investment of all countries, but particularly that from medium-income and fast-growing industrializing nations, as they seek to establish a speedy presence in the most innovatory and dynamic markets of the world. Frequently, firms from developing countries do not have the full range of resources and capabilities to promote a fully fledged 'stand-alone' competitive strategy, and certainly not one which would help them penetrate unfamiliar global markets. Depending on their particular strengths and weaknesses, their liquidity position and the type of assets to which they need access, the mode of foreign involvement by firms is likely to vary between an FDI, a minority joint venture and some form of co-operative alliance. However, *ceteris paribus*, the first of these routes is most likely to be preferred whenever the assets sought are perceived to be critical to protect or advance the core competencies of the investing firms.

As yet, there has been little systematic research into the significance of strategic asset-acquiring FDI, relative to that of other kinds. But, taking inbound FDI in the United States as an example, it is generally agreed by scholars that, although the resurgence of activity by European firms in the 1970s and much of the greenfield investment by Japanese firms in the 1980s reflected the growing O advantages of these firms, relative to those of US firms, many of the transatlantic European M&As in the late 1980s and early 1990s have been geared towards strengthening the O advantages of the investing firms (or diminishing those of their competitors) by buying into US resources and capabilities, and/or markets. One suspects that had it been feasible, there would also have been a substantial amount of M&A activity by US and European firms in Japan during this period.

The presence of strategic asset-acquiring FDI is then tending to raise the level of inward investment of industrialized countries – and particularly those which are the leading repositories of advanced created assets. It is also tending to increase the outward investment of these countries – but not to the same extent as inward investment – while raising the outbound FDI by industrializing developing countries, as they seek to aid and accelerate the entry of their firms into global markets. In short, the presence and growth of asset-acquiring MNE activity is leading to a flattening out of the NOI position of countries, as compared with that suggested by the traditional version of IDP; namely, at lower levels of GNP the net *inward* investment position will be lower, and at high levels of income the NOI position will be lower, than in the absence of such investment.[11] The suggested reshaping of the IDP is portrayed by the dotted line in Figure 5.1.

The emergence of alliance capitalism

Another feature of the last decade has been the growth in non-equity collaborative arrangements of one kind or another. Sometimes, these are being pursued as alternatives to FDI, but, for the most part, they are complementary to it. Increasingly, cross-border *intra*firm FDI and *inter*firm co-operative schemes are being perceived as part of a holistic and multimodal strategy of the leading global players.

It is possible to identify many different kinds of collaborative schemes, but the vast majority fall into two categories. The first take the form of strategic alliances which are specifically intended to gain access (or preclude a competitor from gaining access) to foreign assets or markets. The second embrace a galaxy of international subcontracting relationships, in which interfirm co-operation goes beyond the production of materials, parts and components to the design and development of new materials, parts and components. In each case, too, it would seem that the terms of any collaboration are contained less in a formal contract and more in a sense of agreed mission and mutual commitment.

It is the latter characteristic of interfirm relationships which has led to the coining of the term 'alliance' capitalism.[12] As we have seen, alliance capitalism differs from hierarchical capitalism in that, whereas in the case of the former, the co-ordination of economic activity is determined primarily by arm's-length markets and interfirm co-operation, in the latter it is decided primarily by arm's-length markets and hierarchical *intra*firm fiat.[13]

While alliance capitalism has long since been a prominent feature of many East Asian economies – most noticeably Japan and South Korea -in the mid-1990s it is spreading – albeit in a modified form – to other parts of the world.

This is for three main reasons. The first reflects the lack of experience of hierarchical capitalism by the transition economies of Central and Eastern Europe and China. As these countries struggle to embrace the discipline of free markets, they are finding that the speediest and most effective way to upgrade their natural and created assets is for their newly privatized firms to form co-operative alliances with other domestic, or foreign, firms, rather than to pursue the route of internal economic growth. Second, it reflects the increasing inability of firms to pursue 'stand-alone' strategies in situations in which their core competencies need to be efficiently combined with those of other firms if they – the former – are to be fully effective.

Third, one of the features of the emerging techno-economic paradigm of micro-economic activity, namely flexible and innovation-led production, is that it requires a symbiotic and continuing relationship between the various participants in the production process, and that this is likely to be most effective if it is based on mutually agreed upon goals and on active and purposeful co-operation, rather than on administrative fiat. Thus, although many firms are currently downsizing the range of their activities in order to concentrate on those central to their core competencies, that is, becoming *less* hierarchical, they are also concluding new strategic alliances with their critical suppliers and industrial customers along the value chain, and with their competitors across value chains. This they are doing both to leverage more effectively their own special capabilities and to ensure, by appropriate control procedures, that the goods and services they transact with other firms, and which critically affect these capabilities, are provided at the highest quality and/or the lowest cost.[14]

What are the implications of the advent of alliance capitalism on the international direct investment position of countries and their IDP? Perhaps the main implication is that such non-equity forms of cross-border production are becoming too important to be ignored in discussing the export and import of resources and capabilities, and the way in which their use is influenced either by hierarchical or by co-operative arrangements involving foreign firms. Here what scant evidence we have[15] suggests that, apart from situations in which inbound and/or outbound FDI is disallowed or regulated by governments, cross-border alliance formation to gain access to new technologies and markets, or to exploit the economies of scale and synergy, tends to involve a two-way exchange of resources and capabilities between firms from advanced industrial countries. By contrast, other kinds of alliances, and especially those which involve firms from both developed and developing countries, are primarily concluded in order to facilitate a transfer of resources and capabilities from the former to the latter countries.[16]

Incorporating such alliances into the IDP would then suggest that inbound transfer MNE activity[17] of the poor or middle-income countries would increase, but in the case of the richer countries, one might predict an increase of both inbound and outbound resource transfer. Unfortunately, apart from some data on cross-border interfirm royalties and fees, it is extremely difficult to quantify either the extent to which alliances *do* transfer resources and capabilities, or the consequence of such transfers on the welfare of the exporting and importing countries. As a subject for further research, the relationships between alliance formation, economic structure and development surely demand some degree of priority.

The role of non-market country-specific differences in explaining the IDP

In our earlier testing of the hypothesis that a country's outward and inward FDI is systematically related to its stage of development (Dunning, 1981, 1986, 1988a), we identified a number of contextual variables which could explain why the shape and position of the IDP differs between countries. *Inter alia*, our research showed that industrial or industrializing countries were likely to generate more outward direct investment at any given level of GNP per head than the natural-resource-based economies.[18] At the same time, we made the general assumption that countries – or, more specifically, the governments of countries – pursued market-friendly economic strategies, and intervened as little as possible in the organization and allocation of resources within their jurisdiction.

In retrospect, it is clear that, throughout the last three decades, by a bevy of macro-economic and organizational policies, national governments have considerably affected the structure of the IDP of their countries. This they have done both by specific actions to influence the level and composition of inbound and outbound FDI, and by their general economic and social policies, which affect the attractiveness of their location-bound resources and markets to foreign investors. Moreover, notwithstanding the liberalization and deregulation of many markets over the past decade, national governments continue to exercise a powerful influence on a country's international investment position and the profile of its IDP.

Several country case studies contained in Dunning and Narula (1996) confirm this proposition. It is most obviously seen in the case of centrally planned and East Asian economies. But, as revealed by some quite dramatic shifts in the outward and inward FDI position of particular countries – which have often occurred as a direct result of a reorientation in government economic policy – it is no less evident in economies such as the United Kingdom, France, Sweden, Greece and Portugal in Europe; Chile, Colombia, Argentina, Jamaica, Mexico and Venezuela in Latin America; China, India, the Philippines, Vietnam and South Korea in Asia; Canada in North America; Morocco, Egypt, Nigeria and South Africa in Africa; and in Iran in the Middle East.

There is already a good deal of evidence that the liberalization and privatization of markets, and the attempts by many governments to increase inbound investment, have led to an increased flow and restructuring of inward investment into many countries, and, *pari passu*, an increased flow of outward investment from other countries.[19] It is also apparent that the role of national governments in affecting the price and quality of location-bound resources within their jurisdictions, and the motivation and capabilities of their own firms to be outward investors, is becoming increasingly significant – and especially in so far as inter-Triad strategic asset- and efficiency-seeking investment is concerned. Thus, for example, government policies which aim to upgrade the quality of indigenous resources and capabilities to meet the demands of the international market-place are likely to engage in more cross-border transactions (e.g. FDI, trade and co-operative alliances) than those which are designed to promote economic self-reliance.[20]

It follows from the above paragraphs that the relationship between FDI and income levels using cross-sectional country data may well be expected to vary at different points of time because of changes in the role of governments in affecting inward and outward investment. It is also likely to fluctuate according to the direction and character of technological advances and the country from which they originate. Such advances, by their impact on the competitive advantages of firms of a particular nationality, on the cost-effectiveness of the location-bound resources and capabilities of countries, and on the way in which economic activity is organized, are likely to lead to a repositioning of the IDPs of countries. At the same time, longitudinal data show that variations in the trajectory of a country's IDP may occur because of changes in the actions of national governments. In short, then, although we have some ideas about the interaction of the behaviour of governments and inward and outward investment, we need to explore this in a more systematic and rigorous way.

The theory: some concluding remarks

In this chapter, we have suggested that some of the propositions initially put forward to relate the inward and outward direct investment position of countries to their stages of development need reconsideration. Partly, we have argued that this is because the *raison d'être* and character of FDI has undergone some important changes. Partly it is because other forms of cross-border involvement – and notably co-operative arrangements – by MNEs need to be incorporated in the analysis; and that the interaction between these other forms and the stages of development may well be different from those of FDI. And partly we have suggested this is because differences in national government policies need to be more explicitly identified as an explanatory variable of the international direct investment of countries, before any satisfactory relationship between outbound and inward investment and economic development can be established.

Lastly, we believe that further attention needs to be given to the form and characteristics of the fifth stage of the IDP, namely that in which the outward and inward investment positions – like those of exports and imports – fluctuate around the same level. Here the hypothesis is that the structures of the most advanced industrial economies are both similar and inextricably linked with each other. Although, for a period of time, one nation, through a series of path-breaking technological or organizational advances and/or superior macro-economic or macro-organizational policies, might gain a major competitive advantage over other nations, any marked increase in outbound direct investment may well be tempered by a corresponding rise in inbound strategic asset-seeking investment and alliance formation. Moreover, owing to the increasing ease at which knowledge, information and even organizational techniques can move across national boundaries, any lead by one country is likely to be quite quickly eroded by its competitors, and sometimes the catching-up process itself may be aided and abetted by inbound and outbound FDI and alliance formation.

However, little is known about the mechanism by which this is achieved. Some hints about the dynamic interplay between the O-specific advantages of firms and the L-specific advantages of countries have been given by Tolentino (1993), Dunning (1993) and Narula (1996), while Ozawa (1992) has explored some of the ways in which inbound and outbound Japanese FDI has affected the structure of Japanese economic development. The conditions under which inward and outward FDI[21] can promote the upgrading of a country's resources and capabilities and advantageously restructure its resource allocation have also been explored by several writers,[22] including Cantwell (1989) and Cantwell and Dunning (1991), who used the concepts of virtuous and vicious cycles to explore the interplay between inward FDI and the competitiveness of a particular industrial sector.

While some of the contributions in the Dunning and Narula (1996) volume take this discussion a little further, much remains to be done. Why, indeed, has inbound FDI promoted advantageous structural economic development in some countries (e.g. Singapore and Thailand) but not in others (e.g. Chile and Nigeria)? What determines whether outward direct investment helps a country to upgrade the quality of its indigenous assets, and to promote its dynamic competitive advantage, or, instead, to erode its technological strengths and human resource development? What is the impact of alliance capitalism on both the optimal mode of resource transfer and usage, and on the ways in which these may affect the structure and pace of economic development? It is questions such as these which need the attention of scholars in the years to come.

A STATISTICAL EVALUATION

Structural Changes and the IDP

At the outset it is important to point out that any statistical evaluation of the IDP must necessarily be a tentative one. Any attempt to conduct a thorough empirical analysis of a complex and changing relationship has severe limitations. Given this fact, it is not our intention to develop a rigorous statistical specification and test of the IDP. In fact, our aim is almost exactly the opposite, as we wish to demonstrate that a statistical evaluation of the relationship between FDI and economic development cannot be conducted on an aggregate basis across countries, as the IDP represents a paradigm which is idiosyncratic and country specific, and therefore best analysed on a country-by-country basis. We intend merely to argue that the basic relationships postulated by the IDP are still applicable, and how the lacunae regarding the extent and evolution of natural and created assets as well as the changes in the world economy affect the relationships suggested by the IDP.

Structural Changes in the World Economy

There have been two major developments in the world economy which have affected the character of the IDP. The first is the introduction of Stage 5, which reflects the catching-up and convergence process of the industrialized economies. As we have discussed in the first part of this chapter and elsewhere (Narula, 1993, 1996; Dunning and Narula, 1994), as countries reach Stage 4 and begin to enter Stage 5, the activities and growth of their MNEs are no longer a function of just the economic conditions of their home country, but the various host countries in which they have subsidiaries. The more globalized the operations of a firm, the greater the extent to which its O advantages are likely to be firm specific, rather than determined by the economic, political and cultural conditions of its home country. Moreover, the O advantages of firms will increasingly be dependent on their ability to acquire and develop *created* assets and their ability to organize these assets efficiently in order to exploit the advantages due to common governance, making the MNE less dependent on its home country's natural resources. As such, O advantages become increasingly firm specific as MNEs become more internationalized. The consequence of this is that the outward direct investment position of a country's firms at this stage is no longer entirely dependent on the economic status and competitiveness of their home country, and increasingly affected by the conditions in the various other countries in which they operate. Therefore, after reaching a certain NOI position, a country's investment position will *not* necessarily be proportional to *its income level or relative stage of development*. To put it another way, we hypothesize that, *ceteris paribus*, a Stage 5 country will continue to experience change in its FDI position regardless of whether its relative stage of development or income levels changes. This is readily apparent when examining the NOI position and GDPs of countries like the United States and the United Kingdom which have either remained at the same relative stage of development or fallen, but continue to experience high growth in both their inward and outward position. Indeed, not only has the share of total world-wide inward investment to industrialized countries increased, but a greater extent of outward investment from these countries is being directed towards other industrialized countries. (The current exception is the surge of FDI into China.)

Furthermore, the use of GDP as a proxy for development does not take into account the profound changes in the economic structure of the industrialized countries, which have shown a clear trend towards tertiary (i.e. service) sectors. In other words, while their overall economic growth has slowed over the past two decades, there has been considerable structural adjustment between sectors. This has also had an effect on the composition of their inbound and outbound FDI and, because of this, its geographical composition. Since 1980, for example, much of the growth in inward and outward FDI has been directed to the tertiary sector, and has been between industrialized countries (Narula, 1996). These changes make a statistical evaluation of the relationship between NOI and GDP of Stage 4 and 5 countries an increasingly difficult exercise through an aggregate, cross-sectional test.

The growth of alternative forms of overseas value-added activity such as strategic alliances needs also to be taken into account, especially in high-technology sectors. As suggested in the first part of this chapter, strategic alliances have become an important means by which MNEs from industrialized countries have begun to engage in cross-border activities since the 1980s. The evidence suggests that there is an increasing preference for Triad-based MNEs to utilize non-equity-based co-operative agreements in preference to equity-based agreements (such as joint ventures) in their intra-Triad partnering activities in these sectors[23] (Hagedoorn and Narula, 1994). Such agreements are naturally not reflected in the FDI data, and since well over 95 per cent of all strategic alliances[24] are intra-Triad in scope (Freeman and Hagedoorn, 1994) the use of FDI data for industrialized countries without allowing for the growth of strategic alliances may make the results questionable.

The second consequence of changes in the world economy has been the growing divergence of at least some of the developing economies away from the industrialized economies. The catching-up process described earlier has not occurred among the poorer countries, who have diverged as a group from the wealthier countries and are not exhibiting a tendency to converge in relation to the world leaders (Dowrick and Gemmell, 1991; Dowrick, 1992; Verspagen, 1993), and are in fact 'falling behind'. The effect on the FDI activities of developing countries is that less inward direct investment is from industrialized countries, and those developing countries that are outward investors prefer to invest in the industrialized countries, wherever possible, to acquire created assets. However, the 'falling-behind' effect is associated primarily with Stage 1 and 2 countries, while a handful of developing countries that are regarded as newly industrializing economies (Stage 3) have been shown to be 'catching up' with the industrialized economies. Indeed, data on FDI flows indicate that the four Asian NICs account for 57.6 per cent of total outward flows from non-oil-exporting developing countries between 1980 and 1990, and 83 per cent over 1988–90.

The Idiosyncratic Nature of Countries

Most previous tests of the validity of the IDP have used a cross-sectional study across countries as a surrogate for longitudinal analysis. As various country studies in Dunning and Narula (1996) show, the exact circumstance of each country is unique, and while there are some general similarities between groups of countries, the explanatory power of the 'ideal' IDP based on cross-sectional analysis of a large group of countries is severely limited. This aggregation of countries for a given time period assumes that countries follow a broadly similar IDP, whereas, in fact, each country follows its own particular path which is determined by three main variables: (i) the extent and nature of its created and natural assets; (ii) its strategy of economic development; and (iii) the role of government. These factors essentially determine the nature and extent of the firm-specific assets of both foreign MNEs and domestic firms operating within its borders.

The character of a country's resource endowments

The extent and nature of a country's natural and created assets are determined by two main issues: (i) its resource structure and (ii) its size.

Resource structure A country may possess a significant comparative advantage, or an absolute advantage, in primary commodities. Such a country is likely to spawn domestic firms that possess O advantages in the exploitation of such assets. However, especially if such an advantage is a near absolute one, it is likely to be the recipient of considerable inward investment from MNEs that wish to internalize the supply of primary products to their upstream activities located in other countries, and the extent of this inward investment will almost continue to rise as the other L advantages associated with the host country develop. These L advantages include the availability of skilled labour and other infrastructural facilities, and may lead to sequential vertical investment in upstream activities by both domestic firms and MNEs. As a result, a comparative advantage in a natural-resource-based industry may be sustained even when the income levels rise to developed country standards. Such a scenario would result in an NOI position that continues to be negative even when its economy is developed, as for example in Australia. Any outward investment would also tend to be in industries that are either in or related to the primary sector, but would be dwarfed by the increasing extent of inward investment. Such countries would tend to have a much lower (i.e. negative) level of NOI at considerably advanced stages of development.

The *lack* of a natural resource base (i.e. a comparative disadvantage in primary commodities) would, *ceteris paribus*, result in the opposite effect. Inward investment at earlier stages would be muted, and outward investment might begin at an earlier stage to secure the availability of necessary natural resources. Such a country is also more likely to begin strategic asset-seeking investment at an earlier stage (e.g. Japan). Overall, these countries would become net outward investors at a considerably earlier stage of development than those well-endowed with natural resources.

Market size Countries that possess small domestic market size, such as Hong Kong, Singapore and Switzerland, are likely to have not just limited natural resources such as primary commodities, but limited attraction in terms of market size. Thus the lack of economies of scale will inhibit inward foreign investment in earlier stages. As their human capital and infrastructure improves, some inward investment may occur for export processing purposes. The small populations may mean not just small aggregate consumption, but that domestic firms would need to seek overseas markets in order to achieve economies of scale. This not only would result in outward direct investment at earlier stages of development, but also suggests that as income levels rise, domestic investors that were involved in export-oriented production will seek overseas locations to compensate for the shortage of low-wage human capital for labour-intensive production. Such countries will reach (and remain at) a positive NOI position at a considerably earlier stage of their development. The opposite scenario would apply for large countries, which would attract larger amounts of inward investment due to the attractions of their large markets, and domestic firms may not have as much incentive to seek overseas markets since economies of scale can be achieved at home.

The dynamics of the natural/created asset evolution are primarily determined by those associated with the economic, social and political environment issues that are generally a direct result of the actions of governments. A statistical analysis of the IDP cannot, given the static nature of a cross-sectional test, capture the dynamic development of created assets. The role of government is even more idiosyncratic and peculiar to each country, and it is exceedingly difficult to translate this into a general variable, or to group countries into distinct groups according to the role of governments in influencing the created/natural asset balance. However, since these issues are dealt with in considerable detail in the country studies in Dunning and Narula (1996), we will briefly discuss the two main issues that primarily influence the dynamics of created asset development.

Economic system

The economic orientation of a country may be outward looking, export oriented (OL–EO) or inward looking, import substituting (IL–IS) (Ozawa, 1992). Depending on the orientation of an economy, the use of either (or a hybrid of the two) will substantially affect both economic development and the extent and pattern of FDI, and hence the nature of the path taken by a particular country. An OL–EO regime is likely to achieve faster growth and structural upgrading. Ozawa (1992) argues that an OL–EO regime is a necessary condition for FDI-facilitated development. We suggest here that although it is not a necessary condition for growth in the first two stages, the greater the extent of OL–EO policy orientation, the faster the process of structural adjustment and economic growth and the quicker a country's progress through the stages of the IDP. Our earlier discussion of the various stages assumes an OL–EO type of policy regime beyond the second stage, but not for the first two. IL–IS countries would tend to have relatively little inward and outward FDI activity.

The failure of countries to proceed beyond the second stage is associated with the vicious cycle of poverty (VCP). This, when applied in the traditional sense, is explained as follows: low income levels in less developed countries are associated with low savings rates which, in turn, result in low capital investment, thereby keeping income levels low. In the parlance of the eclectic paradigm there is a lack of ownership advantages of domestic firms and location advantages of the country, as well as an inability to develop or acquire these. The O advantages referred to here include financial assets as well as the Oa and Ot types of advantages, whereas the L advantages are those of infrastructure. This cycle can be broken, *inter alia*, through the infusion of capital through FDI, which allows for technological spillovers and financial capital.

Governments and organization of economic activity

Although the kind of economic system associated with a country broadly determines the path taken by a country, the nature of government policy associated with a particular system can vary between countries with the same economic system and at the same stage of development. There are two main areas of government strategy which directly impinge on the nature of the IDP of a country: macro-economic strategy and macro-organizational strategy (Dunning, 1992). The role of governments in determining macro-economic policy is relatively well defined, and is often associated with the economic system. On the other hand, there is considerable variance among countries in the role of governments in determining macro-organizational strategy. Macro-organizational strategy primarily influences the structure and organization of economic activity, and the nature of the policies most appropriate at a particular stage should, in an 'ideal' situation, change as the economy evolves, reflecting the nature of market imperfections that the policy is designed to circumvent (Hämäläinen, 1993). Essentially, in such a best-world scenario, government plays a market-facilitating role in which its macro-organizational policy dynamically evolves over time. Increasing economic specialization associated with economic development leads to a growth in market failures and increases the potential benefits of government macro-organizational policy (Durkheim, 1964). However, as Hämäläinen (1993) points out, governments may also fail, and society is often faced with a choice between imperfect markets and imperfect governments. Given that macro-organizational policy embraces a wide variety of issues,[25] and the fact that there is little agreement on what the optimal involvement of government should be, the macro-organizational policy stance varies widely among countries. The differences between the macro-organizational strategy of countries at the same stage of development influence both the structure of markets and the extent to which economic activity is efficiently conducted, thereby affecting the specialization and economic structure of the country, as well as the extent of FDI activity associated with it.

Evaluating the IDP

As we have earlier indicated, it is not our intention to develop a rigorous specification of the IDP, but merely to examine whether a causal relationship exists between FDI and economic development for 1992, and to illustrate the deviation from the 'ideal' path due to the extent of natural and created assets, as well as those due to structural changes in the world economy. We shall utilize data on FDI stocks published in UNCTAD (1994). GDP and population data are derived from World Bank (1994). All data are in nominal US dollars. All FDI and GDP figures are normalized by population. Inward FDI per capita is denoted as IWK, outward FDI as OWK, NOI per capita as NOIK, and GDP per capita is denoted as GDPK. In conducting the analysis, we shall also attempt to illustrate that the nature of the relationship varies with the extent of natural and created assets associated with a country.

The extent of natural/created assets is based on a twofold criterion to allow for differences due to resources intensity as well as differences in country size. High natural asset countries are defined as those countries whose primary exports as a percentage of total exports (PRX) are greater than or equal to 50 per cent or whose area is greater than 1.9 million km^2.[26] Since most developing countries tend to have a comparative advantage in primary commodities, the sample tends to consist largely of this group of countries. Although it would be more appropriate to include only those countries which have an absolute advantage in natural resources, rather than those with a comparative advantage, it is exceedingly difficult to find such measure. Low natural asset countries are assumed to represent countries with a high created asset base, or have a potential to become economies with a created asset base. This group is defined as countries for which PRX $\leq$ 20 per cent or area is less than 5000 km^2.

Net outward investment

We examine the relationship between NOI and GDP utilizing a quadratic specification. This allows for the fact that the dependent variable changes over time and stages, but it also assumes that the rate of change is more or less constant. Apart from running regressions for the entire sample (ALL), we also do so for a smaller subsample that excludes the most industrialized countries. This has two purposes. First, since we have not developed a specification for the fifth stage of the IDP, by excluding the countries that are most likely to be in Stage 5, we are able to test whether in fact the J-curve initially proposed by Dunning (1981) is still valid for the pre-Stage 5 countries. Second, by excluding the Stage 5 countries we are able to avoid 'stretching' of the IDP due to the cluster of a large number of developing countries at the origin and the spread of the industrialized countries around the *X*-axis, due to the process of convergence and divergence. This would make the second NOI = 0 point be further to the right than might actually be the case. The cut-off point for this sample is taken to be the first industrialized country with an NOI > 0. Figure 5.2 shows the plot of NOI per capita against GDP per capita for 1992. We also run regressions for two other subsamples, the created asset countries (HI CA) and the natural asset countries (HI NA). These four curves have been superimposed on Figure 5.2 while the results of these regressions are given in Table 5.1. We have not included the results for 1980 here since these are broadly similar to those for 1992. None the less, there are broad differences in the distribution of the observations for the developing countries and the industrialized countries that are due to the catching-up and falling-behind scenarios due to convergence and divergence which have been evaluated using some simple measures in Table 5.2. In the case of the industrialized countries, which dominate much of the graph, there has been an increasing trend towards a wider distribution along the *Y*-axis since 1980. The mean NOI has become more positive, increasing by a factor of 10.2, while the mean GDP has increased by a factor of just 2.1. Furthermore, the ratio of the standard deviation to the mean of NOI has fallen from 9.2 in 1980 to 2.4 in 1992 for industrialized countries, while this ratio for GDP have remained constant at 0.2. This suggests that convergence phenomena regarding GDP have halted, while the NOI positions of these countries have become increasing similar.

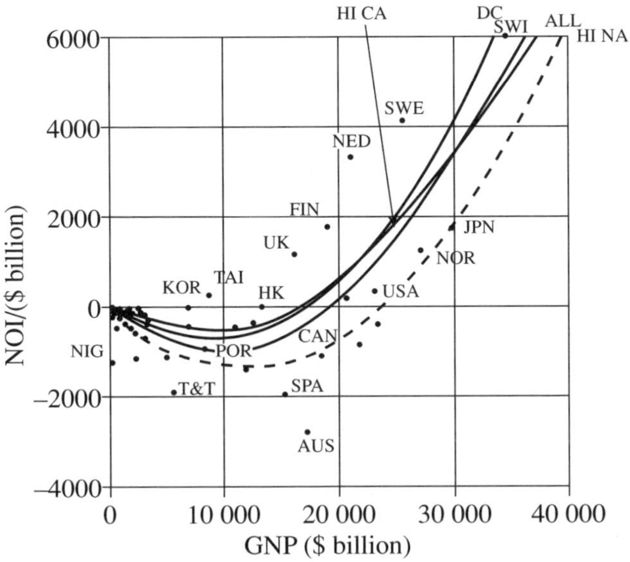

Source: Derived from data published by UNCTAD (1994) and World Bank (1994).

Figure 5.2 Net outward investment and GDP of selected countries, 1992

The high growth rate of NOI relative to GDP for the industrialized countries can be contrasted with that of the non-industrial countries (Table 5.2). The mean NOI levels for the non-industrial countries have become more negative but only by a factor of 2.2, whereas their mean GDP levels have increased by a factor of 1.5. The ratio of the standard deviation to the mean of NOI has decreased only slightly, while that of GDP has increased from 1.2 to 1.4 between 1980 and 1992. This suggests there is an increasing variation in the income levels of these countries as a whole, while their NOI positions have remained at the same level of dispersion.

Table 5.1 Linear regression equations for NOI with GDP based on a quadratic statistical relationship

Sample	GDPK	$GDPK^2$	ADJ.R^2	F-value	N
ALL	–0.1872***	0.957×10^{-5}***	0.542	51.69	88
DC	–0.1767***	0.102×10^{-4}***	0.418	26.35	73
NA	–0.2292***	0.962×10^{-5}***	0.582	36.64	53
CA	–0.1329**	0.789×10^{-5}***	0.579	16.33	24

*** Significant at the 1% level.
** Significant at the 2.5% level.

Table 5.2 International direct investment and GDP for selected countries, 1980 and 1992

	1980			1992				
	Mean ($billion)	Standard deviation	Ratio	Mean ($billion)	Standard deviation	Ratio	Ratio of means	Ratio of standard deviations
	(i)	(ii)	(i)/(ii)	(iii)	(iv)	(iii)/(iv)	(i)/(iii)	(ii)/(iv)
All countries								
Inward FDI	246	386	1.6	783	1 263	1.6	3.2	3.3
Outward FDI	164	533	3.2	721	1 783	2.5	4.4	3.3
NOI	–84	402	–4.8	–62	1 076	–17.4	0.7	2.7
GDP	3 453	4 200	1.2	6 231	8 717	1.4	1.8	2.1
Industrialized countries								
Inward FDI	749	525	0.7	2 671	1 746	0.7	3.6	3.3
Outward FDI	837	985	1.2	3 562	2 717	0.8	4.3	2.8
NOI	87	804	9.2	890	2 157	2.4	10.2	2.7
GDP	10 919	2 167	0.2	22 816	4 804	0.2	2.1	2.2
Non-industrialized countries								
Inward FDI	128	223	1.7	363	574	1.6	2.8	2.6
Outward FDI	6	26	4.2	90	338	3.8	14.8	13.2
NOI	–124	217	–1.7	–273	429	–1.6	2.2	2.0
GDP	1 696	2 088	1.2	2 545	3 533	1.4	1.5	1.7
Stage 3 countries								
Inward FDI	556	789	1.4	2 694	4 414	1.6	4.8	5.6
Outward FDI	40	84	2.1	727	954	1.3	18.2	11.4
NOI	–515	711	–1.4	–1 966	3 815	–1.9	3.8	5.4
GDP	5 402	2 975	0.6	11 118	3 671	0.3	2.1	1.2
Stage 1 and 2 countries								
Inward FDI	97	183	1.9	221	347	1.6	2.3	1.9
Outward FDI 5	5	26	5.5	12	35	2.8	2.6	1.4
NOI	–94	177	–1.9	–208	335	–1.6	2.2	1.9
GDP	1 110	1 095	1.0	1 285	1 182	0.9	1.2	1.1

Note: All values are normalized by population.

Source: Derived from data published by UNCTAD (1994) and World Bank (1994).

However, as Figure 5.2 illustrates, there seem to be two groups of pre-Stage 4 countries. The majority of developing countries seem to be clustered at the origin, while just a handful of countries are more widely distributed, and roughly correspond to the newly industrializing countries (NICs). If we extract this group, we are able to distinguish between the Stage 1 and 2 countries, and the Stage 3 countries, identified separately in Table 5.2. It is readily apparent that much of the growth associated with the entire sample of non-industrialized countries was primarily associated with the NICs. The mean level of GDP for Stage 1 and 2 countries between 1980 and 1992 has shown only a marginal increase even in nominal terms by a factor of just 1.2, implying that there may even have been a decline in real terms. As for the Stage 3 countries, their GDP growth rate was equivalent to that of the industrial countries. The mean NOI level for Stage 1 and 2 countries doubled over the same period, becoming more negative, while NOI for Stage 3 became more positive, growing by a factor of 3.8.

The change in distribution over time lends support to our earlier comments regarding the changes in the world economy. None the less, there are only minor differences in the regressions between 1980 and 1992, and therefore we shall only present those for the most recent period.

The results of the regressions, set out in Table 5.1 and plotted on Figure 5.2, confirm our hypotheses. By excluding the industrialized countries from our analysis, the results of the regressions seem to be weaker. The curve (labelled as 'DC') provides a better estimation of the true relationship between NOI and GDP for non-industrialized countries.

As Figure 5.2 shows, the results of our regressions also confirm our hypotheses regarding the differences in the 'idealized' IDP due to the differences in the extent of natural and created assets. Countries with above-average natural assets tend to demonstrate a lower level of NOI for any given value of GDP relative to the average expected path. Countries with above-average created assets, on the other hand, demonstrate a much higher value of NOI relative to the average expected path, and to the natural-asset-type countries. It is interesting to note, however, that although there are differences in NOI for any given level of GDP between the two groups, the difference narrows considerably at higher levels of GDP.

Inward and outward FDI

The effects noted above regarding changes to the extent of NOI are more apparent when examining the two components of NOI separately. As Table 5.2 shows, the mean outward FDI for the industrialized countries increased by a factor of 4.3 between 1980 and 1992 – twice that of the growth of GDP. The ratio of the standard deviation to the mean has also fallen, implying that the level of outward FDI has tended to converge among this group of countries. The mean inward FDI has also increased by a factor of 3.6, but the level of disparity has remained constant.

For pre-Stage 4 countries, outward FDI grew faster than inward FDI between 1980 and 1992, but even in 1992 the extent of outward investment remained at very low levels. It is interesting to note that the ratio of the standard deviation to the mean for outward FDI for developing countries has fallen from 5.5 to 2.8, implying that a larger number of developing countries have begun to engage in outward FDI since 1980. The Stage 3 countries, on the other hand, have shown an 18-fold increase in their outward investment levels, and a fall in the ratio of the standard deviation to the mean from 2.1 to 1.3. Inward investment into the NICs also grew twice as rapidly as that into other developing countries. Thus, as expected, the Stage 3 countries have demonstrated growth of both inward and outward FDI at a much higher pace than both the developing countries and the industrialized ones. Their GDP has grown at the same rate as that of the industrialized countries, and twice as fast as the developing countries. The ratio of the standard deviation to the mean of GDP for the NICs is almost the same as that for the industrialized countries, implying that, as a group, their levels of GDP have converged.

Table 5.3 Log–linear regression equations for inward and outward FDI against GDP

Independent variable	Sample	Constant	LOGGDPK	ADJ.R^2	F-value	N
LOGOWK	ALL	–11.866***	1.9487***	0.866	342.58	54
LOGOWK	NA	–10.812***	1.8199***	0.809	115.63	28
LOGOWK	CA	–14.572***	2.2457***	0.768	57.35	18
LOGIWK	ALL	–3.7024***	1.1626***	0.746	256.85	88
LOGIWK	NA	–4.2996***	1.2751***	0.705	127.39	54
LOGIWK	CA	–4.166***	1.176***	0.755	68.87	23

*** Significant at the 1% level.
** Significant at the 2.5% level.

In running regressions for gross inward and outward direct investment, we have utilized a log–linear specification as originally suggested by Dunning (1981). We have done so for three samples – all countries (ALL), the natural asset countries (NA) and the created asset countries (CA) and the results are set out in Table 5.3 and graphed against the data in log form on Figures 5.3 and 5.4. Since a large number of developing countries have no outward investment, there is a considerable loss of sample size when outward direct investment per capita (OWK) is logged. As a result of this, the estimated value of the intercept is inaccurate. In the case of inward direct investment per capita (IWK), although theoretically a constant term is not required, since there is no country for which GDP = 0, it is necessary to include one. It is therefore not meaningful to reconvert the data back into linear form. None the less, it is significant to note that the intercept terms for IWK equations are considerably lower than for OWK, which confirms that in fact inward FDI tends to precede outward FDI.

As Table 5.3 shows, the results are highly significant for all six regressions at the 1 per cent level, with values greater than 0.7 in all cases. In the case of

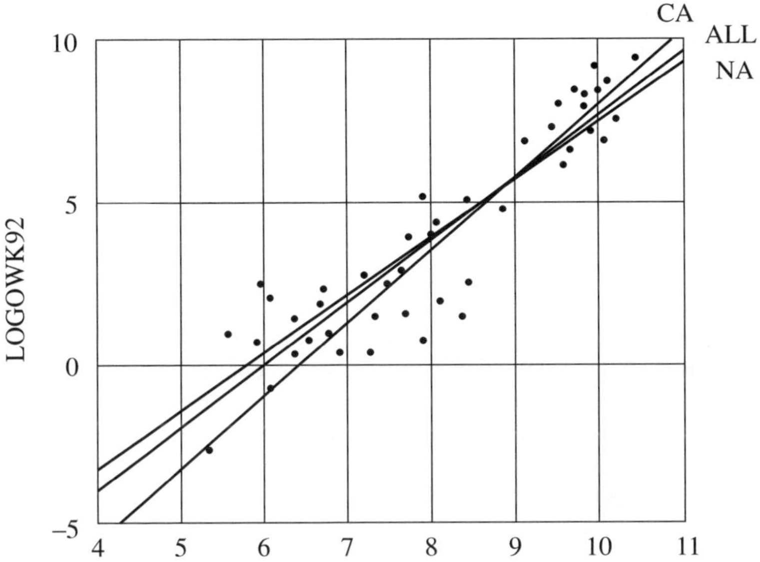

Figure 5.3 Outward foreign direct investment and GDP, 1992 (log–linear)

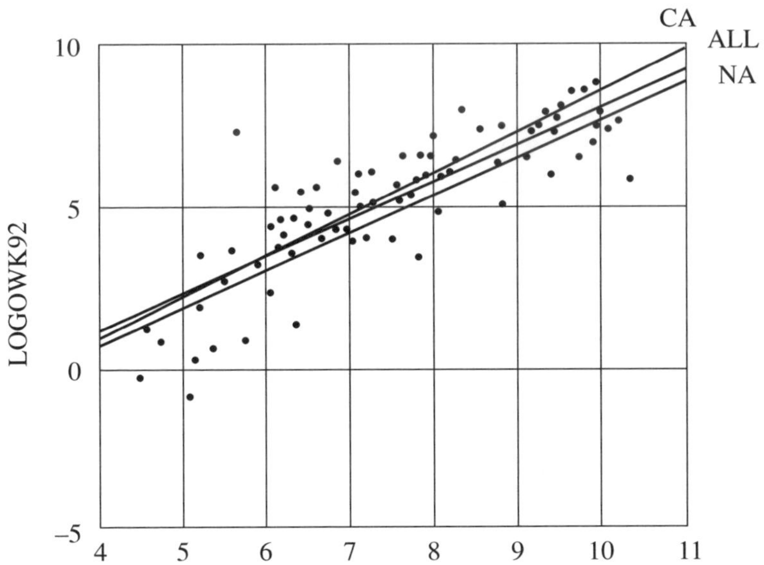

Figure 5.4 Inward foreign direct investment and GDP, 1992 (log–linear)

inward FDI, as hypothesized, created asset countries demonstrate a lower rate of growth of inward FDI than do natural asset countries, while created asset countries have a higher slope for outward FDI than do natural asset countries.

CONCLUSIONS

The current version of the IDP, in introducing dynamic aspects to its framework, represents a paradigm that encapsulates complex phenomena which are exceedingly averse to aggregation. The relationship between FDI and economic development requires the comparison of two phenomena at different levels of economic analysis. While FDI is primarily a micro-economic or firm-specific activity, economic development is a macro-economic or country-specific phenomenon (Gray, 1982). The examination of FDI as a country-specific variable requires the assumption that the activities of domestic and foreign MNEs can be aggregated in terms of their motivation, both within industrial sectors and across industrial sectors. Such aggregation can only be justified in countries where the nature, mode and motivation of MNE activity are relatively homogeneous, and the extent of their value-adding activities remains at relatively low levels, such as in the less developed countries. However, as MNEs become more globalized and engage in more complex investment activity, the importance of firm-7 specific factors in determining the FDI profile of a country becomes increasingly significant. This increasing complexity, together with the differences in measuring FDI between countries, makes any such analysis a hazardous one.

In addition, some of the data reviewed confirm that there have been profound changes in the world economy as a whole, as well as among particular groups of countries and within these countries. The process of catching up and falling behind has resulted in a polarization of countries into three distinct groups. The first group consists of the industrialized countries, which have been shown to have a convergence within the group of income levels, but considerable growth in income levels in the past 15 years. On average, their NOI positions have become increasingly positive, while their levels of gross inward and outward FDI are tending to converge. The second group consists of a handful of economies that can be regarded as being in Stage 3, which are exhibiting high growth in income levels and have become larger net outward investors since the 1980s. Their income levels also show signs of converging as a group, as well as with the industrialized countries. More significantly from our point of view, however, is the fact that their inward and outward FDI has been growing at a rate that outstrips even that of the industrialized countries. The third group consists of the Stage 1 and 2 countries which have experienced a divergence of income levels away from those of the industrialized countries as well as from the Stage 3 countries. Income levels have grown only marginally even in nominal terms, although the extent of FDI activity associated with these countries continues to grow faster than their domestic economies. None the less, their NOI position has become increasingly negative, and both their inward and outward FDI positions have grown at a slower pace than that of either of the other two groups.

Despite the limitations associated with a static analysis of a dynamic phenomenon, and changes in the world economy as well as the large differences between countries, the data reviewed in this chapter indicate that there continues to be a relatively strong causal relationship between FDI activity and economic development. Furthermore, we have also been able to examine, albeit simplistically, the hypotheses regarding how the extent of natural/created assets determines the shape of the IDP. Countries that are relatively well endowed in natural assets have a higher growth rate of inward FDI, but a much lower growth rate of outward FDI, than countries that do not have a strong natural asset position as well as those countries with a strong created asset position. In terms of the traditional J-relationship between NOI and development, the J-curve continues to be valid for pre-Stage 5 countries. Natural-asset-type countries tend to have a considerably higher NOI position relative to the created asset countries at any given income level.

Both parts of this chapter have sought to show that cross-sectional analysis is not an appropriate tool to capture the dynamic character of the IDP. This requires an oversimplification of complex economic activity into a few general and aggregated variables, an exercise which cannot be undertaken without great caution. For instance, if we restrict ourselves to using GDP as a single indicator of development, the process of economic restructuring as well as the growth of the technological competitiveness of countries are not taken into account. Likewise, the growth of strategic alliances as an alternative mode of international value-added activity and the growth of the activities of governments in the organization of economic activity cannot be usefully included in an aggregate analysis across countries.

NOTES

1. See Kumar and McLeod (1981).
2. Earlier called 'cycle'.
3. Or the right to their use.
4. *Natural assets* consists of the 'fruits of the earth' and the stock of unskilled labour. *Created assets* are those derived from the upgrading of natural assets. For further details, see earlier chapters of this volume and Narula (1996).
5. See the article by Reich (1990) for a succinct discussion on this issue.
6. See Gugler (1991).
7. For a review of the various empirical studies, see Narula (1993).

8. Cited, for example, in Dunning (1993), Chs 11–19.
9. As reviewed, for example, in Dunning (1993).
10. Acquisitions accounted for 83.2 per cent of the outlays by foreign direct investors in the United States between 1986 and 1992 (Fahim-Nader and Bargas, 1993).
11. Put another way, in their search for created assets and markets which they perceive necessary to advance their objectives, both firms and countries are acquiring these resources and capabilities by buying out (or investing in) foreign firms, in addition to being bought out (or invested in) by foreign firms. The extent to which these routes are complements to, or substitutes for, each other has not been explored in the literature.
12. Also called 'collective' capitalism (Lazonick, 1992) and the 'new' capitalism (Best, 1990).
13. What one writer (Maister, 1993) has referred to as a 'farmer' rather than a 'hunter' organizational management style.
14. Other motives for strategic outsourcing include the need to capture the specialized professional capabilities of suppliers, to shorten cycle times, and to respond better to customers. Examples of firms engaging in 'close' control procurement strategies include Marks and Spencer, Nike and Honda (Quinn and Hilmer, 1994).
15. Notably from the work of John Hagedoorn and his colleagues at MERIT. For recent contributions see Hagedoorn and Schakenraad (1991, 1992, 1994) and Hagedoorn (1992, 1993).
16. For example, host governments may compel foreign firms to conclude co-operative arrangements with indigenous firms if they wish to produce within their boundaries, and/or force domestic firms to conclude such arrangements with foreign firms if they wish to transfer their O advantages abroad.
17. It is also worth recalling that the greater part of non-equity technology and organizational transference between countries is undertaken by MNEs.
18. Primarily because the *created* to *natural* asset ratio of the former countries was higher.
19. See especially Contractor (1990).
20. This proposition is explored in more detail in Dunning (1992, 1994).
21. Thus to quite a large extent the US net inward investment position in the 1960s has been eroded by the catching up of many European countries, while the seemingly invincible economic prowess of Japan in several sectors is now being challenged by the United States and Europe.
22. For a review of these, see Dunning (1993), especially the writers mentioned in Ch. 10. See also Dunning (1994).
23. Freeman and Hagedoorn (1994) suggest that between 1980 and 1989, almost 70 per cent of strategic technology partnering agreements between Triad firms and developing country firms were equity based, while for intra-Triad agreements, it was less than 50 per cent.
24. These data only cover strategic technology partnering for the period 1980–89.
25. See Dunning (1992, 1993).
26. These data are both derived from the World Bank (1994).

REFERENCES

Abramovitz, M. (1986), 'Catching up, forging ahead, and falling behind', *Journal of Economic History*, **XLVI**: 385–406.

Alam, M.S. (1992), 'Convergence in developed countries: an empirical investigation', *Weltwirtshaftliches Archiv*, **128**: 189–200.

Baumol, W. (1986), 'Productivity growth, convergence, and welfare: what the long-run data show', *American Economic Review*, **76**: 1072–85.

Best, M. (1990), *The New Competition: Institutions of Restructuring*, Cambridge, MA: Harvard University Press.

Cantwell, J. (1989), *Technological Innovation and Multinational Corporations*, Oxford: Basil Blackwell.

Cantwell, J.A. and Dunning, J.H. (1991), 'Multinationals, technology and the competitiveness of European industries', *Aussenwirtschaft*, **46**(1): 45–65.
Cantwell, J. and Randaccio, F. (1990), 'The growth of multinationals and the catching up effect', *Economic Notes*, **19**: 1–23.
Contractor, F. (1990), 'Ownership patterns of US joint ventures abroad and the liberalization of foreign government regulation in the 1980s: evidence from the benchmark *surveys'*, *Journal of International Business Studies*, **21**: 55–73.
Dowrick, S. (1992), 'Technological catch up and diverging incomes: patterns of economic growth 1960–88', *The Economic Journal*, **102**: 600–10.
Dowrick, S. and Gemmell, N. (1991), 'Industrialization, catching up and economic growth: a comparative study across the world's capitalist economies', *Economic Journal*, **101**: 263–75.
Dunning, J.H. (1981), 'Explaining the international direct investment position of countries: towards a dynamic or developmental approach', *Weltwirtschaftliches Archiv*, **119**: 30–64.
Dunning, J.H. (1986), 'The investment development cycle revisited', *Weltwirtshaftliches Archiv*, **122**: 667–77.
Dunning, J.H. (1988a), *Explaining International Production*, London: Unwin Hyman.
Dunning, J.H. (1988b), *Multinationals, Technology and Competitiveness*, London: Unwin Hyman.
Dunning, J.H. (1992), 'The global economy, domestic governance, strategies and transnational corporations: interactions and policy recommendations', *Transnational Corporations*, **1**, December: 7–45.
Dunning, J.H. (1993), *Multinational Enterprises and the Global Economy*, Wokingham, UK, and Reading, MA: Addison Wesley.
Dunning, J.H. (1994), 'Reevaluating the benefits of foreign direct investment', *Transnational Corporations*, **3** February: 23–52.
Dunning, J.H. and Narula, R. (1994), 'Transpacific FDI and the investment development path: the record assessed', *University of South Carolina Essays in International Business*, May, **10**: 69.
Dunning, J.H. and Narula, R. (eds) (1996), *Foreign Direct Investment and Governments*, London and New York: Routledge.
Durkheim, E. (1964), *The Division of Labour in Society*, New York: The Free Press.
Fahim-Nader, M. and Bargas, S.E. (1993), 'US business enterprises acquired or established by foreign direct investors in 1992', *Survey of Current Business*, May: 113–23.
Freeman, C. and Hagedoorn, J. (1994), 'Catching up or falling behind: patterns in international interfirm technology partnering', *World Development*, **22**: 771–80.
Gray, H.P. (1982), 'Macroeconomic theories of foreign direct investment: an assessment', in A. Rugman (ed.) *New Theories of the Multinational Enterprise*, London: Croom Helm.
Gugler, P. (1991), *Les Alliances Stratégiques Transnationales*, Fribourg: Editions Universitaires.
Hagedoorn, J. (1992), 'Organizational modes of inter-firm cooperation and technology transfer', *Technovation*, **10**: 17–30.
Hagedoorn, J. (1993), 'Understanding the rationale of strategic technology partnering: inter-organizational modes of cooperation and sectoral differences', *Strategic Management Journal*, **14**: 371–85.
Hagedoorn, J. and Narula, R. (1994), *Choosing Modes of Governance for Strategic Technology Partnering: International and Sectoral Differences*, MERIT Working Paper Series, No. 94–025.

Hagedoorn, J. and Schakenraad, J. (1991), 'The internationalization of the economy, global strategies and strategic technology alliances', *Nouvelles de la Science et des Technologies*, **9**: 29–41.

Hagedoorn, J. and Schakenraad, J. (1992), 'Leading companies in networks of strategic alliances in information technologies', *Research Policy*, **21**: 163–90.

Hagedoorn, J. and Schakenraad, J. (1994), 'The effects of strategic technology alliances on company performance', *Strategic Management Journal*, **15**: 291–309.

Hämäläinen, T. (1993), *The Evolving Role of Government in Economic Organization*, Newark, NJ: Rutgers University (mimeo).

Kumar, K. and McLeod, M. (eds) (1981), *Multinationals from Developing Countries*, Lexington, MA: D.C. Heath.

Lazonick, W. (1992), 'Business organization and competitive advantage: capitalist transformation in the twentieth century', in G. Dosi, R. Giannetti and P. A. Toninelli (eds) *Technology and Enterprise in a Historical Perspective*, Oxford: Clarendon Press, pp. 119–63.

Maister, D.H. (1993), *Managing the Professional Service Firm*, New York: The Free Press/Macmillan.

Narula, R. (1993), 'An Examination of the Evolution and Interdependence of Foreign Direct Investment and Economic Structure: The Case of Industrialized Countries', PhD Thesis, Newark, NJ: Rutgers University.

Narula, R. (1996), *Multinational Investment and Economic Structure*, London: Routledge.

Ohmae, K. (1987), *The Borderless World*, New York: The Free Press.

Ozawa, T. (1992), 'FDI and economic development', *Transnational Corporations*, **1**: 27–54.

Porter, M.E. (1990), *The Competitive Advantage of Nations*, New York: The Free Press.

Quinn, J.B. and Hilmer, F.G. (1994), 'Strategic outsourcing', *Sloan Management Review*, **35**, Summer: 43–55.

Reich, R. (1990), 'Who is us?', *Harvard Business Review*, January–February: 53–64.

Tolentino, P. (1993), *Technological Innovation and Third World Multinationals*, London: Routledge.

UNCTAD (1993), *World Investment Report 1993, Transnational Corporations and Integrated International Production*, New York and Geneva: UN.

UNCTAD (1994), *World Investment Report 1994, Transnational Corporations Employment and the Workplace*, New York and Geneva: UN.

Verspagen, B. (1993), *Uneven Growth Between Interdependent Economies*, Avebury: Aldershot.

World Bank (1994), *World Development Report 1994*, Oxford: Oxford University Press.

6. The changing dynamics of international production: an economic and strategic approach*

INTRODUCTION

There is a slow, but discernible, convergence between the literature on global strategic management and that of the theory of international production. Though the language and analytical approach of the two schools of thought continues to differ, the message of each is similar. This is demonstrated particularly in the work of some younger scholars who have been trained in, or are at least familiar with, the concepts and techniques of both disciplines.[1]

It is the purpose of this chapter to attempt to review some of the similarities and differences between the approaches of the strategic management analyst and the economic theorist towards explaining the globalization of production, and to consider the possibilities of integrating some of their thoughts and findings. Writing as an economist with a long-standing interest in international business, my views on these particular issues will inevitably reflect my own predilections and prejudices. In particular, this chapter seeks to see how far the economist's approach to understanding the determinants of foreign value-added activities of firms might be improved upon by taking more explicit account of the work of business scholars. No doubt the latter would wish to start from the opposite end, and see how far economic principles might be usefully incorporated into their thinking. Apart from the fact that I do not feel qualified to undertake this latter task, it would probably be accepted by both groups of scholars that the theory of international production is at a rather more advanced stage than the theory of global strategic management.[2]

* Revised version of chapters 3 and 4 in *The Globalization of Business*, London and New York: Routledge, 1993, pp. 51–77.

DIFFERENCES BETWEEN THE ECONOMIST'S AND THE BUSINESS ANALYST'S APPROACH TO EXPLAINING INTERNATIONAL PRODUCTION

The Mainstream Economic Theories

Economists define international production as production owned or controlled by multinational enterprises (MNEs). The MNE is an enterprise which engages in foreign value-added activities and internalizes intermediate product markets across national boundaries. Until comparatively recently, economists were primarily interested in explaining foreign direct investment as a means of transferring resources, e.g. capital, management and technology, between countries but within the same firm. Nowadays, their domain of interest is more focused on the organization of cross-border activities, including non-equity collaborative alliances.

Over the past three decades, a variety of explanations have been forwarded to explain the level and pattern of MNE activity. Recent reviews are contained in Dunning (1989, 1992, 1993) and Cantwell (1991). Some scholars have directed their interest to explaining particular kinds or aspects of MNE related activity. Others have attempted to formulate more general theories or paradigms – either of the MNE or the value-added activities undertaken by such enterprises. Both, to a varying degree, implicitly incorporate strategy related variables in their explanations, but only a few, notably Knickerbocker's 'follow my leader', Graham's 'exchange of threats' and Lessard's and Rugman's 'risk diversification' hypotheses, have focused more explicitly on the strategy of firms as a separately identifiable explanatory variable.[3]

Up to now, most economic theories of foreign production have been directed to explaining such production at discrete points of time rather than its path of change between these points of time. Exceptions include Vernon's product cycle theory (Vernon, 1966, 1979), which relates the changing propensity of firms to engage in foreign direct investment as the product they produced moved from its innovatory to its mature or standardized form; Buckley and Casson's analysis of the optimal timing of a switch in the mode of servicing a foreign market from exports to foreign investment (Buckley and Casson, 1981); and Dunning's investment development cycle or path, which traces the changing propensity of countries to be inward or outward direct investors according to their stages of economic development (Dunning, 1988). Mention might also be made of the exploratory attempts of Mark Casson to incorporate entrepreneurship into the theory of foreign direct investment (Casson, 1987, 1988). At the same time, most of these contributions have paid only passing attention to the alternative strategies open to firms in penetrating foreign markets (apart from the export v. foreign direct investment option); and, like most of the other explanations by economists, they were predicated on the assumption that firms were profit or wealth maximizers.

Since the mid-1970s, there have been three attempts by economists to offer generalized explanations of international production.[4] These might be called the macro-economic, the internalization, and the eclectic paradigmatic explanations. Each should be considered as complementary to rather than competitive with each other, and to the partial explanations earlier put forward. Since the latter two approaches address themselves to the behavior of groups of firms (rather than that of countries), and appear to offer the most promise for incorporating the thinking of the strategic business analyst, we will concentrate our attention on these.[5]

The Internalization School

Scholars of this school of thought are primarily interested in the MNE as a particular kind of multi-activity firm. Their central proposition is that the existence of the cross-border value-added activities by firms stems from the failure of intermediate product markets to operate efficiently. FDI seeks to improve upon the market as a transactional mechanism. The replacement or internalization of such markets by hierarchies leads to an extension of the boundaries of the firm. Most of the internalization literature[6] is concerned with identifying the kinds of cross-border market failure which might lead to, or increase, MNE activity, and with the evaluation of the transactional costs and benefits associated with these alternative organizational routes.

In several respects, the internalization theory of foreign production offers a promising basis for the inclusion of strategic related variables. Like the management analyst, the internalization economist fully embraces the concept of uncertainty in his analysis of market failure; indeed the reduction or counteracting of uncertainty is viewed as one of the critical reasons for the emergence and growth of multinational activity.[7] Like the management analyst too, the internalization economist focuses his attention on the conduct and behavior of the firm as a unit of analysis, and on the alternative strategies open to it in the pursuance of its objectives.[8]

At the same time, the purview of interest of the two groups of scholars is rather different. The internalization economist is primarily interested in explaining the organization of the cross-border value-added activities. The strategic management analyst is interested in evaluating the determinants of all aspects of decision taking to do with the creation and deployment of a firm's competitive advantages in international markets. To the internalization economist, most competitive advantages of MNEs (other than those which derive from their multinationality as such) are taken as given; to the business strategist they are something to be explained. To the internalization economist, the key question is 'Under what situations will multinational hierarchies replace international markets?' To the business strategist it is to analyze why some firms, rather than others, are successful at becoming global players, and sustaining or advancing their global market shares.

The Eclectic Paradigm

The eclectic paradigm of international production sets out a generalized framework for explaining the level and pattern of the cross-border value-added activities of firms. It postulates that, at any given point of time the stock of foreign assets owned and controlled by multinational firms, is determined by (a) the extent and nature of the ownership specific or competitive advantages of those *firms*, *vis-à-vis* those of uninational firms, (b) the extent and nature of the location bound endowments and markets offered by *countries* to firms to create or add further value to these competitive advantages, and (c) the extent to which the market for these advantages, including those which arise from multinationality *per se*, are best internalized by the firm itself, rather than marketed directly to foreign firms.

The paradigm suggests that the configuration of these ownership, location and internalization (OLI) advantages will vary according to country, nature of activity, and firm specific characteristics; but that the propensity of corporations to engage in foreign production will be the most pronounced the greater their (relative) competitive advantages, and the more they find it profitable to create or add value to these advantages themselves from a foreign location. Some of the more important OLI variables identified by the eclectic paradigm are set out in the appendix to this chapter.

Although the eclectic paradigm addresses itself to explaining the foreign production of *firms*, rather than that of a particular firm, and draws on a wider range of economic tools than does internalization theory, in several respects it has more in common with the interests of the strategic management analyst. Most importantly, perhaps, it takes both the competitive advantage of firms and those of countries as something to be explained, although it accepts that some of these former advantages may arise from the common governance of value-added activities and the internalization of cross-border markets. In the identification of these advantages, there is very little difference (except in presentation, emphasis and language) between the kind of ownership specific advantages of firms and locational advantages of countries listed by such scholars as Porter (1986, 1990), Kogut (1983, 1985), Doz (1986, 1988), Ghoshal (1987), Hamel and Prahalad (1987), and those in my own writings.

For reasons already suggested, the attention given to the concept of market failure by the strategic management literature is somewhat less. At the same time, the advantages which arise from the common ownership of activities across national boundaries are fully recognized by business scholars. Porter (1990), for example, distinguishes between *nation* or *location* based advantages and *system* based advantages of firms; while, in an earlier study (Porter, 1986), he identified the *configuration* and *coordination* options open to firms, identifying the latter as those which other scholars would refer to as the economies of common governance or scope. Kogut (1983) explicitly distinguishes between the O specific advantages which are often a necessary prerequisite for the initial act of foreign production, and those which arise as a direct consequence of foreign production, or the growth in it. These latter benefits include the spreading of environmental risk, the capacity to maximize global efficiency by engaging in product and process specialization, and intrafirm trade; the opportunities to arbitrage cross-border information, financial and factor markets, and/or to exercise additional leverage in negotiating with national governments or indigenous economic agents; and the learning and experience gains which may stem from operating in different environments (Kogut, 1985).

In his suggestion for an organizing framework to study the issues of global strategic management, Ghoshal (1987) sets out two matrices. One relates the objectives of firms to different kinds of competitive advantage (p. 428) and the other the economies in product and market diversification to some components of common governance (p. 435). The latter is almost a perfect rationale for the hierarchical coordination of discrete value-added activities to capture the extra market benefits arising from them (Caves, 1980b), while the former sets out some of the gains from geographical diversification, which parallel those identified by Kogut and Porter, but which arise primarily because of the capacity of multinationals to exploit cross-border market imperfections.

There are, however, important differences in emphasis between the eclectic paradigm and the strategic management literature in explaining the globalization of business. The most important among these is that, like most other economic models, the eclectic paradigm is interested in identifying and evaluating the most significant variables affecting the level and patterns of international production, or changes in international production, rather than those affecting the strategic action of firms to achieve such production.

Second, while the eclectic paradigm acknowledges the significance of firm specific characteristics in determining international production, its main focus is on country and industry characteristics. For example, the theory is interested in explaining why there tends to be more globalization of production in the pharmaceutical and petroleum industries than in the iron and steel or railway sectors, or why the industrial or geographical distribution of Japanese and Taiwanese MNEs is different from that of its Canadian or French counterparts. By contrast, the strategic business analyst's attention is more likely to be directed to answering such questions as why the global sourcing strategy of

Toshiba is different from that of BMW, or why the marketing strategy of Nestlé is more 'niche' oriented than that of Unilever. From the economist's perspective, strategy related variables are more often treated as part of the 'unexplained' (or unexplainable) variables, whereas they are the main subject of interest to the business analyst.

Third, the eclectic paradigm is usually couched in static or comparative static terms. Though some attempt has to be made to theorize about the changing international OLI configuration facing, or engineered by, firms or industries over time,[9] for the most part, economists have been content to explain the international allocation of MNE activity at a given point of time or between points of time. Moreover, no real attempt has been made either to explicitly incorporate the interaction between firms into the eclectic framework – and particularly the feedback effects of a firm's actions on the behavior of its competitors – nor to acknowledge the fact that the capabilities of firms in implementing their chosen strategies may be very different. Finally, it is only recently that the eclectic paradigm has acknowledged that firms may invest abroad (particularly via the acquisition and merger route) to protect or gain a competitive position rather than to exploit existing O specific advantages.[10]

INCORPORATING STRATEGY INTO THE ECLECTIC PARADIGM OF INTERNATIONAL PRODUCTION

We now turn to consider how the eclectic paradigm, and, for that matter, internalization theory as well, might better take account of the strategic actions and reactions of firms. We have suggested that, insofar as they directly affect the foreign value-added activities of firms, many of the strategy related variables considered by business analysts have already been identified by the eclectic paradigm; but others, which impact indirectly though affecting the behavior of firms, may require more attention than they have so far been given.[11] What, however, is missing is the incorporation of strategy *per se* as an explanatory variable. How, if at all, might this be done?

First, we would reiterate the point that a firm's choice of options is only a point of issue where the markets in which it competes are imperfect. Such imperfections may be *structural* (i.e. they are brought about by market distorting actions on the part of the participants in the market) or *endemic* (they reflect the inability of the market to fulfil certain tasks required of it). Pure market failure is a situation in which, due to the presence of uncertainty, or to technological imperatives, or to the fact that the consequences of some transaction spillover to institutions or individuals who are not party to those transactions, it is impossible to create the conditions of a perfect market in which each firm produces at its lowest average cost while equating marginal cost to price. Once, however, market failure arises, a firm's range of behavioral options increases. For example, there can be no generalized 'optimal' trade-off between a set of possible outcomes to a firm's strategic behavior and the profits associated with these outcomes because the estimation and valuation of the uncertainties involved are, themselves, likely to be firm specific! Similarly, once the choice of product differentiation is introduced as a possible corporate strategy, one is immediately faced with the possibility of multiple profit or wealth maximizing strategies, e.g. to supply a superior quality product at a higher price versus a lower quality product at a lower price.

The way in which we would suggest strategic choice might be incorporated into the eclectic paradigm of international production is to introduce a 'dynamized add-on' independent variable.[12] The variable we propose to use in our framework of thought is that of strategic change ($\dot{S}_t$). We shall define strategy as a 'change in the conduct of firms designed to advance their long-term objectives, which specifically takes heed of the estimated likely reactions of other decision taking units in response to that change'.

We shall identify two kinds of strategic change. The first is a change in the way in which a firm or group of firms seeks or seek to achieve its (their) long-term objectives, given any particular configuration of any OLI advantages (i.e. a *strategy initiating*, or autonomous strategic, change). The second is a change in strategy occasioned by a change in that configuration (i.e. a *strategy induced* change). To illustrate and simplify our analysis, we shall consider just one period of time, viz. $t - 1 \rightarrow t$; and examine how a strategic variable or set of strategic variables might be incorporated into the tripod of OLI variables affecting the level and structure of foreign production. We shall also assume that the goals of firms remain unchanged over this time, i.e. their reaction to a *given set* of OLI advantages is constant.

Take first the ownership or competitive advantages of a firm. At any given point of time t, these advantages (O_t) represent its current stock of income generating or cost reducing technological and organizational assets, the nature and structure of which are a function of its past ownership advantages, and the overall strategic response to such advantages. Such a response is likely to be multifaceted and to include actions taken with respect to, for example, innovation, organizational structures, acquisitions and interfirm alliances, product diversification, vertical integration, sourcing exchange risks and foreign production. So, assuming just one time period '$t - 1 \rightarrow t$',

$$Ot = f(OLI_{t-1}S_{Ot-1}\ \dot{S}_{Ot-1\rightarrow t})E\dot{X}N_{Ot-1\rightarrow t}) \ldots \qquad (1)$$

where $E\dot{X}N$ represents changes in the value of any exogenous or non-strategic endogenous variables over time $t - 1 \rightarrow t$.

Similarly, the competitive or locational specific attractions of countries for the value-added activities of a firm at time t (L_t) is a function of its OLI configuration in time t – 1 (as each of these variables may interact to affect a firm's locational choice at that time), changes in the locational advantages of countries, as affected by changes in the value of non-strategic related variables, and any changes in the autonomous strategy of a firm which may affect its location. So:

$$L_t f\,(OLI_{t-1}, S_{Lt-1}, \dot{S}_{Lt-1\to t}\; E\dot{X}N_{\,Lt-1\to t}) \ldots \qquad (2)$$

This equation, then, suggests that the geographical distribution of a firm's current production is dependent, in part at least, on changes in either its autonomous locational strategy or that which is the result of changes in non-strategic related variables which may themselves induce a change in its strategy over the time t – 1 → t.

Finally, the way in which a firm organizes the creation or development of its O advantages (or others it may seek to acquire) and relates these to the advantages of countries (i.e. its choice of whether or not to internalize or increase its internalization of cross-border intermediate product markets) will depend upon its transnational deployment of past OLI advantages and any changes in strategy which might occur over the time period under consideration. Hence:

$$I_t = f(OLI_{t-1}\; S_{It-1}\dot{S}_{It-1\to t}\; E\dot{X}N_{It-1\to t}) \qquad (3)$$

Combining the three previous equations and aggregating for all firms, we arrive at a general equation:

$$OLI^*_t = f(OLI^*_{t-1}\; S^*_{OLIt-1}\; \dot{S}_{OLIt-1\to t}\; E\dot{X}N^*_{OLIt-1\to t}) \ldots \qquad (4)$$

where * = all firms.

International production in time t then represents the totality of the strategic responses of firms to past OLI configurations and to changes in these configurations brought about by changes in the external environment and non-strategic endogenous variables. Indeed, the strategic responses of firms to their current (or expected future) OLI variables, together with autonomous strategic changes, will determine their future pattern of international production.

It is worth noting that unless the firm is in equilibrium at time t – 1 and that there are no learning or other strategic responses still in the pipeline at that time (i.e. $S_{OLIt-1\to t}$ is zero), OLI_t will be different than OLI_{t-1}. and hence so also will the level and structure of international production. In this event, any changes in foreign production are assumed to be caused solely by changes in the value of exogenous or non-strategic endogenous variables which might affect the OLI configuration (e.g. a product innovation, a reduction in cross-border transport costs, a more cost-effective advertising campaign, better protection of property rights, a new inroad into the firm's market by its competitors, and so on).

It may also be observed that we have chosen to treat strategic change as a time related variable; but that at a given moment of time, we have not included the response of a firm to its past OLI configuration as an independent variable. This implies that we have assigned objectives to a firm which are independent of the OLI variables affecting these objectives, and that these goals are consistent over time, and similar between firms. For those who feel uncomfortable with this procedure, it would be acceptable to formulate an additional hypothesis which treated foreign production as the independent variable, and the OLI configuration and the goals of firms as dependent variables. Thus, at time t for a group of firms.

$$IP_t = f(OLI_t G_t) \ldots \qquad (5)$$

where G = the goals of the firms at time t. A change in the goals of firms over time $t - 1 \rightarrow t$ could then either be explicitly incorporated into equations 1 through 4, or be assumed to affect their strategic actions and reactions over that time period, and hence its OLI, at time t.

HYPOTHESIZING ABOUT STRATEGY RELATED VARIABLES

Strategy Induced Variables

The primary purpose of the eclectic paradigm is to identify the kind of OLI advantages likely to affect international production, and to hypothesize about the significance of these variables. However, on this second point, much will depend upon the nature of the products produced, by which firms they are produced, and where they are produced. An operationally testable explanation of *resource based* investment will draw upon a different set of OLI variables than will that of *market seeking* investment or an investment which is part of a *global, cost-minimizing or asset acquiring* strategy. Similarly, the relevance of a particular configuration of OLI variables affecting the foreign value-added activities of Italian or Korean MNEs may be different than those influencing Canadian or UK multinationals. Finally, the O specific advantages of firms and the L advantages of countries, and the way in which firms coordinate their cross-border value-added activities based on these advantages, are likely to vary according to such variables as the size of the enterprise, whether the investment is a greenfield or an acquisition, whether it is first-time or sequential, and whether it is just one or one of many foreign ventures.

All this suggests that, within a general paradigmatic framework, a number of self-contained, and for the most part, complementary, operationally testable theories may be generated. Indeed, much of the research of trade and industrial organizational economists has been directed to identifying and evaluating the most significant, explanatory variables, and, it might be added, with some success.[13]

However, all of these studies assume that, faced with the same OLI advantages and normalizing for country, industry and (non-strategic) firm specific characteristics, firms will react in a similar way to these advantages. Implicitly or explicitly, firms are assumed to be wealth or profit maximizers. Neither does any of the empirical research attempt to incorporate strategic variables *per se* into the OLI configuration of firms. Only strategy related theories, such as those already identified and which are designed to answer very specific questions about the oligopolistic behavior of firms, come near to doing this.

Is it then possible to suggest strategy induced variables, which could be incorporated with OLI variables, into the eclectic paradigm; and also to theorize more explicitly about which particular strategy variables are likely to affect particular types of international production? Can one predict ways in which strategic change may affect the (future) value of OLI variables?

Consider, for example, the case of a profit maximizing firm producing a single product (say a pharmaceutical drug) in a monopolistically competitive market. The firm is faced with a particular OLI configuration, on the basis of which it finds it profitable to export part of its output to an independent distributing and marketing outlet in another country. Assume, too, that the firm's cost and pricing strategy is consistent with its long-term economic goals, and that this strategy does not affect its future OLI configuration. Finally, assume that the firm has all the information it needs about domestic and foreign markets, suppliers, customers and government policies, and that it undertakes no innovatory activities. In every sense, then, the firm's output is in equilibrium with its OLI configuration, and the strategy management of that configuration (which in one sense, of course, might be considered as an O advantage in its own right) is consistent with maintaining this equilibrium. This latter assumption is the one built into the eclectic paradigm.

Now suppose this equilibrium is disturbed by the importing country imposing a substantial tariff on the drug supplied by the foreign firm. The immediate effect of this is to decrease the attractiveness of domestic production (i.e. by raising the cost of supplying the foreign market by exports). The question then is, should the firm opt out of the market altogether or try to supply it by other means, and, if the latter, what means? In turn, to answer these questions, other issues need to be explored. Among these are the effect the options may have on the firm's O advantages (e.g. on its ability to exploit scale and scope economies); and if some of these produce negative results, how might they be overcome and at what cost? The primary interest of the international business economist is to identify the way in which the first best solution to these questions affects the level and pattern of global production. Rarely, if ever, is he or she concerned with the path by which a firm makes a choice from the alternative options open to it.

As a first step to incorporating strategy in the OLI paradigm, one then needs to identify the options available to firms in respect of any change in the OLI configuration. However, the real significance of strategy is where the outcome of pursuing alternative options is uncertain, and where there is no clearly identifiable optimum way of achieving particular goals or even of identifying the trade-off between goals. Taking the above example as a case in point, there may be some uncertainty as to the future policy of the importing government, not only towards the purchase of foreign goods, but also towards inward direct investment or licensing. There may be some doubt as to the extent to which local licensors are likely to adhere to any contract for producing the drug under license. There may also be some question over the contestability of domestic markets and the effect of new entrants on the profitability of existing investment. While, in part, the likely response to these uncertainties may be gauged from the existing OLI configuration of firms, it is the latters' idiosyncratic characteristics, and their perception of their position in the strategic groups with which they identify, which is likely to determine the actual strategies pursued.

Consider next a situation in which the value of locational variables changes. A firm may have a set of options open to it to adjust to these changes. Each option is likely to vary according to the type of foreign production being considered. Each option is likely to have a different outcome. Each outcome is likely to generate different costs and benefits which it is impossible to predict in advance. Often, too, the consequences of alternative options are interactive. Only if we know the firm's assessment of the degree of risk involved, and if its trade-off between risk and profitability is known, will it be possible to gauge its optimum locational strategy.

Now, assume there is a change in the firm's O specific advantages. Suppose, for example, it invents a new fermentation process which halves the cost of producing the drug. How might this affect its foreign production? Since the firm is not currently producing overseas it may be that the answer is 'not at all'; it may simply increase its exports. But this will not necessarily be the case. Depending on its price elasticity, the demand for the product might rise in the importing country to allow local production to become economically viable. Or, it could be that, because of the nature of the inputs it requires, the fermentation process can be more economically undertaken in a foreign country than at home. At the same time, it might be in the firm's strategic interest to license, or otherwise collaborate with, a foreign firm to produce the drug. Again, while it is possible to identify the options available to the firm, the strategy it actually chooses will rest on its perception of, and attitude towards, the anticipated costs and benefits of the options, and, not least, how these may impinge upon its main competitors (or potential competitors).

Finally, the circumstances surrounding a firm's I related advantages may change. Suppose, for example, the firm finds that the foreign distributing and marketing company to which it is exporting its products has become unreliable, or the quality of its services has fallen, or it raises its prices. Suppose, too, that, at the same time, the firm's own knowledge and experience of the local market have improved, and/or it perceives that local customers require it to modify its product to meet their particular needs. Then, the firm may decide to undertake the distributing and marketing functions itself. But, again, this might not be its only option and, even if it were, the firm still has a choice as to whether it should set up a greenfield marketing venture or buy an existing venture. Or should it enter into a cooperative alliance with a local competitor or with another marketing and distribution company? What effect might each of these possible actions have on its O advantages, and so on? Each option carries an uncertain outcome, and thus requires some appreciation of the strategy of a firm.

We have introduced the most simple of changes in the OLI configuration of firms; and we have assumed away many of the interesting options open to firms. For example, suppose our pharmaceutical company were producing in an oligopolistic market. Then, not only might its OLI configuration be directly affected by the behavior of its major competitors, but, considering any change in its own strategy, it would have to take account of the likely impact of this strategy on its competitors, and how, in turn, their responses may affect its own competitive position. We have also assumed that the firm is a single product and non-innovating enterprise. Clearly, not only are multi-product and innovating firms likely to have more options in reacting to changes in their OLI variables; the chances are they will also interact with the strategy of a larger number of other firms, both along and between value-added chains.

Strategy Initiating Variables

Up to this point we have considered strategic induced changes being brought about by changes in the configuration of the OLI variables of firms (i.e. those exogenous to their strategies). Earlier in this chapter we also identified strategy initiating changes. These pro-active changes may be made for a variety of reasons, the most common of which are, first, to improve the O specific advantages of firms (to reduce those of competitors); second, to influence the

L attractions of particular countries (in some cases by lobbying governments to take action to help achieve this goal); and third, to reduce the transaction costs of markets and/or improve the transaction efficiencies of single or collaborative hierarchies. Such autonomous changes in strategy are often sparked off by a change in the ownership of the firm or the composition of its senior management. They may be forced on a company by a failure of previous strategies; or they may be made in anticipation of new technological advances or organizational restructuring. Expected changes in the external environment, e.g. a reorientation in government economic policy, may also necessitate a change in strategy. A possible configuration in the structure and composition of competition, and the global strategies of rivals may have a similar effect.

There are two key consequences of strategic initiating changes. The first is that they may result in a particular OLI configuration being responded to in a different way. In this case there will be a direct effect on international production. For example, a greater reluctance to embrace political risks might result in less FDI in politically unstable regimes; while, in anticipation of the effects of the formation of the European Economic Community (EEC) in 1958, many US firms began integrating their production facilities within its six founding members.

Second, they may, themselves, impinge upon the OLI configuration and, by doing so, affect the level and pattern of international production. A conscious decision to invest more in innovatory activities, or to reduce product diversification and specialize in core value-added activities, or to develop a niche marketing strategy, or to boost and/or change the format of advertising campaigns, or to introduce new sourcing policies or wage systems, or to decentralize more decision taking activities to regional offices, are just a few examples of autonomous changes in strategy that may affect OLI configuration and, thus, the foreign production of firms.

To what extent is it possible to generalize about the likely form of strategic initiating changes and their effect on international production? As regards the first question, several writers, e.g. Porter (1986), Doz (1986), Hedlund (1986), Bartlett and Ghoshal (1990) and Teece, Pisano and Shuen (1990), have sought to demonstrate how changes in endogenously determined variables such as the creation and management of technological capabilities and organizational systems, and the revitalization of entrepreneurship, and exogenously determined variables such as the emergence of Japan as a major international competitor, the trend towards less regulated market economies and regional economic integration, and the changing structure of global competition, have affected the direction of the global product and marketing strategies of firms – including their strategies towards foreign production *per se*. Similarly, researchers have identified some of the likely changes in the ownership and locational preferences of firms which have followed, or may be expected to follow, the dismantling of trade barriers in the EEC (UN, 1993); from more relaxed government policies towards inward foreign direct investment (Contractor, 1990); from the competitive pressures to innovate and upgrade the quality of output (Cantwell, 1989); or from the liberalization and deregulation of many service or service related markets (Giersch, 1989; UNCTC, 1988).

As to how these changes are likely to impact on the OLI configuration of firms and, through these, foreign production, there has been less substantial research. There is, however, a great deal of casual evidence. For example, a change in the character and geography of European production by US manufacturing affiliates, following the formation of the EEC in 1958, led to an increase in the competitive advantages of US firms by offering new opportunities for product rationalization and the economies of common governance. At the same time, it also resulted in a shift in the location of production by US firms to the EC from the United States, and increased the extent to which US firms internalized their exports of technology and management skills to their EEC based subsidiaries.

In conclusion, autonomous strategic changes may sometimes affect the level and pattern of international production directly, and sometimes indirectly, through their effect on the firm's OLI configuration. Strategy induced changes are a response to changes in the OLI configuration, which will also impact directly on international production. In each case, strategy is the 'dynamic add-on' variable which links past and current as well as current and future levels of production to existing and future OLI advantages. While changes in international production may and do occur without strategic change, many changes are a direct consequence of it.

Explaining Differences in the Global Strategy of Firms

So far in this chapter we have illustrated some ways in which strategy might be incorporated into the variables influencing the foreign decision by the average or representative firm. In doing so, we have argued that the direction of a firm's future strategy is related to its current OLI configuration (which, in turn, is partly the result of its past strategies). *It follows, then, that if firms possess a different configuration of OLI advantages, they are likely to pursue different strategies towards the deployment of these advantages.* Indeed, a good deal of the management literature has sought to identify and explain these strategies, and to examine how far they can be linked to the particular characteristics of firms.

Consider, first, the kind of strategic initiating changes which different kinds of MNEs might introduce. It may, for example, be reasonable to hypothesize that firms which are leaders in their particular industry in product innovation are likely to opt for a product differentiation strategy, while those which see their main advantage in supplying low cost products are more likely to pursue a cost minimizing strategy (Porter, 1980, 1985). Integrated MNEs which operate in a large number of countries are likely to pursue different finance raising and international sourcing strategies than those which produce in only one or two countries and which organize their affiliates on an 'every tub on its own bottom' basis. New MNEs seeking to establish a global marketing presence in sectors in which there is a surplus of production capacity are likely to follow very different market entry strategies than those in rapidly growing industries. MNEs which have already decentralized their R&D facilities to several foreign countries and/or adapted their products to local needs are likely to evolve different innovating strategies than those which centralize these facilities, and/or aim to produce a world product. Given then, a knowledge about the OLI configuration of firms, it should not be difficult at least to narrow down the likely choice of strategic initiating changes open to it, and indeed, to classify MNEs accordingly.

Similarly, it may be possible to offer some generalizations about the form of the strategic response of firms to changes in the value of non-strategic variables, according to the character and mix of their OLI configuration. Thus, firms which are particularly adept at supplying and marketing low-cost standardized products are likely to respond differently to regional economic integration than those supplying high-quality products to niche markets. MNEs which have a special knowledge of (say) production conditions in Latin America are likely to react differently to locational strategies in respect of changes in these conditions than firms whose main production experience is confined to the Far East. MNEs which compete in a tight oligopolistic market structure, or which have developed close bonds with their industrial customers, are likely to respond differently to a reduction in cross-border market failure than firms which operate in monopolistic competitive markets or which maintain an arm's-length relationship with their customers.

These illustrations could be multiplied many times. They all point to the conclusion that hypothesizing about the factors which may determine strategy is not very different from hypothesizing about the contextual variables which determine the shape of the OLI configuration affecting particular firms. These we have identified as *industry* (or *activity), country* and *firm* specific variables; and the value of each of these is likely to influence both the strategic options open to firms, and their response to them. Alternatively, we might take the OLI configuration as a given variable and relate (future) strategic behavior to that variable. Much depends upon one's starting point of analysis and the extent to which one believes strategic decision taking impacts on the OLI variables or the OLI variables impact on strategy! The answer is likely to be 'both', depending on the time frame one is taking. Thus, we might have:

$$S_{t \to t+1} f(OLI_t) \text{ or } OLI_t = f(S_{t-1 \to t}) \qquad (6)$$

We accept, of course, that an explanation of the differences in the strategic behavior by firms based upon their reactions to a particular OLI configuration may not give a complete explanation of such conduct. However, in the context of global strategy, it does have the major advantage that research has already demonstrated its robustness as a framework for analyzing the international operations of firms.

This brings us to another point. Our main subject of explanation is the *foreign* value-added activities of firms. At the same time, as has been pointed out elsewhere (Dunning, 1977, 1988, 1993), these activities may be influenced by variables which affect the ability of such firms to compete in foreign markets independently of whether they engage in foreign production, and by those which are a direct consequence of internalizing cross-border markets. Indeed, it is an important premise of the internalization paradigm that these latter advantages are both a necessary and sufficient condition for FDI to occur.

Similarly, in explaining the global strategy of firms, it is reasonable for the strategic management analyst to direct his attention to those aspects of their behavior which arise from their multinationality *per se*. Hence, for example, the distinction is made by Doz (1986) between integrated MNEs and nationally responsive MNEs; and much of the author's analysis is concerned with identifying differences in the production and marketing strategies pursued by two types of firms. Likewise, Porter's conceptual framework (Porter, 1986) and Teece's distinction between firms pursuing entrance deterring strategies and those pursuing resource and capabilities enhancing strategies (Teece, Pisano and Shuen, 1990) can be readily applied to identifying the managerial responses to a particular OLI configuration facing MNEs, and how these differ according to the degree of multinationality of such firms and their governance structures. Indeed, in their monograph, Bartlett and Ghoshal (1990) specifically address the way in which the globalization of production by firms might affect their organizational capabilities and mentalities, and how these, in turn, may impact on management structures.

CONCLUDING REMARKS: A FIRST CUT AT A SYNTHESIS

The question then remains, how can strategic behavior best be embodied into the economist's approach to international production? First, we have suggested that at the paradigmatic level, strategy specific variables may be incorporated as 'dynamic add-ons' to the OLI configuration of variables, which currently offer a generalized or eclectic framework for explaining the foreign value-added activities of firms. We have also suggested that it is possible to hypothesize about the autonomous or induced strategies likely to be pursued by MNEs according to the configuration of the OLI advantages with which they are faced.

Second, we have argued that, just as any operationally testable *theory* of international production must specify the *kind* of foreign production being considered,[14] so likewise any attempt to theorize about the effect of strategy on foreign production must do the same. Thus, the strategies of firms considering resource based investment are likely to be different from those considering market seeking, cost minimizing or strategic asset acquiring investments, or from those wishing to acquire new competitive advantages. By the same token, different generic product, innovation or marketing strategies will have a different impact on the future OLI configuration of MNEs.

Third, we have asserted that the significance of particular OLI variables will also vary according to the products being produced, the countries of origin and destination, and firm specific factors. So, too, might the relevance of any combination of strategic variables also vary; and it is the task of the business analyst to identify and evaluate these.

One final problem needs mentioning. Most of the OLI variables (or proxies for them) identified by the eclectic paradigm are, to some degree or another, measurable. Strategic variables are, perhaps, less so. How does one quantifiably compare a cost minimizing strategy with a product differentiation strategy? Or an innovating aggressive as compared with an imitating defensive strategy? Or a segmented compared with a general product line strategy? The fact is that most strategic actions can be measured only indirectly, e.g. by their effects. But this raises another difficulty, namely how to attribute the effect, or effects, associated with a strategic action to that action? Indeed, one can easily fall into the trap of tautological reasoning, viz. the OLI configuration determines strategy yet strategy determines the OLI configuration.

However, by treating strategy as a time related or dynamic variable, this particular trap can be avoided. The challenge which then remains is how to isolate the strategic from the other variables that might affect the future OLI configuration of firms – a problem which most economists avoid by treating strategic success (or failure) as a residual. By the same token, economists, *de facto*, regard the strategic response to a particular OLI configuration as a residual variable in explaining foreign production.

At the end of the day, whether this matters or not obviously rests on the size of the unexplained variable. This, in turn, will depend on how correctly one has identified and specified the appropriate OLI variables and the particular kind of production one wishes to explain.

For example, firms from a particular country or industry which adopt global sourcing strategies are likely to exhibit a very different profile of international production to those which prefer to buy their inputs from local suppliers. The choice of whether to decentralize or centralize R&D facilities is also likely to be closely related to particular innovatory capacities of a firm, which markets it serves, and of how it views the relative advantages of using or internalizing the market for foreign sourced R&D. Firms which engage in product specialization in different countries are likely to be those which have important systemic or common governance advantages, and which supply products which face few barriers to trade and whose transport costs are relatively insignificant. Firms which conclude international coalitions presumably do so because they perceive that this is the best way to exploit or strengthen their existing ownership advantages *vis-à-vis* their competitors. Firms which practice a strategy of international cost leadership are likely to do so because they have strong competitive advantages in either acquiring cheap and efficient factor inputs or in scale economies. The strategies pursued by firms towards human resource recruitment, deployment and training are likely to reflect the relative importance attached to this management function and the capabilities of their personnel managers.

If the above analysis is correct, what is left to be explained is strategy or strategic change *which is unrelated to the existing OLI variables affecting the firm.* Earlier (pp. 184–6) we gave some examples of autonomous strategic change, which leads, rather than reacts to, any given OLI configuration – but, at the same time, may affect the pattern and structure of international production. Of the strategies which it might be difficult to trace back to the OLI configuration, those which are uncertainty or risk related are perhaps the most significant. Even here, however, there are aspects of entrepreneurial risk strategy, e.g. the measurement of risk, and the choice of options to protect against, counteract, or reduce risk, which may be gauged from knowledge about the OLI configuration.

In as much as intelligent entrepreneurship is, itself, a firm specific advantage and is likely to affect corporate attitudes to uncertainty bearing, there remain only those risks which essentially reflect the attitudes of individual decision takers. That these can be important is witnessed by the dramatic changes in both functional and overall management strategies which often follow a change in the senior management (and especially the chief executive) and/or boards of directors of corporations. Indeed, one might hypothesize that, more than any other factor, apart from those strategic related variables embodied in the OLI configuration of firms, the perception of, and attitudes towards, risk taking by the key decision takers in a corporation are the most critical variables determining strategy. And, at the end of the day, because these are, at least partly, culture specific, it may be the difficulty of embodying these in any general theory of the firm – or that of global business strategy – which constrains the extent to which the economist's and strategic analyst's approach to understanding and explaining foreign production can be integrated.

APPENDIX: AN EXTENDED VERSION OF THE ECLECTIC PARADIGM OF INTERNATIONAL PRODUCTION*

1. *Ownership-Specific Advantages* (of enterprise of one nationality [or affiliates of same] over those of another)
   a. Property right and/or intangible asset advantages.
      Product innovations, production management, organizational and marketing systems, innovatory capacity, noncodifiable knowledge, 'bank' of human capital experience, marketing, finance, knowhow, etc.
   b. Advantages of common governance.
      i. Those that branch plants of established enterprises may enjoy over *de novo* firms.
         Those due mainly to size, product diversity and learning experiences of enterprise, e.g. economies of scope and specialization. Exclusive or favored access to inputs, e.g. labor, natural resources, finance, information. Ability to obtain inputs on favored terms (due, e.g. to size or monopsonistic influence). Exclusive or favored access to product markets. Access to resources of parent company at marginal cost. Synergistic economies (not only in production, but in purchasing, marketing, finance, etc. arrangements).
      ii. Those that specifically arise because of multinationality. Multinationality enhances operational flexibility by offering wider opportunities for arbitraging and production shifting. More favored access to and/or better knowledge about international markets, e.g. for information, finance, labor, etc. Ability to take advantage of geographic differences in factor endowments, government intervention, markets, etc. Ability to diversify or reduce risks, e.g. in different currency areas and creation of options and/or political and cultural scenarios. Ability to learn from societal differences in organizational and managerial processes and systems. Balancing economies of integration with ability to respond to differences in country specific needs and advantages.

2. *Internalization Incentive Advantages* (i.e. to protect against or exploit market failure)
   Avoidance of search and negotiating costs.
   To avoid costs of moral hazard and adverse selection, and to protect reputation of internalizing firm.

* These variables are culled from a variety of sources, but see especially Dunning (1981, 1988, 1993) and Ghoshal (1987).

To avoid cost of broken contracts and ensuing litigation.
Buyer uncertainty (about nature and value of inputs [e.g. technology] being sold).
When market does not permit price discrimination.
Need of seller to protect quality of intermediate or final products.
To capture economics of interdependent activities (see b. above).
To compensate for absence of future markets.
To avoid or exploit government intervention (e.g. quotas, tariffs, price controls, tax differences, etc.).
To control supplies and conditions of sale of inputs (including technology).
To control market outlets (including those which might be used by competitors).
To be able to engage in practices, e.g. cross-subsidization, predatory pricing, leads and lags, transfer pricing, etc. as a competitive (or anticompetitive) strategy.

3. *Location Specific Variables* (these may favor home or host countries)
Special distribution of natural and created resource endowments and markets.
Input prices, quality and productivity, e.g., labor, energy, materials, components, semifinished goods.
International transport and communications costs.
Investment incentives and disincentives (including performance requirements, etc.)
Artificial barriers (e.g. import controls) to trade in goods and services.
Societal and infrastructure provisions (commercial, legal, educational, transport and communication).
Cross-country ideological, language, cultural, business, political, etc. differences.
Economics of centralization of R&D production and marketing.
Economic system and policies of government: the institutional framework for resource allocation.

4. *Dynamic 'Add-on' Strategy Related Variables* (Some illustrations)	Extent and form of innovation – and in what direction? Is the firm aiming to develop core or diversified competencies?
Technology and Innovation	Is the firm primarily an innovator or an imitator? Does the firm internalize or externalize the R&D function? To centralize or decentralize R&D? Nature of foreign R&D activities. Form and nature of technology transfer.

Product	Degree of product specialization or diversification. High quality or low cost product? Product line broadening or upgrading? Degree of vertical integration. Degree of geographical specialization of plants. Extent to which products arc adapted for local consumption.
Sourcing	The 'make' or 'buy' decision. Single or multiple sourcing? To source locally or import? Form of relationship with suppliers. Quality control exercised over intermediate products.
Production	Methods of manufacturing (batch, mass production, flexible manufacturing). Extent to which production processes are adopted in foreign subsidiaries. Work practices. Quality control and inspection procedures
Human Resource Management	Recruitment policy (e.g. extent to which this is centralized or decentralized). Patterns of industrial relations. Methods of wage payments, productivity incentives, and fringe benefits. Worker participation in decision making process. Training programs. Policy towards employment of local nationals in foreign subsidiaries.
Marketing and Distribution	Geographical market orientation. Broad liner, innovator, nicher or synergist. Distribution channels. 'Do it yourself' or use agents? Control over markets served by foreign subsidiaries. Extent of intrafirm trade. Advertising *et al.* promotional techniques
Organization	M, U or matrix form? Ethnocentric, polycentric or geocentric attitudes towards foreign operations.

	Multidomestic, global or transnational orientation of MNEs towards foreign affiliates.
	Organizational structure of foreign affiliates.
	Degree of control or influence exerted over decision taking by affiliates.
	How far are local managers included in centralized decision taking process?
Finance and Accounting	Techniques of capital budgeting and evaluation of investment projects.
	Sourcing of finance.
	Transnational accounting, budgetary, and planning control procedures.
Ownership	Extent of ownership of foreign subsidiaries.
	Policies towards strategic alliances – with whom and what form?
	Strategy towards joint ventures and non-equity associations.
Locational Issues	Attitudes towards foreign production and geographical risk diversification Leverage and arbitrage opportunities.
	Behavior of competitors, suppliers, customers, etc.
	Nature of interface with home and foreign governments; negotiating and bargaining strengths and tactics of the two parties.

NOTES

1. See, for example, the work of Doz (1986), Ghoshal (1987), and Kogut (1985, 1989, 1990), Kogut and Singh (1988) and Porter (1980, 1985, 1986, 1990).
2. For an analysis of the state of the art of this latter theory, see a special issue of the *Strategic Management Journal*, Vol. 12, 1991.
3. See Knickerbocker (1973), Graham (1978), Lessard (1977) and Rugman (1979).
4. These are compared and contrasted more fully in Dunning (1993).
5. Business scholars, however, do well to acquaint themselves with macro-economic theories of foreign direct investment, of which that of Kiyoshi Kojima (Kojima, 1978, 1982) is the best known. The particular merit of Kojima's approach is that it looks at the issue of outward and inward investment from a *country*'s viewpoint, and attempts to argue that it is the *comparative* locational or competitive advantages of countries which should determine the amount, form and structure of international business operations. To this extent, there is some parallel between the attributes of competitiveness identified by Porter in his latest book (1990), and those analyzed by Kojima. However, Kojima pays only limited attention to the market

replacing, or systemic advantages of multinational firms, as his whole analysis if strongly neoclassical, and based on the principle that cross-border markets are (or should be) (near) perfectly competitive.

6. For reviews of this literature see especially Buckley and Casson (1985), Casson (1987), Hennart (1986), Teece (1985) and Rugman (1986).
7. For example, with respect to the behavior of suppliers, customers or competitors of the investing firm (Vernon, 1983) and of environmental volatility (Kogut, 1985).
8. For example, both Stuckey (1983), in his study of vertical integration in the aluminum industry, and Hennart (1988), in his comparison of the organization of the international aluminum and tin industries, discuss the alternative strategies which MNEs may adopt towards minimizing their cross-border transaction costs. For a more general analysis of the choice of organizational strategies within hierarchies when market failure exists, see Anderson and Gatignon (1986) and Kogut (1988).
9. See especially Chapters 3 and 6 of Dunning (1988).
10. As explained more fully in Dunning (1993).
11. These include both firm specific variables (e.g. attitude of decision takers to risk, time profile of earnings, innovation, age, segments of market served, long term objectives) and exogenous factors (e.g. corporation taxes, R&D subsidies, training grants, presence of related industries, and demand patterns).
12. Cf. Caves (1980a), who argues that the concept of strategic groups and mobility barriers 'do not add up to a tight formal model ... but serve as a dynamized add-on to the traditional structure–conduct–performance paradigm'.
13. For recent surveys of some of these findings, see Clegg (1987), Kumar (1990), Dunning (1993) and UNCTC (1992).
14. Although they vary, classification of different types of international production itself requires careful research and analysis.

REFERENCES

Anderson, E. and Gatignon, H. (1986), 'Models of foreign entry: A transaction cost analysis and propositions', *Journal of International Business Studies*, **17**, Fall: 1–16.

Bartlett, C.A., and Ghoshal, S. (1990), *Managing Across Borders: The Transnational Solution*, Boston, MA: Harvard Business School Press.

Buckley, P.J. and Casson, M.C. (1981), The optimal timing of a foreign direct investment' *Economic Journal*, **91**, March: 75–87.

Buckley, P.J. and Casson, M.C. (1985), *The Economic Theory of the Multinational Enterprise*, London: Macmillan.

Cantwell, J. (1989), *Technological Innovation and Multinational Corporations*, Oxford: Basil Blackwell.

Cantwell, J. (1991), 'Theories of international production' in Pitelis, C. and Sugden, R. (eds), *The Nature of the Transnational Firm*, London: Routledge.

Casson, M.C. (1987), *The Firm and the Market*, Oxford: Basil Blackwell.

Casson, M.C. (1988), *Entrepreneurship as a Cultural Advantage*, University of Reading Discussion Papers in International Investment and Business Studies No. 124, November.

Caves, R.E. (1980a), 'Industrial organization, corporate strategy and structure', *Journal of Economic Literature*, **XVIII**: 64–92.

Caves, R.E. (1980b), 'Investment and location policies of multinational companies', *Schweiz Zeitschrift für Volkwirtschaft und Statistik*, **116**: 321–327.

Clegg, J. (1987), *Multinational Enterprises and World Competition*, London: Macmillan.

Contractor, F.J. (1990), 'Ownership patterns of U.S. joint ventures abroad and the liberalization of foreign government regulations in the 1980s. Evidence from the bench mark surveys', *Journal of International Business Studies*, **21**: 55–74 .

Contractor, F.J. and Lorange, P. (eds) (1988), *Cooperative Strategies in International Business*, Lexington, MA: Lexington Books.

Douglas, S.P. and Rhee, Dong Kee (1989), 'Examining generic strategy types in US and European markets', *Journal of International Business Studies*, **20**: Fall: 437–63.

Doz, Y. (1986), *Strategic Management in Multinational Companies*, Oxford: Pergamon Press.

Doz, Y. (1988), 'International industries: fragmentation versus globalization', in Guile, B.R. and Brooks, H. (eds) *Technology and Global Industry*, Washington: National Academy Press.

Dunning, J.H. (1977), 'Trade location of economic activity and the multinational enterprise: A search for an eclectic approach', in Ohlin, B., Hesselborn, P.O., and Wikman, P.M. (eds), *The International Allocation of Economic Activity*, London: Macmillan: pp. 395–418.

Dunning, J.H. (1981), *International Production and the Multinational Enterprise*, London: Allen and Unwin.

Dunning, J.H. (1988), *Explaining International Production*, London: Unwin Hyman.

Dunning, J.H. (1989), 'The theory of international production', in Fatemi, K. (ed.) *International Trade*, New York: Taylor and Francis.

Dunning, J.H. (1990), 'The eclectic paradigm of international production: A personal perspective', in Pitelis, C. and Sugden, R. (eds), *The Nature of the Transnational Firm*, London: Routledge, pp. 117–36.

Dunning, J.H. (1992), *The Theory of Transnational Corporations*, Vol. 1 of UN Library on Transnational Corporations, London and New York: Routledge.

Dunning, J.H. (1993), *Multinational Enterprises and the Global Economy*, Reading, MA: Addison-Wesley.

Flowers, E.B. (1976), 'Oligopolistic reaction in European and Canadian direct investment in the U.S.', *Journal of International Business Studies*, **7**: 43–55.

Ghoshal, S. (1987), 'Global strategy: An organizing framework', *Strategic Management Review*, **8**: 425–40.

Giersch, H. (ed.) (1989), *Services in World Economic Growth*, Tübingen: J.C.B. Mohr.

Graham, E.M. (1978), 'Transatlantic investment by multinational firms: A rivalistic phenomenon', *Journal of Post Keynesian Economics*, **1**: 82–99.

Graham, E.M. (1990), 'Strategic interaction among multinational firms and foreign direct investment', in Pitelis, C. and Sugden, R. (eds), *The Nature of the Transnational Firm*, London: Routledge, pp. 155–67.

Hamel, G. and Prahalad, C.K. (1987), 'Creating global strategic capability', in Hood, N. and Vahlne, J. E. (eds), *Strategies in Global Competition*, London: Routledge, pp. 5–39.

Hedlund, G. (1986), 'The hypermodern MNC: A heterarchy human resource', *Human Resource Management*, Spring: 9–35.

Hennart, J.F. (1986), 'What is internalization?', *Weltwirtschaftliches Archiv*, **122**: 791–804.

Hennart, J.F. (1988), 'Upstream vertical integration in the aluminum and tin industries: A comparative study of the choice between market and intra-firm coordination', *Journal of Economic Behavior and Organization*, **9** (3): 281–300.

Knickerbocker, F. (1973), *Oligopolistic Reaction and the Multinational Enterprise*, Cambridge, MA: Harvard University Press.

Kogut, B. (1983), 'Foreign direct investment as a sequential process', in Kindleberger, C.P. and Audretsch, D. (eds), *The Multinational Corporation in the 1980s*, Cambridge, MA: MIT Press.

Kogut, B. (1985), 'Designing global strategies: profiting from operational flexibility', *Sloan Management Review*, Fall: 27–37.

Kogut, B. (1989), 'A note on global strategies', *Journal of International Business Studies*, **10**: 383–9.

Kogut, B. (1990), *The Permeability of Borders and the Speed of Learning Among Countries*, Lund: The Crafoord Lectures, 1989.

Kogut, B. and Singh, Harbir (1988), 'The effects of national culture on the choice of entry mode', *Journal of International Business Studies*, Fall: 411–32.

Kojima, K. (1978), *Direct Foreign Investment: A Japanese Model of Multinational Business Operations*, London: Croom Helm.

Kojima, K. (1982), 'Macro economic versus international business approach to foreign direct investment', *Hitosubashi Journal of Economics*, **23**: 1–19.

Kumar, K. (1990), *Multinational Enterprises in India*, London: Routledge.

Lessard, D.G. (1977), 'International diversification and foreign direct investment', in Eitman, D. and Stonehill, A. (eds), *Multinational Business Finance*, 4th edn, Reading, MA: Addison-Wesley.

McGee, J. and Thomas, H. (1986), 'Strategic groups: Theory research and taxonomy', *Strategic Management Journal*, **7**: 141–60.

Porter, M.E. (1980), *Competitive Behavior*, New York: Free Press.

Porter, M.E. (1985), *Competitive Advantage*, New York: Free Press.

Porter, M.E. (ed.), (1986), *Competition in Global Industries*, Boston, MA: Harvard Business School Press.

Porter, M.E. (1990), *The Competitive Advantage of Nations*, New York: Free Press.

Robbins, L. (1928), 'The Representative Firm', *Economic Journal*, **38**: 387–404.

Rugman, A M. (1975), 'Motives for foreign investment: The markets imperfection and risk diversification hypothesis', *Journal of World Trade Law*, **9**: 567–73.

Rugman, A.M. (1979), *International Diversification and the Multinational Enterprise*, Lexington, MA: Lexington Books.

Rugman, A.M. (1986), 'New theories of the multinational enterprise: An assessment of internalization theory', *Bulletin of Economic Research*, **38**: 101–18.

Stuckey, J. (1983), *Vertical Integration and Joint Ventures in the Aluminum Industry*, Cambridge, MA: Harvard University Press.

Teece, D.J. (1984), 'Economic analysis and strategic management', *California Management Review*, **XXVI**: 87–110.

Teece, D.J. (1985), 'Transaction cost economics and the multinational enterprise: An assessment', *Journal of Economic Behavior and Organization* **7**: 21–45.

Teece, D.J., Pisano, G. and Shuen, A. (1990), *Firm Capabilities, Resources and the Concept of Strategy*, Berkeley, CA: University of California (mimeo).

UN (1993), *From the Common Market to EC 92. Regional Integration in the European Community and Transnational Corporations*, New York: UN Transnational Corporations and Management Division.

UNCTC (1988), *Transnational Corporations and World Development*, New York: United Nations, No. E88 II A8.

UNCTC (1992), *The Determinants of Foreign Direct Investment*, New York: United Nations.

Vernon, R. (1966), 'International investment and international trade in the product cycle', *Quarterly Journal of Economics*, **80**: 90–207.

Vernon, R. (1979), 'The product cycle hypothesis in the new international environment', *Oxford Bulletin of Economics and Statistics*, **41**: 255–67.

Vernon, R. (1983), 'Organizational and institutional responses to international risk', in Herring, R. J. (ed.), *Managing International Risk*, Cambridge: Cambridge University Press, pp. 191–256.

7. The eclectic paradigm of international production: a restatement and some possible extensions*

INTRODUCTION

When the concept of the eclectic paradigm of international production was first put forward by the author in 1976 at a presentation to a Nobel Symposium in Stockholm on *The International Allocation of Economic Activity*,[1] the intention was to offer a holistic framework by which it was possible to identify and evaluate the significance of the factors influencing both the initial act of foreign production by enterprises and the growth of such production. The choice of the word eclectic was an ambitious, yet deliberate one. It was meant to convey the idea that a full explanation of the transnational activities of enterprises needs to draw upon several strands of economic theory; and that foreign direct investment is just one of a number of possible channels of international economic involvement, each of which is determined by a number of common factors.

It is accepted that, precisely because of its generality, the eclectic paradigm has only limited power to explain or predict particular kinds of international production; and even less, the behaviour of individual enterprises.[2] But this deficiency, if it is a deficiency, which some critics have alleged, could no less be directed at attempts to formulate a general, but operational testable, paradigm of international trade. The classical and neoclassical theories of trade, for example, while still having wide explanatory powers for most kinds of inter-industry trade, are quite inadequate to explain much of intra-industry trade.[3] Indeed, it is perhaps worth emphasizing that the point at which the Heckscher–Ohlin–Samuelson (HOS) theory of trade fails is precisely that at which the modern paradigm of international production starts, that is, the point at which there are positive transaction costs in intermediate goods markets.[4] The difference between the neotechnology and other modern theories of trade, and those of international production, is that, while the former *implicitly* assume that all goods are exchanged between independent buyers and sellers across national frontiers, the latter *explicitly* postulate that the transfer of intermedi-

* From *Journal of International Business Studies*, **19**(1) (1988), 1–31.

ate products is undertaken with the same enterprises. In other words, without international market failure, the *raison d'être* for international production disappears. But once it exists, explanations of trade and production may be thought of as part of a general paradigm, based upon the international disposition of factor endowments, and the costs of alternative modalities for transacting intermediate products across national boundaries. This, indeed, is the central theme of this chapter.

CRITICISMS OF THE ECLECTIC PARADIGM

Are Competitive or Ownership Advantages Necessary to Explain International Production?

In its original form, the eclectic paradigm stated that the extent, form and pattern of international production were determined by the configuration of three sets of advantages as perceived by enterprises.[5] First, in order for firms of one nationality to compete with those of another, by producing in the latter's own countries, they must possess certain production or transactional advantages specific to the nationality of their ownership. These advantages must be sufficient to compensate for the costs of setting up and operating a foreign value-adding operation in addition to those faced by indigenous producers or potential producers.

In our 1976 contribution, which is reproduced in Chapter 2 of this volume, we identified three types of ownership specific (O) advantages: (1) those which stem from the exclusive privileged possession of, or access to, particular income generating assets; (2) those which are normally enjoyed by a branch plant compared with a *de novo* firm; and (3) those which are a consequence of geographical diversification or multinationality *per se*.[6] In a later typology (Dunning, 1983), we distinguished between the *asset* (*Oa*) and *transaction* (*Ot*) advantages of multinational enterprises (MNEs).[7] While the former arise from the proprietary ownership of specific assets by MNEs *vis-à-vis* those possessed by other enterprises (i.e. of type (1) above, which can only occur in a situation of structural market distortions),[8] the latter mirror the capacity of MNE hierarchies, *vis-à-vis* external markets, to capture the transactional benefits (or lessen the transactional costs) arising from the common governance of a network of these assets, located in different countries.

The distinction between *structural* and *transactional* market imperfections is an important one (Dunning and Rugman, 1985). Clearly the relevance of each in determining the O advantages of MNEs will vary according to the characteristics of firms, the products they produce and the markets in which they operate; and whether the competitive process is viewed from a static or dynamic perspective. Certainly, the earlier analysts of foreign direct investment – particularly those of the Hymer (1960, 1976) tradition – tended to emphasize the former kind of imperfection; but likewise, so do contemporary economists working in the area of innovation and technological development (e.g. Pavitt, 1987; Cantwell, 1986), and business analysts seeking to identify the systemic advantages of globally oriented enterprises (e.g. Prahalad and Doz, 1987; Kogut, 1983, 1985a). By contrast, the modern theory of the MNE *qua* MNE (e.g. as summarized by Teece, 1986 and Casson, 1987) tends to emphasize transactional market failure as the main *raison d'être* for international production. The two kinds of imperfection are, of course, often inter-related, particularly in a dynamic market setting;[9] and there is a growing consensus that the most successful MNEs are those which are best able to nurture and exploit *both* asset and transactional ownership advantages.

The second condition for international production is that it must be in the best interests of enterprises which possess *O* advantages to transfer them across national boundaries *within* their own organizations rather than sell them, or their right of use, to foreign based enterprises. This immediately suggests that MNEs perceive that the international market place is not the best modality for transacting intermediate goods or services. The reasons for the internalization of markets have been explored in considerable detail in the literature.[10] Suffice to reiterate here that three main kinds of market failure are usually identified, viz. (1) those which arise from risk and uncertainty as, for example, those succinctly analysed by Vernon (1983); (2) those which stem from the ability of firms to exploit the economies of large scale production, but only in an imperfect market situation and (3) those which occur where the transaction of a particular good or service yields costs and benefits *external* to that transaction, but which are not reflected in the terms agreed by the transacting parties.[11] The desire by firms to integrate different stages of the value-added chain, to engage in product diversification, or to capture the economies of the use of complementary assets (Teece, 1987), originate from the presence of one or other of these forms of transactional market failure, even though the motives for internalization may be expressed rather differently (e.g. to safeguard supplies of essential inputs, to ensure quality control of end products, to guarantee markets, to protect property rights, to allow price discrimination, to spread the costs of shared overhead and so on). The greater the perceived costs of transactional market failure, the more MNEs are likely to exploit their competitive advantages through international production, rather than by contractual agreements with foreign firms. By contrast, the higher the administrative costs of hierarchies and/or the external diseconomies (or disbenefits) of operating a foreign venture (e.g. as shown by the Bhopal disaster), the more probable it is that the latter vehicle, or at least a jointly shared equity stake, will be preferred.

In such cases, where there is no external market for the competitive advantages of MNEs, the distinction between ownership and internalization advantages may seem irrelevant. Indeed, some writers, notably Buckley and Casson (1985) and Casson (1987), have argued that the failure of international intermediate product markets is both a necessary and sufficient condition to explain the *existence* of MNEs. Yet, we believe it is not only useful, but logically correct, to distinguish between the capability of MNEs to internalize markets and their willingness to do so. For, while the latter may explain why hierarchies, rather than external markets, are the vehicle by which transactional ownership advantages (*Ot*) are transferred across national boundaries, it is the former which explains why these advantages are exploited by one group of MNEs rather than another, or by MNEs rather than firms indigenous to the country of production.[12] The eclectic paradigm also assumes that market imperfections, without which firm specific proprietary advantages could not persist, are endogenous to MNEs, unlike the internalization rubric which assumes them to be exogenous (Buckley, 1987).[13] When, however, one examines the dynamics of international business growth, and especially why some MNEs prosper and others do not, the two approaches are more easily reconcilable with each other.

Certainly in the exploitation of specific intangible assets (*Oa*), such as a patent or trade mark, firms often have a choice between using the external market or not. Here the distinction between asset *generation*, or *acquisition*, and asset *usage* is an important one. We would accept, with Rugman (1981), that, if an ownership advantage is either created by, or becomes the exclusive property of, a particular enterprise, it has, in some sense, 'internalized' the market for its use;[13] but we believe this to be a questionable extension of the interpretation of a term which originally, and quite specifically, was intended to convey a response to transactional, rather than structural, market failure.[14]

Locational Advantages: Structural and Transactional Market Failure

The third strand of the eclectic paradigm is concerned with the 'where' of production. Enterprises will engage in foreign production whenever they perceive it is in their best interests to combine spatially transferable intermediate products produced in the home country[15] with at least some immobile factor endowments, or other intermediate products, in another country. While, in the eclectic paradigm, the advantages or disadvantages of particular locations are treated separately from the *O* advantages of particular enterprises, as are the reasons for the internationalization of these advantages, the decision on where to site a mine, factory or office is not independent of the ownership of these assets, nor of the route by which they or their rights are transacted. For example, the ability of an enterprise to choose the correct location or organize its assets efficiently may itself be considered an *O* advantage. Similarly, the choice of location may be prompted by spatial market failure: historically, the imposition of trade barriers has led to a lot of foreign manufacturing investment of MNEs. At the same time, a reduction in transport costs and the formation of customs unions or regional trading blocs, e.g. EEC and LAFTA, have prompted greater regional specialization of production by MNEs (Dunning, 1988).

Once more, a distinction needs to be drawn between the different kinds of market imperfections which may influence the locational decisions of MNEs. Structural market distortions, including those arising from some (but not all) kinds of government intervention,[16] and which affect the costs and/or revenues of producing in different locations, may either encourage or discourage inward direct investment (Guisinger, 1985). On the other hand, even without such distortions, MNE activity would still occur wherever there are transaction gains likely to result from the common governance of activities in different locations. Such advantages include enhanced arbitrage and leverage opportunities, the reduction of exchange risks and better co-ordination of financial decision-taking, the protection afforded by a hedged marketing or multiple sourcing strategy, and the possibility of gains through transfer price manipulation, leads and lags in payments, and so on (Kogut, 1985b).

The ability to generate and sustain such *O* advantages itself strengthens the competitive position of MNEs *vis-à-vis* uninational firms. But, because transactional market failure is sometimes country specific, it has locational implications as well. To this extent, Rugman is on the right lines when he refers to MNE as 'internalising exogenous spatial imperfections' (Rugman, 1981); but this analysis better explains the common *ownership* of MNE subsidiaries in different locations, rather than why *particular* subsidiaries are located where they are.

Specific versus General Theories of International Production

It is then the juxtaposition of the *O*-specific advantages of firms contemplating foreign production, or an increase in foreign production, the propensity to internalize the cross-border markets for these, and the attractions of a foreign location for production which is the gist of the eclectic paradigm of international production. But the identification and value of the specific ownership, location and internalization (*OLI*) parameters which will influence individual MNEs in any particular production decision will vary according to the motives underlying such production. The parameters influencing an MNE to invest in a copper mine in New Guinea are unlikely to be the same as those influencing investment by a Japanese colour television company in the United States; while those determining the pattern of rationalized production in the EEC by a large and geographically diversified US motor vehicles MNE will be different from an investment by a Korean construction management company in Kuwait.

However, the eclectic paradigm does allow one to go a step further by relating the *OLI* configuration facing MNEs to a number of structural or contextual variables. Elsewhere (Dunning 1979), we have identified the more important of these as *country*, *industry* (or activity) and *firm* specific. For example, the asset advantages *(Oa)* of particular MNEs may be expected to vary according to the factor endowments and other characteristics of the countries from which they originate and/or in which they operate, and the technological and other features of the activities in which they engage. The fact that such assets may be the exclusive property of particular firms, and be mobile across national boundaries, does not negate the possibility that their source may be explained by the international disposition of country specific and immobile endowments. To this extent, one is back to HOS-type theory, except for two differences: the first is that the goods and services traded are intermediate rather than final products, and the second is that the eclectic paradigm allows for the role of governments in affecting – by the political systems they operate and the economic policies they pursue – the real (as opposed to the potential) value of resources within their boundaries.[17] Several writers, e.g. Franko (1976), Ergas (1983), Davidson (1976) and Pavitt (1987), have demonstrated that the kind of innovatory advantages generated by MNEs reflect the resource endowments, markets, culture, attitudes and the institutional framework of their home countries.[18]

It requires a small extension of the 'modified' factor endowment approach to explain why some types of economic activity are more prone to internationalization than others. Again the spatial disposition of resource endowments and international transport costs are the key variables. If the capacity to create a particular asset is ubiquitous, and the right to its use can be disseminated at zero cost, then international production is unlikely; it is also improbable where the competitive advantages of firms rest not in the exclusive possession of specific assets, but in the access to immobile but non-specific factor endowments on favourable terms. Thus a combination of the resource requirements of particular economic activities, their geographical disposition and the transfer costs of their output helps to explain some of the operations of MNEs.

But only some! For example, it does little to explain the cross-hauling of investment in the same industries by MNEs of different nationalities, or the fact that some countries display similar patterns of international production. The explanation is limited because it ignores transactional market failure, which itself varies between countries and types of economic activities. Without such failure, but with an uneven distribution of resource endowments, trade in intermediate products would be conducted through external markets. With an even distribution of resource endowments, but with market failure, then the only advantage which MNEs *qua* MNEs possess is their capability to overcome international transactional imperfections better than their uninational rivals.

Does the Eclectic Paradigm Insufficiently Allow for Firm-Specific Behavioural Differences?

We now turn to consider a structural variable which some business analysts regard as the most crucial of all in influencing the level and pattern of international production. This is the strategic response of decision-takers within MNEs to a set of economic and other variables, and the way the idosyncratic behaviour of firms might influence and respond to cross-border market failure.

A cursory review of the international profiles of the leading MNEs identified by Stopford (1982) reveals that in some sectors, e.g. consumer electronics, motor vehicles, pharmaceuticals, etc., there are as many differences between the characteristics of MNEs in the same sector as there are between MNEs in different sectors. Moreover, since these firms rarely supply identical products or the same range of products, or produce on the same (or similar) points of the value-added chain, or sell in the same markets, and since too, they have differing capabilities for, and a need of, international production, it follows that not only are they faced with a different set of strategic options, but that their evaluation of these options, and the risks attached to them, will vary. Indeed, the risk diversification thesis (Rugman, 1979) asserts that different firms may view identical investment opportunities offered by a particular country differently, *inter alia*, according to the distribution of their existing portfolios and their attitudes towards uncertainty. For these, and other reasons identified in the business literature, firm-specific characteristics may be a crucial determinant of the response by MNEs to any particular *OLI* configuration.

While there have been some attempts to model strategic behaviour of firms towards their foreign operations,[19] they have not generally been incorporated into the mainstream of international production theory. The exceptions are the product-cycle, oligopolistic-strategy and risk-minimization models. The first two (Vernon, 1974; Knickerbocker, 1973) look upon much of foreign production as a strategy by firms to protect or gain an *O* advantage *vis-à-vis* their rivals, the implication being that, in a more competitive and less risky environment, firms would have less impetus to engage in international direct investment (Vernon, 1983). Evidence of such strategies of oligopolists includes the bunching of the timing of foreign investment in some sectors (Dunning, 1986a; Knickerbocker, 1973; Graham, 1978, 1985; Lake, 1976a, 1976b). The risk-minimization hypothesis argues that, other things being equal, firms will prefer to diversify the geographical portfolio of their investments. This concept may be extended to incorporate non-financial portfolio behaviour. Clearly, whether or not a firm adopts a global product or marketing strategy, or chooses to engage in multiple sourcing (Kogut, 1983, 1985b) reflects not only its ability to do so (which *inter alia* will be a function of its size, product structure and existing overseas commitments), but its perceptions of the resulting costs and benefits.

To what extent can differences in the behaviour of firms be embraced by the *OLI* framework? The answer is they can, in so far as it is possible to identify and evaluate systematic patterns of such behaviour. Purely random or idiosyncratic actions by particular MNEs cannot be so easily incorporated. But no less is this true if one was attempting a generalized theory of the uninational firm. Such theories as abound in the literature are really theories of the behaviour of *firms*, in the sense that it is not the behaviour of any particular firm they are trying to predict, but that of a group of firms, or of a representative (or average) firm of that group. They usually assume two things: first, that firms have broadly similar goals; and second, that they respond to economic signals to advance these goals in a rational and consistent way. When neither condition exists, it is not possible to offer any generalized explanations of behaviour, which, indeed, is exactly what some business analysts would claim.

We do not accept that such a drastic course is either desirable or justifiable; indeed, we believe that, in most firms, that part of business conduct which is purely idiosyncratic is probably very small. However, we are persuaded that the interface between the economic and behavioural theories of the firm does not need more explicit and systematic analysis. While there is general agreement about the main *country* and *industry* characteristics likely to influence each of the main components of the eclectic paradigm, much less attention has been given to identifying the key attributes of firms – and especially those which might be identified as operational or strategically based – which may affect their response to any particular configuration of *OLI* parameters.

There are now signs of this happening. Some of the recent literature on the global dimensions of business is replete with attempts to identify the strategically related characteristics of firms most likely to be associated with a robust international posture.[20] These include their long-term goals and perspectives, the nature and scope of their core assets, their attitude to innovation and change (are they leaders or followers in their industry, are they innovators or imitators?), the range and segment of critical markets served, their attitude to risk and uncertainty, their operational flexibility, their organizational and cultural ethos, the entrepreneurial initiative of their chief decision-takers and their willingness and capacity to conclude cross-border alliances.

Apart from the studies of Knickerbocker (1973), Flowers (1976) and Graham (1975, 1978) on oligopolistic behaviour, there has been little empirical research on behavioural-related variables which might influence the extent and pattern of international production. Horst (1972a, 1972b) concluded that, apart from size, he could identify no firm-specific variable which satisfactorily explained the degree of multinationality of US owned firms across industries and countries. A later study undertaken on the *modes* of transferring technology between countries but within firms (Davidson and McFeteridge, 1984, 1985) revealed that such variables as existing overseas commitment, research intensity, and degree of product diversification were positively and significantly correlated with the extent of a firm's internalization. More recently still, Porter (1986) has developed a model which relates the extent to which different types of firms seek to co-ordinate their international value-adding investments with the propensity to centralize or decentralize the location of these investments. Porter describes a globally or geocentrically oriented MNE as one which operates an extensive network of foreign affiliates, the activities of which are subject to a high degree of centralized co-ordination. Such an MNE is to be distinguished from a multi-domestic company which through its affiliates – which are largely autonomous in their decision taking – pursues a series of country-centred strategies, or indeed from one which adopts a simple global strategy with a geographically concentrated configuration of activities.[21]

In conclusion, it may well be that there are some behavioural-related variables of firms which have not been successfully incorporated into the eclectic paradigm. In so far as it is possible to identify those which might influence the response of groups of enterprises to be given *OLI* configuration, there is no reason why this could not be done. But where no general systematic or consistent response of firms to changes in exogenous variables can be discovered, any attempt to generalize about the causes of international production is thwarted from the start.

The Aliber Theory of Foreign Direct Investment

Let us now briefly turn to Robert Aliber's dissatisfaction with the eclectic paradigm (Aliber, 1983), and, indeed, with all theories that take some measure of the foreign activities of enterprises as their starting point of interest. This reflects his view that the key attribute of an MNE is not the fact that it engages in foreign production, but that it finances at least part of this production in its home currency. He is, then, primarily interested in the export of direct investment as a means of financing foreign capital expenditure rather than as a channel by which an enterprise transfers non-financial resources between countries, and controls the use of such resources once transferred. He would appear to believe that the extra-territorial expansion of firms *per se* raises no issues not addressed by the theory of the domestic firm. Rather the uniqueness of the MNE is its ability to dominate its geographically dispersed assets in different currencies, and by so doing, to take advantage of structural or transactional imperfections in international capital and foreign-exchange markets; and particularly the existence of 'strong' and 'weak' currencies.

Inasmuch as scholars are entitled to study subjects of interest to them, we have no dispute with Aliber. We would, however, challenge his implicit assumption that while differences *in kind* exist between national and international financial markets, this is not the case for non-financial markets, such as those for technology and management services. Moreover, it seems to us that Aliber restricts his consideration of foreign direct investment to situations in which enterprises invest in different currency areas. While this may be usually the case, it is by no means universally so.

In any event, we do not find Aliber's thesis incompatible with the eclectic paradigm. The very fact that firms, by their presence overseas, may be able to denominate their assets and goods in different currencies, could give them (as a group) *O* advantages over uninational firms. These advantages will be the more pronounced the greater the degree of structural or transactional failure in international capital and/or exchange markets, and the better equipped MNEs are to internalize these markets. Yet, by themselves, these advantages are not sufficient to explain either the amount or distribution of FDI. For example, expected profits (other than those resulting from the internalization of imperfect financial markets) are not independent of the locations in which investments are made, nor of the ability of MNEs to appropriate economic rent by internalizing non-financial markets.

It is not our purpose to offer a detailed critique of the Aliber hypothesis,[22] but rather to suggest that, in so far as imperfections do exist in the markets in which he is interested, these may affect both the way in which capital expenditure by MNEs is financed, and the geographical distribution of international production. Similarly, the factors identified in the eclectic paradigm as influencing the foreign activities of firms may, directly, by their impact on capital and exchange markets and, indirectly, by affecting the total capital expenditure by MNEs, have no less a bearing on their financing of these activities. We would then assert that, in support of his own theory, Professor Aliber must take cognizance of the non-financial aspects of the international operations of firms.

The Kojima Hypothesis[23]

As originally propounded, Professor Kojima's theory of foreign direct investment (Kojima, 1978, 1982) is an extension of the neoclassical theory of trade to embrace cross-border transactions of intermediate products, e.g. technology, management skills etc. It is primarily a normative theory, and views the MNE as an instrument by which the comparative trading advantage of nation states may be better advanced. Hence his prescription that a *home* country should invest abroad in sectors which require intermediate (but internationally mobile) products which it is comparatively well suited to supply, but which need to be combined with non-transferable inputs in which the *host* country is relatively well endowed. In this case, foreign direct investment acts both as a catalyst to trade and as an arbitrager for improving the international allocation of economic activity.

Kojima criticizes the eclectic paradigm for being too micro- or business oriented, and claims it is of limited use for policy formation by home or host countries. But, as we have sought to demonstrate from the perspective of the UK (Dunning, 1988), many of the normative implications of our paradigm are entirely consistent with Kojima's recommendations. This is particularly the case for resource-based and import substitution investment, where the export of intermediate products by MNEs to countries best suited to engage in further value-added activities either circumvents artificially imposed impediments to trade, or better promotes the dynamic comparative advantage of the participating countries.

However, even as a prescriptive macroeconomic model, the Kojima approach is deficient in two major respects. First, since it is neoclassical in its stance, it can neither explain nor evaluate the welfare implications of those types of foreign direct investment prompted by the desire to rationalize international production and to benefit from the common governance of cross-border activities (i.e. *Ot* advantages). The eclectic paradigm can and does embrace such international production. Second, and related to the first, Kojima largely ignores the essential characteristic of MNE activity – that is, the internalization of intermediate product markets – and where he does take this into account, he always seems to assume that the resulting allocation of resources is less desirable than that which would have been dictated by the market (Kojima, 1978, Ch. 9). This is because Kojima is locked into a neoclassical paradigm of perfect competition which negates the very possibility of market failure. In his scenario, the MNE can *never* be the most efficient agent for transferring resources across national boundaries, simply because its very existence implies a second best transactional situation.

Again, this does not seem to be of much practical value to governments in their formulation of policy towards MNEs. Firms do not exist in a riskless or timeless vacuum; many individual transactions do give rise to external costs or benefits; the exploitation of economies of scale may not be possible without the presence of some structural market distortion; some product differentiation may be desirable; and some property rights may require at least temporary protection against their infringement or dissipation, if they are supplied at all.[24] The question at issue is surely that, *given the viable alternatives and over an appropriate time period*, can the resource allocation between countries be improved by FDI or the operation of MNEs?

Empirically, the alleged dichotomy between the patterns of Japanese and US direct investment is a false one. As Mason (1980) has well argued, such differences as do exist reflect the different stages in the evolution of Japanese and

US MNEs as much as anything else. The eclectic paradigm would suggest that, in a world free of trade restrictions, the initial act of foreign direct investment would normally occur in those sectors which use intermediate products in which the investing country has a comparative advantage. This act would be welfare creating wherever the price charged for the intermediate output fairly reflected its social opportunity cost, and the resources released within the home country are deployed in a way consistent with the principle of comparative advantage. We would accept that most Japanese foreign investment of the 1960s and 1970s was of this kind. However, as firms become more multinational and take a more global perspective of their foreign operations, their ownership advantages become less based on the exclusive possession of particular intangible assets, which are country specific in origin, and more on their ability successfully to co-ordinate and manage a network of geographical activities. These transaction costs minimizing advantages – which tend to be firm rather than country specific in origin – were largely the property of the larger US and European MNEs in the 1960s and 1970s; only now, in the later 1980s, are they beginning to be exploited by their Japanese counterparts.

A RESTATEMENT OF THE ECLECTIC PARADIGM

So much for some of the criticisms of the eclectic paradigm. In consideration of these, and on further reflection, we are now fully persuaded that any holistic theory of international production must draw upon two inter-related strands of economic analysis. The first is the neoclassical theory of factor endowments, extended to embrace intermediate products, and to allow for the possibility that some endowments are mobile across national boundaries. *Ceteris paribus*, the more uneven the geographical distribution of factor endowments, the more international production is likely to take place. The nature of such production will resemble that of HOS trade in that it is inter-industry in character. The second strand is the theory of market failure, which is relevant to explaining not only the location of some kinds of economic activity across national boundaries, but also the division of that activity between multinational and uninational firms.[25] *Ceteris paribus*, the higher the transaction costs of using the market as a transactional mode, and the greater the efficiency of MNEs as co-ordinators of geographically dispersed activities, the more international production is likely to take place. Such production may be either inter- or intra-industry in character; but that based on *Ot* advantages alone is more likely to be of the latter kind.

In Figure 7.1, we set out the relationship between these two intellectual strands and the analytical constructs set out in this paper. We believe this figure is self-explanatory and needs no further elaboration. Table 7.1 illustrates the relevance of these two basic elements of the eclectic paradigm in explaining the three main kinds of international production. We would also reiterate an earlier observation, that as an enterprise develops a network of foreign affiliates, which it treats as part of a global system of activities, the relative importance of factor endowments in explaining changes in international production is likely to decrease, and that of market failure likely to increase.[26]

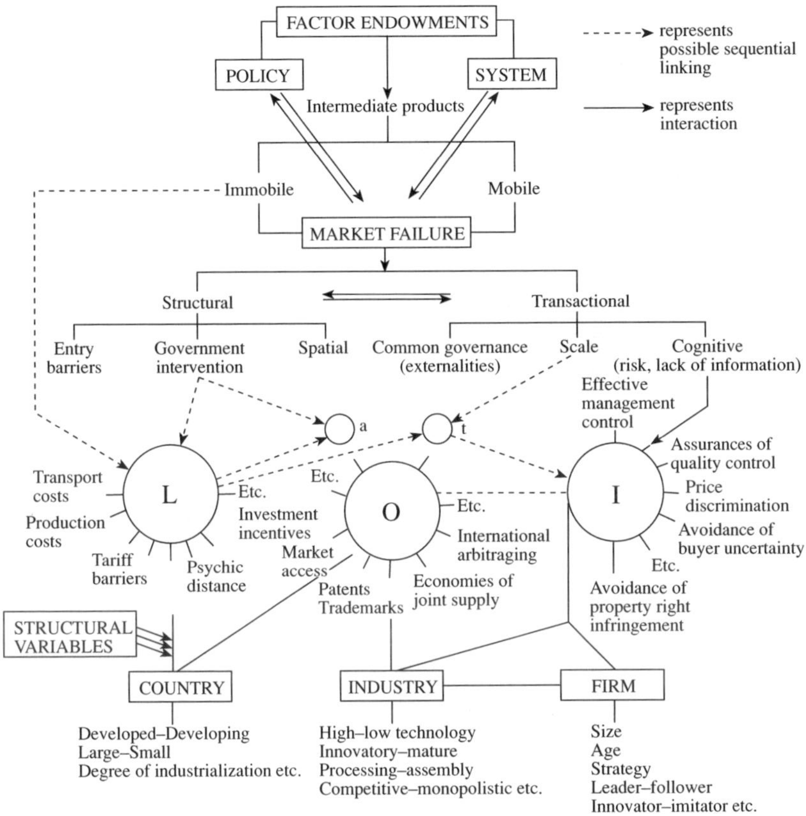

Figure 7.1 The endowment/market-failure paradigm of international production

SOME POSSIBLE EXTENSIONS OF THE ECLECTIC PARADIGM

It is our contention that the eclectic paradigm provides a rich and robust framework not only for analysing and explaining the determinants of interna-

Table 7.1 Illustration of the use of factor-endowment/market-failure paradigm in explaining three main forms of international production

Main types of international production	Factor endowments (affecting geographical distribution of *L*)	Market failure	
		Structural (affecting *L* and *Oa*)	Transactional (affecting *Ot*, *L* and *I*)
1 Market seeking (import substituting)	Home country for creation of *Oa* (= mobile endowments/intermediate products) Host country advantage in immobile endowments with which *Oa* have to be used, e.g. natural resources, some kinds of labour Market size and character	Firm specific = proprietary *Oa* (e.g. knowledge) Privileged access to inputs Restrictions on trade in goods (a) natural (transport costs) (b) artificial (import controls) Oligopolistic market structure	Search and negotiating costs Protection against misrepresentation or infringement of property rights Economics of bulk purchasing Part of international portfolio to spread risks Protection against actions of competitors
2 Resource seeking (supply oriented)	Home country (as above but also market size and character) Host country. Availability of resources, natural, labour (export processing), technology (e.g. investment by IDES in DCS)	As above, but also privileged access to markets Incentives offered by governments to FDI (also relevant for 1 and 3) Oligopolistic market structure	Avoidance of risks of breach of contract and interruption of supplies Absence of future markets Economies of vertical integration
3 Efficiency seeking (rationalized investment)	Vertical Mainly as 1 and 2 above Horizontal Usually distribution of factor endowments not very relevant, as international production in countries with similar resource structures Lateral Of limited importance in effect	As above but investment influenced more by supply than market considerations Government induced structural imperfections likely to be of considerable importance, e.g. tax differentials, investment incentives, performance requirements etc. Note that, as above, regional integration and reduction of trade barriers aid rationalized investment	As with 2, above Economies of scale and scope Risk reduction through product diversification As above, but in respect of ancillary activities, e.g. various services – shipping, consultancy etc.

tional production and how this varies between firms, industries, and countries, and over time, but also for our understanding of a wide variety of other MNE-related issues. In this section, we illustrate six possible directions in which work on the paradigm might be further developed.

A More Formal Modelling of the Paradigm

There is need for a more systematic and rigorous modelling of the explanation of different types of international production by the use of specifically and operationally testable *OLI* parameters.[27] Given these types, the variations within them may be explained by structural variables as identified by empirical research.[28] Some work by trade economists, notably Ethier (1986), Markusen (1984) and Helpman (1984), is currently proceeding in this direction. There is also need for formal modelling of the MNE as an organizational mechanism and/or choice of modality of resource transfer. Again some progress has been made by Grosse (1985), Casson (1985) and Horstman and Markusen (1986, 1987), but more work requires to be done. Finally, there is need for a more systemic approach to examining the strategic behaviour of MNEs (using, for example, such tools as game-theoretic and network analysis).

Dynamic and Development Aspects of International Production

Some commentators, e.g. Vernon (1985), have alleged that the eclectic paradigm is couched in static terms and is unable to explain the dynamics or the process of change of international production. Dynamics can be interpreted and modelled in various ways; Vernon's particular concern is that the eclectic paradigm fails to allow for the behavioural interaction between international oligopolists, which both affects and is affected by their foreign activities. In other words, faced with the same set of *OLI* parameters, not only would the response of MNE vary according to their strategic postures, but this response might also trigger reactions on the part of their competitors, which themselves may cause a change in one or other of these parameters. In the real world of uncertainty about future markets, the actions of government, the conduct of competitors, suppliers, consumers and labour unions, firms – and particularly those which are geographically or industrially diversified – have a variety of strategic options, simply because they do not know with certainty what is their best option. This is a very different scenario from the one assumed by the neoclassical models, where, once the value of the relevant parameters is known, the first best solution is both identifiable and assumed always to be adopted by firms.

The literature identifies various factors likely to influence the strategy of MNEs towards their foreign operations. These include the structure of their existing investment portfolios and risk exposures, their competitive strengths and weaknesses, their bargaining power with governments, their product portfolios, their liquidity position and so on. However, these are, at best, partial behavioural explanations. The crucial question is whether a general theory of business strategy can be devised which can be used alongside the eclectic paradigm to explain the actions of MNEs in a dynamic situation. Perhaps the best hope for progress here lies in some of the concepts in industrial organization theory, e.g. that of dynamic market contestability;[29] and for the transactional model itself to embrace the type of market failure inherent in interactive behavioural situations.

A somewhat different, but nonetheless related, interpretation of dynamics might suggest that the eclectic paradigm should embrace the economics of entrepreneurship and technological innovation and change. Mark Casson (1986a) has forcefully argued that any satisfactory explanation of the dynamics of ownership advantage must rest on the reinstatement of the role of the entrepreneur to a central position in the theory of the firm. Like Casson, Cantwell (1986) and Dunning and Cantwell (1986) view the economy as an evolutionary system, and have applied the eclectic paradigm to analyse the way in which MNEs both generate and respond to technological change. Business historians, too, are making a useful contribution to our understanding of the growth of individual MNEs, especially using a transaction-cost approach (Nicholas, 1986).

Viewing growth and development from the perspective of countries rather than firms, more progress has been made, using mainly the tools of the development economist. Here, the concept of an investment development path or cycle, as first set out by this author in 1979, and subsequently modified and presented in Chapter 6, is especially relevant.[30]

The basic hypothesis of the investment development path or cycle is that a country's propensity to engage in outward direct investment, or be invested in by foreign firms, will vary according to (1) its stage of economic development, (2) the structure of its factor endowments and markets, (3) its political and economic systems, and (4) the nature and extent of market failure in the transaction of intermediate products across national boundaries. It suggests that, as a country's economic development proceeds, its international direct investment position will pass through a number of stages. In the first stage, there will be neither inward nor outward MNE activity, partly because its markets and factor endowments are insufficient to attract either import substituting or resource-based inward investment; and partly because its political, commercial and technological infrastructure is unable to generate the kind of support services required by foreign direct investors (or, for that matter, by indigenous firms engaged in similar activities). As the infrastructure improves, then, depending on the economic structure of the country and government policy, intermediate products will start to be imported; however, because of the high transaction costs of using external markets, these will tend to be internalized by the foreign suppliers. In this first stage of inward investment, the ownership advantages of MNEs are more likely to derive from the possession of individual intangible assets (*Oa*) (*vis-à-vis* those of indigenous firms), rather than on the economies of co-ordinating multiple activities (*Ot*), but this will partly depend on whether the MNE already has related investments in other countries and the extent of its intra-firm trade.

The third stage of development is marked by the ability of a developing country's firms to generate their own ownership-specific advantages, which, initially at least, are likely to reflect the structure of the country's factor endowments. Depending on the nature of these advantages, the relative attractions of a foreign location, and their strategic priorities, these firms may go abroad as market or resource seekers. However, whereas in their early ventures abroad firms from industrialized countries normally sought natural resources and low-cost labour, in which their home country was disadvantaged, those from developing countries are currently seeking to acquire technology (i.e. the resource in which they are comparatively poorly endowed).[31] Alternatively, developing countries may export the kind of intermediate products which require endowments in which they have comparative advantage; in the case of South Korea, Turkey and the Philippines, for example, this has sometimes involved the export of unskilled labour services – notably of construction workers – an intermediate product traditionally thought to be immobile across frontiers.

It should be noted that the point at which a country reaches the third stage of the investment development cycle – if indeed it is reached at all – rests largely on the structure of its resource endowments, and the attitudes of its government towards international economic involvement in general, and inward and outward direct investment in particular.[32] A country such as India, with its sights set on industrial self-sufficiency, might well prefer to indigenize activities initially undertaken by foreign affiliates rather than participate in an international division of labour in which its own firms become foreign investors. By contrast, economies such as Singapore, Hong Kong and Taiwan would seem to favour building up a comparative advantage in the production of intermediate products, which, in part at least, may best be used in conjunction with immobile resources in other countries, while, at the same time, they seek to foster inward investment in activities which require immobile resources in which they are evolving (e.g. via appropriate education, training and innovating policies) a comparative advantage.

The fourth stage of the investment development cycle occurs when a country becomes a net outward investor. Since, by definition, the outward capital stock or investment flows of all countries must equal the inward capital stock or investment flows of all countries, it follows that, at a given moment of time, only some countries can be *net* outward investors. Therefore, any correlation between net outward investment and economic development can only hold good when making cross-country comparisons. Using time-series data, the correlation may be positive for some countries but not for others. This problem, however, may be overcome by normalizing the per capita income of particular countries by the average per capita for all countries.

But how far can the eclectic paradigm predict *which* countries will become net outward investors, and/or the point on the investment development cycle that this will occur? And how far can it explain the *reduction* in the net outward investment position of some high (and rising) income countries, e.g. the USA, in recent years? The answers lie in the changing international distribution of factor endowments, especially those which are transferable across national frontiers, and in the changing efficacy of hierarchies and markets as transnational modes. As a general hypothesis, the less evenly assets (which help produce mobile intermediate products) are distributed across national boundaries, and the greater the transactional failure of markets in these products, the wider will be the dispersion of the net outward investment position of countries (around a zero net outward investment position).[33] The more evenly resources are distributed, and the less the transactional market failure, the narrower the dispersion in the net outward investment position of countries is likely to be.

The gradual convergence of per capita income levels and the economic structure of the advanced industrialized economies, together with some harmonization of government policies, are making for more symmetrical trans-border direct investment patterns. The phenomenon is associated with the growth of intra-industry production. Like intra-industry trade, such production reflects less the disposition of factor endowments and more the advantages of scale economies in production and marketing, together with differences in consumer tastes between countries (although, *within* some sectors, e.g. consumer electronics, there may continue to be some international division of labour based on the distribution of country-specific endowments).[34] Like inter-industry production it sometimes replaces trade (e.g. where it is prompted by import restrictions), and sometimes complements, or changes the pattern of, trade (e.g. where there is specialization of products or production processes in different locations). Again in this latter case, the competitive advantages of the participating firms are less those of the rent-seeking kind, and more those which arise from the common oversight of complementary assets. The fact, too, that intra-industry production is largely in the hands of large and diversified multinational oligopolists adds further to this likelihood.

The case of Japan is a particularly interesting application of the investment development path, in spite of (or perhaps because of) the fact that intervention by the Japanese government deliberately curtailed the role of inward investment for most of the second stage of the cycle. In terms of the *OLI* paradigm, Japan initially disallowed the internalization of most intermediate products (especially technology) markets by foreign MNEs; instead, it acquired these products in other ways, or promoted their indigenous production. This process continued until the Japanese economy had evolved a strong indigenous technological capability, and its firms distinctive ownership advantages in world markets. At the same time, and partly as a consequence of this process, Japan's locational attractions began to change. Rising real wages reduced the competitive edge of its unit labour costs; technology-intensive and material-saving activities became comparatively more attractive. The net result of these changes was that Japan both needed to export mobile resources and intermediate products to help to relocate the kind of production which required immobile resources in which her comparative advantage was falling, and to import mobile resources and intermediate products which could be used with immobile resources in which her comparative advantage was rising. But, for its own firms to become multinational, it also had to accept the presence of foreign MNEs. Moreover, the type of mobile resources it required were often not forthcoming via the non-equity route; in consequence, over the years, Japanese policy towards inward direct investment has been liberalized.

In the mid-1980s, Japan entered the fifth stage of the development cycle.[35] This point is reached where two things happen. First the ownership-specific advantages of a country's MNEs become more *firm* specific (i.e. of a transaction cost minimizing kind) and less *country* specific (i.e. asset based); and second, the locational decisions by both foreign and domestic MNEs become less based on the comparative advantage of factor endowments, and more on the strategies of competitors supplying regional or global markets, the desire to fully exploit the economies of large scale production, the need to reduce market instabilities and uncertainty, and the incentive to reap the gains from integrating related activities over space. To these features another may be added, which rests less on the development stage of a country, and more on its economic position *vis-à-vis* that of other countries. Here, the proposition is that as countries converge in their income levels and economic structures, the more symmetrical cross-investment flows are likely to be. The relatively faster growth of European and Japanese direct investment in the US than of US direct investment in Europe and Japan in the 1970s and the early 1980s lends support to this proposition; while the dramatic improvement of US economic performance in the mid-1980s, the accelerated path of technological advance, and the realities of global competition are causing a resurgence of foreign activity by US MNEs.

The fact that Japanese participation in European and US manufacturing industry is currently growing very quickly, and especially in those sectors, e.g. electronics and motor vehicles, which tend to be dominated by MNEs, and that European and US firms in similar industries are forming alliances with the Japanese in their home markets (Ohmae, 1985), suggests that the structure of Japanese outward direct investment is now increasingly resembling that of US and European countries. And, indeed, it may be reasonably predicted that as the Japanese economy becomes an increasingly high-wage and technology intensive economy, yet more internationally oriented, the character of Japanese MNEs will change in two ways. First, a higher proportion of their investments will be directed to the developed world and be within similar sectors to those invested in by foreign companies in Japan. Second, their competitive strengths will come to depend more on their ability to operate successfully a global network of inter-related activities than on the favoured possession of particular assets. At the same time, while there is some suggestion (Dunning, 1986) that Japanese manufacturing MNEs are currently concentrating their high-value activities in their home plants, a need to tap and monitor the latest technological advances in such sectors as biotechnology and telematics is encouraging these same MNEs to set up (or share with local firms) research, development and design facilities in Europe and the US (Ohmae, 1985).

Explaining Different Forms of International Economic Involvement

The third direction in which the eclectic paradigm of international production might be extended is for it to incorporate other forms of international business transactions, notably arm's-length trade, joint ventures and non-equity contractual agreements. To date, however, while some progress has been made in embracing the latter two subject areas[36] (indeed, some authors, e.g. Casson, 1986b) would go so far as to argue that the contractual relationship, be it part of an equity or non-equity form of business association, is the key to our understanding of international business involvement), only limited headway has been made in unifying explanations of trade and production.[37] We suggest there are two main reasons for this. The first is that the modern theory of international production derives its analytical framework from the theories of the firm and industrial organization rather than from the theory of international trade; and, implicitly, at least, all tradable activities are assumed to be conducted between independent buyers and sellers.[38] Second, while the latter theory takes as its unit of interest the nation state, the focus of interest of students of the MNE is the firm, or group of firms.

It is true that several of the modern theories of trade – particularly those designed to explain intra-industry transactions – explicitly acknowledge the role of market imperfections as determining factors; but the emphasis of interest is strongly directed to structural rather than transactional imperfections (Krugman, 1981, 1983). Much of neotechnology and monopolistic competitive trade may be explained by the spatial distribution of resources which gave rise to ownership-specific advantages, but which are used by firms in conjunction with immobile resources located in the *home* country. When a firm goes abroad, it exports these intangible assets or their rights, and uses them in conjunction with foreign resources which it can obtain at lower cost than at home. However, the implications of transactional market failure which make for the common ownership of assets across national boundaries and which, in turn, may impinge on the trading competitiveness of firms, have been largely neglected by trade theorists. It is here where an integrated approach to international production and trade offers particular promise.

Historically, there are many parallels in the way in which the patterns of trade and international production have evolved. To start with, most trade was inter-sectoral and largely explainable by the international distribution of factor endowments. Likewise, as we have already suggested, although an element of market failure is necessary to explain the ownership of international production, its structure and location initially follow the dictates of the HOS paradigm as applied to intermediate products. Later, as trade became more intra-sectoral, new explanations were sought and found (Grubel and Lloyd, 1975; Tharakan, 1984). Intra-sectoral production also possesses many of the attributes of intra-industry trade, but with additional market imperfections (notably those which are unique to the common ownership of assets in different countries and the internalization of trade in intermediate products). Moreover, unlike intra-industry trade, intra-industry production implies intra-*firm* trade as well. Indeed, the ability of a firm to trade internally may itself afford that firm certain advantages over its competitors (e.g. the possibility of gains from specialized sourcing or transfer price manipulation). It is not, then, surprising that the more multinational a firm becomes, the more it is inclined to engage in internalized trade (Dunning and Pearce, 1985).

The economic theory of intra-firm trade, and how it differs from inter-firm trade, is now beginning to receive some attention in the literature, but again, mostly by scholars interested in the organization of transactions, rather than transactions *per se*. Normatively, in so far as intra-firm trade is market replacing, it has been viewed with some suspicion by welfare economists; and is commonly perceived as a means through which MNEs manipulate transfer prices in a way inimical to the interests of one or other (or both) of the trading countries. Though the organization of trade *need* not affect its extent, pattern or terms, the country-specific differences in the perceived gains which transfer pricing manipulation may offer may encourage MNEs to locate production in countries in which the gains are thought to be most likely. On the other hand, MNEs may engage in intra-firm international trade for exactly the same reason as domestic firms engage in intra-firm national trade (that is, to internalize the external economies of individual transactions). Whether this benefits or adversely affects the distribution of international economic activity and/or the welfare of the participating countries depends on the nature of the market failure being internalized, the consequences of such internalization, and how the gains or losses resulting from it are distributed. But there is no a priori reason to suppose that intra-firm trade in final goods products is less beneficial to international resource allocation than either *inter*-firm trade conducted in imperfectly competitive markets or *intra*-firm trade in intermediate products.

The fact that an optimal solution (in the Pareto sense) is so difficult to identify is that, because market failure exists, one is forced to compare a number of second best alternatives. Once matters such as the distribution of benefits over time, risk and government intervention enter the equation, one's criteria for judging optimality inevitably become multifaceted. While, in principle, transactions between different parts of a domestic firm pose identical problems, the gains or losses resulting from the transactions are at least contained in that country. In the case of trade within hierarchies across national boundaries, inter-country distributional questions cannot be ignored; just as governments may judge internal allocative efficiency in terms of their own economic and social goals, so they will evaluate the impact of MNEs on the extent and pattern of trade flows.

Before concluding this section, brief reference may be made to one of the fastest growing forms of institutional arrangements: the cross-border non-equity collaborative venture at a product or project level between MNEs, and particularly those operating in the OECD area. These have arisen for a variety of economic and strategic reasons, but as several contributors to a recent symposium on the subject (Contractor and Lorange, 1988) demonstrated, the exploitation of complementary ownership advantages by horizontal or vertical integration is not only consistent with the premises of the eclectic paradigm, but points to a need for broadening its scope to embrace quite specific, and perhaps temporary, international alliances between enterprises as part and parcel of their wider international strategies.

The Locus of Decision-Taking

One subject area, normally considered outside the domain of the economist, but one in which we believe the eclectic paradigm offers a useful conceptual framework, concerns the geographical locus of decision-taking within the MNE. Let us focus on the question why and under what conditions are decisions on the way in which resources are allocated by foreign affiliates of MNEs controlled or influenced by managers located in the parent company?[39] This question may be broken down into the 'where' and 'who' aspects of decision-taking. The former is mainly an issue of locational economics, and concerns the price and efficiency of decision-taking (including support) resources in different countries, and the costs of trans-border inter- and intra-firm transactions (e.g. especially administration and communication costs) in which managers are involved. Here a factor endowment model is the appropriate tool of analysis.

The 'who' aspect may be divided into two components which parallel two questions asked earlier in this chapter: 'Why does an MNE undertake production in a foreign country rather than an indigenous firm in that country?' and 'Why does an MNE choose to internalize the market for the cross-border transfer of intermediate products?' The competitive advantage of centralized decision taking rests in the capacity to take (what are perceived to be) the right decisions for the MNE as a whole. If, for one reason or another, such capacity cannot be efficiently transferred to foreign affiliates – either through the training of local managers or by exporting expatriates – then the decision-taking resources will be located in the home country. Clearly, the more the specificity, idiosyncrasy or non-codifiable nature of information and related managerial assets, the more difficult it is to ensure an efficient use of them in a foreign affiliate, while the greater the advantages of scale economies or benefits of centralized decision taking which accrue to the MNE *in toto*, the less likely decision taking is to be delegated. On the other hand, the more decisions require to be customized to local needs, or depend on indigenous support facilities and expertise for their efficient execution, e.g. with respect to personnel management, industrial relations, distribution and public relations, the more likely they are to be decentralized.

But, even assuming there is capacity in the host country to assimilate the transfer of ownership-specific advantages, unless there is a mutuality of interests between managers at headquarters and their agents in the affiliates, decision taking may still be centralized. When might this occur? Two possibilities arise. The first is wherever, as a consequence of the actions of an affiliate, there are costs and benefits which accrue to the *rest* of the organization of which it is part; and the second is where there is a different perception of objectives and/or risks by local and central management. Take a simple example. Suppose a US MNE operates two manufacturing plants, one in the US and the other in France. Assume the aim of each is to maximize local profits, and that each acts as an independent decision-taking unit. Then, as long as the locational advantages favour the siting of managerial resources in France, and these resources are efficiently used, decisions will be decentralized. Now suppose the parent plant adopts a new strategy aimed at maximizing *group profits*. To do so, it *may* need (and the situation is comparable to a takeover by one firm of another) to centralize decisions so as both to rationalize resource allocation and to capture any benefits external to either of the production units but internal to the organization as a whole. In this way, by centralizing decision taking, the MNE is undergoing a hierarchical process very similar to that which follows the internalization of intermediate product markets.

Using the *OLI* framework, then, it may be possible to construct an economic theory of the locus of decision taking (and as a variant of this, within a location, the nationality of the decision-taker).[40] The hypothesis is that decision taking will be more centralized (1) the greater the uniqueness, specificity and non-codifiable nature of decision-taking advantages emanating from the home country; (2) the greater the likelihood of a conflict of interests between the parent company and the subsidiary, with respect especially to (a) risk perception and (b) externalities; and (3) the more the locational costs of decision-taking resources favour the home country, which might reflect both difficulties in transferring management attitudes and practices, and the price of management and management-related services.

These elements will clearly vary according to *country-*, *industry-* and *firm-*specific factors, and also according to the decision-taking functions. The tendency to centralize decisions relating to research and development, capital budgeting and accounting methods, but to decentralize those relating to personnel matters and sourcing arrangements might be explained in these terms. Some illustrations of the use of this approach are contained in Dunning (1986b), which examines the locus of decision taking as between US parent companies and their UK subsidiaries in the 1950s and their Japanese counterparts in the 1980s.[41]

Divestment by MNEs

A fifth possible area for further study relates to our understanding of divestment or a reduction of foreign production by MNEs. Some progress along these lines has been made by Boddewyn (1979, 1983) and Casson (1986c), but, by and large, the literature has so far treated divestment as a discrete act of asset disposal (i.e. the reverse of acquisition) rather than part and parcel of a continual reappraisal of the amount and disposition of the assets a firm wishes to hold. The process of a reduction or disintegration of foreign production is different from an initial act of entry in two ways. First, it requires the absence of only one of the three *OLI* variables, and second, there may be certain barriers to exit which do not correspond to barriers to entry.[42]

Using the 'Mark 2' version of the eclectic paradigm set out earlier in this chapter, we might predict that MNEs would wish to reduce their presence in a particular country or sector under two circumstances. First, where a change in the distribution of factor endowments (or the efficiency with which these are used) (1) weakens their competitive advantages relative to those of firms in host countries, or (2) causes them to switch production from the host to home (or indeed, other host) countries.[43] Second, where the net transactional benefits (costs) of using the external markets for the exploitation of these competitive advantages increase (fall) *relative* to those offered by administered hierarchies.[44]

As a starting point for an integrated approach to an understanding of changes in interactional production, let us assume that, once a firm is established abroad, its sequential investment decisions are organically related to the size and pattern of its existing investments; and to its views about (a) its existing, and likely future competitive strengths and weaknesses, (b) its expectations about technological and market opportunities, and (c) its perception of its competitors' reactions to (a) and (b). In a dynamic situation, this is likely to result in a continual reassessment, relocation and reorganization of its activities. As a firm's competitive position changes; as new core skills replace existing ones; as new management strategies evolve; as new markets open up and others die; and as the balance of advantage between using internal and external markets shifts, so will the level and structure of its international production. Although in some cases, this may lead to a divestment of the entire foreign assets of a firm, more often, it will result in a restructuring of its portfolio, with a sale of assets in some countries or sectors helping to finance an increase of assets in others. Integration and disintegration within MNEs often go hand in hand, just as do the birth and death of firms.[45]

The realignment of the *OLI* advantages of the leading international investors in the last two decades provides ample confirmation of the relevance of the factor endowment component of the eclectic paradigm. The emergence of Japan as a significant international investor has resulted in a fall of the share of US and European MNEs in several industrial sectors, notably automobiles and consumer electronics. The growth of offshore manufacturing in some developing countries in the 1970s to take advantage of an apparently changing international division of labour helped accelerate the decline of labour-intensive domestic sectors (both of multinational and uninational companies) in developed countries. However, recent technological advances, while placing a premium on skilled labour, have at the same time reduced the significance of labour costs in many manufacturing processes. This has resulted in a return home of these activities.[46] Within some of the more rapidly developing industrializing developing countries, e.g. South Korea, Taiwan and Singapore, one has also seen divestment in low value-added and new investment in high value-added activities. In some primary sectors, mainly at the insistence of host governments, one has witnessed a market decline in inward investment; in others, and particularly in some service industries, domestic and/or international vertical integration has sharply increased. Just as the volume and pattern of trade of a firm or country is affected by changes in the distribution of factor endowments, so will that of international production.

The question of the changing *ownership* of assets in particular countries is, perhaps, more interesting. Why should MNEs sell assets and acquire others? Clearly, changes in the relative transaction costs of individual capital and foreign exchange markets (not least those reflecting new uncertainties about interest and exchange rates) will cause MNEs to reappraise their international financial portfolios. But what about long-term real forces? The answer must be that, where incentives for the direct investment are reduced or advantages of common governance disappear, so divestment will occur, *providing* that the exit costs, which themselves involve transaction costs, do not outweigh the savings of using the market. The transaction costs of exit require further study, but anything which reduces the risk and uncertainty of external markets, lessens the importance of scale economies in production, or reduces the externalities particular transactions will make for divestment.[47]

This shifting of the balance of advantages of hierarchies and external markets as cross-border transactional vehicles, together with the emergence of new contractual arrangements which possess some of the characteristics of each (Oman, 1984; Casson, 1986b), has led to frequent realignments of the functions and boundaries of MNEs. While vertical integration has noticeably increased in some sectors (e.g. vehicles and electronics) and fallen in others (e.g. hotels and shipping),[48] the general trend has been towards new collaborative arrangements built around a group of core technologies. This has elsewhere been termed quasi-integration (Contractor and Lorange, 1988). At the same time, technological and organizational advances have increasingly linked investment in services with investment in goods; the information industry is a classic example. In secondary industry, new alliances between firms along the value-added chain have been fostered to exploit complementary technologies, and to the link of computer aided design of components with that of later manufacturing processes (Hayes and Wheelwright, 1984). On the other hand, the sizeable amounts of capital involved and the danger of an integrated firm being locked into one particular source of supply increases the risk of internalization.[49]

Similarly, the *raison d'être* of horizontal integration may change as the importance of synergistic ownership advantages shifts with advances in technology and information. The extent of cross-hauling of hierarchical or quasi-hierarchical arrangements in the technologically advanced sectors between the US and Japan is testimony of this. Indeed the growth of global industries, characterized by a substantial amount of intra-industry and intra-firm production and an interlocking network of cross-border alliances, is a feature which industrial organization economists and business strategists are only just starting to get to grips with. But here, too, an organic approach to both divestment and investment by MNEs is required.

The Consequences of MNE Activity

One final area in which the eclectic paradigm can be a useful framework for analysis is in examining the impact of MNE activity on home and host country economic goals. Let us illustrate from the viewpoint of a *host* country.

The argument runs something like this. Inward direct investment is welcomed for the resources and/or access to markets it brings to the recipient country, and the way it may promote the upgrading and better deployment of existing indigenous endowments. The concern over this particular vehicle of importing intermediate products is twofold. First, that because of its strong bargaining power, the investing firm is able to capture an undesirably high share of the value added created by its subsidiary in the host country; and second, that decisions taken about the amount and kind of resources transferred, and about the use of these resources, may yield less benefit to the recipient country than that which might arise from some other pattern of resource allocation.

In the one case, the MNE is regarded as an organizational mechanism by which intermediate products, which are unavailable or costly to produce in the host country, are efficiently acquired and used; in the other, as a vehicle of economic rationalization and economic power, which it may use to promote its global goals in a way which distorts or inhibits the desired disposition of resources by the host country.

The debate over the impact of inward direct investment on host countries is now entering a new phase as markets and production are become increasingly internationalized. Moreover, not only are MNEs taking a global view of their strategies – and view the location attributes of countries from this perspective – but countries, too, are beginning to recognize that their industrial strategies and competitive postures must take on an international dimension. Since the industries which most countries view as strategically desirable are largely dominated by MNEs, it follows that conflict between multinational oligopolies pursuing global economic strategies and countries pursuing domestic political strategies (and both within a changing and increasingly competitive international environment) is inevitable, and, in part, irreconcilable. In the 1950s and 1960s, the interest centred largely on whether the types of resources provided by MNEs were appropriate to needs of recipient countries; and if, compared with alternative routes of acquiring these resources, their benefits exceeded their costs. The current debate is much more to do with the way in which MNEs use their worldwide assets to achieve their long term economic goals; and whether the resulting allocation of activity is consistent with that which the countries in which they operate are seeking to achieve. As a framework for analysing these questions, we believe that the eclectic paradigm has a great deal to offer.

CONCLUSIONS

This chapter has sought to demonstrate that, a decade after its inception, the eclectic paradigm remains a useful and robust general framework for explaining and analysing not only the economic rationale of international production but many organizational and impact issues relating to MNE activity as well. Conceptually, there are close parallels between the main tenets of the paradigm and that of modern theory of business strategy,[50] though neither approach is sufficient to explain the international profile of any particular MNE. It is likely, however, that new theorizing in the next decade will take a different form to that of the last ten years, if for no other reason than that the character and organization of international production are themselves undergoing fundamental change. More especially, we foresee a more systematic effort by trade economists to incorporate transactional market failure into more general theories of international economic involvement, while industrial and business economists are likely to become more interested in the dynamics of the OLI configuration, and its impact on the strategy of individual firms, through such techniques as game theoretic analysis and network models (Johanson and Mattson, 1987a, 1987b). We expect more attention to be paid to the determinants and effects of collaborative ventures now being formed between MNEs from advanced countries (Contractor and Lorange, 1988), and between MNEs and their customers and suppliers.

We foresee a renewed interest in identifying and evaluating the *O* advantages of firms, with a particular focus on entrepreneurship, the ability of management to identify and co-ordinate a range of core skills and assets through a variety of organizational routes, and to promote operational flexibility in a volatile world environment; global marketing networks; the creation and use made of computer-related information and communications technology; and a variety of cross-cultural management-related issues. As Chapter 9 will examine in more detail, we would perceive a gradual interweaving of the approaches of the economist, business analyst and organizational theorist to our understanding of international production, although within these and related disciplines, theorizing and empirical work will become both more technically sophisticated and more policy oriented.

NOTES

1. International production is defined as production financed by foreign direct investment and undertaken by multinational enterprises. The proceeds of the symposium were published under the editorship of Ohlin, Hesselborn and Wijkman (1977).
2. See also pp. 205–7 of this chapter.
3. For a recent review of the literature on intra-industry trade, see Tharakan (1984).
4. For an elaboration of this thesis see Dunning (1988), Ch. 7.
5. As set out in Chapter 2.
6. Dunning (1981b), p. 27.
7. Teece (1983) uses a rather different terminology: *production* and *transaction* advantages.
8. For example as identified by Bain (1956) as monopoly power, product differentiation, absolute cost barriers and government intervention.
9. See, for example, an interesting paper by Buckley (1986) presented to the London meeting of the Academy of International Business in November 1986.
10. See especially Casson (1979), Buckley and Casson (1985), Teece (1981a, 1981b, 1986), Hennart (1982, 1986) and Rugman (1986). The word 'failure' is an unfortunate one as it

implies that there is an alternative transactional mechanism which is superior to the market. This is not necessarily the case.

11. As, for example, occurs in the case of 'natural monopolies' and in industries with high sunk or developmental costs.
12. For example, in the UK, Japanese affiliates dominate the colour TV sector partly because their parent companies prefer this route of entry rather than licensing their competitive advantages to UK producers; but partly, too, because they are more successful at internalizing intermediate product transactions than are their UK counterparts.
13. Another difference between the eclectic and internalization paradigms is that the former seeks to explain the international production of *firms*, not of *a* firm. This means that variables which are exogenous to the behaviour of individual firms, e.g. market structure, may become endogenous when perceived from the viewpoint of a group of firms. This is an important point not always appreciated by scholars of the MNE.
14. We would also accept with Hennart (1982, 1986) that a privileged access to technology or capital may enable a firm to internalize cross-border intermediate product markets. We would, however, suggest that the privileged access *per se* arises because of an *operational* rather than an *organizational* failure of that market, in the sense that it discriminated in favour of particular groups of transactors, rather than it failed as a transactional mode cf. some other mode, e.g. a firm.
15. For a useful distinction between transferable and non-transferable intermediate products, see Lall (1980).
16. For example, it is possible for government intervention to be directed to reducing the transaction costs associated with market failure.
17. The concept of 'created' or 'managed' comparative advantage is gaining strength in the literature (see, e.g. Scott and Lodge, 1985; Teece 1987). It suggests that at a given moment of time, a country's productive assets consist not only of its natural resources (defined in the HOS sense) but the accumulated man-made assets of the past, the way in which these are organized and the attitudes of its people towards wealth creation and distribution, and towards the rest of the world. The literature further suggests that government plays a major role in determining the institutional mechanism of resource allocation, of the pattern of income distribution, and the ideological and work ethos of its population.
18. Sometimes referred to as the environment, systems and policy (ESP) paradigm. See Koopmans and Montias (1971) and Dunning (1981).
19. See, as summarized, for example, by Robock and Simmonds (1983) and Rugman, Lecraw and Booth (1985).
20. See particularly Porter (1985, 1986), Hamel and Prahalad (1987), Lahdenpaa and Ansoff (1987). The difference between the firm-specific variables identified by these scholars and those of their predecessors is that the latter concentrated on the *structural* characteristics of firms (e.g. size, age, product composition etc.) while the former focus on *operational*, i.e. strategic related, characteristics, such as those identified above.
21. It is one of the more irritating characteristics of academic researchers (and the present author is no exception!) that they sometimes invent their own nomenclature for concepts which are familiar under different names to other researchers. Thus Porter's concept of configuration is to all intents and purposes the same as our location advantage; while his co-ordination dimension is similar to those aspects of internalization which relate to the common governance of cross-border value-adding activities. Finally, Porter's competitive advantages make up a major part of what we call ownership advantages. The only difference is that *O* advantages might embrace characteristics of firms which are better described as monopolistic rather than competitive.
22. Some of these were identified by the author when Aliber's thesis (Aliber, 1970) was first put forward (Dunning, 1971). See also more recent criticisms by Gray (1982) and Teece (1986).
23. For a more extended analysis of the differences and similarities between the Kojima and the eclectic and internalization paradigm see Buckley (1983a, 1985) and Gray (1985).
24. Unless the asset is sold outright in the first place.

25. This suggests that economists interested in explaining the international allocation of activity both by firms and countries needed to be versed in modern trade and location theory, industrial organization theory and the theory of the firm and on the way in which each interact with the other. Both Casson (1985) and Norman and Dunning (1985) take up and illustrate this point.
26. See Kogut (1983).
27. A first attempt to do this by use of cluster analysis was made in Dunning (1981), Ch. 5.
28. For example, while it may be possible to identify the major variables influencing all import substitution FDI, there may be additional factors specific to (say) Swedish investment in the Thai car industry.
29. See, for example, some work on these lines by Graham (1986) and Johanson and Mattson (1987a, 1987b).
30. For a full explanation see Chapters 4 and 5 of this volume. The term cycle was used in that it was predicated that a country both started as a zero net outward and, at a later stage in its development, returned to that position when its inward direct investment stake was balanced by its (growing) outward direct investment stake. In retrospect, the term 'path' might have been a better word to describe the process of change in a country's international direct investment position.
31. Hence the acquisition or part acquisition of European and US high technology firms (particularly those in difficult financial straits) by e.g. Indian, Middle Eastern and Chinese firms.
32. The role of government is one of the most idiosyncratic to evaluate. In the 1970s and 1980s for example there have been quite dramatic swings in the policies of individual countries to inward investment, according to the government in power. In so far as it is possible to generalize, the more right wing the ideology of a government is, the more liberal its attitude is likely to be towards inward and outward foreign direct investment and, indeed, to private enterprise as a whole.
33. Most countries are, in fact, negative net outward investors, i.e. net inward investors.
34. For example, MNEs may continue to concentrate their high value, e.g. research and development, activities in countries which have a comparative advantage in the supply of highly trained manpower, while locating the low value-added activities in countries which have a comparative advantage in the supply of low or semi-skilled labour.
35. Not considered in the original version of the theory. For an elaboration see Chapter 5 of this volume.
36. For a review of the literature see Oman (1984) and Buckley and Casson (1985).
37. With some noticeable exceptions, e.g. the work of Hirsch (1976), Gray (1982), Ethier (1986) and Markusen (1986).
38. And no distinction appears to be made between multi-activity and single-activity trading firms.
39. Using managers as a generic term for decision takers.
40. For example, why are most Japanese manufacturing subsidiaries in the UK headed by a Japanese expatriate whereas most US subsidiaries have a UK national as chief executive?
41. See also some interesting work on the structure of decision taking in UK subsidiaries in the 1970s by Young, Hood and Hamill (1985).
42. Porter (1980) identifies six of these: the presence of specialized assets, fixed costs, strategic exit barriers, information constraints, managerial emotions and pride, and government-related barriers.
43. The question of a reduction in foreign production *in toto* and that in a particular country and/or sector needs more careful distinction than it has been given up to now.
44. We use the term net benefits and costs because there are often costs *and* benefits of using both routes for transacting goods and services.
45. It is interesting that there is abundant literature on the theory of the growth of the firm (which, in practice, often occurs as a result of the expansion of *part* of a firm's activities) but very little on the decline of the firm. Yet, particularly in times of rapid technological change, growth and decline are handmaidens to each other.
46. Ohmae (1985) suggests that while labour costs in many developing countries are only one-third of those in developed countries, the direct labour costs in the major competitive manufacturing companies represent less than 10 per cent of total costs. The savings on costs

in producing in developing countries are often more than outweighed by the transport costs between developing and developed countries. Moreover, as real wage costs rise in developing countries, these savings are likely to fall.

47. It is worth emphasizing at this point that internalization is not without its costs and multinationality may bring diseconomies, external to particular affiliates and internal to the MNE.
48. See Casson (1986a, 1986b). In both these latter cases, contractual agreements of one kind or another have enabled the contractor to gain many of the benefits of integration without the costs.
49. For a summary of some interesting work on the integration of information systems in manufacturing see de Meyer and Ferdows (1984). For a general view of changing corporate strategies in a time of technological change see Ergas (1985).
50. As for example set out by Porter (1980, 1985, 1986) and Kogut (1985a). The expression competitive advantage may be interpreted as ownership-specific advantage, while the comparative advantage of countries appears synonymous with our location advantage. While the business strategy approach gives more emphasis to the positioning of firms in the sectors in which they compete, the eclectic paradigm places more stress on the organizational form of transactional relationships.

REFERENCES

Aliber, R.Z. (1983), 'Money, multinationals and sovereigns', in Kindleberger, C.P. and Audresch, D.B. (eds), *The Multinational Corporation in the 1980s*, (Cambridge, MA: MIT Press).

Bain, J. S. (1956), *Barriers to New Competition*, (Cambridge, MA: Harvard University Press).

Boddewyn, J.J. (1979), 'Foreign divestment: magnitude and factors', *Journal of International Business*, **10**, Spring/Summer, 21–7.

Boddewyn, J.J. (1983), 'Foreign divestment theory. Is it the reverse of FDI theory?' *Weltwirtschaftliches Archiv*, **119**, 345–55.

Buckley, P.J. (1983a), 'Macroeconomic versus international business approach to direct foreign investment: a comment on Professor Kojima's interpretation', *Hitosubashi Journal of Economics*, **24**, 95–100.

Buckley, P.J. (1986), *The Limits of Explanation: Tests of the Theory of the Multinational Enterprise*. Paper presented to Academy of International Business Annual Meeting, London, November.

Buckley, P.J. (1987), *The Theory of the Multinational Enterprise* (Uppsala: Acta Universitas Upsalienis; Almqvist and Wiksell International).

Buckley P.J. and Casson, M.C. (1985), *The Economic Theory of the Multinational Enterprise*, (London: Macmillan).

Cantwell, J.A. (1986), *Technological Innovation and International Production in the Industrial World: A Study of the Accumulation of Capital in International Networks*, Ph.D. Thesis, University of Reading.

Casson, M.C. (1979), *Alternatives to the Multinational Enterprise*, (London: Macmillan).

Casson, M.C. (1985), 'The theory of foreign direct investment', in Buckley, P.J. and Casson, M.C. (eds), *The Economic Theory of the Multinational Enterprise*, (London: Macmillan).

Casson, M.C. (1986a), 'General theories of the multinational enterprise: a critical examination', in Hertner, P. and Jones, G. (eds), *Multinationals: Theory and History* (Aldershot and Brookfield, VT: Gower).

Casson, M.C. (1986b), *Alternative Contractual Arrangements for Technology Transfer: New Evidence from Business History*, University of Reading, Discussion Papers in International Investment and Business Studies, no. 95, May.

Casson, M.C. (1986c), 'Foreign divestment and international rationalization: the sale of Chrysler (UK) to Peugeot', in Coyne, J. and Wright, N. (eds), *Divestment and Strategic Change*, (Oxford: Philip Allan).

Casson, M.C. (1987), *The Firm and the Market*, (Oxford: Basil Blackwell).

Contractor, F. and Lorange, P. (1988), *Cooperative Strategies in International Business* (Lexington, MA: D.C. Heath).

Davidson, W.H. (1976), 'Patterns of factor saving innovation in the industrialized world', *European Economic Review*, **8**, 207–17.

Davidson, W.H. and McFeteridge, D.G. (1984), 'International technology transactions and theory of the firm', *Journal of Industrial Economics*, **32**, 253–64.

Davidson, W.H. and McFeteridge, D.G. (1985), 'Key characteristics in the choice of international transfer mode', *Journal of International Business Studies*, **XVI**, Summer, 5–23.

Dunning, J.H. (1981), *International Production and the Multinational Enterprise*, (London: Allen & Unwin).

Dunning, J.H. (1983), 'Market power of the firm and international transfer of technology', *International Journal of Industrial Organisation*, **1**, 333–51.

Dunning, J.H (1986), *Japanese Participation in British Industry*, (London: Croom Helm).

Dunning, J.H. (1988), *Multinationals, Technology and Competitiveness*, (London: Allen & Unwin).

Dunning, J.H. and Cantwell, J.A. (1986), *The Changing Role of Multinational Enterprises in the International Creation, Transfer and Diffusion of Technology*, University of Reading Discussion Papers in International Investment and Business Studies, no. 101, December.

Dunning, J.H. and Pearce, R.D. (1985), *The World's Largest Industrial Enterprises 1962–83*, (Aldershot: Gower).

Dunning, J.H. and Rugman, A. (1985), 'The influence of Hymer's dissertation on theory of foreign direct investment', *American Economic Review*, **75**, May, 228–32.

Edelstein M. (1982), *Overseas Investment in the Age of High-Imperialism: the United Kingdom 1850–1914* (New York: Columbia University Press).

Ergas, H. (1983), 'Corporate strategies in transition', in Jacquemin, A. (ed.), ' *Industrial Policy and International Trade*, (London: Cambridge University Press).

Ethier, W.J. (1986), 'The Multinational Firm', *Quarterly Journal of Economics*, **101**, 806–33.

Flowers, E.B. (1976), 'Oligopolistic reaction in European and Canadian direct investment in the US', *Journal of International Business Studies*, **7**, 43–55.

Franko, L.G. (1976), *The European Multinationals*, (New York: Harper).

Graham, E.M. (1975), *Oligopolistic Imitation and European Direct Investment in the United States*, DBA Dissertation, Harvard University, unpublished.

Graham, E.M. (1978), 'Transatlantic investment by multinational firms: a rivalistic phenomenon', *Journal of Post Keynesian Economics,* **1**, Fall, 82–99.

Graham, E.M. (1986), *Internal Economies, Oligopoly Reaction and Dynamic Contestability in Global Industries: A First Cut at a Synthesis*, mimeo.

Gray, H.P. (1982), 'Towards a unified theory of international trade, international production and direct foreign investment', in Black, J. and Dunning, J.H. (eds), *International Capital Movements*, (London: Macmillan), pp. 58–83.

Gray, H.P. (1985), 'Multinational corporations and global welfare: an extension' of Kojima and Ozawa', *Hitosubashi Journal of Economics*, **26**, December, 125–32.
Grosse, R. (1985), 'An imperfect competition theory of the MNE', *Journal of International Business Studies*, **16**, Spring, 57–80.
Grubel, H.G. and Lloyd, P.J. (1975), *Intra-Industry Trade, the Theory and Measurement of International Trade in Differentiated Products*, (London: Macmillan).
Guisinger, S. (1985), Investment Incentives and Performance Requirements, (New York: Praeger).
Hamel, G. and Prahalad, C.K. (1987), 'Creating global strategic capability', in Hood, N. and Vahlne J. E. (eds), *Strategies in Global Competition*, (Chichester and New York: John Wiley).
Hayes, R.H. and Wheelwright, S.C. (1984), *Restoring our Competitive Edge: Competing through Manufacturing*, (Chichester and New York: John Wiley).
Helpman, E. (1984), 'A simple theory of international trade with multinational corporations', *Journal of Political Economy*, **92**, 451–67.
Hennart, J.F. (1982), *A Theory of Multinational Enterprise*, (Ann Arbor: University of Michigan Press).
Hennart, J.F. (1986), 'What is internalization', *Weltwirtschaftliches Archiv*, **122**, 791–804.
Hirsch, S. (1976), 'An international trade and investment theory of the firm', *Oxford Economic Papers*, **28**, July, 258–70.
Horst, T. (1972a), 'Firm and industry determinants of the decision to invest abroad: an empirical study', *Review of Economics and Statistics*, **54,** August, 258–56.
Horst, T. (1972b), 'The industrial composition of US exports and subsidiary sales to the Canadian market', *American Economic Review*, **62**, March, 37–45.
Horstman, I. and Markusen, J.R. (1986), *Licensing v Direct Investment: A Model of Internalization by the Multinational Enterprise*, University of Western Ontario, mimeo.
Horstman, I. and Markusen, J.R. (1987), 'Strategic investments and the development of multinationals' *International Economic Review*, **28**, 109–21.
Johanson, J. and Mattson, L.G. (1987a), 'Internationalization in industrial systems – a network approach', in Hood, H. and Vahlne, J. E. (eds), *Strategies in Global Competition*, (Chichester and New York: John Wiley).
Johanson, J. and Mattson, L.G. (1987b), 'Interorganizational relations in industrial systems: a network approach compared with a transaction-cost approach', *International studies of Management and Organization*, **xvii**, pp. 34–48.
Kogut, B. (1983), 'Foreign direct investment as a sequential process', in Kindleberger, C.P. and Audretsch, D. (eds), *The Multinational Corporation in the 1980s*, (Cambridge, MA: MIT Press), pp. 38–56.
Kogut, B. (1985a), 'Designing global strategies: corporate and competitive value-added chain', *Sloan Management Review*, **25**, Summer, 15–28.
Kogut, B. (1985b), 'Designing global strategies: profiting from operational flexibility', *Sloan Management Review*, **26,** Fall, 27–38.
Kojima, K. (1978), *Direct Foreign Investment: A Japanese Model of Multinational Business Operations*, London: Croom Helm.
Kojima, K. (1982), 'Macroeconomic versus international business approach to foreign direct investment', *Hitosubashi Journal of Economics*, **23**, 1–19.
Knickerbocker, F.T. (1973), *Oligopolistic Reaction and the Multinational Enterprise*, Cambridge, MA: Harvard University Press.

Koopman, K. and Montias, J.M. (1971), 'On the description and comparison of economic systems', in Eckstein, A. (ed.), *Comparison of Economic Systems*, (California: University of California Press).

Krugman, P.R. (1981), 'Intra-industry specialization and the gains from trade', *Journal of Political Economy*, **89**, 959–73.

Krugman, P.R. (1983), 'The new theories of international trade and the multinational enterprise', in Kindleberger, C.P. and Audretsch, D. (eds), *The Multinational Corporation in the 1980s*. (Cambridge, MA: MIT Press).

Lake, A.W. (1976a), *Foreign Competition and UK Pharmaceutical Industry*, New York: NBER Working Paper 127, March.

Lake, A. (1976b), *Transnational Activity and Market Entry in the Semiconductor Industry*, New York: NBER Working Paper No. 126, March.

Lall, S. (1980), 'Monopolistic advantages and foreign involvement by US manufacturing industry', *Oxford Economic Papers*, **32**, March, 102–22.

Markusen, J.R. (1984), 'Multinationals, multi-plant economies and the gain from trade', *Journal of International Economics*, **16**, 205–16.

Mason, R.H. (1980), 'Comment on Professor Kojima's Japanese type versus American type of technology transfer', *Hitosubashi Journal of Economics*, **20**, 42–52.

Nicholas, S. (1986), 'The theory of multinational enterprise as a transactional mode', in Hertner, P. and Jones, G. (eds), Multinationals; Theory and History, (Aldershot: Gower).

Norman, G. and Dunning, J.H. (1985), 'Intra-industry foreign direct investment: its rationale and trade effects', *Weltwirtschaftliches Archiv*, **120**, 522–40.

Ohlin, B., Hesselborn, P.-O. and Wijkman, P. M. (eds) (1977), *The International Allocation of Economic Activity*, (London: Macmillan).

Ohmae, K. (1985), *Triad Power*, (New York: The Free Press).

Oman, C. (1984), *New Forms of International Investment in Developing Countries*, (Paris, OECD).

Pavitt, K. (1987), 'International patterns of technological accumulation', in Hood, N. and Vahlne, J. E. (eds) *Strategies in Global Competition*, (Chichester and New York: John Wiley).

Porter, M.E. (1980), *Competitive Strategy*, (New York: The Free Press).

Porter, M.E. (1985), *Competitive Advantage*, (New York: The Free Press).

Porter, M. E. (1986), (ed.) *Competition in Global Industries*, (Boston: Harvard Business School Press).

Prahalad, C.K. and Doz, Y.L. (1987), *The Multinational Mission*, (London and New York: The Free Press). '

Robock, S.F. and Simmonds, K. (1983), *International Business and the Multinational Enterprise*, 3rd edn (Homewood, IL: R.D. Irwin).

Rugman, A.M. (1979), *International Diversification and the Multinational Enterprise*, (Lexington, MA: Lexington Books).

Rugman, A.M. (1981), *Inside the Multinationals: The Economics of Internal Markets*, (London: Croom Helm).

Rugman, A.M., Lecraw, D.J. and Booth, L.D. (1985), *International Business: Firm and Environment*, (New York: McGraw Hill).

Stopford, J. (1982), *The World Directory of Multinational Enterprises*, (Basingstoke: Macmillan).

Teece, D.J. (1981a), 'The multinational enterprise: market failure and market power considerations', *Sloan Management Review*, **22**, 3–18.

Teece, D.J. (1981b), 'The market for know-how and the efficient international transfer of technology', *The Annals of the Academy of Political and Social Science*, **458**, 81–96.

Teece, D.J. (1986), 'Transaction cost economics and the multinational enterprise: an assessment', *Journal of Economic Behaviour and Organisation*, **7**, 21–45.

Teece, D.J. (1987), 'Profiting from technological innovation: implications for integration, collaboration, licensing and public policy', in Teece, D.J. (ed.), *The Competitive Challenge*, (Cambridge, MA: Ballinger).

Tharakan, P.K.M. (1984), *The Economics of Intra-Industry Trade*, (Amsterdam: North Holland).

Vernon, R. (1974), 'The location of economic activity', in Dunning, J. H. (ed.), *Economic Analysis and the Multinational Enterprise*, (London: Allen & Unwin), pp. 89–114.

Vernon, R. (1983), 'Organizational and institutional responses to international risk', in Herring, R.J. (ed.), *Managing International Risk*, (Cambridge, MA: Cambridge University Press), pp. 191–216.

Vernon, R. (1985), 'Comment on Chapter, by Dunning, J.H. and Norman, G.', in Erdilek, A.(ed.), *Multinationals as Mutual Invaders*, (London: Croom Helm).

Young, S, Hood, N. and Hamill, J. (1985), *Decision making in Foreign Owned Multinational Subsidiaries in the United Kingdom*, Geneva: ILO Working Paper no. 35.

8. Some historical antecedents to the eclectic paradigm*

INTRODUCTION

This chapter represents an attempt to resolve an apparent paradox in the theory and history of international production. Until recently, most economists have believed that international production was of little importance in the world economy before the Second World War. If this were so, it would explain why it is only in the last two decades that we have seen the emergence of a separate theory of the multinational enterprise (MNE), the major institution through which international production is organized.

However, as has been demonstrated elsewhere (Dunning, 1993), international production was both absolutely and relatively more important before 1914 than at any other time until at least the 1960s. 'Why, then, was it not incorporated into theoretical analysis before 1914? As we mention below, there was some discussion in the literature, around the turn of the century, of international cartels, and of the export of capital in general. Yet this lay largely outside the mainstream of economic thought, in which international production was not treated as an issue worthy of separate attention.

We shall argue that a closer inspection of the theory and history of international production helps us to answer this question. On the historical side, there has been a major shift in the geographical and industrial composition of international production, as well as in the organizational capacities of the MNE, which now make it impossible to treat as a 'special case' of certain more general economic phenomena. On the theoretical side, as illustrated by Table 8.1, the development of neoclassical theory after 1870, at the time when the modern MNE had begun to emerge, meant that most economists treated the firm as a 'black box' which could be subsumed within a general analysis of markets.

One of the strengths of the modern theory of international production is that it enables us to contrast the approach of earlier economists to this topic with more recent views, and thereby to situate each in its historical context. Modern theories of the MNE are comprehensively surveyed by Caves (1982) and Calvet

* Jointly authored with J.A. Cantwell and T.A.B. Corley in P. Hertner and G. Jones et al., *Multinationals, Theory and History*, Farnborough, Hants: Gower Press, 1986, pp. 19–44.

(1980); however, their elements may be summarized within the structure of an eclectic framework as set out in earlier chapters in this volume. This suggests that firms will engage in international production under the following conditions. First, there must be *location* (*L*) advantages to foreign production in a given host country compared with exporting to the host country from the home country. These have to do with the costs of organizing production in different countries, as well as the international structure of wage rates, material costs, taxes, tariffs, and so on. Second, MNEs must have *ownership O* advantages *vis-à-vis* other firms wishing to supply a similar market, which represents a range of competitive strengths that are essential to their continued growth, and ultimately to their survival.

It is helpful to distinguish two categories of *O* advantages. The first are the unique intangible assets possessed by each firm, which consist of new product and process innovations, as well as managerial and marketing skills; these have been called asset or production cost advantages.[1]

The second category of such advantages is generally known as governance or transaction-cost advantages, and these advantages refer essentially to economies of integration within the firm, achieved, that is, through the common ownership of separate value-adding activities. Where these activities are located in more than one country, they may confer additional advantages which are unique to firms engaging in international production. These latter kinds of ownership advantages reflect the ability of firms to exploit market failure. The term *internalization* (*I*) *advantage* embraces the gains arising from co-ordinating the use of complementary assets as well as the benefits of replacing the markets for the first kind of advantage relative, for example, to the licensing of the right of their use within the independent foreign firms.

In terms of the history of economic theory, as set out in Table 8.1, we may try to explain the existence of *L* advantages for a given pattern of international production through the theories of capital movements, trade or location; *O* advantages through the theories of industrial organization, innovation, and the firm; and *I* advantages through theories of the firm and markets. It follows that different schools of economic thought, partly considered by the different historical circumstances surrounding their origins, may be expected to have varying approaches to explaining international production (in so far as they consider it worthy of attention at all).

In the earliest days of the expansion of commerce between the sixteenth and eighteenth centuries, what international production there was followed the trading companies and their associated colonial settlements. At this time, international trade and production was clearly locationally determined, and the theoretical explanation of Adam Smith captured this well, as we describe below. Later economic changes following in the wake of the industrial revolution gave rise to business enterprises founded around ownership and internalization

Table 8.1 Development of the theory of international production

Factors underlying international production: May follow the pattern suggested by the				Location advantages			Ownership advantages	Internalization advantages
Central concerns of period	Main features of international production	Period	Theory of capital movements	Theory of trade	Theory of location	Theory of industrial organization	Theory of innovation	Theory of the firm
International commerce and exchange	Trading companies, especially in colonies	Mercantilist period (16th century–18th century)	Early mercantilists: prohibition on export of money needed to accumulate national wealth Later mercantilists: flow of money regulated by balance of trade	Later mercantilists (Mun): government sponsored stimulation of export industries and carrying trade to accumulate national wealth	Later mercantilists: more expensive industrial manufacturers at home, cheaper raw materials in colonies			
Value, capital accumulation and income distribution	Resource-based especially in dependent territories, manufacture by individual entrepreneurs of expatriate investors	Classical period (1776–1870)	Regulated by differential profit rates Ricardo, J.S. Mill: barriers to international capital movements Hume's specie-flow mechanism equalized money prices	Smith: absolute advantage conditioned by position in development cycle. Manufacturers traded for certain products of land. Free trade ensured profits productively re-invested Ricardo: comparative labour cost. Free trade in wage goods meant higher domestic and continued accumulation	Smith, von Thünen: early consideration of transport costs Smith: advantages of natural circumstances, and acquired advantages through development Ricardo, J.S. Mill: comparative advantages through natural endowments and technological capabilities	Little analysis of market structure or behaviour of firms	Smith: evolutionary view of technological progress with expansion of market Marx: application of science to large-scale manufacture through machine technology. Major and minor innovations incorporated	Marx: concentration and centralization of capital. Hierarchic organization of labour process in firm

Static resource allocation	Emergence of international production as an extension of the domestic activities of firms in resource-based and import-substituting sectors	Neo-classical period (1870–1920)	Regulated by differential interest rates Fisher: human knowledge and physical capital distinguished	Marshall: reciprocal demand. Technology moves to where most appropriately used Heckscher: comparative advantage of relative factor endowments	Weber: industries transport-oriented, labour-oriented (i.e. decentralized or agglomerated in centres)	General assumption of perfect competition. Monopoly due to artificial restrictions	Outside neoclassical tradition: Schumpeter: major (disequilibrating) innovations undertaken by individual entrepreneurs in accordance with expectations	Marshall: 'trees in the forest' varying around representative firm. American institutionalist critics: Veblen: control of large businessmen decisive to direction of modern industry
Markets not perfectly self-adjusting (thus economics of disequilibrium or less than full employment equilibrium): as illustrated by Keynesian demand management and the theory of imperfect competition	Increase in import-substituting investment. Later followed by rise in intra-industry investment, appearance of globally integrated MNE, and increase in joint venture and licensing activity.	Modern period (1920 up to 1950s)	Regulated by differential interest rates Short-term capital movements may be destabilizing	HOS model: factors, movements and trade may be substitutes Later critical models: trade greatest between similarly endowed countries: attempts to explain intra-industry trade	Ohlin: locational factors (e.g. transport costs) strongly influence pattern of interregional and international trade Lösch: firms control spatial markets Hotelling: agglomeration of activities through locational interdependence	Chamberlin, J. Robinson theory of monopolistic, imperfect competition Bain: barriers to entry in concentrated industries Bye: real and financial size	Usher: emphasis on continuous minor technological improvements	Sraffa, Kaldor, E.A.G. Robinson: limits to the size of firm Coase: transaction costs of participating in markets compared with costs of internal co-ordination of activities Plummer: unification of control

advantages. The latter became increasingly important for the establishment of international production as firms matured in their organization of economic activity.

However, while *O*, and to some extent *I*, advantages were known to be critical to business success and failure, purely locational accounts of the aggregate pattern of international trade and production continued to predominate. This is because, until the 1950s, the bulk of international production was organized by developed-country firms in the less-developed world, while the industrial structure of each country's exports was significantly different from the structure of its imports. Moreover, the classical and neoclassical theories of trade assumed that trade took place under conditions of perfect competition, and that in so far as the firm was concerned at all, it was assumed to engage in only a single product or activity (i.e. engaged in no intra-firm transactions). The incorporation of *O* and *I* advantages in theoretical work had to await the massive growth of US foreign direct investment (FDI) in European manufacturing after 1945, based largely on technological ownership advantages, and the spread of globally integrated MNEs across the industrialized countries thereafter. The rapid growth of intra-industry trade between developed countries likewise gave rise to new theories of international trade after 1960.[2] It was only when the *O* and *I* advantages of firms were integrated into the analysis that a distinct theory of international production emerged.

With this in mind we will sketch out what earlier economists had to say about the state of international production in their day. We shall also occasionally show how their reasoning may be related to the modern theory of international production, as a relevant extension or application of their models in today's conditions. After an introductory discussion, three periods will be examined: the period to 1914; from 1914 to 1960; and from 1960 to 1980.

THE EMERGENCE OF THEORY WITH THE GROWTH OF INTERNATIONAL PRODUCTION

Part of the explanation of the divergence between history and theory of international production is that the theory of the firm was little developed before the interwar period. As befitted his time, Adam Smith dealt with individual entrepreneurs rather than corporations, whose activities, he maintained, were co-ordinated through markets. Most economists writing after 1870 adopted an analytical framework which assumed that entrepreneurial and productive activity depended upon the conditions of market co-ordination. They therefore chose to ignore the growing importance of the direct co-ordination of economic activities by firms without the intermediation of markets.

Others, such as Marshall, despite their awareness of institutional facts, did not seem to believe the international firm worthy of separate theoretical consideration. Technology transfer within the firm was probably seen as a special case of general international technology transfer. British economists especially regarded outward direct investment as an extension of domestic economic activity: a highly ethnocentric attitude, but an understandable one as the British colonies accounted for a good proportion of such investment before 1914, where the interests of investing countries and firms were assumed to coincide (Svedberg, 1981). As Archer (1986) and Dunning and Archer (1987) have shown, many UK companies confined their overseas investments to the dominions prior to 1914, and it was only in the 1960s that they made the transition to the more diverse range of experience across quite disparate countries and markets.

British economists in particular, unlike the American institutionalists, chose to neglect the more rapid development of corporate structures in the US, which, together with Germany, had, by the turn of the century, become the home of a new group of dynamic industries and companies (Chandler, 1977). Moreover, although the USA was more resource-sufficient than the UK, it had built up a significant stock of foreign direct investment by 1914, and by 1939 the value of its foreign manufacturing subsidiaries' output was twice that of its export of manufactures.

Yet, until the 1920s, no government regularly collected data on direct investment flows or stocks, or on the activities of either their own MNEs or foreign companies in their midst. Official inquiries were only conducted irregularly and limited to obtaining data on the stock of FDI. The US Department of Commerce published its first foreign investment study in 1929, and others followed in 1936, 1940 and 1950. Since 1950 annual figures have been published. Before the Second World War, only Canada published FDI flow data. Not until 1962 did the UK government start to publish a regular series of FDI flows, and only in 1963 were the activities of foreign companies separately identified in the UK Census of Production. As to world-wide data, even as recently as 1960 there was no overall estimate of the amount of foreign direct capital invested globally.

Moreover, theoretical and empirical research is interactive, and governments do not usually go to the trouble and expense of collecting economic data unless they are likely to be useful (e.g. for taxation or planning purposes) or unless the precise extent of the problem (e.g. for a royal commission) needs to be established. Even then, there seems to be a time-lag between new economic problems emerging and serious attention being paid to them. Until economists were obliged to adjust their theoretical frameworks to distinguish international production, empirical evidence on the topic was sparse.

INTERNATIONAL PRODUCTION BEFORE 1914

The Scope of MNE Activity in 1914

Tables 8.2 and 8.3 present our estimates of the value of the outward and inward FDI stocks between 1914 and 1983. Not surprisingly, it was the most developed countries that accounted for the bulk of FDI in 1914. Britain, the USA, Germany and France contributed nearly 87 per cent. As to the recipients, developing countries received about 70 per cent – mainly Latin America, Asia and Russia – but the USA received over 10 per cent; Britain's share of total inward investment was about 1.5 per cent.

Table 8.2 Estimated stock of accumulated foreign direct investment by country of origin, 1914–83

	1914		1938		1960		1973		1983	
	$m	%	$m	%	$bn	%	$bn	%	$bn	%
Developed countries	14 302	100.0	26 350	100.0	62.9	99.0	204.4	97.1	555.2	97.4
North America										
USA	2 652	18.5	7 300	27.7	31.9	48.3	101.3	48.1	227.0	39.6
Canada	150	1.0	700	2.7	2.5	3.8	7.8	3.7	29.1	5.1
Western Europe										
UK	6 500	45.5	10 500	39.8	10.8	16.3	26.9	12.8	95.4	16.7
Germany	1 500	10.5	350	1.3	0.8	1.2	11.9	5.7	40.3	7.0
France	1 750	12.2	2 500	9.5	4.1	6.2	8.8	4.2	29.9	5.2
Belgium					1.3	2.0	2.2	1.0	6.7	1.2
Italy					1.1	1.7	3.2	1.5	9.8	1.7
Netherlands	1 250	8.7	3 500	13.3	7.0	10.6	15.8	7.5	36.5	6.4
Sweden					0.4	0.6	3.0	1.4	10.1	1.8
Switzerland					2.3	3.5	7.2	3.4	19.8	3.5
Other developed countries										
Russia	300	2.1	450	1.7	neg	neg	neg	neg	neg	neg
Japan	200	0.1	750	2.8	0.5	0.8	10.3	4.9	32.2	5.6
Australia					0.2	0.3	0.5	0.2	3.0	0.4
New Zealand	180	1.3	300	1.1	a	a	a	a	a	a
South Africa					a	a	2.1	1.0	6.5	1.1
Other	neg	neg	neg	neg	2.5	3.8	3.4	1.6	9.0	1.2
Developing countries	neg	neg	neg	neg	0.7	1.1	6.1	2.9	17.6	2.6
TOTAL	14 482	100.0	26 350	100.0	66.1	100.0	210.5	100.0	572.8	100.0

Note: a = included in Other.

Sources: as set out in Dunning (1983, pp. 74–5).

Table 8.3 Estimated stock of accumulated foreign direct investment by recipient country or area

	1914		1938		1960		1973		1983	
	$m	%	$m	%	$bn	%	$bn	%	$bn	%
Developed countries	5 235	37.2	8 346	34.3	36.7	67.3	121.3	72.9	416.9	75.5
North America										
USA	1 450	10.3	1 800	7.4	7.6	13.9	17.3	10.4	128.3	23.2
Canada	800	5.7	2 296	9.4	12.9	23.7	27.6	16.8	56.6	10.2
Europe										
Western Europe:	1 100	7.8	1 800	7.4	12.5	22.9	60.8	36.5	197.8	35.8
of which UK	(200)	(1.4)	(700)	(2.9)	(5.0)	(9.2)	(14.8)	(8.9)	(50.2)	(9.1)
Other Europe	1 400	9.9	400	1.6	neg	neg	neg	neg	neg	neg
of which Russia	(1 000)	(7.1)	–	–	–	–	–	–	–	–
Australasia and										
South Africa	450	3.2	1 950	8.0	3.6	6.6	16.7	10.0	–	–
Japan	35	0.2	100	0.4	0.1	0.2	1.3	0.8	4.1	0.7
Developing countries	8 850	62.8	15 969	65.7	17.6	32.3	45.2	27.1	135.6	24.5
Latin America	4 600	32.7	7 481	30.8	8.5	15.6	20.9	12.5	70.0	12.6
Africa	900	6.4	1 799	7.4	3.0	5.5	4.8	2.9	12.1	2.2
Asia	2 950	20.9	6 068	25.0	4.1	7.5	8.0	4.8	39.8	7.2
of which: China	(1 100)	(7.8)	(1 400)	(5.8)	(neg)	(neg)	(neg)	(neg)		
India and Ceylon	(450)	(3.2)	(1 359)	(5.6)	(1.1)	(2.0)				
Southern Europe					0.5	0.9				
Middle East	400	2.8	621	2.6	1.5	2.8				
International and unallocated	neg	neg	n.a.	n.a.	n.a.	n.a.	–	3.9		
TOTAL	14 085	100.0	24 315	100.0	54.5	100.0	166.7	100.0	552.6	100.0

Sources: As set out in Dunning (1983, pp. 74–5).

In this FDI pattern, there were two separate but interlinked strands. The first were mainly resource-based investments, to supply the home country with food and raw materials.[3] Typically, therefore, the host countries were colonial territories: either actual colonies or *de facto* ones such as the 'honorary dominions' of Latin America. Associated investments often took place on infrastructural projects, for example, railroad networks and public utilities. This type of FDI, leading to 'supply-oriented' MNEs, represented by far the greatest type, perhaps as much as 85 per cent, of total FDI in 1914. The second type, leading to 'market-oriented' MNEs, was import-substituting manufacturing investment, usually located in the most developed countries, but also in those on the brink of 'take-off' such as tsarist Russia and the white British dominions. This type became significant only in the period 1870–1914.

Between the 1870s and 1914, large multi-unit enterprises grew up, both in the USA and in Europe. Integrating mass production with mass distribution, they built up a coordinated system of goods flow from raw materials, via production, to the retailer and the final consumer (Chandler, 1977). From the outset, such enterprises were associated with the possession of strong ownership advantages. Import-substituting production abroad was a response to increasingly rigorous tariffs and patent laws, especially in North America, France, Germany and Russia (Chandler, 1977; Wilkins, 1970; Stopford, 1974). International cartel arrangements were also common by the 1900s. By 1914, MNEs, operating in conditions either of intense competition or of collaboration, were prevalent in many parts of the world.

Explanations of FDI by Economists before 1914

Practical men of affairs knew well the extent of MNE activity. Several British works published in 1901–2 on the 'American invasion' pointed out that many leading US firms had set up factories in Britain,[4] while in the USA and continental Europe there was a widespread recognition of the role of FDI in scaling tariff barriers.

However, those economists who did consider the question of FDI before 1914 tended to think of it in terms of colonialist policies.[5] If the home country lacked the primary products concerned, it had to go out and obtain them. The mercantilists (who flourished from the sixteenth to the eighteenth centuries) and the classical economists (from Adam Smith in 1776 to the 1870s) put their analyses in macroeconomic terms; for them, international production would simply have been a special case of the theory of international trade.

Mercantilists

Perhaps the most noteworthy exponent of mercantilism – which proclaimed the doctrine that a favourable balance of trade was essential for a nation's prosperity – was Thomas Mun, a director of the East India Company (Mun, 1664, reprinted in 1928). To him, international production, as for instance undertaken by the trading companies of his time, would help to provide raw materials for the home country and to give work to the domestic labour, which made them up into fashioned goods for export. However, since the mercantilists saw national wealth as being created through international trade rather than production, the activities of trading companies were explained through the pattern of locational advantages of countries, in terms of their export potential. The ability of the companies to conduct such operations arose from the authority of the home country state rather than internally generated ownership advantages.

Adam Smith

Smith's treatment of the macroeconomic locational advantages was a more sophisticated one, and his theory of trade is more interestingly related to modern discussions of international production, once the theory of the firm is taken into account (Smith, 1776). Smith put forward a dynamic theory of domestic and international trade as part of the development or growth process which lay at the root of his analysis. For Adam Smith, as for the mercantilists, trade occurred because of absolute advantages arising from differences in climate, fertility and other natural and acquired location advantages of particular countries (Bloomfield, 1975). However, unlike the mercantilists, as trade was seen to be supportive of the growth of production rather than vice versa, Smith was able to view trade as mutually beneficial to the countries concerned. An undeveloped country was likely to have an advantage in some specific agricultural areas to which its natural endowments could be adapted, while a development cycle led developed countries towards the production of more refined manufactures.

Smith seemed to believe that the development cycle for nations was an extension of that followed within a country, as between the urban and rural areas. A surplus above the subsistence needs of producers first arose in agriculture, and the town afforded a market for this surplus produce; while, through the division of labour, it supplied manufactures for the countryside with a smaller quantity of labour than if they had been produced in the country itself. The emergence of urban areas was also responsible for the appearance of good government and the accumulation of wealth by merchants and manufacturers, who, when under the pressure of competition, were parsimonious by comparison with the prodigal landlords (Rosenberg, 1975). Hence, by redistributing the value of surplus produce, trade assisted in increasing capital accumulation.

Once a country became sufficiently rich and was set on a course of rapid growth, international trade and foreign investment were encouraged by a falling rate of profit arising from a surplus of capital rather than simply a surplus of produce over subsistence needs. In the same way, as the emergence of towns introduced law and good government in the older countries, colonial settlers were able to bring such benefits of experience with them to the newer countries. These might be thought of as *I* advantages at a country level, assisting the agricultural development of colonies through trade and investment, in return for which the colonial power received such goods as tobacco and raw cotton, which could not be produced at home, for its own consumption or re-export. There is also an early consideration of *O* advantages here in that colonists took abroad with them the skills which had earlier been developed in the home country, and applied them on the more spacious fertile land of the colonies (i.e. combined them with the locational advantages of producing abroad).

It was in the interest of the colonies to concentrate their efforts on agriculture, which set a greater productive labour into motion and laid the foundation of lasting improvement in national wealth. Refined manufactures could be imported from the home country, widening its market, furthering the division of labour in manufacturing, and strengthening the capital accumulation of both trading participants.

If Smith's development process is translated into an expansion of firms, it is consistent with Vernon's product-cycle thesis (Vernon, 1966) as firms engage in FDI to take advantage of changing locational advantages offered by countries (e.g. from the US to Europe in the 1960s).[6] It is likewise related to the current Kojima or Ozawa idea of a macroeconomic or trade-creating type of FDI, following what is perceived to be the dynamic comparative advantages of countries (from Japan to South East Asia in the 1970s) (Kojima, 1978, 1982; Ozawa, 1981a, 1981b).

Although Smith's model incorporated only the rudimentary type of international production that existed in his day, its theoretical structure is highly relevant to recent discussions in international economics. The locational aspects of Smith's development cycle can also be linked with a view of dependent development later compassed by Hymer (1972). According to Hymer, the MNE perpetuates an existing state of uneven development by locating its activities in a spatial hierarchy (from the urban centres of the developed countries to the rural less developed countries). This would have received a sympathetic ear from Smith, who 200 years earlier had argued that since merchants and manufacturers were better able to collude than other classes, they might succeed in obtaining an artificially high rate of profit, partly through colonial restrictions on trade, in their interest, which had rendered a potentially beneficial increase in trade 'destructive to several unfortunate countries'. European countries were regarded as being equally hindered if they embarked upon trade, and the foreign activities required to support it, before establishing a firm agricultural base of their own. For this reason, Smith was sceptical of foreign investment, and he poured scorn on what he saw as the economically harmful activities of the chartered trading companies in erecting forts and garrisons which were often unnecessary and sometimes paid for by government subsidies.

However, Smith's formulation of a macroeconomic locational framework for the analysis of international trade deserves reappraisal by contemporary economists, in view of its capacity to accommodate the role of international production once the firm is more explicitly introduced into the discussion.

David Ricardo

Whereas Smith had based his theory of trade on the absolute advantages of countries, and admitted to overseas capital movements, Ricardo rested his on the comparative advantages, and emphasized international factor immobility; or more precisely, he asserted that the emigration of capital or labour was sufficiently limited or 'checked' for the proposition to hold (Ricardo, 1817). Capital owners, he maintained – reasonably in the conditions of 1817 – were loath to take the risk of allowing their capital to go out of their immediate control, and were equally disinclined – should they contemplate accompanying their capital – to forsake their homeland and submit themselves to strange regimes and unfamiliar laws, even with the prospect of more favourable returns.

Unlike the neoclassical economists, Ricardo accepted that comparative advantages might arise from technological differences as well as natural endowments (O'Brien, 1975). However, he assumed that capital and labour moved together; differences arose in overall productivities rather than the varying availability of capital internationally, as in the much later Heckscher–Ohlin–Samuelson model of trade (see below).[7] Like Smith, Ricardo objected to outward investment, fearing untoward consequences for capital accumulation in Britain itself. Relying as he did on Say's law of markets, he could not accept the possibility of excess capital at home.

J.S. Mill

While adhering to the Ricardian international trade theory framework, Mill saw positive benefits for a home country (if relatively advanced) from investment overseas. To him such investment both absorbed part of the increased capital that was the cause of falling domestic profitability, and provided for the home country cheap food and raw materials, thereby increasing opportunities for the lucrative employment of capital at home (Mill, 1848, reprinted 1909). At the same time, he was dismissive of the supposed advantages, put forward by Smith, of extending the market by foreign investment, since he regarded the gains from trade (including enhanced efficiency) as the consequence of receiving imports advantageously in barter terms.

Like Ricardo, Mill assumed some degree of – but not complete – capital immobility. Capital could not move to remote parts of the world as 'readily and for so small an inducement' as to another quarter of the same town: hence the varying rates of profit on capital in different countries. However – writing in 1848 – he accepted that there was already a tendency for capital to be shifted around the world, and as the capital itself became more cosmopolitan, he foresaw customs and institutions would converge, and suspicion of foreigners would diminish. Therefore, he continued, 'both population and capital now move from one of these (more developed) countries to another on much less temptation than heretofore'.

Alfred Marshall

In his unpublished 'Theory of Foreign Trade', which probably dates from the late 1870s, Marshall discussed in realistic terms 'the migration of capitalists in company with their capital'. He cited Bagehot's comment that international capital movements had become one of the greatest instruments of world-wide trade (Stevas, 1978). He also spoke of 'a few prominent cases' where English capitalists had set up branch establishments for making textiles on the continent of Europe, and for iron manufacture in America (Whitaker, 1975). Yet these instances did not lead him to shift his Ricardian views on international trade (Marshall, 1923).

The Role of Ownership and Internalization Advantages in the Thinking of pre-1914 Economists

Some ownership advantages

As shown above, the early classical economists stressed advantages in productive activity at a country or regional level, within which firms as institutions were not differentiated. A possible exception was Cournot, who considered the firm as a centre for planning and decision making. However, with the growing importance of technological change and mass marketing techniques, Marx, Schumpeter and other critics more clearly translated these into ownership advantages at the company level through the competitive adoption by enterprises of innovations and differentiated products.

Clearly, the geographical disposition of immobile resources was still an important factor contributing to international location of economic activity, but by the latter part of the nineteenth century it was no longer the whole explanation. Advantaged foreign firms were motivated to set up production facilities by high tariffs in the USA and continental Europe, and by slow technical progress in Britain after 1870, which laid it open to technologically advanced US firms. In the rapidly industrializing pre-1914 Russia, entrepreneurs, sponsored by interested investors, commissioned home-based scientists and engineers to undertake detailed studies of indigenous industrial techniques in Russia. In contrast with the assumption of the conventional location framework, the factor they looked at was not so much the average profitability of the foreign industry, as what ownership advantages over indigenous competitors could be discovered (McKay, 1970).

The origin of *O* advantages considered by economists before 1914 can be discussed under the headings of innovation and entrepreneurship.

Innovation

In contrast with the disequilibrating theory of Schumpeter, Adam Smith's theory of innovation was an evolutionary one, in which all firms were expanding more or less in line with the total growth of the market. The benign workings of the invisible hand would bring about an adaptation of industrial structure and emerging new technology to the fresh opportunities being created by the extension of the market.

Unlike Smith, Marx was perhaps the first to predict a trend towards the creation of large firms, enjoying ownership advantages based on the application of science in technology, especially machine technology. The motive for innovation he put forward was the social pressure of competition, in a world of rapid technical change; this was in contrast with the later view of Schumpeter, that innovations arose from individual decisions, based on expectations.

The neoclassical period after 1870, with its emphasis on optimization of the use of fixed resource endowments, gave little incentive for exploring the ownership advantages of individual firms. Even Marshall, who for the first time – in mainstream economics – devised a realistic theory of the firm by bringing together supply and demand aspects, did not explore the possibility that better-than-representative firms might possess ownership advantages useful for opening up production overseas to set alongside his strictly locational views.

Entrepreneurship

Like innovation, entrepreneurship is highly relevant to the formation of ownership advantages. Of the entrepreneur's functions, that of innovation was initially set out by Schumpeter in 1911.[8] Those of organization and the bearing of uncertainty had been covered by Say in the early nineteenth century (Koolman, 1971). By contrast, Adam Smith portrays only a rather shadowy entrepreneur, or 'undertaker', in line with his evolutionary process generally.

Internalization advantages

We have to look to Marx and – from a very different perspective – some institutional writers in the USA and Europe for any serious discussion of what we would now call the internalization advantages within the firm. Marx gave a central place to the planning of the firms, mainly through the promotion of technical progress as a means of achieving higher productivity and hence higher profits. Marx was thus addressing the same issues of *I* advantages as did the later Coasian theory of transaction costs, which has become such an integral part of the modern theory of international production.

A classical interpretation of *I* advantages with reference to Marx is presented in Cantwell (1984). Wakefield (1833) was the only earlier classical economist to have insisted that if colonial settlers engaged in subsistence farming rather than combining to produce tradable commodities, then they could not be regarded as expatriate investors, as implicitly suggested by Smith. Marx commended Wakefield on this point for seeing how the internalization of labour markets to create profits required the subordination of the worker to the organizer of production, that is, the entrepreneur (Marx, 1867, reprinted 1959).

Meanwhile, in the USA, the institutionalists were putting forward a rather different view of the capitalist process. Although Veblen (1904) and Mitchell (1913) wrote in this general area, perhaps of greater interest is the contribution of J.R. Commons (1924), whose basic ideas were formulated in the formative years of managerial capitalism. In his *Legal Foundations of Capitalism*, he forcefully took the neoclassical economists to task for neglecting non-market transactions. Although the bulk of his work was descriptive and historical, Commons never ceased to emphasize a holistic approach to the economic activity in general; in this sense, he is a worthy antecedent to Coase, Williamson and Chandler.

On the continent of Europe, the movement in German industry towards concentration and cartels between 1880 and 1910 gave rise to a remarkable series of studies on monopolies and their activities, notably by Liefmann (1897), Levy (1911) and Hilferding (1910). As a precursor to the later literature on the theory of the firm and its transaction cost minimizing functions, there was a lively recognition that, in the pre-1914 developed world, international production was an alternative to the cross-border cartel agreements, and that both, in the words of Levy (1971), 'attempt to draw back the destructive forces of international competition'.

Hilferding (1910) argued that the gradual rise of tariffs would facilitate international cartels as much as FDIs, and especially those cartels based on the allocation of geographical markets and price agreements. These were extensions and/or consortia of national cartels already well established behind protective barriers. This is a valuable argument inasmuch as it relates the spread of international cartels to an increasingly restrictive trading environment in the inter-war years, while noting their absence after 1945 when trade was flourishing.

While Hilferding's general explanation of the export of capital was a traditional locational one of equalizing national rates of profit, he did distinguish between cartels and MNEs, the latter of which, by producing in two protected countries, could earn higher profits than if they exported from just one country under free trade. Liefmann's contribution was to show how international cartels could help prevent dumping and permit overseas firms to penetrate a high tariff country, and in so doing act as imperfect substitutes for international production.

INTERNATIONAL PRODUCTION, 1914–60

The Growth of MNE Activity, 1914–60

The radical changes which took place in the composition of international production during this period were largely confined to its two final decades. In 1938, as Tables 8.2 and 8.3 show, nearly two-thirds of FDI was still being directed to developing countries, and to Latin America and Asia in particular.

By 1960, the share of the world direct capital stock provided by the USA had leapt to 49 per cent, while that of Britain had fallen to 16 per cent. The recipient areas had also changed markedly, with developed countries now accounting for two-thirds of global FDI, due largely to the substantial growth of US manufacturing investment in Canada and Western Europe in the 1950s.

Explanation by Economists

Throughout this period, *O* and *I* advantages were essential to those firms engaged in business activity abroad. However, it was only in the 1950s, when the locational pattern of FDI (and trade) underwent a major shift towards the industrialized world, that it became clearer how these advantages affected not just the fortunes of individual firms, but were an integral part of any general explanation of international production. *O* advantages were obviously crucial in the rise of technology-intensive FDI, which could not be described in purely locational terms. However, until 1960 economists continued to focus on locational factors since it appeared possible to them to treat FDI as a special case of international capital movements.

Locational advantages

The most comprehensive work on international production in the interwar period is to be found in various mainly descriptive studies such as that of Frank Southard (1931), which listed a wide range of locational advantages enjoyed by US firms producing in Europe. At the same time, import restrictions encouraged a good deal of defensive direct investment by US firms in European industry in these years.

The main development in trade theory was the evolution of what became the Heckscher–Ohlin–Samuelson (HOS) model, in which trade is held to arise from the fact that different countries have different factor endowments: countries that are rich in capital will tend to export capital-intensive goods, while those with abundant labour will export labour-intensive goods. For trade to follow this pattern, the Ricardian factor-immobility condition is essential. Yet if we examine the antecedents of the model, namely the separate works of Heckscher (1919), Ohlin (1933) and Stolper and Samuelson (1941), none of them provides a convincing analysis of why international production takes place (as an alternative to trade) in the absence of frictions. In a later work, Ohlin (1977) recognized that the weakness of seeing factor movements across frontiers and trade as simple substitutes – e.g. in the HOS model as developed by Mundell (1957) – is that factor movements alter the pattern of production and trade through time. In that work he acknowledges that he should also have considered differences in technology of the type retained only in certain countries or firms.

Perhaps Ohlin's main contribution to the theory of international production was to expand location theory into the international arena (Ohlin, 1933). J.H. von Thunen, acknowledged to be the father of location theory, evolved his ideas from a similar standpoint to the trade theorist, in seeking to establish where each commodity would be produced with a given distribution of resources (von Thunen, 1876). As in any simple model of import-substituting FDI, he looked at substitution between transport and non-transport costs, so that agricultural goods (on which he concentrated his analysis), which were cheaply cultivated but cost a lot to transport, would be produced close to the market (the town), while goods with high production costs but easy to transport would be produced in more distant locations.

Alfred Weber (1929) generalized that location theory, making allowances for variations in real wages and productivity between locations. Industries could be placed in one of three categories: transport-oriented, labour-oriented and those relying on more integrated operations with agglomerating advantages in the town or centres of activity. In the first two cases, there were decentralizing tendencies, leading to multiple production locations: a vital prerequisite of any international production theory.

A somewhat different perspective to location theory was taken by Hotelling (1929), who postulated that the interdependence of economic agents' activities could influence the pattern of location, and thus create a further motive for Weber's case of the agglomeration of certain types of firm at the centre of a market area. This work is interesting in that it may be regarded as a natural antecedent for later oligopolistic explanations of the MNE, e.g. Knickerbocker (1973).

The firm was brought more specifically into location theory by the market area school, notably by Lösch (1940), who sought to determine the spatial features of a firm's market through a process similar to imperfect or monopolistic competition, but using spatial rather than product differentiation.

Ownership advantages

J.H. Williams was one of the few interwar economists who appeared to recognize the emergence of international production, and the role played by *O* advantages – at least of countries, if not of firms. In his classic article in the *Economic Journal* (Williams, 1929), he cited an 'impressive' array of basic industries, from oil to match manufacture, which had expanded 'in disregard of political frontiers'. He went on to observe that sometimes this projection of one country's economic presence into others took the form of the export of tangible and intangible capital 'along the lines of an industry and its market, as against the obvious alternative of home employment in other lines'. In other cases, the direct investment represented an 'international assembling of capital and management for world enterprises, ramifying into many countries'. He also made the perceptive comment that these enterprises provided very strikingly 'an organic interconnection of international trade, movement of productive factors, transport and market organization'. However, Williams did not attempt to incorporate these ideas into a new theory of international trade organized by firms with ownership advantages.

One of the first economists to recognize the importance of the 'centralized and unified control' of foreign activities by a single firm was Alfred Plummer (1934). His interest was in international trusts which he defined as 'a complete merger and ownership of the constituent undertakings in two or more countries'. In retrospect, however, it is clear that his conception of an international trust was very similar to that of the modern-day multinational enterprise. Some quotations from his work (as recorded by Fieldhouse, 1986) are illuminating.

> International concerns and trusts developed first from the desire to have branches – factories, warehouses and offices – in two or more countries, a line of advance which is no doubt attributable partly to the pressure of heavy import duties and partly to the desire to have a closely controlled unit 'on the spot' making a study of the local market requirements and peculiarities. (Plummer, 1934, p. 26)

and again:

> While one international trust may bring together under unified control a number of existing undertakings, another may begin as a single national undertaking and spread *itself* and its activities out into other countries. This type of international business does not have to achieve unified control for control is unified from the beginning, but it has to create its foreign undertakings before it can control them. (Plummer, 1934, p. 41)

Unfortunately Plummer did not elaborate on these points, and the remainder of his book is concerned with more general issues to do with international combines.

The development of the theory of the firm by Edwin Chamberlin (1933) and Joan Robinson (1933) at last provided a basis for exploring *O* advantages, which had been more or less lost sight of in the earlier preoccupation with the market as the sole organizer of economic activity. In particular, the concept of market power was brought firmly into the analysis, while the work of Joe Bain, both on barriers to entry (Bain, 1954, 1956) and on industrial economics generally (1959), helped to work out the implications of these theories on an industry-wide scale.

Edith Penrose's theory of the growth of the firm (Penrose, 1958) brought back the entrepreneur (of the Schumpeterian innovative kind) into the analysis with her twin concepts of managerial limits to growth and managerial slack as a springboard for growth. Moreover, her analysis of corporate diversification has analogies with international involvement as firms gain experience of transferring ownership advantages across national frontiers just as they do across industries. Earlier, Penrose had published a pathbreaking article on foreign direct investment in Australia (Penrose, 1956) in which she pre-dated Hymer in the idea that such investment is better seen in terms of the theory of the growth of the firm rather than that of international capital movements.

Internalization advantages

In a pathbreaking article, Ronald Coase (Coase, 1937) contrasted how resources were transferred through the market by relative prices with the way in which the price mechanism was superseded within the firm, so that resources move by the fiat of the entrepreneur. This theme was first systematically applied to international production by McManus (1972) and Buckley and Casson (1976). However, prior to this, Maurice Bye (1958) had observed that the key feature of the international firm was its ability to control many factors internally that would be exogenous to the small firm. Bye, in fact, coined the term multi-territorial firm, and used the case of the international oil industry to demonstrate that 'real and financial size enables firms to cross varying thresholds of growth either by extension or integration, and so assure them of a certain bargaining position' (Bye, 1958, p. 161). Bye traces the concept of the firm as a centre of planning and decision back to Cournot, and is one of the first economists to acknowledge the importance of the common governance of activities as an *O* advantage.

For the more formal development of the theory of internalization, Coase's substantive achievement was to introduce into the analysis the costs of coordinating marketing and management across different activities, namely relating costs to the structure and extent of the firm's diversification. Oliver Williamson's *Markets and Hierarchies*, which has been the inspiration for much subsequent research on internalization in MNEs by organizational economists, drew both on Coase and on the earlier emphasis by Commons on transactions as the fundamental unit of economic investigation (Williamson, 1975).

Although economists had not yet appreciated its significance for the theory of international trade and production, the transition of giant corporations from the unitary to the multidivisional form gave rise to a new wave of thinking by organizational theorists, notably Herbert Simon (1947, 1955).

INTERNATIONAL PRODUCTION, 1960–80

The Scope of MNE Activity, 1960–80

Developments in international production since 1960 have been narrated by Stopford and Dunning (1983). Some statistical data are also set out in Tables 8.2 and 8.3. Perhaps most notably, the rise of US FDI in the 1950s and 1960s has in the 1970s been matched by an increase in FDI by West Germany and

Japan. Very recently, in the 1980s, MNEs have emerged from some of the newly industrialized countries, e.g. South Korea, Hong Kong and Singapore.

Related to the trend of FDI being largely between developed countries, cross-investment or intra-industry FDI has emerged: a comparatively rare phenomenon before 1945. Consequently, as between source countries, the industrial pattern of international investment (like trade) has tended to converge.

Analysis by economists

These developments in the 1960s and 1970s have strongly influenced the direction of the growing body of research into international production. Some of these are well summarized by Fieldhouse (1986), who also reminds his readers that it was David Lilienthal, then chief executive of the Development and Resources Corporation of New York, who first coined the term 'Multinational Corporations' in an address he gave in April 1960 to the Carnegie Institute of Technology. In particular, the increasingly prevalent phenomenon of cross-investment could not be adequately explained either by location or international capital theory. The focus of discussion therefore shifted to ownership advantages of firms, first clearly articulated in the work of Hymer (1960), who laid the foundations of the modern theory of international production.

Vernon helped to show the interaction between *O* and *L* advantages in his product-cycle model (Vernon, 1966). This drew on a theory of innovation to demonstrate the country-specific ownership advantages of firms alongside the location advantages of countries. An interpretation of the product-cycle model set within the eclectic framework is discussed by Dunning and Cantwell (1981).

This novel emphasis on the *O* advantage of firms in international economics drew in some authors who had started from trade theory (Hirsch, 1976) and some who started from industrial economics (Caves, 1971). It also fitted in with the arguments of those who feared the 'American challenge' to Europe, in contending that US firms were engaged in monopolistic rent-seeking through the exploitation of their ownership advantages.

During the 1970s, when emphasis shifted from explaining FDI to explaining the activities of MNEs, i.e. firms which had diversified their value-adding activities outside their natural boundaries, so did the theoretical underpinning of international production. Canadian, Swedish and UK economists working independently focused attention on the *raison d'être* of the MNE in terms of the advantages of internalizing cross-border intermediate product markets.[9] In particular this explanation was used to explain FDI taking place in high-technology-intensive manufacturing industries, where firms were increasingly integrating their research and development with their production and marketing activities. A further development in the 1970s was the emergence of global multinationality through rationalized or efficiency-seeking investment, which sought to capture the benefit of coordinating the activities of its subsidiaries within the regional blocs such as the EEC, or sometimes across greater distances.

Towards an Interdisciplinary Approach

Finally, the last two decades have seen an increasingly interdisciplinary approach being taken to the theory of international production. Suffice to mention here that the most significant theoretical advance in explaining MNE activity in the 1970s and 1980s has undoubtedly been that to do with the economics of organizations. We have already mentioned Coase's perception of private hierarchies as market-replacing mechanisms in a world of imperfect competition, limited information and exchange frictions; but no less influential to our understanding of organizations have been the contributions of Simon (1947, 1955), in his analysis of the human psychology of decision making under a situation of bounded rationality, and that of Alchian (1950), in his explanation of organizational structure and survival in terms of a biological system that is largely independent of decision taking at a micro level (Moe, 1984).

Much of the contemporary transaction costs literature on the economics of information, the contractual paradigm and the principal–agent model associated with scholars such as Williamson (1975, 1981, 1986), Alchian and Demsetz (1972), Ross (1973), and Jensen and Meckling (1976) can be traced to the writings of these earlier scholars.

CONCLUSIONS

Our survey of the views (mainly since 1776) of interested authors on international production suggests that those who were most aware of this activity were men of affairs – such as Bagehot – businessmen or civil servants such as consular officials. Not until the 1950s, when US firms began to undertake massive FDI in Europe, were economists compelled to revise their purely locational approach towards international trade and capital movements, with international production as a special case.

Up to 1870 economists used a macroeconomic approach, in line with classical economic thought generally, and locational considerations were naturally of the greatest interest as long as the bulk of FDI was resource-based and often located in colonial or dependent territories, regarded often as offshoots of home production. Outside these areas, international production was organized by individual entrepreneurs, again attracted by the advantages of foreign locations.

From the 1870s onwards, both the composition of FDI and the tenor of economic thought underwent a change. The modern MNE began to evolve and increasingly undertook, as well as resource-based investments, market-oriented and import-substituting investments to supplement their domestic value-adding activities. A corresponding theory of microeconomic location advantages was therefore required: this took a number of decades to be formulated.

In the freer trading conditions after 1945, when cross-investment on a vast scale grew up between countries, the ownership advantages specific to firms have become clearer. More recently, the fall in the share of import-substituting investment, owing to the rise of joint ventures in developing countries, on the one hand, and of internationally integrated investment in industrialized countries on the other, has helped to focus attention on internalization advantages.

The modern theory of international production has thus moved away from reliance on country-oriented advantages in production towards firm-specific (ownership and internalization) advantages. We suggest that this is also related to a maturing of firms whose ownership advantages are now less dependent on the characteristics of their home country, and more on their multinationality *per se*. This is associated with intra-industry FDI, and a new organizational efficiency of MNEs which itself aids them in their international expansion in its own right.

These factors help to explain why a distinct theoretical framework for the analysis of international production has grown up only recently. Economists attempt to adapt existing paradigms to explain new developments, and it is only when the adaptations required are so drastic as to undermine the original framework that new paradigms emerge. This stage appears to have been reached in international economics: neoclassical models grounded on the assumption that the technical conditions of production are everywhere the same cannot hope to account for current trends in the international division of labour.

In this chapter we have stressed the growing importance of the theory of the firm to an understanding of international trade and production. However, given that the modern MNE is increasingly mobile in its allocation of economic activity, we have also moved back towards a Smithian world with regard to the international location of production. In a very real sense, then, the wheel has turned full circle.

NOTES

1. See Chapters 2 and 7 of this volume, and Teece (1983).
2. As, for example, are described in Chapter 7 of this volume.
3. As described in Edelstein (1982).
4. As, for example, described in Dunning (1958) and Wilkins (1970).
5. As reviewed in Svedberg (1981a, 1981b).
6. See also Vernon (1979) and Dunning and Cantwell (1981).
7. For a further discussion of the relevance of Ricardo on trade theory to the modern theory of international production, see Cantwell (1984).
8. See his book, *Theorie der wirtschaftlichen Entwicklung* (1911), which was translated as *The Theory of Economic Development* (Cambridge, MA, 1934), p. ix.
9. See especially, Liefmann (1897), later enlarged upon in Liefmann (1932), Levy (1911), Hilferding (1910, English translation 1981).

REFERENCES

Alchian, A. (1950), 'Uncertainty, Evolution and Economic Theory', *Journal of Political Economy*, **58**, June, 211–21.

Alchian, A. and Demsetz, H. (1972), 'Production, information costs and economic organisation', *American Economic Review*, **62**, December, 777–95.

Archer, H.J. (1986), An eclectic approach to the historical study of UK multinational enterprises, PhD. dissertation, Reading, UK.

Bain, J.S. (1954), 'Economies of scale, concentration and the condition of entry in twenty manufacturing industries', *American Economic Review*, **44**, 15–39.

Bloomfield, A.I. (1975), 'Adam Smith and the theory of international trade', in Kinner, S. and Wilson, T. (eds), *Essays on Adam Smith*, (London).

Buckley, P.J. and Casson, M.C. (1976), *The Future of the Multinational Enterprise*, (London: Macmillan).

Bye, M. (1958), 'Self-financed multiterritorial units and their time horizon', *International Economic Papers*, **8**, 147–78.

Calvet, A.L. (1980), *Markets and Hierarchies: Towards a Theory of International Business*, PhD. thesis, Sloan School of Management, Cambridge, MA.

Cantwell, J.A. (1984), *The Relevance of the Classical Economists to the Theory of International Production*, University of Reading Discussion Papers in International Investment and Business Studies, No. 79.

Caves, R.E. (1982), *Multinational Enterprise and Economic Analysis*, (Cambridge: Cambridge University Press).

Chamberlin, E.H. (1933), *The Theory of Monopolistic Competition*, (Cambridge, MA).

Chandler, A.D. Jr, (1977), *The Visible Hand: The Managerial Revolution in American Business*, (Cambridge, MA: Harvard University Press).

Coase, R.H. (1937), The nature of the firm', *Economica (New Series)*, **4**, November, 386–405.

Commons, J.R. (1924), *Institutional Economics: Its Place in Political Economy*, New York: Macmillan.

Dunning, J.H. (1958), *American Investment in British Manufacturing Industry*, (London: Allen & Unwin) (reprinted by Arno Press, New York, 1976).

Dunning, J.H. (1988), *Explaining International Production*, (London: Allen & Unwin).

Dunning, J.H. and Archer, H. (1987), 'The eclectic pradigm and the growth of UK multinational enterprise 1870–1983', *Business and Economic History*, Second Series, **16**, 1–28.

Dunning J.H. (1993), *Multinational Enterprises and the Global Economy*, Wokingham, Berkshire: Addison Wesley.

Dunning, J.H. and Cantwell, J.A. (1981), *Inward Direct Investment from the US and Europe's Technological Competitiveness*, mimeo, University of Reading Discussion Papers in International Investment and Business Studies, No. 85.

Fieldhouse, D. (1986), 'The Multinational: a Critique of a Concept' in Teichora, A., Levy-Lebeyer, M. and Nussbaum, H. (eds), *Multinational Enterprise in Historical Perspective*, (Cambridge: Cambridge University Press) pp. 9–29.

Heckscher, E.F. (1919), 'The effect of foreign trade on the distribution of income', *Economisk Tidskrift*, 497–512, reprinted in *AEA Readings in the Theory of International Trade*, (London, 1950), pp. 272–300.

Hilferding, R. (1910), *Finance Capital; a Study of the Latest Phase of Capitalist Development*, English translation (London, 1981).

Hirsch, S. (1976), 'An international trade and investment theory of the firm', *Oxford Economic Papers*, **28**, July, 258–70.

Hotelling, H. (1929), 'Stability in competition', *Economic Journal*, **29**, 41–57.
Hymer, S. (1960), *The International Operations of National Firms: A Study of Direct Investment*, Ph.D. Thesis, MIT: published by MIT Press under same title in 1976.
Jensen, M.C. and Meckling, W. (1976), 'Theory of the firm: managerial behavior, agency costs, and ownership structure', *Journal of Financial Economics*, **3**, October, 305–60.
Knickerbocker, F.T. (1973), *Oligopolistc Reaction and the Multinational Enterprise*, Cambridge, MA: Harvard University Press.
Kojima, K. (1978), *Direct Foreign Investment: A Japanese Model of Multinational Business Operations*, London: Croom Helm.
Kojima, K. (1982), 'Macroeconomic versus international business approach to foreign direct investment', *Hitosubashi Journal of Economics*, **23**, 1–19.
Koolman, G. (1971), 'Say's conception of the role of the entrepreneur', *Ecoonomica*, **38**, 269–86.
Levy, H. (1911), *Monopoly and Competition: a Study in English Industrial Organisation* (English Translation, London).
Liefmann, R. (1897), *Die Unternehmerverbaende*, later enlarged in Liefmann, R., *Cartels, Concerns and Trusts* (London: Methuen 1932).
Lösch, A. (1940), Die Raeumliche Ordnung der Wirtschaft, translated as *The Economics of Location*, (New Haven, CT: Yale University Press, 1954).
Marshall, A. (1923), *Money, Credit and Commerce*, (London: Macmillan).
Marx, K. (1867), *Capital*, **1**, reprinted 1959, London: Lawrence & Wishart.
McKay, J.P. (1970), *Pioneers for Profit: Foreign Entrepreneurship and Russian Industrialisation, 1885–1913*, (Chicago, IL: University of Chicago Press).
McManus, J.C. (1972), 'The theory of the multinational firm', in Paquet, G. (ed.), *The Multinational Firm and the Nation State*, (Toronto: Collier-Macmillan).
Mill, J.S. (1848), *Principles of Political Economy*, London, reprinted 1909.
Mitchell, W.C. (1913), *Business Cycles*, Berkeley, CA: University of California Press.
Moe, T.M. (1984), 'The new economics of organization', *American Journal of Political Science*, **28**, November, 739–73.
Mundell, R.A. (1957), 'International trade and factor mobility', *American Economic Review*, **47**, 321–35.
Mun, T. (1664), *England's Treasure by Foreign Trade*, reprinted in London 1928.
O'Brien, D.P. (1975), *The Classical Economists*, (Oxford: Oxford University Press).
Ohlin, B. (1933), *Inter-regional and International Trade*, (Cambridge, MA: Harvard University Press, rev. edn 1967).
Ohlin, B. (1977), 'Some aspects of the relations between international movements of commodities, factors of production and technology', in Ohlin, B., Hesselborn, P.-O. and Wijkman, P. M. (eds), *The International Allocation of Economic Activity* (London: Macmillan), pp. 25–56.
Ozawa, T. (1981a), 'International investment and industrial structure: new theoretical implications from the Japanese experience', *Oxford Economic Papers*, **31**, March, pp. 72–92.
Ozawa, T. (1981b), *The Japanese Experience with the 'New' Forms of Investment. A Preliminary Exploration*, unpublished paper for OECD (Development Centre) meeting 2–6 March.
Penrose, E.T. (1956), 'Foreign investment and growth of the firm', *Economic Journal*, **60**, 220–35.
Penrose, E.T. (1958), *The Theory of the Growth of the Firm*, (Oxford: Basil Blackwell) (rev. edn published 1979).
Plummer, A. (1934), *International Combines in Modern History*, (London: Pitman).

Ricardo, D. (1817), *On the Principles of Political Economy and Taxation* (London) reprinted Harmondsworth 1971.

Robinson, Joan (1933), *The Economics of Imperfect Competition*, (London: Macmillan).

Rosenberg, N. (1975), 'Adam Smith on Profits: Paradox Lost and Regained', in Skinner, A. S. and Wilson, T. (eds) *The Market and the State: Essays on Adam Smith* (Oxford: The Clarendon Press).

Ross, S.A. (1973), 'The economic theory of agency: the principal's problem', *American Economic Review*, **12**, May, 134–39.

Simon, H.A. (1947), *Administrative Behavior*, (New York: Macmillan).

Simon, H.A. (1955), 'A behaviorial model of rational choice', *Quarterly Journal of Economics*, **69**, February, 118.

Smith, A. (1776), *An Inquiry into the Nature and Causes of the Wealth of Nations* (London, reprinted in Cannon, E. (ed.) (New York, 1937).

Southard, F.A. Jr. (1931), *American Industry in Europe*, (Boston, MA: Houghton Mifflin).

Stevas, N.S. (ed.) (1978), *Collected Works of Walter Bagehot*, (Economic Essays, London).

Stolper, W.F. and Samuelson, P.A. (1941), 'Protection and real wages', *Review of Economic Studies*, 58–73.

Stopford, J.M. (1974), 'The origins of British-based multinational manufacturing enterprises', *Business History Review*, **48**, 303–35.

Stopford, J.M. and Dunning, J.H. (1983), *Multinationals: Company Performance and Global Trends*, (London: Macmillan).

Svedberg, P. (1981a), 'Colonial enforcement of foreign direct investment', *Manchester School of Economic and Social Studies*, **50**, 21–38.

Svedberg, P. (1981b), 'Colonialism and foreign direct investment profitability', in Dunning, J.H. and Black, J. (eds), *International Investment and Capital Movements*, (London: Macmillan).

Teece, D.J. (1983), 'Technological and organizational factors in the theory of the multinational enterprise', in Casson, M.C. (ed.), *Growth of International Business*, (London: Allen & Unwin).

Veblen, T.B. (1904), *The Theory of Business Enterprise*, (reprinted New Brunswick, 1978).

Vernon, R. (1966), 'International investment and international trade in the product cycle', *Quarterly Journal of Economics*, **80**, 90–207.

Von Thunen, J.H. (1876), *Der Isolierte Staat:* English translation in Hall, P., (ed.), *Von Thunen's Isolated State*, (Oxford, 1966).

Wakefield, E.G. (1833), *England and America: A Comparison of the Social and Political State of Both Nations*, 2 vols (London).

Weber, A. (1929), *Ueber den Standort der Industrien*, translated as *The Theory of Location of Industries*, (Chicago).

Whitaker, J.K. (1975) (ed.), *The Early Economic Writings of Alfred Marshall, 1867–1890*, London.

Wilkins, M. (1970), *The Emergence of Multinational Enterprise: American Business Abroad from the Colonial Era to 1914*, (Cambridge, MA: Harvard University Press).

Williams, J.H. (1929), 'The theory of international trade reconsidered', *Economic Journal*, **39**, 195–209.

Williamson, O.E. (1975), *Markets and Hierarchies: Analysis and Antitrust Implications* (New York: The Free Press).

Williamson, O.E. (1981), 'The modern corporation: origins, evolution, attributes' *Journal of Economic Literature*, **19**, 1537–68.

Williamson, O.E. (1986), *Economic Organisation*, (Brighton: Wheatsheaf Books).

9. Towards an interdisciplinary explanation of international production*

INTRODUCTION

For the most part, the approach taken so far in this volume to analysing the determinants of international production has been that of the economist. Such an approach has its serious limitations. In particular, economists in general are extremely prone to taking an exogenous or 'given' the environment in which economic phenomena occur and in which institutions operate, and to make such statements as 'we are not competent to analyse these non-economic factors' when pressed to give more attention to them. Even in dealing with activities of firms within a country this is becoming an increasingly dubious position, as technology – which is the economists favourite 'given factor' – is becoming the key ingredient for determining economic success and failure.[1] But in the context of the reasons for the internationalization of business where differences in the non-economic factors, and especially the role of governments, play such a crucial role in influencing the value of the OLI variables facing firms, the economist – and particularly the international economist – is in danger of not being taken seriously if he persistently fails to incorporate these forces in his paradigms and theories.

It is for this reason that the task of this chapter is to consider the extent to which it is desirable and possible to widen the theoretical framework we have adopted to consider the same subject matter from an interdisciplinary perspective. The hypothesis is that since, at the end of the day, we are trying to explain an economic phenomenon – the foreign production of firms – it is entirely appropriate to use the logic and techniques of economic science. At the same time, since we are also trying to understand the way in which institutions behave in differing political and cultural environments, and both fashion and react to non-economic phenomena, we must accept that the variables affecting decisions on FDI are not solely economic; neither, indeed, should economists assume they have the monopoly of understanding the techniques which might explain the rationale of economic decision-taking. For these reasons, then, it is not only

* From J.H. Dunning, *Explaining International Production*, London: Unwin Hyman, 1988, pp. 306–26.

acceptable but desirable for the economist to trespass into other disciplines to see what they may offer him in his quest to explain international production.

At this point, we should perhaps emphasize that we are *not* proposing that economists or business analysts should abandon their unidisciplinary specializations and become multidisciplinary generalists. We are, however, persuaded that only an interdisciplinary approach to the study of international business will capture the richness of its characteristics and consequences; and that scholars from the various interested disciplines should be encouraged to pool their talents in order to improve their theorizing about international production, and, where appropriate, to suggest policy prescriptions.

The following sections of this chapter seek to do two things. First, we present a brief overview of some of the work now being done by scholars in disciplines other than economics which bear directly on, and add to, our understanding about the determinants of international production. Second, we shall examine the extent to which it is possible to offer a unifying interdisciplinary paradigm which might be used as a framework by which all the relevant variables affecting international production may be better identified, interpreted and evaluated.

AN INTERDISCIPLINARY APPROACH

It is not long before, in his attempts to explain international production, the economist needs to draw upon the help of other disciplines. This is for a number of reasons all to do with characteristics of the subject matter to be explained. In discussing these we will distinguish those which are primarily (i) external (or exogenous) to firms; and (ii) those which are internal (or endogenous)[2] to firms.

The External Environment

Of the non-economic variables which make up the *external environment*, and which a reading of the literature suggests are most likely to affect international production, the political and legal aspects are among the most important. Domestic firms, seeking to invest in their own country, take as given the legal, ideological and political environment; that is to say the role played by those non-economic forces, including the effect which they have on efficiency of international intermediate product markets, is assumed to be the same for all firms.[3] Once firms enter a different geography and national jurisdiction, these variables become relevant in affecting both their competitive advantages and the modality of their foreign involvement. In some cases, these non-economic differences may be of little significance; in other cases they may be crucially important.

To identify non-economic variables affecting international production and to hypothesize about their impact on FDI needs the help of various disciplines. At first sight this may not seem to be so; indeed in all international business texts, the political system, language, business customs, and the legal framework are mentioned as factors influencing the location of value-added activity. Most surveys on the factors influencing investment decisions put these non-economic variables at the top of the list; and economic determinants only become relevant after the initial screening of possible production sites on non-economic grounds has been made. However, beyond generalities, the economist soon gets out of his depth. Thus *political* issues embrace the interplay between sectoral or interest groups making up society, the objectives of these constituents and the extent to which they conflict or are in harmony with each other, their relative strengths and weaknesses, and the institutional mechanisms by which they are able to make their views known. The authority and stability of the central government; the nature of the political fabric and the degree of bureaucracy; the balance of influence between agrarian and urban sectors in influencing the development process; the role of trade unions; lobbying capabilities of large corporations; the power of the central bank and financial institutions: all of these affect not only the attractiveness of a country to foreign investors, but the competitiveness of foreign compared with indigenous firms, the way in which an MNE might organize its production in that country, and how they relate to the world-wide activities.

The *legal* environment is no less relevant. The failure of the least developed countries to attract much FDI is not only due to their small markets, or lack of trained manpower and communications infrastructure, but also to inadequate protection of property rights; or an unacceptable law of contract; or a convoluted litigation procedure; or unacceptable disclosure requirements about a subsidiary's operations; or lack of legal recourse available to foreign firms against breach of contract by local suppliers or governments; or lack of provision for compensation in the case of nationalization. In some countries foreign-owned subsidiaries may be discriminated against in the courts. The role of legislation with respect to industrial relations, injury compensation, consumer rights, and environmental pollution may be no less important. In addition, there is the controversial question of extra-territorality, and the extent to which the laws of the host and home countries affecting MNE activity are in harmony or conflict with one another. Again such issues are likely to affect the competitive position of foreign firms (e.g. whether or not cross-border patent agreements are respected), the location of activity (e.g. what is expected of a company with respect to drug testing and clinical trials), and, perhaps, most important of all, the form and organization of contracts negotiated between foreign affiliates and local firms and/or employees.

Social, cultural and ideological issues are difficult both to evaluate and to pinpoint to a particular discipline. Yet several authors (e.g. Lodge and Vogel, 1987) have underlined their importance in explaining international production. For example, it is widely accepted that attitudes to wealth creation and income distribution, economic incentives, work and authority, are crucial in any explanation of the economic prowess of particular nations, and of the level and pattern of consumption. Variations in cultural heritage, religious perspectives, political ideologies and moral values fashion such attitudes. Work systems, social norms and patterns of leisure differ not only between developed and developing countries, but within these countries; while the character of societal relationships and the extent to which these have been subject to foreign domination or influence in the past, may strongly influence a country's attitude towards inward direct investment, and particularly the extent to which it prefers to conclude equity partnerships with foreign firms rather than accept 100 per cent-owned foreign affiliates.

Each of the issues so far identified interact with each other. Attitudes to entrepreneurship, authority and work may affect the industrial policies of a country; those towards foreigners may influence the nature of its external economic relationships; those towards thrift, economic security and leisure may help fashion a government's fiscal and social programme and income distribution policy; those towards authority and leadership may constrain or encourage the growth of private or public hierarchies; those towards women in a society, the level and pattern of its educational budget and employment legislation.

There are other disciplines which relate to the environment in a less central way. The *regional and urban geographer*, for example, is a specialist whose interest is in the spatial distribution of economic activity. His special skills relate more to the logistics of traversing space and the location of value-adding activity within particular countries. He is much more interested in the determinants and efficiency of inter-spatial linkages, both between producers along a value-added chain and across value-added chains. His field of study touches upon many of the non-economic factors mentioned above; and often planned regional development and associated incentives and penalties may enhance, or compensate for the lack of, natural resources in a region. Primarily the regional scientist is interested in explaining the 'where' of production; but in so far as spatial costs are regarded as a form of market failure, they may impinge on the competitive advantages and organizational modalities of firms. The extent to which the internationalization of production requires special treatment essentially depends on the extent to which the traversing of national boundaries introduces a new spatial dimension. Yet from the regional geographer's viewpoint this may not matter; the geographical, climatic and transportation differences *within* the USA, for example, are greater than between Holland and Belgium. Political borders do not necessarily coincide with geographical boundaries.

Factors Internal to the Firm

As in decisions relating to domestic production, the interaction between economic, organizational, financial, marketing and management variables affecting international production is a complex one and is sometimes difficult to disentangle. However, when an enterprise engages or contemplates engaging in value-adding activity in different countries, a new order of complexity enters into the three main areas of decision-taking (as traditionally identified by business schools) viz organization, management and marketing.

Management is, at the same time, the easiest and most difficult to deal with: easiest because, in its approach to an understanding of business conduct, performance and strategy, it embraces many of the concepts of the industrial economist; the most difficult because of the generality and lack of theoretical underpinning of many of the issues discussed in the literature (the discipline of strategic management is especially prone to this). As far as the determinants of international production are concerned, business analysts such as Doz, Prahalad, Stopford, Porter and Hamel, most of whom are attached to the top business schools in their countries, have done much to enrich our understanding of the nature and significance of management-related ownership advantages of MNEs; while an earlier generation of scholars, notably, Fayerweather, Robinson, Vernon and Stobaugh, greatly advanced our perceptions about the way in which the management of MNEs interacted with the environment in which they operated.[4]

Recent work on management has strongly oriented itself to identifying and evaluating the competitive advantages of MNEs and the management-related variables which make for a foreign location. Porter's work (1986) is a synthesis of a generation of scholars, which varies from the general to the very specific. Of the latter, we might mention the efforts of Prahalad and Doz (1987a, 1987b) to identify some of the key managerial attributes to successful MNEs; that of Doz (1979, 1985) in his study of the interaction between government policies and the management strategy of MNEs; that of Kogut (1985a, 1985b) who relates the management of foreign economic involvement to the volatility of the international environment; and that of Teece (1981a, 1983, 1987) who marries management, organizational and economic issues to consider the way in which firms manage the organization of assets and transactions. Other scholars have emphasized country-specific differences in managerial perceptions and behaviour (Negandhi, 1983); and some promising work has been done on assessing the role of culture on managerial values. The global challenges to management have also engaged the attention of researchers such as Hamel and

Prahalad (1984) and Porter (1986). Only to a limited extent have intra-firm organizational issues been of interest to scholars of management; except in so far as the strategy of ownership is itself regarded as a management tool. A lot of useful work has also been done on the management of risk and of joint ventures; the management-related factors influencing the choice of organizational form (e.g. Stopford and Wells, 1971); and on the management of technology strategy (Friar and Horwitch, 1984; Ching-Sung Wu, 1987).

By contrast – and as one might expect – the way in which firms organize themselves to supply goods for sale to foreign markets or engage in value-added activities outside national boundaries has been central to the interest of organizational theorists. We might mention four organizational issues which directly bear on the international production decision. The first is the form of organization (both formal or informal) which might influence the way in which investment decisions are taken. These break down into components such as: 'What modifications are required to the form of hierarchial organization as a consequence of being international?' 'Which of the various variants of M structure are suitable for which types of overseas operations?' 'How might these vary over time and according to the type of value-added activity being undertaken?' 'To what extent are adaptations required to the organizational culture or an enterprise when it produces abroad?' and 'How far do the costs of these adaptations affect the way it penetrates foreign markets?' Here, work by such organizational theorists as Ouchi (1980), Wilkins and Ouchi (1983) and Nonaka (1994) is particularly relevant.

The second organizational issue concerns the locus of decision-taking within hierarchies, and the rationale of alternative governance structures. 'To what extent, and in which functional areas are decisions most likely to decentralize?' Bridging the first and second issues is the way in which particular functional activities are organized across national boundaries. Work now being done on the ways in which firms acquire and develop technology and organize their innovating activities by such scholars as Ghoshal and Bartlett (1987), Friar and Horwitch (1984) and Bartlett and Ghoshal (1988) amply illustrates the interaction between strategic and economic goals, and the way in which each impinges on the structure of decision-taking and the location of R&D.

One important conclusion of these latter groups of scholars is that, while the capacity to innovate remains a key competitive advantage of firms, no less important is their capability to integrate new innovations with existing technological assets, and to be able to use these with other resources of the firm to capture operational synergies and scope and scale economics. As Bartlett and Ghoshal (1988) put it, 'the "challenge" (to the global competitors) of the late 1980s is much more one of developing the appropriate organisational capabilities than one related to technological skills or resource allocation'. In pleading for a holistic approach to innovatory responsibilities, they echo the argument of Teece (1987) that the successful commercialization of new products and processes is contingent upon the availability and effective deployment of complementary assets, e.g. marketing skills, flexible manufacturing systems, an adaptable labour force, etc., all of which help to lower the transaction lists associated with the use of innovations. As technologies become multi-purpose and inter-related in character, the pressures on these complementary assets are likely to become even greater.

The third organizational question of interest to FDI scholars relates to the vertical or horizontal interaction between the participating stakeholders in organizations, and especially on the manner by which work is organized, performance is monitored and conflicts of interest resolved (Alchian and Demsetz, 1972); and the fourth the way in which internal and external contractual relationships are handled (Williamson, 1975). Once again country-specific differences would suggest that cross-border organizational relationships may differ in substance, if not in kind, from those facing the purely domestic firm.

The contribution of *marketing* scholars to our understanding of international production has greatly widened over the years. In the 1960s, interest was largely confined to examining the mechanics of international market penetration, and the extent to which products needed to be customized to meet the needs of foreign buyers. Currently, there would seem to be three main streams of analytical thought. The first is typified by the work of two groups of scholars. It comprises that of the Swedish marketing analysts Mattson (1985), Forsgren (1985), Håkansson (1982), Johanson and Vahlne (1977) and Johanson and Mattson (1987a, 1987b). While the initial focus of attention was on the process of internationalization, this has more recently been directed to an analysis of industrial markets as a network of relationships between firms. This analysis – which is closely allied to the fourth interest of the organizational scholars mentioned above – embraces both final and intermediate goods markets, and includes all forms of organizational modes from equity investment to subcontracting.[5] The research questions pursued by these scholars is essentially related to the way MNEs forge and sustain a network of relationships with foreign firms, and how this affects, and is affected by, the internationalization process *per se*, including the transition from exporting or licensing to FDI. This approach contrasts with the internalization theory in that it argues that a firm's *O* advantages will depend no less on the success of its external relationships with other firms in the network. To quote from Johanson and Mattson (1987b), 'The multinational firm may use its network position to effectively "externalize" some of its activities without losing control of its crucial intangible assets.' They go on to point out that the internalization of markets is often best regarded as a process by which network positions are established and changed, the result of which may substantially influence the MNEs product, marketing and purchasing strategies.

A second, and rather different approach to network analysis has been taken by a group of Japanese scholars working at Hitosubashi University in Tokyo. (See, for example, Imai, Nonaka and Takeuchi, 1984 and Imai and Itami, 1984). Their interest is more in networks as a form of organizational relationship between firms, and as a means of overcoming the differences of the allocation of resources by pure markets or pure hierarchies. Like the Swedish scholars, they prefer to think of firms as mutually related units, usually located in linked positions, rather than standing as completely independent units. Interpenetration of market and organization is thus the theoretical foundation of the network organization.

The Japanese scholars stress the importance of information accumulating among transacting participants in leading to strong ties between firms producing at different stages of the value-added chain. In the Japanese context, they view a large firm (or lead manufacturer) at the core of the hierarchical network. At the next level, there are the primary contractors with which the lead manufacturer has a strong tie and an orderly and planned exchange of information. The information flows between the lead manufacturer and the secondary subcontractor are also channelled through the primary subcontractor, who thus plays an important linking role (Imai, 1985).

No less important are the forms of relationships which exist in the network. Here, Imai and Itami (1984) contrast the relationships between US firms, which tend to be based on a formal, hierarchical or contractual relationship, and that between Japanese firms, based more on mutual trust, respect and integrity. Moreover, since, in Japan, the primary subcontractor usually bears most of the economic risks of the relationship (and has most to lose by severing the relationship), an important governance cost commonly faced by US and European contracting firms is removed, and hence the Japanese networking system brings with it an organizational advantage to the firms at the hub of the network. Whether or not the advantage can be transferred by Japanese MNEs outside their national boundaries is a subject engaging the attention of scholars. A useful comparative analysis of the organizational characteristics of Japanese and US MNEs in Taiwan has recently been published by Yeh and Sagafi-nejad (1987).

The second and more recent strand of marketing literature is illustrated by the writings of Anderson and Gatignon (1986), who have addressed themselves primarily to the *raison d'être* for different modes of foreign penetration, both in respect of sales and production ventures. Here the emphasis, so far at least, has been on identifying the appropriate channels of entry with *L*-specific variables being considered as an independent rather than a dependent variable. A third interest of marketing scholars relates to the international marketing strategy of firms, both in respect of the type of products which different markets may require, and of the scope of markets (e.g. general or niche) which companies should aim to cultivate. Here, the work being done parallels that of the business analysts, in that the objective of the exercise is to identify and evaluate the competitive strategies most likely to be successful. As such, the work of this group of scholars is of direct interest to economists in identifying the main *O*-specific advantages of MNEs.

We next turn to consider *the finance* literature. In general, after contributing a great deal to our understanding about FDI in the 1960s and 1970s, finance theory has had very little to say about the determinants of MNE activity in the later 1970s and 1980s. This may be because, as earlier chapters have shown, the interests of scholars have switched from explaining the act of FDI *per se* to explaining the cross-border expansion of firms in which the relevant variable to be explained is value-added rather than the currency in which capital expenditure is financed. Following the pioneering work of Grubel (1968), Agmon and Lessard (1977) and Rugman (1979) to explain the geographical distribution of the financing of foreign capital expenditure by MNEs in terms of an international portfolio model, and that of Aliber (1970, 1971) who explained FDI in terms of capital and exchange-market imperfections, the main interest of finance scholars has been more to do with the management of short-term capital flows, long-term debt and exchange-rate fluctuations. As firms become more multinational, their options for financing their capital expenditures become wider; and there is little evidence to suggest that, in the absence of government intervention, firms have been constrained in their foreign production and decisions by the lack of cost of finance in their home countries; they will simply seek funding from the least expensive or least risky source (Eitman and Stonehill, 1986).

In some ways, it is strange that financial analysis has not had more to contribute to the way in which firms organize their trans-border transactions. The relative advantages of different degrees of equity investment and between equity investment and non-equity capital rest on the balance between financial risk and control. The lower the former relative to the importance of the latter, the more internal hierarchies will be preferred to external relations with independent firms. Yet, apart from some sophistication of political and foreign risk exposure analysis in which economists, no less than financial analysts, are interested, and a contribution to the debate on principal–agent analysis, which is central to students of both economics and organizational behaviour, there have been few advances in financial theory germane to our understanding of international production.

Finally, brief mention should be made of the burgeoning literature of *business history*. Following the pioneering work of Chandler (1962, 1977) on the growth of the large managed enterprise, and Wilkins (1970, 1974) on the emergence and maturing of US MNEs, there has been a great deal of research – mainly by

European scholars – on the history of international business activity. This research has ranged from attempts to formulate a general paradigm about the reasons why firms extend their territorial boundaries to detailed case studies of the history of individual MNEs from particular countries.[6] As the unit of analysis for most business historians is the individual enterprise, it is not, perhaps, surprising that transaction cost minimizing and strategic type explanations have emerged as the dominant analytical tools. While increasing attention is now being paid to entrepreneurship as an engine of growth, most discussions on competitive advantages by business historians have tended to centre on the ability of enterprises to coordinate their value-added activities across national boundaries and over time. The issue of the 'where' of international business activity does not seem to have captured the interest of business historians.

APPROPRIATE INTERDISCIPLINARY PARADIGMS

Up to this point, we have described some of the contributions of scholars in disciplines outside mainstream economic analysis and business behaviour to an explanation of international production. We have suggested both those which purport to examine non-economic changes in the external environment in which business operates, and those to do with the decision-taking process within hierarchies, impinge on the capacity and willingness of firms to be internationally involved, and on the modality and location of that involvement.

The question now arises: 'What, if any, is the analytical interface between these different disciplinary strands?' Is there a unifying paradigm which links the explanations? A priori, we might suppose that each unidisciplinary explanation for international production might draw upon the ideas, logic and techniques of its own school of thought. But our perception of what has been happening in recent years is that each discipline has been drawing upon quite similar concepts and thought forms, but modifying these to suit its own sphere of interest. The consequence is that some very robust interdisciplinary paradigms are beginning to emerge, which offer a degree of intellectual rigour and richness; and which promise well for a fuller understanding of the nature and determinants of international production.

Throughout this volume, we have suggested that the eclectic paradigm offers a cohesive and systematic framework for hypothesizing about the economic causes of international production. To what extent can one widen the paradigm to embrace non-economic variables? Is it simply a matter of identifying political, legal, organizational, marketing and other variables and adding these to those encompassed in economic models; or does one need to look for a new, or new paradigms?

It is our belief that there is a great deal of mileage in integrating the kind of analysis used in this book with that used by other disciplines to answer the kind of questions raised in this chapter. The basic reason for this is that the *OLI* configuration described by the eclectic paradigm both has applications outside of economics, and draws upon the ideas and concepts of other disciplines. Chapter 2 has suggested that the kernel of the modern theory of international production rests in the distribution of country-specific factor endowments and the theory of organization, especially that of market failure. If, in the former, we incorporate non-economic variables, notably those under the control of governments,[7] and in the latter, we extend market failure to cover all forms of organizational relationships both within and between firms – then one has the makings of a genuinely interdisciplinary theory of international business behaviour. To those who assert that the eclectic paradigm is already too general and/or is little more than a listing of the variables which may or may not affect the extent and form of a firm's international involvement, we would reply that the purpose of a dominant paradigm is not to offer a set of operationally testable explanations of any observed phenomena, but to provide an organizational framework by which the interaction between the phenomenon to be explained and other phenomena can be analysed.

Table 9.1 sets out the kind of interdisciplinary approach we have in mind. We are suggesting that each of the unidisciplinary explanations for international production can be interpreted in terms of the *OLI* configuration of relationships.[8] More particularly, to a greater or lesser extent, we believe it is possible to evaluate the role of managerial, marketing, financial, organizational, political and legal factors in the competitive advantages of firms, the locational advantages of countries and the way in which firms organize the resources within their control and/or those they seek to obtain from other firms. Recent technological advances and particularly the emergence of a number of generic technologies, e.g. information and communications technology, robotics, biotechnology, etc., together with the rapid growth of strategic alliances among firms, are having a marked impact on our thinking about the nature and growth of firms, and the form of their cross-border organizational relationships. But the particular point of issue here is that, by their nature and impact, these advances are forcing scholars to take a more interdisciplinary approach to explaining international production, and to form strategic alliances among themselves, so as to better understand and evaluate the various aspects of this phenomenon.

The 'Why' Sub-paradigm – O Advantages

The competitive advantages of firms are not only economic; and they are certainly not determined by the firms themselves. Country-specific political, legal, ideological and cultural differences may fundamentally affect the ability of firms to generate and sustain competitive advantages. Let us give just a few

Table 9.1 An interdisciplinary approach to the eclectic paradigm

	Ownership advantages	Location advantages	Internalization advantages
1. Management (Porter, Doz, Hamel, Negandhi, Prahalad)	• Management, culture, experience, strategy • Quality of management • Product quality • Economies of scope • Coordinating options	• Comparative resource endowments • Configuration options • Oligopolistic strategy	• Form of involvement as part of a firm's competitive posture/strategy • Strategic partnering
2. Organization (Williamson, Simon, Teece, Chandler, Ouchi, Ghoshal, Bartlett)	• Organizational culture/ resources/structure • Complementary assets to core advantages • Synergistic economies • Nature of external relationships (e.g. networking)	• Environmental complexity • Ease of transferring organizational structures and external relationships	• Transaction costs: both inter- and intra-firm • Strategic partnering • Markets'/hierarchies' clan options • Cultural differences affecting organizational forms
3. Marketing (Goodnow, Terpstra, Keegan, Mattson, Anderson/Gatignon)	• Product characteristics • Segmented markets • Goodwill/brand names • Control of distribution • Network advantages	• Inter-country social and cultural differences • Physical distances • Need for product customization	• Transaction costs with respect to a) entry modes b) agency costs c) supplier relationships
4. Finance (Lessard, Aliber, Rugman)	• Access to finance capital on favourable terms • Portfolio diversification across national boundaries	• Exchange rates • Controls on sourcing, capital and dividend, remissions, etc.	• Market failure in capital/ exchange markets • Agency costs • Network analysis

5. Political science and international relations (Nye, Kobrin, Moran, Boddewyn)	• Cultures, ideologies as affecting '*O*' advantages • Economic systems • Structure of government • Lobbying ability/bargaining power	• Role of power groups (e.g. trade unions) • Politically induced incentives and barriers to FDI • Inter-country political relations	• Transaction costs arising from political risk • Negotiating/bargaining • Government intervention
6. Regional science (Dicken, Taylor, Thrift)	• Multiplant economies • Ability to improve or reduce cost of transport, • Information/communications	• Spatial distance • Transport costs	• Spatial costs of organizing hierarchies
7. Law (Vagts, Folsom, Gordon and Spagnole)	• Legal infrastructure • Patent/contract/company law	• Extraterritorality • Restrictive practices legislation • Codes of conduct	• Litigation procedures • Efficiency of contract law (in protecting property rights)
8. Economic and business history (Chandler, Wilkins, North, Jones, Nicholas)	• Entrepreneurship • Economics of vertical integration • Organizational forms. • Access to resources/markets • Interpersonal relationships	• Tariffs and other import controls • Size of markets • Government regulations • State's role in enforcing contracts • Behavioural norms	• To capture economics of common governance • Quality control • Agency costs • Cost of enforcing contracts

examples. Competition and anti-trust legislation (a legal instrument) in one country might prevent firms from merging or forming collaborative alliances, but in another it may allow it. Assuming such mergers and alliances to be beneficial to the firms' attempt to capture international markets, firms may have their competitive advantages increased or lowered as a result. Similarly, as we have seen, a firm's competitive prowess may be directly related to its ability to minimize the cost of transactions associated with different organizational relationships both within or across national boundaries. A full appreciation of cross-border differences in the way in which subcontracting is organized, and in consumer perceptions, preferences and reactions to different marketing techniques, may be the crucial ingredient to success in some sectors; in others, competitive advantage might rest more on the way in which firms handle their incentive systems and employee relations. And to gain access to knowledge and understanding of the local legal, political and cultural environment has always been a potent reason for concluding joint ventures when penetrating foreign markets.

It is interesting that, in the management literature, a distinction is made between management as a specific asset in its own right (Prahalad and Doz, 1987), and the capability of the owners of a firm (or their immediate agents i.e. the board of directors) effectively to coordinate separate value-adding activities, i.e. internalize horizontal, or vertical markets. These organizational advantages again are of two kinds (those related to the organization of single activities and those concerned with multiple activities) but, as we shall see later, both reflect the interaction between market failure and the distribution of factor endowments. However, what most of the literature fails to do is to offer a unifying explanation for the *O* advantages it identifies. *Why* is one firm better able to manage assets, e.g. technology, than another? Why does another have superior coordinating capabilities? Why are some firms able to market their products more effectively? Why do others manage their labour force so successfully? Why does the capacity to minimize the costs of contractual relationships vary so much between firms? To a certain extent, economic models of the distribution of factor endowments and market failure can help. Thus some competitive advantages turn out to be largely industry- or country-specific (i.e. determined by production or product characteristics and the availability and cost of immobile factor endowments). If one includes the role of government as one of these latter (Boddewyn, 1986), then the factor endowment model can be extended further. Moreover, one could possibly treat attitudes, ideologies and cultures, as they affect entrepreneurship and investment motivation in the same way. Alternatively non-economic *O* advantages might reflect market distortions or failure. Discriminatory non-tariff barriers and purchasing policies by public authorities would be examples of the first kind;

having access to a network of suppliers, bound together by social and cultural mores, as well as economic self-interest, is an example of the second.

The 'Where' Sub-paradigm

Second, there is much in common between the various interdisciplinary attempts to explain the 'where' of international production. The variables considered by the modern economic geographer and regional scientist are virtually the same as those as the earlier researchers on FDI – e.g. Southard (1931), Barlow (1953), Robinson (1961), Behrman (1962) – but the techniques of analysis are now considerably more sophisticated.[9] The business analyst is inclined to pay more attention to industry- and firm-specific characteristics and the behaviour of competitors affecting the targeting of foreign markets, the location of different kinds of production and the timing of the FDI. Work by Porter (1986) on the configuration of the activities by MNEs, by Knickerbocker (1973) and Graham (1975, 1978) on the bunching of FDI in particular countries, and by Kogut (1985a, 1985b) on the role of environmental volatility as it affects the coordinating advantages of geographically diversified activities, is also relevant.

Political scientists and legal scholars generally seek to identify, but not to measure, the politically and legally oriented variables likely to favour the choice of production sites. Indeed, as a general observation, with the possible exception of seeking to quantify economic risk and the general political climate of a country, there have been few attempts to subject political or legal variables to statistical testing.[10]

Perhaps the most comprehensive acknowledgement of the whole range of non-economic factors affecting the location of MNE activity is the efforts of the international banks and specialist institutions, e.g. BERI, Frost and Sullivan (the World Political Risk Forecast), Business International and Data Resources Inc. (Policon), which seek, on behalf of their clients, to rank countries by their perceived suitability to foreign direct investment. However, the weights applied to the variables identified as making up the attractiveness are completely subjective, and, to the best of our knowledge, there has been no systematic attempt to test the relationship between changes in their values with flows of direct investment or changes in international production.[11]

Most of the efforts to assess the significance of locational variables by non-economists have been cross-sectional; the major exception is by marketing scholars who have looked into the timing of the different stages of the internationalization process, and how an appropriate marketing strategy might vary according to changes in the size and character of a country's market and the policies pursued by host governments. Management scholars have also examined the role of cultural specific variables in affecting the location of subsidiaries by MNEs of different nationalities (Negandhi, 1983),[12] while the locus of decision taking and of subcontracting has particularly interested some organizational theorists. Some geographers have also concerned themselves with the location of MNE activity *within* particular regions or countries (Dicken, 1982; Dicken and Lloyd, 1980; and Hall et al., 1987).

Once again, we are fully persuaded that the factor endowments and market failure paradigm can be used to explain the interface between non-economic factors and the location of value-adding activities, and also of the way in which firms are likely to respond to change in the value of these variables.

The 'How' Sub-paradigm

It is, however, in the examination of the organization of international economic activity by firms that the most exciting analytical advances have been made outside economics. Here, without question, the dominant mode of thought has been the transaction-cost paradigm, which is at the heart of explaining and identifying the characteristics of market failure. Indeed, some commentators feel that the main tenets of the paradigm, as developed mainly by economists, have been inappropriately applied by scholars in other disciplines to explain situations it was not intended to explain (Robbins, 1985).

As one might expect, the transaction-cost paradigm has been most widely adopted by *organizational theorists* to explain the kind of questions identified on page 264. In other words, it has been taken out of the context of examining the appropriate mode of exchanging goods, assets and rights to explaining the nature and form of organizational structures *within* hierarchies and the relationships *between* hierarchies. Although, for the most part, organizational scholars have not explicitly made use of the paradigm in their examination of cross-border organizational relationships, implicitly, a lot of the literature on subsidiary–HQ relationships, and on comparative Japanese, European and US systems, deals with the economics of different forms of governance.

In principle, there seems no reason why the choice of the appropriate administrative mode for transacting resources should not be influenced by similar factors as the choice between markets and hierarchies. However, to be of operational value the transaction-cost paradigm may need to be used in conjunction with the principal–agent model. The argument runs like this. Where external markets fail to give the result that a firm using the market wishes, that firm may consider replacing that market by its own decision-taking process. In a sense, this is saying that the market as an agent for the firm has not performed in the firm's best interests. But, in many cases, this is not surprising, as there are always two parties to an exchange and, where each has a competing objective, there is. no presumption that the market will better serve one of the parties to the transaction more than the other. Exceptions include collaborative alliances, and some customer–supplier relationships. However, within a hierarchy, most decisions performed by the market are decentralized to agents of the owners (or principals) of the firm. Where the internal coordinating mechanism is working efficiently, this implies that the agent is behaving in a way consistent with the owner's wishes; *inter alia* this implies that the agent is both capable and rightly motivated. The structure of a principal–agent system is, of course, highly complex; and, within most hierarchies, agents are also principals in their own right. Moreover, there may be collective as well as individual agents.

The transaction-cost paradigm is useful in identifying situations in which the structure of the principal–agent relationship is appropriate. Viewed in this way, a purchase of a component from a supplier is no different from purchasing an hour's work from a mechanic. In both cases, a firm measures the intra-hierarchical transaction (or agency) costs in terms of the incentives and policing costs necessary to ensure quality control, optimum delivery schedules etc. Inasmuch as organization theory can help us identify and measure costs between production units in different countries, it can add much to our understanding of the 'how' of international production.

Marketing theory is also using a transaction cost approach to identify modes of penetrating new markets. Here an excellent representention of contemporary thinking is contained in a well-received paper by Anderson and Gatignon (1986, 1987). To an extent, their work suggests that disciplinary labels are meaningless, for the concepts and techniques used to evaluate the modes of entry into a particular market, which vary along a continuum from non-equity to 100 per cent subsidiaries, are exactly those which economists and business analysts might have been expected to deploy. At the same time, the authors bring the marketing perspective and orientation to their work, which does have some distinctive properties.

As indicated earlier in this chapter, *economic and business historians* have focused especially on the growth of international production as a form of cross-border vertical or horizontal integration. In recent years, they too have increasingly used a transaction-cost paradigm on their studies. Douglass North (1985), in an extremely perceptive article, has traced the history of organized exchanges in terms of the interplay between the costs of transacting and the institutional framework of society. In the pre-modern world, the cost of enforcing contracts was often prohibitive; most transactions were highly personalized, and the role of the state as a contract-enforcement agency was limited. By contrast, over the past two centuries, the costs of transacting have been substantially reduced as a result of the development of uniform weights and measures, contract law, new behavioural norms, and improvements in both market coordinating and hierarchical exchange mechanisms. Quite differently, but no less interestingly, Nicholas (1982, 1983, 1986), in his study of the history of British MNE activity, has used the transaction-cost paradigm to explain the replacement of foreign distribution and marketing agents by sales subsidiaries of the exporting firms.

We now turn to *the political scientist*. He, too, is concerned with forms of governance; and the whole issue of public bureaucracy has overtones of the transaction costs and principal–agent paradigm. In the context of explaining the modes of international production, his main interest is the extent to which the external political environment (in the way identified) may affect the transaction costs and/or forms of internal governance by MNEs, and of how this might vary between countries. 'Would the establishment and operational costs of dealing with bureaucracy be lower in a joint venture compared with a 100 per cent subsidiary?' 'What are the costs of obtaining the necessary approval to set up a production facility in a foreign country rather than licensing a local firm to produce the same product?'[12] 'To what extent do governments discriminate against MNE subsidiaries that do not engage in local subcontracting?' These are all issues which involve an analysis of the political costs of engaging in alternative exchange relationships.

Finally, the *legal dimension*. The extent to which firms prefer full control over their affiliates or are willing to relinquish *de jure* control to external agents may rest on the legal provisions for protecting the firm against an abuse of the agent's position. Indeed, the failure of markets to operate efficiently may be directly related to the uncertainty of the participants as to any legal obligations each may bear to the other about the nature of the good, service or right transacted, and to the capability and fairness of the legal system to redress breaches and/or abuses of contract as and when they occur. Similarly, the extent to which firms may wish to conclude strategic alliances may be affected by the provisions of the anti-trust legislation. Translated into the international dimension, the issues of extra-territorality and the insurance against political risk – insofar as each affects the transaction costs of both hierarchies and markets – are of direct relevance to the way in which firms may organize their trans-border activities.

CONCLUSIONS

Although this chapter has been little more than a thumbnail sketch of the contribution of disciplines other than economics to our understanding of the nature and determinants of international production, it is hoped that it has demonstrated the interest and interdisciplinary nature of the subject under examination, and also the similarity of analytical approaches now being adopted by scholars. The second half of the chapter has suggested that the eclectic paradigm is robust enough to embrace non-economic variables (implicitly it does so already); and for the underlying theoretical rationale of the structure of the *OLI* configuration

– the distribution of factor endowments and the theory of market failure – to be usefully applied to answering questions of interest to the non-economist.

Clearly, we are only at the start of this particular approach to explaining international production, and it may be it will take quite a different direction to that implied by the author in this chapter. It may be that we have overstressed the convergence of analytical tools of the separate disciplines, or have underestimated the differences in perspectives taken by scholars from different powerful integrating forces at work. Scholars from organization, management and marketing are increasingly talking the same language and are publishing in each others' journals. Papers at professional conferences are increasingly being given by participants whose main sphere of interest is in another subject area. More specifically, on the questions which we have sought to address in this chapter, while much of the detailed empirical testing of specific hypotheses may continue to be unidisciplinary, we believe that the broad-canvas approach to our understanding of the nature and causes of international production will increasingly take on an interdisciplinary stance. And it is in promoting this approach that we believe that the paradigm explored in this chapter offers a powerful tool of analysis.

NOTES

1. We except from this criticism the very considerable body of knowledge now developing on the economics of technological innovations. For a survey of this literature as it relates to our understanding of the determinants of international production, see Cantwell (1986).
2. These, of course, overlap, in that factors internal to the firm which 'directly' affect production decisions may themselves have been influenced by external factors. In turn, internal circumstances may affect the way in which a firm reacts to exogenous change.
3. That is not to say these factors do not influence investment decisions, but simply that, in any decision about where to invest within a country, they are unlikely to be significant.
4. Indeed the original student of FDI and/or the MNE came from a variety of disciplines, especially economics, management and marketing, but they quickly interacted through their common interest in the international dimension. In the last ten years or so there has been a tendency for research on international business to be more closely identified with particular functional areas in business schools.
5. For an analysis of some of these relationships see Karlsson (1987).
6. The literature is too extensive even to be summarized here. Besides the work of Chandler and Wilkins quoted above, the reader should consult two volumes which well summarize the main streams of thought: Hertner and Jones (1985) and Teichova et al. (1986). Vol. 16 (1987) of the *Journal of Business and Economic History* also contains some useful articles on international business history.
7. One attempt to embrace both economic and political variables in a single explanatory model is that of Schneider and Frey (1985).
8. In even a casual reading of the management/organization/marketing literature, it is quite clear that the borders between these disciplines are very fuzzy; indeed, they frequently overlap particularly when questions relating to the process of a firm's decision-taking are being analysed.

9. For example, less use is made of field surveys and more of such statistical techniques as multiple discriminant and factor analysis. For a critical analysis of these and other political assessment models see de la Torre and Neckar (1986).
10. One exception being Schneider and Frey (1985). See also Root and Ahmed (1982).
11. In addition to the compilation of attractiveness compiled by the banks and large MNEs and specialist institutions, there have been other efforts to compile a compendium of economic and non-economic variables which might affect the location of investment. (See, for example, Bornschier and Heintz, 1979.)
12. Several authors in a special edition of *Journal of International Business Studies* (Vol. 14, Fall issue, 1983) devoted to cross-cultural management issues touch upon the impact of culture on locational variables, e.g. the work ethic, attitudes to authority and responsibility, the objectives of managers etc.

REFERENCES

Agmon, T. and Lessard, D.R. (1977), 'Investor recognition of corporate international diversification', *Journal of Finance*, **32** (September): 1049–55.

Alchian, A. and Demsetz, H. (1972), 'Production, information costs and economic organisation', *American Economic Review*, **62**, December, 777–95.

Aliber, R.Z. (1970), 'A theory of foreign direct investment', in Kindleberger, C.P. (ed.) *The International Corporation*, (Cambridge, MA: MIT Press).

Aliber, R.Z. (1971), 'The multinational enterprise in a multiple currency world', in Dunning, J.H. (ed.) *The Multinational Enterprise*, (London: Allen & Unwin).

Anderson, E. and Gatignon, H. (1986), 'Modes of foreign entry: a transaction cost analysis and propositions', *Journal of International Business Studies*, **17**, Fall, 1–26.

Barlow, E.R. (1953), *Management of Foreign Manufacturing Subsidiaries*, (Cambridge, MA: Harvard University Press).

Bartlett, C.A. and Ghoshal, S. (1988), 'Managing innovations in the transnational Corporation' in Bartlett, C.A., Doz, Y. and Heglund, G. (eds), *Research on Multinational Management*, (London: Addison Wesley).

Behrman, J.N. (1962), 'Foreign associates and their financing', in Mikesell, R. (ed.), *US Private and Government Investment Abroad*, (Oregon: Oregon University Press).

Boddewyn, J.J. (1986), *International Political Strategy. A Fourth Generic Strategy*, paper presented to the Academy of International Business, London meeting, November, 1986.

Bornschier, V. and Heintz, P. (1979), A source-book of data based on the study of MNCs economic policy and economic development, *Soziologisches Institut der Universitat Zurich Bulletin*, Zurich, March.

Cantwell, J.A. (1986), *Technological Innovation and International Production in the Industrial World: A Study of the Accumulation of Capital in International Networks*, Ph.D. Thesis, University of Reading.

Chandler, A.D. Jr. (1962), *Strategy and Structure: The History of American Industrial Enterprise*, (Cambridge, MA: MIT Press).

Chandler, A.D. Jr. (1977), *The Visible Hand: The Managerial Revolution in American Business*, (Cambridge, MA: Harvard University Press).

Ching-Sung Wu (1987), *Strategic Alliances in Global Competition: Cases of Computers, Telecommunications and Semi-Conductor Industries*. (Mimeo).

De la Torre, J. and Neckar, D.H. (1986), *Forecasting Political Risk for International Operations*, Fontainbleau: INSEAD Working Research Paper No. 86/08.

Dicken, P. (1982), 'Foreign direct investment in European manufacturing industry; the changing position of the United Kingdom as a host country', *Geoforum II*, 289–313.

Dicken, P. and Lloyd, P.E. (1980), 'Patterns and process of change in the spatial distribution of foreign controlled manufacturing employment in the United Kingdom 1963–1975', *Environment and Planning, A*, **12**, 1405–26.

Doz Y. (1979), *Government Control and Multinational Strategies*, (New York: Praeger).

Doz, Y. (1985), *Strategic Management in Multinational Companies*, (Oxford: Pergamon Press).

Eiteman, D.K. and Stonehill, A. (1986), *Multinational Business Finance*, Reading, MA: Addison Wesley.

Forsgren, M. (1985), *The Foreign Acquisition Strategy – Internalization or Coping with Strategic Interdependencies in Networks*, Uppsala, Centre for International Business Studies, Working Paper 1985/2.

Friar, J. and Horwitch, M. (1984), 'The current transformation of technology strategy' (Mimeo).

Ghoshal, S. and Bartlett, C.A. (1987), *Organising for Innovations: Case of the Multinational Corporation*, Fontainebleau, INSEAD Working Papers. No. 87/04.

Graham, E.M. (1975), 'Oligopolistic Imitation and European Direct Investment in the United States', D.B.A. Dissertation, Harvard University, unpublished.

Graham, E.M. (1978), 'Transatlantic investment by multinational firms: a rivalistic phenomenon', *Journal of Post Keynesian Economics*, **1**, Fall, 82–99.

Grubel, H.G. (1968), 'Internationally diversified portfolios, welfare gains and capital flows', *American Economic Review*, **58**, December, 1299–314.

Håkansson, L. (ed.) (1982), *International Marketing and Purchasing of Industrial Goods: An Interaction Approach*, (Chichester: Wiley).

Hall, P., Breheny, M., McQuaid, R. and Hart, D. (1987), *Western Sunrise*, (London: Allen and Unwin).

Hamel, G. and Prahalad, C.K. (1985), 'Do you really have a global strategy?', *Harvard Business Review*, **63**, 139–48.

Hertner, P. and Jones, G. (1986), *Multinationals: Theory and History*, (Aldershot and Brookfield, VT: Gower).

Imai, K. (1985), *Network Organisation and Incremental Innovation in Japan*, Institute of Business Research, Hitosubashi Discussion Paper no. 122, July.

Imai, K. and Itami, H. (1984), 'Interpenetration of organisation and market: Japan's firm and market in comparison with the US', *International Journal of Industrial Organization*, **2**, 284–310.

Imai, K., Nonaka I. and Takeuchi, H. (1984), *Managing the New Product Development Process: How Japanese Companies Learn and Unlearn*, paper presented at the Harvard Business School Colloquium on Productivity and Technology, Boston, MA.

Johanson, J. and Vahlne, J.E. (1977), 'The internationalisation process of the firm – a model of knowledge development and increasing foreign market commitments'. *Journal of International Business*, **8**, Spring/Summer, 23–32.

Johanson, J. and Mattson, L.G. (1987a), 'Internationalization in industrial systems – a network approach', in Hood, H. and Vahlne, J.E. (eds), *Strategies in Global Competition* (Chichester and New York: John Wiley).

Johanson, J. and Mattson, L.G. (1987b), 'Interorganizational relations in industrial systems: a network approach compared with a transaction-cost approach', *International studies of Management and Organization*, **xvii**, 34–48.

Karlsson, C. (1987), 'Corporate families to handle galloping technology', in Hood, N. and Yahlne, J.E., *Strategies in Global Competition*, (Chichester and New York: John Wiley).

Kogut, B. (1985a), 'Designing global strategies: corporate and competitive value-added chain', *Sloan Management Review*, **25**, Summer, 15–28.

Kogut, B. (1985b), 'Designing global strategies: profiting from operational flexibility', *Sloan Management Review*, **26**, Fall, 27–38.

Knickerbocker, F.T. (1973), *Oligopolistic Reaction and the Multinational Enterprise*, Cambridge, MA: Harvard University Press.

Lodge, G.C. and Vogel, E.F. (eds) (1987), *Ideology and National Competitiveness*, (Boston, MA: Harvard Business School Press).

Mattson, L.G. (1985), 'An appreciation of a network approach to marketing: defending and changing market positions', in Dhalakia, N. and Arndt, J. (eds), *Alternative Paradigms for Widening Marketing Theory*, (Greenwich, CT: JAI Press).

Negandhi, A.R. (1933), 'Cross cultural management research: trends and future directions', *Journal of International Business Studies*, **14**, Fall, 91–114.

Nicholas, S.J. (1982), 'British multinational investment before 1939', *Journal of European Economic History*, **II**.

Nicholas, S.J. (1983), 'Agency contracts, institutional modes and the transition of foreign direct investment by British manufacturing multinationals before 1939', *Journal of Economic History*, **43**, 675–86.

Nicholas, S. (1986), 'The theory of multinational enterprise as a transactional mode', in Hertner, P. and Jones, O. (eds), *Multinationals: Theory and History*, (Aldershot: Gower).

Nonaka (1994), 'A dynamic theory of organizational knowledge creation', *Organizational Science*, **5** (1) 14–37.

North, D. (1985), 'Transaction costs in history', *Journal of Economic History*, **42**, 566–76.

Ouchi, W.G. (1980), 'Markets, bureaucracies and class', *Administrative Science Quarterly*, **25**, 129–41.

Porter, M.E. (ed.) (1986), *Competition in Global Industries* (Boston, MA: Harvard Business School Press).

Porter, M. and Fuller, M.B. (1986), 'Coalitions and global strategy', in Porter, M.E. (ed.), *Competition in Global Industries*, (Boston, MA: Harvard Business School Press).

Prahalad, C.K. and Doz, Y.L. (1987), *The Multinational Mission*, (London and New York: The Free Press).

Robbins, J.A. (1985), 'Organisations and economics. Some logical problems of transaction costs analysis', *Academy of Management Proceedings*, 181–5.

Robinson, H.J. (1961), *The Motivation and Flow of Private Foreign Investment*, Stanford, CA Stanford Research Institute.

Root, F.R. and Ahmed, A. (1978), 'The influence of policy instruments on manufacturing direct foreign investment in developing countries', *Journal of International Business Studies*, **9**, Winter, 81–93.

Rugman, A.M. (1979), *International Diversification and the Multinational Enterprise*, (Lexington, MA: Lexington Books).

Sauvant, K. (1986), *International Transactions in Services*, (Boulder, CO and London: Westview Press).

Southard, F.A. Jr. (1931), *American Industry in Europe*, (Boston, MA: Houghton Mifflin).

Stopford, J.M. and Wells, L.T. (1972), *Managing the Multinational Enterprise*, (New York: Basic Books).

Teece, D.J. (1981a), 'The multinational enterprise: market failure and market power considerations', *Sloan Management Review*, **22**, 3–18.

Teece, D.J. (1981b), 'The market for know-how and the efficient international transfer of technology', *The Annals of the Academy of Political and Social Science*, **458**, 81–96.

Teece, D.J. (1983), 'Technological and organizational factors in the theory of the multinational enterprise', in Casson, M.C. (ed.), *Growth of International Business*, (London: Allen & Unwin).

Teece, D.J. (1987), 'Profiting from technological innovation: implications for integration, collaboration, licensing and public policy', in Teece, D.J. (ed.), *The Competitive Challenge*, (Cambridge, MA: Ballinger).

Teichova, A., Levy-Leboyer, M. and Nussbaum, H. (eds) (1986), *Multinational Enterprise in Historical Perspective*, (Cambridge: Cambridge University Press).

Wilkins, A. and Ouchi, W.G. (1983), 'Efficient cultures exploring the relationship between culture and organizational performance', *Administrative Science Quarterly*, **25**, 468–81.

Wilkins, M. (1970), *The Emergence of Multinational Enterprise: American Business Abroad from the Colonial Era to 1914*, (Cambridge, MA: Harvard University Press.

Wilkins, M. (1974), *The Maturing of Multinational Enterprise: American Business Abroad from 1914 to 1970*, (Cambridge, MA: Harvard University Press).

Williamson, O.E. (1975), *Markets and Hierarchies: Analysis and Antitrust Implications* (New York: The Free Press).

Yeh Rhy-song and Sagafi-nejad, T. (1987), 'Organizational Characteristics of American and Japanese firms in Taiwan', *Academy of Management Best Papers Proceedings*, pp. 111–15.

10. Reappraising the eclectic paradigm in an age of alliance capitalism*

INTRODUCTION

Over the last decade or so, a number of events have occurred that, viewed collectively, suggest that the world economy may be entering a new phase of market-based capitalism – or, at least, changing its trajectory of the past century. These events recognize no geographical boundaries, and they range from changes in the way in which individual firms organize their production and transactions to a reconfiguration of location-specific assets and the globalization of many kinds of economic activity.

The pre-eminent driving force behind these events has been a series of systemic technological and political changes, of which a new generation of telecommunication advances and the demise of central planning in Eastern Europe and the renaissance of the market economy in China are, perhaps, the most dramatic. But no less far reaching has been the economic rejuvenation of Japan and the emergence of several new industrial powers – especially from East Asia – whose approach to market-based capitalism – both at a socio-institutional and a techno-economic level (Freeman and Perez, 1988; Ruigrok and Van Tulder, 1995) – is very different from that long practised by Western nations.

The interrelated and cumulative effects of these phenomena have compelled scholars to re-examine some of their cherished concepts about market-based capitalism, and to do so in two major respects. The first is the growing acceptance that, by themselves, competitive market forces do not necessarily ensure an optimum innovation-led growth path in a dynamic and uncertain world. This is partly because technology is an endogenous variable – not an exogenous one as assumed in the received literature – and partly because the pressures of frequent and unpredictable technological and political changes do not permit a Pareto-optimal allocation of resources (Pigou, 1932). With the acceleration of technological change, and a growing emphasis on institutional learning and continuous product improvement, both the concepts and the policy prescriptions of our forefathers are becoming less relevant each day.

* From *Journal of International Business Studies*, **26** (3) (1995): 461–89.

The second revered concept that is now under scrutiny is that the resources and competencies of wealth-creating institutions are largely independent of each other, and that individual enterprises are best able to advance their economic objectives, and those of society, by competition rather than by co-operation. Unlike the first idea, this concept has only been severely challenged over the last decade, although, for more than a century, scholars have acknowledged that the behaviour of firms may be influenced by the actions of their competitors (Cournot, 1851), while Marshall (1920) was one of the first economists to recognize that the spatial clustering or agglomeration of firms with related interests might yield agglomerative economies and an industrial atmosphere external to the individual firms, but internal to the cluster.

It is the purpose of this chapter to consider some of the implications of the changes now taking place in the global market-place for our understanding of the determinants of multinational enterprise (MNE) activity, and especially the eclectic paradigm of international production.[1] The main thrust of our argument is that, although the autonomous firm will continue to be the main unit of analysis for understanding the extent and pattern of foreign-owned production, the OLI configuration determining transborder activities is being increasingly affected by the collaborative production and transactional arrangements between firms, and that these need to be more systematically incorporated into the eclectic paradigm. But, prior to subjecting this idea to closer examination, we briefly outline the underlying assumptions of the extant theory of MNE activity in the mid-1980s.

HIERARCHICAL CAPITALISM

For most of the present century, the deployment of resources and capabilities in market-oriented economies has been shaped by a micro-organizational system known as Fordism and a macro-institutional system known as hierarchical capitalism.[2] The essential characteristic of both these systems is that the governance of production and transactions is determined by the relative costs and benefits of using markets and firms as alternative organizational modes. In conditions of perfect competition, where exchange and co-ordination costs are zero and where there are no externalities of production or consumption, all transactions will be determined by market forces. Business entities will buy their inputs at arm's-length prices from independent firms and households, and sell their outputs at arm's length prices to independent purchasers.

In practice, such a governance structure has rarely existed; to some degree, all markets contain some impurities. Such impurities are of two kinds. The first is structural market failure, which arises from the actions of participants in or outside the market to distort the conditions of demand or supply. The second is endemic or natural market failure, where either, given the conditions of supply and demand, the market *qua* market is unable to organize transactions in an optimal way, *or* it is difficult to predict the behaviour of the participants. Such endemic market failure essentially reflects the presence of uncertainty, externalities, and the inability of producers to capture fully increasing returns to scale in conditions of infinite demand elasticity. It also accepts that bounded rationality, information asymmetries and opportunism are more realistic principles governing economic conduct (Williamson, 1985, 1993) than perfect cognition and profit- or utility-maximizing behaviour on the part of the transactors in the market.

It is partly to avoid or circumvent such market imperfections, and partly to recoup the gains of a unified governance of interrelated activities, that single-activity firms choose to internalize intermediate product markets and, in so doing, become diversified firms. To co-ordinate these different activities, the administrative system takes on the guise of a hierarchy, and as Chandler (1962, 1990) has well demonstrated, as US firms internalized more markets in the last quarter of the nineteenth century, so hierarchical capitalism came to replace 'arm's-length' capitalism.

Throughout most of the present century, as economic activity has become increasingly specialized and more complex, and as technological advances and political forces have created more endemic market imperfections, the role of large hierarchies, relative to that of markets, as an organizational modality has intensified. At the firm level, the fully integrated production facilities of enterprises such as the Ford Motor Company[3] in the 1960s epitomized the *raison d'être* for, and the extreme form of, hierarchical capitalism; hence the coining of the term 'Fordism'. At a sectoral level, the proportion of output from most industrial countries supplied by vertically integrated or horizontally diversified firms rose throughout most of the twentieth century.[4] Until the late 1970s, scholars usually considered co-operative modes of organizing economic activity as *alternatives* to hierarchies or markets, rather than as part and parcel of a micro-organizational *system*, in which interfirm and intrafirm transactions complement each other. This, in part, reflected the fact that, in the main, economists viewed the boundary of a firm as the point at which its owners relinquished *de jure* control over resource harnessing and usage, and, to a large extent, this boundary was thought to be coincident with a loss of majority equity ownership. It is not surprising, then, that, for the most part, minority joint ventures were regarded as a second-best alternative to full ownership. At the same time, most contractual arrangements were considered as market transactions – even in situations in which there was some element of a continuing and information-sharing relationship between the parties to the exchange.

We would mention two other important features of twentieth-century hierarchical capitalism. The first is that it implicitly assumes that the prosperity of firms depends exclusively on the way in which their managements internally organize the resources and capabilities at their disposal. These include the purchased inputs from other firms and the marketing and distribution of outputs. Admittedly, the behaviour of such firms might be affected by the strategies of other firms, for example oligopolistic competitors, monopolistic suppliers, large customers, and labour unions. But, with these exceptions, in hierarchical capitalism, the external transactions of firms are assumed to be *exogenous*, rather than *endogenous*, to their portfolio of assets and skills, and to the way in which these assets and skills are combined with each other to create further value-added advantages.

The second characteristic of hierarchical capitalism is that firms primarily react to endemic and structural market failure by adopting 'exit' rather than 'voice'-type strategies. Hirschman (1970) first introduced this concept of exit and voice to explain the responses of firms and nation states to threats to their economic sovereignty. He postulated two such responses: 'exit' to a better alternative, and 'voice', which he defined as any attempt at all to change, rather than escape from, an objectionable state of affairs (p. 30). Borrowing from Hirschman's terminology, we might identify two reactions of firms to the presence of market failure. These are: (i) to 'exit', where the response is to replace the market by internal administrative fiat, and (ii) to 'voice', where the response is to work with the market (in this case the buyers of its products or the sellers of its purchases) to reduce or eliminate market failure.

Our reading of the *raison d'être* for hierarchical capitalism, particularly its US brand, is that it was (and still is) an 'exit' reaction to market failure.[5] To a limited extent, 'voice' strategies are evident in joint equity ventures and contractual agreements, and in compensatory institutional instruments (e.g. futures and insurance markets). But, in general, collaborative production, marketing or innovatory projects or problem solving are eschewed. Contract disputes are usually resolved by litigation procedures rather than by propitiating attempts to remove the cause of the disputes. Competition and adversarial relations, rather than co-operation and synergistic affinities, are the hallmarks of hierarchical capitalism, and this is evident in the conduct of both interfirm and intrafirm co-ordination procedures and transactions. Hierarchical capitalism rarely interprets the roles of firms and governments as being complementary to each other (World Bank, 1991).

It is beyond the scope of this chapter either to trace the factors that led to hierarchical capitalism and the scale system of production, or to describe its characteristics in any detail. (The reader is invited to consult Oman, 1994 and Ruigrok and Van Tulder, 1995 on these matters.) Suffice to mention that, between the mid-1870s and the early 1970s, a series of technological, organizational and financial events occurred that helped reduce the transaction and co-ordination costs of multi-activity hierarchies relative to those of arm's-length intermediate product markets. Moreover, in contrast to the craft system of production which preceded it, the main impact of the mass production system was felt in the fabricating or assembling, rather than in the processing, sectors. And, it was in the former sectors where – in order to co-ordinate better the stages of production, to reduce the risks of supply irregularities, and to ensure quality control over downstream operations – firms began to internalize intermediate product markets and to engage in vertical integration and horizontal diversification in order to capture the economies of scope and scale.

We have already asserted that mainstream economic and organizational theorists paid only scant attention to this phenomenon until the post-war period,[6] and that much of the credit for such work as was done must go to scholars interested in the explanation of the growth of MNEs.[7] In the 1950s, both Edith Penrose (1956) and Maurice Bye (1958) sought to explain the extension of a firm's territorial boundaries in terms of the perceived gains to be derived from vertical and horizontal integration. Later, Penrose formulated a more general theory of the growth of firms (Penrose, 1959), but her penetrating insights into the advantages of internalized markets (although she never used this term)[8] had to wait many years before they were adequately acknowledged.[9]

Since the mid-1970s, there has been a plethora of academic papers and monographs that have tried to interpret the existence and growth of MNEs in terms of the benefits that such firms are perceived to derive from internalizing cross-border intermediate product markets.[10] Although several scholars have considered co-operative arrangements as alternatives to fully owned affiliates, and as forms of quasi-internalization,[11] for the most part, they have been accommodated in a market/hierarchies transaction costs model, with such arrangements being perceived as a point on a continuum between arm's-length markets and complete hierarchies.

The eclectic paradigm, first put forward by the present author at a Nobel Symposium in 1976, is different from internalization theory[12] in that it treats the competitive (so called O-specific) advantages of MNEs, apart from those which arise from the act of cross-border internalization, as *endogenous* rather than as *exogenous* variables. This means that the paradigm is not just concerned with answering the question of why firms engage in FDI, in preference to other modes of cross-border transactions. It is also concerned with why these firms possess unique resources and competencies – relative to their competitors of other nationalities – and why they choose to use at least some of these advantages jointly with a portfolio of foreign-based immobile assets.

At the same time, as so far enunciated, the eclectic paradigm is embedded within a socio-institutional framework of hierarchical capitalism, which, as stated earlier, presumes that the wealth-creating and efficiency-enhancing properties of an MNE are contained within the jurisdiction of its ownership. Thus, using the OLI nomenclature, except where they are acquired by M&As,

the O advantages of firms are presumed to be created and organized quite independently of their dealings with other firms; the L advantages of countries are assumed to reflect the scope and character of their unconnected immobile assets, and the way in which hierarchies and markets determine their use; and the propensity of firms to internalize intermediate product markets is based primarily on the presumption that most kinds of market failure[13] faced by firms are generally regarded by them as immutable (i.e. exogenous). Currently, the eclectic paradigm only peripherally embraces the ways in which the participation of firms in collaborative arrangements, or in networks of economic activity, affect the configuration of the OLI variables facing firms at a given moment of time, or on how this configuration may change over time. Partly (one suspects) this is because the value of such arrangements is difficult to quantify; and partly because interfirm transactions have been perceived to be of only marginal significance in the techno-economic production system of Fordism and in the socio-institutional paradigm of hierarchical capitalism.

ALLIANCE CAPITALISM

As suggested in the introduction, a series of events over the last two decades has led several scholars to suggest that the world is moving to embrace a new trajectory of market capitalism. This has been variously described as alliance, relational, collective, associate and the 'new' capitalism.[14] A critical feature of this new trajectory – which is essentially the outcome of a series of landmark technological advances and of the globalization of many kinds of value-added activity – is that it portrays the organization of production and transactions as involving both co-operation and competition between the leading wealth-creating agents.[15] This view is in marked contrast to that which has dominated the thinking of economists since Adam Smith, whereby collaboration among firms is viewed as a symptom of *structural* market failure,[16] rather than as a means of reducing *endemic* market failure. And, it would be a bold scholar who would argue that most agreements concluded between firms over the last hundred years have been aimed at facilitating rather than inhibiting competition.

But our reading of the literature suggests that both the *raison d'être* for concluding interfirm alliances and their consequences for economic welfare have significantly changed over the last two decades. We would at least hypothesize that a powerful contemporary motive for concluding such arrangements is to reduce the transaction and co-ordinating costs of arm's-length market transactions, and to leverage the assets, skills and experiences of partner firms. Another motive is to create or extend hierarchical control, which may also prompt firms to engage in M&As. However, co-operative arrangements differ from M&As in three respects. First, the former usually involve only a part – and sometimes a minor part – of the collaborating firms' activities. Second, they may entail no change in the ownership structure of the participating firms; and third, whereas the hierarchical solution implies an 'exiting' by firms from the dictates of the market-place, the alliance solution implies a 'voice' strategy of working within these dictates to maximize the benefits of the joint internalization of interrelated activities.

The choice between a hierarchical and alliance modality as a means of lessening arm's-length market failure clearly depends on their respective costs and benefits. The literature on the rationale for joint ventures and non-equity transactions – *vis-à-vis* markets and hierarchies – is extensive and well known, and will not be repeated here.[17] It is, however, generally accepted that the choice rests on a trade-off between the perceived benefits of sharing risks and capital outlays on the one hand, and the costs of a loss of control associated with a reduced (or no) ownership on the other. Partly, the outcome will be influenced by the success of the 'voice' strategy between the participants, as illustrated, for example, by the exchange of information, the division of managerial and financial responsibility, and the distribution of profits. But, in the main, most scholars view the choice as being determined by the most cost-effective way of organizing a portfolio of resources and capabilities.

Another reason for collaborative arrangements, however, has less to do with reducing the co-ordinating and transaction costs of alternative organizational modalities, and more to do with protecting existing – or gaining new – proprietary, or O-specific, advantages. Co-operative alliances have a parallel with strategic asset-acquiring FDI: according to several researchers, over the past decade, the principal incentives for alliance formation have been to lower transaction costs, develop new skills and overcome or create barriers to entry in national or international markets.[18] Sometimes, these alliances take the form of shared ownership, that is, the merging of firms, or the setting up of greenfield joint ventures. But, since the early 1980s, the great majority of interfirm associations have tended to be less formal in structure and more specific in scope and purpose. According to research undertaken at MERIT (Hagedoorn, 1993a), the goal of most strategic alliances has been to gain access to new and complementary technologies, to speed up innovatory or learning processes and to upgrade the efficiency of particular activities – for example, research and development (R&D), marketing and distribution, manufacturing methods, etc. – rather than to enhance the overall prosperity of the participating firms.

It is perhaps worth rehearsing some of the reasons for the spectacular growth of competitiveness-enhancing alliances since 1980. Essentially, these reduce to the impact that technological advances and the globalization of the market economy have had on the organization of economic activity. The consequences of the former – a supply-side phenomenon – have been fivefold: first, to raise the fixed – and particularly the learning and innovatory – costs of a wide range of manufacturing and service activities; second, to increase the interdependence between distinctive technologies that may need to be used jointly to supply a particular product;[19] third, to enhance the significance of multi-purpose, or core, technologies, such as robotization, informatics and biotechnology; fourth, to truncate – and sometimes dramatically so[20] – the product life cycle of a particular product; and fifth, which is partly a consequence of the other four characteristics and partly a result of the changing needs of consumers, to focus on the upgrading of core competencies of firms, and on the way these are organized, as a means of improving global competitive advantage.

One of the main consequences of the globalization of economic activity described earlier has been to force firms to be more dynamically competitive. This is particularly the case for firms from advanced industrial countries, and it is demonstrated in two main ways: first, a more determined effort to raise the efficiency with which they produce their existing products, and second, by the successful innovation of new products and the upgrading of assets and skills throughout their value chains.

This combination of global supply and demand pressures on competitiveness has caused firms – and particularly large hierarchies – to reconsider both the scope and organization of their value-added activities. In particular, the 1980s and early 1990s have seen three major responses. First, there has been a fairly general movement by firms towards the shedding or disinternalization of activities both along and between value chains, and towards the specialization on those activities that require resources and capabilities in which firms already have (or can acquire) a perceived competitive advantage. This is a *concentrate on critical competency response*. At the same time, because of the interdependence of technological advances (e.g. computer-aided design and manufacturing techniques), firms find that they need to assure access to the products over which they have now relinquished control. Firms may also wish to exercise some influence over the quality and price of these products, and over the innovation of new products. This means that disinternalization is frequently replaced, not by arm's-length transactions, but by controlled interfirm co-operative arrangements. Such agreements are particularly noticeable between firms and their subcontractors in the more technologically advanced and information-intensive sectors (Hagedoorn, 1993b).[21]

Second, because of competitive pressures, the huge and rising costs of R&D and speedier rates of obsolescence, firms – particularly in high-technology sectors – have been increasingly induced to engage in cross-border alliances. Freeman and Hagedoorn (1992) traced 4192 of these alliances between 1980 and 1989. They found that 42 per cent were organized through R&D pacts; that 90 per cent were between companies from the Triad; and that 63 per cent were formed during the second half of the 1980s. The majority of the alliances involved large firms competing as oligopolies in global markets.[22] The need, on the one hand, for operational participation and, on the other, for complementarity, shared learning and an encapsulation of the innovation time span has combined to make the 'voice' strategy of co-operative ventures a particularly suitable mode for sustaining and advancing competitive advantage.[23] At the same time, to be successful, an *asset-seeking alliance response* does have implications for governance structures, a point we will take up later in this chapter.

The third response of firms to recent events has been to try to widen the markets for their core products, so as to benefit fully from the economies of scale. This is, itself, a cost-reducing strategy. It serves to explain much of market-seeking and strategic asset-acquiring FDI – especially between firms servicing the largest industrial markets – as well as those of minority-owned foreign joint ventures and non-equity arrangements that are intended to gain speedy entry into unchartered and unfamiliar territories. Thus, of the 4192 alliances identified by Freeman and Hagedoorn, 32 per cent were geared towards improving access to markets. As might be expected, such alliances were particularly numerous among firms with Japanese partners. Such a 'voice' strategy might be termed a *market-positioning alliance response*.

Each of the three responses identified has widened the sphere of influence of the firms participating in external partnerships. Such actions have also caused a heightened degree of dependence on firm partners for their own prosperity. Thus, the resources and capabilities of companies such as Philips, IBM and Toyota – each of which has several hundred interfirm alliances – cannot be considered in isolation. Gomes-Casseres and Leonard-Barton (1994) have identified some eighty recently established learning, supply and positioning partnerships in the personal digital assistants (PDA) sector alone.[24] One must also consider the impact that these alliances have had on their internally generated O-specific advantages. The design and performance of the next generation of automobiles, microchips and computers critically depend not only on the advances in innovatory and manufacturing capabilities of the leading assembling companies, but also on the way these capabilities interact with those of their suppliers. Boeing's competitive advantages in producing the next breed of large passenger aircraft are likely to rest as much on the interaction it has with its suppliers and its customers (e.g. the airlines) as it does on its own technological and commercial strengths. Siemens – a leading producer of mainframe computers – relies heavily on cutting-edge technology supplied by Fujitsu. In its venture to explore the sea bed, Kennecott's mining consortium brings together a large number of firms supplying very different, but interrelated, technologies from many different sectors. Lorenzoni and Baden Fuller (1995) give several examples of organizations which view their subcontractors as partners in innovation and skill development.[25]

Of course, interfirm co-operation is not a new phenomenon. What is, perhaps, new is its relative significance as an organizational form, whereby the success of the firms involved is being increasingly judged by each party's ability to generate innovation-led growth; by the range, depth and closeness of the interaction between themselves and their alliance or networking parties; and by the effect that such alliances are having upon overall industrial performance. It is the combination of these factors, taken together with the twin forces of the dis-internalization of hierarchical activities and the impressive growth of M&As to gain access to complementary assets,[26] which leads us to suggest – along with Gerlach (1992) – that the term *alliance* capitalism might be a more appropriate description of the features of innovation-led capitalism now spreading through the globalizing economy, than the term *hierarchical* capitalism.

A distinctive feature of alliance capitalism is its governance structure. Within a hierarchy, decisions rest on a pyramid of delegated authority. In establishing and strengthening relationships with other firms, customers and labour unions, success is usually judged by the extent to which the hierarchy is able to obtain its inputs at the least possible cost, and to sell its output at the most profitable price. Relationships between firms and within firms are normally defined by a written contract.

In alliance capitalism, decisions are more likely to rest on a consensus of agreement between the participating parties, and there is rarely any formal structure of authority. Such an agreement is based upon a commitment, on the part of each party, to advance the interests of the alliance, and upon mutual trust, reciprocity and forbearance between the partners. In the modern factory practising flexible manufacturing or Toyota-like production methods, labour is not thought of as a cog in the wheel, as it is in traditional Fordism, but as a partner in the wealth-producing process. Suppliers are not just expected to produce goods to agreed specifications, but to work actively with the purchasing firms to upgrade continually the quality and/or lower the price of their outputs. Even within the hierarchical firm, technological and organizational imperatives are requiring each function, activity and stage of production to be closely integrated with the other. Thus, for example, the purchasing and R&D departments may be expected to work with the manufacturing departments on the design and development of new products and production methods. The personnel, finance and production departments each need to be involved in the introduction of new working procedures and incentive arrangements. At the same time, industrial customers and large wholesale and retail outlets may be expected to play an increasingly significant role in determining the direction and pattern of product improvement.

The growing significance of interfirm co-operative transaction arrangements would suggest that 'voice', relative to 'exit', strategies are becoming more cost-effective. This, of course, could be due either to the 'push' factor of the increasing net costs of hierarchical control, or to the 'pull' factor of the reduced costs of alliances. It is likely that both factors have been at work in recent years, but it can surely be no accident that the thrust towards alliance capitalism first originated in Japan, whose culture, like that of many other Eastern nations, especially values such qualities as teamwork, trust, consensus, shared responsibility, loyalty and commitment, which are the essential ingredients of any successful partnership. These qualities – together with the recognition that, by improving quality control throughout the value chain and cutting inventories to the minimum – enabled Japanese producers, particularly in the fabricating sectors, to break into their competitors' markets, and to adopt the production strategies and working practices that conformed to the resource and institutional advantages of their home countries. Indeed, most researchers are agreed that the two most significant competitive advantages of Japanese firms that evolved during the post-war period were, first, the way they restructured their production and intrafirm transactions, and second, the way they managed and organized their vertical and horizontal relationships with other firms.[27]

Before considering the implications of the new trajectory of market-based capitalism for our theorizing about MNE activity, we would mention three other trends in economic organization that are also favouring more, rather than less, interfirm co-operation. The first concerns the renewed importance of small and medium-sized firms in the global economy.[28] This has led some commentators, notably Naisbitt (1994), to assert that yesterday's commercial behemoths are tomorrow's dinosaurs. The reasoning behind this assertion that 'small is beautiful' is that modern production methods, accelerating technological advances, more demanding consumers and the growing importance of services are all eroding the advantages of large plants based on a continuous, scale-friendly and relatively inflexible production system.

While accepting that there is some evidence for this contention (e.g. much of the growth in employment now taking place in the advanced industrial countries is in small to medium-sized firms) we, like Harrison (1994), are not convinced that the strategic influence of large firms is diminishing. We would prefer to suggest that any restructuring of the activity of large firms reflects their preferences for replacing hierarchical with alliance relationships, and that an increasing number of small firms are, in fact, part of *keiretsu*-like networks, which, more often than not, are dominated by large, lead or flagship firms (D'Cruz and Rugman, 1992, 1993; Rugman and D'Cruz, 1995) or as Lorenzoni and Baden Fuller (1995) put it, 'strategic centers'. Many small firms, too, are either spin-offs of large firms, or owe their prosperity to the fact that the latter are frequently their main clients and suppliers of critical assets. The kinds of example one has in mind are the hundreds of second- or third-tier suppliers to the large Japanese automobile companies;[29] the intricate web of horizontal relationships between the various associated companies of the Japanese 'soga shosa'; the extensive outsourcing of both hardware and software development by the Japanese video game producer Nintendo; the network of knitwear firms in the Modena region of Northern Italy; the many hundreds of Asian subcontractors to the giant footwear and apparel firms (e.g. Nike and Benetton).[30] The competitive advantages of the firms in these and similar groups are closely dependent on the exchange of skills, learning experiences, knowledge and finance between the firms in the network, and on the example and lead given by the flagship firms.

The second trend is related to the first. It is the growth of spatial clusters of economic activities that offer external or agglomerative economies to firms located within the cluster. The idea, of course, is not new. Marshall paid much attention to it in his study of UK industry in the early twentieth century (Marshall, 1920). Recently, it has been given a new lease of life by Porter (1990), who considers the presence of related industries as one of the four key determinants of a country's competitive assets, and by Krugman (1991), who believes that such economies largely explain the geographical specialization of value-added activities. While the evidence on the subnational spatial concentration of particular activities is still fragmentary, what information we have (including that documented in a new book by Kenichi Ohmae, 1995), such as it is, suggests that, in the technology and information-intensive sectors, not only are MNEs creating multiple strategic centres for specialized activities, but such clusters are becoming an increasingly important component of competitiveness (Enright, 1994). The form and extent of the clusters may differ.[31] Sometimes, they relate to a range of pre-competitive innovatory activities (e.g. science parks); sometimes to very specific sectors (e.g. auto assemblers and component suppliers);[32] and sometimes to entrepreneurial or start-up firms and co-operative research organizations (e.g. SEMITECH). Sometimes the local networks are contained in a very small geographical area (e.g. financial districts in London and New York); sometimes they spread over a whole region (e.g. the cluster of textile firms in North Italy).

The third trend is the growth of industrial networks. Interfirm alliances can range from being simple dyadic relationships to being part of complex, and often overlapping, networks consisting of tens, if not hundreds, of firms. The literature on industrial networks is extensive;[33] but, up to now, the subject has been mainly approached from a marketing or an organizational, rather than from an economic, perspective. This is, perhaps, one reason why internalization theory and the eclectic paradigm of international production have sometimes been portrayed as alternative approaches to network analysis. But to the economist, a network is simply a web of interdependent dyadic relationships. One must admit, this makes theorizing about the behaviour of the participants very difficult, but no more so than theorizing about the behaviour of oligopolists. It is also true that the economist is primarily concerned with the firm as a unit of analysis, but this in no way should inhibit him (or her) from considering the implications for the firm when it is a part of a network of related firms.

What is clear, however, is that, as networks of alliances become more important, the composition and behaviour of the group of firms becomes a more important determinant of the foreign production of the individual firms comprising the network. Nowhere is this more clearly seen than in the role played by the *keiretsu* in influencing both the competitive advantages of its member firms, and in the way in which these advantages are created, upgraded and used.

REAPPRAISING THE ECLECTIC PARADIGM

We now turn to consider the implications of alliance capitalism for our theorizing about the determinants of MNE activity, and, more particularly, for the eclectic paradigm. In brief, the implications are threefold. First, the concept of the competitive, or O-specific, advantages of firms, as traditionally perceived, needs to be broadened to take *explicit* account of the costs and benefits derived from interfirm relationships and transactions (both at home and abroad), and particularly those that arise from strategic alliances and networks. Second, the concept of location (or L) advantages of countries (as traditionally perceived) needs to give more weight to the following factors: (i) the territorial embeddedness of interdependent immobile assets in particular geographical areas;[34] (ii) the increasing need for the spatial integration of complex and rapidly changing economic activities; (iii) the conditions under which interfirm competitiveness-enhancing alliances may flourish; and (iv) the role of national and regional authorities in influencing the extent and structure of localized centres of excellence.

Third, the idea that firms internalize intermediate product markets, primarily to reduce the transaction and co-ordination costs associated with them, needs to be widened to encompass other – and, more particularly, dynamic and competitiveness-enhancing – goals, the attainment of which may be affected by micro-governance structures. The incorporation of external alliances into the theory of internalization presents no real problems, other than semantic ones. Either one treats a non-equity alliance as an extension of intrafirm transactions, and accepts that the theory is concerned less with a *de jure* concept of hierarchical control and ownership, and more with the *de facto* ways in which interdependent tangible and intangible assets are harnessed and leveraged, or one treats the interfirm alliance as a distinctive organizational mode, and more specifically one which is complementary to, rather than a substitute for, a hierarchy. Partly, of course, the choice will depend on the unit of analysis being used. Is it the alliance or the network, *per se*, in which case the idea of 'group internalization' may be a relevant one? Or, is the unit of analysis the individual enterprises that comprise the alliance or network? For our purposes, we shall take the individual enterprise as the unit of analysis.[35]

Let us now be more specific about the modifications that alliance capitalism seems to require of the eclectic paradigm. We consider each of its components in turn. On the left-hand side of Table 10.1, we set out some of the more important OLI variables that scholars traditionally have hypothesized to influence the level and structure of MNE activity. Research has shown that the composition and significance of these determinants will differ according to the value of four contextual variables: (i) the kind of MNE activity being considered (*market, resource, efficiency* or *strategic asset seeking*); (ii) the portfolio of location-bound assets of the countries from which the FDI originates, and in which it is concentrated; (iii) the technological and other attributes of the sectors in which it is being directed; and (iv) the specific characteristics (including the production, innovatory and ownership strategies) of the firms undertaking the investment.

The variables identified in Table 10.1 are more than a checklist. They are chosen because a trilogy of extant economic and behavioural theories – namely, *the theory of industrial organization and market entry, the theory of location*[36] and *the theory of the firm*[37] – suggests that they offer robust explanations of the ownership structure of firms, the location of their activities, and the ways in which they govern the deployment of resources and capabilities within their control or influence. However, until very recently, none of these theories has paid much attention to the role of co-operative agreements in influencing MNE activity.

On the right-hand side of Table 10.1, we identify some additional OLI variables which we believe, in the evolving era of alliance capitalism, need to be incorporated into our theorizing about MNE activity. The table shows that not all of the OLI variables listed require modification. Thus, of the Oa-specific variables, we would not expect the formation of strategic partnerships to influence greatly the internal work processes of the participating firms, although technological advances, and the need for continuous product improvement, are likely to demand a closer interaction between related value-adding activities, and may well enhance the contribution of shop-floor labour to raising process productivity. Nor would we expect the proprietary rights of brand ownership, favoured access to suppliers, or the financial control procedures of firms to be much affected by co-operative agreements.

By contrast, Oa advantages stemming from a firm's ability to create and organize new knowledge, to maintain and upgrade product quality, to seek out and forge productive linkages with suppliers and customers, especially – in unfamiliar markets – to externalize risk, to manage successfully a complex portfolio of core assets and value-creating disciplines, and to internalize the skills and learning experiences of other organizations, may be strongly

Table 10.1 A reconfiguration of the eclectic paradigm of international production

1 Ownership-specific advantages (of enterprise of one nationality (or affiliates of same) over those of another)	
Hierarchical-related advantages	Alliance or network-related advantages
(a) Property right and/or intangible asset advantages (Oa) Product innovations, production management, organizational and marketing systems, innovatory capacity, non-codifiable knowledge: 'bank' of human capital experience; marketing, finance, know-how, etc.	(a) *Vertical alliances* (i) Backward access to R&D, design engineering and training facilities of suppliers. Regular input by them on problem solving and product innovation on the consequences of projected new production processes for component design and manufacturing. New insights into, and monitoring of, developments in materials, and how they might impact on existing products and production processes
(b) Advantages of common governance, i.e. of organizing Oa with complementary assets (Ot) (i) Those that branch plants of established enterprises may enjoy over *de novo* firms. Those due mainly to size, product diversity and learning experiences of enterprise, e.g. economies of scope and specialization. Exclusive or favoured access to inputs, e.g. labour, natural resources, finance, information. Ability to obtain inputs on favoured terms (due, for example, to size or monopsonistic influence). Ability of parent company to conclude productive and co-operative interfirm relationships, e.g. as between Japanese auto assemblers and their suppliers. Exclusive or favoured access to product markets. Access to resources of parent company at marginal cost. Synergistic economies (not only in production, but in purchasing, marketing, finance, etc., arrangements)	(ii) Forward access to industrial customers, new markets, marketing techniques and distribution channels, particularly in unfamiliar locations or where products need to be adapted to meet local supply capabilities and markets. Advice by customers on product design and performance. Help in strategic market positioning (b) *Horizontal alliances* Access to complementary technologies and innovatory capacity. Access to additional capabilities to capture benefits of technology fusion, and to identify new uses for related technologies. Encapsulation of learning and development times. Such interfirm interaction often generates its own knowledge feedback mechanisms and path dependencies
(ii) Which specifically arise because of multinationality. Multinationality enhances operational flexibility by offering wider opportunities for arbitraging, production shifting and global sourcing of inputs. More favoured access to and/or better knowledge about international markets, e.g. for information, finance, labour, etc. Ability to take advantage of geographic differences in factor endowments, government intervention, markets, etc. Ability to diversify or reduce risks, e.g. in different currency areas, and creation of options and/or political and cultural scenarios. Ability to learn from societal differences in organizational and managerial processes and systems. Balancing economies of integration with ability to respond to difference in country-specific needs and advantages	(c) *Networks* (i) of similar firms: Reduced transaction and co-ordination costs arising from better dissemination and interpretation of knowledge and information, and from mutual support and co-operation between members of network. Improved knowledge about process and product development and markets. Multiple, yet complementary, inputs into innovatory developments and exploitation of new markets. Access to embedded knowledge of members of networks. Opportunities to develop 'niche' R&D strategies, shared learning and training experiences, e.g. as in the case of co-operative research associations. Networks may also help promote uniform product standards and other collective advantages. (ii) business districts: As per (i) plus spatial agglomerative economies, e.g. labour market pooling. Access to clusters of specialized intermediate inputs, technological spillovers, and linkages with knowledge-based institutions, e.g. universities, co-operative R&D establishments etc.

2 Internalization incentive advantages (i.e. to circumvent or exploit market failure)	
Hierarchical-related advantages	Alliance or network-related advantages
Avoidance of search and negotiating costs To avoid costs of moral hazard, information asymmetries and adverse selection, and to protect reputation of internalizing firm To avoid costs of broken contracts and ensuing litigation Buyer uncertainty (about nature and value of inputs (e.g. technology) being sold) When market does not permit price discrimination Need of seller to protect quality of intermediate or final products To capture economies of interdependent activities (see (b) above) To compensate for failure or absence of future markets To avoid or exploit government intervention (e.g. quotas, tariffs, price controls, tax differences, etc.) To control supplies and conditions of sale of inputs (including technology) To control market outlets (including those which might be used by competitors) To be able to engage in practices, e.g. cross-subsidization, predatory pricing, leads and lags, transfer pricing, etc., as a competitive (or anti-competitive) strategy	While, in some cases, time-limited interfirm co-operative relationships may be a substitute for FDI, in others they may add to the I incentive advantages of the participating hierarchies, R&D alliances and networking which may help strengthen the overall competitiveness of the participating firms. Moreover, the growing structural integration of the world economy is requiring firms to go outside their immediate boundaries to capture the complex realities of know-how trading and knowledge exchange in innovation, particularly where intangible assets are tacit and need speedily to adapt competitive-enhancing strategies to structural change Alliances or network-related advantages are those which prompt a 'voice' rather than an 'exit' response to market failure; they also allow many of the advantages of internalization without the inflexibility, bureaucratic or risk-related costs associated with it. Such quasi-internalization is likely to be most successful in cultures in which trust, forbearance, reciprocity and consensus politics are at a premium. It suggests that firms are more appropriately likened to archipelagos linked by causeways rather than self-contained 'islands' of conscious power. At the same time, flagship or lead MNEs, by orchestrating the use of mobile O advantages and immobile advantages, enhance their role as arbitragers of complementary cross-border value-added activities

3 Location-specific variables (these may favour home or host countries)	
Hierarchical-related advantage	Alliance or network-related advantages
Spatial distribution of natural and created resource endowments and markets Input prices, quality and productivity, e.g. labour, energy, materials, components, semi-finished goods International transport and communication costs Investment incentives and disincentives (including performance requirements etc.) Artificial barriers (e.g. import controls) to trade in goods Societal and infrastructure provisions (commercial, legal, educational, transport and communication) Cross-country ideological, language, cultural, business, political, etc., differences Economies of centralization of R&D production and marketing Economic systems and policies of governments: the institutional framework for resource creation and allocation	The L-specific advantages of alliance formations arise essentially from the presence of a portfolio of immobile local complementary assets, which, when organized within a framework of alliances and networks, produce a stimulating and productive industrial atmosphere. The extent and type of business districts, industrial or science parks and the external economies they offer participating firms are examples of these advantages which, over time, may allow foreign affiliates and cross-border alliances and network relationships better to tap into, and exploit, the comparative technological and organizational advantages of host countries. Localized networks may help reduce the information asymmetries and likelihood of opportunism in spatially linked markets. They may also create local institutional thickness, and foster interfirm learning economies and social embeddedness. Note that globalization, while heightening the mobility of some O-specific advantages, is also increasing some distance-related transaction costs, and leaning to more 'sticky' places (Markusen,1994)

influenced by some kinds of co-operative arrangements. Moreover, each of these advantages may better enable a firm both to engage in transborder activities and to seek out appropriate agreements to strengthen and consolidate its competitive competencies.

The literature identifies two groups of competitive Ot advantages arising from the way in which a firm combines its own resources and capabilities with those of other firms. The first are those which a firm gains from being a multi-activity enterprise, independently of where these activities are located. Such economies of common governance may enable an established firm of one nationality to penetrate a foreign market more easily than a single-activity competitor of the same or of another nationality. The second type of Ot advantage arises as a direct consequence of foreign production.[38] The impact of alliance capitalism is to offer an additional avenue for firms to acquire and build up both types of advantages – and, normally, to do so with less financial outlay and risk than hierarchical capitalism might involve.[39]

It is, however, the second kind of Ot advantage that is the quintessence of both the multi-activity and the multinational firm. The implication is, then, that any decline in hierarchical activity reflects a diminution in the net benefits of internalized markets, which may lead to a *concentrate on core competency strategy*. It is also implied that other ways of obtaining the advantages are becoming more attractive (e.g. as a result of a reduction of other kinds of market failure). In our present context, the switch in organizational form is a reflection of a shift in the techno-economic system of production. As we have already argued, this tends to favour a 'voice', rather than an 'exit', response to the inability of markets to cope with the externalities of interdependent activities in the first place.

It is too early to judge the extent to which the economies of synergy (and operational flexibility) are being realized in a more cost-effective way by external partnerships, rather than by hierarchical control. In any event, as we have already stated, many – indeed, perhaps, the majority of – strategic business alliances identified by scholars should not be regarded as substitutes for FDI, as they are directed to achieving very specific purposes.

Turning next to the internalization advantages (I) of MNE activities, it is perhaps here where the co-operative interaction between Japanese firms is most clearly demonstrated as a viable alternative to the full ownership and control favoured by US firms. Here, too, it is not so much that interfirm agreements add to the internalization incentives of firms. It is rather that they may help to achieve the same objective more effectively, or spread the capital and other risks of the participating firms. In other words, interfirm agreements may provide additional avenues for circumventing or lessening market failure where the FDI route is an impractical option.

Clearly, the impact of alliance capitalism on the organization of economic activity will vary according to the type of market failure being considered; it is also likely to be highly industry and country specific. Institutional structures, learning paths, the extent of social and territorial embeddedness, cultural values, and national systems of education and innovation are likely to play an especially important role. In some countries, such as Japan, there is less incentive by firms to internalize markets in order to avoid the costs of broken contracts, or to ensure the quality of subcontracted products. The reason is simply because these types of market failure are minimized by the 'voice' strategies of buyers and sellers, which are built upon mutual interest, trust and forbearance. The *keiretsu* network of interfirm competitive interaction – sometimes between firms in the same sector and sometimes across sectors – is perhaps one of the most frequently quoted alternatives to hierarchical internalization. Although there is frequently some minority cross-ownership among the networking firms, the relationship is built upon objectives, values and strategies that negate the need for the internalization of some kinds of market failure. At the same time, the extent and pattern of *keiretsu* ties is likely to vary between industrial sectors. It is, for example, most pronounced in the fabricating sectors (where the number and degree of complexity of transactions are the most numerous) and the least pronounced in the processing sectors. And it is a fact that Japanese FDI in Europe – relative to its US counterpart – is concentrated in those sectors in which interfirm, rather than intrafirm, transactions are the preferred modality of counteracting market failure in Japan.

While it would be inappropriate to generalize from this example, it is nevertheless the case that – again due to the adoption of new and flexible production techniques – American firms in the auto and consumer electronic sectors are disinternalizing parts of their value chains. At the same time, they are reducing the number of major suppliers and delegating more design and innovatory functions to them.[40] Moreover, Japanese-owned auto assemblers in the United States are replicating or modifying the *keiretsu*-type relationships of their parent companies as more Japanese suppliers have been setting up subsidiaries, or engaging in co-operative agreements with US firms to supply components to the assemblers (Banjerji and Sambharya, 1996).

Most certainly, a 'voice' response to market failure is raising the profile of strategic partnerships in the organizational strategies of MNEs. Nevertheless, it is the case that some kinds of benefits of cross-border value-added activity can only be effectively realized through a full hierarchical control over such operations. Examples include situations in which path dependency, learning experience and the global control over financial assets and key technologies and competencies bring their own O-specific advantages, which, because of possible conflicts of interest, would not be realizable from interfirm agreements. Such agreements, then, would probably be confined to very specific areas of a firm's value-added activities, and, noticeably, those that are outside its core competencies need specialized proficiencies or require to be closely monitored for quality control, and are too costly to produce internally (Quinn and Hilmer, 1994). But, to achieve and sustain many of the most valuable O-specific advantages of multinational operations, hierarchical control probably will remain the principal mode of internationalization, and this applies as much to the Japanese as it does to US- and European-based MNEs.

We finally consider how the advent of alliance capitalism is affecting the location-specific variables influencing international production. We have already indicated that the received literature generally assumes these variables to be exogenous to individual firms, at least at a given moment of time, although, over time, such firms may affect the L advantages of particular countries or regions.

There are essentially two main ways in which alliance capitalism may affect, or be affected by, the presence and structure of immobile assets. The first is that it may introduce new L-specific variables, or modify the value of those traditionally considered by location theory. The second is that the response of firms to economic geography may be different because of the impact that external alliances may have upon their competitive strengths and global strategies.

Let us first deal with the first type of effect. Chief among the L variables affecting MNE activity – and that surveys have revealed have become more significant in the past decade – is the availability of resources and capabilities that investing firms believe are necessary both to upgrade and make best use of their core O-specific advantages. In some cases, these complementary assets, or the rights to their use, can be bought on the open market (e.g. power supplies and transport and communication facilities), but, in others, and noticeably in regimes of rapid technological progress (Teece, 1992), the 'continuous handshake' of an alliance relationship rather than the 'invisible hand' of the market is favoured (Gerlach, 1992). Since frequently FDI requires the establishment of several of these bilateral relationships, it follows that the positioning of a constellation of related partners becomes a prime locational factor. Where part or all of the constellations are sited in close proximity to each other, then additional benefits may arise. These include not only the static agglomerative economies earlier identified, but also the dynamic externalities associated with the gathering and dissemination of information, and the cross-fertilization of ideas and learning experiences.

The attention given by governments of host countries – or of regions in host countries – to the building of a critical mass of interrelated activities, which is consistent with the perceived dynamic comparative advantage of their location-bound assets, and to the use of FDI in order to create or upgrade core competencies to advance this goal, is just one illustration of the growing benefits to be derived from interfirm linkages.[41] These serve as an L-pull factor. Casual empiricism, both past and present, provides ample examples of how the presence of spatially related business networks attracts new investors, and recent evidence unearthed by Wheeler and Mody (1992), Harrison (1994), Lazerson (1993), Herrigel (1994), Audretsch and Feldman (1994) and Enright (1994) confirms these impressions. It also reveals that an innovation-driven industrial economy, which seeks to be fully integrated into world markets, needs to focus more attention on the development of clusters of interfirm linkages, of intelligent regions and of local institutional thickness (Amin and Thrift, 1994).

Chapter 2 of volume 2 of these essays will give attention to some of the paradoxes of the emerging globalized economy. One of these relates to the apparent contradiction between the truncation of geographical space, for example in the financial services industries, brought about by advances in telecommunications and information technologies, and the growth of new local or regional economic districts, made up of economic activities which need to be in close propinquity of each other. We believe that the key to this paradox lies in the changing significance of different kinds of distance-related transaction and co-ordination costs. While recent innovations and organizational changes have enhanced the cross-border mobility of many kinds of goods, services and assets, they have also led to new rounds of specialization and 'stickiness' in economic activity, such that 'vast areas of substantively complex, irregular, uncertain and extremely time dependent transactions have been created' (Storper and Scott, 1995, p. 508). These transactions are not only unstructured and highly sensitive to distance; they also confer substantial interactive learning benefits on the participating firms. Examples of such closely knit economic clusters of activity are given in Enright (1994), Markusen (1994) and Storper and Scott (1995).

The new trajectory of capitalism has other implications for the locational requirements of MNE investors. Some of these are set out in Table 10.1. As a generalization, while traditional production-related variables generally are unaffected or becoming less important, those to do with minimizing transaction and co-ordination costs of markets or the dysfunctioning of hierarchies, those specific to being part of a group or cluster of related activities, and those that help protect or upgrade the global competitiveness of the investing firm, are becoming more important.[42]

Turning now to the second type of effect that alliance capitalism has on L advantages, we ask the following question: how far, and in what ways, are the responses of MNEs to the L advantages of countries themselves changing because of the growing pluralism of corporate organizations? The answer is that such pluralism allows firms more flexibility in their locational strategies, and that the immobile assets of countries will affect not only the extent and pattern of foreign participation, but also its organizational form. Thus, on the one hand, the opportunities for networking in a specific country may increase FDI. This is particularly the case when an MNE acquires a firm that is already part of a network. On the other hand, networking may also reduce FDI, as it may allow a foreign firm to acquire the complementary assets it needs without making an equity stake.

Of the two scenarios, the one which is more likely to occur will, of course, depend on a host of industry-, firm- and country-specific circumstances. But, our point will have been made if it is accepted that the hypotheses of scholars about the responses of firms to at least some L-specific variables may need to be modified in the light of the growing significance of non-equity-based co-operative arrangements, and of networks of firms with related interests. We also believe that the ways in which MNEs choose to leverage and use a portfolio of interrelated location-bound assets, with those of their own O-specific advantages and the complementary competencies of external partners, are, themselves, becoming an increasingly important competitive advantage of such firms.

CONCLUSIONS

This chapter has suggested that the socio-institutional structure of market-based capitalism is undergoing change. The catalyst is a new wave of multi-purpose generic technological advances and the demands of knowledge-based production, which are compelling more co-operation among economic agents. Though part of that co-operation is 'bought' by firms through M&A activity, the growing significance of interfirm partnering and of networking is demanding a re-examination of traditional approaches to our understanding of the extent and form of international business activity.

Our discussion has concentrated on only one of these approaches, namely the eclectic paradigm of international production, and has suggested that its explanatory framework needs to be modified in three main ways. First, the role of innovation in sustaining and upgrading the competitive advantages of firms and countries needs to be better recognized. It also needs to be more explicitly acknowledged that firms may engage in FDI and in cross-border alliances in order to acquire or learn about foreign technology and markets, as well as to exploit their existing competitive advantages. *Inter alia*, this suggests a strengthening of its analytical underpinnings to encompass a theory of innovation – as, for example, propounded by Nelson and Winter (1982) and Cantwell (1989, 1994) – that identifies and evaluates the role of technological accumulation and learning as O-specific advantages of firms, and the role of national education and innovation policies affecting the L advantages of countries.

Second, the paradigm needs to recognize better that a 'voice' strategy for reducing some kinds of market failure – and particularly those to do with opportunism and information impactness by participants in the market – is a viable alternative to an 'exit' strategy of hierarchical capitalism, and that, like hierarchies, strategic partnerships are intended to reduce endemic market failure, and may help to advance innovatory competitiveness rather than inhibit it. Among other things, this suggests that theories of interfirm co-operation or collective competition, which tend to address issues of static efficiency (Buckley, 1993), need to be widened to incorporate questions of dynamic efficiency, for example market positioning.

Third, the eclectic paradigm needs to acknowledge that the traditional assumption that the capabilities of the individual firm are limited to its ownership boundaries (and that, outside these boundaries, factors influencing the firm's competitiveness are exogenous to it) is no longer acceptable whenever the quality of a firm's efficiency-related decisions is significantly influenced by the collaborative agreements it has with other firms. The concept of decision taking has implications that go well beyond explaining FDI and international production; indeed, it calls into question some of the fundamental underpinnings of the theory of industrial organization.

Much of the thrust of this chapter has been concerned with suggesting how these three evolving concepts – innovation-led growth, a 'voice' reaction to market failure, and co-operation as a competitiveness-enhancing measure – affect the OLI configuration facing firms engaging, or wishing to engage, in cross-border transactions. In doing so, it has thrown up a number of casual hypotheses as to the kinds of O-specific advantages that are most likely to be affected by interfirm alliances and networks, and about how the opportunities to engage in such alliances or networks may affect, and be affected by, the portfolio of interrelated location-specific assets. The analysis has also sought to identify some of the implications of the gathering pace of innovation-led production, and of alliance capitalism, for the organization of economic activity. In doing so, it has suggested that the internalization paradigm still remains a powerful tool of analysis, as long as it is widened to incorporate strategic asset-acquiring FDI and the dynamic learning activities of firms, and to take account more explicitly of the conditions under which a 'voice' strategy of interfirm co-operation may be a preferable option to an 'exit' strategy for reducing the transaction and co-ordination costs of arm's-length markets, and building interactive learning-based competitiveness.[43]

There has been some exploratory empirical testing, using both field and case study data, of the impact of alliances and networks on the performance of locational and organizational strategies of participating firms. Studies by Gomes-Casseres (1994, 1995) on the global computer and electronics industries; by Gomes-Casseres and Leonard-Barton (1994) on the multimedia sector; by Mowery (1988) on the commercial aircraft industry; by Brooks et al. (1993) on the container transport industry; by Shan and Hamilton (1991) and Whittaker and Bower (1994) on the pharmaceutical industry; by Peng (1993) on the role of network and alliance strategies in assisting the transition from a collectivist to a market-based economy; by Helper (1993) on the 'exit' and 'voice' sourcing strategies of the leading auto assemblers; by Enright (1993, 1994), Glaismeier (1988), Henderson (1994), Lazerson (1993), Piore and Sabel (1984), Saxenian (1994) and Scott (1993) on the rationale for regional clusters and specialized industrial districts in Europe and the United States; and multiple case studies by a number of authors on the roles of *keiretsu*-based transactions and relational contracting as alternatives to hierarchies (e.g. Lincoln, 1990) are just a few examples.

But much more remains to be done. Indeed, it is possible that the basic contention of this chapter – that innovation-led production systems and co-operative interfirm agreements are emerging as the dominant form of market-based capitalism – is incorrect. At the same time, it would be difficult to deny that important changes – and, for the most part, irreversible technological changes – are afoot in the global economy, and that these changes are requiring international business scholars to re-examine at least some of the concepts and theories that have dominated the field for the last two decades or more.

NOTES

1. As set out, most recently, in Dunning (1993a, Ch. 4).
2. See, for example, Dunning (1994a) and Gerlach (1992) for a more extensive analysis of this proposition.
3. Especially at River Rouge (USA), where its empire included ore and coal mines, 70 000 acres of timberland, saw mills, blast furnaces, glass works, ore and coal barges, and a railway (Williamson, 1985).
4. As, for example, is shown by data published in the US Census of Manufactures and the UK Census of Production (various issues).
5. For full details, see Chandler (1962) and Dunning (1994a).
6. At the time it was published (1937), Coase's article on 'The nature of the firm' was treated as an 'aberration' by his fellow economists (Williamson, 1993). As Coase himself acknowledged (1993), in the 1980s there was more discussion of his ideas than during the whole of the preceding 40 years.
7. I do not know for sure which particular scholar first used the concept of market failure to explain the existence and growth of the MNE. I first came across the concept of internalization in the early 1970s in a chapter by John McManus entitled, 'The theory of the multinational firm', in an edited volume by Pacquet (McManus, 1972).
8. It is also of some interest that Penrose did not cite Coase in any of her work.
9. There were, I think, two reasons for this. The first was that mainstream micro-economists were strongly influenced (one might almost say hidebound) by the static equilibrium models of Chamberlin (1933) and Robinson (1933); and the second was that Penrose had not formalized her theory in a manner acceptable to her colleagues.
10. Among the most frequently quoted scholars are Buckley and Casson, Hennart, Rugman and Teece. A summary of the views of the internalization school is contained in Dunning (1993a). See also Rugman (1981), Hennart (1982), Buckley and Casson (1985) and Casson (1987).
11. See, for example, the contributions to Buckley's edited volume (1993).
12. Elsewhere (Dunning, 1993b), we have suggested paradigm is a more appropriate term to apply to explain the reactions of firms to cross-border market failure.
13. Exceptions include structural market failure deliberately engineered by firms and the extent to which they may be able to influence the content and degree of market failure, for example

by lobbying for particular government action, and by the setting up of compensating institutions, for example insurance and future markets, to reduce risk.

14. See especially Best (1990), Gerlach (1992), Lazonick (1991, 1992), Michalet (1991), Dunning (1994a) and Ruigrok and Van Tulder (1995).
15. Here, we think it appropriate to make the point that the expression *alliance capitalism* should be perceived partly as a socio-cultural phenomenon and partly as a techno-organizational one. The former suggests a change in the ethos and perspective towards the organization of capitalism and, in particular, towards the relationships between the participating institutions and individuals. The latter embraces the formal structure of the organization of economic activity, including the management of resource allocation and growth. Alliance capitalism is an eclectic (*sic*) concept. It suggests both co-operation and competition *between* institutions (including public institutions) and between interested parties *within* institutions. *De facto*, it is also leading to a flattening out of the organizational structure of decision taking of business enterprises, with a pyramidal chain of command being increasingly replaced by a more heterarchical interplay between the main participants in decision taking. Finally, we would emphasize that we are not suggesting that alliance capitalism means the demise of hierarchies, but rather that the rationale and functions of hierarchies require a reappraisal in the socio-economic climate of the global market-place now emerging.
16. In the words of Adam Smith (1776), 'people of the same trade seldom meet together, even for merriment and diversion, but the conversation ends in a conspiracy against the public, or in some contrivance to raise prices'.
17. See especially Buckley and Casson (1988), Contractor and Lorange (1988), Kogut (1988), Hennart (1988, 1989) and Hagedoorn (1993a, 1993b).
18. The facts are documented in various publications, for example Freeman and Hagedoorn (1992), Hagedoorn (1990, 1993a, 1993b), Gomes-Casseres (1993) and UNCTAD (1993, 1994).
19. Some examples are set out in Dunning (1993a, pp. 605ff.): 'Optoelectronics, for example, is a marriage of electronics and optics and is yielding important commercial products such as optical fibre communication systems [Kodama, 1992]. The latest generation of large commercial aircraft, for example, requires the combined skills of metallurgy, aeronautical engineering and aero-electronics. Current medical advances often need the technological resources of pharmacology, biotechnology, laser technology, and genetic engineering for their successful commercialization. The design and construction of chemical plants involves innovatory inputs from chemical, engineering and materials sectors. New telecommunication devices embrace the latest advances in carbon materials, fibre optics, computer technology, and electronic engineering. Modern industrial building techniques need to draw upon the combined expertise of engineering, materials and production technologies. In its venture to explore the sea-bed, Kennecott's consortium brings together a large number of technical disciplines and firms from many different industrial sectors [Contractor and Lorange, 1988]. Since both the consumption and the production of most core technologies usually yield externalities of one kind or another, it follows that one or the other of the firms involved may be prompted to recoup these benefits by integrating the separate activities, particularly those which draw upon the same generic technology.'
20. Examples include the rapid obsolescence of successive generations of computers and the information-carrying power of microchips.
21. One particularly good example is the pharmaceutical industry, where the large drug companies are increasingly disinternalizing the most novel and risky types of biotechnology innovations to small specialist firms. In the words of two British researchers (Whittaker and Bower, 1994): 'The large pharmaceutical companies no longer view themselves as the primary innovators in the industry. ... The biotechnology companies take on the role of supplier of innovatory activity.' The authors go on to illustrate the symbiotic supplier/buyer relationship that is developing between the two groups of firms. 'The large drug company needs technologically novel products to market and the biotechnology company needs finance, sometimes some ancillary technical expertise in later-stage process development and formulation, skill in handling regulatory agreements and marketing forces' (p. 258). However, it should be pointed

out that in the last two years there have been some significant acquisitions of biotechnology companies by pharmaceutical MNEs.

22. For example, of the alliances identified by Freeman and Hagedoorn, 76.3 per cent were accounted for by 21 MNEs, each of whom had concluded 100 or more alliances.
23. At the same time, MNEs have increased the R&D intensity of their foreign operations, and have set up technological listening posts in the leading innovating countries.
24. The authors assert that such alliances result from the fusion of technologies from computer communications and consumer electronics; and that because no single firm had (or has) the internal capabilities or the time needed to produce a PDA, it was necessary to form a cluster of 'matching' alliances.
25. In their words, 'Competitive success requires the integration of multiple capabilities (e.g., innovation, productivity, quality, responsiveness to customers) across internal and external organizational boundaries' (p. 151).
26. Not to mention to preclude competition from gaining such assets.
27. See, for example, several chapters in an edited volume by Encarnation and Mason (1994).
28. As shown by a variety of indices.
29. See, for example, Banjerji and Sambharya (1996).
30. For further illustrations, see Hamel (1991), Harrison (1994), Stopford (1995), Whittaker and Bower (1994) and Lorenzoni and Baden Fuller (1995).
31. For an interesting discussion of the differing nature of business districts both in the United States and in other countries, see Markusen et al. (1991).
32. It is estimated that 70 per cent of all Toyota's suppliers are within 100 miles (160 km) of Toyota's main assembling complex in Tokyo.
33. See, particularly, Forsgren and Johanson (1991), Håkansson and Johanson (1993), Johanson and Mattsson (1987, 1994) and Johanson and Vahlne (1977).
34. In the words of Amin and Thrift (1994), and in the context of the globalizing economy, 'centers of geographical agglomeration are centers of representation, interaction and innovation within global production filieres'. It is their 'unique ability to act as a pole of excellence and to offer to the wide collectivity a well consolidated network of contacts, knowledge, structures and institutions underwriting individual entrepreneurship which makes a center a magnet for economic activity' (p. 13)
35. For an examination of the alliance as a unit of analysis, see Gomes-Casseres (1994).
36. Where country-specific characteristics are regarded as endogenous variables, then the theory of international economics becomes relevant. This is the position of Kojima (1978, 1990), who is one of the leading exponents of a trade-related theory of MNE activity.
37. In particular, the transaction cost theories of Coase and Williamson. The resource-based theory of the firm (Wernerfelt, 1984; Barney, 1991; Peteraf, 1993) is much broader and, in many respects, closer in lineage to industrial organization theory, as it is concerned with explaining the origin of a firm's sustainable competitive advantages in terms of resource heterogeneity, limits to competition and imperfect resource immobility.
38. It is these latter advantages that internalization economists claim *follow* from foreign-owned production, rather than *precede* it; although, of course, once established, these advantages may place the MNE in a more favoured position for sequential investment.
39. Of course, in some instances (e.g. jointly funded R&D projects), the resulting economic rents may also have to be shared.
40. Stopford (1995), drawing upon the World Automotive Components supplement published by the *Financial Times* on 12 July 1994, gives several examples of this phenomenon.
41. As is amply realized by the national governments of foreign investment agencies in their attempts to attract foreign firms to locate in their territories.
42. We accept that it may be difficult to separate the specific effect of alliance capitalism from the other forces influencing the L advantage of countries. This, indeed, is a fertile area for empirical research.
43. According to Storper (1994), those firms, sectors, regions and nations that are able to learn faster and more efficiently become competitive because knowledge is scarce and, therefore, cannot be imitated by new entrants or transferred by codified and formal channels to other firms, regions or nations.

REFERENCES

Amin, A. and Thrift, N. (eds) (1994), *Globalization, Institutions and Regional Development in Europe*, Oxford: Oxford University Press.

Audretsch, D.B. and Feldman, M.P. (1994), 'External economies and spatial clustering', in P. R. Krugman and A. Venables (eds), *The Location of Economic Activity: New theories and evidence*, London: Centre of Economic Policy Research (CPER).

Banjerji, K. and Sambharya, R.B. (1994), 'Vertical keiretsu and international market entry: The case of the Japanese automobile industry', *Journal of International Business Studies* **27**(1): 89–114.

Barney, J.B. (1991), 'Firm resources and sustained competitive advantage', *Journal of Management*, **17**: 99–120.

Best, M. (1990), *The New Competition: Institutions of Restructuring*, Cambridge, MA: Harvard University Press.

Brooks, M.R., Blunder, R.G. and Bidgood, C.I. (1993), 'Strategic alliances in the global container transport industry', in R. Culpan (ed.) *Multinational Strategic Alliances*, New York and London: The Haworth Press, pp. 221–50.

Buckley, P.J. (ed.) (1993), *Cooperative Forms of TNC Activity*, UNCTC Library on Transnational Corporations, Vol. 13, London and New York: Routledge.

Buckley, P.J. and Casson, M.C. (1985), *The Economic Theory of the Multinational Enterprise*, London: Macmillan.

Buckley, P.J. and Casson, M.C. (1988), 'A theory of cooperation in international business', in F.J. Contractor and P. Lorange (eds) *Cooperative Strategies in International Business*, Lexington, MA: D.C. Heath, pp. 31–53.

Bye, M. (1958), 'Self-financed multiterritorial units and their time horizon', *International Economic Papers*, **8**: 147–78.

Cantwell, J.A. (1989), *Technological Innovation and Multinational Corporations*, Oxford: Basil Blackwell.

Cantwell, J.A. (ed.) (1994), *Transnational Corporations and Innovatory Activities*, United Nations Library on Transnational Corporations, Vol. 17, London: Routledge.

Casson, M.C. (1987), *The Firm and the Market*, Oxford: Basil Blackwell.

Chamberlin, E. (1933), *The Theory of Monopolistic Competition*, Boston, MA: Harvard University Press.

Chandler, A.D. Jr. (1962), *Strategy and Structure*, Boston, MA: Harvard University Press.

Chandler, A.D. Jr. (1990), *Scale and Scope: The Dynamics of Industrial Capitalism*, Cambridge, MA: Harvard University Press.

Coase, R.H. (1937), 'The nature of the firm', *Economica*, **4**, November: 386–405.

Coase, R.H. (1988), *The Firm, the Market and the Law*, Chicago and London: University of Chicago Press.

Coase, R.H. (1993), 'The nature of the firm: meaning and influence', in O.E. Williamson and S.G. Winter (eds), *The Nature of the Firm*, New York and Oxford: Oxford University Press, pp. 34–74.

Contractor, F.J. and Lorange, P. (1988), *Cooperative Strategies in International Business*, Lexington, MA: D.C. Heath.

Cournot, A.A. (1851), *Researches into Mathematical Principles of the Theory of Wealth*, trans. N.T. Bacon, New York: Macmillan.

D'Cruz, J.R. and Rugman, A.M. (1992), 'Business networks for International Business', *Business Quarterly*, **54**, Spring: 101–7.

D'Cruz, J.R. and Rugman, A.M. (1993), Business networks for global competitiveness, *Business Quarterly*, **57**, Summer: 93–8.

Dunning, J.H. (1993a), *Multinational Enterprises and the Global Economy*, Wokingham: Addison Wesley.

Dunning, J.H. (1993b), *Globalization of Business*, London and New York: Routledge.

Dunning, J.H. (1994a), *Globalization, Economic Restructuring and Development*, The Prebisch Lecture for 1994, Geneva: UNCTAD.

Dunning, J.H. (1994b), 'The strategy of Japanese and US manufacturing investment in Europe', in M. Mason and D. Encarnation (eds), *Does Ownership Matter? Japanese Multinationals in Europe*, Oxford: Clarendon Press, pp. 59–86.

Encarnation, D. and Mason, M. (eds) (1994), *Does Ownership Matter? Japanese Multinationals in Europe*, Oxford: Clarendon Press.

Enright, M.J. (1993), 'Organization and coordination in geographically concentrated industries', in D. Raff and N. Lamoreaux (eds), *Coordination and Information: Historical Perspectives on the Organization of Enterprise*, Chicago: Chicago University Press, pp. 103–146.

Enright, M.J. (1994), 'Regional clusters and firm strategy', Paper presented to Prince Bertil Symposium on *The dynamic firm: The role of regions, technology, strategy and organization*, Stockholm, June.

Forsgren, M. and Johanson, J. (eds) (1991), *Managing Networks in International Business*, Philadelphia, PA: Gordon & Breach.

Freeman, C. and Hagedoorn, J. (1992), *Globalization of technology*, Maastricht Research Institute on Innovation and Technology (MERIT), Maastricht: Working Paper 92.013.

Freeman, C. and Perez, C. (1988), 'Structural crises of adjustment, business cycles, and investment behavior', in G. Dosi, C. Freeman, R. Nelson, G. Silverberg and L. Soete (eds), *Technical Change and Economic Theory*, London: Pinter.

Gerlach, M.L. (1992), *Alliance Capitalism: The Social Organization of Japanese Business*, Oxford: Oxford University Press.

Glaismeier, A. (1988), 'Factors governing the development of high tech industry agglomeratives: a tale of three cities', *Regional Studies*, **22**: 287.

Gomes-Casseres, B. (1993), 'Computers, alliances and industry evolution', in D.B. Yoffie (ed.), *Beyond Free Trade: Firms, Governments and Global Competition*, Boston: Harvard Business School Press, pp. 62–74.

Gomes-Casseres, B. (1994), 'Group versus group: How alliance networks compete', *Harvard Business Review*, July–August.

Gomes-Casseres, B. (1995), *Collective Competition: International Alliances in High Technology*, Boston, MA: Harvard University Press.

Gomes-Casseres, B. and Leonard-Barton, D. (1994), *Alliance Clusters in Multimedia: Safety Net or Entanglement*?, Boston, MA: Harvard Business School (mimeo).

Hagedoorn, J. (1990), 'Organizational modes of inter-firm cooperation and technology transfer', *Tecknovation*, **10**(1): 17–30.

Hagedoorn, J. (1993a), 'Understanding the rationale of strategic technology partnering: inter-organizational modes of cooperation and sectoral differences', *Strategic Management Journal*, **14**: 371–85.

Hagedoorn, J. (1993b), 'Strategic technology alliances and modes of cooperation in high technology industries', in G. Grabher (ed.), *The Embedded Firm*, London: Routledge, pp. 116–37.

Håkansson, H. and Johanson, J. (1993), 'The network as a governance structure', in G. Grabher (ed.) *The Embedded Firm*, London: Routledge, pp. 35–51.

Hamel, G. (1991), 'Competition for competence and inter-partner learning with international strategic alliances', *Strategic Management Journal*, **12**: 82–103.
Harrison, B. (1994), *Lean and Mean: The Changing Landscape of Power in the Age of Flexibility*, New York: Basic Books.
Helper, S. (1993), 'An exit-voice analysis of supplier relations: the case of the US automobile industry', in G. Grabher (ed.), *The Embedded Firm*, London: Routledge, pp. 141–60.
Henderson, V. (1994), 'Externalities and industrial development', in P. Krugman and A. Venables (eds), *The Location of Economic Activity: New Theories and Evidence*, London: Centre of Economic Policy Research (CPER).
Hennart, J.F. (1982), *A Theory of the Multinational Enterprise*, Ann Arbor, MI: University of Michigan Press.
Hennart, J.F. (1988), 'A transaction costs theory of equity joint ventures', *Strategic Management Journal*, **9**: 361–74.
Hennart, J.F. (1989), 'Can the new forms of investment substitute for the old forms? A transaction costs perspective', *Journal of International Business Studies*, **XX**: 211–33.
Herrigel, G.B. (1994), 'Power and the redefinition of industrial districts: the case of Baden Wurttemberg', in G. Grabher (ed.) *The Embedded Firm*, London: Routledge, pp. 227–52.
Hirschman, A.O. (1970), *Exit Voice and Loyalty*, Cambridge, MA: Harvard University Press.
Johanson, J. and Mattsson, L.G. (1987), 'Internationalization in industrial systems – network approach', in H. Hood and J.E. Vahlne (eds), *Strategies in Global Competition*, Chichester and New York: John Wiley.
Johanson, J. and Mattsson, L.G. (1994), 'The markets-as-networks tradition in Sweden', in G. Laurent, G.L. Lilien and B. Pras (eds) *Research Traditions in Marketing*, Dordrecht and Boston: Kluwer, pp. 321–46.
Johanson, J. and Vahlne, J.E. (1977), 'The internationalization process of the firm – a model of knowledge development and increasing foreign market commitments', *Journal of International Business Studies*, **8**, Spring/Summer: 23–32.
Kodama, F. (1992), 'Japan's unique capability to innovate: technology, fusion and its international implications', in T.S. Arrison, C.F. Bergsten and M. Harris (eds), *Japan's Growing Technological Capability: Implications for the US Economy*, Washington, DC: National Academy Press.
Kogut, B. (1988), 'Joint ventures: theoretical and empirical perspectives', *Strategic Management Journal*, **9**(4): 319–22.
Kojima, K. (1978), *Direct Foreign Investment: A Japanese Model of Multinational Business Operations*, London: Croom Helm.
Kojima, K. (1990), *Japanese Direct Investment Abroad*, Mitaka, Tokyo: International Christian University, Social Science Research Institute Monograph Series 1.
Krugman, P.R. (1991), *Geography and Trade*, Leuven: Leuven University Press and Cambridge, MA: MIT Press.
Lazerson, M. (1993), 'Factory or putting out? Knitting networks in Modena', in G. Grabher (ed.), *The Embedded Firm*, London: Routledge.
Lazonick, W. (1991), *Business Organization and the Myth of the Market Economy*, Cambridge: Cambridge University Press.
Lazonick, W. (1992), 'Business organization and competitive advantage: capitalist transformation in the twentieth century', in G. Dosi, R. Giannetti and P.A. Toninelli (eds), *Technology and Enterprise in a Historical Perspective*, Oxford: Claendon Press, pp. 119–63.

Lincoln, J. (1990), 'Japanese organization and organizational theory', *Research and Organizational Behavior*, **12**: 255–94.

Lorenzoni, G. and Baden Fuller, C. (1995), 'Creating a strategic center to manage a web of partners', *California Management Review*, **37**(3): 146–63.

Markusen, A. (1994), *Sticky Places in Slippery Spaces: The Political Economy of Post-War Fast Growth Regions*, New Brunswick Center for Urban Policy Research, Rutgers University Working Paper No. 79.

Markusen, A., Hall, P., Deitrick, S. and Campbell, S. (1991), *The Rise of the Gunbelt: The Military Remapping of Industrial America*, New York and Oxford: Oxford University Press.

Marshall, A. (1920), *Principles of Economies*, London: Macmillan.

McManus, J.C. (1972), 'The theory of the multinational firm', in G. Paquet (ed.), *The Multinational Firm and the Nation State*, Toronto: Collier Macmillan.

Michalet, C.A. (1991), 'Strategic partnerships and the changing international process', in L.K. Mytelka (ed.), *Strategic Partnerships: States, Firms and International Competition*, London: Pinter.

Mowery, D.C. (1988), *International Collaborative Ventures in US Manufacturing*, Cambridge, MA: Ballinger.

Naisbitt, J. (1994), *Global Paradox: The Bigger the World Economy, the More Political its Smallest Players*, New York: William Morrow.

Nelson, R.R. and Winter, S.G. (1982), *An Evolutionary Theory of Economic Change*, Cambridge, MA: Harvard University Press.

Ohmae, K. (1995), *The End of the Nation State: The Rise of Regional Economies*, London: Harper Collins.

Oman, C. (1994), *Globalization and Regionalization: The Challenge for Developing Countries*, Paris: OECD Development Centre.

Peng, M.W. (1993), *Blurring Boundaries: The Growth of the Firm in Planned Economies in Transition*, Washington Center for International Business Education and Research, University of Washington (mimeo).

Penrose, E.T. (1956), 'Foreign investment and growth of the firm', *Economic Journal*, **60**: 220–35.

Penrose, E.T. (1959), *The Theory of the Growth of the Firm*, Oxford: Basil Blackwell.

Peteraf, M. (1993), 'The cornerstones of competitive advantage: a resource based view', *Strategic Management Journal* **14**: 179–91.

Pigou, A.C. (1932), *The Economics of Welfare*, 4th Edition, London: Macmillan.

Piore, M.J. and Sabel, C.F. (1984), *The Second Industrial Divide: Possibilities for prosperity*, New York: Basic Books.

Porter, M. (1990), *The Competitive Advantage of Nations*, New York: The Free Press.

Quinn, J.B. and Hilmer, F.G. (1994), 'Strategic outsourcing', *Sloan Management Review* Summer: 43–55.

Robinson, J. (1933), *The Economics of Imperfect Competition*, London: Macmillan.

Ruigrok, W. and Van Tulder, R. (1995), *The Logic of International Restructuring*, London and New York: Routledge.

Rugman, A.M. (1981), *Inside the Multinationals: The Economics of Internal Markets*, London: Croom Helm.

Rugman, A.M. and D'Cruz, J.R. (1995), *The Five Partners Business Network Model*, Toronto: University of Toronto (mimeo).

Saxenian, A.L. (1994), *Regional Advantage: Culture and competition in Silicon Valley and Route 128*, Cambridge, MA: Harvard University Press.

Scott, A.J. (1993), *Technologies: High-technology industry and regional development in Southern California*, Berkeley and Los Angeles: University of California Press.
Shan, W. and Hamilton, W. (1991), 'Country-specific advantage and international co-operation', *Strategic Management Journal*, **12**(6): 419–32.
Smith, A. (1776), *An Inquiry into the Nature and Causes of the Wealth of Nations*, Vol. 1 (1947 edition published by Dent, London).
Stopford, J.M. (1995), 'Competing globally for resources', *Transnational Corporations*, **4**: 34–57.
Storper, M. (1944), *Institutions of a Learning Economy*, Los Angeles School of Public Policy and Social Research, UCLA.
Storper, M. and Scott, A.J. (1995), The wealth of regions', *Futures*, **27**(5): 505–26.
Teece, D.J. (1992), 'Competition, cooperation and innovation', *Journal of Economic Behavior and Organization*, **18**: 1–25.
UNCTAD (1993), *World Investment Report 1993: Transnational Corporations and Integrated International Production*, New York and Geneva: UN.
UNCTAD (1994), *World Investment Report 1994: Transnational Corporations, Employment and the Workplace*, New York and Geneva: UN.
Wernerfelt, B. (1984), 'A resource-based view of the firm', *Strategic Management Journal*, **5**(2): 171–80.
Wheeler, K. and Mody, A. (1992), 'International investment and location decisions: the case of US *firms'*, *Journal of International Economics*, **33**: 57–76.
Whittaker, E. and Bower, D. Jane (1994), 'A shift to external alliances for product development in the pharmaceutical industry', *R&D Management*, **24**(3): 249–60.
Williamson, O.E. (1985), *The Economic Institutions of Capitalism*, New York: The Free Press.
Williamson, O.E. (1993), 'The logic of economic organization', in O.E. Williamson and S.E. Winter (eds), *The Nature of the Firm*, New York and Oxford: Oxford University Press.
World Bank (1991), *The World Development Report*, New York and Oxford: Oxford University Press.

11. What's wrong – and right – with trade theory?*

INTRODUCTION

What distinguishes international from intranational economic transactions? How much and to what extent do national boundaries matter? Is the globalizing economy eroding such boundaries? Why do we need – if indeed we do need – a separate theory of cross-border trade and direct investment of firms? What is the justification for international economics, or for that matter international business,[1] as a distinct area of study?

Economics is, if nothing else, a pragmatic social science. Its primary purpose is, or should be, to explain, in the most rigorous way possible, the way in which scarce resources are allocated between alternative uses, and to suggest ways and means of improving this allocation. Some of our braver – but not necessarily wiser – colleagues also engage in predicting future economic events. But, for most of us, we are content to be judged on our ability to explain the real world as it is. The late nineteenth-century economist could hardly have anticipated the supersonic aircraft, the microchip or laser surgery, much less the geopolitical and cultural scenario of the late twentieth century. The happenings of the last century – or even the last two decades – surely confirm that economists must be prepared to modify their paradigms, theories or models to meet the needs of the time.

In some areas of economics, creditable progress has been made – particularly in development theory, macro-economics and industrial economics – but in other areas, such changes have been minimal. Relative to the demands placed on economists by changes in the world economic environment, international economics – especially international micro-economics – must take the 'booby' prize, with the possible exception of work on the new theory of trade[2] and foreign direct investment (FDI) (Helpman, 1984; Helpman and Krugman, 1985; Krugman, 1990, 1991; Markusen, 1995; Markusen and Venables, 1995; Dunning, 1988b, 1993a; Froot, 1993) to which we shall return later. For

* From *International Trade Journal*, **X** (2) (1995): 153–202.

example, it was not until the 1950s that trade theorists gave any attention at all to technology, market imperfections and differential consumer tastes.

Why is it then, that, apart from some advances in model building, the textbooks on international trade are more or less the same as they were 30 or 40 years ago? Is it because economists believe that the old paradigms – particularly when modified to embrace new variables – are still a good – if not the best – explanation of today's cross-border transactions? Is it that they are well aware of the deficiencies of orthodox theory, but do not know how to remedy them? Is it because the real world poses analytically awkward challenges to traditional modes of thought? Or, is it because the *distinctive* features of international economics as a subject for study no longer merit the attention of economists, because there are more exciting research opportunities?

We believe that each of these explanations has some truth in it. But, we wish to suggest another, and look at this in some detail in the chapter.[3] This is that the nature and character of international transactions have so much changed in recent years (and, indeed, are continuing to do so in the 1990s) that the traditional intellectual apparatus of the international economist is, by itself, no longer adequate to explain real-world phenomena, and that only by drawing upon the tools of other branches of economics – notably industrial, institutional and techno-growth economics – can contemporary cross-border flows of goods, services and assets be properly understood. But, with few exceptions, intra-disciplinary alliances between economists are rare. A cursory look at journals on, for example, international, business and regional economics reveals little spreading of the interest of trade scholars beyond the narrow confines of their subject. The writings of Ray Vernon, Charles Kindleberger, Richard Caves, Giovanni Dosi, Luc Soete, and most recently Paul Krugman and James Markusen stand out as beacons in an otherwise dimly lit territory. Others, notably Michael Porter, have been critical of traditional theoretical constructs, but have offered only limited guidance as to what should replace them. As to trade-related topics, that of international direct investment is particularly interesting, not only in its own right, but because it acts as an intellectual bridge between mainstream trade theory as it is and how it ought to be in explaining what is really going on in the world economy.

We find it astonishing that, in a global economy in which (i) the sales of the foreign affiliates of MNEs exceeds that of trade; (ii) the great bulk of trade (nobody knows the exact figure – it is thought to be between 60 and 70 per cent) is directly or indirectly connected to FDI; and (iii) where upwards of one-half of trade is either within the same organizational entity, or between parties which engage in some kind of medium- to long-term co-operative relationship (e.g. subcontracting, strategic alliances), most trade economists still give almost all their attention to analysisng traditional cross-border arms length transactions.

WHY HAS INTERNATIONAL ECONOMICS NOT KEPT UP WITH THE TIMES?

Several reasons might be adduced for the apparent lack of attention given by orthodox trade theorists to non-traditional cross-border transactions. These include a lack of knowledge or understanding about their importance, and the belief that such 'connected' transactions[4] can be satisfactorily explained by arm's-length trade theory; that is, connectedness *per se* is perceived to be of only marginal importance in explaining trade.

The latter reason is worthy of particular attention. At the end of the day, its validity must rest on whether or not it is supported by the facts. Here, as shown by a wealth of empirical studies, the evidence is mixed. Some kinds of trade (i.e. those in natural-resource-intensive products between resource-poor and resource-rich countries) are well explained by Heckscher–Ohlin (H–O) factor endowment models; others (i.e. most intraindustry trade between advanced industrial nations in sophisticated high-technology products) need a quite different kind of explanation. Most of the efforts of trade theorists in the last 30 years, under various guises (i.e. neo-factor, neo-technology, 'neo-neo'-technology,[5] monopolistic competition, scale, product cycle, product differentiation theories, etc.), have been directed to resolving these issues, and especially to explain trade among countries with similar economic structures.

While it is generally recognized that it is difficult – if not impossible – to construct satisfactorily a single comprehensive *theory* – as opposed to paradigm – of international trade, none the less each of the newer (i.e. post-1950) theories – with a couple of exceptions – has made use of the analytical tools of the international economist. By contrast, advances in the theory of FDI have primarily stemmed from the work, and made use of the tools, of industrial economics and the theory of the firm. Why the difference in approach?

In a chapter of a book co-authored with George Norman several years ago (Dunning and Norman, 1985), reprinted in Dunning (1988a), we set out a 3×3 matrix. This matrix has been modified for this chapter and is presented as Figure 11.1. It depicts nine different kinds of international economic transactions. Each kind is distinguished by two criteria. The first is the degree of similarity between the goods and services imported and exported by a country. This is presumed to vary along a continuum from zero to complete substitutability. Second, each transaction is classified by its organizational mode. This, also, is assumed to vary along a continuum from that of an intrafirm (or hierarchical) transaction through a variety of cooperative arrangements to arm's-length trading.[6] The top left-hand cell of the matrix – characterized by trade between independent parties in completely different products – essentially depicts Ricardian or H–O trade. Diagonally opposite, the bottom right-hand cell – characterized by intrafirm transactions in substitutable products – essentially

			ORGANIZATION OF TRANSACTIONS		
			Spot markets	Inter-firm alliances and networks	Hierarchies
COMPOSITION OF TRANSACTIONS	Interindustry	Assets	Arm's-length transactions Different assets traded Porfolio investments	Licensing, management contracts, strategic alliances, etc. between 'relational' firms	Internalized intermediate production markets
		Products	Neo-technology and neo-factor trade	Product or process specialization between 'relational' firms and within networks	Intrafirm trade
	Inter/intra-industry	Assets	Some cross-hauling of similar assets	As above	Vertical and horizontal FDI to reduce transaction and/or co-ordination costs of markets
		Products	Trade in similar products	As above	Intrafirm trade
	Intraindustry	Assets	Cross-hauling of similar assets	Cross-hauling of closely similar assets between firms or within networks	Intrafirm trade and horizontal FDI
		Products	Not applcable / Oligopolies trading in similar products	Cross-hauling of similar products between firms or within networks	Intrafirm trade among MNE oligopolies

Note: Broadly speaking the evolution has proceeded from left to right and diagonally downwards, though in the last decade, there has been some movement from the bottom right-hand corner to the bottom middle section of the matrix.

Figure 11.1 The evolution of international transactions of assets and products

represents trade in knowledge-intensive products internalized by MNEs (i.e. that associated with FDI). The rest of the matrix into which other forms of cross-border transactions can be fitted, embraces different combinations of organizational modes and kinds of products traded. The matrix attempts to illustrate the assertion that any paradigm – let alone theory – of trade must embrace both a *theory of organization* and a *theory of the location of economic activity*.

In our analysis of the evolution of trade patterns, George Norman and I suggested that for much of the nineteenth and early twentieth century, trade was of a type depicted by the top left-hand section of the matrix. Since the Second World War, it has increasingly been of an intraindustry, intrafirm character, as best illustrated by the bottom right-hand sections of the matrix. In turn, these trade types reflect the kinds of micro-techno-economic and macro-socio-institutional systems operating at the time. Nineteenth-century trade was mainly conducted within the discipline of the gold standard, with relatively little direct government intervention in economic affairs, and by firms producing under the craft or batch systems of production. For most of the present century, the techno-economic system has been dominated by scale or Fordist production, while relative to market forces, governments and hierarchies have played a more important organizational role in influencing the level and pattern of trade. As this century draws to a close, we are entering into a new trajectory, or age, in capitalism, which at the micro-organizational level has been referred to as flexible, or post-Fordism, value-adding activity; and at a macro-institutional level we refer to as alliance (rather than hierarchical) capitalism. For reasons which shall be explained later, this latest era of capitalism is likely to shift the dominant pattern of trade to the left of the bottom right-hand corner of the matrix.

The feature about most received trade theory is that, at best, it considers as neutral and, at worst, it ignores altogether the co-ordination and relational costs and benefits associated with the *production* and *consumption* of tradable products, and those associated with the *transactions* of those products, as relevant explanatory variables of the amount and pattern of trade. While more recent theories, notably strategic trade models and Krugman's foray into geography (Krugman, 1991), have incorporated some of the analytical tools of industrial and locational economics,[7] none adequately embraces either the organizational or institutional characteristics of demand and supply, or those associated with alternative modes of exchange.[8] The assumption continues to be made that the entities engaging in trade are single-activity firms, and that there is no incentive for these firms *not* to use the market as an exchange mechanism. In neo-classical theory, at least, each trading firm is presumed to be operating on its optimum production function;[9] and because it supplies only one product, and produces on one point of the value chain, it is also presumed to engage in no intermediate transactions. Issues of interfirm alliances or the clustering of firms to gain agglomerative economies are disregarded altogether.

But, an even greater criticism of trade theory is that the act of exchanging goods and services in the open market is assumed to be costless.[10] When one thinks about this, it is an incredible assumption. It implies that buyers and sellers have full and symmetrical information both about each other's motives and capabilities, and about the characteristics and quality of the goods and services being transacted. Each party to any exchange is presumed to behave towards the other with complete honesty and transparency, and there is a complete absence of opportunism. H–O theory also explicitly assumes zero spatial costs, but we suspect that even had these been included, no attention would have been paid to such transaction costs as failed delivery dates.

Micro-economists from Ronald Coase (1937) onwards have been well versed in these concepts; but, is it not odd that the transaction cost paradigm has been used primarily to explain the growth of multi-activity and multinational firms rather than the level and pattern of international trade? Are we, then, to assume that the size and character of transactional costs makes no difference to the amount of a good or service traded? In practice, we know this is not true. Indeed, is it arguable that one of the most powerful facilitators of the cross-border division of labour (and hence trade) is a reduction in transaction costs brought about by the establishment of an acceptable legal and commercial system and by the reduction of cross-border psychic and physical distance? And what is the function of such institutions as GATT and the newly formed World Trade Organization (WTO) if it is not to reduce market failure in products traded across national borders?

In short, both neo-classical and much of modern trade theory gives short shrift to the firm as an organizing unit. The location of economic activity, and hence trade arising from it, is assumed to be entirely dependent on location-bound, country-specific characteristics, although some attention is given by Helpman and Krugman (1985) and Markusen (1995) to the distinction between firm-level and plant-level scale economies, and on the distribution of intrafirm value-added activities, for example headquarters, services and subsequent production processes.[11] The doctrine of comparative advantage – that each country should allocate its resources to the production of goods which require inputs for which it is comparatively well endowed, and trade these for goods and services which require resources in which it is relatively poorly endowed – follows quite logically from the assumptions underlying the theory which, it should be noted, are essentially *normative*, rather than *positive*, in character. According to H–O logic, the comparative advantage of a country is entirely determined by the *allocative* efficiency of its value-added activities. Questions relating to *technical* or *scale* efficiency or to the competitive advantage of firms are regarded as predetermined or irrelevant! And, only comparatively recently has the ability of a country to adjust its pattern of resources and capabilities to changing demand and supply conditions been embraced by trade theorists.

Table 11.1 Alternative scenarios for theorizing about determinants of trade in goods and services

Scenario I Neo-classical trade (NCT) theory 1950	Scenario II Modern trade theory plus direct investment (DI) theory 1950–90	Scenario III Emerging theory of international transactions in the age of alliance capitalism 1990
• No unique competitive (O) advantages of firms	• Unique competitive (O) advantages of individual firms	• As for DI theory, plus those advantages external to individual firms, but as influenced and/or co-ordinated by those firms
• Immobility of natural resources	• Mobility of created assets	• Less mobility of created assets because of increasing significance of agglomerative (i.e. clustering) economies
• Allocation of economic activity mainly based on allocation of natural resources and finance capital	• Allocation of economic activity based on disposition of natural and created assets	• Allocation of economic activity as for DI theory, but also influenced by economies of subnational agglomeration, e.g. business districts
• Government activity largely ignored; supranational regimes considered superfluous	• Government activity viewed as an asset (or liability!). Role of supranational regimes acknowledged	• As for DI theory, but also as embracing cross-border alliances and interfirm networking
• Single-activity firms	• Multi-activity firms	• More concentration on 'core' competences of individual firms, but growing significance of multi-activity networks
• Transactions mainly of an interindustry character	• Transactions mainly of an intraindustry character	• As for DI theory
• All transactions conducted between independent firms	• Transactions conducted between related firms or within multinational hierarchies	• As for DI theory, but more focus on intranetwork activities
• No endemic market failure, hence zero transaction costs	• Endemic market failure overcome by hierarchical internalization	• Endemic market failure reduced (or overcome) by interfirm co-operation (quasi-integration)
• No attention given to co-ordinating costs and benefits of related activities	• Gains and costs from co-ordinating cross-border activities specifically acknowledged	• As for DI theory, but greater plurality of organizational forms for co-ordinating economic activity
• Perfect competition	• Imperfect competition	• As for DI theory, but fewer imperfections in intermediate product markets involving co-operation among firms

Once, however, one accepts that there are different modalities of organizing economic activity, and that each of these involves costs and benefits, it is no longer acceptable to assume that the market is necessarily the most beneficial way of organizing resources. In particular, the role of other organizing agents (e.g. hierarchies, networks, consumer groups and governments) may legitimately be considered. Sometimes, these roles and/or their outcomes may conflict with those of markets; sometimes they are complementary to them, or provide the infrastructure for markets to operate effectively. This does not mean that non-market forms of organization (e.g. hierarchies, networks or governments) will necessarily be more cost effective than markets; this may or may not be the case. Moreover, over time, the net benefits of alternative organizational modes may change. But what it does mean is that, in order for markets to perform effectively at a future date, for example $t + 1$, $t + 2$, etc., some extra-market supporting or enabling mechanism might be required in time t. Hence, for example, before the market can work even moderately well in China or Russia, an efficient legal, institutional, financial and commercial infrastructure – not to mention a market culture – needs to be established, which, unaided, private enterprise system may be unable to achieve. As a conclusion to this part of our chapter and as an introduction to what follows, it may be useful to compare and contrast three different scenarios assumed by economists in their attempts to explain international transactions. These are set out in Table 11.1.

The first scenario contains the assumptions underlying the traditional theories of trade put forward up to around 1950, while those marked with an asterisk (*) are also assumed by post-1950 trade theories. The second scenario contains the assumptions which scholars versed in FDI theory have used to explain both the foreign value-added activities of MNEs and the trade of these enterprises.

The third scenario looks to the future. It sets out the kind of real-world situations which several analysts believe will condition the pattern of future international transactions. We have already described this scenario as one of 'alliance' capitalism – to contrast it with the scenario of 'hierarchical' capitalism, which typified the economies of the Western world in much of the twentieth century.

It may be inferred from Table 11.1 that each of these scenarios requires very different explanations for the extent and pattern of international transactions. But do they? There are three aspects of the changing world environment that we believe have not been given the attention they deserve by traditional trade economists. The three aspects are:

1. The significance of micro-organizational costs and benefits.
2. The growing mobility of firm-specific assets.
3. The role of national governments in the macro-organization of economic activity.

THE RELEVANCE OF MICRO-ORGANIZATIONAL COSTS AND BENEFITS

What is the main organizational task of firms? Surely, it is to co-ordinate the use of separate – including those bought from other firms – inputs in such a way that, when taken together, they maximize the value added of the output they help to create. That is to say, although firms create value through production, in order to best achieve this goal, managers need effectively to co-ordinate the contributions of various inputs into the production and marketing process.

Indeed, one of the earliest conceptions of the firm was that it is a co-ordinated unit of decision taking. Yet, only in the last 20 years or so has the co-ordinating role of the firm been explicitly considered – and this largely from an intra-rather than an interfirm perspective. It is true that neo-classical economists have always accepted that there are alternative ways of utilizing available factor inputs, but basically this is presumed to rest on the quality and costs of the inputs, rather than on the costs of co-ordination *per se*. Most economics textbooks pay only passing attention to the organizing function of firms. Implicitly, they are presumed to buy their inputs at arm's-length on the open market, and that even when they have some choice over the conditions of purchase, the costs of search and negotiation surrounding these choices are assumed to be zero. Although when it comes to international trade, textbooks switch their focus of interest from the firm to the country, implicitly at least the same assumptions about co-ordinating costs apply.

Consider for a moment what has occurred in the nature of trans-border production and transactions over the past two decades. We would point to three features which have especially affected the organizing principles of resource allocation. The first is the rising co-ordinating costs of an increasingly complex division of labour. This is partly a reflection of the nature of the products produced and partly that of the underlying demand and supply conditions. Thus, more specialization of economic activity tends to raise a firm's co-ordination costs, by increasing the number and specificity of tasks and of information links. It may also raise transaction costs, as the likelihood of information asymmetry and opportunistic behaviour increases. Second, specialization may yield benefits from the common governance of activities which require similar inputs or which yield economies of scope. Third, the outcome of decisions associated with various kinds of value activities has increasingly affected economic entities beyond the participants involved in any particular transaction.

Each of these factors – by raising the costs of using arm's-length markets and/or using the benefits of other (notably intra- or interfirm) co-ordinating mechanisms – has resulted in the co-ordination of value-added activities, which were previously undertaken separately and independently. Except in the factor and final goods markets, and for much of the twentieth century, hierarchical transactions have gradually assumed greater importance. In the last decade or so, as markets have become increasingly liberalized and deregulated, and as firms have downsized the range of their activities, various interfirm and governmental arrangements, including networks, have replaced some intrafirm hierarchies, although, other than in the primary goods sector, pure arm's-length transactions of intermediate products remain the exception rather than the rule.

The greater costs of using arm's-length markets have then changed both the structure of firms and the relationships between them. This has not only affected patterns of trade or exchange within countries, but also between countries. Indeed, international transactions are likely to incur their own specific co-ordination and transaction costs. Some of these reflect a lack of information about, or unfamiliarity with, foreign markets, or uncertainty about institutions, organizational structures, business customs and actions of foreign governments. To be sure, trade economists have embraced, and have examined the effect of, structural market failure (e.g. that brought about by the imposition of import barriers), apart from the presence of scale and some aspects of vertical integration on trade patterns. However, they have largely ignored the role of *endemic* market failure, in so far as it has affected both the underlying demand and supply conditions under which tradable goods and resources are produced, and the costs and benefits of alternative forms of organizing their cross-border exchange.[12]

How then does the presence of endemic market failure affect our theorizing about trade patterns? It is, we suggest, possible to consider five possible responses by traders to the incorporation of such variables as bounded rationality, increasing returns to scale, externalities and uncertainties into the 'terms' of trading. The first is simply to cease trading. Thus, an unaccountably high risk of non-, or late, delivery, or the unreliable quality of intermediate products, may result in the buyer ceasing to trade in those products. Whether no trade is better than second- or third-best trade is a moot point!

The second response to cross-border market failure is to try to reduce market failure. This Hirschman 'voice'-type strategy (Hirschman, 1970) is usually accomplished by an exchange of views and information between buyers and sellers; by each seeking to establish and maintain a climate of trust, forbearance and commitment; and, in the case of interfirm transactions, by the parties to the exchange working together to reduce transaction and co-ordination costs, and to upgrade the quality and/or lower the cost of the intermediate products. Sometimes, such transaction costs can be best reduced by establishing formal contractual relationships (a kind of half-way house between arm's-length trade and hierarchies), and sometimes by establishing less formal but none the less binding ties between the trading parties, for example of a *keiretsu* kind. The initial costs of creating such relationships may be quite high, particularly where the trading cultures of the parties are different, or when there is information asymmetry about the quality of products. However, over time, these may be expected to fall as a congenial working ethos is built up and as this ethos spreads to competitors and other suppliers alike.

As we have already indicated, the main market-facilitating or sustaining costs considered in the trade literature are those to do with the removal of *structural* market distortions, for example trade barriers and monopoly power. And yet, not only throughout history have the costs of *endemic* market failure acted as impediments to trade (and some of these have fallen as a result of telecommunication advances) but others (and especially those to do with asymmetries in knowledge) have risen sharply as economic activity has become more complex and multi-faceted.

The third reaction to market failure is for firms to try to reduce the costs of arm's-length transactions by internalizing international product markets. Vertical and horizontal intrafirm trade then replaces interfirm trade. The subject of intrafirm (as opposed to intraindustry) trade is a very underresearched topic. While a great deal has been written on *why* firms may wish to internalize cross-border markets,[13] much less attention has been given to the ways and extent to which the level and pattern of hierarchical trade differs from arm's-length trade, or, indeed, if and when the former is more efficiency enhancing than the latter. In some cases, intrafirm trade may be structurally distorting, as, for example, when firms seek to exploit or extend their monopoly power (*à la* Hymer, 1960). But in others, where hierarchical trade replaces trade previously conducted under conditions of endemic market failure, it may improve economic welfare. And while it is possible to identify situations when the second hypothesis is likely to be more plausible than the first, virtually no attention has been paid to whether or not a hierarchical internalization of market failure is the most cost-effective way of responding to that failure.

The fourth possible response to market failure is for some kind of non-market agency (e.g. government) to step in to try to simulate a perfect or near-perfect market, or to encourage the participants in the market to behave in a way which has similar results to those which would have been brought about by a perfect market. Finally, traders may accept the transaction or co-ordinating costs associated with arm's-length markets, on the basis that any alternative organizational mode of exchange would be less cost efficient.

It is worth observing that each of these reactions will vary according to both the nature of the goods or services being traded and the participants involved in the trade. Less directly, but no less importantly, it will depend on the techno-economic characteristics of production and the socio-institutional framework of the macro-economic system. Thus, while a scale production system and hierarchical capitalism tended to encourage the third type of response to endemic market failure, the advent of flexible production and alliance capitalism is leading to a greater emphasis on the formation of interfirm co-operative relationships and networks. This is partly because it is perceived that at least some of the benefits of internalized markets can be captured by non-equity alliances, and partly because, in recent years, the Japanese experience has shown that a 'voice' rather than an 'exit' approach to market failure (i.e. an attempt to reduce, rather than bypass, arm's-length transaction costs) may be a more cost-effective response. In so far as this kind of reaction is taking root, some of the assumptions of neo-classical theory about the characteristics of markets are becoming *more*, rather than *less*, apposite than they once were.

In their explanation of why firms engage in intrafirm trade, scholars versed in direct investment theory usually focus on two kinds of cross-border transactions. The first is that of intangible assets which essentially comprise both the rationale and ingredients of FDI; and the second is the intermediate or finished (but not final) products traded between commonly owned affiliates located in different countries. In both cases, the relative significance of intra- (compare interfirm) trade is likely to vary according to *what* is being traded and with *whom* the trade is being conducted. It follows, then, that the effect of cross-border market failure on the international division of labour will be, to some extent at least, country and activity (or industry) specific. But, even if a relatively few markets are imperfect, the substitution of hierarchical for arm's-length trade may, none the less, affect the *comparative* advantages of the constituent countries – and hence an explanation of *which* countries trade in *which* goods.

Let us illustrate what we mean. Assume a Swiss MNE discovers a cost-effective cure for AIDS, and that it alone has the right to produce the drug. Assume too that the firm's only option for selling the drug to a foreign market is to export it from a home production base. In choosing to export, not only is its own competitive advantage affected, but so is the structure of the revealed comparative advantage of Switzerland (i.e. it increases in pharmaceuticals and decreases in other products). Suppose next it is discovered that it is possible to manufacture the drug more cheaply in another country, say in Brazil. However, suppose that the Swiss firm is not prepared to sell the knowledge about the drug (i.e. the intangible asset) to a Brazilian firm at either arm's-length prices – because it fears opportunism on the part of the buyer – or through an interfirm co-operative agreement – because it is not able to gain the economies of co-ordination between its Brazilian activities and those of the rest of its organization,[14] or because it cannot ensure cross-effective quality control of the Brazilian product. In this instance, the locational advantages of Brazil – and the consequential restructuring of the comparative advantage of both Brazilian and Swiss location-bound resources[15] – is outweighed by endemic market failure. In seeking ways to reduce such failure, let us finally assume the Swiss firm decides to set up, or acquire, a subsidiary in Brazil in the expectation that, by so doing, it can capture both the gains of a Brazilian location and those of minimizing its co-ordination and transaction costs.

The kind of scenario just outlined will cause trade in pharmaceutical products between Switzerland and Brazil (and possibly elsewhere in the world) to be different than that which would have occurred had cross-border exchanges been limited to arm's-length transactions. Exactly how much and in what way will depend on the nature and extent of the market failure. Similarly, the structure of hierarchically related trade described in our example would, itself, be different from that which might have arisen had the drug (produced by the Swiss subsidiary in Brazil) been supplied by a Brazilian firm which was part of a co-operative network of activities in which both it and the Swiss firm were members. Again, the critical issue is how significant are such organizational modes as compared with other possible determinants in explaining international trade in the AIDS-curing drug?

In short, any paradigm of intercountry patterns of trade and direct investment needs to embrace both the co-ordinating costs and benefits of engaging in multiple activities – or the same activity – in more than one country, and it must embrace the transaction-related costs of the alternative routes of organizing trade. Such costs and benefits will be partly country specific; indeed, we shall argue later in this chapter that the capability of a country to organize its production and exchange efficiently may be considered as a competitive advantage in its own right. Hence, countries with a well-ordered system of markets, and those whose institutions are appropriate to optimizing production and cross-border exchanges, are likely to be in a better position to supply products which are transaction cost intensive, or to engage in interrelated activities which yield high externalities and/or co-ordinating benefits. Costs and benefits will also be partly sector specific; hence, the trading patterns of countries which specialize in the kind of activities and exchanges which are transaction and/or co-ordinating cost intensive are likely to be more affected than those which do not, by the incorporation of such costs.

THE GROWING MOBILITY OF FIRM-SPECIFIC ASSETS

Among the assumptions, or presumptions, of extant trade theory, perhaps the two least appropriate to the reality of the global economy of the 1990s are, first, that resources consist of location-bound natural assets – notably land and unskilled labour – and, second, that these assets are equally available to all firms to acquire and utilize in their production processes. In the 1990s, not only are most assets 'created' from natural resources[16] – information, knowledge capital, innovatory and organizational capacity, experience, and institutional infrastructure are examples – but a significant proportion of these assets are, at least at a particular point in time, the proprietary right of particular firms, that is, not equally available to all producing entities. Moreover, unlike natural assets, many created assets are intangible. These include such location-bound assets as the culture of a country and the economic policies of its government.[17]

The growing importance of *created*, relative to *natural*, assets in the explanation of the competitive and comparative advantages of countries is impelling economists to rethink some of their cherished notions about the determinants of trade. For example, since at least some created assets are footloose across national boundaries, it follows that a country's comparative advantage in a global economy is as much determined by the structure of inbound and outbound direct investment as by that of trade. To some extent, the mobility of assets was embraced in an extension to H–O theory introduced by Mundell (1957), when he argued that the movement of (finance) capital could be assumed to substitute for the movement of goods. The question arises as to whether this idea can be extended to other forms of assets – and especially those which are the privileged possession of particular firms.

The idea that a firm might possess, or have access to, unique assets denied to its competitors is fundamentally alien to traditional trade theory, which asserts that the competitive advantage of any particular country is entirely dependent on the way in which its indigenous resources are allocated among different uses. The theory argues that to optimize this advantage, these resources should be distributed to sectors in which the country – relative to other countries – has a *comparative* advantage. That the firm is treated as a 'black box' naturally follows from the presumption that trade is (or should be) conducted under perfectly competitive conditions. This, in turn, negates the possibility of structural market distortions, and/or of differentiated or dynamic products (Gray, 1994). Yet, it is these latter products, rather than the more standardized goods and services with which H–O theory is concerned, which make up much of world trade, and especially intraindustry trade between the Triad nations. And, it is precisely these products which are likely to be 'created asset' intensive in their production; whose locational needs are likely to be 'footloose'; and which are produced under conditions of endemic market failure.

In short, trade and investment patterns of dynamic products are as much likely to be determined by the structure and distribution of *firm-specific created assets* as they are by that of *country-specific natural assets*. We shall address the role of these former assets in affecting the pattern of trade and investment in the next section. For the moment, we would observe that, *de facto*, even in the most market-oriented economies, the role of non-market institutions (e.g. governments and supranational agencies such as GATT) can critically affect how, and in what way, endemic market failure may be overcome, and hence our thinking about the determinants of trade.

But, even accepting the fact that firm-specific advantages do exist, what difference does this make to our theorizing about trade patterns? The previous section dealt with issues surrounding the governance of firms and markets;[18] and, in particular, how the presence of co-ordination and transaction costs might affect the structure and ownership of international activity. In this section, we shall be primarily concerned with the way in which the distribution of the ownership of assets among firms may affect the geography of their creation and usage.

Here, apart from some foraging by Helpman and Krugman (1985) and Markusen (1984, 1995), we are largely in uncharted territory – and there are several separate questions we might wish to explore. We shall attempt to examine only two, and in doing so will adopt a step-by-step approach in our reasoning. The first question is, in what way does the principle of comparative advantage need to be modified to take account of the existence of firm-specific advantages? Let us concentrate on just two such advantages:[19] the privileged possession of a specific piece of technology, say a chemical formula protected by patent; and a branded product which is perceived by consumers to be uniquely different from that of its nearest substitute. Although both advantages confer at least a degree of temporary monopoly power on the firm possessing them, both may also help upgrade product quality and/or widen consumer choice, and hence advance economic welfare. However, without knowledge of the utility functions of consumers, it is impossible to say whether the social benefits of this situation are more or less than those resulting from perfect competition, since the latter is simply not equipped to deal with variables other than price and quantity.

Now, to some extent, post-H–O–S trade theories implicitly take account of these firm-specific characteristics, but each assumes that their origin stems from the resources and markets *exogenous* to the firms but endogenous to their home countries. Thus, US firms in the computer industry may have an advantage over UK firms, simply because the United States offers a more supportive technological infrastructure and economic environment than does the United Kingdom. Michael Porter (1990) would appear to support this hypothesis, although his interpretation of the term economic environment goes well beyond that of most trade economists.[20] However, in today's globalizing economy, this proposition is less persuasive than it used to be for two reasons. The first is that firms – and especially MNEs with significant foreign operations – may, directly or indirectly, derive some of their competitive advantages from tapping into the created assets and markets of other countries. And second, the business literature suggests that firms develop their own particular trajectories of technological, managerial and marketing capabilities and experiences, which are as much fashioned by their own strategic objectives and organizational cultures as they are by the location-bound characteristics of their home countries. This is particularly likely to be the case in the more dynamic sectors of industry, and where competition between firms is oligopolistic.[21] In such cases, then, one needs a separate theory of business strategy to explain fully why countries trade with each other.

The second step in the reasoning is to allow for the mobility of intangible assets. This is precisely what Ray Vernon and his colleagues did in their exposition and empirical testing of the product cycle,[22] which is now explicitly acknowledged by FDI theory. Indeed, it is generally accepted that MNEs are the main vehicles for transferring non-financial assets across national boundaries, and that, in so doing, they affect both the competitive advantages of firms in the exporting and importing countries, and the comparative advantages of location-bound resources in both home and host countries.

Taking this analysis to its logical extreme, if all assets were completely mobile across national boundaries, a critical conclusion of the neo-classical trade theory, namely that all countries can benefit from engaging in trade, would fall to the ground. This is because, in response to market forces, assets may choose an 'exit' rather than a 'voice' strategy, by moving rather than being utilized (or reallocated) within a country. History is, indeed, replete with examples of the *absolute* decline of nation states, which – in theory, at any rate – is inconsistent with the principle of comparative advantage. It follows, then, that countries whose current comparative advantages rest largely in their possession of mobile-created, firm-specific assets are likely to be more vulnerable to exogenous economic forces than those whose advantages rest on the possession of immobile country-specific assets. At the same time, as the experience of the Japanese and Singaporean economies has shown, the opportunities of countries dependent on created assets to upgrade and restructure their comparative advantages are just as promising as, if not more promising than, those reliant on their natural resources.

Of course, in practice, not only are some resources completely location bound (e.g. land and (most) buildings), but most (e.g. labour, R&D laboratories and culturally sensitive intangible assets) are only partially mobile. Hence, the principle of comparative advantage may still hold good – particularly when it incorporates firms and non-market (e.g. government) related variables, and is viewed from a dynamic, rather than a static, perspective. Yet, while it is difficult to fault the proposition that, viewed from a *country's* perspective, its resources and capabilities should concentrate on producing goods and services which the international market-place deems it is comparatively best suited to produce, this should not be taken to mean that it is necessarily in the best interests of the *owners* of those resources and capabilities to deploy those assets in any one specific location.[23] This, to our mind – and this is especially true in a situation of global structural unemployment – is why the notion of countries competing with one another is not quite the mindless obsession Krugman (1990) claims it to be.[24]

THE ROLE OF NATIONAL GOVERNMENTS IN THE MACRO-ORGANIZATION OF ECONOMIC ACTIVITY

Up to this point, we have been primarily concerned with two main organizing entities of the structure of economic activity, namely firms and markets. We now turn to consider a third, that is national governments and supranational economic regimes. Once again, we shall argue that the globalization of economic activity is requiring a reappraisal of the role of non-market institutions as both pro-active and reactive players in the determination of the pattern and distribution of international activity. To give more focus to our argument, we shall give specific consideration to the role of national governments and supranational agencies as fashioners of the economic environment for cross-border transactions. Elsewhere,[25] we have examined the consequences of government actions on the competitiveness of firms and countries. Here, we shall confine our attention to their impact on the received theories of trade and FDI.

For the last two centuries, the main body of international economics has taken as axiomatic that the level and pattern of cross-border trade is best left to free market forces. On efficiency grounds, government interaction is thought legitimate in only two cases. The first is that, in order to promote a country's dynamic comparative advantage, it might be necessary to protect potentially competitive, but fledgling, firms and industries from their more robust foreign competitors. For the last two centuries, such protection has been widely practised by many governments; indeed, the 'infant industry' argument is often used to justify the resuscitation of well-established firms and industries. The second rationale for government intervention is to counter anti-competitive or other forms of structurally distorting behaviour practised by one or other of the participants in the market – including foreign governments. Although not expressed in these terms, neo-classical economists accept this rationale of government intervention – as long as it is directed to facilitating the workings of the free market, *and* as long as such intervention is cost effective. Of course, it is also recognized that governments might intervene to achieve goals other than that of economic efficiency, but an examination of these is normally considered outside the purview of the economist.

At the same time, it is a fact that, in the pursuance of their macro-economic and macro-organizational policies, governments *do* strongly influence trade patterns. It is our contention not only that the globalizing economy is requiring national administrations to take a more active stance as the guardian of the well-being of their constituents, but also that their willingness and ability to do this efficiently should, itself, be perceived as a public good in its own right.

Our justification for this last statement is basically an extension of the argument of the previous two sections. There it was asserted that the way in which each firm organizes its value-added activities is as much a factor in influencing its trading capabilities as is its ability to innovate new products or production processes.[26] In this section, we shall argue that the way in which governments organize the resources, capabilities and markets within their jurisdiction – and this includes the extent to which they are prepared to delegate this responsibility to private hierarchies, groups of firms or markets – is a critical determinant of the pattern of international transactions.

At first sight, it might be supposed that globalization – driven by technological imperatives and facilitated by market-supporting economic policies – is fashioning a scenario more in accord with the tenets of neo-classical trade theory than those which it replaced. And, it is difficult to deny that, by and large, the structural impediments to many kinds of international transactions in the 1990s are fewer than those in the 1970s, while advances in telecommunications and informatics are dramatically reducing the costs of physical and psychic distance. At the same time, as we have already observed, there are suggestions that, as the techno-institutional fabric of society becomes more complex and interwoven, various forms of endemic market impurities – such as those associated with asset specificity, information impactness and bounded rationality – increase, and that, at the very least, governments have the responsibility to their constituents for ensuring that the cost of these impurities is minimized.[27]

Earlier in this chapter, we distinguished between *natural* and *created* assets, and between assets which would normally be supplied by the private sector in response to, or in anticipation of, market signals, and those which take the form of public goods – which, because of their high fixed and low variable costs, or the uncertainties associated with their supply, are more likely to be produced, or at least financed by, the public sector. Secondary school education and pre-competitive R&D are two examples. To exploit their full value, many of these assets (e.g. roads and airports) require to be used jointly with privately owned assets; and it is the way firms co-ordinate the use of both sets of assets – and any other assets which they may acquire – which will determine their competitiveness in global markets. Indeed, it is the quality of complementary assets available to firms – and the way in which they are packaged – which is a major element of the co-ordinating and transaction costs earlier described (Teece, 1992).

Another aspect of globalization which requires a response by governments is the increasing ease with which assets are able to move across national boundaries. Firms, like people, can 'vote with their feet'.[28] *Inter alia*, this is demonstrated by the sharp increase in all kinds of MNE activity and in interfirm co-operative arrangements (UNCTAD, 1993). At the same time, there are strong suggestions that the kinds of international transactions which have grown the most rapidly in the last decade are those which are determined less by the availability, price and quality of location-bound natural assets and more by those of location-bound *created* assets – the production of which governments, directly or indirectly, influence a great deal. Each of these latter assets, together with a culture which favours entrepreneurship, innovation, wealth creation and the acquisition of new markets, helps to lower the transaction or hassle costs of economic activity, and furnishes firms with the ability and the motivation to organize efficiently their value-adding activities.

How might the actions of governments be incorporated into traditional trade theories? One possibility is to treat government as an additional location-bound factor of production. However, apart from the difficulty of identifying and measuring either its input or output, there is little reason to suppose that more government leads to better macro-organizational management or lower production and transaction costs.[29] At the same time, there is reason to suppose that the *quality* of government action is an important element in determining both the competitiveness of firms and the comparative advantage of countries. Indeed, just as organizational competence is an essential prerequisite for corporate competitiveness, so it is a critical precondition for successful government intervention. *Inter alia*, this means governments should know *when* to intervene, *how much* to intervene and in *what ways* they should intervene. The most noticeable feature of the economic success of East Asian nations like Hong Kong, Singapore, Japan, Taiwan and Korea is not the extent or form of government intervention – this has differed considerably between these nations – but the fact that, in each case, the visible hand of government has been aimed at facilitating the invisible hand of markets and promoting the dynamic comparative advantage of their resources and capabilities. Although it cannot be denied that such government action was (and still is, to some extent) sometimes market distorting, the main thrust of such intervention has been to aid the structural adjustment of indigenous resources and capabilities, and of consumer needs, and to facilitate its firms to behave in a way that is consistent with long-term market needs.

All this is not to ignore the strategic role of governments in helping to ensure that their own firms, *vis-à-vis* their competitors, are not penalized in international markets; nor, indeed, to ignore the deliberate aggressive actions of national administrations to capture the maximum economic rent from the activities of their firms outside their boundaries and from foreign firms within their national boundaries. Like it or not, such actions are increasing – and not only through measures directly targeted to influencing trade and investment patterns, but also by a gamut of other measures – notably industrial, environmental, competition and tax policies – which indirectly affect both the ability and motivation of their own firms and resources to be competitive in world markets. Sometimes such measures are market facilitating, and sometimes market distorting. One thing is certain, however; in the global economy of the 1990s, the concept of commercial policy needs to embrace all actions by governments which affect the organization of economic activity, and hence on the structure of a country's comparative advantage.

But, to what extent does the incorporation of the actions of governments – and particularly those to do with macro-organizational policy – improve the predictions of traditional trade theory? This is essentially an empirical question which can, at least, be partially answered by reference to history. Here, the answer is a mixed one. There have been times (e.g. the late nineteenth century and the 1960s) when the market-facilitating role of governments has probably outweighed its market-distorting impact, and in these years, such intervention has helped improve trade patterns. On other occasions (e.g. the interwar years, and during the 1970s) when import-substituting policies on the part of governments were at their zenith, the reverse has been the case.

In the global economy of the 1990s, we venture to suggest that the power and responsibility of national governments to exercise each of these functions have intensified, and this in spite of the growth of international economic regimes (e.g. GATT) and regional economic blocs (e.g. the EC). This is because of the growing role of government-influenced co-ordination and transaction costs in affecting trade and investment, and particularly that of an intraindustry character. Those governments which, by their macro-organizational policies, can successfully lower these costs – or exploit the benefits of agglomerative and other forms of market externalities – are those most likely to induce trade patterns which are consistent with dynamic comparative advantage. By the same token, however, the power of national governments to distort structurally the cross-border allocation of resources has also risen.

In spite of fears about the emergence of regional fortresses or blocks, we believe that the pressures of globalization are disciplining national governments to adopt policies that are more, rather than less, conducive to optimizing trade patterns. These pressures are essentially twofold. The first is the outcome of the widespread liberalization and deregulation of markets, and the privatization of state assets over the past decade.[30] The second – which is still largely in its infancy – is the recognition of the need for the strengthening of multilateral and supranational mechanisms which set the rules of the game for national government actions.

Already, in the area of macro-economic policy, the G7 have played a major (though admittedly not always successful) role in discouraging 'beggar my neighbour' exchange rate policies by national governments which might have negative externalities for the rest of the world, and in encouraging monetary and fiscal policies which might promote positive externalities. And, of course, the IMF, in its monetary and financial strategies, and GATT, in its trade strategies, are designed to minimize the global disbenefits and maximize the global benefits of world trade, and of a stable monetary and financial regime.[31]

However, increasingly, the adequacy and scope of these institutions in a global economy are being questioned. This is because of the growing externalities of an increasing range of national government policies, which do not come within the purview of existing multinational regimes. Indeed, most of the macro-organizational policies – including, incidentally, FDI policies – currently implemented by national administrations are subject to no supranational governance at all.[32]

It is the concern that, as national macro-*economic* policies become more circumscribed, national macro-*organizational* policies may be increasingly deployed by governments to promote domestic economic interests, which have negative externalities for the rest of the world – and thus promote a vicious circle of retaliatory actions on the part of other governments. This is leading both economists and politicians to urge for a widening of the rubric of existing supranational regimes, and/or the creation of new regimes to embrace such issues as competition, FDI, technology and environmental policies. Unless this is done, it is feared that the gains from the renaissance of market economy will be negated by the rent-seeking activities of national governments. By contrast, if supranational regimes[33] – both public and private – are successful in reducing endemic market failure, they may help to promote, rather than inhibit, an efficient international allocation of resources, and thus uphold, rather than support, the principle of comparative advantage – as modified to take account of the actions of non-market institutions.

We believe that Michael Porter (1990) is wrong when he argues that the principle of comparative advantage is no longer useful in explaining the pattern of international trade. What, however, does need to be reconsidered is the composition of the location-bound factor endowments of a country, and their relevance in determining the competitiveness of a country's firms.[34] Richard Lipsey (1991), for example, has suggested that a country's culture might be considered as an input into economic activity, and that countries differ in the ability and willingness to supply culturally intensive products.[35] Likewise, it is possible to think of the macro-economic and organizational actions of governments as a location-bound variable which affects not only the competitiveness of all economic activity, but different activities to a greater or lesser degree. Thus, government actions which lower the transaction and co-ordinating costs of production and exchange would particularly favour those activities in which these costs were relatively the most important, and thus would affect the *comparative* as well as the competitive advantage of firms and countries. The actions of supranational, or multilateral, regimes may be evaluated in a similar way.

It is indeed a paradox that, as the world economy becomes more integrated, the role of non-market supranational institutions in facilitating the efficient operation of cross-border markets may become increasingly important. Moreover, paraphrasing Albert Hirschman (1970), as and when 'market exit' hierarchies are replaced by 'market voice' interfirm relationships, these, too – depending on the nature and content of the relationships – might be more in tune with the dictates of competitive markets than with those they replace.

At the same time, the increasing mobility of assets between countries, and the almost permanent disequilibrium in the use and allocation of resources between countries in an innovation-led global economy, considerably reduces the plausibility of the assumptions underpinning much of traditional trade theory. Just as within a country, there is no assurance that a particular county or region will fully share in the prosperity of the rest of the country – and that it may be to the advantage of the country as a whole if resources move out of that region to other regions – so in a world of 'quicksilver' assets, the principle of absolute, rather than comparative, advantage becomes a reality. To this extent, and in the presence of the underutilization of resources in a country, the idea of countries (or governments of countries) competing with each other for resources and markets does make sense – particularly where the industrial structure of the countries is very similar. Taken to its extreme, if all resources were completely mobile, much of the rationale for trade theory as a separate branch of economics would disappear. However, as long as there is at least *one* completely location-bound resource, and/or there is some component of immobility in that or other resources, there is some justification for studying intercountry transactions of goods and services.

While the operationalization of the actions of national governments – not to mention supranational or multilateral regimes – may tax the minds of scholars, there can surely be no doubt that, in the last 30 years – both in respect of a particular country over time and between countries at a given time – these actions have varied a great deal – as have the competitiveness and trading patterns of nations. Surely, it should not be beyond the collective wisdom of international economists – perhaps with a little help from their colleagues in industrial economics and choice theory – to devise a measure which relates a particular type, or types, of government action to economic success, and to the promotion of a particular kind of trading advantage. We repeat, it is *not* primarily the question of the level of government expenditure or the amount of intervention which is at issue, but the willingness and ability of the government to superintend efficiently the organization of economic activity – including that in which it is, itself, directly engaged.

CONCLUSIONS

Let us now pull the threads of this chapter together. We have suggested that what's wrong is the failure of trade theory to address techno-economic micro- and macro-organizational issues, and particularly, the effect on trade of co-ordinating resources and transacting across exchanges by alternative modalities. In particular, we have asserted that the globalizing of the world economy is affecting the pattern of trade in three main ways. First, the increasing mobility of assets is widening the options of firms in their engagement in international commerce. In particular, FDI and strategic alliances have replaced trade as the main form of international transaction. The second is the declining significance of arm's-length transactions, relative to those conducted between related parties.[36] The third is the increasing role of national governments and supranational regimes in the management of trade, and in influencing the disbursement of 'quicksilver' assets and the competitiveness of locationally immobile resources and capabilities.

At the same time, we have argued that, *de facto*, technological, political and economic changes of the past two decades, which have virtually destroyed the credibility of any theory which assumes that firms are 'black boxes' and that governments play no role in affecting trade and investment, have led to a restructuring of economic activity which, in general, has been more in keeping with the extant tenets of the neo-factor and scale theories of trade than that which it replaced. This is because the internalization of arm's-length markets by hierarchies, the growth of strategic alliances, and the macro-organizational strategies of governments have not only been the response to the pressures of global competition, but often helped promote allocative and dynamic competitiveness. Even if, to some observers, this is a hypothetical, rather than proven, statement, it suggests that, far from being dead and buried, there is a good deal of life left in traditional trade paradigms, which aver that, given a chance and over time, market forces do work.

We would not want to press our argument too far, or to deny that there are some firm- or government-specific patterns of behaviour which run counter to the principles of neo-classical economics. Examples include strategies to promote rent seeking or to gain or exploit an oligopolistic or monopolistic position. But our reading of the forces now making for globalization is that they are making such strategies more difficult to achieve – except, perhaps, at a regional level. For the moment, we would aver that many of the propositions of received trade theory are being upheld by the very organizational forces which they tend to neglect.

NOTES

1. However, for the purposes of this chapter, we shall be concentrating on international economic issues.
2. And especially the attention given to increasing returns as a determinant of trade.
3. This in no way denies the need for further theoretical extension of both traditional and newer trade models as, for example, set out by Bensel and Elmslie (1992) and Krugman (1990).

4. We use the adjective 'connected' to embrace transactions other than those conducted at arm's length. They include all intrafirm trade and trade between separately owned entities which arise from contractual agreements.
5. See especially the work of Dosi et al. (1990), which links technological accumulation theories of growth to those of dynamic comparative advantage.
6. We accept that the idea of a continuum of transactional relationships may fail to capture the complex realities of exchange, and in the words of Walter Powell (1990) is 'too quiescent and mechanical'. However, for the purposes of this chapter, I find it useful to delineate the main organizational routes for conducting trade.
7. Notably models of oligopolistic competition. For a review of these theories, see Krugman (1986).
8. The nearest, perhaps, is Markusen's recent attempts to examine the relationship between the boundaries of MNEs and the modern theories of trade (Markusen, 1995).
9. It is unclear in more recent trade theories whether or not firms are presumed to be producing with zero X inefficiency!
10. These costs should embrace any and all costs which can be traced to a particular transaction, including those incurred before or after the transaction takes place.
11. According to Markusen (1995, p. 175), MNEs are 'exporters of the services of firm-specific assets'. Earlier models constructed by Helpman (1984) and Markusen (1984) separated the headquarters or firm-level activity such as R&D from the rest of the production process of firms. In both models, the MNE headquarter's activity is modelled as a joint input such that adding additional plants (at home or abroad) does not reduce the value of the input to existing plants. Later work by Brainard (1993) and Horstman and Markusen (1992) demonstrated that MNEs are supported in equilibrium wherever firm-specific fixed costs and spatial barriers are large relative to plant-level economies. The researchers also showed that MNEs are more likely to exist in equilibrium when the trading countries are large and when they have similar factor endowments. This view is generally supported by the voluminous empirical evidence on FDI and MNE activity (Dunning, 1993a).
12. Again, the work of Markusen is an exception, and in one of his most recent papers (Markusen, 1995) he explicitly considers such market imperfections as information asymmetry, the 'free rider' problem, buyer uncertainty and moral hazard in his analysis.
13. For a recent review of the literature, see Dunning (1993a) and Gray (1993).
14. These might include economies of risk diversification, marketing synergies, common sourcing, standardization of financial and accounting techniques, the feedback of know-how, and the easy transfer of learning and experience.
15. And, indeed, of other trading partners of both countries.
16. For a discussion of the role of technology in international trade, see Vernon (1966, 1970).
17. Which, in some instances, may be a liability rather than an asset! See Dunning (1994).
18. This is especially true of firms from smaller nations, whose growth and prosperity largely rests on the foreign operations of the MNEs.
19. For a discussion of the gains arising from access to HQ administrative, managerial and administrative services, see Helpman and Krugman (1985) and Markusen (1984, 1995).
20. See also later sections of this chapter.
21. For a further exposition of the role of the firm in explaining trade in dynamic goods, see Gray (1994).
22. See especially Vernon (1966) and Wells (1972).
23. Hence, as shown by Dunning (1988b), in the case of the United Kingdom, and Lipsey and Kravis (1987), in the case of the United States, it is quite possible for *firms* of a particular nationality to improve their international competitiveness as a result of their foreign value-adding activities while, at the same time, the competitiveness of the location-bound resources of their home countries might be declining.
24. See Dunning, 1997.
25. See especially Dunning (1993b, 1994 and 1997).
26. For a more general exposition of the importance of organizational advantages in affecting the competitiveness and growth of firms, see Chandler (1962, 1990).
27. As, for example, identified in Dunning (1993b, 1994).

28. An expression first coined by public choice theorists to illustrate that, in the last resort, individuals can respond to an unacceptably high tax burden by emigrating. Similarly, if the net tax burden imposed on firms by the government of one country is higher than that imposed by another, this might result in a relocation of production away from the first to the second country (Gray, 1994).
29. Indeed, quite the reverse. In a study carried out for the IMF, Ostry (1993) found little evidence that even selective interventionism by East Asian governments was positively correlated with superior growth performance. Instead, high domestic savings and investment ratios, an emphasis on the upgrading of human capital, flexible labour markets and an unrestricted access to foreign resources, capabilities and markets are among the shared factors in the success of Asian economies.
30. Again, neo-classical economics, with its concentration on economic man (or woman), dismisses the idea that the work ethic and the culture of competitiveness may differ in their desire to upgrade the choice and quality of goods and services available – particularly if this means harder or less congenial work or the sacrifice of leisure.
31. For a discussion of the external consequences of domestic economic policies on global economic welfare, see Eden and Hampson (1990) and Currie and Vines (1992).
32. Apart, that is, from those promised by national authorities which are part of a regional customs union or community. For a review of the ways in which supranational institutions may promote the convergence of national innovation, competition and financial market regulation, see Ostry (1991).
33. In addition to the more obvious supranational institutions, there are a host of other private, or semi-public, multilateral agencies or clubs, for example the World Intellectual Property Organization (WIPO) and the International Organization for Standardization (ISO). Depending upon their *raison d'être* and their power or influence over their members, each of these can either simulate efficient markets, or as in the case of many cartels (OPEC), structurally distort markets.
34. A similar view is held by Adrian Wood (1993), who argues for a re-examination of the H–O thesis in terms of factor endowments which are both immobile and (in the short run at least) non-reproducible. In his model of North/South trade, Wood excludes financial capital, but includes knowledge embodied in people and social infrastructure.
35. In other words, anything other than a 'perfect' culture for competitiveness could be considered a cost. This cost could vary from zero to one which was so high that no production, trade or investment was economically feasible.
36. We might also mention that FDI and trade are becoming increasingly complementary to, rather than substitutable for, each other (UNCTAD, 1996).

REFERENCES

Bensel, T. and Elmslie, B.T. (1992), 'Rethinking international trade theory: a methodological appraisal', *Weltwirtschaftliches Archiv*, **128**(2): 249–65.

Brainard, S.L. (1993), 'A simple theory of multinational corporations and trade with a trade-off between proximity and concentration', Cambridge, MA: NBER Working Paper No. 4269, February.

Chandler, A.D. Jr. (1962), *Strategy and Structure: The History of American Industrial Enterprise*, Cambridge, MA: MIT Press.

Chandler, A.D. Jr. (1990), *Scale and Scope: The Dynamics of Industrial Capitalism*, Cambridge, MA: Harvard University Press.

Coase, R.H. (1937), 'The nature of the firm', *Economica* (New Series) **4**, November: 386–405.

Currie, D.A. and Vines, D. (1992), 'A global economic policy agenda for the 1990s: is there a special British role?', *International Affairs*, **68**(4): 585–602.

Dosi, G., Pavitt, K. and Soete, L. (1990), *Technical Change and International Trade*, New York: Harvester Wheatsheaf.

Dunning, J.H. (1988a), *Multinationals, Technology and Competitiveness*, London: Unwin Hyman.

Dunning, J.H. (1988b), *Explaining International Production*, London and Boston, MA: Unwin Hyman.

Dunning, J.H. (1993a), *Multinational Enterprises and the Global Economy*, Workingham, UK, and Reading, MA: Addison Wesley.

Dunning, J.H. (1993b), *Globalization of Business: The Challenge of the 1990s*, London and New York: Routledge.

Dunning, J.H. (1994), *Globalization: The Challenge for National Economic Regimes*, Dublin: The Economic and Social Research Council.

Dunning, J.H. (1999), *Alliance Capitalism and Global Business*, London and New York: Routledge.

Dunning, J.H. and Norman, G. (1985), 'Explaining intra-industry international production', in A. Erdilek (ed.), *Multinationals as Mutual Invaders*, London: Croom Helm.

Eden, L. and Hampson, F.O. (1990), *Clubs are Trumps: Towards a Taxonomy of International Regimes*, Ottawa Center for International Trade and Investment Policies, Carleton University, C/TQS, 90–102.

Froot, K.A. (ed.) (1993), *Foreign Direct Investment*, Chicago and London: University of Chicago Press.

Gray, H.P. (ed.) (1993), *Transnational Corporations and International Trade and Payments, UN Library on Transnational Corporations*, Vol. 8, London and New York: Routledge.

Gray, H.P. (1994), *A Firm Level Theory of International Trade in Dynamic Goods*, Newark, NJ: Rutgers University (mimeo).

Helpman, E. (1984), 'A simple theory of trade with multinational corporations', *Journal of Political Economy*, **92**: 451–71.

Helpman, E. and Krugman, P.R. (1985), *Market Structure and Foreign Trade*, Cambridge, MA: MIT Press.

Hirschman, A. (1970), *Exit Voice and Loyalty*, Cambridge, MA: Harvard University Press.

Horstman, I. and Markusen, J.R. (1992), 'Endogenous market structures in international trade', *Journal of International Economics*, **32**: 109–29.

Hymer, S. (1960), 'The international operation of national firms: a study of direct investment', PhD Dissertation, MIT (published by MIT Press in 1976).

Krugman, P. (ed.) (1986), *Strategic Trade Policy and the New International Economics*, Cambridge, MA: MIT Press.

Krugman, P. (1990), *Rethinking International Trade*, Cambridge, MA: MIT Press.

Krugman, P. (1991), *Geography and Trade*, Cambridge, MA: MIT Press.

Lipsey, R. (1991), *Economic Growth: Science and Technology and Institutional Change in the Global Economy*, Toronto: Canadian Institute for Advanced Research, CIAR Publication No. 4, June.

Lipsey, R.G. and Kravis, I.B. (1987), 'The competitiveness and comparative advantage of US multinationals 1957–1984', *Banca Nazionale del Lavoro Quarterly Review*, **16** (June): 147–65.

Markusen, J.R. (1984), 'Multinationals, multi-plant economics, and the gains from trade', *Journal of International Economics*, **16**: 205–26.

Markusen, J.R. (1995), 'The boundaries of multinational enterprises and the theory of international *trade'*, *Journal of Economic Perspectives*, **9**(2): 169–89.
Markusen, J.R. and Venables, A. (1995), *Multinational Firms and the New Trade Theory*, Cambridge: NBER Working Paper No. 5036, February.
Mundell, R. (1957), 'International trade and factor mobility', *American Economic Review*, **47**: 321–35.
Ostry, S. (1991), 'Beyond the border: the new international policy arena', in *Strategic Policies in a Global Economy*, Paris: OECD International Futures Program.
Ostry, J. (1993), 'Selective government interventions and economic growth: a survey of the Asian experience and its applicability to New Zealand', Paper on Policy Analysis and Assessment, Washington: IMF.
Porter, M. (1990), *The Competitive Advantage of Nations*, New York: The Free Press.
Powell, W.W. (1990), 'Neither market nor hierarchy: network forms of organization', in B.M. Staw and L.M. Cummings (eds), *Research in Organizational Behavior*, Vol. 12, Greenwich, CT: JAI Press, pp. 295–316.
Teece, D.J. (1992), 'Competition, cooperation and innovation', *Journal of Economic Behavior and Organization*, **7**: 1–25.
UNCTAD (1993), *World Investment Report 1993: Towards an Integrated Production System*, New York and Geneva: UN.
UNCTAD (1996), *World Investment Report 1996: Transnational Corporations, Trade and International Production*, New York and Geneva: UN.
Vernon, R. (1966), 'International investment and international trade in the product cycle', *Quarterly Journal of Economics*, **80**: 190–207.
Vernon, R. (1970), *The Technology Factor in International Trade*, New York: Columbia University Press.
Wells, L.T. (ed.) (1972), *The Product Life Cycle and International Trade*, Cambridge, MA: Harvard University Press.
Wood, A. (1993), *Give Heckscher and Ohlin a Chance*, Sussex: Institute of Development Studies, Chance, Sussex (mimeo).

12. Toward a general paradigm of foreign direct and foreign portfolio investment*

INTRODUCTION

Until the early 1960s, the theory of foreign investment was essentially a theory of international portfolio or indirect capital movements. Capital flowed across national borders, mainly (though not exclusively) through the intermediation of the international capital market; and it did so in search of higher interest rates (discounted for exchange and other risks) and/or higher profits relative to those which could be earned at home. The types of financial device that were involved in these cross-national flows of capital were bonds and notes from the public and private sectors, equities, money market instruments and financial derivatives.[1]

Capital also crossed borders in the form of direct investments (FDI). FDI historically has been the dominant form of international *private* capital transfers and has represented a significant proportion of all investment. As can be seen in Figure 12.1 and Appendix 12.1,[2] from 1980 to 1995, FDI accounted for 38.7 percent of all inbound foreign investment to all countries in the International Monetary Fund's *Balance of Payments Statistics Yearbook*, with a slightly higher proportion (43.4 percent) occurring in the first half of the period than in the second half (32.6 percent).[3]

Figures 12.2 and 12.3, and Appendix 12.2 show that the vast majority of FDI and foreign portfolio investment (FPI)[4] is directed towards developed countries. During the early 1980s, FDI to developing countries was quite small and showed little sign of growth; it has only been in the late 1980s through 1995 that FDI to developing countries has trended upward and has been increasing relative to FDI to developed countries. A similar pattern appears for (FPI) although the proportion of FPI going to developed countries is much higher than that for FDI. This phenomenon is due in large part to the inclusion of government securities as well as equities in the IMF data on portfolio investment, both of which have large, well-developed markets in developed countries.

* Written with John Dilyard. From *Transnational Corporations*, **8** (1) (1999): 1–53.

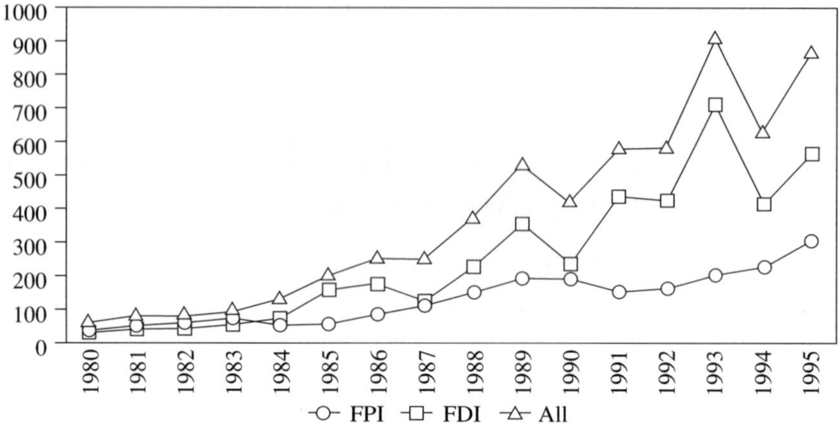

Source: World Bank (1997a).

Figure 12.1 Inbound foreign investment, 1980–95

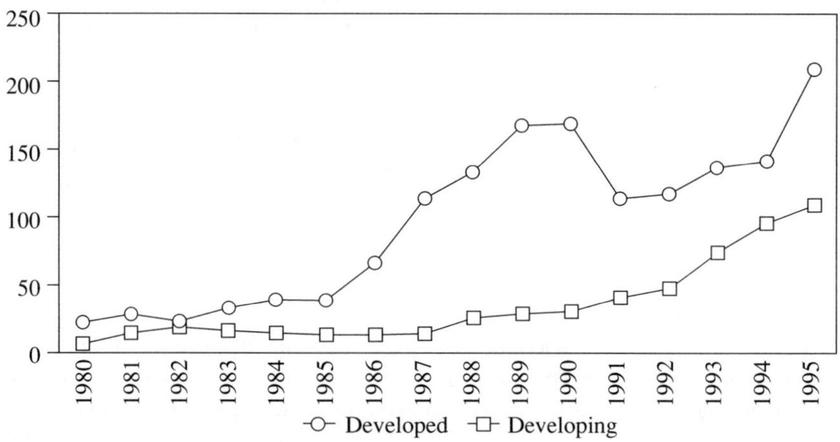

Source: World Bank (1997a).

Figure 12.2 Inbound foreign direct investment, 1980–95

Traditionally, FDI has been differentiated from FPI in four ways. The first is that, unlike FPI, FDI involves the transfer of non-financial assets, notably technology and intellectual capital, in addition to financial assets.

The second is that, in the case of FPI, there is a change in ownership of the assets transferred; this is not so in the case of FDI. Third, FDI is more lumpy

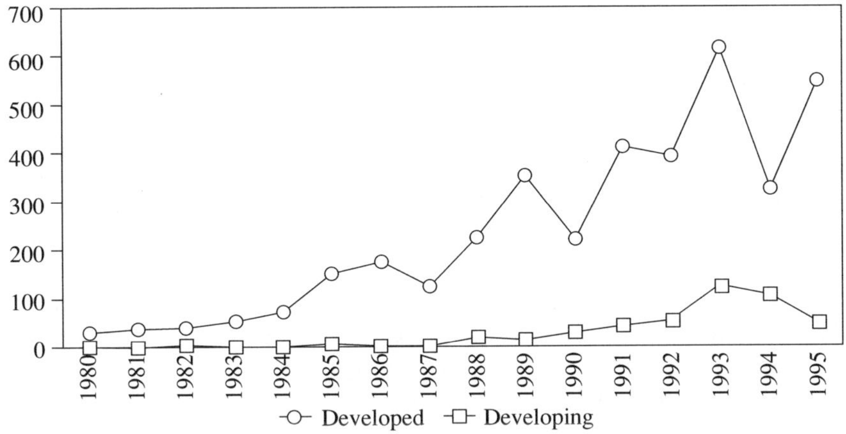

Source: World Bank (1997a).

Figure 12.3 Inbound foreign portfolio investment, 1980–95

(or indivisible) and less fungible than FPI, and is undertaken mainly by corporations, which control the deployment of the assets transferred, rather than by individuals and institutions, which exercise little control or influence over those assets. Fourth, unlike FPI, which is primarily prompted by higher foreign interest rates, FDI is motivated by the opportunity of achieving a better economic performance than that currently earned by competitor firms. For this to be achieved, the investing firms need to have some competitive advantage, either prior to, or in consequence of, their foreign activities, over and above that possessed by their foreign rivals, and for this advantage to be transferable across national boundaries.

There is now a well-established body of theory of FDI which, for the most part, is not concerned with explaining intrafirm capital movements *per se*, but rather that of the foreign value-adding activities of firms in which they have a financial stake sufficient enough to allow them some control or influence over such activities. While, *de jure*, such control is only achievable with a majority equity ownership, in practice most national authorities take a 25 percent, or even, in some cases a 10 percent equity stake, as indicative of some influence on the decision-making of the invested-in firm by the investing firm.[5]

Unlike the theory of FPI, that of FDI is concerned chiefly with explaining why firms extend their territorial boundaries outside their home countries, and why they do so by setting up new subsidiaries or acquiring existing foreign value-added activities, rather than by exports from their domestic production units, or by selling the right to use their competitive advantages, especially non-financial assets, through intermediate product markets. In doing so, it draws upon and integrates several branches of economic theory, including the theory of the firm and those of trade, of location and of market structure (Dunning, 1993a, 1999 and 2000).

Yet, in their discussion of why firms should wish to internalize cross-border intermediate product markets, economists have been almost exclusively concerned with real, rather than financial, assets (as for example summarized in Dunning, 1993b and Caves, 1996). For example, while much has been written on the reasons why firms prefer to exploit a particular technological advantage (e.g. the ownership of patents) themselves, rather than license another firm to do so, virtually no attention has been given to why firms prefer to internalize the market for international capital (i.e. engage in foreign direct investment, rather than in foreign indirect investment). This, we believe, is partly because the two phenomena have been treated largely as substitutes for each other, but also because they have been considered as quite different and independent modalities of capital exports.

It is the contention of this chapter that this is a mistaken view and that, in our contemporary globalizing economy, portfolio and direct foreign investment can best be considered as components of a common paradigmatic approach to explain all kinds of private capital flows. We believe that, although essentially a financial act, FPI can be viewed in the same way as arm's-length trade of any other asset; and that in discussing its relative merits, *vis-à-vis* FDI, one can use many of the tenets of internalization theory, first put forward to explain the intra- rather than interfirm (or market) exchange of non-financial assets.

However, there is a more important reason for our search for a general paradigm of private foreign investment. This is the growing interconnectedness between FDI and FPI – particularly when one takes a dynamic perspective. Historically, FPI – both private and public – has tended to precede FDI. Much of the early nineteenth-century European investments in the United States took the form of loans or minority equity stakes by institutions and/or individuals to one of the United States, and loans or minority equity stakes in publicly owned utilities or privately owned railroads, rather than by the direct ownership of United States assets by European firms (Wilkins, 1989). Yet, as the United States economy matured, often with the help of inbound direct investment, its own capital markets evolved to absorb new portfolio capital inflows by European institutional and individual investors. In this way, history is now repeating itself in the emerging economies of Asia and Latin America, as successful FDI is helping to foster domestic capital markets, which, in turn, draw in more portfolio investment.

The current interconnections between FDI and FPI are, however, a good deal more complex than those of the nineteenth century. Thus, the FDI by a Chinese multinational enterprise (MNE) in an Australian mining venture may be financed by a loan to the former by a foreign bank, or an international lending agency or a foreign government. An acquisition of a French telecommunications company by a United States corporation may – if successful – lead to an inflow of FPI into the acquired company. A strategic alliance between a Canadian and a Brazilian company in which, in exchange for Canadian processing knowledge, the Brazilian company will share its marketing and distribution capabilities with the Canadian firm, may be accompanied by a minority investment of the former in the latter company.

To illustrate this point further, consider three hypothetical cases.

Case 1

Company A, a consumer products company, wants to expand globally and has targeted country X, an emerging market with demand for the products company A has to offer, as a likely place to start. Inside country X is company B, a distributor of consumer products with a strong regional presence in the most populated, economically developed area of the country. Company B would like to expand but is short of capital. Company A's strategic analysts agree that it is expensive to establish a greenfield distribution network and that it would be difficult to compete with company B in its regional market because of its extensive local knowledge and experience. Company A approaches company B about a cooperative venture in which company A will utilize B's distribution system and help expand it nationally by providing the necessary financing. This financing is made through a loan from company A to company B. The transaction does not alter company B's ownership structure, nor is a separate company established to house the venture.

Case 2

A consortium of three technology companies has developed a new generation of processing micro-chips and is looking for a location in which the chips can be mass produced at competitive costs. Country D, with a highly skilled but relatively cheap labor pool, has a state-owned chip processing plant with significant overcapacity. To attract foreign capital, country D has embarked on a privatization programme. The consortium and country D's government reach an agreement whereby the consortium acquires 48 percent of the company's stock (each member of the consortium acquires 16 percent) and sets up a management structure to control the newly privatized company.

Case 3

A diversified global conglomerate has targeted country Y as a location for expansion of one of its businesses. To test the market, this business acquires

100 percent of a small domestic company. Because the acquired company seems to be run efficiently and profitably, and is similar in most respects to other companies owned or managed by the acquiring company, no changes are anticipated in the way the acquired company is run. If it looks like the business can be expanded in country Y, the acquiring company intends to invest more capital. If expansion does not appear to be profitable, the acquired company will be sold.

To all intents and purposes, Case 1 is a direct investment by company A. However, it does not fit the prevailing definition of a direct investment and could be interpreted as a portfolio investment by company A. Case 2, on the other hand, is a clear example of a direct investment. Case 3, on paper, also is an example of direct investment, but, as far as management is concerned, it is entirely portfolio in nature.

At the same time, some FDI is increasingly taking on the characteristics of FPI. Thus, a firm rich in liquid assets may acquire the ownership, or part ownership, of a foreign corporation purely as a financial investment (i.e. there is no transfer of non-financial assets). Many of the capital exports by oil-rich countries to Europe and the United States in the 1970s were of this kind. Much more significant, however, is the strategic asset-seeking FDI of the late 1980s and 1990s, the purpose of which is less to exploit a particular competitive advantage of the investing firm by adding value to it in a foreign location, and more to protect or augment that advantage. Here, there is a direct parallel to FPI, viz. to tap into the resources and capabilities of foreign firms; although one of the main differences between FDI and FPI investment remains, viz. that the former transfers ownership rights to the investor while the latter does not.

The character of FPI is also changing as, increasingly in a knowledge-based global economy, *de facto* control over asset creation and asset usage rests less on the ownership of finance capital and more on that of all kinds of intellectual capital. Thus, in the last 15 years or so, in addition to FDI as a mode of exploiting or augmenting the competitive advantages of firms, we have seen a huge growth in cross-border non-equity alliances and networking relationships. The motives for such alliances are many and varied (for recent studies of alliances, see Duysters and Hagedoorn, 1995; Hagedoorn, 1985; and Beamish, 1998) but they all have one thing in common, viz. they involve the international transfer of assets – both financial and non-financial – without any FDI on the part of the parties to the alliance or the participants in the network. Sometimes the alliances are intended to exploit a competitive advantage of the contracting firm by way of a written or tacit agreement with a foreign partner, e.g. franchising in the hotel and fast-food sector, licensing agreements in the flat-glass industry, a turnkey project in the petrochemicals industry, and subcontracting arrangements in the textiles, shoe and electronics industries. Each of these collaborative ventures usually involves: (i) an ongoing non-equity association between two or more firms of different nationalities; and (ii) a transfer of assets or rights between the partners to the association.

In other cases, however, strategic alliances, like strategic asset-seeking FDI, may be geared towards accessing new knowledge or new sources of capital, or better exploiting a foreign market. Sometimes, too, they may be motivated by the need to share financial and non-financial assets and/or speed up the process of efficient asset creation or usage.

The critical feature of the plethora of cross-border arrangements now spanning global commerce is that each involves the transfer and/or governance of a single asset or combination of assets without the formal ownership rights afforded by FDI. Yet, *de jure*, while each transaction is akin to an arm's-length or portfolio transfer of wealth-creating assets or rights – *de facto* they may have many of the governance characteristics of FDI.[6]

All these examples point to two main conclusions, the analysis and implications of which are the main topic of this chapter. The first is the growing complementarity between FDI and FPI as agents of economic growth and development. Sometimes, this complementarity may be simultaneous; in other cases it may be sequential. But, whatever the time scale might be, the value of the one is enhanced by the other. Hence it is appropriate that, at least at one level of analysis, the determinants of each are considered as part of a whole, rather than separately.

The second conclusion is that, with the increasing cross-border mobility of many firm specific assets, or rights to assets, and the ever widening channels by which such assets are transferred, the boundaries between FDI and other modalities of asset transfer, including FPI, are becoming more difficult to delineate. Because of this, we believe there is some merit in considering whether a more holistic explanation of international asset movements – in this case FDI and FPI – is appropriate to those currently offered by the literature.

The rest of this chapter proceeds as follows. The next section discusses the changing characteristics of private FDI and FPI over the past century, and particularly over the last two decades. It goes on to offer a general paradigm within which it is suggested that more specific, or operational, explanations of FDI and FPI may be accommodated. Then, it goes on to give examples of how FDI and FPI have interacted in the past, and interact today, with each other. This is followed by a description of capital flows between the United Kingdom and the United States, both past and present, and another look at what is happening in emerging economies. The conclusion sets out some general hypotheses which we believe emerge from the 'new' paradigm of foreign investment.

FDI AND FPI: ARE THEY REALLY DIFFERENT PHENOMENA?

Earlier in this chapter we identified the main analytical differences between FDI and FPI. FDI essentially represented a modality by which a package of created assets[7] is transferred across national boundaries within the jurisdiction of the transferring firm. From a balance-of-payments viewpoint, outbound investment flows embrace all new equity and loan capital supplied by the investing company in the foreign organization over which it has a *de facto* controlling interest,[8] plus the reinvested profits of the foreign subsidiary and intracompany financial transfers.[9] The stock of FDI is more easily defined. It consists of the share of the total assets (usually valued at book value, but sometimes at replacement value) of the foreign subsidiary owned or financed by the investing company less its current liabilities. It, therefore, comprises both equity capital and long-term debt financed from foreign sources.

Private FPI includes the flow of both equity and long-term debt (bonds and loans) between individuals and/or institutions domiciled in different countries.[10] This is achieved either indirectly through the capital market, or directly in a foreign company, as long as the financial stake is below that which constitutes a direct investment. Such investment may be channelled across national boundaries in several different ways. Historically, the most common of these was through the international capital market, and, in recent years, as the section 'The sequential relationship between FPI and FDI' below will show, there has been a marked increase in the flow of FPI from and between developed countries, and the emergence of developing countries as new players in that market. Second, FPI might take the form of minority equity investments of one corporation in another and/or loans made between two or more corporations. Third, capital may be directly invested by institutions and/or individuals in non-publicly quoted private companies and/or in public or semi-public bodies.

While, in the last two examples of FPI, there is a direct transfer of funds, the *de jure* right to deploy the capital loaned or invested is transferred to the recipient institution. *De facto*, however, as we have already seen and will demonstrate in more detail in the section on the sequential relationship between FPI and FDI, depending on the amount of the minority equity capital[11] and/or the terms and conditions attached to it or to any loan, the investing individual or institution may be able to exert considerable influence over the use made of that capital, for example as part of a franchising, technical service, or subcontracting agreement. As these, and other contractual agreements are becoming an increasingly important component of the global exploitation and harnessing of resources and capabilities, the *de facto* line between FDI and FPI is becoming an increasingly difficult one to draw.[12] Because of this, and the fact that sequentially FDI and FPI may be closely linked to each other, this chapter seeks to see how far it is possible to establish a general framework for determining both forms of foreign capital transfer. It is important to keep in mind that, for the most part, we do not view FPI as being in competition with FDI. Rather, we see the two as sometimes complementary or, possibly, alternative modes of investment that are, as a result, capable of being described under a common paradigm.

TOWARDS A GENERAL PARADIGM OF FOREIGN INVESTMENT

We start our analysis by reiterating one of the most widely accepted paradigms of FDI – or more particularly the value-added activities resulting from FDI. The eclectic paradigm (Dunning, 1977, 1988, 1993a, 1995, 1998a, 1999, 2000) avers that the amount and pattern of foreign production by firms – i.e. production financed by FDI – will depend on the value of three sets of variables:

1. The competitive advantage of the investing (or potentially investing) firms, which are specifically the result of the nationality of their ownership (so-called ownership or O specific advantages), relative to those possessed by firms of other nationalities of ownership; and the ability of the investing firms to transfer, exploit or augment these advantages outside their national boundaries.
2. The absolute and relative attractions of different spatial areas (e.g. a country or region within a country) as a location (L specific advantages), both for the creation or acquisition of new O advantages, and for the usage of the O specific advantages. Essentially, the L specific advantages of particular spatial areas rest on the ability of national or subnational markets, and of governments, to provide a unique set of immobile assets necessary for investing firms – both domestic and foreign – to optimize the deployment of their mobile assets.
3. The relative merits, to the investing firms, of coordinating their O specific advantages with the L advantages of particular spatial areas, via arm's-length markets, or internally through their own hierarchies, or by some intermediate route (e.g. an interfirm alliance or network of alliances). Where a firm chooses to replace the market for these advantages, or the rights to them by its own administrative fiat (i.e. via the modality of FDI), it is presumed to possess internalization (I) advantages. Where some form of alliance capitalism is preferred to the external market, or internal hierarchies, when it may or may not involve some FPI, it is presumed that their advantages rest with quasi-internalized or quasi-market interfirm transactions.

The eclectic, or OLI, paradigm suggests that the greater the O and I advantages possessed by firms and the more the L advantages of creating, acquiring (or augmenting) and exploiting these advantages from a location outside its home country, the more FDI will be undertaken. Where firms possess substantial O and I advantages but the L advantages, as described above, favor the home country, then domestic investment will be preferred to FDI, and any foreign markets will be supplied by exports. Where firms possess O advantages which are best acquired, augmented and exploited from a foreign market, but by way of interfirm alliances or by the open market, then FDI will be replaced by both a transfer of at least some of the assets normally associated with FDI (e.g. technology, capital, management skills, etc.) and a transfer of ownership of these assets or the right to their use. One of these assets is the equity or loan capital which comprises FPI.

The extent to which the OLI configuration favors FDI, or some other mode of international economic involvement, will be strongly dependent on a number of contextual variables, and it is when the eclectic paradigm is explicitly related to these variables that the paradigm can be translated into a number of operationally testable theories. These contextual variables are essentially fourfold. The first is the *raison d'être for* the FDI. Four motives, or types of FDI, are usually distinguished in the literature[13] – each is designed to further the economic prosperity of the investing firm (see, for example, Dunning, 1993a).

The first is to seek and secure natural resources, e.g. minerals, raw materials, or unskilled labor for the investing company (i.e. resource seeking FDI), the second is to identify and exploit new markets for its finished products (i.e. market seeking FDI); the third is to restructure its existing investments (of the first and/or second kind) so as to achieve an efficient allocation of international economic (i.e. rationalized or efficiency seeking FDI); and the fourth is to protect or augment its existing O specific advantages in order to sustain or advance its global competitive position (strategic asset seeking FDI). The *components* and *configuration* of the OLI advantages facing firms falling into each of these categories is likely to be very different; so, too, then will be the explanatory variables contained in any operationally testable theory of FDI.

Second, within the eclectic paradigm, the determinants of FDI may be different according to the home countries making the FDI (cf., e.g. Japan with Canada) and the host countries receiving the FDI (cf., e.g. Nigeria with Switzerland). Third, the precise configuration of the OLI variables explaining FDI is likely to be sector or activity specific. Thus, for example, the importance of patents, wage rates, government intervention, cross-border transport costs, and agglomerative economies in influencing the extent and pattern of MNE activity in the computer software and pharmaceutical sectors is likely to be very different from that in the iron and steel or building and contracting industry. Fourth, even within the same industry, the extent and structure of the OLI advantages of particular firms, and their response to particular OLI configurations may vary according to such contextual variables as their size, history, product range, degree of vertical integration, and location of their foreign operations; and also, too, to their managerial strategy (e.g. with respect to knowledge creation and market penetration). Clearly, then, the eclectic paradigm, though a tool offering an analytical foundation to explaining FDI, needs a good deal of contextualization before its principles can be subject to empirical testing.

It will be observed that – like its near counterpart, the internalization theory or paradigm – the eclectic paradigm of FDI is concerned with the extent to which, and the form in which, firms allocate their assets across national boundaries. Indeed, it is not a theory of FDI *per se*.[14] Rather, it draws upon and integrates several separate strands of microeconomic theory – most notably the resource and evolutionary theories of the firm,[15] the theory of location, the theory of economic organization (including the theory of internalization), the theory of international trade, and the theory of risk management. Implicitly or explicitly, it also incorporates a theory of business strategy, i.e. how firms might respond to a given OLI configuration, in terms of the alternative product-marketing innovation strategies open to them.[16] By contrast, the theory of FPI has traditionally drawn on macroeconomic financial variables, notably interest rate differentials and exchange rate fluctuations. If, however, indirect investment is viewed as a transfer of wealth similar to that of an arm's-length transfer of technology, plant and equipment, or human capital, then it would be legitimate to consider its determinants, *vis-à-vis* an internalized transfer of capital, in exactly the same way as the third component of the eclectic paradigm, viz. the I component, the purpose of which is to distinguish between the relative advantages of FDI and the market (or quasi-market) as a vehicle for transferring and coordinating the use of non-financial assets.

This, indeed, will be the underlying thrust of this chapter, viz. to treat FPI[17] as the cross-border transfer of assets through the open market, or by a non-equity interfirm agreement, rather than within the investing institution; and to see how far one can use the microeconomic and/or strategy-related theories of FDI to explain FPI – and, by inference, foreign investment in toto. This we do in the full recognition that there are certain features about FPI – notably its divisibility into small financial units – which FDI, almost by definition, cannot possess.

Let us, first, consider the three main tenets of the OLI paradigm and see how far we can apply them to FPI.

(1) O Specific Advantages

It is self-evident that for FPI to occur, the lending, or investing, entity must have capital to invest. This, in itself, may be regarded as an advantage over other entities that do not possess that asset, or do not possess as much of it. In addition, unless perfect markets exist, and assuming that the advantage is sustainable over time, the entity must have some knowledge about both the prospects of the firm or firms in which the investment is being made and that of alternative foreign investment opportunities and their likely success. Where an intermediary is being used (e.g. an investment broker or mutual fund), such knowledge would also include that about competent sources of advice.

Such O specific advantages are the minimum required for successful FPI in cases where the investment is unconditional and the investing entity has no influence over the outcome of the investment. It embraces most individual and institutional loans, and minority equity investments channelled through the international stock market. However, as we have already seen, in other cases, FPI may be part and parcel of a package of assets transferred (e.g. as in the case of a franchising agreement) or have terms and conditions over its use set by the lending or investing entity, even though the foreign investor has no controlling equity ownership of the recipient entity's capital. In such cases, the O advantages attached to the FPI may be similar to those associated with (some kinds of) FDI. Thus, for example, in the hotel sector, long-term loans may be made by a hotel chain to a foreign hotel with which the chain has concluded a franchising agreement or management contract. The FPI is then conditional upon the terms of the agreement or contract, which will normally involve some non-equity transfer of technology, managerial skills and marketing expertise from the contractor to the contractee. O advantages associated with that kind of FPI may then be similar to those associated with a full-fledged FDI by the same hotel chain in a foreign hotel.[18] In other words, in such cases, FPI cannot be considered as an arm's-length or a stand-alone transfer of financial capital, but as part of a more systemic or integrated package of resource transference – but one which does not involve an equity stake which constitutes an FDI.

(2) L Specific Advantages (of Countries or Regions)

If the 'how is it possible' for FPI to occur rests upon the possession of capital, knowledge about investment opportunities, the extent and structure of existing investments, and, in some cases, O advantages of a non-financial kind, the 'where' of FPI will reflect the likely opportunities for securing a good rate of return (in the form of interest, dividends and capital appreciation) of the capital loaned or invested. Where the expected rate of return, discounted for risk,[19] is higher in the home country than elsewhere, domestic investment will be preferred to foreign investment. Where the reverse is the case, the choice between different foreign locations can be assessed by exactly the same criteria as those used to evaluate the choice of location for FDI, with the sole exception that in the case of FPI one is looking at L advantages from the angle of how they affect the prosperity of the recipient entity, rather than that of the investing company – as in the case of an FDI.

We do not propose to rehearse the locational attractions of particular countries, or regions within countries, to domestic corporations in which, directly or indirectly, there is some FPI. For the most part, these will be similar to those facing the subsidiaries of MNEs, except that their industry composition may be different, as may be their respective 'embeddedness' (e.g. with respect of research and development activity), in the local economy, and their propensity to engage in international transactions. But variables such as raw material and labor costs, taxes, quality of infrastructure, size and character of the local market and managerial efficiency, as they affect the prosperity of indigenous firms, are as much likely to affect the location of inbound portfolio investment as that of direct investment.

At the same time, it may be hypothesized that FPI will be more responsive to changes in the value of L specific variables of countries and regions than will FDI. This is partly because the latter tends to be both more indivisible and spatially 'sticky'[20] than the former,[21] and partly because international capital markets are likely to be more volatile than are the internal workings of TNCs. Indeed, it is this very volatility[22] which may lead to the replacement of these markets by FDI or some form of interfirm agreement in the first place.

(3) The Internalization Theory of FDI

This theory (see, for example, Buckley and Casson, 1976, 1985 and Hennart, 1982, 1986) argues that the foreign production of firms arises because of the failure of cross-border markets to transact intermediate goods and services at a cost below that which would be achieved if these transactions were undertaken within the same firm. The market most commonly taken to illustrate the *raison d'être* for FDI is that of intangible assets, and especially technology and all kinds of information. Thus, for example, technology will be bought and sold on the open market, i.e. externalized, as long as the net costs of doing so are less than those of organizing the transactions within the same firm. This, in fact, is only likely to be the case where the technology is reasonably standardized, where there are large numbers of buyers and sellers, and where there is little information asymmetry or avenues for opportunism. But, as often as not, these conditions do not exist, in which case the market will either be internalized or be translated into a specific agreement between the parties to the exchange.

In principle, there is no reason why (the services of) finance capital should not be treated like that of any other intangible asset, or part of a group of intangible assets.[23] In practice, of course, finance capital is more fungible (i.e. can be put to many uses than can intangible real assets), although this fungibility may be constrained where conditions or terms are placed on its deployment. It is also more divisible; hence the large number of individuals engaging in FPI. Such fungibility and divisibility, together with the homogeneity of finance capital (in the sense that one dollar or pound sterling is identical to another), are just some of the reasons why the market for FPI is likely to involve fewer transaction or coordination costs than that of the market for real intangible assets; and why, indeed, the volume of FPI greatly exceeds the value of cross-border interfirm flows of the latter assets (as opposed to claims to intangible assets).

Although in reality (e.g. where they are undertaken by different investors, such as individuals compared to institutions, or to achieve different goals), FPI and FDI may not be viable alternatives for each other, the internalization paradigm may still offer a robust analytical framework for evaluating the choice of one kind of investment over another; and this is so notwithstanding the fact that the composition and value of the individual I specific variables determining that choice may be different from those used to explain the mode by which other intangible assets are transferred across national boundaries.

To further consider the relationship between FDI and FPI, we first identify the major actors involved in FPI; second, how the OLI variables facing direct investors need to be modified to explain FPI; and third, how the particular advantages available to private portfolio investors are translated into an FPI. Table 12.1 sets out the major actors and their objectives. The actors are placed in three categories – viz. mutual funds; banks; and other investors such as corporations, investment banks, insurance companies, pension funds and individuals other than those channelled through the first two actors. Table 12.2

Table 12.1 Major actors and their objectives in private portfolio investment

Investor	Objective
Institutional investor	Yield
	Capital gain
	Diversification
	Speculation
	Market knowledge/access
Bank holding companies	Yield
	Capital gain
	Market knowledge/access
	Diversification
Non-financial firms	Yield
	Capital gain
	Speculation
	Market knowledge/access
	Diversification

Table 12.2 A description of ownership, location and externalization (OLE) variables for foreign portfolio investment

Ownership (origin of investment)	Location (direction of investment)	Externalization (reason for using external markets rather than internal markets for transferring capital)
Size of investible funds	Political stability of countries in which investments are made	Correlation of returns with other markets, especially home markets
Number of different funds, such as geography-based or sector-based[a]	Commitment to a market economy	Lower transaction costs
Access to new/additional investible funds	Degree of market openness and integration with global or regional markets[b]	Divisibility, transparency, fungibility of finance capital
Ease of transferability of investment among funds	Level of market sophistication or maturity	Possession of propietary or non-public information
Research capabilities and access to information about other markets/countries	Level of government support for portfolio investment	
Experience and capabilities of fund managers	Ease with which returns or gains can be repatriated	
Client preference for and attitude to risk	Ease of capital repatriation and/or dividend remission	
Risk-management capabilities, including use of derivative products	Condition of financial market infrastructure (e.g. banking system)	
Electronic funds transfer and communication capabilities	History of or prospects for economic growth	

Notes:

[a] The institutionalization of savings on OECD countries in the last decade is an example of this. Where and how these savings are invested is dependent on many other factors within the OLE framework.

[b] The liberalization of financial markets, particularly in emerging and developing economies, has expanded the location options of FPI.

cross-references the objectives with the ownership, location and *externalization* advantages (OLE) of FPI identified earlier, and Table 12.3 describes how the advantages are manifested in actions.

While each type of lender or investor has similar objectives, the criteria each uses in making its investment decisions are likely to be different. Diversification, for instance, will have a different meaning for each investor, depending on the structure of the portfolio and the diversification strategies used. An international bond fund will diversify differently from an international stock fund, and both will diversify differently from, say, a single product high-technology

Table 12.3 The execution of OLE advantages in foreign private portfolio investment

Advantage	How executed
Ownership	Choice of investment (e.g. debt or equity), including amount, term, yield, location (geographic and sector), and covariance with other similar investments in other locations.
Location	Investment made to pursue firm and client diversification objectives, as well as to meet client preferences for country and/or sector exposure. Knowledge-gathering investment. To take advantage of favourable tax and/or dividend/repatriation policies.
Externalization	Selective participation in countries, geographic regions or sectors to pursue portfolio structure objectives, as well as the movement among and between countries, regions and sectors.

firm looking for a minority interest in a foreign firm to help it find new markets for its existing product lines. It is quite possible, of course, that each of these investors may hold the same kind of investment. In fact, if direct investment is included, all types of investor might hold the same asset. In case 2 above, for instance, this situation could occur if the government of country D continues to privatize its 52 percent interest in the company. As a result, and as cases 1, 2 and 3 illustrate, little can be known about the intent of an investment just by looking at what it is.

As a framework for later discussion, let us first identify the ownership, location and externalization advantages specifically applicable to portfolio investors. Ownership advantages include the size of the portfolio, the investment, risk management and learning capabilities and experience of the portfolio managers, the existing stock of FPI,[24] and market information and knowledge (or the ability to access/acquire market information). All of these are things that can (and do) differ from investor to investor. Location advantages refer both to those provided by the home base and foreign locations (actual or desired). Thus, access to funds and a regulatory and policy-framing environment that is conducive to the marshalling and investing of funds domestically and abroad are locational advantages. Externalization advantages – the counterpart of internalization advantages of FDI – of using markets to support ownership and location advantages include the ability to take advantage of investments whose returns have limited covariance with the existing stock of investments;

the ability of the market to provide the necessary information of investors to exercise their preferred options and investment strategies; and also the lower costs of managing a large number of relatively standard transactions, cf. those incurred by firms.

Diversification, as used in Table 12.1 refers to the diversification (reduction) of risk as well as the structure of the entire investment portfolio. This can be achieved by diversifying the type of investment made (e.g. stocks in different industries, bonds from different countries, mixing stocks and bonds, etc.) or by selecting investments that have little covariance within and across sectors. The expertise and market knowledge of portfolio managers, displayed in the ability of portfolio managers to research, locate and act upon investment opportunities, and the ability to marshal funds to invest, determine in large part how much the portfolio can be diversified. It is an ownership advantage because that expertise, market knowledge and access to funds can be unique to each type of investor.

The location advantage of having easy access to investible funds and a regulatory, financial and economic environment that eases the marshalling of funds for investment help a mutual fund seek other markets outside its home market. This is not the same thing as simply investing foreign source funds from investors, which would represent a capital outflow from those foreign sources. Rather, it is establishing a foreign base in which those foreign source funds are accumulated for real investment. The mode in which the base is established can take the form of direct investment (e.g. setting up a branch office), portfolio investment (e.g. purchasing a minority interest in a domestic fund in return for access to funds and/or clients), or an arm's-length transaction (e.g. buying funds). Access to funds is not the same thing as the ownership advantage of having investible funds. For instance, all mutual funds in the United States share the same locational advantage created by the regulatory and investment climate of the United States, but not all mutual funds have the same level of assets, the same investment objectives and the same mix of investors.

The same rationale for market-seeking actions applies to banks and other investors. Banks, however, also engage in client-following and client-seeking investment behavior. The role locational advantage plays here is clear: the institutions want to be near their clients and would like to attract new clients. Given the highly regulatory nature of the banking industry, the most effective way foreign banks can get close to existing and potential clients is by being where the clients are (see Sagari, 1989). This could be accomplished through direct investment (branch offices) or portfolio investment (joint ventures or partnerships with domestic banks). Both of these advantages could enhance an existing ownership advantage, the former by strengthening ties with clients and attracting more investible funds, and the latter by attracting more investible funds.

One could argue with a fair amount of strength that certain other investors, such as investment banks, also engage in client-following and client-seeking behavior. For investment banks, however, once capital is mobile across borders, the incentive for them to establish a foreign office simply to be near their existing clients is weakened. A better way to characterize their behavior, and that of other investors such as pension funds, is resource seeking. Functionally, resource-seeking behavior is the same as the client-seeking behavior of banks in that the objective (i.e. securing more investible funds) is similar. The distinction is in the underlying purpose of using the locational advantage. For banks, it is primarily in establishing a relationship that may result in funds to invest; for non-banks, on the other hand, it is gaining access to funds. As with the client-seeking and client-following behavior of banks, the resource-seeking behavior of non-banks can be achieved through either direct or portfolio investment.

Because the advantages of using the international capital market rather than internalizing that market are defined in terms of portfolio structure and strategic outlook (attitude towards risk), they will influence the yield-seeking and capital gain-seeking behavior of all three types of investor. The overall return of an entire portfolio will be affected by the degree of covariance among the assets (see Markowitz, 1959). Volatility of returns will be greater when covariance is high. The amount of total risk in a portfolio therefore will depend a great deal on the level of covariance. Investors comfortable with volatility (risk seeking) will build a portfolio of assets differently from risk-averse investors who are not comfortable with such greater volatility, but both will build portfolios in accordance with the desired structure of those portfolios.

The possibility of a link between diversification and yield-seeking and capital gain-seeking behavior comes immediately to mind. Obviously, the overall yield of a portfolio and the amount of risk inherent in it will depend on how much the portfolio is diversified and how much covariance is present. In a sense, then, the ultimate performance of a portfolio will depend on the interplay of the various ownership, locational and externalization advantages. The size, type and nature of a portfolio and the way it is managed from a cash-flow and risk perspective (ownership) depends on the assets in the portfolio. The way in which new assets are acquired to meet specific growth objectives (for the individual portfolio or the investing company) depends on the use to which locational advantages are put. Performance (yield and capital gains) objectives, which in turn influence the type of asset acquired or sought, then depend on the strategic outlook of the investor.

The variables and contexts identified in Tables 12.1 and 12.2 are self-explanatory. Each is firmly grounded in the theory of FDI, of portfolio capital movements, and of locational economics. From these, and taking a medium- to long-term perspective, it is possible to formulate a series of operationally testable hypotheses as to: (a) when FDI and FPI are complements to each other; and (b) if they are substitutes, or are independent of each other, what are the variables likely to determine the final choice or modality of financial asset transfer. While we shall offer some hypotheses later in this chapter, we shall not seek to formally test them. Instead, we shall offer some illustrations of how, in the past, and in today's globalizing economy, FDI and FPI have been, and are, related to other, in terms of their respective – sometimes similar, sometimes different – OLI or OLE configurations.

THE SEQUENTIAL RELATIONSHIP BETWEEN FPI AND FDI

While, at a given moment of time, FPI and FDI may appear to be independently determined and undertaken for different reasons, it is quite possible that over time they may be closely related to each other. History is full of examples of FPI, both in developed and developing countries, laying the ground work for FDI. Usually, and especially in the case of infrastructure investment in countries subject to political or economic volatility, the FPI will be financed by public authorities or international agencies (e.g. the World Bank), or protected by an investment guarantee scheme. In other instances (e.g. as on the American continent in much of the nineteenth century), private foreign capital was steered, mainly through the international capital market, to state governments and/or to state-supported ventures. No less today do foreign direct investors expect host countries to provide the human, technological and institutional infrastructure with which their O specific intangible assets may be successfully combined. Frequently, however, especially in some developing and transitional economies, local savings are insufficient to finance these assets and the capital has to be imported, usually by grants from foreign governments, by foreign loans, and/or (minority) equity investments from international agencies and corporations.

At the same time, it is clear from the emergence and dramatic growth of domestic capital markets in several Asian and Latin American countries that FPI may follow, as well as precede, FDI. But most post-FDI portfolio capital flows are quite differently sourced and directed than are pre-FDI portfolio flows. Whereas the former tend to be financed by national governments and international lending agencies and directed to infrastructural projects – and hence are not our immediate concern – the latter are primarily initiated by individual and institutional investors and are directed to (potentially) profitable and/or growth-oriented sectors in the recipient countries – including some infrastructure projects. Furthermore, while pre-FDI portfolio capital flows normally precede the presence of a flourishing domestic economy and capital market, post-FDI flows are drawn largely by these phenomena.

In today's global economy, however, the sequential interaction between FPI and FDI can be both more indirect and more varied than that just described. For example, it is perfectly possible that part of inbound portfolio capital flows may be used to finance outbound direct investment[25] or, for FDI, in a particular sector, to stimulate competitors to seek FPI – often jointly with other intangible assets to upgrade their own core competencies. In their global search for resources and capabilities, MNEs themselves frequently draw on loan capital from both national and international capital markets; and, in the case of alliances with foreign firms, they may exchange loans and/or equity stakes. Sometimes, too, foreign-owned banks will make long-term loans to indigenous firms, which are used to finance their own international operations; or, in the case of wholesale traders and distributors, to help finance a joint venture with a foreign exporting company. Renewed confidence in an economy, or in a particular sector or region in an economy, which may have been greatly assisted by the activities of foreign subsidiaries, may lead to more FPI in that economy, sector and industry.[26] By contrast, lack of confidence in an economy, region or sector, as demonstrated for example by falling stock prices, might lead not only to a reduction of FPI, but – in the longer run – of FDI as well. More generally, there is some suggestion that, over time, the economic progress of an economy, region or sector will parallel all kinds of foreign and domestic investment quite closely.[27]

The following two sections illustrate the changing interaction between FDI and FPI, using the framework of the eclectic paradigm. The first considers the evolving form and structure of capital flows between the United Kingdom and the United States over the past century or more; and the second does the same – but for a more recent period, viz. 1972 to 1995 – in respect of foreign capital flows into two emerging regions, East Asia and Latin America.

United Kingdom–United States Capital Flows

The history of foreign investment in the United States up to 1914 has been well documented by Mira Wilkins (1989). Here we will seek to emphasize a few highlights of that history from the perspective of United Kingdom FDI and FPI.

Applying the concept of the investment development path[28] (Dunning and Narula, 1996), most of the created assets (e.g. capital, technology and organizational capacity, etc.) for the economic development of colonial America initially came from Europe, and especially the United Kingdom. Partly by way of migration of human and physical capital, partly by grants and loans from the mother country, and partly by some embryonic American businesses financed by foreign direct or portfolio investment, foreign assets, when combined with the rich natural resources of the Eastern seaboard, helped create the colony's own location (L) advantages, and its firms to generate a unique set of O specific competencies.[29]

In the post-revolutionary period, foreign capital flowed into the United States. The first half of the century was a time when the new Republic was both making huge investments of roads, canals, ports and railroads, and evolving its own distinctive economic structure, based largely on the comparative advantage of its natural assets and its emerging created assets, the latter being primarily designed to upgrade the value of the former (Wright, 1990). Such circumstances combined to create an OLI (or OLE) configuration in which the major vehicles for transferring financial and real assets (or rights) between the United Kingdom and the United States were: (a) migration of human capital; (b) the transfer of knowledge via the export of goods and licensing agreements; and (c) the international capital market (see Wilkins, 1989). In 1853, according to a United States Treasury Department Survey, of the $222 million of foreign investment stocks held in the United States, 72 percent was directed to government securities and another 21 percent to the bonds of railroad, canal and navigation companies. The main FDIs of the time were confined to trading and banking and insurance activities. There was also some United Kingdom ownership of the early railroad companies, but FDIs in manufacturing industry were, according to Mira Wilkins (1989), 'few and far between' (p. 88).

The marked preference for United Kingdom and other European indirect, rather than direct, investments in the United States reflected primarily the (relatively) efficient workings of the international capital market, and partly the (relatively) high trans-Atlantic transaction and coordination costs of operating a United States subsidiary of a United Kingdom company. In addition, the most capital-intensive sectors in the United States economy were those in which foreign companies were reluctant to hold a major equity stake (viz. public utilities). By contrast, FPI in United States government securities was generally thought to be a relatively safe investment, particularly when they were recommended by a leading United Kingdom merchant banking house.

Technological and organizational advances of the 1870s and the maturing of many United States enterprises dramatically changed the scenario for inbound foreign investment. Although, right up to the First World War, the bulk of such investment was portfolio, rather than direct,[30] the advent of managerial capitalism and the lowering of intracompany spatial transaction and coordination costs favored the territorial expansion of foreign firms into the United States, particularly in those sectors in which they were perceived to have an O advantage over their United States counterparts. At the same time, there was a great deal of syndicated FDI in these years,[31] which, in its intent at least, has more in common with FPI. By 1910, too, the sectoral preference of United Kingdom investors had switched from government securities to railway stocks and bonds and commercial ventures. According to Sir George Paish (1911), the former accounted for 85.2 percent of the $3.3 billion of United Kingdom investments in the United States in 1910, while investments in industrial companies, mining, land and public utilities accounted for most of the balance. Of these latter investments, about two thirds took the form of direct investments, as it was in these sectors that the net transaction costs of markets, relative to administrative hierarchies, were most evident.[32]

During and after the First World War, a sizeable proportion of United Kingdom investments in the United States were sold, while the late 1920s saw the collapse of the international capital market. However, while United Kingdom investors lost some of their O advantages as suppliers of finance capital, United Kingdom firms continued to lead the outflow of FDI, and by 1938 they accounted for two fifths of global FDI. During these years, however, United Kingdom firms lost ground to their United States counterparts, particularly in FDI intensive sectors, while new locational attractions were being offered by Commonwealth countries, notably Canada and Australia. The net result of these events was that although the flow of United Kingdom investment into the United States did recover somewhat in the 1930s, this recovery was almost wholly the result of new FDI designed to exploit the growth of the United States market and overcome trade and transaction related barriers.

For much of the first 20 years following the end of the Second World War, there was very little United Kingdom portfolio investment in the United States capital market. Indeed, it was only in 1958 that sterling became fully convertible. FDI was also limited because of the lack of competitive advantages of United Kingdom, cf. United States, firms and because of the high costs of production in the United States relative to those in the United Kingdom. Gradually, however, United Kingdom industrial competitiveness recovered, often aided by the capital, technology and managerial skills transferred via FDI from the United States to the United Kingdom (Dunning, 1958); and by the early 1980s United Kingdom and continental European FDI in the United States was rising at twice to three times the rate of United States FDI in Europe (Dunning, 1993b, chap. 7). By 1982, the United Kingdom FDI stake in the United States once more exceeded that of the United States in the United Kingdom, and by the early 1990s it was one half as much again.

While part of this renewed interest by United Kingdom MNEs in the United States can be explained by the extant theories of FDI, since the early 1980s an increasing proportion of FDI has taken the form of takeovers and mergers which has been geared less to exploiting the existing competitive advantages of the investing companies and more to augmenting these advantages.[33] To this extent, the motives of United Kingdom FDI in the United States have begun to parallel those of FPI – viz. to invest in the economic strength of a foreign company, country or region in a country. This has been particularly well demonstrated in the high-technology sectors, where FDI by United Kingdom firms in the United States has been complemented by interfirm alliances between United States and United Kingdom firms. Sometimes such alliances have involved an export of loan or equity capital from the United Kingdom to the United States; but, more usually, the main vehicle of financial involvement by individual and institutional investors in the more competitive United States sectors has been through the capital market, for example, by the purchase of unit trusts, mutual funds, and by purchases of stock of United States companies or of United Kingdom MNEs with FDIs in the United States.

Table 12.4 FDI flows from the United Kingdom into the United States, 1972–95 ($ billions)

Years	FDI	Per cent growth	GNP	Per cent growth
1972–74	0.36		1350	
1973–75	0.56	55.9	1478	9.5
1974–76	0.58	2.4	1619	9.5
1975–77	0.63	9.9	1792	10.7
1976–78	0.76	19.8	2011	12.2
1977–79	1.26	66.7	2257	12.2
1978–80	2.04	61.9	2506	11.0
1979–81	3.20	56.6	2776	10.8
1980–82	4.26	33.1	2995	7.9
1981–83	4.52	6.2	3226	7.7
1982–84	5.08	12.4	3472	7.6
1983–85	4.86	–4.3	3763	8.4
1984–86	6.22	28.0	4044	7.5
1985–87	10.35	66.2	4292	6.1
1986–88	15.05	45.5	4577	6.6
1987–89	19.19	27.5	4900	7.1
1988–90	14.51	–24.4	5227	6.7
1989–91	9.71	–33.1	5503	5.3
1990–92	2.10	–78.4	5839	6.1
1993	13.23	530.8	6564	12.4
1994	11.12	–15.9	6932	5.6
1995	22.08	98.5	7247	4.5

Note: Data are not available on United Kingdom FPI into the United States.

Source: Calculated from various issues of United States Department of Commerce, *Survey of Current Business*. These data include reinvested profits from existing investments.

Table 12.4 sets out the trend of United Kingdom FDI flows in the United States and the United States gross national product from 1972 to 1995. We have presented the data as three-year moving averages to iron out at least some of the sharp changes in foreign investment brought about by mergers and acquisitions and/or short-term speculative reasons. Table 12.5 presents the trend of all FDI and FPI flows to the United States and the United States' gross national product over the same period, also as three-year moving averages. The figures show, first, that both kinds of foreign investment have increased at a faster rate than gross national product; second, that FPI and FDI have broadly parallelled one another, but especially so since the early 1980s; and third, that, although for the period as a whole, the share of FPI in total foreign investment has risen, it has also fluctuated more noticeably than FDI.

Table 12.5 Trends in all FDI and FPI flows into the United States, 1972–95 ($ billions)

Period	FDI	Per cent change	FPI	Per cent change	All foreign	
					Investment	Per cent change
1972–74	2.8		5.9		8.7	
1973–75	3.4	19.8	3.0	–48.6	6.4	–26.4
1974–76	3.9	15.0	2.9	–3.8	6.8	6.3
1975–77	3.6	–8.9	11.0	278.3	14.6	114.7
1976–78	5.3	49.3	12.0	8.6	17.3	18.5
1977–79	7.1	33.8	11.4	–4.8	18.5	6.9
1978–80	11.5	61.8	6.8	–40.1	18.3	–1.1
1979–81	17.3	50.7	9.3	37.1	26.6	45.4
1980–82	18.7	8.0	11.7	25.2	30.4	14.3
1981–83	17.1	–8.8	8.7	–25.3	25.8	–15.1
1982–84	17.1	–0.1	12.2	38.9	29.3	13.6
1983–85	18.8	10.3	31.5	159.3	50.3	71.7
1984–86	26.1	38.4	58.2	84.7	84.3	67.6
1985–87	31.6	21.2	70.8	21.7	102.4	21.5
1986–88	44.3	40.2	73.0	3.0	117.3	14.6
1987–89	55.7	25.6	77.6	6.4	132.3	12.8
1988–90	57.6	3.6	63.9	–17.8	121.5	–8.2
1989–91	45.9	–20.4	58.4	–8.5	104.3	–14.2
1990–92	29.2	–36.4	50.5	–13.5	79.7	–23.7
1993	43.0	47.4	111.0	119.7	154.0	93.2
1994	49.8	15.7	139.5	25.7	189.3	22.9
1995	60.2	21.0	236.2	69.4	296.4	56.6

Source: IMF (1996), *Balance of Payments Statistical Yearbook, 1996* (Washington, DC: IMF).

In terms of the eclectic paradigm, the rising share of foreign investment in the United States' gross national product – and incidentally of the total gross fixed capital formation in the United States[34] – is consistent with two somewhat conflicting propositions. The first is that the O specific advantages of foreign-owned firms are rising relative to those of United States' owned firms, and hence the firms' ability to invest in the United States is that much greater. The second is that the foreign firms are investing in the United States to protect or augment their existing competitive advantages. This second proposition is consistent with the view of portfolio investors that the United States' economy is a good place in which to invest their capital. Clearly, which of these two propositions is most applicable is likely to be industry and, indeed, firm specific. But from a casual examination of the comparative growth and profitability data on the leading United States and United Kingdom firms (Dunning and Pearce, 1985), and data from the United States Department of Commerce and the industrial distribution of the United Kingdom FDI in the United States – including FDI in research and development ventures – it would seem that, while the former proposition may hold good for the less knowledge- but more marketing-intensive industries (especially food, drink and tobacco), the latter proposition better explains the growth of the United Kingdom (and for that matter other European and Japanese) FDI in the high-technology industries, noticeably the biotechnology and the telematics industries).

Over the last two or more decades, the L advantages of United States-based assets have been most evident in two kinds of activity. The first, as witnessed especially by Japanese FDI in the United States, has been in those industries in which the global O advantages of the foreign investors are particularly evident, yet which are best exploited from a United States location. The second has been in those industries in which foreign firms perceive they need a presence in the United States to gain access to specific resources and capabilities, including institutional capital, and/or to augment their own advantages by acquiring, or engaging in an alliance with, United States firms. This latter kind of FDI has been particularly noticeable in research and development, knowledge-intensive manufacturing and in the service industries. It is also worth observing that both foreign and domestic investment in these industries has tended to favor particular states in the United States – notably California, Massachusetts, New Jersey, South Carolina and Texas – each of which has an above average share of knowledge-intensive manufacturing and service industries.

For the most part, then, we conclude that, normalizing for industry and firm specific differences, discounting short-term factors affecting stock market performances and apart from differences in cross-border transaction and transport costs which only affect FDI, that the L advantages of the United States in attracting inbound portfolio and direct investment are broadly the same. However, within the United States, there is some suggestion that foreign subsidiaries do portray different locational preferences than their indigenous competitors (Ulgado, 1996; Shaver, 1998).

While in some cases the premises of the internalization paradigm can be used to explain why FDI is preferred to FPI, much of United Kingdom FPI now directed to the United States is not directly substitutable for FDI, but rather is complementary to it. This is primarily because it is undertaken by different economic agents and the unit size of the investment is, on average, much smaller. In the case of individual (i.e. personal) lenders or investors, for example, the choice is not between FPI and FDI, but between FPI in the United States[35] or in United States firms, and that in other countries or in non-United States firms; this, for example, especially applies to FPI in United States Government securities. At the same time, indirectly and over time, there is some suggestion that FDI and FPI are sometimes alternative and sometimes complementary ways of achieving this goal. Certainly since the late 1980s they have tended to parallel the fortunes of the United States economy. Many non-equity United Kingdom–United States strategic alliances are also part of the global strategy of foreign firms with major foreign interests in the United States, and are intended to protect or add to the value of these interests. At the same time, FPI invested in United States MNEs may help such firms not only to finance (say) joint research and development or marketing ventures with foreign firms, but to better penetrate new foreign markets, either by way of outbound direct investment or by some form of interfirm collaboration.

FDI and FPI in Emerging Economies

The last two decades have seen a remarkable increase in the level of private capital flows into developing countries, with the fastest growth occurring in FPI. The entire period from 1975 to 1995 can be divided up into three seven-year subperiods: 1975–81; 1982–88, and 1989–95. These periods coincide roughly with three stages of private capital flows: the pre-debt crisis stage (1975–81); the debt crisis and its aftermath stage (1982–88); and the recovery and boom stage (1989–95). Table 12.6 presents data on the annual average inbound flows of FDI and FPI during these stages for all developing countries, and shows the proportional share of FDI in these flows.[36] The initial stage is indexed at 100.0 to provide a gauge for the changing magnitude of each type of investment. (Further details on the year-to-year FDI and FPI to all developing countries are provided in Appendix Table A.12.2.)

The effect of the debt crisis on FPI from 1982 to 1988 resulted in a slightly negative ($169 million) net flow. Two factors caused the downturn in private FPI. First, some private debt was either restructured or was converted to public debt which, in turn, was guaranteed by a third party (such as the United States Treasury Department or the IMF) to both forestall economic collapse of the debtors and to protect the lenders.[37] Second, the flow of new private debt slowed as the effects of the debt crisis spread across developing countries, making lenders cautious about extending credit until conditions improved.[38] Net flows of FDI, on the other hand, increased by 167 percent during the debt-crisis stage.

Table 12.6 Net flows of private investment to all developing countries in three stages, 1975–95 ($ billions)

Stage	FDI	Index Stage 1 = 100	FPI	Index Stage 1 = 100	Total	FDI as per cent of total
1: 1975–81	7 035	100.0	7 866	100.0	14 901	47.2
2: 1982–88	11 764	167.2	–169	–2.1	11 595	101.5
3: 1989–95	53 037	753.9	35 671	453.5	88 707	459.8

Source: Calculated from World Bank (1997a).

Table 12.7 Private investment in East Asia and Latin America as compared to that in all developing countries during three stages, 1975–95 ($ billions)

Stage	FDI	Per cent of all FDI	FPI	Per cent of all FPI	Total	Per cent of total
1: 1975–81	5 679	80.7	6 212	79.0	11 891	80.0
2: 1982–88	8 519	72.4	–475	281.4	8 044	69.4
3: 1989–95	41 264	77.8	29 439	82.5	70 704	79.7

Source: Calculated from World Bank (1997a).

These private investment flows, however, were not spread uniformly across developing countries. As can be seen in Table 12.7 two geographic regions – East Asia and Latin America – attracted the largest share of private investment throughout the entire period.[39] From 1975 through 1995, these two regions averaged over 77 percent of all FDI directed to developing countries, and well over 100 percent of all FPI (around 80 percent, excluding the debt-crisis stage) directed to developing countries. In terms of combined private flows, and considering that FPI in Latin America during the debt crisis saw a net outflow, these two regions averaged 76 percent of all private flows going to developing countries from 1975 through 1995. Table 12.8 describes the effect these two regions had on the changes in flows from stage to stage, and Table 12.9 indexes FDI and FPI flows to the first stage for East Asia, Latin America and all other regions.

The main features of Tables 12.6 through 12.9 can be summarized as follows:

- In the initial, pre-debt-crisis stage, average FPI actually exceeded average FDI in all developing countries, $7.9 billion versus $7.0 billion.
- Most of this FPI is presumed to be in the form of commercial bank loans rather than bonds or equity.
- The proportion of all FDI to all private foreign investment has risen from stage to stage, taking into account the impact of the debt crisis.
- The proportion of FDI to all private foreign investment is generally higher in East Asia than Latin America.
- Following the debt crisis, average FDI, $41.3 billion, exceeded average FPI, $35.7 billion, for all developing countries.
- Of the stage-to-stage change in average flows of FDI, 60.1 percent went to East Asia and Latin America from stage 1 to stage 2, and 79.3 percent from stage 2 to stage 3.
- Of the stage-to-stage change in average flows of FPI, 116.3 percent of the change from stage 1 to stage 2 was explained by flows to East Asia and Latin America, and 81.3 percent from stage 2 to stage 3.
- East Asia experienced higher indexed growth rates than all developing countries in FDI and FPI across all stages.
- Latin America experienced lower indexed growth rates than all developing countries in FDI and FPI across all stages (except for the debt-crisis stage).

The last two points indicate that although East Asia and Latin America combined have attracted the largest share of private foreign investment going to developing countries, the pattern of flows to each region differs. Comparing data in Tables 12.7, 12.8 and 12.9 shows that, in terms of indexed growth, both FDI and FPI in Latin America lagged behind East Asia and all developing countries in stages 2 and 3. Even so, the share of average FDI going to Latin America in stages 2 and 3 was 42.3 percent and 35.6 percent, respectively (versus 30.1 percent and 36.5 percent for East Asia), and the share of average FPI was 46.1 percent in stage 3, versus 36.5 percent for East Asia.[40] The reasons for this difference are two-fold. First, Latin America started from a much higher base in both FDI and FPI than did East Asia; in 1975, it attracted $3.3 billion in FDI and $3.0 billion in FPI, compared to East Asia's $1.0 billion in FDI and FPI (see Appendix Table A.12.3). Second, more markets were opening up to FDI in East Asia than in Latin America, particularly from 1989 to 1995, the years in which China began to open its markets to foreign participation.[41]

Another feature distinguishing the East Asian and Latin American regions is their deeper and richer history of foreign capital inflows as compared to other regions. This being so, they offer a useful case study of how the extension of

Table 12.8 Change in private investment in East Asia and Latin America from stage 1 to stage 2 and stage 2 to stage 3 as compared to that in all developing countries ($ billions)

East Asia and Latin America						
Stage	Change in FDI	Per cent of all change	Change in FPI	Per cent of all change	Change in total	Per cent of total change
From 1 to 2	2 840	60.1	–6 687	83.2	–3 847	116.3
From 2 to 3	32 746	79.3	29 914	83.5	62 660	81.3

All developing countries			
Stage	Change in FDI	Change in FPI	Change in total
From 1 to 2	4 728	–8 035	–3 307
From 2 to 3	41 273	35 839	77 112

Source: Calculated from World Bank (1997a).

Table 12.9 Net flows of private investment to East Asia and Latin America in three stages, 1975–95 ($ billions)

East Asia						
Stage	FDI	Index Stage 1 = 100	FPI	Index Stage 1 = 100	Total	FDI as per cent of total
1: 1975–81	1 174	100.0	843	100.0	2 017	58.2
2: 1982–88	3 539	301.4	938	111.3	4 477	79.0
3: 1989–95	26 592	2 264.5	13 011	1 544.3	39 603	67.1

Latin America						
Stage	FDI	Index Stage 1 = 100	FPI	Index Stage 1 = 100	Total	FDI as per cent of total
1: 1975–81	4 518	100.0	5 370	100.0	9 887	45.7
2: 1982–88	4 980	110.2	–1 413	–26.3	3 567	139.6
3: 1989–95	14 672	324.8	16 429	306.0	31 101	47.2

Source: Calculated from World Bank (1997a).

the eclectic paradigm to embrace FPI might help explain the changing composition of inbound foreign investment in the last 20 years.

If we start with the premise that the ownership variables for portfolio investors described in Table 12.2 already are present, the choice of outlet for FPI would depend on location (L) and externalization (E) variables. Several studies of FPI in East Asia and Latin America have concluded that a broad range of macroeconomic reforms and conditions (such as the realignment of exchange rate and monetary controls, reduced restrictions on capital flows and a commitment to a market economy, including privatization) have helped pull portfolio investment to those areas (Lim and Siddall, 1997; Chudnovsky, 1997; Frischtak, 1997; World Bank, 1997a and 1997b). These pull factors coincide with a reconfiguration of the location variables for FPI set out in a section on the general paradigm of foreign investment (Chuhan, Claessens and Mamingi, 1993; Bekaert, 1995; Fernandes-Arias and Montiel, 1995). At the same time, declining interest rates in developed economies, particularly the United States, and higher expected rates of return in the developing markets of East Asia and Latin America, combined with a low correlation of returns between developed and developing markets, helped push FPI to those markets in which attractive investment opportunities were present (Harvey 1995; Calvo, Leiderman and Reinhart, 1993 and 1996). These push factors are consistent with those found in the externalization variable explaining FPI.

The amount of direct and portfolio investment in East Asia and Latin America during the first stage of the past two decades, viz. 1975 to 1981, can be used as a base from which changes in the pattern of investment flows within and between regions can be assessed. From Table 12.9 it is evident that Latin America provided more opportunities for both FDI and FPI than did East Asia in that stage, which is consistent with the former's broader and deeper level of economic development, especially in Mexico, Brazil and Argentina.[42] Given this higher base, it would be likely that the relative rate of increase in FDI and FPI in East Asia would be higher than that found in Latin America even if, in absolute terms, the level of both kinds of flows is higher in Latin America.

In both regions, the increase in L specific advantages sought by foreign MNEs, coupled with the appropriate O and I specific advantages, led to increases in FDI. As might be expected, the rate of increase in FDI in East Asia has been considerably higher than in Latin America, particularly in stage 3 (1989–95), which saw the opening up of China as a major new location for FDI.

At the same time, FPI in many East Asian economies grew rapidly in response to the combination of the increasing openness of their political regimes and their rapid industrialization. The differing pattern of FPI flows in East Asia and Latin America is also worth discussing. In stage 2, growth in FPI in East Asia, as indexed to stage 1, outpaced FPI growth in Latin America.[43] Given the Mexican debt crisis and its impact on other Latin American countries in the

1980s, it is not surprising that FPI in Latin America was negative. It is interesting to note, however, that the outflow in FPI from Latin America was not matched by a corresponding increase in FPI either in East Asia or any other region.

This phenomenon can be explained within the context of the eclectic paradigm as applied to FPI. Using the terminology of L specific variables in the section on the general paradigm of foreign investment, this crisis was sparked off by a deterioration in basic financial infrastructure, which was exacerbated by over-borrowing and foreign-exchange problems. The degree to which replacements to the 'lost' investment in Latin America could be found elsewhere rested on the opportunities for such investment. However, the fact that developing countries as a whole experienced a net outflow of FPI in stage 2, and that FPI was only marginally higher than stage 1 in East Asia, points to the apparent lack of suitable locational advantages found in other developing countries and regions.[44]

The different pattern of FPI flows in East Asia and Latin America from stage 2 to stage 3 also can be described within the context of the eclectic paradigm if one first thinks about how ownership and location advantages for FPI are exercised. The modality of FPI is one of externalization – viz. using the financial markets to pursue the objectives enabled by ownership and location advantages – as opposed to internalizing them as in the case of FDI. As financial markets develop and mature in more places, outlets for potential direct and/or portfolio investment should increase, as should the volume of investible funds. One should expect, therefore, an increase in both types of investment.

How FDI and FPI change in relation to each other depends in large part on the forces of supply and demand. It can be argued that the supply of opportunities for FDI will begin to decline before similar opportunities for FPI begin to decline. Presumably, then, the volume of FPI flows should increase relative to FDI, and perhaps, at some point, surpass it. Taking into consideration that stage 1 FPI consisted mostly of bank loans rather than the 'purer' bond and/or equity form of FPI, and the effect of the 1980s debt crisis, this relationship between FPI and FDI has been the case in East Asia and Latin America. In the former region, the ratio of FDI to FPI declined from roughly 4 to 1 in the 1980s to roughly 2 to 1 in the 1990s; in the latter the ratio of FDI to FPI was about 7 to 8. And in both regions the volume of FDI grew dramatically, by a factor of nearly 8 in East Asia from stage 2 to stage 3, and by a factor of around 4 in Latin America. In other words, the evidence strongly suggests that the factors favoring the externalization of the market for O specific advantages have increased faster than those favoring internalization.

While this analysis uses data prior to the Asian financial crisis of 1997, brief reference to that crisis should be made. In a nutshell, the Asian financial crisis was caused and exacerbated by financial systems that were neither as strong nor as secure as they seemed, and the over-extension of those financial systems that FPI helped to cause. In particular, unlike the Mexican debt crisis some years earlier, the Asian crisis was initiated by the calling in of a very large number of debts over a short period of time (i.e. it was a liquidity crisis). To some extent, this helps support the arguments made here about the applicability of the eclectic paradigm to portfolio investment. For what has happened in Asia, as in Latin America in the 1980s, has been a change for the worse in a key location variable which has resulted in the decision to not externalize existing ownership or other L specific advantages in the form of portfolio investment.[45]

SUMMARY AND CONCLUSIONS

This chapter has sought to extend one of the mainstream themes of FDI, viz. the eclectic paradigm of international production, to embrace FPI, and in particular to examine the situations in which FPI and FDI are substitutable or complementary forms for exploiting or augmenting the ownership specific advantages of investing institutions and/or individuals. After setting out an analytical framework for discussing these issues and offering some tentative suggestions about the real determinants of FPI, the chapter went on to illustrate how, first, in the role of foreign (and particularly United Kingdom) investment in the development of the United States economy, and second, in the recent explosive growth in FDI and the emergence of domestic capital markets in some developing countries, FDI and FPI have interacted with each other, and how such interaction may be at least partly explained by the tenets of the eclectic paradigm.

In particular, the eclectic paradigm would seem to provide a good analytical framework for explaining (a) the level and pattern of long-term FPI – and particularly that undertaken by corporations and by institutions and private investors investing in commercial institutions, and (b) the choice between FPI and FDI – and particularly where FDI is made to augment existing corporate competitive strengths, and where FPI is part and parcel of a transfer of other real resources.

In addition, this chapter has offered some casual, statistical and other evidence which suggests that inbound FPI tends to follow FDI as countries proceed along their IDPs. At some point in that path, however, the flows appear to be more complementary to each other as countries become increasingly integrated through both intra- and inter-firm transfers of global resources and capabilities across national boundaries.

The ability to test our assertions in the previous section about the patterns of FDI and FPI in the more advanced emerging economies will depend on further study and more refined methods of collecting data. In particular, detailed analysis of capital transfers, including the type of transfer and the parties involved, is needed to determine, for instance, how much a firm or sector receiving FDI flows also makes use of FPI flows. Because developing countries will continue to be a target for FDI and FPI, and as a result of the problems in East Asia during the summer of 1997, these flows will attract greater attention, which means that more and better data should become available. A more rigorous analysis of our conclusions, therefore, will be possible.

Finally a word about the policy implications of this chapter. While, in some cases, national or subnational governments seeking foreign resources and capabilities to help them advance their economic objectives might view FPI (combined with inter-firm technology et al. transfers) and FDI as competitive modalities, increasingly they would be advised to take a more holistic stance towards their competitive-enhancing strategies and to arrange their domestic economic affairs so as to attract (the right kind of) both FPI and FDI. This is because, as we have shown, FPI and FDI are becoming increasingly complementary to each other, both in their determinants and in their effects. In general. recent economic events have shown that the key economic role of governments in a globalizing knowledge-based economy is first to facilitate an efficient market-based economic system, and second to ensure that the appropriate legal, institutional, and moral infrastructure is in place for this to be accomplished.

APPENDIX

Table A12.1 All inbound foreign investment, 1980–95 ($ billions)

Year	FDI	Portfolio	Total	Percent direct
1980	29.1	30.1	59.2	49.1
1981	45.6	39.9	85.4	53.3
1982	44.0	39.2	83.1	52.9
1983	48.9	55.7	104.6	46.8
1984	53.7	74.4	128.1	41.9
1985	51.0	153.8	204.8	24.9
1986	78.8	177.9	256.8	30.7
1987	126.9	125.4	252.3	50.3
1988	156.8	226.3	383.1	40.9
1989	193.8	356.7	550.6	35.2
1990	201.2	236.1	437.3	46.0
1991	153.8	442.2	596.0	25.8
1992	165.9	434.1	599.9	27.6
1993	210.3	727.5	937.7	22.4
1994	231.0	417.4	648.4	35.6
1995	316.4	583.7	900.2	35.2

Source: IMF, *Balance of Payments Statistical Yearbooks*, 1987–96.

Table A12.2 Distribution of inbound FDI and FPI between developed and developing countries, 1980–95 ($ billions)

	FDI						FPI					
Year	Developed	Percent	Developing	Percent	Total	Percent	Developed	Percent	Developing	Percent	Total	Percent
1980	23.8	81.8	5.3	18.2	29.1	100.0	28.6	95.0	1.5	5.0	30.1	100.0
1981	29.9	65.6	15.7	34.4	45.6	100.0	37.2	93.2	2.7	6.8	39.9	100.0
1982	24.2	55.1	19.7	44.9	43.9	100.0	35.0	89.5	4.1	10.5	39.1	100.0
1983	33.3	68.1	15.6	31.9	48.9	100.0	53.1	95.3	2.6	4.7	55.7	100.0
1984	38.5	71.6	15.3	28.4	53.8	100.0	71.6	96.2	2.8	3.8	74.4	100.0
1985	38.5	75.5	12.5	24.5	51.0	100.0	149.5	97.2	4.3	2.8	153.8	100.0
1986	66.4	84.3	12.4	15.7	78.8	100.0	177.0	99.4	1.0	0.6	178.0	100.0
1987	113.2	89.2	13.7	10.8	126.9	100.0	124.9	99.6	0.5	0.4	125.4	100.0
1988	132.1	84.2	24.8	15.8	156.9	100.0	216.8	95.8	9.4	4.2	226.2	100.0
1989	166.5	85.9	27.3	14.1	193.8	100.0	349.9	98.1	6.8	1.9	356.7	100.0
1990	169.6	84.3	31.6	15.7	201.2	100.0	213.6	90.5	22.5	9.5	236.1	100.0
1991	112.9	73.4	40.9	26.6	153.8	100.0	410.9	92.9	31.3	7.1	442.2	100.0
1992	117.7	70.9	48.2	29.1	165.9	100.0	385.3	88.8	48.8	11.2	434.1	100.0
1993	136.5	64.9	73.8	35.1	210.3	100.0	613.4	84.3	114.1	15.7	727.5	100.0
1994	139.5	60.4	91.4	39.6	230.9	100.0	316.2	75.7	101.3	24.3	417.5	100.0
1995	208.9	66.0	107.5	34.0	316.4	100.0	541.5	92.8	42.2	7.2	583.7	100.0

Source: IMF, *Balance of Payments Statistical Yearbooks*, 1987–96.

Table A12.3 Annual flows of FDI and FPI to all developing countries, 1975–95 ($ billions)

Year	FDI	FPI
1975	7 309.7	4 857.2
1976	3 461.0	3 979.6
1977	6 107.2	5 527.2
1978	7 015.7	5 564.7
1979	7 429.3	7 248.6
1980	5 092.3	9 216.0
1981	12 832.6	18 668.5
1982	11 335.3	5 706.7
1983	8 424.3	451.2
1984	9 129.3	(998.0)
1985	11 103.4	(1 695.4)
1986	9 464.3	(1 407.8)
1987	13 506.7	(1 388.5)
1988	19 382.4	(1 849.8)
1989	23 168.0	3 847.0
1990	24 549.0	13 285.0
1991	33 478.0	15 740.0
1992	43 644.0	30 704.0
1993	67 214.0	63 931.0
1994	83 716.0	56 548.0
1995	95 489.0	65 639.0

Note: Parentheses indicate negative flows.

Source: World Bank (1997a).

Table A12.4 Annual flows of FDI and FPI to East Asia and Latin America, 1975–95 ($ billions)

	East Asia				Latin America			
Year	FDI	Per cent of total	FPI	Per cent of total	FDI	Per cent of total	FPI	Per cent of total
1975	969.1	13.3	971.0	20.0	3 274.0	44.8	3 039.0	62.6
1976	962.0	27.8	787.0	19.8	1 760.0	50.9	2 130.0	53.5
1977	983.0	16.1	762.0	13.8	3 159.0	51.7	2 872.0	52.0
1978	979.0	14.0	162.9	2.9	4 082.0	58.2	3 089.0	55.5
1979	920.0	12.4	563.6	7.8	5 205.0	70.1	4 625.0	63.8
1980	1 312.0	25.8	1 030.0	11.2	6 148.0	120.7	6 000.0	65.1
1981	2 001.0	15.6	1 620.9	8.7	7 996.0	62.3	15 833.0	84.8
1982	2 403.0	180.0	1 532.3	26.9	6 345.0	475.2	4 020.0	70.4
1983	2 820.0	33.5	1 481.8	328.4	3 614.0	42.9	(1 917.0)	NM
1984	2 837.0	31.1	1 067.3	NM	3 234.0	35.4	(2 035.0)	203.9
1985	2 949.0	26.6	373.0	NM	4 373.0	39.4	(2 079.0)	122.6
1986	3 115.0	32.9	(83.5)	5.9	3 556.0	37.6	(1 877.0)	133.3
1987	3 908.0	28.9	554.2	NM	5 788.0	42.9	(2 229.0)	160.5
1988	6 740.0	34.8	1 640.2	NM	7 949.0	41.0	(3 773.0)	204.0
1989	8 330.0	36.0	5 370.0	139.6	8 138.0	35.1	(2 296.0)	NM
1990	10 179.0	41.5	9 022.0	67.9	8 121.0	33.1	3 603.0	27.1
1991	12 706.0	38.0	7 150.0	45.4	12 504.0	37.3	8 921.0	56.7
1992	20 923.0	47.9	9 351.0	30.5	12 740.0	29.2	18 739.0	61.0
1993	38 128.0	56.7	16 692.0	26.1	14 066.0	20.9	39 779.0	62.2
1994	44 105.0	52.7	18 366.0	32.5	24 238.0	29.0	24 531.0	43.4
1995	51 776.0	54.2	25 123.0	38.3	22 897.0	24.0	21 724.0	33.1

Note: Parentheses indicate negative flows.

Source: World Bank (1997a).

NOTES

1. The latter have been included in the IMF's *Balance of Payments Statistics Yearbook* (IMF, various years) only recently and are recorded only for the 1990s. They represent a small fraction of total portfolio capital.
2. Prior to 1980, the IMF recorded portfolio investment as the net of inbound and outbound investment, even though records of direct and portfolio investment go back to 1970. Also, data from IMF sources differ from those used by the World Bank (and used elsewhere in this chapter) for two reasons. First, although economists in both institutions continually analyse the data for accuracy and make adjustments as necessary, the World Bank data go further back in time. Second, portfolio investment includes public-sector securities and other investments, in addition to the private investments that are focused on later.
3. Inbound investment reflects all direct and portfolio investment, including government bonds and other public debt, that is going into a country and is therefore a better measure of investment flows than outbound investment, which reflects the source of investment flows. The vast majority of outbound investment comes from developed countries.
4. *Editor's note:* In balance-of-payments statistics, foreign investment consists of three components: direct, portfolio and *other* investment. In this chapter, the authors treat portfolio and other investments together as one single entity, and call this entity 'portfolio investment'.
5. The World Bank, for example, distinguishes between direct and portfolio (or indirect) investment by using the 10 percent ownership rule. It is not the purpose of this chapter to debate the appropriate level of equity ownership by which a portfolio investment becomes a direct one. In any event, the vast majority – probably 80–90 percent of all FDI takes place in enterprises in which the foreign investor has a majority, i.e. 51 percent or above equity shareholding.
6. As, for example, are written into many management contracts in the hotel sector, or franchising agreements in the case of franchisors in the fast food sector, e.g. McDonalds or Kentucky Fried Chicken.
7. For a distinction between created assets, e.g. capital, knowledge, technological capacity, entrepreneurship and natural assets, e.g. land and unskilled labour, see Dunning (1992).
8. Which, itself, is made up of outflows of capital to finance acquisitions and/or greenfield investment, and/or changes in inter-company capital transaction.
9. Although not all countries report such data.
10. Including loans with bonds and equity as a form of portfolio investment is done for two reasons. First, the credit circumstances of firms or die condition of domestic financial markets (especially in developing countries) may be such that loans are the only available source of long-term debt. Second, prior to 1989, data from the World Bank do not distinguish between loan and bond categories of private long-term debt on a consistent basis, categorizing it as loans only.
11. I.e. up to 49 percent or the total equity stake.
12. Both absolutely and relative to that of other portfolio investors.
13. E.g. to advance its overall profitability, long-term growth, market share, etc.
14. A point frequently made by some commentators, notably Robert Aliber (1970, 1971).
15. As these theories have evolved over the past two decades or so. On the resource-based theory see especially Penrose (1959), Barney (1991), Collis (1991), Peteraf (1993). On the evolutionary theory, see Nelson and Winter (1992), Dosi et al. (1988), and Cantwell (1989). On the concept of the eclectic paradigm being an 'envelope' of several economic and business context specific theories, see Dunning (2000).
16. Strategy is a variable which need only be introduced when time and uncertainty enter into the determinants of FDI. For our own interpretation of how this variable may be incorporated into the eclectic paradigm, see Dunning (1993b), chs 3 and 4.
17. Portfolio knowledge is that transferred on the open market or between independent buyers and sellers (i.e. inter-firm transfers), as opposed to knowledge transferred within the same firm (i.e. intra-firm transfers).

18. To the best of our knowledge, there have been no estimates made of the kind of FPI being described.
19. Which may differ between companies according to their managerial strategies, time preferences and attitude toward risk and uncertainty. In theory, however, it is possible to use financial formula, e.g. net present value or other formulae of the discounted rate of return, to collate alternative locations.
20. *Inter alia* because of its investment in firm specific fixed assets.
21. Exceptions include some kinds of footloose manufacturing investment and some non-capital intensive service investment. Of course, as a last resort an FDI can always be sold to an indigenous firm.
22. *Inter alia* because of its investment in firm specific fixed assets.
23. We specifically mention groups of products as very rarely does FDI internalize the market for a specific product, but rather a package of complementary intangible assets (e.g. technology, entrepreneurship, organization skills, learning experience, marketing expertise).
24. It is possible also that investment portfolios will include domestic investments as well.
25. For example, a joint Chinese/Australian venture for mineral exploitation in Australia is being financed partly by a loan from the World Bank to the Chinese partner. For other examples, see Zhan (1995).
26. As, for example, has occurred in the United Kingdom auto industry since the mid-1980s.
27. As shown, for example, in the stock prices of publicly quoted companies in the world's capital markets, GNP data and trends in foreign investment and domestic capital formation.
28. The investment development path suggests that as countries develop their propensity to engage in FDI, or be invested in by foreign firms, changes. At an early stage of development, countries tend to be substantial net importers of FDI; later, as the competitive advantages of their own firms increase, they also become capital exporters.
29. Here, it is worth distinguishing between two separate economies in colonial America, viz. that of the North, based on textiles, shipbuilding and the fishing industry; and that of the South, based on cotton and tobacco plantations.
30. Estimates of the relative significance of FDI vary a great deal. According to Cleona Lewis (1938), some 86 percent of United Kingdom investments in the United States in 1914 represented the purchase of United States securities and the balance was direct investments in controlled enterprises. Elsewhere (Dunning, 1988) we have estimated that $1450 million, or 21 percent, of the stock of all long-term foreign investments in the United Suites were FDIs. For an alternative assessment of the portfolio composition of FDI see Svedberg (1978).
31. For example, in brewing and distilleries, and in the flour milling sector.
32. For a more detailed analysis of United Kingdom investments in the United Stales in 1910–14, see Corley (1994a, 1994b).
33. For example, by harnessing new technologies and/or management capabilities, fostering synergistic economies, planning the financial risks and reducing the time of innovatory activities, enabling economies of scale and scope to be both exploiting, strengthening global marketing networks, etc.
34. In 1976–80, the ratio of all inbound FDI flows to gross fixed capital formation in the United States was 2.0 percent, by 1981–85 it had risen to 2.9 percent, by 1984–89 to 5.8 percent and by 1990–94 to 41 percent (Dunning, 1997; UNCTAD, 1996).
35. Including that in United Kingdom mutual funds specializing in United States securities.
36. The reader may note a difference in the level of flows reported in this table versus that in Appendix Table A12.1. The data shown in the tables of this section represent inbound flows to developing countries only. Appendix Table A12.1 presents inbound flows to all countries from all countries and as such includes investments made in developed countries as well as developing countries.
37. This does not mean that net flows of public or guaranteed debt increased during this period. Rather, this category of debt fell virtually steadily from a high of $60.3 billion in 1982 to $41.4 billion in 1988. Also, some FPI was converted to FDI as part of the debt restructuring (World Bank, 1997a).

38. This overall decline in private debt was not universal and was confined mostly to Latin America. Some regions, such as East Asia, actually saw an increase in the average flow of private debt from the pre-debt-crisis period.
39. The World Bank divides all developing countries into six geographic regions: East Asia and the Pacific; Latin America; South Asia; Eastern Europe and Central Asia; Middle East and North Africa; and, sub-Saharan Africa. *Editor's note*: The World Bank definition of developing countries differs substantially from the definition used by UNCTAD. The most notable difference is that, in UNCTAD's categorization, Central and Eastern Europe does not belong to the developing world.
40. In stage 2, the high level of average net outflows of FPI in Latin America, $1.4 billion, was greater than all average net inflows to all other regions.
41. FDI to China increased from $3.4 billion in 1989 to $35.8 billion in 1995, growing from 41 percent to 69 percent of all FDI going to East Asia. FPI to China in 1995, on the other hand, totalled only $3.3 billion, or only 13 percent of all FPI to East Asia (World Bank, 1997a).
42. East Asian flows exclude Singapore and Taiwan Province of China, both of which are excluded from the World Bank definition of developing countries.
43. Stage 2 actually saw a net outflow of FPI from Latin America, but some of this outflow was caused by the conversion of private debt to public or publicly guaranteed debt.
44. Interestingly, the 1997 financial crisis in East Asia also has its root in the financial services industry. While the effects of the crisis have been felt most profoundly in East Asia, the threat of contagion is more widespread than that found in the Mexican/Latin America debt crisis. This is partly due to a greater degree of market integration between the Asian markets and other developed and developing markets caused by the FPI in that region.
45. In the last 18 months, primarily due to actions taken by their governments, the L advantages of several Asian countries, and especially Korea, have improved considerably. As a result FDI has been stable and FPI, to some extent, has started to flow back into the region. For further details see UNCTAD (1999).

REFERENCES

Aliber, R.Z. (1970), 'A theory of foreign direct investment', in C.P. Kindleberger (ed.), *The International Corporation*, Cambridge, MA: MIT Press.

Aliber, R.Z. (1971), 'The multinational enterprise in a multiple currency world', in J.H. Dunning (ed.), *The Multinational Enterprise*, London: Allen & Unwin.

Barney, J.B. (1991), 'Firm resources and sustained competitive advantage', '*Journal of Management*, **17**, 99–120.

Beamish, P.W. (ed.) (1998), *Strategic Alliances*, Cheltenham: Edward Elgar, pp. 49–56.

Bekaert, Geert (1995), 'Market integration and investment barriers in emerging equity markets', *The World Bank Economic Review*, **9** (1), 75–107.

Buckley, P.J. and Casson, M.C. (1976), *The Future of the Multinational Enterprise*, London: Macmillan.

Buckley, P.J. and Casson, M.C. (1985), *The Economic Theory of the Multinational Enterprise*, London, Macmillan.

Calvo, Guillermo A., Leiderman, L. and Reinhart, C.M. (1993), 'Capital inflows and the real exchange rate appreciation in Latin America: the role of external factors', *IMF Staff Papers*, **40** (1), 108–51.

Calvo, Guillermo A., Leiderman, L. and Reinhart, C.M. (1996), 'Inflows of capital to developing countries in the 1990s', *Journal of Economic Perspectives*, **10** (2), 123–39.

Cantwell, J. (1989), *Technological innovation and multinational corporations*, Oxford: Blackwell.

Caves, R.E. (1996), *Multinational Enterprise and Economic Analysis*, Cambridge: Cambridge University Press.

Chudnovsky, D. (1997), 'Beyond macro-economic stability in Latin America', in J.H. Dunning and K.A. Hamdani (eds), *The New Globalisation and Developing Countries.* Tokyo and New York: United Nations University Press.

Chuhan, Peter, Claessens, S. and Mamingi, N. (1993), 'Equity and bond flows to Asia and Latin America', Working Paper 1160, Policy Research Department, Washington, DC: World Bank.

Collis, D.J. (1991), 'A resource based analysis of global competition: the case of the bearings industry', *Strategic Management Journal*, **12**, pp. 49–68.

Corley, T.A.B. (1994a), 'Foreign direct investment and British economic deceleration 1870–1914', in H. Pohl (ed.), *Transatlantic Investment from the 19th Century to the Present*, Stuttgart: Franz Steiner Verlag.

Corley, T.A.B. (1994b), 'Britain's overseas investments in 1914 revisited', *Business History*, **36** (1), pp. 71–87.

Dosi, G., Freeman, C., Nelson, R., Soete, L. and Silverberg, G. (eds) (1988), *Tecnical Change and Economic Theory*, Cambridge: Cambridge University Press.

Dunning, J.H. (1958), *American Investment in British Manufacturing Industry*, London: George Allen and Unwin.

Dunning, J.H. (1977), *United Kingdom Transnational Manufacturing and Resource Based Industries and Trade Flows in Developing Countries*, Geneva: UNCTAD.

Dunning, J.H. (1988), *Explaining International Production*, London: Unwin Hyman.

Dunning, J.H. (1992), 'The global economy, domestic governance, strategies and transnational corporations; interactions and policy recommendations', *Transnational Corporations*, **1** (3), 7–46.

Dunning, J.H. (1993a), *Multinational Enterprises and the Global Economy*, Wokingham: Addison Wesley.

Dunning, J.H. (1993b), *The Globalization of Business*, London and New York: Routledge.

Dunning, J.H. (1995), 'Reappraising the eclectic paradigm in the age of alliance capitalism', *Journal of International Business Studies*, **26** (3), 461–93.

Dunning, J.H. (1997), 'Globalization and the new geography of foreign direct investment', *Oxford Development Studies*, **26** (1), 47–69.

Dunning, J.H. (1998a), 'Location and the multinational enterprise: a neglected factor?', *Journal of International Business Studies*, **29** (1), 45–56.

Dunning, J.H. (1999), 'Globalization and the theory of MNE activity', in N. Hood and S. Young (eds), *The Globalization of Multinational Enterprise*, London: Macmillan.

Dunning, J.H. (2000), 'The Eclectic Paradigm as an Envelope for Economic Business Theories of MNE Activity', *International Business Review*, **9**, 163–90.

Dunning, J.H. and Narula, R. (eds) (1996), *Foreign Direct Investment and Governments*, London and New York: Routledge.

Dunning, J.H. and Pearce, R.D. (1985), *The World's Largest Industrial Enterprises 1962–83*, Farnborough: Gower.

Duysters, G. and Hagedoorn, J.H. (1995), 'Strategic groups and inter-firm networks in international high-tech industries', *Journal of Management Studies*, **32** (3), 359–81.

Fernandes-Arias, E. and Montiel, P.J. (1995), 'The surge in capital inflows to developing countries', World Bank Policy Research Working Paper, 1473 (June).

Frischtak, C.R.L. (1997), 'Latin America', in J.H. Dunning (ed.), *Governments, Globalization and International Business*, Oxford: Oxford University Press, pp. 431–54.

Hagedoorn, J.H. (1986), 'Trends and patterns in strategic partnering since the early seventies', *Review of Industrial Organisation*, **11**, 601–16.
Harvey, Campbell R. (1995), 'The risk exposure of emerging equity markets', *The World Bank Economic Review*, **9** (1), 19–50.
Hennart, J.F. (1982), *A Theory of Multinational Enterprise*, Ann Arbor, MI: University of Michigan Press.
Hennart, J.F. (1986), 'What is internalization?', *Weltwirtschaftliches Archiv*, **122**, 791–804.
International Monetary Fund (IMF) (various years), *Balance of Payments Statistics Yearbook*, Washington, DC: IMF.
Lewis, C. (1938), *America's Stake in International Investment*, Washington, D.C.: Brookings Institution.
Lim, Linda Y.C. and Siddall, N.S. (1997), 'Investment dynamism in Asian developing countries', in J.H. Dunning and K.A. Hamdani (eds), *The New Globalisation and Developing Countries*, Tokyo and New York: United Nations University Press, pp. 79–124.
Markowitz, Harry M. (1959), *Portfolio Selection: Efficient Diversification of Investments*, New Haven, CT: Yale University Press.
Nelson, R. and Winter, S. (1992), *An Evolutionary Theory of Economic Change*. Cambridge, MA.: Harvard University Press.
Paish, G. (1911), 'Great Britain's capital investments in individual colonial and foreign countries', *Journal of the Royal Statistical Society*, **74**, 2, 167–211.
Penrose, E.T. (1959), *The Theory of the Growth of the Firm*, Oxford: Basil Blackwell.
Peteraf, M. (1993), 'The cornerstones of competitive advantage: A resource based view', *Strategic Management Journal*, **14**, 179–91.
Rugman, A.M. (1980), 'Internalization as a general theory of foreign direct investment, a reappraisal of the literature', *Weltwirtschaftliches Archiv*, **116** (2), 365–79.
Rugman, A.M. (1986), 'European multinationals: an international comparison of size and performance', in K. Macharzina and W.H. Staehle (eds), *European Approaches to International Management*, Berlin and New York: Walter de Gruyter.
Sagari, S. (1989), 'U.S. direct investment in the banking sector abroad', Washington, DC: World Bank, mimeo.
Shaver, J.M. (1995), 'Do foreign-owned and U.S.-owned establishments exhibit the same location pattern in United States manufacturing industries?', *Journal of International Business Studies*, **29** (3), 469–92.
Svedberg, P. (1978), 'The portfolio direct composition of private foreign investment in 1914 revisited', *Economic Journal*, **88**, 763–77.
Ulgado, F. (1996), 'Location characteristics of manufacturing investments in the United States: a comparison of American and foreign based firms', *Management International Review*, **36** (1), 7–26.
UNCTAD (1996), *World Investment Report 1996: Investment, Trade and International Policy Arrangements*. New York and Geneva.
UNCTAD (1997), *World Investment Report 1997: Transnational Corporations, Market Structure and Competition Policy*. New York and Geneva.
UNCTAD (1999), *World Investment Report 1999: Foreign Direct Investment and the Challenge of Development*. New York and Geneva.
United States Department of Commerce (various years), *Survey of Current Business*, Washington, DC: Department of Commerce.
Wilkins, M. (1989), *The History of Foreign Investment in the United States to 1914*, Cambridge, MA: Harvard University Press.

World Bank (1996), *World Debt Tables, Volumes I and II*, Washington, DC: The World Bank.

World Bank (1997a), *Global Development Finance, Volumes I and II*, Washington, DC: The World Bank.

World Bank (1997b), 'Financial flows and the developing countries', quarterly reports, mimeo.

Wright, G. (1990), 'The origins of American industrial success, 1879–1940', *American Economic Review*, **80**, 651–68.

Zhan, J.X. (1995), 'Transnationalization and outward investment: the case of Chinese firms', *Transnational Corporations*, **4** (3), 67–100.

13. Globalization and the theory of MNE activity*

INTRODUCTION

This chapter seeks to answer the question 'To what extent, and in what ways, does the globalization of economic activity require a reappraisal of existing paradigms and theories of international production?'[1] More specifically, 'Are the motives, determinants and organizational modes of international business activity, as identified by scholars in the 1960s and 1970s, relevant and applicable to our contemporary world scenario? Are drastic changes called for, or is it simply that our ideas, propositions and paradigms[2] need to be fine-tuned to accommodate the events of the late 1990s?'

The chapter will proceed in the following way. First, it will place the current unease about the state of our theorizing about MNE activity within the context of two previous watersheds in the development of scholarly thinking, viz. those of the early 1960s and of the late 1970s, and it will pinpoint such watersheds by both the events of the time and the advent of new analytical insights. Second, it will consider how contemporary thinking is affecting our understanding about different types of FDI – and particularly that of Third World MNEs, and that directed to augmenting the competitive advantages of the investing firms; and, third, it will consider how far, and in what ways, economic and behavioural theories of MNE activity need to be integrated if they are to adequately explain the dynamics of international production.

However, three other introductory points should be made at this stage. The first is that globalization is best considered as a *process* towards the deepening of economic interdependence between institutions and/or countries. For the most part, the world economy of the late 1990s is not *globalized*, although some types of value-added activities and corporate functions, some countries and some regions are more globalized than others. What, however, is clear from a plethora of statistics[3] is that economic activity is becoming more globalized – or at least regionalized[4] – and that the pace and extent of this movement has increased dramatically over the last decade or so.

* From N. Hood and S. Young (eds), *The Globalization of Multinational Enterprise Activity*, London: Macmillan (1999), pp. 21–54.

The second point is that it is difficult to consider the impact of globalization in isolation from the other events which have fashioned the structure of the contemporary world economy. Indeed, there are good reasons for asserting that globalization is not *the* critical parameter encouraging scholars to reappraise the theory of MNE activity. For, while the removal or reduction of cross-border barriers to the movement of goods, services and people has helped facilitate a new international division of labour and new patterns of MNE activity, the engine of that change has been the dramatic technological advances of the last two or three decades. Several scholars, for example Perez (1983) and Lipsey (1997), have argued that we are now witnessing the beginning of a new Kondratieff cycle, which is promoting a new and different kind of cross-border specialization of production both within and between corporations. Though it is difficult to pinpoint a single path-breaking innovation,[5] few would deny that the critical attributes of contemporary technology, viz. its complexity and multiple uses, its cost and its rate of obsolescence, are very different from those of even 20 years ago.

Elsewhere (Dunning, 1998b), the present author has argued that the world is moving into a new phase of market-based capitalism, which is marked by three characteristics. First, the main source of wealth creation has moved from land in the seventeenth century, through machines and finance in the nineteenth and most of the twentieth century, to knowledge as embodied in human beings, in physical hardware and in intangible assets, for example patents, learning capabilities and organizational structures. Second, in the last years of the previous millennium, the spatial context of both asset creation[6] and asset usage has widened from the sub-national, through the national to the macroregional[7] and global. Third, the 'typical' organizational form of a firm has progressed from that of the individual entrepreneur or family business, through a managerial hierarchy to a system of corporate governance which, *inter alia*, involves a myriad of interfirm cooperative agreements.

The late twentieth-century capitalism is then knowledge-based, regional or global in its scope, and involves more intra- and interinstitutional alliances than any of its predecessors. It is a combination of these three features which is heralding a new trajectory of economic development and demanding a reappraisal of our theorizing about MNE activity.

Third, it should be recognized that although there are many theories and several paradigms about FDI and MNE activity, the majority are complementary to, rather than substitutable for, each other. This is because they are seeking to explain different aspects of international production, or are based on different units of analysis (the firm, industry or country), or offer a different disciplinary perspective. It can be claimed that globalization is leading to more, rather than less, convergence in the conceptualization and analysis of MNE activity among scholars – especially at a paradigmatic level.[8]

THE THREE LANDMARKS IN THEORIZING ABOUT MNE ACTIVITY

The First Half of the 1960s

Before 1960, there was no unique theory or paradigm of the determinants of foreign direct investment (FDI). However, in the 1950s there was a surge of outbound investment by US corporations, especially in Europe.[9] Some of the economic implications of this phenomenon were explored by the present author in his 1958 book (Dunning, 1958), but it was left to Stephen Hymer (1960) of MIT and Ray Vernon of Harvard (1962, 1966) to offer a formal explanation of it.

Neither found the answer in received theory. In his PhD thesis, Hymer, for example, argued that the theory of foreign (portfolio) investment could not explain the territorial expansion of firms, because the essence of this expansion was the transfer of real, not financial, assets; and that it occurred not in perfect, but in imperfect, markets. He used Joe Bain's concept of barriers to entry (Bain, 1956) to explain how a competitive advantage protected by such barriers was a necessary condition for US FDI; and why such FDI was concentrated in certain industries. In a later article, Hymer (1968) more explicitly adopted a Coasian concept of internalization to explain why US firms preferred to engage in FDI rather than cross-border licensing activities.

Quite independently of Hymer, Ray Vernon (1966) was interested in explaining the process of, rather than the reason for, the deepening internationalization of US firms. Initially, he turned to trade theory for an explanation, but found it wanting because of its constrained assumptions of perfect competition, immobile factor endowments and product homogeneity. Nevertheless, he did use the tenets of neoclassical economics to explain why, in the 1960s, the US had a comparative advantage in *innovating* particular products; and why other countries had a comparative advantage in *adding value* to these innovations.

In explaining the migration of market-seeking US firms abroad, Vernon used a micro-marketing concept, namely the product cycle. In doing so, he took for granted that US firms possessed some (home) country-specific advantages, *vis-à-vis* their foreign competitors, and sought to explain the changing location of their value-added activities as they moved from the product innovation to the product maturation state of the cycle. In retrospect, one of Vernon's critical insights was to distinguish between the asset creation and asset usage functions of firms; and the recognition that each might require a different portfolio of location-specific endowments for their efficient production.

The combined value of Hymer and Vernon's contributions (though not analysed in the literature in this way) was the first major breakthrough in theorizing about MNE activity. Both, however, were scholars of their time, and their explanations were strongly contextual.[10] Both tended to deal with first-time – rather than sequential – *US* direct investment. Both tended to view each act of FDI as a discrete and 'stand-alone' phenomenon. Both assumed that firms ventured abroad to exploit an existing set of monopolistic or competitive advantages. Moreover, both sought to explain foreign-owned production in a world economy in which cross-border trade was substantially restricted by natural and artificial barriers.

The same limitations applied to the other theories of international production which were put forward in this era, though most were directed to explaining particular kinds of FDI and their contexts changed as more countries became outward investors, and as firms became more multinational. Some of the newer explanations came from finance scholars, for example Alan Rugman's (1982) risk-diversification theory and Robert Aliber's (1970) capital-markets imperfections theory.[11] Others, notably Frederick Knickerbocker's (1973) 'follow my leader' theory, Edward Graham's (1978) 'tit for tat' theory, and later work by Ray Vernon (1974) emphasized the importance of firm-specific issues – and especially the strategies of firms engaged in oligopolistic competition.

The 1960s and early 1970s yielded several valuable empirical studies on both the determinants and effects of MNE activity. These, in the main, sought either to establish reasons why US foreign investors tended to favour some sectors rather than others; or why they chose to site their value-added activities in some countries rather than others. Such partial explanations of FDI and international production were exactly that. Compared, for example, to the study of international trade, there was no overarching or unifying paradigm within which the contextually specific theories could be accommodated.

The Second Half of the 1970s

This second major advance in our understanding about the determinants of MNE activity came in the mid-1970s with the emergence of two closely related (but distinct) paradigms;[12] and also an attempt by the Japanese economist – Kiyoshi Kojima – to formulate a normative theory of FDI to parallel that of trade (Kojima, 1978). Since Kojima's theory was primarily an extension of the extant theory of comparative advantage to embrace the trade in intermediate products (and particularly technology), and took no account of whether the cross-border markets for these products were internalized or not, the author's view is that this was not a paradigm of MNE activity *per se*.[13] Moreover, the application of Kojima's theory was strongly contextual in that it specifically focused on the differences between the structure and determinants of US and Japanese FDI.

Most certainly, the publication of John McManus's classic article on the theory of the multinational firm (1972), and that of Peter Buckley and Mark

Casson's monograph *The Future of the Multinational Enterprise* (1976), introduced a new dimension into scholarly thinking; and with the strong, yet for the most part independent, contributions of Jean-François Hennart (1982), Alan Rugman (1982) and Birgitta Swedenborg (1979), the focus of attention switched from the foreign value-added production by firms to the very *raison d'être* of the MNE *qua* MNE.

The theory of internalization is a simple yet profound one. It avers that firms exist because they can coordinate the deployment of discrete, yet complementary, resources and capabilities at lower costs than can the external market. In a perfectly competitive situation, the transaction costs of using the market to perform this task are zero. Hence production is undertaken either by the owners of the resources themselves or by a firm engaging in a single value-added activity.[14] In an imperfect market, transaction costs are positive. As a consequence, the opportunity for alternative coordinating mechanisms arises. Firms exist and grow where they can undertake the transactional and coordinating functions of economic activity more efficiently than can arm's-length markets.

It will be quickly appreciated that this understanding about the nature of the firm is independent of its geography. Certainly, too, most of the market failures initially identified by Buckley and Casson (1976) were not unique to multinational compared to uninational firms. Indeed, as has been argued elsewhere (Dunning, 1998a), internalization economists have in general paid relatively little attention to cross-border market failure *per se*.[15] A recent monograph by Klaus Meyer (1998) does just this.

In retrospect, this author would aver that the major contribution of internalization theory is to offer a formal explanation of why firms internalize the markets for the intermediate products they own, or wish to acquire, rather than choose some other organizational modality. It is acknowledged that some scholars would like to argue that all the monopolistic or competitive advantages of firms derive from the internalization of factor or product markets. We believe that to do so devalues the analytical core of the theory, and that it is not only useful, but essential, to distinguish between the nature and content of the advantages possessed by firms and the way in which these are deployed.

The eclectic paradigm tries to do just this and also to factor in the spatial aspect of MNE activity. When the paradigm was first put forward in 1977 (Dunning, 1977) it was fully recognized that its contents were an amalgam of the partial theories of the MNE and of MNE activity of the previous 15 years. It was also acknowledged that its analytical foundation rested on three sets of economic theory, viz. the theory of industrial organization (including market structure), which seeks to explain *how it is possible* for one group of firms to acquire and sustain a competitive advantage (or set of advantages) relative to another group of firms;[16] the theory of the firm, which aims to explain the organizational mode by which firms create, augment or use these advantages;

and the theory of location, which explains where firms choose to locate their value-adding activities.

Like the internalization paradigm, the basic proposition of the OLI paradigm is very simple. It is that, at any given moment of time, the extent, ownership and pattern of MNE activity depends upon the configuration of the competitive (or ownership(O)-specific) advantages of MNEs relative to those of non-MNEs, the competitive (or location(L)-specific) attractions of one country or region relative to those of another, and the benefits to firms of exploiting these two sets of advantages by internalizing the market for the O-specific advantages (including those arising directly from FDI), that is internalization (I) advantages.

Over the last two decades, the author has made various modifications to the original formulation of the paradigm mainly to accommodate advances in scholarly thinking and to take account of recent economic events.[17] At the same time, there have been several attempts both to test the propositions of the internalization and eclectic paradigms, and to offer alternative explanations of the growth of MNEs or MNE activity. But, as regards the latter, most, like those of the 1970s, continued to address specific issues. Thus the *stages of internationalization* approach, favoured by a group of Swedish and Finnish economists,[18] was primarily a spatially oriented paradigm. It was also directed at explaining a particular kind of FDI (namely, market-seeking FDI), even though the timing of the transition from exports and/or licensing to foreign production was partly determined by the nature of the competitive advantages of firms in question.

By contrast, both the *resource-based* and the *evolutionary* theories of the firm which were first articulated in the 1980s (the former by management scholars,[19] and the latter by economists[20]), even when discussed within the context of MNE activity,[21] were concerned with identifying and evaluating particular competitive or O-specific advantages of firms, not only at a given moment of time, but over time. Like their industrial organizational colleagues, the resource-based scholars averred that to create and sustain new competitive advantages, markets could not be fully contestable – at least in the short run. However, unlike them they focused more on *firm*-specific competencies and strategies to generate unique and non-imitable assets, and the capabilities to coordinate these with those of other firms. The evolutionary theorists went a further step and argued that not only was the firm a 'bundle of resources and capabilities', but that bundle represented an accumulation of past created assets which was itself strongly path-dependent.

Though not direct descendants of the eclectic paradigm, both the resource-based and evolutionary theories steered it along a new trajectory. When first put forward, both the eclectic and internalization paradigms were essentially designed to explain the locational and organizational deployment of *existing* competitive advantages – even though it was acknowledged that those advantages had to be created in the first place. The evolutionary theory reoriented the attention of scholars to the upgrading of competitive advantages through innovation; while the resource-based theory emphasized the significance of firm-specific resources, rather than that of country-specific endowments; and of the capabilities of firms to design and implement the strategies which would best advance the competitiveness of these resources.

The emphasis on 'knowledge' as a competitive asset has itself become more pronounced over the last decade; and, as indicated earlier, it is now acknowledged as the principal engine of *increased* wealth of both firms and countries. And, it is the case that most empirical studies have shown that FDI, and particularly that of US MNEs, tends to be concentrated in knowledge-intensive sectors. At the same time, all these studies, including the eclectic paradigm, have tended to presume that firms create (or acquire) their assets in their home countries, *prior* to engaging in FDI, rather than from the countries receiving the investment. This was notwithstanding the findings of several early empirical studies (for example Dunning, 1958; Reddaway, Potter and Taylor, 1968) that the R&D undertaken by the UK affiliates of US firms and the foreign affiliates of UK firms resulted in a valuable feedback of knowledge to their parent companies.

The 1990s

The year 1989 saw the fall of the Berlin Wall. Together with the introduction of more market-oriented policies of the leading industrial nations, the opening up of Chinese economic space, and the transparent economic success of the newly industrializing Asian countries in upgrading and restructuring their indigenous resources and capabilities to meet the dictates of the international marketplace, these events have combined to deepen the economic interdependence between nations. They are also challenging much of extant thinking about the determinants of MNE activity. In particular, three of these challenges are mentioned here.

The first is that existing theories continue to explain a good deal of contemporary FDI. Take, for example, market-seeking FDI. While the value of some of its determinants – for example investment incentives, labour productivity, communication costs, the physical infrastructure and the presence of related firms influencing (say) US FDI in China and India – may be different than those influencing such investment in Brazil or Germany, for the most part the economic models of the 1970s and 1980s are broadly relevant to explaining such investment in the 1990s. Similarly, most of the OLI variables which have long determined FDI in the natural resource sectors are no less applicable today. Much of the rationale for rationalized or efficiency-seeking FDI prompted, for example, by the completion of the internal market of the European Union, also stems from the work of economists in the 1970s.

But, second, it is true that even in these cases the increasing extent and geographical diversity of FDI by many firms is fashioning a new and more integrated international division of labour.[22] At the same time, the technological complexity of many products and production processes, and the changing needs of consumers, are reconfiguring locational priorities. In particular, some types of related value-added activities are becoming more spatially interdependent. This especially affects the level and structure of MNE activity designed to augment home-based competitive advantages. In such cases it is fairly obvious that the availability of local technological capability becomes a more important *pull* factor for FDI. This point is subsequently considered further.

The third challenge of the globalizing economy stems from the increasing geographical dispersion of knowledge-intensive assets; and from the need of firms to tap into the core competencies of foreign firms, which are synergistic or complementary to their own. Moreover, in a world of rapidly changing technologies there is increasing pressure on firms to quickly access a variety of tacit intangible assets (for example, ideas and learning experiences) which again are frequently located outside their home countries. Thus, in addition to adding value to their existing O-specific advantages, firms are increasingly engaging in FDI to seek out and harness complementary created assets.

Several scholars have begun to explore the concept of asset-augmenting FDI. In 1993, in *Multinational Enterprises and the Global Economy* (Dunning, 1993), a fourth category was added to the motives of the market, resource and efficiency-seeking FDI traditionally delineated in the literature. This was named strategic-asset-seeking FDI, which it was argued was undertaken to 'add to the acquiring firm's existing portfolio of assets others which they perceive will either sustain or strengthen their overall competitive position, or weaken that of their competitors' (Dunning, 1993, p. 60). Tom Wesson, in his PhD thesis, developed a model of asset-augmenting FDI (Wesson, 1993, 1997), and this model has been extended by Makino (1998) who also emphasizes the need of firms, particularly from developing countries, to gain access to new technologies and organizational capabilities. In his various writings, Teece[23] has also stressed the need of firms to harness and efficiently deploy assets complementary to their own if they are to make the best use of their own core competencies.

There have been several case studies of the growing significance of asset-seeking or asset-complementing FDI. Kuemmerle (1996) found that an increasing proportion of foreign-based research by the leading MNEs in the pharmaceutical and electronics sectors was designed to gain new knowledge rather than to exploit existing knowledge. Almeida, in an analysis of patenting in the US semiconductor industry, reported that foreign affiliates tended to use local patents more frequently than did their indigenous competitors (Almeida, 1996); while in a field study of the US biotechnology industry, Shan and Song

(1997) showed that the primary purpose of foreign firms investing in this sector was to gain access to advanced technology owned by local firms. In this author's analysis of the sources of competitiveness of 150 of the largest industrial companies listed in *Fortune*, it was not only clear that the executives providing data perceive that a fairly high proportion (between one-third and two-fifths) of their global resources and capabilities were directly derived from their foreign operations, but that this percentage was closely correlated with the degree of a firm's multinationality, and was increasing over time (Dunning, 1996).

All these, and other, studies point to a very different kind of FDI than that traditionally examined in the literature; although there is some parallel with natural-resource-seeking FDI, inasmuch as this, too, is prompted by investors seeking to augment their domestic O-specific advantages. The parallel, however, ceases when one considers that strategic asset-seeking investment is very much a feature of our contemporary globalizing, knowledge-based economy. Moreover, it is part and parcel of the need of firms to sustain and augment their own created assets by acquiring those of other firms; and to tap into the complementary but immobile assets of the host economy.

To what extent can asset-augmenting FDI be explained by existing paradigms or theories of international production? The answer, we believe, is that while new context-specific theories may be required – if for no other reason than the motivation of asset-augmenting FDI is very different from asset-exploiting FDI – the dominant paradigms of international production, and notably the eclectic paradigm, can quite comfortably accommodate it. To explain why this is so, the next subsection deals very briefly with how each of the components of the paradigm is affected, that is what are the 'add-on' variables. The differences between the scenario of the 1970s and 1990s are summarized in Table 13.1.

Ownership-specific advantages

- As globalization facilitates, and competitive pressures and technological advances compel, firms to engage in efficiency-seeking FDI, so the unique and sustainable O-specific advantages of such firms are increasingly resting on their capability to manage complex and geographically dispersed created assets. This is particularly true of MNEs in knowledge-intensive sectors which, according to Doz, Asakawa, Santos and Williamson (1997), is leading to the emergence of the 'metanational' corporation. This they identify as a corporation which is able to 'simultaneously access, meld and leverage locally-bound and context-dependent knowledge from throughout the world'.
- Because of the widening dispersal of knowledge-based assets, and the growing specialization in their asset-enhancing activities, the need of firms to tap into complementary and synergistic assets from outside their

Table 13.1 The changing characteristics of paradigms and theories: some stylized facts

1970s–1980s	1990s
• FDI mainly to exploit O-specific advantages of investing firm; one-way flow of resources and capabilities	• Multiple motives for FDI; more global sourcing of assets
• Largely greenfield FDI and sequential FDI financed by reinvested profits	• FDI (particularly in Triad) largely in form of acquisitions and mergers and reinvested profits
• O advantages largely based on privileged possession of (home) country-specific assets (Oa)	• O advantages more firm-specific and related to degree of multinationality and ability to harness and utilize created assets throughout the world
• Clear-cut choice between alternative modalities of exploiting O advantages (licensing compared to FDI, and so on)	• Systemic approach to organization of MNE activities; alternative modalities often complementary to each other; more institutional pluralism
• O-specific advantages (for example unique resources and capabilities) internal to firms	• Recognition of importance of complementary resources and capabilities external to firms (including the quality of institutional and social capital), and how these are coordinated with internally generated O advantages
• Comparatively little foreign-based innovatory activity; foreign affiliates less embedded in the host countries	• Considerable foreign-based innovatory activity (carried out mainly in advanced industrial countries) and/or via strategic alliances with foreign firms
• Significant inter-country barriers to both trade and FDI	• Reduced barriers to trade and FDI
• Clear-cut international division of labour based on H- and O-type distribution of factor endowments	• International specialization of MNEs based more on Schumpeterian type and FDI
• Locational choices made mainly in respect to asset usage	• Locational choices also made with respect to asset augmentation

• Relatively little attention paid to 'spatial' market failure and location-specific external economies	• More attention paid to gains arising from being part of a complex, or cluster, of firms, and from spatially linked learning economies
• Static nature of major paradigms	• Better appreciation of need to consider the dynamic nature of OLI variables; and to extend the theory to embrace path-dependent asset-creation and learning capabilities
• Hierarchical organizational structure of MNEs	• Flattened pyramids; more heterarchical structures; more delegation of responsibilities to line managers
• Most strategies towards market failure 'exit' rather than 'voice' strategies	• More voice strategies towards market failure; and particularly towards capturing dynamic externalities of common governance
• Cautious attitudes by many governments to FDI	• Welcoming attitude to FDI by most governments
• Few attempts to integrate interdisciplinary approaches to understand MNE activity	• Recognition of need to draw upon interdisciplinary theories to construct a meaningful and robust systemic paradigm of MNE activity

national boundaries is growing. The capability to successfully identify the sources of such assets, to acquire them in the most productive way,[24] and to coordinate them with their existing core competencies is becoming a more significant competitive advantage.

- The choice of an optimum portfolio of locations for asset augmentation and asset usage is also becoming a more critical capability, as firms engage in an increasing proportion of value-added activities outside their national boundaries, and/or conclude more alliances with foreign firms.
- With the need to complement their core competencies with those of other firms, the ability of a firm's management to identify and evaluate such partners, to conclude the appropriate collaborative agreements with them, and to ensure that the results of any agreement (be it, for example, a subcontracting, joint research or customer-related design project) is in its best interests, is also becoming more important. To be realized, such advantages require the MNE to learn from, and work effectively with, partner firms – and, indeed, with other institutions in the foreign country, for example governments, labour unions and consumer representatives – in many different cultures, and to gain the maximum benefits from such coalitions.[25]

Location-specific advantages

Some of the consequences of globalization on the location of economic activity, and particularly that of MNEs, have been articulated in a recent paper by the present author (Dunning, 1998a). Here one or two basic points are made:

- With advances in telecommunications and lowering barriers to trade, the locational options open to firms to engage in both asset-augmenting and asset-exploiting activities have considerably widened. At the same time, the need of countries to attract knowledge-related assets to sustain and upgrade the competitiveness of their own firms and indigenous resources is becoming more acute. Increasingly, as the economic structure of many countries is converging, national governments are seeking to identify and promote the distinctive and non-imitable immobile resources and capabilities within their midst.[26] Moreover, notwithstanding the lessening of their intervention in the asset-deployment activities of firms, their role as enablers of asset-creating activities is increasing via, for example, the provision of infrastructure and their human-resource development, technology, trade and investment policies.[27]
- Although globalization is widening the options open to MNEs to locate in different countries, *within* countries there is suggestion that at least some kinds of value-added activities – and particularly asset-augmenting activities – are becoming more concentrated, and are favouring sites

which have a cluster of related firms. In short, the externalities of spatially proximate linked activities -first identified by Marshall many years ago[28] (Marshall, 1920) but more recently extended to embrace dynamic learning economics and asset-upgrading activities (Florida, 1995; Krugman, 1995; Storper, 1995; Storper and Scott, 1995) – are becoming a more important locational benefit to firms and, indeed, to microregions as they seek to attract mobile investment to their borders. Examples of such clusters abound.[29] Although by no means confined to high-tech sectors, they are expanding particularly rapidly in these sectors, which are also those in which both FDI and cross-border alliances are assuming greater significance.[30]

- The paradox of 'sticky places within slippery space', as articulated by Markusen (1996), is particularly pertinent to the knowledge-based globalizing economy. Its successful resolution depends on the ways in which both firms and governments react to its challenges. On the part of firms, the gains of efficiency-seeking FDI in multiple locations, and those arising from agglomerative economies, are those most likely to promote competitiveness. On the part of national and subnational governments, the need is to provide and publicize a unique set of immobile assets pertinent to the types of economic certainty they wish to attract and retain, *vis-à-vis* those offered by other countries; and also to promote market-facilitating measures which might foster the formation of efficient subnational clusters of related activities. This may require them to reconsider the scope and effectiveness of their fiscal and investment incentive policies (UNCTAD, 1996); and, indeed, for scholars to reappraise the value of these policies as instruments for attracting inbound FDI.

Internalization advantages

Perhaps, the single most important impact of globalization on the organization of cross-border value-adding activities by firms is that on the costs and benefits of alternative modalities to acquire, create and utilize created assets and intermediate products. More specifically, we believe that the emphasis on the costs of individual transactions as the main determinant of the internalization of intermediate-product markets needs to be broadened to allow for the systemic economies of governance of global operations, and the dynamic coordination costs and benefits arising from the accessing of cross-border assets and learning capabilities. In particular, we would emphasize that four attributes of the globalizing economy are worthy of emphasis:

1. The increasing interaction between related cross-border and intra-border spatial markets. Such externalities suggest that a more holistic approach is needed in analysing the transaction costs of economic activity (both from

an intra-firm and an inter-firm perspective), and that more attention should be given to those transactions which are specifically associated with the global division of labour fostered by MNEs.

2. The static and dynamic benefits of alternative organizational modes. Almost, by definition, there are static externalities to be obtained from the common governance of related activities; and there is little doubt that globalization offers a new range of benefits. But, more than this, in an innovating and alliance-based economy there are likely to be substantial *dynamic* external benefits, for example to do with learning capabilities and the exchange of tacit knowledge. It is at least possible that such economies associated with (say) inter-firm alliances may more than compensate for any static transaction costs associated with such alliances.
3. The increasing significance of distance-related transaction costs in explaining both the international and intra-national distribution of economic activity, and particularly that of knowledge-intensive sectors. The idea of regions as 'loci of untraded interdependencies', and the emergence of new spatial clusters of value-added activities designed to capture the benefits of interrelated trading and learning economies between the clustering firms, has been set out in Storper (1995), Storper and Scott (1995), and more recently by Dunning (1998c).
4. The implications of asset-seeking FDI. When first introduced, the theory of internalization by firms was primarily directed to explaining the modality of cross-border asset deployment. Indeed, it was (and still is) rather better at explaining the existence of firms than their growth. Nor can it comfortably encompass strategy-related issues within its framework; in essence, it is an extension of the neoclassical theory of the firm.

In seeking to identify the optimum transactional vehicle of firms seeking to add to, rather than exploit, their core competencies, a different set of organizational variables needs to be considered. More particularly, the investing firm must believe that the benefits arising from the internalization of the market for the asset(s) it is acquiring, less the transaction costs involved, are greater than those which could have been obtained through some other vehicle of entry. Moreover, even when the market for them is internalized, the benefits arising from the acquired assets are frequently uncertain and likely to be spread over time. The costs, and there must be some costs otherwise all knowledge acquisition would take place through FDI, will be partly the normal costs of governance, and partly those to do with integrating the acquired assets and learning capabilities into the firm's existing portfolio of assets. These, like the costs of any acquisition or technological transfer, are unlikely to be negligible, although some at least are common to inter-firm and arm's-length transactions.

In short, then, the globalizing economy requires some reconstruction of the theory of internalization. Partly, this should be in the direction of a more systemic approach which acknowledges that as technology and organization of value-added activities become more complex, the costs and benefits of individual transactions become more interwoven. Partly it should give more attention to the specific features of cross-border transactions – particularly those to do with exchange rate uncertainty and cultural differences. And, partly, it needs to view its choices of organizational options, in terms not only of minimizing its efficiency-related transaction costs, but of upgrading its distinctive wealth-creating capabilities and any future income streams arising from these.

SOME IMPLICATIONS OF THE REVISED PARADIGM OF INTERNATIONAL PRODUCTION

There are implications for scholarly research which can be drawn from the analysis so far presented in this chapter. Two of these are selected for consideration. The first concerns the relevance of, and interface between, some of the leading economic and behavioural theories of the MNE and MNE activity. We shall offer an extremely encapsulated view on this issue. The second relates to the empirical significance of this analysis for explaining FDI between different groups of countries[31] or regions.

Implications for Extant Theories

As one might expect, most of the extant theories require some modification in the light of the kind of revisions to the OLI paradigm which have been suggested. In the case of some, however (for example, the product-cycle model), it is difficult to see how either asset-seeking or efficiency-seeking FDI can be accommodated. In others, for example Knickerbocker's 'follow my leader' hypothesis (Knickerbocker, 1973), the acquisition and merger (A&M) mania of the last decade well illustrates how an asset-seeking FDI by one firm might be followed by others. Graham's 'exchange of threats' thesis (Graham, 1978) similarly stands the test of time well, though less for efficiency-seeking than for asset-seeking FDI. The recent application of signalling theory suggests that where there is imperfect or asymmetrical information, a successful FDI by one firm may act as a signal to other firms to invest[32] (Liu, 1998). At the same time, compared with the early 1970s, there are many more strategic options open to firms in the ways in which they may augment their assets; and what is appropriate to one firm may be inappropriate to another.

What of the contemporary relevance of the exchange and capital imperfections model of Aliber (1970) or the risk-diversification model of Rugman?

Since Aliber's theory was originally devised to explain the timing of acquisitions of domestic firms by foreign investors, and why the latter should assign a higher value to the assets of the former than other domestic investors, it might be thought to have some relevance to contemporary asset-seeking FDI. At the same time, it cannot adequately explain why the A&Ms of recent years have been two-way in character, that is the purchases of European assets by US firms have gone side by side with the purchases of US assets by European firms. It is difficult, however, to see how the risk-diversification hypothesis can be used to explain such A&M, which are usually firm- rather than country-specific. Perhaps at the margin, where the required assets are broadly similar in (say) a German and US firm, the existing locational portfolio of the assets may be of some relevance. The Rugman hypothesis can, however, be used to explain the distribution of efficiency-seeking FDI within free trade areas and customs unions. One reason given by Japanese manufacturers for targeting France as an investment outlet since the late 1980s is that they believed that their assets were too concentrated in the UK, and that it would be politically judicious for them to spread them more widely.

Turning to two of the leading theories of the firm in the 1980s – the resource-based and evolutionary theories – both can be comfortably accommodated within the revised framework of international production. This is particularly the case with respect to identifying and evaluating the critical O advantages of knowledge-based firms, and the appropriate modality for exploiting, or adding to, these assets. Together with organizational theories, these strategic-cum-managerial approaches have greatly enhanced our understanding of the endogenous variables affecting MNE activity. In the eclectic paradigm, those specific to individual firms are treated as contextual variables influencing asset-exploiting FDI. Nevertheless, there is no reason to suppose such variables are any the less important in explaining asset-seeking as distinct from asset-exploiting FDI.

In the past decade, the interaction between scholars favouring evolutionary and resource-based theories and those espousing internalization theory has been an uneasy, if not a confrontational, one. To a large extent such uneasiness has been unwarranted, and such confrontation counterproductive. For the most part the authors have been aiming to explain different phenomena, or have offered complementary perspectives on the same phenomena.[33] Moreover, where disagreements have occurred they have been largely of emphasis rather than of substance. One exception is that while internalization theory is geared to identifying the optimum mode for organizing existing assets and capabilities, both the resource and evolutionary theories are focused on ways in which new assets and capabilities are generated, and of how the competitive advantage arising from these may be sustained.[34] However, two of the leading proponents of internalization theory (Casson and Buckley), accept that once one takes on board *dynamic* market failures, the incorporation of *new* O-specific advantages into any theory or paradigm of the MNE becomes appropriate. And, it is the origin and content of these advantages which is the central interest of the evolutionary and resource-based scholars.

The author believes that the current state of our theorizing about MNE activity and the parameters of our contemporary globalizing economy is demanding a reconsideration of the relationship between these three theoretical perspectives, which, between them, embrace the O and I facets of the OLI trilogy. In this chapter it has been suggested that a reconciliation of the approaches is possible if the internalization theory is dynamized and its determinants are widened to embrace the innovatory and developmental benefits of alternative organizational forms, as well as their short-term transactional costs and benefits. If this is done, not only would the distinction between O and I components of the eclectic paradigm become sharper; the I component would also become a more comprehensive explanation of both asset-seeking and asset-exploiting FDI.[35]

The Geography of FDI

The changing motives for, and determinants of, FDI identified in this chapter have not affected all regions or countries alike. More than ever, this author believes models and theories of MNE activity need to be set within a specific geographical context. Let us illustrate by considering how globalization is requiring us to modify our explanations of:

1. FDI by developed-country firms in developing countries;
2. FDI by developed-country firms in other developed countries;
3. FDI by developing-country firms in developed countries; and
4. FDI by developing-country firms in other developing countries.

In making these geographical classifications and the subsequent comments, it is readily conceded that apart from their stages of development[36] there may be as many significant economic differences *within* developed and developing countries as between them.[37]

1. The main impact of globalization on MNE activity from developed to developing countries has been to increase the amount of market-seeking and efficiency-seeking FDI. For the most part, the push factor, viz. the exploitation of O-specific advantages of MNEs from the Triad, has been relatively unaffected by recent economic events, save that competitive pressures have forced firms to export some of their more labour-intensive activities to Asian and Latin American locations.[38] However, there remains comparatively little North–South asset-augmenting FDI; and only a small

proportion of cross-border strategic alliances or A&Ms have involved developing-country firms.[39] Rather more changes have occurred in the *pull* determinants, as governments from almost all developing countries have adopted more investment-friendly policies, and have sought to develop 'clusters' of related activities based upon their (perceived) comparative advantages.

2. It has been estimated that over the decade 1986–95, three-fifths of the FDI among developed countries took the form of A&M, and that such activities were largely concentrated in the knowledge-intensive manufacturing and service sectors (UNCTAD, 1997). At the same time, four-fifths of the cross-border strategic alliances (and an even higher proportion of those in R&D) have been concluded between firms from the Triad countries. As indicated earlier, there is a general perception among high-tech MNEs that they need to have a substantial presence in each of the major advanced markets of the world, viz. the USA, Japan and Western Europe; and while much of FDI by these MNEs continues to be asset-exploiting, an increasing proportion is of an asset-seeking kind. The ability of the investing firms to successfully coordinate their own core competencies with those of the firms they acquire, or conclude non-equity alliances, is itself one of critical advantages of the contemporary global corporation (Doz, Asakawa, Santos and Williamson, 1997).

   The *push* factor driving intra-Triad FDI then needs reappraising, as static theories of MNEs are losing some of their robustness. The *pull* factor also requires reconsideration, as asset-augmenting FDI is increasingly drawn to locations which offer more advanced, or at least similar, created assets to those possessed by the home countries, in contrast to asset-exploiting FDI which tends to seek out a different set of resources and capabilities.

   There is, indeed, an interesting parallel here between the rationale for different kinds of FDI and trade. For example, FDI designed to add value to a home-based competitive advantage is likely to parallel inter-industry trade, and be best explained by traditional factor endowment (for example, Heckscher–Ohlin) theory. By contrast, FDI intended to gain access to new created assets is likely to parallel intra-industry trade, which is best explained by scale or neo-technology (for example Schumpterian) theories of trade – or, indeed, strategy-related theories (Krugman, 1986). We have also suggested that knowledge-intensive FDI is likely to favour those locations within host countries which offer not only attractive investment opportunities, but also a cluster of firms engaged in complementary or synergistic activities.

3. The difference between intra-developed country FDI and that by MNEs from developing countries into developed countries lies principally in the O-specific advantages possessed by each; and the relative L-specific

advantages of the home, *vis-à-vis* potential host countries. The nature and extent of these differences has led several scholars to question whether traditional theories of FDI based on the comparative advantage of the investing country in asset creation and that of the recipient country on asset usage hold good in the case of Third World FDI in industrialized countries. This author's view is they can do, but only if the theories are modified. On the one hand, and agreeing with Lall (1983), it is important not to understate the distinctive competencies of Third World MNEs, particularly where part of these competencies are derived from technical and other agreements with First World MNEs. At the same time, it must be accepted that many of the early competitive advantages of Korean, Taiwanese and other Asian MNEs specifically stemmed from their home-country characteristics and, in particular, their lower real labour costs.

Explaining developing-country FDI in developed countries then rests as much on the *pull* as well as the *push* factors. Some of these can be accommodated within received theory, including the 'stages' of development paradigm of Ozawa (1992).[40] Others – notably the need of investing firms to be in close proximity to their major competitors, and to gain access to European and US intellectual capital and learning experiences (with a view to upgrading their O-specific advantages) – cannot; and it is here where the asset-augmenting theory is again most relevant.[41]

Whether as a result of their FDI in developed countries, MNEs from developing countries can upgrade their O advantages sufficiently to outweigh the increased labour and other costs of producing in the former countries remains to be seen. But certainly, to be successful, such a strategy requires 'a deep pocket' of financial resources. The recent depreciation of Asian currencies looks certain to undermine this strategy, at least for the immediate future. Indeed, this could well mean that for Asian firms the mode of acquiring advanced resources and capabilities will revert back to inbound, rather than outbound, MNE activity.[42]

4. The data (UNCTAD, 1997) show that FDI among developing countries is growing faster than either between developed countries or among developed and developing countries. A major reason for this is, of course, the huge growth in MNE activity between mainland China, Taiwan, Singapore and Hong Kong.[43] At the same time, the share of inbound FDI stock of South, East and Southeast Asia originating from that region rose from 25 per cent of total inward FDI stock in 1980, to nearly 40 per cent in 1995 (UNCTAD, 1997, p. 82). Most certainly, there are very unique ethnic and cultural ties between the countries in Asia (and particularly among the Chinese communities) compared with the rest of the world. At the same time, other kinds of South–South FDI are also growing. There is, for example, a major Indian presence in sub-Saharan Africa; three-fifths of Chilean FDI is located

elsewhere in Latin America; while Singapore was the largest foreign investor in Myanmar in 1994.

Much of this FDI can be explained by received theory. It is, for example, entirely consistent with the proposition of the investment development path (Narula, 1996; Dunning and Narula, 1996) and the notion that FDI tends to be initially directed to countries with the closest psychic, ethic or economic ties. It is, however, worth noting that regional integration schemes are leading to a fall in defensive import-substituting FDI, and an increase in efficiency-seeking FDI. In most main respects, however, the determinants of South–South MNE activity are similar to those of North–South MNE activity. However, one suspects that as the more advanced developing countries upgrade their resources and capabilities, there may be more South–South asset-augmenting FDI. This, indeed, is already occurring in the case of Singaporean MNEs as they seek to develop new clusters of high-value activity in Malaysia.[44]

CONCLUSIONS

The following conclusions of this chapter are highlighted:

1. The characteristics of the globalizing economy of the late 1990s are sufficiently different from those of earlier years to suggest that international business scholars should be prepared to reconsider received paradigms and theories of MNE activity. This suggestion is compounded by the belief that contemporary events are helping to foster the integration of a number of theories from different business disciplines which were first put forward in the 1970s and 1980s.
2. In the past, there have been two major watersheds in the development of international business theory. The first of these, which dominated scholarly thinking between 1960 and the mid-1970s, produced a variety of theories of 'first-time' FDI and international production. Each of these was tailored to explain particular aspects of FDI or types of FDI. The second was the emergence of a general paradigm of MNE activity in the 1970s, and also some new theories designed to explain 'sequential' FDI, the increasing integration of MNE activity, and the sustainability of the competitive advantages arising from such activity.
3. In examining the implications of the globalizing economy for the paradigms and theories of the early 1990s, it has been suggested that both the motives for, and the determinants of, international production have changed – or are in the process of being changed. Foremost among the former has been the increasing significance of asset-augmenting FDI, and among the latter, the

rising importance of a knowledge-supporting human and physical infrastructure as a locational *pull* to mobile investment.

4. The author believes, however, that while new explanations are necessary for some kinds of MNE activity, and other explanations need to be modified as the significance of particular explanatory variables change, the eclectic paradigm of international production remains sufficiently robust and flexible to accommodate most of these changes. Indeed, 22 years after it was first propounded we would like to think of it as a more, rather than less, useful systemic framework for evaluating the kinds of explanations of MNE activity now emerging.[45] However, it is accepted that the paradigm does need to be broadened and dynamized to better take account of current developments in the evolutionary and resource-based theories of the firm; to embrace current thinking on the interface between trade and FDI theory (Markusen, 1995), and on subnational clustering of asset-creating activities; to better acknowledge the role of institutional capital and the social context in influencing the O-unique advantages of firms; and to incorporate the specific characteristics of the emerging metanational corporation as identified by some organizational scholars.

NOTES

1. Defined as value-added activity financed by foreign direct investment (FDI) and undertaken or controlled by multinational enterprises (MNEs). We adopt the threshold definition of an MNE as an enterprise which owns or controls value-added activities outside its home country.
2. In this chapter a paradigm is defined as an overarching systemic framework which comprises a set of general assumptions and boundary conditions, and offers some general propositions into which operationally testable theories can be incorporated. As long as new phenomena can be integrated within this framework, without infringing upon the paradigm core assumptions, then they need not threaten its long-term viability (Foss, 1996).
3. Some of which are set out in UNCTAD (1996, 1997) and Dunning (1998a).
4. The issue of whether regionalization is best regarded as a stepping stone towards globalization or a substitute to it is not debated here. For the purposes of this chapter, the word globalization is used to encompass regionalization wherever it is not in direct conflict with the spirit of globalization.
5. Although, generically speaking, the advent of the microchip and biotechnology are two major advances which have given rise to a whole new generation of technological advances.
6. The word asset is used to encompass a stock of resources and capabilities capable of generating a future income stream.
7. A macroregion is defined as a collection of countries in a particular geographical area; and a microregion as a geographical area within a particular country.
8. For example, as between economists and organizational theorists; and as between the explanations of economic geographers and trade economists.
9. The stock of US direct investment in all foreign countries increased by two-and-a-half times in the 1950s; and that in Europe by more than three times.
10. Related to a particular context of, for example, time, place, activity, or type of FDI; and viewed from a particular disciplinary perspective, for example finance, marketing, and so on.
11. For a review of these theories see Rugman (1982, 1996), Dunning (1993) and Caves (1996).

12. Although neither was called a paradigm at the time.
13. Indeed, in the original version of his theory Kojima made no clear distinction between inter-firm and intra-firm trade in technology – the latter being the essence of FDI. Later he incorporated the unique attributes of intermediate trade, undertaken *within* the same firm, in his model (see Kojima, 1992).
14. Since in neoclassical theory firms do exist in perfect markets, yet transaction costs are zero in such markets, it must be presumed that firms either engage in no transactions or do so at no cost. In practice, then, the markets vs firms paradigm relates to the extent to which a firm engages in more than one activity, for example by vertical integration or product diversification.
15. As identified, for example, in Behrman and Grosse (1990).
16. This is the critical reason for distinguishing O from I advantages. O advantages relate to those possessed by one firm relative to another; I advantages refer to those possessed by firms relative to the market.
17. These included the distinction between asset and transaction-cost ownership advantages (Oa and Ot); some suggestions of how strategic variables can be incorporated into a dynamic version of the paradigm; the application of the paradigm to explain the (international) investment development path of countries; the recognition that the O advantages of firms need to incorporate the way in which firms tap into and utilize the O advantages of other firms and the L advantages of countries; and the acceptance that over time the OLI components of the paradigm are all closely interlinked. See especially Dunning (1988, 1993, 1995).
18. Notably Johanson and Wiedersheim (1975), Johanson and Vahlne (1977,1990) and Luostarinen (1979).
19. See, especially, the work of Wernerfelt (1995), Conner (1991) and Barney (1991).
20. See, especially, the writings of Nelson and Winter (1982), Dosi, Freeman, Nelson, Silverberg and Soete (1988) and Saviotti and Metcalfe (1991).
21. Most notably by Cantwell (1989, 1991, 1994) and Kogut and Zander (1993).
22. In contrast to a multi-domestic structure in which each affiliate replicates (often in truncated form) the activities of its parent company; and there is relatively little intra-firm trade either between the parent and its affiliates or among the affiliates.
23. See, especially, Teece (1987) and Teece, Pisano and Shuen (1997).
24. This includes achieving a balance between minimizing transaction costs, and ensuring that the dynamic learning capabilities associated with the acquisition are maximized.
25. This choice, of course, depends on the relative costs and benefits of alternative modalities, which are better dealt with under the I component of the eclectic paradigm.
26. Various scholars have written about the increasing parallels between corporations and governments as both seek to evolve their unique competitive advantages – the one ownership, the other locational – in a globalizing economy. The notion of Singapore Inc. explored by Haley, Low and Toh Mun-Heng (1996) is now being extended to other small nation-states, and/or regions within nation states, both large and small. So far, however, the author has not seen any scholarly work on the resource-based theories of the firm as applied to countries.
27. The changing role of national government in the global economy is summarized in Dunning (1998b) and explored in more detail by several authors in Dunning (1997).
28. These included technological spillovers and access to pooled skilled labour, industry-specific inputs and consumers. Much earlier in history Adam Smith was also very aware of such external economies.
29. Among those most frequently quoted are Silicon Valley in California, the Bader-Württemburg region in Germany, the Solingen Cutlery industry, the cork and port wine industry of Northern Portugal, the watch industry of Geneva, the City of London in the UK, Toyota City in Japan, the Prato wool textile industry and the tomato canning industry of Naples in Southern Italy. For a detailed examination of the *raison d'être* and effects of these and other clusters see Enright (1993, 1994).
30. But mostly it appears in order to gain access to new assets, rather than to exploit existing assets (Birkinshaw and Hood, 1996).
31. Equally this chapter might have examined the implications of the revised paradigm for particular sectors, or particular sizes of firms, or for government policy. There is, indeed, a rich panoply of research waiting to be done!

32. Incidentally, signalling theory may act as a bridge between internalization and strategic oligopolistic behavioural theories.
33. Each, for example, is concerned with different aspects of market failure; and, therefore, it is to be expected each offers different solutions.
34. However, it is true that until recently the resource-based theory has paid little attention to the ways in which the resources and capabilities of a particular firm may be augmented by their association with other firms; or of how they relate to the institutional fabric and social context in which they operate. In a recent paper, Oliver (1997) has explored some of the exogenous factors influencing the sustainable competitiveness of firms (for example incentive systems that nurture competency-sharing, decision-support systems that diffuse resource innovations, training programmes that facilitate resource adoption and learning), and concludes that 'firms need both resource capital and institutional capital for their longer term competitive advantage' (p. 709).
35. At the same time, we have to admit that, generalizing about the behaviour of firms which are pursuing a variety of strategies, and which view a given configuration of OLI variables in a very different light, is much more difficult than under the more constrained contextual assumptions of the internalization economists.
36. Usually measured in terms of gross national product per head. But here the boundary line is sometimes difficult to draw as some rich oil states and Singapore and Hong Kong (usually classified as developing countries) are among the 30 richest countries in the world.
37. With respect, for example, to economic structure, degree of openness, government economic policy, political ideology, culture or ethnic composition, and so on.
38. Not all of these have been low-skill activities, for example office service centres in the Caribbean and computer software in India.
39. According to Narula and Sadowski (1998), only 6.2 per cent of the strategy technology partnering agreements identified by MERIT and concluded between 1980 and 1994 involved firms from developing countries.
40. In which he links the role of inbound and outbound MNE activity to the structural upgrading and economic growth of developing countries. In doing so he identifies three stages of development, which he respectively calls factor-driven, investment-driven and innovation-driven.
41. Although Ozawa (1992) did recognize the 'technology seeking' (his words) motive for FDI in the third phase of his 'stages' paradigm.
42. The optimum way for a firm to acquire created assets – for example by inward or outward FDI, by cross-border alliances, by arm's-length trade in knowledge-intensive products, or by its own innovatory activities – is a subject worthy of more attention by international business scholars.
43. In 1995, such FDIs accounted for over four-fifths of intra-developing-country FDI (UNCTAD, 1995, p. 64).
44. See, for example, a chapter on Singapore by Chia Siow Yue (1998) in a forthcoming monograph edited by Charles Oman and published by the OECD Development Centre on *Regional Incentives and FDI* (provisional title).
45. The concept of the eclectic paradigm as a systemic framework for accommodating context-specific explanations of MNEs was introduced in the author's original Nobel symposium paper (Dunning, 1977).

REFERENCES

Aliber, R.Z. (1970), 'A Theory of Foreign Direct Investment', in C.P. Kindleberger (ed.), *The International Corporation* (Cambridge, MA: MIT Press).

Almeida, P. (1996), 'Knowledge Sourcing by Foreign Multinationals: Patent Citation Analysis in the US Semi-conductor Industry', *Strategic Management Journal*, vol. 17 (Winter), 155–65.

Bain, J. (1956), *Barriers to Competition* (Cambridge, MA: Harvard University Press).

Barney, J.B. (1991), 'Firm Resources and Sustained Competitive Advantage', *Journal of Management*, vol. 17, 99–120.

Bartness, A. and K. Cerny (1993), 'Building Competitive Advantage through a Global Network of Capabilities', *California Management Review*, vol. 35 (Winter), 78–103.

Behrman, J.N. and R. Grosse (1990), *International Business and Governments*, (Columbia, SC: University of South Carolina Press).

Birkinshaw, J. and N. Hood (1996), *Foreign Direct Investment and Industry Cluster Development: The Characteristics of Subsidiary Companies in Different Types of Industry Clusters*, (Stockholm and Strathclyde: Stockholm School of Economics and University of Strathclyde, mimeo).

Buckley, P.J. and M.C. Casson (1976), *The Future of the Multinational Enterprise*, (London: Macmillan).

Cantwell, J. (ed.) (1994), 'Transnational Corporations and Innovatory Activities', *United Nations Library on Transnational Corporations*, vol. 17, (London and New York: Routledge).

Cantwell, J. (1991), 'The Theory of Technological Competence and its Application to International Production', in D.G. McFetridge (ed.), *Foreign Investment, Technology and Economic Growth*, (Calgary: University of Calgary Press).

Cantwell, J. (1989), *Technological Innovation and Multinational Corporations*, (Oxford: Basil Blackwell).

Caves, R. (1982 and 1996), *Multinational Firms and Economic Analysis* 1st and 2nd edns (Cambridge: Cambridge University Press).

Conner, K. (1991), 'A Historical Comparison of Resource Based Theory and Five Schools of Thought within Industrial Organization Economies. Do We Have a New Theory of the Firm', *Journal of Management*, vol. 17, 121–54.

Conner, K.R. and C.K. Prahalad (1996), 'A Resource Based Theory of the Firm: Knowledge versus Opportunism', *Organizational Science*, vol. 7, no. 5, 477–501.

Dosi, G., C. Freeman, R. Nelson, G. Silverberg and L. Soete (eds), (1988) *Technical Change and Economic Theory*, (London: Pinter).

Doz, Y.L., K. Asakawa, J.F.P. Santos and P.J. Williamson (1997), *The Metanational Corporation*, INSEAD Working Paper 97/60/SM, Fountainebleau, France.

Dunning, J.H. (1998a), 'Location and the Multinational Enterprise: A Neglected Factor', *Journal of International Business Studies*, vol. 29, no. 1, 45–66

Dunning, J.H. (1998b), 'The Changing Nature of Firms and Governments in a Knowledge-Based Globalizing Economy', Discussion Papers on International Investment and Business Studies, no. 250, (Reading: Reading University Department of Economics).

Dunning, J.H. (1998c), *Regions, Globalization and the Knowledge Based Economy: The Issues Stated*, (Reading: Reading University), June, mimeo.

Dunning, J.H. (ed.) (1997), *Governments, Globalization and International Business* (Oxford: Oxford University Press).

Dunning, J.H. (1996), 'The Geographical Sources of Competitiveness of Firms: The Results of a New Survey', *Transnational Corporations*, vol. 5, no. 3 (December), 1–30.

Dunning, J.H. (1995), 'Reappraising the Eclectic Paradigm in the Age of Alliance Capitalism', *Journal of International Business Studies*, vol. 26, 461–91.

Dunning, J.H. (1993), *Multinational Enterprises and the Global Economy*, (Wokingham, UK, and Reading, MA: Addison Wesley).

Dunning, J.H. (1988), *Explaining International Production*, (London: Unwin Hyman).

Dunning, J.H. (1977), 'Trade Location of Economic Activity and the Multinational Enterprise: A Search for an Eclectic Approach', in B. Ohlin, P.O. Hesselborn and P.M. Wikman (eds), *The International Allocation of Economic Activity*, (London: Macmillan), pp. 359–418.

Dunning, J.H. (1958), *American Investment in British Manufacturing Industry*, (London, George Allen & Unwin). (New, revised and updated edition, London, Routledge, 1998).

Dunning, J.H. and R. Narula (eds) (1996), *Foreign Direct Investment and Governments*, (London and New York: Routledge).

Enright, M.J. (1994), 'Regional Clusters and Firm Strategy', paper presented to Prince Bertil Symposium on *The Dynamic Firm, The Role of Regions, Technology, Strategy and Organization*, Stockholm, 12–15 June.

Enright, M.J. (1993), *Geographic Concentration and Industrial Organization*, PhD dissertation (Cambridge, MA: Harvard).

Florida, R. (1995), 'Towards the Learning Region', *Futures*, vol. 27, no. 5, 527–36.

Foss, N.J. (1996), 'Research in Strategy, Economics and Michael Porter', *Journal of Management Studies*, vol. 1, 1–24.

Graham, E.M. (1978), 'Transatlantic Investment by Multinational Firms: a Rivalistic Phenomenon', *Journal of Post Keynesian Economics*, vol. 1, 82–99.

Haley, U.C.V., L. Low and Mun-heng Toh (1996), 'Singapore Incorporated: Reinterpreting Singapore's Business Environments through a Corporate Metaphor', *Management Decision*, vol. 34, no. 9, 17–28.

Hennart, J.F. (1982), *A Theory of Multinational Enterprise*, (Ann Arbor, MI: University of Michigan Press).

Hymer, S.H. (1968), 'La Grande Firme Multinationale', *Revue Economique*, vol. 14(b), 949–73.

Hymer, S.H. (1960), *The International Operations of National Finns: A Study of Direct Investment*, PhD thesis (Cambridge, MA: MIT Press).

Johanson, J. and J.E. Vahlne (1990), 'The Mechanism of Internationalization', *International Marketing Review*, vol. 7, no. 4, 11–24.

Johanson, J. and J.E. Vahlne (1977), 'The Internationalization Process of the Firm – a Model of Knowledge Development and Increasing Market Commitments', *Journal of International Business Studies*, vol. 8, 23–32.

Johanson, J. and P.P. Wiedersheim (1975), 'The Internationalization Process of the Firm – Four Swedish Case Studies', *Journal of Management Studies*, (October), 305–22.

Kim, W.S. and E.G. Lyn (1990), 'FDI Theories and the Performance of Foreign Multinationals Operating in the US', *Journal of International Business Studies*, vol. 21, no. 1, 41–54.

Knickerbocker, F.T. (1973), *Oligopolistic Reaction and the Multinational Enterprise* (Cambridge, MA: Harvard University Press).

Kogut, B. and I. Zander (1993), 'Knowledge of the Firm and the Evolutionary Theory of the Multinational Corporation', *Journal of International Business Studies*, vol. 24 no. 4, 625–45.

Kojima, K. (1992), 'Internalization vs. International Business Approach to Foreign Direct Investment', *Hitosubashi Journal of Economics*, vol. 23, 630–40.

Kojima, K. (1978), *Direct Foreign Investment: A Japanese Model of Multinational Business Operations*, (London, Croom Helm).

Krugman, P. (1995), *Development, Geography and Economic Theory*, (Cambridge, MA: MIT Press).

Krugman, P. (ed.) (1986), *Strategic Trade Policy and the New International Economics*, (Cambridge, MA: MIT Press).

Kuemmerle, W. (1996), *The Drivers of Foreign Direct Investment into Research and Development: An Empirical Investigation*, Working Paper no. 96: 062 (Boston, MA: Harvard Business School).

Lall, S. (1983), *The New Multinationals*, (Chichester and New York: Wiley).

Lipsey, R.E. (1997), 'Globalization and National Government Policies: An Economist's View', in J.H. Dunning (ed.), *Governments, Globalization and International Business* (Oxford: Oxford University Press).

Liu, S.X. (1998), *Foreign Direct Investment and the Multinational Enterprise. A Reexamination Using Signaling Theory*, (Westport, CT: Greenwood Publishing).

Luostarinen, R. (1979) *Internationalization of the Firm*, (Helsinki Acta Acadamie Oeconomicae, Helsinki School of Economics).

Makino, S. (1998), *Toward a Theory of Asset Seeking Foreign Direct Investment* (Hong Kong: The Chinese University, mimeo).

Markusen, A. (1996), 'Sticky Places in Slippery Space: A Typology of Industrial Districts', *Economic Geography*, vol. 72, no. 3, 293–313.

Markusen, J.R. (1995), 'The Boundaries of Multinational Enterprises and the Theory of International Trade', *Journal of Economic Perspectives*, vol. 9, no. 2, 169–89.

Marshall, A. (1920), *Principles of Economics*, 8th edn (London: Macmillan).

McManus, J.C. (1972), 'The Theory of the Multinational Firm', in G. Paquet (ed.), *The Multinational Firm and the Nation State*, (Toronto: Collier Macmillan).

Meyer, K. (1998), *Direct Investment in Economies in Transition*, (Cheltenham, UK and Lyme, US.: Edward Elgar).

Narula, R. (1995), *Multinational Investment and Economic Structure*, (London: Routledge).

Narula, R. and B. Sadowski (1998), *Technological Catch-up and Strategic Technological Partnering in Developing Countries*, Occasional Paper 2/98–002, (Maastricht: Maastricht Economic Research Institute on Innovation and Technology, MERIT).

Nelson, R. and S. Winter (1982), *An Evolutionary Theory of Economic Change*, (Cambridge, Belknap, MA, Harvard University Press).

Oliver, C. (1997), 'Sustainable Competitive Advantage: Combining Institutional and Resource Based Views', *Strategic Management Journal*, vol. 18 no. 9, 697–713.

Ozawa, T. (1992), 'Foreign Direct Investment and Economic Development', *Transnational Corporations*, vol. 1, 27–54.

Penrose, E.T. (1959), *The Theory of the Growth of the Firm*, (Oxford: Basil Blackwell).

Perez, C. (1983), 'Structural Changes and the Assimilation of New Technologies on the Economic and Social System', *Futures*, vol. 15, 357–75.

Perlmutter, H.V. (1969), 'The Tortuous Evolution of the Multinational Corporation', *Columbia Journal of World Business* (January–February), 9–18.

Reddaway, N.B., S.T. Potter and C.T. Taylor (1968), *The Effects of UK Direct Investment Overseas*, (Cambridge, MA: Cambridge University Press).

Rugman, A.M. (1996), *The Theory of Multinational Enterprise*, vol. 1 (Cheltenham: Edward Elgar).

Rugman, A.M. (ed.) (1982), *New Theories of the Multinational Enterprise*, (London: Croom Helm).

Saviotti, P.P. and J.S. Metcalfe (eds) (1991), *Evolutionary Theories of Economic and Technological Change – Present Statistics and Future Prospects*, (Harwood Academic Publishers).

Schumpeter, J.A. (1934), *The Theory of Economic Development*, (Cambridge, MA: Harvard University Press), originally published in German in 1911.

Shan, W. and J. Song (1997), 'Foreign Direct Investment and the Sourcing of Technological Advantage: Evidence from the Biotechnology Industry', *Journal of International Business Studies*, vol. 28, no. 2, 267–84.

Storper, M. (1995), 'The Resurgence of Region Economies: Ten Years Later: The Region as a Nexus of Untraded Interdependencies', *European Urban and Regional Studies*, vol. 2, no. 3, 191–221.

Storper, M. and A.J. Scott (1995), 'The Wealth of Regions', *Futures*, vol. 27, no. 5, 505–26.

Swedenborg, B. (1979), *The Multinational Operations of Swedish Firms: An Analysis of Determinants and Effects*, (Stockholm: Industriens Utredningsinstitut).

Teece, D. (1987), 'Profiting from Technological Innovation: Implications for Integration Collaboration, Licensing and Public Policy', in D. Teece (ed.), *The Competitive Challenge*, (Cambridge, MA: Ballinger Publishing).

Teece, D.J., G. Pisano and J. Shuen (1997), 'Dynamic Capabilities and Strategic Management', *Strategic Management Journal*, vol. 18, no. 7, 509–33.

UNCTAD (1997), *World Investment Report 1997, Transnational Corporations, Market Structure and Competition Policy*, (Geneva and New York, UN).

UNCTAD (1996), *Investment Incentives*, (New York and Geneva: UN).

UNCTAD (1995), *World Investment Report 1995: Transnational Corporations and Competitiveness*, (New York and Geneva: UN).

Vernon, R. (1974), 'The Location of Economic Activity', in J.H. Dunning (ed.), *Economic Analysis and the Multinational Enterprise*, (London: Allen & Unwin).

Vernon, R. (1966), 'International Investment and International Trade in the Product Cycle', *Quarterly Journal of Economics*, vol. 80, 190–207.

Vernon, R. (1962), 'The Trade Expansion Act in perspective', in *Emerging Concepts in Marketing*, American Marketing Association, 384–9.

Wernerfelt, B. (1995), 'The Resource Based View of the Firm: Ten Years After', *Strategic Management Journal*, vol. 16, 171–4.

Wesson, T. (1997), 'A Model of Asset Seeking Foreign Direct Investment', Proceedings International Business Division, *The Administrative Sciences Association of Canada*, vol. 18, no. 8, 110–20.

Wesson, T.J. (1993), *An Alternative Motivation for Foreign Direct Investmen*t, PhD dissertation (Cambridge, MA: Harvard University).

Yue, C.S. (1998), 'Singapore', in C. Oman (ed.), *Regional Incentives and Foreign Direct Investment*, (Paris: OECD Development Center).

14. The eclectic paradigm as an envelope for economic and business theories of MNE activity*

INTRODUCTION: THE CONTENTS OF THE ECLECTIC PARADIGM

For more than two decades, the eclectic (or OLI[1]) paradigm has remained the dominant analytical framework for accommodating a variety of operationally testable economic theories of the determinants of foreign direct investment (FDI) and the foreign activities of multinational enterprises (MNEs).[2]

The eclectic paradigm is a simple, yet profound, construct. It avers that the extent, geography and industrial composition of foreign production undertaken by MNEs is determined by the interaction of three sets of interdependent variables, which themselves comprise the components of three sub-paradigms. The first is the competitive advantages of the enterprises seeking to engage in FDI (or increase their existing FDI), which are specific to the ownership of the investing enterprises, i.e. their ownership (O) specific advantages. This sub-paradigm asserts that, *ceteris paribus*, the greater the competitive advantages of the investing firms, *relative to those of other firms* – and particularly those domiciled in the country in which they are seeking to make their investments – the more they are likely to be able to engage in, or increase, their foreign production.

The second is the locational attractions (L) of alternative countries or regions, for undertaking the value adding activities of MNEs. This sub-paradigm avers that the more the immobile, natural or created endowments, which firms need to use jointly with their own competitive advantages, favor a presence in a foreign, rather than a domestic, location, the more firms will choose to augment or exploit their O specific advantages by engaging in FDI.

The third sub-paradigm of the OLI tripod offers a framework for evaluating alternative ways in which firms may organize the creation and exploitation of their core competencies, given the locational attractions of different countries or regions. Such modalities range from buying and selling goods and services

* From *International Business Review*, **9** (1) (2000): 163–90.

in the open market, through a variety of inter-firm non-equity agreements, to the integration of intermediate product markets, and an outright purchase of a foreign corporation. The eclectic paradigm, like its near relative, internalization theory,[3] avows that the greater the net benefits of internalizing cross-border intermediate product markets, the more likely a firm will prefer to engage in foreign production itself, rather than license the right to use the intangible assets transferred, e.g. by a technical service or franchise agreement, to a foreign firm.

The eclectic paradigm further asserts that the precise configuration of the OLI parameters facing any particular firm, and the response of the firm to that configuration, is strongly contextual. In particular, it will reflect the economic and political features of the country or region of the investing firms, and of the country or region in which they are seeking to invest; the industry and the nature of the value-added activity in which the firms are engaged; the characteristics of the individual investing firms, including their objectives and strategies in pursuing these objectives; and the *raison d'être* for the FDI.

Regarding this last contextual variable, scholars have identified four main types of foreign-based MNE activity:[4]

1. That designed to satisfy a particular foreign market, or set of foreign markets, viz. *market seeking*, or demand oriented, FDI.
2. That designed to gain access to natural resources, e.g. minerals, agricultural products, unskilled labor, viz. *resource seeking*, or supply oriented FDI.
3. That designed to promote a more efficient division of labor or specialization of an existing portfolio of foreign and domestic assets by MNEs, i.e. *rationalized or efficiency seeking* FDI. This type of FDI, though related to the first or second kind, is usually sequential to it.
4. That designed to protect or augment the existing O specific advantages of the investing firms and/or to reduce those of their competitors, i.e. *strategic asset seeking* FDI.

Combining our knowledge of the individual parameters of the OLI paradigm with that of the economic and other characteristics of home and host countries, and of the investing, or potentially investing, firms, it is possible to derive a wide range of fairly specific and operationally testable *theories*. Thus, it may be hypothesized that some sectors, e.g. the oil and pharmaceutical sectors, are likely to generate more FDI than others, e.g. the iron and steel or aircraft sectors, because the characteristics of the former generate more unique O advantages, and/or because their locational needs favor production outside their home countries, and/or because the net benefits of internalizing cross-border intermediate product markets are greater.

Similarly, it is possible to predict that the significance of outward FDI will be greater for some countries, e.g. Switzerland and the Netherlands, than for others, e.g. Russia and India, simply by knowing about their economic histories, the core competencies of their indigenous firms, the size of their home markets, their experience in foreign markets, and the locational attractions of their immobile resources and capabilities, relative to those of other countries. Finally, some firms, even of the same nationality and from the same industry, are more likely to engage in FDI than others. Sometimes, this might reflect their size – on the whole, large firms tend to be more multinational than small firms; sometimes their attitude to risk – particularly those associated with foreign ventures and of foreign partnerships with foreign firms; and sometimes their innovating product, marketing, locational, or FDI strategies.

The extent and pattern of foreign owned production will depend on the challenges and opportunities offered by different kinds of value-added activity. Thus the growth of existing, and the emergence of new, markets, e.g. in China, over recent years, has led to a considerable expansion of various kinds of market seeking FDI – particularly in fast growing industries, e.g. telecommunications. By contrast, the rate of expansion of several natural resource sectors has been less impressive, as many products have become less resource intensive, due, for example, to the innovation of new alloys, improved recycling techniques, the miniaturization of components, and the replacement of natural by synthetic materials. The reduction of both transport costs and artificial barriers to most forms of trade has led to more efficiency seeking FDI – both among developed countries and between developed and developing countries.[5] While as some kinds of technology have become more standardized and/or more codifiable, licensing agreements and management contracts have replaced FDI, e.g. in the hotel and fast foods sectors, in the more knowledge and trade intensive industries, e.g. pharmaceuticals, industrial electronics and management consultancy, the economies of global integration have made for a dramatic increase in merger and acquisition (M&A) activity (UN, 1998).[6] Moreover, the advent of call centres and electronic commerce is not only heralding the end of the geography of some financial and information markets, but is revolutionizing the organization of intra-firm production and trade.[7]

The content and predictions of the eclectic paradigm are firmly embedded in a number of different economic and business theories. Although, *taken separately*, none of these offers a comprehensive explanation of the growth and decline of MNE business activity,[8] *taken together*, i.e. as a group, they do so. Most of the theories, too, are complementary to, rather than substitutable for, each other. Some tend to focus on particular kinds of FDI, but not others. Others are designed to explain different aspects of international production, e.g. its ownership, structure, its locational profile or its organizational form. Thus, location theory forms the basis of the 'where' of MNE activity; industrial organization and resource based theories of the firm offer some reasons 'why' foreign owned affiliates may have a competitive edge over their indigenous competitors; while the concept of the firm as a 'nexus of treaties' (Williamson, 1990) is critical to an understanding of the existence of MNEs, and of why firms prefer to engage in FDI rather than sell their O specific assets, or the rights to use them, to independent foreign producers.

Much of this chapter will, in fact, seek to demonstrate how, and in what ways, these approaches are complementary to each other; and of how the eclectic paradigm offers both an envelope of these theories and a common analytical framework within which each can be accommodated and fully enriched in their application.[9]

Finally, the relevance of the individual components of the eclectic paradigm, and the system of which they are part, will depend on whether one is seeking to explain the static or dynamic determinants of MNE activity. For example, one of the earliest theories of FDI, viz. the product cycle theory, put forward by Raymond Vernon (1966), was concerned not only with explaining the *process* by which firms deepened and widened their markets,[10] but also how their locational needs might change as they moved from the innovatory to the standardized stage of production. By contrast, much of extant location theory and internalization theory seeks to identify and explain the optimum spatial and organizational dimensions of the existing resources and capabilities of firms and nations. Knickerbocker's 'follow my leader', and Graham's 'tit for tat' thesis (Knickerbocker, 1973; Graham, 1975) also contain a longitudinal dimension, which, for the most part, is absent in most variants of industrial organization theory, for example as originally propounded by Hymer (1960) and Caves (1973). Initially, too, the eclectic paradigm primarily addressed static and efficiency related issues (Dunning 1977), but more recently has given attention to the dynamic competitiveness and locational strategy of firms, and particularly the path dependency of the upgrading of their core competencies (Dunning 1995, 1998, 1999).

The kernel of this chapter is directed to examining the changes in the boundaries, constraints and structure of the eclectic paradigm over the past 20 years;[11] and those now being demanded of it by contemporary world events and scholarly thinking. In doing so, it will pay especial attention to the emergence of alliance capitalism[12] and the growth of asset augmenting FDI (Wesson, 1993, 1997; Makino, 1998; Kuemmerle, 1999). In particular, it will set its analysis in the context of four significant happenings of the 1980s and 1990s, viz.:

(a) the maturation of the knowledge-based economy;[13]
(b) the deepening integration of international economic and financial activity, including that fostered by electronic networks (Kobrin, 2000);
(c) the liberalization of cross-border markets, and the flotation of the world's major currencies; and

(d) the emergence of several new countries as important new players on the global economic stage.

The next three sections will examine how the main intellectual thrust in explaining each of the OLI triumvirate of variables has evolved over this time. In particular, it will argue that, as the dynamic composition of these variables has assumed more significance, so the value of the eclectic paradigm has increased relative to the sum of its parts, with the contribution of each becoming increasingly interdependent on the others. Finally, the chapter will give especial attention to the contribution of strategic cum managerial approaches to understanding the growth and composition of MNE activity, while averring that the relevance and richness of these is enhanced if set within the overarching construct of the eclectic paradigm.

The Ownership Sub-paradigm

In explaining the growth of international production, several strands of economic and business theory assert that this is dependent on the investing firms possessing some kind of unique and sustainable competitive advantage (or set of advantages), relative to that (or those) possessed by their foreign competitors. Indeed, some would argue that in traditional neoclassical theory, in which the firm is a 'black box', no FDI is possible – as all firms have equal access to the same resources and capabilities *within* their own countries, while there is complete immobility of resources and capabilities *between* countries.

When the eclectic paradigm was first put forward (in 1977),[14] it was assumed that such competitive or O specific advantages largely reflected the resources and capabilities of the home countries of the investing firms; and that FDI would only occur when the benefits of exploiting, i.e. adding value to, these advantages from a foreign location outweighed the opportunity costs of so doing.

Since the 1960s, the extant literature has come to identify three main kinds of firm or O specific competitive advantages.

1. Those relating to the possession and exploitation of monopoly power, as initially identified by Bain (1956) and Hymer (1960) – and the industrial organization (IO) scholars (e.g. Caves, 1971, 1980; Porter, 1980, 1985). These advantages are presumed to stem from, or create, some kind of barrier to entry to final product markets by firms not possessing them.
2. Those relating to the possession of a bundle of scarce, unique and sustainable resources and capabilities, which essentially reflect the superior technical efficiency of a particular firm relative to those of its competitors.[15] These advantages are presumed to stem from, or create, some kind of barrier to entry to factor, or intermediate, product markets by firms not possessing

them. Their identification and evaluation has been one of the main contributions of the resource-based and evolutionary theories of the firm.[16]

3. Those relating to the competencies of the *managers* of firms to identify, evaluate and harness resources and capabilities from throughout the world, and to co-ordinate these with the existing resources and capabilities under their jurisdiction in a way which best advances the long-term interests of the firm.[17] These advantages, which are closely related to those set out in (2), are especially stressed by organizational scholars, such as Prahalad and Doz (1987), Doz, Asakawa, Santos and Williamson (1997) and Bartlett and Ghoshal (1989, 1993). They tend to be *management*, rather than *firm*, specific in the sense that, even within the same corporation, the intellectual et al. competencies of the main decision-takers may vary widely.

The *relative* significance of these three kinds of O specific advantages has changed over the past two decades, as markets have become more liberalized, and as wealth creating activities have become more knowledge intensive. In the 1970s, the unique competitive advantages of firms primarily reflected their ability to internally produce and organize proprietary assets, and match these to existing market needs. At the turn of the millennium, the emphasis is more on their capabilities to access and organize knowledge intensive assets from throughout the world; and to integrate these, not only with their existing competitive advantages, but with those of other firms engaging in complementary value-added activities. Hence the emergence of alliance capitalism, and the need of firms to undertake FDI to protect, or augment, as well as to exploit, their existing O specific advantages (Dunning, 1995). Hence, too, the growing importance of multinationality, *per se*, as an intangible asset in its own right.

The question at issue, then, is whether the changing character and boundaries of the O specific advantages of firms can be satisfactorily incorporated into the eclectic paradigm, as it was first put forward. We would argue that as long as they do not undermine the basic tenets of the paradigm, and are not mutually inconsistent, they can be, although most certainly they do require some modification to existing sub-paradigms and theories.

In Table 14.1 we set out some of the models and hypotheses which have been sought to explain the origin, nature and extent of O specific advantages. We divide these into two categories, viz. those which view such advantages as the income generating resources and capabilities possessed by a firm, at a given moment of time, i.e. *static* O advantages; and those which treat such advantages as the ability of a firm to sustain and *increase* its income generating assets over time, i.e. *dynamic* O advantages. Both kinds of advantages tend to be context specific, e.g. with respect to industry or country; and related to the kinds of competitive advantages (as identified earlier) which firms seek to attain or sustain. While over the past two decades, changes in the world economic

Table 14.1 Theories explaining O specific advantages of firms

A: Group 1 **Explaining static O advantages**	(1) MS	(2) RS	(3) ES	(4) SAS
1. **Product cycle theory** Vernon (1966, 1974, 1979)	• Country (largely US) specific resources and capabilities of firms. • All asset-exploiting FDI. • Further hypothesizes that competitive advantages of firms are likely to change as product moves through its cycle.			
2. **Industrial organization theories** Hymer (1960, 1976), Caves (1971, 1974, 1996), Dunning (1958, 1993), Teece (1981, 1984)	• Largely Oa advantages initiated, or protected, by entry and/or mobility barriers to product markets. These include patent protection and marketing, production and financial scale economies. • All asset-exploiting FDI. • Little attention paid to asset-augmenting FDI.		• Oa advantages based on efficiency of investing firms also described in various empirical studies from Dunning (1958) and Safarian (1966) onwards.	
3. **Multinationality, organizational and risk diversification theories** Vernon (1973, 1983), Rugman (1979), Kogut (1983, 1985), Kogut and Kulatilaka (1994), Doz et al. (1997), Rangan (1998)	• Mainly Ot advantages, but also some Oa advantages arising from presence of investing firms in countries with different economic political, cultural circumstances. Ot advantages include ability to access, harness and integrate differences in distribution of natural and created assets and of organizational and managerial experience related to these. • FDI primarily asset exploiting, but also some asset augmenting. • (Potentially could be extended to include why markets for sustaining or increasing O specific advantages are best internalized.)			

4. **Internalization theory** Buckley and Casson (1976, 1985, 1998a, 1998b),Hennart (1982, 1989), Rugman (1982, 1996)	• Entirely confined to Oa and Ot advantages arising from internalization of intermediate product markets. • All asset-exploiting FDI. • Largely, though not exclusively, a static theory, though some acknowledgement that relative transaction costs of markets and hierarchies may vary as firms seek to exploit dynamic market imperfections	
5. **Capital imperfections theory** Aliber (1971)	• Largely independent of type of FDI. The theory argues that firms from countries with strong exchange rates or which discount capital at higher rates of interest will be tempted to invest, often by M&As, in countries which are economically weaker. The theory, as initially put forward, has no time (t) dimension; and, in essence, is a financial variant of internalization theory.	
6. **Follow my leader, tit for tat theory** Knickerbocker (1973), Graham (1975, 1990, 1998), Flowers (1976)	• Mainly concerned with explaining FDI as a space related strategy among competing oligopolists. The main hypothesis is that FDI will be bunched in particular regions or countries over time; and that there is likely to be an interpenetration of the territories occupied by the oligopolists. Though originally applied to explain asset-exploiting FDI, it is now also being used to explain some asset-augmenting FDI.	
7. **Resource-based theory** Wernerfelt (1984, 1995), Conner (1991), Helleloid (1992), Montgomery (1995), Conner and Prahalad (1996)	• As initially formulated, mainly concerned with identifying and evaluating variables influencing sustainability of competitive advantages of firms. Less attention given to traditional barriers to entry and more to such variables as specificity, rareness and non-imitatability of resources, and the capabilities of firms to create and utilize them. Mainly concerned with asset-exploiting FDI and only limited recognition of Ot advantages.	• FDI designed to augment domestic-based resources and capabilities (Wesson, 1993, 1997; Makino, 1997; Dunning, 1996; Chen and Chen, 1999; Kuemmerle, 1999)

Table 14.1 continued

B: Group 2 **Explaining dynamic O advantages**	(1) MS	(2) RS	(3) ES	(4) SAS
1. **Evolutionary theory** Nelson and Winter (1982), Nelson (1991), Cantwell (1989, 1994), Cantwell, Dosi, Freeman, Nelson, Silverberg and Soete (1988), Saviotti and Metcalfe (1991), Teece, Pisano and Shuen (1997)	• A holistic and time-related approach, mainly directed to identifying and evaluating dynamic Oa advantages of firms. Basic proposition relates to the path dependency of accumulated competitive advantages, and that the more efficient firms are in managing these advantages, the more likely they will have the capability to engage in asset exploiting and asset augmenting FDI.			
2. **Organizational (management-related) theories** Prahalad and Doz (1987), Bartlett and Ghoshal (1989, 1993), Porter (1991), Doz and Santos (1997), Doz, Asakawa, Santos and Williamson (1997)	• Essentially explain O advantages in terms of ability of managers to devise appropriate organizational structures and techniques to effectively access, co-ordinate and deploy resources and capabilities across the globe. These theories, in recent years, have especially focused on the cross-border sourcing of intellectual assets and the co-ordination of these assets with those purchased within the MNE.			

Oa = ownership advantage based on the possession or privileged access to a specific asset:
Ot = ownership advantages based on capabilities to organize assets, both internal and external to the investing firm, in the most efficient way.
(1) Market-seeking
(2) Resource seeking
(3) Efficiency-seeking
(4) Strategic-asset-seeking

scenario and knowledge about MNE activity have led to a *relative* decline in market-seeking (MS) and resource-seeking (RS) FDI – both of which tend to be based on the static O advantages of the investing firms – they still help to explain a major part of first-time FDI, particularly in developing countries (Dunning 1999).

However, one of the key characteristics of the last two decades has been the increasing significance of FDI based on the possession of, or need to acquire, dynamic O advantages. Thus, rationalized or efficiency-seeking (ES) FDI is only viable if: (a) the investing firm is already producing in at least one foreign country; and (b) both intermediate and final product trade is relatively unimpeded by natural or artificial cross-border barriers. Strategic asset-seeking (SAS) FDI is dependent on intellectual capital being located in more than one country, and the proposition that it is economically preferable for firms to acquire or create these assets outside, rather than within, their home countries.

To successfully explain dynamic and alliance related O specific advantages, each of the particular theories of FDI identified in Table 14.1 requires some modification. Thus, the *resource-based* theory needs to reexamine the content and significance of existing resources and capabilities of the firm in terms of:

(i) their ability to sustain and/or upgrade these advantages;
(ii) their ability to harness and influence the quality and price of complementary assets, and to efficiently co-ordinate these with their own innovating competencies; and
(iii) their ability to locate their value-added activities in countries and regions which offer the optimum portfolio of immobile assets, both for creating or acquiring new O specific advantages, and for exploiting their existing advantages. *Inter alia*, such immobile assets may reflect the bargaining and negotiating skills of MNEs in their dealings with foreign governments (Rugman and Verbeke, 1998).

While accepting much of the content of *resource-based* theory, the *evolutionary* theory of the firm pays more attention to the *process* or *path* by which the specific O advantages of firms evolve and are accumulated over time. In contrast (or in addition) to internalization theory, it tends to regard the firm as an innovator of created assets, rather than a 'nexus of treaties'. It is, by its nature, a dynamic theory, which, like the resource-based theory, accepts the diversity of competencies between firms; however, unlike the latter, it focuses on the firm's long-term strategy towards asset accumulation and learning capabilities, and its implications both for established routines and the development of new ones (Nelson and Winter, 1982; Nelson, 1991; Foss, Knudsen and Montgomery, 1995, Teece, Pisano and Shuen, 1997).

Zeroing down to management as the unit of analysis, contemporary organizational scholars, such as Prahalad and Doz (1987), Doz, Asakawa, Santos and Williamson (1997), and Bartlett and Ghoshal (1989, 1993) are paying increasing attention to the harnessing, leveraging, processing and deployment of knowledge-based assets as a core competence. While the subject of interest is similar to that of the resource and evolutionary theories, the emphasis of this kind of approach is on the capabilities of management to orchestrate and integrate the resources it can internally upgrade or innovate, or externally acquire, rather than on the resources themselves. But, as with the resource-based and evolutionary theories, the objective of the decision-taker is assumed to be as much directed to explaining the growth of firm specific assets, as to optimizing the income stream from a given set of assets.

The question now arises, to what extent are the theories relating to the origin and content of O specific advantages, as set out in Table 14.1 – and particularly their contemporary versions – consistent with, or antagonistic to, each other? Our reading is that, when the eclectic paradigm was first propounded, they were largely aimed at explaining different phenomena, or offered complementary, rather than alternative, explanations for the same phenomena. It is true the unit of analysis was frequently different; and that the underlying philosophy and some of the assumptions of industrial organization theory were different than those of resource-based theories (Pauwells and Matthysenns, 1997). But, in general, within their specified analytical framework, the predictions of the various theories were consistent with those of a general 'envelope' paradigm, and also the more specific predictions of the O sub-paradigm about the kind of competitive advantages likely to be possessed by MNEs, and the industrial sectors and countries in which their affiliates were likely to record superior levels of performance relative to those of their indigenous competitors (Dunning, 1993; Caves, 1996).

The Locational Sub-paradigm of Countries (and Regions)

For the most part, until recently, neither the economics nor the business literature gave much attention as to how the emergence and growth of the cross-border activities of firms might be explained by the kind of location-related theories which were initially designed to explain the siting of production within a nation state; nor, indeed, of how the spatial dimension of FDI might affect the competitiveness of the investing entities. In the last decade or so, however, there has been a renaissance of interest by economists (e.g. Audretsch, 1998; Krugman, 1991, 1993, 1998; Venables, 1998), and industrial geographers (e.g. Scott, 1996; Storper, 1995; Storper and Scott, 1995) in the spatial concentration and clustering of some kinds of economic activity; by economists in the role of exchange rates in affecting the extent, geography and timing of FDI (Cushman,

1985; Froot and Stein, 1991; Rangan, 1998); and by business scholars (Porter, 1994, 1996; Enright, 1991, 1998, 1999) in the idea that an optimum locational portfolio of assets is a competitive advantage in its own right.

The eclectic paradigm has always recognized the importance of the locational advantages of countries as a key determinant of the foreign production of MNEs (Dunning, 1998).[18] Moreover, since the 1930s, at least, there have been numerous context specific theories of the geographical distribution of FDI and the siting of particular value-added activities of firms.[19] Some of these 'partial' theories are set out in Table 14.2. They include the locational component of Vernon's product cycle theory (Vernon, 1966), and that of Knickerbocker's 'follow my leader' theory (Knickerbocker, 1973), which was one of the earliest attempts to explain the geographical clustering of FDI; and Rugman's risk diversification theory, which suggested that MNEs normally prefer a geographical spread of their foreign investments to having 'all their eggs in the same (locational) basket' (Rugman, 1979).[20]

However, for the most part, the question of *where* to locate a particular FDI, given the configuration of the O and I variables, was not thought to raise new issues of interest to students of the MNE. At the same time, throughout the last three decades, there have been many *empirical* studies on the determinants of both the export vs FDI choice of corporations, and the spatial distribution of MNE activity.[21]

Once again, in conformity with our earlier analysis, and as Table 14.2 shows, these explanatory variables are seen to differ according to the' motives for FDI, its sectoral composition, the home and host countries of the investing firms, and a variety of firm specific considerations. But, in the main, scholarly research has extended, rather than replaced, standard theories of location to encompass cross-border value-added activities. In particular, it has embraced new locational variables, e.g. exchange rate and political risks, the regulations and policies of supra-national entities,[22] inter-country cultural differences; and has placed a different value of other variables common both to domestic and international locational choices.[23] However, these add-on or re-valued variables could be easily accommodated within the extant analytical structures.[24] This marked off most pre-1990 explanations of the location (L) specific advantage of nations from those of the O specific advantages of firms.

The emergence of the knowledge-based globalizing economy and asset-augmenting FDI is compelling scholars to take a more dynamic approach to both the logistics of the siting of corporate activities, and to the competitive advantages of nations and/or regions. In the former case, firms need to take account not only of the presence and cost of traditional factor endowments, of transport costs, of current demand levels and patterns, and of Marshallian type agglomerative economies (Marshall, 1920); but also of distance related transaction costs (Storper and Scott, 1995), of dynamic externalities, knowledge

Table 14.2 Theories explaining L specific advantages of countries

	(1) MS	(2) RS	(3) ES	(4) SAS
1. **Traditional location theories** Hoover (1948), Hotelling (1929), Isard (1956), Lösch (1954), Lloyd and Dicken (1990), Weber (1928)	• Demand-related variables, e.g. size, character and potential growth of local and adjacent markets. • Presence of competitors.	• Supply-oriented variables, e.g. availability, quality and price of natural resources, transportation costs, artificial barriers to trade.	• Supply-oriented variables, especially those related to comparative advantages of immobile assets, e.g. labor, land and infrastructure.	• Location and price of created assets, including those owned by firms likely to be acquired. • Exchange rates
2. **Theories related to the process of internationalization** Anderson and Gatignon (1986), Buckley and Cavusgil (1980), Daniels (1971), Forsgren (1989), Hirsch (1976), Johanson and Vahlne (1977, 1990), Luostarinen (1979), Vernon (1996), Welch and Luostarinen (1988)	• Mainly MS and RS, using traditional locational variables, but also several firm specific variables and transaction costs. • Emphasis on role of psychic distance, particularly in exploiting knowledge-based O advantages (Daniels, 1971; Johanson and Vahlne, 1977, 1990).			• Some attention given to FDI as a learning activity.
3. **Theories related to agglomeration of economic activity** Audretsch (1998), Enright (1991, 1998, 1999), Forsgren (1989), Krugman (1991, 1993, 1998), Malmberg, Sölvell and Zander (1996), Porter (1994, 1996), Storper (1995), Cantwell and Piscitello (1997)	• Some clustering of products for convenience of consumers, including industrial consumers. • Economies of scale and scope.	• Supply-related clusters, based on static external economies, e.g. pooled labor markets. • Economies of scale and scope.		• Supply-related clusters based on asset-augmenting activities, local accumulation of knowledge, and exchange of information and learning experiences.

4. **Theories related to spatially specific transaction costs** Florida (1995), Scott (1996), Storper and Scott (1995)	• Given production and transport costs, external ties and scale economies, spatially related transaction costs are hypothesized to lead to a clustering of related activities. (a) to reduce overall costs and (b) to maximize benefits of inter-related innovating and learning activities.			
5. **Theories related to complementary assets** Teece (1992), Teece, Pisano and Shuen (1997), Chen and Chen (1998, 1999)	• The presence of related activities which help lower transport costs and promote joint economies in innovation, production and marketing.			• As for MS, RS and ES, but directed to asset-augmenting activities, and strategic networking.
6. **Theories related to government induced incentives** Loree and Guisinger (1995), UNCTAD (1996a)	• Especially fiscal and other incentives leading to increase in demand for products of MNEs.	• Supply-related incentives, concessionary rights for exploitation of natural-resource-based sectors; intellectual property rights, tax advantages for RS and ES.		• Mainly incentives to promote innovation-driven alliances, and the upgrading of existing O advantages of investing firms.
7. **Theories related to oligopolistic behavior and product cycle** Graham (1978, 1998), Knickerbocker (1973), Vernon (1974)	• Follow my leader and other forms of oligopolistic behavior may apply to all four forms of international production, although incentives and pressures for such behavior are likely to be context specific.			

Table 14.2 continued

	(1) MS	(2) RS	(3) ES	(4) SAS
8. **Theories of risk diversification** Agmon and Lessard (1977),Rugman (1979)	• Types of location specific risk vary with kind of FDI, but theory suggests that firm will diversify their portfolios to minimize their risk exposures, which include exchange, political and economic risks.			• Risks of SAS FDI also relate to inappropriate timing (especially for M&As) and insufficient knowledge about the assets being acquired.
9. **Exchange rate theories** Aliber (1971), Cushman (1985), Froot and Stein (1991), Blonigen (1997), Rangan (1997)	• Theories which assume exchange rates or changes in exchange rates, suitably discounted for risk, capture most of the differences in cross-border locational costs, and also expectations of investors about the future course of exchange rates. These embrace all kinds of FDI, but particularly that of the timing of M&As.			
10. **Knowledge-enhancing (dynamic) theories of location** Dunning (1997), Kogut and Zander (1993), Kuemmerle (1996), Porter (1994, 1998), Chen and Chen (1998, 1999)	• See also SAS column, for 1–7 above. More specifically, dynamic theories are directed to explaining locational strategy in terms of sustaining and promoting location specific advantages in a world of uncertainty, learning and continuous innovation and upgrading of products. Applies especially to research and development activity of all kinds of FDI. The need to exploit dynamic locational advantage especially pronounced in high-technology sectors.			• Theory is that firms will invest in those countries which offer the greatest opportunity for upgrading their existing core competencies and that such a locational strategy is path dependent.

accumulation, and interactive learning (Enright, 1991, 1998, 1999; Florida, 1995; Malmberg, Sölvell and Zander, 1996), of spatially related innovation and technological standards (Antonelli, 1998; Sölvell and Zander, 1998), of the increasing dispersion of created assets, and of the need to conclude cross-border asset augmenting and/or asset exploiting alliances (Dunning, 1995, 1998).

Contemporary economic events are suggesting that the nature and composition of a country or region's comparative advantage, which has been traditionally based on its possession of a unique set of immobile *natural* resources and capabilities, is now more geared to its ability to offer a distinctive and non-imitable set of location bound *created* assets, including the presence of indigenous firms with which foreign MNEs might form alliances to complement their own core competencies. Recent research not only reveals that some nation states are not only becoming increasingly dependent on the cross-border activities of their own and foreign-based corporations for their economic prosperity (Dunning, 1996; UNCTAD, 1998);[25] but that the competitiveness of these corporations is becoming increasingly fashioned by the institutional framework within which they operate (Oliver, 1997; Doremus, Keller, Pauly and Reich, 1998). In particular, both nation states and sub-national authorities are becoming more aware of the need to provide the appropriate economic and social infrastructure, both for their own firms to generate the O specific assets consistent with the demands of world markets, and for foreign investors to engage in the kind of value-adding activities which advances the dynamic comparative advantage of the immobile assets within their jurisdiction (Porter, 1994; Peck, 1996; Dunning 1998).

As yet, business strategists, organizational, and marketing scholars have paid little attention to how their own explanations of the timing and geographical profile of international business activity need modifying in the light of the new forms of FDI and of alliance capitalism. There is, for example, little treatment of spatially related factors in either the resource-based or the evolutionary theories of the firm; although the role of spatially related agglomerative economies is being increasingly recognized as an important source of learning and innovating capabilities. Indeed, Michael Porter has gone as far as to say that, in the modern global economy, 'anything that can be moved or sourced from a distance is no longer a competitive advantage' (Porter, 1998, p. 29), and that 'the true advantages today are things that are sticky, that is not easily movable' (ibid., p. 29). If this is correct, it may be inferred that as the dynamic gains from spatial clustering and network linkages become more pronounced,[26] so will the locational choice of firms become a more critical strategic variable. It also follows that national and regional authorities should pay more attention to the fostering of immobile complementary assets and cluster-related public goods as part of their policies to attract and retain mobile investment.

As in the case of O specific advantages, scholarly research on the kind of L advantages most likely to explain the 'where' of international production has taken on a new trajectory over the past decade. More particularly, the dramatic increase in cross-border mergers and acquisitions[27] has reflected the availability and price of assets that firms wish to acquire or tap into to protect or augment their competitive advantages. While the exchange rate might certainly affect a timing of the FDI, the extent to which the acquired assets – together with the business environment of which they are part – advances the competitiveness and strategic trajectories of the investing firms, are the critical locational determinants.

Finally, we would observe that, although several strands of intellectual thought contribute towards our understanding of the locational dynamics of MNE activity, these offer complementary, rather than alternative, explanations. This is not to deny that there are differences of emphasis or methodology among scholars,[28] but we believe that they are not substantive enough to preclude their incorporation into any revised paradigm of international production.

The Internalization Sub-paradigm

Given that a firm has a set of competitive or O specific advantages, and the immobile assets of a foreign country are such as to warrant locating value-adding or asset-augmenting activities there, what determines whether such activities are undertaken by the firms possessing the advantages, or by indigenous producers buying the advantage, or the right to its use, in the open market, or acquiring them by some other means?[29] Orthodox internalization theory offers a fairly straightforward answer, viz. as long as the transaction and co-ordination costs of using external arm's-length markets in the exchange of intermediate products, information, technology, marketing techniques, etc. exceed those incurred by internal hierarchies, then it will pay a firm to engage in FDI, rather than conclude a licensing or another market-related agreement with a foreign producer. In general, the transaction costs of using external markets tend to be positively correlated with the imperfections of those markets. Over the last two decades, an extensive literature has identified a whole range of market failures, such as those associated with bounded rationality, and the provision of public and jointly supplied products and common intangible assets, and which permit opportunism, information asymmetries, uncertainty, economies of scale, and externalities of one kind or another.[30]

In explaining why firms choose to engage in FDI rather than buy or sell intermediate products in some other way (the third question which any international business theorist must answer), internalization theory has provided the dominant explanation over the past two decades. Yet it has not gone unchallenged. The major criticisms have been of three kinds. The first is that it is an incomplete theory in that it ignores other functions which a firm may perform, other than those which are transaction related; and other reasons, apart from short-run profit maximization, why firms may wish to engage in value-added activities outside their national boundaries. For example, firms have abilities of learning, memory adaptation and the capabilities to produce – tasks which markets cannot emulate. Many cross-border M&As are undertaken to gain new resources and/or to access to new capabilities, markets, or to lower the unit costs of production, or to gain market power, or to forestall or thwart the behavior of competitors.

Such objectives fit less comfortably with the conception of a firm as a 'nexus of treaties', and more with that of a firm as a 'collection or bundle of resources' (Barney, 1991), or as a 'repository of knowledge and capabilities' (Kogut and Zander, 1993; Madhok, 1996). This does not destroy the validity of internalization theory *per se*. It does, however, suggest that its contents should be widened to incorporate *all* costs and benefits associated with corporate activities; and not only those which are transaction related![31] Contemporary writings, both by resource-based and evolutionary scholars, have refocused attention on the unique characteristics of the firm[32] *vis-à-vis* those of other institutions, viz. as a unit of production, whose function is to efficiently convert a given set of resources into economically rewarding products.

The second criticism of orthodox internalization theory is that it is a static theory, and gives little guidance as to how a firm may best organize its activities to create future assets, rather than optimize the use of its existing assets. The increasing role of innovation in the contemporary global economy, and the need of firms to tap into, and exploit, resources and capabilities outside their home countries, is requiring a reappraisal of the rationale for, and economics of, extending the boundaries of a firm. It is also requiring scholars to judge the success of managerial strategy less on the criteria of short-run profitability, and more on that of long-run asset appreciation. To be relevant in a dynamic context, extant internalization theory needs to explain why firm specific transaction costs are likely to be less than market specific transaction costs in the *creation*, as well as in the *use*, of resources and capabilities.

Third, the growth of a range of inter-firm coalitions is resulting in *de facto* internalization, but without equity ownership. This is most evident in two cases. The first is where the competitive advantage of a firm is based on its ownership of a set of proprietary rights, the use of which it can effectively control and monitor through a contractual agreement. The second is that where firms engage in collaborative agreements for a very specific purpose, which is usually time limited, e.g. a research and development project or a joint marketing arrangement in a particular country or region. Here, full internalization, which, in essence, addresses ownership issues, is not a realistic option for the participating firms. At the same time, most strategic partnerships now being formed

Table 14.3 Theories explaining why firms choose to own foreign value-added facilities

	(1) MS	(2) RS	(3) ES	(4) SAS
1. **Orthodox internalization theory**	• To capture co-ordinating and transactional benefits of common governance of related activities; to benefit (mainly through M&As) from innovating, production or marketing scale/scope economies.			
(i) Resource or productivity-enhancing Caves (1996), Dunning (1993)				
(ii) Cost reduction Anderson and Gatignon (1986), Aoki, Gustafson and Williamson (1990), Buckley and Casson (1976, 1985, 1998a, 1998b), Hennart (1982, 1989), Rugman (1982, 1996)	• To reduce transaction and co-ordinating costs of arm's-length markets and/or non-equity contractual relations. Such costs include opportunism and shirking, and those designed to protect the reputation of the contractor. Most empirical work relates to entry modes. See, for example, Anderson and Gatignon (1986).			
(iii) Risk reduction Vernon (1993)	• To reduce organizational and related risks implicit in (ii) above.			
2. **Dynamic internalization theory** Ghoshal, Hahn and Moran (1997), Buckley and Casson (1998a)				• To tap into learning and experience-related assets and to speed up the innovation process. To capture the advantages of Schumpeterian integration and the common governance of R&D-related activities

3. **Agency theory** Eisenhardt (1989), Jensen and Meckling (1976), Strong and Waterson (1987)	• As with internalization theory, but primarily to reduce risks of external agents behaving against the interests of the principals. • To reduce moral hazard and adverse selection.	
4. **Market power theories** Hymer (1960, 1976), Gowling and Sugden (1987)	• Growth by M&As intended to increase market power, rather than to upgrade efficiency.	
5. **Efficiency-related theories** Caves (1982, 1996), Teece (1981, 1984)	• To capture scale-related production economies. To raise dynamic technical efficiency through shared knowledge, learning experiences and management expertise.	
6. **Knowledge acquisition and sharing theories** Antonelli (1998), Kogut and Zander (1993), Makino (1998), Wesson (1993, 1997), Teece, Pisano and Shuen (1997)		• To augment existing intellectual assets, thereby increasing competitive prowess • To capture synergies of knowledge creation and augmenting activities

cannot be construed as arm's-length transactions as the participants have a continuing knowledge sharing relationship with each other (Dunning, 1995; UN, 1998). The advent of alliance capitalism, which may be perceived as a variant of hierarchical capitalism, offers opportunities for new inter-firm organizational modalities, the rationale for which internalization theory can only partly explain.

In Table 14.3, we set out some of the mainstream theories which have attempted to explain why, given a set of O and L specific advantages, firms prefer to own their foreign value-added or creating activities, rather than lease the right to use their O advantages to independently owned foreign firms. It is our contention that changing world economic events, the growing multinationality of many foreign investors, and the need for firms to engage in highly specific cross-border alliances and in asset-augmenting FDI, are necessitating both a reappraisal of static organizational theories and an integration between 'production based', 'innovation based' and 'transaction based' theories of the firm.

Again, we do not think these approaches to internalization are mutually exclusive. At the end of the day, managers will take decisions which in any particular context (including those of competitor firms) will come closest to meeting an amalgam of short-term and long-term objectives. Yet, to be effective, these decisions need to take account of, and resolve in a holistic way, conflicts between very specific objectives. It is extremely unlikely, for example, that any one firm will be successful, at one and the same time, in minimizing short-run transaction costs, maximizing short-run and long-run productive efficiency, accessing new markets, optimizing the net benefits of asset creation and asset-augmenting activities, and pursuing a variety of cost-effective strategies to improve its competitive position *vis-à-vis* that of its main rivals – all within a macro-economic environment of uncertainty and volatility.

This, then, suggests that any comprehensive explanation of the existence and the growth of the contemporary MNE must almost inevitably be 'judiciously pluralistic' (Foss, 1996), unless the context in which the explanation is being made is very narrowly delineated. And, it is a fact that most new explanations of the territorial expansion of firms tend to be incremental to extant theories, rather than a replacement of them. Any conflict between alternative theories or models is, as likely as not, to be about the relevance of, or emphasis placed on, these theories or models, rather than about their logical construction.

We would make one other point. In discussing alternative interpretations of the I component of the OLI triumvirate, organizational scholars such as Chris Bartlett, Sumantra Ghoshal, Yves Doz and C.K. Prahalad focus on the individual manager – rather than on the firm – as their main unit of analysis. This results in a somewhat different analytical perspective towards the rationale for existence of hierarchies and the internalization of markets, than that offered by Oliver

Williamson (1985, 1986, 1990), notwithstanding the fact that, in his various writings, he incorporates the concept of managerial discretion as an explanation for the behavior of firms. Moreover, for the most part, Williamson's analysis tends to be concerned with the efficiency of asset exploitation, rather than that of asset augmentation. Because of this, his focus is more on the optimal mode of co-ordinating the use of existing resources and capabilities, rather than on that of upgrading such resources and capabilities, by innovating and other means.

CONCLUSIONS: THE ECLECTIC PARADIGM AS AN ENVELOPE FOR COMPLEMENTARY THEORIES OF MNE ACTIVITY

In the three previous sections of this chapter, we have suggested that, for the most part, the many and varied explanations of the extent and structure of FDI and MNE activity are complementary to, rather than substitutable for, each other, and are strongly context specific. We have further observed that, as the international production by MNEs has grown and taken on new patterns, as the world economic scenario has changed, and as scholars have better understood the *raison d'être* for FDI, so new explanations of the phenomena have been put forward, and existing explanations have been modified and, occasionally, replaced.

According to Kuhn (1962) and Foss (1996, 1997), an existing paradigm can accommodate several contrasting theoretical models as long as these are not addressing exactly the same questions or addressing these in the same context.[33] At the same time, a paradigm that leaves no issues unresolved is of dubious value as a guide to further theorizing (Loasby, 1971). By contrast, a paradigm shift may be required when new phenomena arise which cannot be addressed within the existing paradigm, or where there are serious and irreconcilable conflicts among the theories contained in the paradigm.

However, we believe that the criteria for a successful paradigm are more demanding. More specifically, we would mention three of these. The first is that the sum of the value of the constituent theories must be greater than the whole. This suggests that there are intellectual interdependencies or externalities to each of the theories, which a paradigm can 'internalize' through its integrated approach. It follows then that the more any general paradigm of international production can advance understanding about the determinants of its constituent parts, the more successful it may be judged. Viewed in this way, we would aver that dynamizing the eclectic paradigm, and recognizing the interdependence of the OLI components not only adds value to its original conception, but helps point the way to improving a variety of the individual theories it embraces.

Second, we would assert that the strength of a paradigm also depends on the extent to which it can offer some generic hypotheses, or, indeed, predictions about the phenomena being studied. In the case of the earlier versions of the eclectic paradigm, we offered some general hypotheses about the nature of the relationship between the O, L and I variables and FDI (Dunning, 1977, 1980). However, we did not think it appropriate to put forward specific hypotheses about the relationship between particular OLI variables and particular kinds of FDI – as the paradigm itself was not context specific.

In the case of the contemporary version of the paradigm, which embraces alliance related and asset augmenting MNE activity, even generic hypotheses are harder to make without knowing whether a firm is contemplating an FDI to exploit a competitive strength or to overcome, or counteract, a competitive weakness. Only by treating the search for, and acquisition of, competitive advantages as part of the dynamic and cumulative process of sustaining and advancing O specific advantages (rather than a discrete and once-and-for-all transaction) can this conundrum be resolved. This, then, suggests that the eclectic paradigm might better address itself to explaining the *process* of international production, than to its level and composition at a particular moment of time.

Third, a paradigm may be judged to be robust if it continues to address relevant problems and offers a satisfying conceptual structure for resolving them (Loasby, 1971), and if there are no serious contenders to it. Here, it would be foolish to deny there are not other paradigms which seek to offer general explanations of the internationalization process of firms and/or their international management strategies. But, for the most part, we would not consider these to be competing paradigms.

Managerial-related paradigms, for example, are interested in explaining the behavior of managers in harnessing and utilizing scarce resources, not the overall level and pattern of FDI or MNE activity. Moreover, unlike FDI theories, they tend to be process oriented, unlike most FDI theories (Buckley, 1996). Organizational paradigms are directed to evaluating the costs and benefits of alternative institutional mechanisms for organizing a given set of resources and capabilities, independently of the location of these assets. Paradigms offered by marketing scholars usually focus on the process and/or form of international market entry and/or growth (Johanson and Vahlne, 1977; Luostarinen, 1979; Welch and Luostarinen, 1988; Anderson and Gatignon, 1986). Technologically related paradigms of international production (Cantwell, 1989, 1994; Kogut and Zander, 1993) come nearest to our own approach, but cannot comfortably explain FDI in developing countries and in some service sectors. With a few exceptions (notably Gray, 1999; Markusen, 1995), modern paradigms of international trade ignore or downplay the significance of firm specific advantages.

Finance-related paradigms can offer only limited insights into the growth of corporate networks and cross-border strategic alliances.

We conclude, then, that an add-on dynamic component to the eclectic paradigm, and an extension of its constituent parts to embrace both asset augmenting and alliance-related cross-border ventures can do much to uphold its position as the dominant analytical framework for examining the determinants of international production. We believe that recent economic events, and the emergence of new explanations of MNE activity, have added to, rather than subtracted from, the robustness of the paradigm. While accepting that, in spite of its eclecticism, there may be some kinds of foreign owned value-added activities which do not fit comfortably into its construction, we do believe that it continues to meet most of the criteria of a good paradigm; and that it is not yet approaching its own 'creative destruction' (Foss, 1996).[34]

ACKNOWLEDGEMENT

I am grateful to Jean Boddewyn, John Daniels, Mira Wilkins, Stephen Young and two anonymous referees for their helpful comments on an earlier draft of this chapter.

NOTES

1. Ownership, Location and Internalization.
2. As described, for example, in Caves (1982, 1996) and Dunning (1993). For the purposes of this chapter we use FDI and international production, viz. production financed by FDI, as interchangeable terms.
3. As, for example, set out in Buckley and Casson (1976, 1985, 1998a, 1998b), Hennart (1982, 1989) and Rugman (1982, 1996).
4. For an elaboration of these and other kinds of FDI (e.g. escape, support, and passive investments), see Dunning (1993), ch. 3, pp. 61–3.
5. The former mainly in the form of the growth of horizontal, i.e. product specialization and the latter in the growth of vertical, i.e. process specialization.
6. Such activity is estimated to have accounted for between 55 percent and 60 percent of all new FDI flows over the period 1985 to 1997 (UN, 1998).
7. As witnessed, by the growth of intra-firm trade both of intermediate and of final products, documented, for example, by UN (1996b).
8. The explanation of foreign direct *di*vestment by MNEs is exactly the reverse of that of foreign direct investment. It may be brought about by a decline in their O specific advantages and/or the L advantages of foreign countries, and/or a reduced motive by firms to internalize the cross-border market for buying or selling intermediate products (Boddewyn, 1985; Dunning 1988).
9. Throughout our analysis, we shall proceed on the assumption that paradigmatic and model building theoretic structures to understanding international business activity are complementary rather than alternative scientific methodologies (Buckley and Casson, 1998b). While accepting the need for rigorous theorizing and the empirical treating of specific hypotheses,

we also believe that encompassing related hypotheses into an open-ended and comprehensive conceptual framework, which not only identifies and evaluates the interaction between the theories, but makes its own generic predictions, provides a useful, and in many cases, an essential, foundation to these theories. We, therefore, view the eclectic paradigm as a systemic framework which provides a set of general assumptions and boundary criteria in which operationally testable theories, germane to FDI and MNE theory, can be comfortably accommodated. It is, perhaps, the most expressive of the research tradition in international business which has evolved over the past two decades (Weisfelder, 1998). For an elaboration of the concept of a research tradition, see Laudan (1977).

10. See also the writings of the Scandinavian school on the internalization process (e.g. Johanson and Vahlne, 1977; Luostarinen, 1979; Welch and Luostarinen, 1988).
11. For a longer-term perspective, and particularly for an appreciation of the evolution of the O advantages of firms, and their changing locational patterns and organizational modalities, see two classic studies by Mira Wilkins (Wilkins, 1970, 1974).
12. A generic term which suggests that the wealth of firms and countries is increasingly dependent on the kind and quality of alliances they form with other firms and countries. This concept is explored in more detail in Dunning (1995).
13. Which elsewhere (Dunning, 1997) we suggest represents a new stage in the development of market-based capitalism, the previous two stages being land-based and machine-based capitalism.
14. The origins of the paradigm date back to 1958, when the distinction between the O advantages of firms and the L advantages of countries was first made, in a study by the present author, of American investment in British manufacturing industry (Dunning, 1958, revised 1998). The I component was not explicitly added until 1977, although some of the reasons why firms prefer to engage in FDI rather than cross-border licensing et al. agreements were acknowledged by the author and other scholars in the early 1970s. (See the 1998 revised edition of Dunning, 1958, ch. 11.)
15. Implicitly or explicitly, this assumes some immobility of factors of production, including created assets, and that factor markets are not fully contestable. Much earlier, several kinds of competitive advantages specific to *foreign* owned and *domestic* firms were identified by such scholars as Dunning (1958), Brash (1965) and Safarian (1966).
16. For a full bibliography, see Barney (1991), Conner (1991), Conner and Prahalad (1996), Cantwell (1994), Dosi, Freeman, Nelson, Silverberg and Soete (1988), Foss, Knudsen and Montgomery (1995) and Saviotti and Metcalfe (1991). See also the writings of David Teece (1981, 1994, 1992) and of Teece, Pisano and Shuen (1997).
17. Which includes minimizing the transaction costs and of maximizing the benefits of innovation, learning and accumulated knowledge.
18. Unlike with internalization theory, where the locational decision is normally taken to be independent of the modality of resource transference.
19. One of the first of these studies was that of Frank Southard in 1931 on the locational determinants of US FDI in Europe (Southard, 1931).
20. Earlier, Agmon and Lessard (1977) had suggested that US MNEs commanded a higher price than their uninational counterparts because individual investors looked on the former as a means of internationally diversifying their investment portfolios.
21. For a survey of these studies, see, for example, Dunning (1993) and Caves (1996).
22. See particularly the impact of WTO agreements and dispute settlements on the locational decisions of MNEs, as documented by Brewer and Young (1999).
23. Notably, wage levels, demand patterns, policy-related variables, supply capabilities and infrastructure.
24. As set out in textbooks on location theory, e.g. Lloyd and Dicken (1977) and Dicken (1998).
25. Especially small states like Switzerland, Belgium and Sweden.
26. Chen and Chen (1998, 1999) have argued that the access to foreign located networks would both augment the O specific advantages of the investing firms, and enable firms which otherwise do not engage in FDI, so to do. The authors back up their assertion that FDI might act as a conduit for strategic linkages by drawing upon the experiences of Taiwanese firms.

27. Which, within the triad of countries, are estimated to have accounted for around three-fifths of all new FDI between 1985 and 1995 (UNCTAD, 1997).
28. For example, there are several socio-economic and geographical theories of the rationale for industrial clustering; see, for example, Storper (1995).
29. E.g. by a subcontracting, or turn-key, agreement.
30. For two recent explanations of the various kinds of market failure and the response of firms and governments to these, see Lipsey (1997) and Meyer (1998).
31. I am grateful for one reviewer of this chapter who pointed out that orthodox internalization theory addresses a single question, viz. 'where are the boundaries of the firm drawn?' I agree. But, up to now, this particular question has been approached mainly from a transaction cost perspective, which, I would argue, cannot cope with all the issues raised by it.
32. As compared with markets.
33. Thus, for example, although the transaction cost and resource-based theories of the firm offer alternative predictions of the behavior of firms, they, in fact, are addressing different aspects of that behavior, e.g. the former is concerned with defining the boundaries of a firm's activities and the latter with the origins of its competitive advantages.
34. For a somewhat different, and highly refreshing, approach to some of the concepts dealt with in this chapter, see a recently published article by Boddewyn and Iyer (1999).

REFERENCES

Agmon, T. and Lessard, D.R. (1977), 'Investor recognition of corporate international diversification', *Journal of Finance*, **32**, September, 1049–55.

Aliber, R.Z. (1971), 'The multinational enterprise in a multiple currency world', in Dunning, J.H. (ed.), *The Multinational Enterprise*, London: Allen & Unwin, pp. 49–56.

Anderson, E. and Gatignon, H. (1986), 'Modes of foreign entry: transaction costs and propositions', *Journal of International Business Studies*, **17**, 1–26.

Antonelli, C. (1998), 'Localized technological change and the evolution of standards as economic institutions', in Chandler, A. D. Jr., Hagström, P. and Sölvell, O. (eds), *The Dynamic Firm*, Oxford: Oxford University Press.

Aoki, M., Gustafson, B. and Williamson, O.E. (eds) (1990), *The Firm as a Nexus of Treaties*, London and Newbury Park, CA: Sage Publications.

Audretsch, D.B. (1998), 'Agglomeration and the location of economic activity', *Oxford Review of Economic Policy*, **14** (2), 18–29.

Bain, J.S. (1956), *Barriers to New Competition*, Cambridge, MA: Harvard University Press.

Barney, J.B. (1991), 'Firm resources and sustained competitive advantage', *Journal of Management*, **17**, 99–120.

Bartlett, C.A. and Ghoshal, S. (1989), *Managing Across National Borders: The Transnational Solution*, Cambridge, MA: Harvard Business School Press, 23–46.

Barlett, C.A. and Ghoshal, S. (1993), 'Beyond the M-form: towards a managerial theory of the firm', *Strategic Management Journal*, **14** (1).

Blonigen, B.A. (1997), 'Firm-specific assets and the link between exchange rates and foreign direct investment', *American Economic Review*, **87** (3), 447–65.

Boddewyn, J.J. (1985), 'Foreign divestment theory: Is it the reverse of FDI theory?', *Weltwirlschaftliches Archiv*, **119**, 345–55.

Boddewyn, J.J. and Iyer, G. (1999), 'International business research: Beyond déjà vu', *Management International Review*, **39** (2), 161–84.

Brash, D.T. (1966), *American Investment in Australian Industry*, Canberra: Australian University Press.

Brewer, T. and Young, S. (1999), *The Effects on Firms' Strategic Choices of the WTO Trade Investment Regime*, paper presented to a conference on the Locational Determinants of Multinational Firms, Paris, June.

Buckley, P.J. (1996), 'The role of management in international business theory: a meta-analysis and integration of the literature on international business and international management', *Management International Review*, **36** (1), Special Issue, 7–54.

Buckley, P.J. and Casson, M.C. (1976), *The Future of the Multinational Enterprise*, London: Macmillan.

Buckley, P.J. and Casson, M.C. (1981), 'The optimal timing of a foreign direct investment', *Economic Journal*, **91**, 75–87.

Buckley, P.J. and Casson, M.C. (1985), *The Economic Theory of the Multinational Enterprise*, London: Macmillan.

Buckley, P.J. and Casson, M. C. (1998a), 'Models of the multinational enterprise', *Journal of International Business Studies*, **29** (1), 21–44.

Buckley, P.J. and Casson, M.C. (1998b), 'Analyzing foreign market entry strategies: extending the internalization approach', *Journal of International Business Studies*, **29** (3), 539–62.

Cantwell, J.A. (1989), *Technological Innovation and Multinational Corporations*, Oxford: Basil Blackwell.

Cantwell, J.A. (ed.) (1994), '*Transnational Corporations and Innovatory Activities*', United Nations Library on Transnational Corporations, Vol. 17, London: Routledge.

Cantwell, J.A. and Piscitello, L. (1997), *The Emergence of Corporate International Networks for the Accumulation of Dispersed Technological Competence*, Reading: Department of Economics, Discussion Paper 5 in *International Investment and Management* Series B *X*, No. 238, October.

Caves, R.E. (1971), 'Industrial corporations: the industrial economics of foreign investment', *Economica*, **38**, 1–27.

Caves, R.E. (1974), 'Causes of direct investment: foreign firms, shares in Canadian and United Kingdom manufacturing industries', *Review of Economics and Statistics*, **56**, August, 272–93.

Caves, R.E. (1982 & 1996), *Multinational Firms and Economic Analysis*, Cambridge: Cambridge University Press, 1st and 2nd editions.

Cavusgil, S.T. (1980), 'On the internationalization process of the firm', *European Research*, **8** (6), 273–81.

Chen, Homin and Chen, Tain-Jy (1998), 'Network linkages and location choice in foreign direct investment', *Journal of International Business Studies*, **29** (3), 445–68.

Chen, Tain-Jy and Chen, Homin (1999), *Resource Advantages and Resource Linkages in Foreign Direct Investment*, Paper Presented to 7th International Conference on the MNEs, Taipei Chinese Culture University, December.

Conner, K. (1991), 'A historical comparison of resource based theory and five schools of thought within industrial organization economies. Do we have a new theory of the firm?', *Journal of Management*, **17**, 121–54.

Conner, K.R. and Prahalad, C.K. (1996), 'A resource based theory of the firm: knowledge versus opportunism', *Organizational Science*, **7**(5), 477–501.

Cowling, K. and Sugden, R. (1987), *Transnational Monopoly Capitalism*, Brighton: Wheatsheaf.

Cushman, D.O. (1985), 'Real exchange rate risk, expectations and the level of direct investment', *Review of Economics and Statistics*, **67**, May, 297–308.

Daniels, J.D. (1971), *Recent Foreign Direct Investment in the United States*, New York: Praeger.
Dicken, P. (1998), *Global Shift* (Third edition), New York and London: The Guilford Press.
Doremus, P.N., Keller, W.W., Pauly, L.W. and Reich, S. (1998), *The Myth of the Global Corporation*, Princeton, NJ: Princeton University Press.
Dosi, G., Freeman, C., Nelson, R., Silverberg, G. and Soete, L. (eds) (1988), *Technical Change and Economic Theory*, London: Pinter Publishers.
Doz, Y.L. and Santos, J.F.P. (1997), *On the Management of Knowledge: From the Transparency of Collocation and Cosetting to the Quandary of Dispersion and Differentiation*, Fontainebleau, France: INSEAD, mimeo.
Doz, Y.L., Asakawa, K., Santos, J.F.P. and Williamson, P.J. (1997), *The Metanational Corporation*, Fontainebleau, France: INSEAD Working Paper 97/60/SM.
Dunning, J.H. (1958), *American Investment in British Manufacturing Industry*, London: George Allen and Unwin (New, revised and updated edition, London: Routledge, 1998).
Dunning, J.H. (1977), 'Trade, location of economic activity and the MNE: A search for an eclectic approach', in Ohlin, B., Hesselborn, P. O. and Wijkman, P.M. (eds), *The International Allocation of Economic Activity*, London: Macmillan, pp. 395–418.
Dunning, J.H. (1980), 'Towards an eclectic theory of international production: some empirical tests', *Journal of International Business Studies*, **11**(1), Spring/Summer, 9–31.
Dunning, J.H. (1988), *Explaining International Production*, London: Unwin Hyman.
Dunning, J.H. (1993), *Multinational Enterprises and the Global Economy*, Wokingham, Berkshire: Addison Wesley.
Dunning, J.H. (1995), 'Reappraising the eclectic paradigm in the age of alliance capitalism', *Journal of International Business Studies*, **26**, pp. 461–91.
Dunning, J.H. (1996), 'The geographical sources of competitiveness of firms: the results of a new survey', *Transnational Corporations*, **5**(3), December 1996, 1–30.
Dunning, J.H. (1997), 'Technology and the changing boundaries of firms and governments', in OECD (ed.), *Industrial Competitiveness and the Global Economy*, Paris: OECD, pp. 53–68.
Dunning, J.H. (1998), 'Location and the multinational enterprise: a neglected factor', *Journal of International Business Studies*, **29**(1), 45–66.
Dunning, J.H. (1999), 'Globalization and the theory of MNE activity', in Hood, N. and Young, S. (eds), *The Globalization of Multinational Enterprise Activity*, London: Macmillan, pp. 21–54.
Eisenhardt, K.M. (1989), 'Agency theory: an assessment and review', *Academy of Management Review*, **14**(1), 57–73.
Enright, M.J. (1991), *Geographic Concentration and Industrial Organization*, Cambridge, MA: Ph.D. Dissertation, Harvard.
Enright, M.J. (1998), 'Regional clusters and firm strategy', in Chandler, A.D. Jr., Hagström, P. and Sölvell, O. (eds), *The Dynamic Firm*, Oxford: Oxford University Press, pp. 315–43.
Enright, M.J. (1999), 'The globalization of competition and the localization of competitive advantage', in Hood, N. and Young, S. (eds), *The Globalization of Multinational Enterprise Activity*, London: Macmillan, pp. 303–31.
Florida, R. (1995), 'Towards the learning region', *Futures*, **27**(5), 527–36.
Flowers, E.B. (1976), 'Oligopolistic reaction in European and Canadian direct investment in the United States', *Journal of International Business Studies*, **7**, 43–55.

Forsgren, M. (1989), *Managing the Inlernalizalion Process: The Swedish Case*, London and New York: Routledge.

Foss, N.J. (1996), 'Research in strategy, economics and Michael Porter', *Journal of Management Studies*, **33**(1), 1–24.

Foss, N.J. (ed.) (1997), *Resources, Firms and Strategies*, Oxford: Oxford University Press.

Foss, N.J., Knudsen, C. and Montgomery, C.A. (1995), 'An exploration of common ground: integrating resource based and evolutionary theories of the firm', in Montgomery, C.A. (ed.), *Resource Based and Evolutionary Theories of the Firm: Towards a Synthesis*, Boston, MA and London: Kluwer Academic Publishers.

Froot, K.A. and Stein, J.C. (1991), 'Exchange rates and foreign direct investment: an imperfect market's approach', *Quarterly Journal of Economics* **106**, November, 1191–1217.

Ghoshal, S., Hahn, M. and Moran, P. (1997), *Management Competence, Firm Growth and Economic Progress*, Fontainebleau, France: INSEAD Working Paper 97/21/SM.

Graham, E.M. (1975), 'Oligopolistic Imitation and European Direct Investment in the United States', D.B.A. Dissertation, Harvard University, unpublished.

Graham, E.M. (1990), 'Exchange of threats between multinational firms as an infinitely repeated non-cooperative game', *International Trade Journal*, **4**(3), 259–77.

Graham, E.M. (1998), 'Market structure and the multinational enterprise: a game-theoretic approach', *Journal of International Business Studies*, **29**(1), 67–84.

Gray, H. Peter. (1999), *Global Economic Investment*, Copenhagen: Copenhagen Business School Press.

Helleloid, D. (1992), *A Resource Based Theory of the Multinational Enterprise*, Seattle, WA: University of Washington, mimeo.

Hennart, J.F. (1982), *A Theory of Multinational Enterprise*, Ann Arbor, MI: University of Michigan Press, pp. 81–116.

Hennart, J.F. (1989), 'The transaction cost theory of the multinational enterprise', in Pitelis, C.N. and Sugden, R. (eds), *The Nature of the Transnational Firm*, London: Routledge.

Hirsch, S. (1976), 'An international trade and investment theory of the firm', *Oxford Economic Papers*, **28**, 258–70.

Hoover, E.M. (1948), *The location of Economic Activity*, New York: McGraw Hill.

Hotelling, H. (1929), 'Stability in competition', *Economic Journal*, **29**, 41–57.

Hymer, S.H. (1960), *The International Operation of National Firms: A Study of Direct Investment*, Ph.D. dissertation, M.I.T. (Published by M.I.T. Press in 1976).

Isard, W. (1956), *Location and the Space Economy*, New York: John Wiley.

Jensen, M. and Meckling, W. (1976), 'Theory of the firm: managerial behavior, agency costs, township structure', *Journal of Financial Economics*, **3**, 305–60.

Johanson, J. and Vahlne, J.E. (1977), 'The internationalization process of the firm – a model of knowledge development and increasing market commitments', *Journal of International Business Studies*, **8**, 23–32.

Johanson, J. and Vahlne, J.E. (1990), 'The mechanism of internationalization', *International Marketing Review*, **74**(4), 11–24.

Knickerbocker, F.T. (1973), *Oligopolistic Reaction and the Multinational Enterprise*. Cambridge, MA: Harvard University Press.

Kobrin, S. (2000), 'Development after industrialization: Poor countries in an electronically integrated economy', in Hood, N. and Young, S. (eds), *The Globalization of Multinational Enterprise Activity and Economic Development*, Basingstoke: Macmillan, pp. 133–54.

Kogut, B. (1983), 'Foreign direct investment as a sequential process', in Kindleberger, C.P. and Audretsch, D. (eds), *The Multinational Corporation in the 1980s*, Cambridge, MA: MIT Press, pp. 38–56.

Kogut, B. (1985), 'Designing global strategies: profiting from operational flexibility', *Sloan Management Review*, **26**, Fall, 27–38.

Kogut, B. and Kulatilaka, N. (1994), 'Operational flexibility, global manufacturing and the option value of a multinational network', *Management Service*, **40** (1), 123–39.

Kogut, B. and Zander, U. (1993), 'Knowledge of the firm and the evolutionary theory of the multinational corporation', *Journal of International Business Studies*, **24**(4), 625–46.

Krugman, P.R. (1991), *Geography and Trade*, Cambridge, MA: MIT Press.

Krugman, P.R. (1993), 'On the relationship between trade theory and location theory', *Review of International Economics*, **1**(2), 110–22.

Krugman, P.R. (1998), 'What's new about the new economic geography?' *Oxford Review of Economic Policy*, **14**(2), 7–17.

Kuemmerle, W. (1999), 'The drivers of foreign direct investment into research and development: an empirical investigation', *Journal of International Business Studies*, **30**(1), 1–24.

Kuhn, T.S. (1962), *The Structure of Scientific Revolutions*, Chicago: Chicago University Press.

Laudan, L. (1977), *Progress and its Problems: Towards a Theory of Scientific Growth*, Berkeley, CA: University of California Press, pp. 73–113.

Lipsey, R.G. (1997), 'Globalization and national government policies: an economist's view', in Dunning, J.H. (ed.), *Governments, Globalization and International Business*, Oxford: Oxford University Press.

Liu, S.X. (1998), *Foreign Direct Investment and the Multinational Enterprise. A Re–examination Using Signaling Theory*, Westport, CT: Greenwood Publishing.

Lloyd, P. and Dicken, P. (1977), *Location in Space*, London: Harper and Row.

Loasby, B.J. (1971), 'Hypothesis and paradigm in the theory of the firm', *Economic Journal*, **81**, 863–85.

Loree, D.W. and Guisinger, S.E. (1995), 'Policy and non-policy determinants of US equity foreign direct investment', *Journal of International Business Studies*, **26**(2), 281–99.

Lösch, A. (1954), *The Economics of Location*, (English translation by Woglom, W.H. and Stolper, W.F.), New Haven: Yale University Press.

Luostarinen, R. (1979), *Internationalization of the Firm*, Helsinki Acta Acadamie Oeconomicae, Helsinki School of Economics.

Madhok, A. (1996), 'The organization of economic activity: transaction costs, firm capabilities and the nature of governance', *Organizational Science*, **7**(5), September/October, 577–90.

Makino, S. (1998), *Toward a Theory of Asset Seeking Foreign Direct Investment*, Hong Kong: The Chinese University (mimeo).

Malmberg, A., Sölvell, O. and Zander, I. (1996), 'Spatial clustering, local accumulation of knowledge and firm competitiveness', *Geographical Annals*, **78B**(2), 85–97.

Markusen, J.R. (1995), 'The boundaries of multinational enterprises and the theory of international trade', *Journal of Economic Perspectives*, **9**(2), 169–89.

Marshall, A. (1920), *Principles of Economics*, London: Macmillan (eighth edition).

Meyer, K. (1998), *Direct Investment in Economies in Transition*, Cheltenham, UK, Lyme, US: Edward Elgar.

Montgomery, C.A. (ed.) (1995), *Resource Base and Evolutionary Theories of the Firm: Towards a Synthesis*, Boston, MA and London: Kluwer Academic Publishers.

Nelson, R.R. and Winter, S. (1982), *An Evolutionary Theory of Economic Change*, Cambridge: Belknap Press.

Nelson, R.R. (1991), 'The role of firm differences in an evolutionary theory of technical advance', *Science and Public Policy*, **18**(6), 347–52.

Oliver, C. (1997), 'Sustainable competitive advantage: combining institutional and resource based views', *Strategic Management Journal*, **18** (9), pp. 697–713.

Pauwells, P. and Matthyssens, P. (1997), 'De-internationalization: a search for a theoretical framework', paper presented at Round-table on *Globalization and the Small Open Economy*, Antwerp: Centre for International Management and Development, May 29.

Peck, F.W. (1996), 'Regional development and the production of space: the role of infrastructure in the attraction of new inward investment', *Environment and Planning*, Series A, 28, 327–39.

Porter, M.E. (1980), *Competitive Strategy*, New York: The Free Press.

Porter, M.E. (1985), *Competitive Advantage*, New York: The Free Press.

Porter, M.E. (1991), 'Towards a dynamic theory of strategy', *Strategic Management Journal*, **12**, Special Issue, Winter, 95–117.

Porter, M.E. (1994), 'The role of location in competition', *Journal of Economics of Business*, **I**(1), 35–39.

Porter, M.E. (1996), 'Competitive advantage, agglomerative economies and regional policy', *International Regional Science Review*, **19**(1 and 2), 85–94.

Porter, M.E. (1998), 'Location, clusters and the 'new' microeconomics of competition', *Business Economics*, **33**, Jan. 7–13.

Prahalad, C.K. and Doz, Y.L. (1987), *The Multinational Mission: Balancing Local Demands and Global Vision*, New York: The Free Press.

Rangan, S. (1998), 'Do multinationals operate flexibly? Theory and evidence', *Journal of International Business Studies*, **29**(2), 217–38.

Rugman, A.M. (1979), *International Diversification and the Multinational Enterprise*, Lexington, MA: Lexington Books.

Rugman, A.M. (ed.) (1982), *New Theories of the Multinational Enterprise*, London: Croom Helm.

Rugman, A.M. (1996), *The Theory of Multinational Enterprises: The Selected Scientific Papers of Alan A. M. Rugman*, Vol. 1, Cheltenham: Edward Elgar.

Rugman, A.M. and Verbeke, A. (1998), 'Multinational enterprises and public policy' *Journal of International Business Studies*, **29**(1), 115–36.

Safarian, A.E. (1966), *Foreign Ownership of Canadian Industry*, Toronto: University of Toronto Press.

Saviotti, P.P. and Metcalfe, J.S. (eds) (1991), *Evolutionary Theories of Economic and Technological Change – Present Statistics and Future Prospects*, Chur: Harwood Academic Publishers.

Scott, A.J. (1996), 'Regional motors of the global economy', *Futures*, **28**(5), 391–411.

Sölvell, O. and Zander, I. (1998), 'International diversification of knowledge: isolating mechanisms and the role of the MNE', in Chandler, A. D. Jr., Hagström, P. and Sölvell, O. (eds), *The Dynamic Firm*, Oxford: Oxford: University Press, pp. 402–16.

Southard, F.A. Jr. (1931), *American Industry in Europe*, Boston, MA: Houghton Mifflin.

Storper, M. (1995), 'The resurgence of region economies: ten years later: the region as a nexus of untraded interdependencies', *European Urban and Regional Studies*, **2**(3), 191–221.

Storper, M. and Scott, A.J. (1995), 'The wealth of regions', *Futures*, **27**(5), 505–26.
Strong, N. and Waterson, M. (1987), 'Principals, agents and information', in Clarke, R. and McGuiness, A. (eds), *The Economics of the Firm*, Oxford: Blackwell, pp. 18–41.
Tallman, S.B., Geringer, J.M. and Li, E. (1995), *A Strategic Management Model of the Multinational Enterprise* (mimeo).
Teece, D.J. (1981), 'The multinational enterprise: market failure and market power considerations', *Sloan Management Review*, **22**, 3–18.
Teece, D.J. (1984), 'Economic analysis and strategic management', *California Management Review*, **26**, Spring, 87–108.
Teece, D.J. (1992), 'Competition, cooperation, and innovation: Organizational arrangements for regimes of rapid technological progress', *Journal of Economic Behavior and Organization*, **18**, 1–25.
Teece, D.J., Pisano, G. and Shuen, A. (1997), 'Dynamic capabilities and strategic management', *Strategic Management Journal*, **18**(7), 509–33.
UNCTAD (1996a), *Incentives and Foreign Direct Investment*, Geneva and New York: UN.
UNCTAD (1998), *World Investment Report 1998: Investment, Trade and International Policy Arrangements*, Geneva and New York: UN.
UNCTAD (1998), *World Investment Report 1997, Transnational Corporations: Trends and Determinants*, Geneva and New York: UN.
Venables, A.J. (1998), 'The assessment: trade and location', *Oxford Review of Economic Policy*, **14**(2), 1–6.
Vernon, R. (1966), 'International investment and international trade in the product cycle', *Quarterly Journal of Economics*, **80**, 190–207.
Vernon, R. (1973), *Sovereignty at Bay*, Harmondsworth: Penguin.
Vernon, R. (1974), 'The location of economic activity', in Dunning, J.H. (ed.), *Economic Analysis and the Multinational Enterprise*, London: Allen and Unwin, pp. 89–114.
Vernon, R. (1979), 'The product cycle hypothesis in the new international environment', *Oxford Bulletin of Economics and Statistics*, **41**.
Vernon, R. (1983), 'Organizational and institutional responses to international risk', in Herring, R.J. (ed.), *Managing International Risk*, Cambridge, MA: Cambridge University Press, pp. 191–216.
Weber, A. (1929), *The Theory of Location of Industries* (English translation by Friedrich), Chicago: University of Chicago Press.
Weisfelder, C.J. (1998), *Foreign Production and the Multinational Enterprise: Development of a Research Tradition from 1960 to 1990*, Bowling Green, OH: Bowling Green State University (mimeo).
Welch, L.S. and Luostarinen (1988), 'Internationalization: evolution of a concept', *Journal of General Management*, **14**(2), Winter, 34–55.
Wernerfelt, B. (1984), 'A resource-based view of the firm', *Strategic Management Journal*, **5**(2), 171–80.
Wernerfelt, B. (1995), 'The resource based view of the firm: ten years after', *Strategic Management Journal*, **16**, 171–74.
Wesson, T.J. (1993), *An Alternative Motivation for Foreign Direct Investment*, Cambridge, MA: Ph.D. dissertation, Harvard University.
Wesson, T.J. (1997), 'A model of asset seeking foreign direct investment', *Proceedings International Business Division. The Administrative Sciences Association of Canada*, **18**(8), 110–20.
Wilkins, M. (1970), *The Emergence of Multinational Enterprise: American Business Abroad, From the Colonial Era to 1914*, Cambridge, MA: Harvard University Press.

Wilkins, M. (1974), *The Maturing of Multinational Enterprise, American Business Abroad, From 1914 to 1970*, Cambridge, MA: Harvard University Press.
Williamson, O.E. (1985), *The Economic Institutions of Capitalism*, New York: The Free Press.
Williamson, O.E. (1986), *Economic Organization: Firm, Markets and Policy Control*, Brighton: Wheatsheaf Books.
Williamson, O.E. (1990), *Organization Theory*, New York: Free Press.

15. The challenge of electronic markets for international business theory*

1. INTRODUCTION

The study and research of International Business and E-commerce has both many similarities and some differences. E-commerce touches many of the same disciplines as International Business (IB) (Boddewyn and Iyer, 1999), such as economics, political science, law, sociology, and psychology; as well as several functional or professional areas, such as management, marketing, and finance, etc., which apply concepts, models and variables derived from these disciplines. We have observed how the network properties of the Internet and E-commerce have encouraged International Business, but not necessarily the amount and internal relatedness of foreign direct investment associated with business models of the mid-1990s (Beck et al., 2000).

Similar to Vernon's (1994) cited difficulties in truly understanding the structures, motivations and strategies of multinational enterprises, we are once again confronted with these problems with the emergence of global E-commerce companies, but now have much less history to guide us. Much of the earlier research in E-commerce focused on descriptive case studies, recounting what happened and why (Netscape, Yahoo, etc.), particularly in the US market, rather than taking the lead from the more careful theoretical analysis of Bartlett and Ghoshal (1993) in their evaluation of the major organisation changes then being introduced in such MNEs as ABB. We must attempt to introduce the IB discipline and the eclectic analytic process to analyse the new realities of globally networked businesses. This requires a basic understanding of the reality of business in the new economy and a great deal of imagination necessary to develop creative theoretical solutions to unstructured and undetermined problems.

Since the 1970s, the eclectic paradigm (Dunning, 1977, 1988, 1995, 2000) has sought to integrate the mainstream economic and behavioural theories to explain aspects of FDI and/or foreign-owned production. The paradigm offers a conceptual framework for incorporating a number of context-specific and operationally testable theories, each of which seeks to explain a particular

* Written with Cliff Wymbs. From *International Journal of the Economics of Business and Economics*, **8**(2) (2001): 273–301.

component of the internationalisation process (Dunning, 2000). Expansion of the paradigmatic framework to E-commerce can help us formulate contextual and operationally testable theories. More specifically, this chapter examines the extent to which the tenets of the eclectic paradigm can be applied to E-commerce development, and reviews some of the mainstream theories related to IB to establish this link.

The chapter will address two main issues:

1. *The specific impact of E-commerce on the framework of the eclectic paradigm of international production and some of the economic and behavioural theories that make up the paradigm*

Much like the steam engine, the telegraph, the telephone, the railroad and the highway system before it, the Internet is a facilitating technology that serves as a catalyst for new business combinations, permutations and mutations (Wymbs, 2000a). Each of the above technologies was network-based and required a minimum number of users before its true economic benefit and a period of increasing returns could be realised (Bernstein, 1998). Gates (1999) states that what is different about the Internet as a modality of service delivery is the speed at which its widespread use has followed its initial commercial introduction, namely, in approximately five years as compared with a decade or more earlier in the case of other communication technologies. This time compression will highlight some of the unique dislocations and discontinuities caused by or associated with E-commerce (Iansiti and MacCormack, 1997; Yoffie and Cusumano, 1999).

Although we will analyse it in more detail later, the basic tenets and predictions of the eclectic paradigm (Dunning, 1988, 1993, 2000) appear to hold with respect to the Internet. Firms will seek to leverage Internet technology to sustain or augment rare, inimitable and immutable ownership (O) advantages both from a scale and scope perspective. They will seek efficient organisational structures and internalise asset-creating and value-added activities using electronic commerce when markets fail. In addition, firms will seek to invest in locations around the world where they can either best exploit their core competences or add to them.

The information technology revolution, however, is like an iceberg, the largest and most interesting part of which is below the paradigmatic water line. With regard to firm-, industry- and country-specific issues, key questions include: how will Internet technology affect the boundaries of firms, and how will firms mutate, combine, dissolve and spontaneously regenerate the resources and capabilities to take advantage of a new range of information- and transaction-related economies? How may common cross-industry processes replace industries as the most appropriate classification of groups of firms?

How may governments, both within countries and across countries, attempt simultaneously to encourage E-commerce development, yet limit some of its less desirable effects, including the sub-optimal behaviour of firms experiencing increasing returns on a global scale? We believe that the answers to these questions can be productively explored by using the methodology and contents of the eclectic paradigm.

2. *How contextual variables (industry, country and firm characteristics) affect OLI theory in an E-commerce world*

Fundamental to exploring this issue is the need to answer the following basic question: is it correct to think of E-commerce as a trajectory shift in our analysis of the determinants of international business (IB) activity?

The answer is both 'Yes' and 'No'. Technological advances are helping to transform our lives by inventing new, undreamed of products and producing them in new, undreamed of ways (Dicken, 1998; Tomkins, 1999; Reedy et al., 2000). Richard Lipsey (1997), among others, believes that the world is undergoing a deep structural adjustment in response to the advent of dramatically new information and communications technologies. Unlike structuralist scholars, such as Freeman and Perez (1988), who combine technology, structure and economic performance in one overarching concept, the so-called techno-economic paradigm, Lipsey and Bekar (1995) treat the three components separately and distinctly. We agree, and believe that the contemporary debate with respect to the impact of the Internet today is not so much about technology *per se* (we all expect a geometric increasing in computing power, transmission capacities and fast packet switching), but rather how the facilitating infrastructure will channel and nourish E-commerce growth; and how, and to what extent, the superior economic performance will flow to firms embracing new, increasing return business strategies, that both redefine existing markets, and create new ones.

Steve Kobrin (2000) expands on Lipsey and Bekar's propositions by asserting that cyberspace is a marketplace unlike that of any other in history. Potentially, no physical product crosses geographic borders, no paper currency changes hands, and there is no tangible record of the transaction (Kobrin, 1999). Policy makers, technologists and managers must confront the political and economic implications of digitisation. There appears to be an emerging asymmetry between economics and politics (Strange, 1997). The former is becoming global rather than trans-border, and is being organised via the use of electronic networks, while the latter is overwhelmingly local and geographic.

The intangible aspect of cyberspace means that a transaction can no longer be mapped into two-dimensional space. Borders and jurisdictions are irrelevant, rather than ambiguous. The unique power of national governments to tax, punish and require participation is based on the idea of a national territory. Kobrin (1999) asserts that the basic disconnect between geographic space and cyberspace raises fundamental questions about the concept of national economic jurisdiction and/or control.

From an individual firm perspective, it is important to understand its implications on the three main modes of internationalisation, namely, trade, foreign direct investment and international strategic alliances (Wymbs, 1997). Few would argue with the proposition that the new information economy is reducing most forms of spatial transaction and coordination costs, and is thereby facilitating both more, and less costly cross-border commerce. However, as Coase and Petzinger (1999) have observed, it is by no means clear which organisational entity is best equipped to own, control or access E-commerce. On the one hand, lower transaction costs would appear to favour a market – though not necessarily an arm's-length market – solution; on the other, lower intra-firm coordinating costs and the potential for exploiting firm specific scale and scope economies would seem to favour a hierarchical solution. This particular trade-off of Internet advantages is one of the most challenging questions now exercising the minds of organisational and IB scholars.

2. THE IMPACT OF ELECTRONIC COMMERCE ON IB THEORY

As a context setter, this section first provides a brief overview of the eclectic paradigm. It then systematically analyses and applies each of the OLI components of the paradigm, and their related theories of IB, to E-commerce development.

2.1 The Eclectic Paradigm

In brief, the eclectic paradigm – also known as the OLI paradigm – states that the extent, pattern and form of IB activity will depend on the juxtaposition behaviour of three sets of advantages. The first is the competitive advantage or ownership(O)-specific advantages of firms engaging in or contemplating value-added activities outside their national boundaries. The second is the locational (L) attractions of particular regions or countries in which firms might either create or augment these O advantages, or add value to them. The third advantage is the extent to which firms possessing O advantage will choose to coordinate these advantages with the L advantages of foreign countries through internalising (I) the former's cross-border markets for intermediate products, rather than engaging in arm's-length transactions or contractual agreements with foreign firms.

The paradigm was first put forward at a Nobel Symposium in Sweden in 1976 (Dunning, 1976), and over the past 25 years it has been frequently modified and extended in the light of scholarly criticism and the changing world economic landscape.[1] In 1995, the OLI paradigm, originally developed during an era of hierarchical capitalism, was extended to incorporate alliance-related modalities. In this contribution, we propose another update to the paradigm to reflect the emerging E-commerce world. For example, Table 15.1 compares the three temporal snapshots of the paradigm, while the discussion of the E-commerce parameters follows. Specifically, in this chapter we ask the question: to what extent can Internet-related IB activities be accommodated within the framework of the paradigm? After briefly indicating some of the modifications that seem to be required to the OLI configuration of firms resulting from the advent of E-commerce, we then proceed to consider how some of the specific theories which reference the eclectic paradigm need to be reconfigured.

2.2 Theories Explaining O-Specific Advantages of Firms

We initially address ownership-specific advantages of the firm as they relate to the eclectic paradigm and then discuss four important related theories of the firm, i.e. the resource-based view evolutionary theory, organisational theory and economic strategic theory.

(i) The eclectic paradigm O advantage

The eclectic paradigm clearly identifies two types of ownership advantages. The first pertains to the resources (asset) structure of the firm, which relates to property rights and/or intangible asset advantage (Oa), while the second pertains to the advantage of common governance, that is, of organising Oa with complementary assets (Ot), i.e. transaction cost minimising advantage.

Oa advantages We believe that, while E-commerce is changing the context and scope of the core competences of firms, if anything, such advantages are becoming a more important discriminator in their strategic positioning and commercial success. At the same time, the Internet is creating quite a varied set of such opportunities, from Amazon.com establishing a relational community of over 22 million customers (Helft, 2000) to Chemdex.com putting hundreds of thousands of speciality chemicals online (Muehlbauer, 2000), to GE creating an auction supply network (Margherion, 1998), to DoubleClick using Internet usage data to create databases that target specific customer segments for clients (DoubleClick, 2000). Each venture leverages network attributes of market space

Table 15.1 *An extension of the eclectic paradigm of international production*[4]

1. Ownership-specific advantages (of enterprises of one nationality (or affiliates of same) over those of another)

Hierarchical advantages
*c.*1993

- Property right and/or intangible asset advantages (Oa)
- Advantages of common governance, i.e. of organising Oa with complementary assets (Ot)
  - (i) Those that branch plants of established enterprises may enjoy over *de novo* firms
  - (ii) Which specifically arise because of multinationality. Multinationality enhances operating flexibility, more favoured access and/or better knowledge of international markets, ability to take advantage of geographic differences in factor markets and the ability to diversify or reduce risk

Alliance advantages
*c.*1995

- Vertical alliances
  - (i) Backward access to R&D and suppliers
  - (ii) Forward access to industrial customers and new markets
- Horizontal alliances
  - (i) Access to complementary technologies and innovative capacity
- Networks of similar firms
  - (i) Reduced transaction and coordination costs arising from better dissemination and interpretation of knowledge and information
  - (ii) Business districts
    As per (i) plus spatial agglomerative economies

E-commerce advantages
*c.*2001

- Oa property right advantages based on technology, e.g. Cisco Systems Internet switches
- Oa property right advantages based on standards, e.g. Microsoft's operating system
- Oa property right advantages based on preferred customer interface, e.g. AOL and Amazon.com
- Ot advantage based on E-commerce experience, e.g. Amazon.com's horizontal integration into CDs
- Vertical alliances, e.g. commission paid based on sales referral
- Vertical alliances, e.g. creating business partners to handle auctions (FreeMarkets.com)
- Horizontal alliances, e.g. GM & Ford partnering to create a purchasing system.
- Business districts, e.g. Silicon Valley, Silicon Glen

Table 15.1 continued

2. Internalization incentive advantages (i.e. to circumvent or exploit market failure)

Hierarchical advantages

- Avoidance of search and negotiating costs
- To avoid costs of moral hazard, information asymmetries and adverse selection
- To avoid costs of broken contracts and ensuing litigation

Alliance advantages

- Alliances or network-related advantages are those which prompt a 'voice' rather than 'exit' response to market failure; they also allow many of the advantages of internalisation without the inflexibility or the risk-related costs associated with it
- The growing structural integration of the world economy is requiring firms to go outside their immediate boundaries to capture the complex realities of knowledge exchange in innovation

E-commerce advantages

- Disintermediation: the ability to substitute information technology for various components of an existing vertical value chain, e.g. auto manufacturers taking orders over the Web, bypassing dealers and Chemdex.com replacing catalogues
- Re-intermediation: becoming an agent for buyers, seeking the lowest electronic price
- Outsourcing: reduced transaction costs
- Specialisation: size of core functions can grow owing to reduced coordination costs

3. Location-specific variables (these may favour home or host countries)

Hierarchical advantages

- Spatial distribution of natural and created resource endowments and markets
- Economic systems and policies of governments
- Input prices (land, labour and capital, components)

Alliance advantages

- The L advantage of alliances arises from the presence of a portfolio of immobile local complementary assets, which, when organised within the framework of alliances and networks produce a productive and stimulating environment

E-commerce advantages

- The L advantage arises from:
  (i) State-of-the-art telecommunications infrastructure
  (ii) Flat rate access
  (iii) Government adopting a minimalist market policy
  (iv) Agglomerative economies associated with financing and technology

(which may be domestic or international) and attempts to exploit first mover and increasing return advantages to preclude or inhibit market entry by competitors or potential competitors (Rayport and Sviokla, 1998). Interesting relationships are also being forged between large retailers such as K-Mart and WalMart who, initially, did not embrace the Internet, and by leading market space providers like Yahoo and AOL. In many ways, these alliances are similar to options taken by MNEs in the 1980s in an attempt to expand their territorial boundaries (Kogut, 1985). What is different today is that firms are expanding in cyberspace rather than in the marketplace, and are more likely to use the market to access resources and capabilities rather than to extend their ownership of these same resources and capabilities (Standard, 1999; Rifkin, 2000).

Ot Advantages At the same time, the organisational advantages of firms are becoming increasingly important. They are associated with the ability of firms to learn the business of electronic commerce, and how its various components can be replicated and/or coordinated in diverse industries. For example, in the late 1990s, Priceline.com developed an auction model that initially worked well for the low-cost procurement of the excess capacity of airlines (*The Economist*, 2000a). It then leveraged the information system and management practices to establish itself in the related hotel industry. However, its next move, viz. creating an auction market for grocery items, was in a product area that was far removed from travel (Priceline, 2000). Unlike the historical and functional linkages between the airline and hotel industries, this new linkage is based on the relatedness of processes (auctions) in ubiquitous marketspace (the Internet).

Another important Ot advantage is the ability to work efficiently and harmoniously with other enterprises, e.g. competitors, suppliers and customers, to innovate enterprises more productively or speedily, and/or more effectively utilise existing production and marketing opportunities. In addition to providing its proprietary online auction service functions, e.g. searchable databases, billing and collection, etc., e-Bay's value web includes electronic linkages with its customers, competitors such as Yahoo who route customers to e-Bay's site, but also provides a competing auction site, complementors such as banks that provide credit card verification and suppliers that provide software, hardware and network services (Cartwright and Oliver, 2000). The Internet dramatically increases the amount of specialisation of value-adding activity that can economically take place in creating customer services. It also reduces the importance of the physical location of any particular value activity, and blurs the corporate lines between competitors, co-providers, and strategic partners for any particular service.

(ii) Resource-based view

The resource-based theory suggests that a firm's competitive advantages are internally generated rather than being determined by the industry of which they are part (Capron and Hulland, 1999). It assumes that each firm has rare, sustainable and imperfectly imitable resources and that the firm uses these resources to obtain differential advantage (Barney, 1991). As a general theory, the resource-based view (Wernerfelt, 1984, 1995; Conner and Prahalad, 1996) holds that firms are concerned with identifying and evaluating those assets that afford them a sustainable competitive advantage. However, unique, rare and non-imitable assets identified in the current literature are those primarily based on physical resources, and the capabilities of firms to organise these effectively. In the electronic marketspace knowledge creation and innovation are replacing physical processes as value-adding activities (Cartwright and Oliver, 2000).

The competences associated with E-commerce are likely to include such intangibles as specialisation, speed, the ability to harness and deploy critical assets, and to network efficiently. In particular, the experience gained by first mover firms learning to operate in this new, information-driven and increasing returns environment is likely to become a key component of their future competitive advantages. Because there are relatively low barriers to entry, the creating of sustainable and non-imitable advantages becomes a serious problem for many start-up firms. However, a robust acquisition market for underperforming firms has developed, and when their capabilities are combined with their new owner's resources, a knowledge synergy can take place which helps to generate a new set of unique assets, e.g. Amazon.com buying PlanetAll so that Amazon can marry its customer preference data for 22.5 million customers with PlanetAll's gift suggestion software (Gimein and Lash, 1998). Also, because of low exit costs, the same team can quickly re-form around new ideas with new funding (Laseter et al., 2000). The creative applications of human capital, organisational learning and the network of relationships internal and external to the organisation are becoming the new rare and non-imitable assets of an electronic economy (Cartwright and Oliver, 2000).

(iii) Evolutionary theory

Evolutionary theory's basic proposition relates to path dependency and the accumulated competitive advantages of firms. More particularly, the theory asserts that the more efficient firms are in creating, accessing and managing these advantages, the more likely they will have the capability to engage in asset-exploiting and asset-augmenting FDI (Nelson and Winter, 1982; Cantwell, 1989, 1994; Nelson, 1991; Teece et al, 1997). Not surprisingly, IBM has leveraged its computer and network skills and GE has leveraged its procurement network to become significant E-commerce players.

There are several components of E-commerce that are evolutionary, and most particularly, the building of a network infrastructure to provide high-speed, low-cost digital connectivity to all its users or potential users, and of a customer coverage that permits this infrastructure to be efficiently and economically exploited. Firms have been electronically evolving by replacing expensive private procurement systems like EDI with the Internet. Also, firms that have implemented the Intranet usually evolve and develop gateways to allow their internal user community to access their external users via the Extranet. The Intranet/Extranet migration significantly increases communication efficiency with little incremental communication cost. Once, however, one goes beyond these substitution effects, the next stages of E-commerce are likely to increase focus on using electronic information to target customers, having customers create virtual communities and having customers use intelligent agents to deliver product information. Entrepreneur-related literature (Timmons, 1990; Sahlman, 1996) indicates that these revolutionary changes are more likely to come from smaller firms not wedded to ingrained organisational processes and staid corporate cultures. But as these new Internet business models and processes become more widely established, they will create their own trajectories and path-dependent competitive processes (Hill, 1997). Also, the Internet allows firms to better coordinate related asset-creating activities and exploit dynamic internalisation advantages.

(iv) Organisational (management-related) theories

In the early years of the present millennium, managers will be required to devise appropriate organisational structures to harness and coordinate assets, processes and routines around the world. Information technology and the Internet will dramatically facilitate this process (Prahalad and Doz, 1987; Bartlett and Ghoshal, 1989, 1993; Doz et al., 1997). We would expect the value-added attributes of firms to undergo a fundamental change, with many non-core functions being increasingly contracted out (GE, 1999). Similarly, Coase and Petzinger (1999) believes that this process will result in greater Smithian type specialisation and an enlarged size of specialist firms. When the most successful Internet start-up firms begin to earn profits, this will put increasing pressure on their competitors, in their search for both financial and human assets, to seek more leverage for their intangible assets, and to outsource their less profitable value activities. Indeed, a case has been made that, in the future, physical assets will be reduced to the status of commodities, and that the only assets that will be able to make monopolistic profits will be intellectual and relational (Evans and Wurster, 1997). This suggests that organisational management structures will need to be flexible enough to simultaneously manage both Smithian growth resulting from the division of labour specialisation and Schumpeterian growth resulting from innovation of business processes.

(v) Economic theory – follow my leader, 'tit for tat' strategy

This model based on Knickerbocker (1973) and Graham (1990) appears to be particularly relevant in an E-commerce environment. This is best illustrated by the behaviour of two large US Internet portal suppliers, Yahoo and Lycos, who appear to be chasing each other around the globe – with India being their most recent target country (Manzar, 1999). As stated previously, many of the new companies entering cyberspace are facing increasing returns on their O-specific assets (Arthur, 1996). In fact, the main reason for the high initial public offering prices for these firms is an expectation that they will be able to corner a specialised segment of the consumer market before others do so (Desmet, 2000). This mini-monopoly will then either be exploited directly by the founding firm or sold to a larger player, such as Amazon.com, who is looking to become the anchor tenant in the biggest mall on earth (Gimein and Lash, 1998). Given the current monitoring and control by national governments, monopolies do not sit well from a public policy perspective. Therefore, the best these first movers can hope for is to leverage the increasing returns of their businesses, and to share their economic rents among a few global market players.

2.3 Theories Explaining L-Specific Advantages of Firms

The L-specific advantages of the firm as they relate to the eclectic paradigm are first addressed followed by several important partial theories of the firm that relate to complementary assets, government-induced incentives and knowledge-enhancing dynamics.

(i) The eclectic paradigm L advantage

The competitive advantage of countries or regions relates to the ability of locations (regions, countries or subregions) to offer the immobile assets necessary for the mobile assets of domestic and foreign firms to be used more efficiently – both to add value to those assets and to create (through innovation or tapping into indigenous capabilities) new assets. The locational (L) component of the eclectic paradigm is complex and must be addressed along several dimensions. The first deals with the separation of goods with a high digital content from those without. While it is true that every product has to be produced and consumed at a specific point of space, the physical, intellectual and information path that it takes to get there is becoming increasingly complicated (Kobrin, 1999). For high digital content products, such as CDs and software, there has been a replacement of the physical products with 'virtual' ones. Even for goods without a high digital content, there appears to be a split developing between their tangible and intangible value chains. While, for example, the physical components of a car, e.g. the engine, transmission, etc., still have locational space, the information properties relating to these components can appear only in cyberspace. Databases that contain product-specific design information can be sited in any country that has a server on the Internet, and can be accessed from anyone with a computer and network access. What gives the information value is its connectivity to other parts of the network, rather than where it is stored. Physical access points to the information can be identified, but the value associated with the traditional process of car design is the synergy of the parts working together (Henson, 2000).

The second locational dimension depends on whether the firm is an 'E-commerce firm' or an 'Existing firm using E-commerce'. E-commerce firms are network based and, as such, experience, in most cases, increasing rather than decreasing returns when they produce additional or sell existing products in new markets. Many of these firms seek horizontal integration – e.g. Amazon entering into auctions, toys, CDs markets and geographic expansion, and Yahoo is currently (2000) seeking to develop its international operations by accessing new resources and capabilities where it makes sense, and using its leverage to gain market share where it does not (Larsen, 2000) – and, by so doing, to spread their high initial fixed costs over greater revenue streams and gain economies of scale and scope. Unlike old-economy firms, these E-commerce firms enter foreign markets instantaneously when their services are posted on the Internet. Of course, each firm can expend resources to adapt its site culturally to a particular region; however, in almost all cases, the cost of serving foreign markets is dramatically lower than those associated with the traditional product expansions of the 1990s.

Locational choice decisions by existing firms using E-commerce centre mostly on the opportunities for horizontal or vertical integration that affect the economics of FDI and trade. The Internet reduces both internal coordination (favouring FDI) and market transaction costs (favouring trade) so the relative rate of cost reduction becomes important, and this is likely to be firm and industry specific. The cultural predisposition of firms within a particular location also affects the above trade-off. For example, Toyota, which is part of the GM/Ford/Daimler Benz auction network, is choosing only to put out to bid non-essential supply chain components, while the other auto makers are including most of their essential auto components. Japanese companies in general, and Toyota specifically, have greater cultural bonds with their suppliers that militate against pure market solutions (Dunning, 1993). However, if GM/Ford/Daimler Benz experience significant cost reductions in their supply chains because they have put critical components out to auction, Toyota may have to forsake cultural bounds out of global competitive necessity.

The third locational dimension pertains to domestic government policies toward the basic telecommunication and operating legal environment. Clearly, the quality of the telecommunication infrastructure is the driver of the information revolution (Bond, 1998) and such a structure once established tends to be location bound. Low-cost, flat-rate access stimulates Internet traffic, while E-commerce knowledge-intensive centres *à la* Porter (1998) are developing first around the USA and slowly across the world. The legal environment is a key locational determinant of E-commerce growth. For example, the US model that uses advertising to subsidise much of the cost of new Internet services would not be as effective in the European Union (EU) because E-commerce consumers have the right not only to know about any personal data files kept by companies, but to see, change and delete them, and to collect damages in cases of data abuses (Standard, 2000a). Also, tax laws, as they relate to immediate realisation of personal income when stock options are granted (as opposed to when they are exercised as is the custom in the USA), could dramatically affect location choice of a firm (Sprenger, 2000).

(ii) Theories related to complementary assets

Home and host complementary and location bound assets comprising the telecommunication infrastructure of countries are key to helping E-commerce firms add to and exploit their O advantages (Applegate, 1995). Countries that have low flat-rated telephone access, such as the USA, record a much higher Internet penetration than those that have high, variably priced access. Ubiquitous, country-wide Internet connectivity and a high penetration of personal computers are also key complementary assets to the use of business-to-consumer retail E-commerce applications. With regard to specific technologies, the presence of an upgradable fibre-optic infrastructure, both within and between countries, facilitates the exploitation of high-speed transmission of video-related E-commerce. For online delivery of digital products, the contemporary communication infrastructure is the counterpart of the roads and rails of a past generation, while the information bits are equivalent to the products carried by the trucks and trains. The critical difference, however, is that the bits do not go through customs as they cross borders.

(iii) Theories related to government-induced incentives

To a large extent, national governments provide the basic rules of the game for the conduct of service transactions, though supra-national entities, e.g. WTO and the European Union are likely to play a more important role in the future. To date, most governments have allowed the existing body of commercial law – including that of intellectual property rights, to apply to electronic commerce (Arrow, 1999). This is likely to become increasingly strained, particularly in the area of taxes, privacy, pornography, uniform contracts and intellectual property rights (Kobrin, 1999). However, Peterson (1986) cautions that government intervention could be a heavy-handed solution to a relatively minor problem. Most policies set by governments are national (some are regional like the EU), but could dramatically affect the ability of indigenous firms to compete on a global basis (Kobrin, 2000). However, government policy can, on occasion, enhance the competitiveness of indigenous firms' competitiveness. For example, the establishment of European Union GSM cellular standard allowed firms in the region to lead the development of M-commerce, cellular-based Internet business.

There appears to be significant opportunity for the creation of private–public partnerships. One such example is the authorising by the Chinese government to be a key information site for companies looking to do business in China. Another example of a company working with a government agency is e-Bay consulting with the Better Business Bureau to limit fraud copyright infringements on the Internet. As commerce on the Internet grows, business will increasingly identify areas where it will seek out government assistance to help create order in the virtual E-commerce world (Lessig, 1999).

(iv) Knowledge enhancing (dynamic) theories of location

In the last decade, the attractiveness of particular locations has been increasingly explained by their ability to help investing firms upgrade their knowledge and learning experiences. Such asset-augmenting theories of FDI, as, for example, put forth by Dunning (1997), Kogut and Zander (1993), Florida (1995), Kuemmerle (1999), Porter (1994, 1998) and Wesson (1993, 2001), are particularly applicable to our understanding of the location of E-commerce-related activities. At least four areas of the USA appear to be distinguishing themselves as Internet knowledge centres, i.e. Silicon Valley, MIT media lab in Boston, New York's Silicon Alley and Microsoft's Seattle (Florida, 1998; IDA, 1999), significant E-commerce development is taking place in and about London, and the Scandinavian countries, particularly Finland, are developing M-commerce products and services.

The US entrepreneurial culture and deep venture capital market are also greatly facilitating additional investment in these areas (Dunning and Wymbs, 1999). Though physical in location, each knowledge centre's value added is composed almost entirely of intangible resources, e.g. people with ideas, organisational modalities of firms that readily respond to market needs, funding mechanisms that encourage firm growth and entrepreneur profits and universities that provide positive externalities associated with knowledge spillover. However, as real estate rents for physical space in these knowledge locations increase, many start-ups are choosing to locate in spoke communities around these knowledge centres and use their previous relationships and the Internet to serve as virtual bridges.

(v) Risk diversification theories

Risk diversification – a motive for foreign direct investment, identified and analysed by such scholars as Vernon (1973, 1983), Rugman (1979) and Kogut (1985) – appears to be increasing on a strategic product basis, but decreasing on a locational basis. Firms are now hedging between electronic and bricks-and-mortar applications, e.g. the *New York Times* and the *Wall Street Journal* have electronic editions, Merrill Lynch launched Internet trading, while Barnes and Noble has an online book-selling operation (Henry, 1999). Access to these electronic applications requires only a phone line and a computer, and can occur 24 hours a day, 7 days a week and 365 days a year on a global basis. Also, the recent market shake-out has permitted established firms to execute a relatively low-cost product diversification strategy by buying assets of failing dot coms for cents on the dollar. With regard to physical location, the new knowledge economy is unlike the old economy because it is based on intangible assets that are mobile, rather than tangible assets that are fixed. With information being stored in many places throughout networks, there is less need to diversify a firm's assets geographically to reduce transaction, translation and asset exposure risk.

2.4 Theories Explaining I-Specific Advantages of Firms

The I-specific advantages of the firm as they relate to the eclectic paradigm are first addressed followed by several important partial theories of the firm.

(i) The eclectic paradigm I advantage

With regard to internalisation (I) theory, the impact of E-commerce is likely to have the greatest short-term effects by reducing the transaction and coordinating costs of economic activity, particularly in the business sector. In the past, large businesses have spent billions of dollars using private Electronic Data Interchange (EDI) networks to lower transaction costs (Henry, 1999). Today, the Internet can be used to construct EDI-like networks at a fraction of the price, and in so doing, opens up these economies to virtually all business customers. Increasing access to markets dramatically increases competition, lowers prices and enhances innovation. This is particularly true where producers have been able to set up auctions to induce competitors in real time to bid against one another (Turban, 2000). The range of projects is quite broad, and embraces everything from municipal bond underwriting to the sale of aircraft and vehicle parts to the creation and supply of electronic money (Cohen, 2000).

At this point, it may be instructive to look at how the Internet has changed the main drivers of transaction cost economics as, for example, identified by Buckley and Casson (1976, 1985); Rugman (1981); Hennart (1982); Williamson (1985). Simply stated, transaction cost economics asserts that the firm is an avoider of market costs that result from exchange. It will internalise the markets for those intermediate products which it perceives will derive greater benefit from this modality than from an arm's-length transaction. The three most often cited reasons for internalisation are information asymmetry, bounded rationality and asset specificity. Information asymmetry is predicated on the fact that one of the parties in any transaction lacks information relative to the other. Clearly the Internet network dramatically increases the amount of information available to all parties for informed market decisions. Bounded rationality deals with a human inability to process all information in making a decision. When used correctly, the Internet permits relevant information to be obtained, distilled and transferred in a timely fashion. As cited above, the creation of auctions is a market solution to the bounded rationality problem. Asset specificity pertains to having to commit a large sum of capital to produce a specialised product. To the extent that the Internet permits increased specialisation of activities along the value chain, it may help reduce asset specificity required for each component. In fact, much of the value-adding processes associated even with the production of physical products is not capital intensive, e.g. marketing, R&D, interfirm coordination. For many leading firms in industries, the capital intensive components have been outsourced, e.g. auto parts, PC production, sneakers, etc.

On the other hand, asset specificity might increase if firms focused more on their core competences, and these were interrelated with those of other firms. However, the assets that drive these core competences are mostly intangible (people and relational) resources. Because these assets are more mobile than physical assets, they are less likely to cause asset specificity problems.

Simultaneously, information technology is reducing the coordinating costs within and between organisations, thereby permitting much larger firms to evolve. In consequence, firms using E-commerce tend to be more focused on their core competences, and outsource a higher proportion of their non-core activities. There appears to be a fundamental reordering of firms using the Internet world, based on whether market-specific transaction costs are decreasing as fast as firm-specific coordination benefits are increasing.

(ii) Orthodox internalisation theory

Orthodox internalisation theory, which is essentially concerned with maximising the economic rent of a *given* set of O-specific advantages, explains why firms coordinate these advantages with the L advantages of countries through internal fiat rather than using external markets (Buckley and Casson, 1976; Hennart, 1982, 1989; Anderson and Gatignon, 1986; Caves, 1996). We now consider a number of issues arising from E-commerce in question form, which we aver, in question form, orthodox internalisation theory needs to address.

- *What are the differences between E-commerce and non-E-commerce, and how do they affect the propensity of firms to internalise the cross-border market for Internet-related services?*

The willingness and ability of firms to internalise markets depends on the type of intermediate products and end products being supplied. In supplying products directly to the final consumer, companies like Amazon.com or Priceline.com find that there is a tremendous potential to expand horizontally and internalise heretofore different markets (Taylor, 1999). This they do, for example, by creating a customer database, developing a business model or recipe, and attempting to replicate this model in as many markets as are appropriate. Priceline.com gets bids on airline tickets as well as groceries while Amazon.com has expanded into toys, auctions and CDs (Watson et al. 1998).

The business-to-business (B2B) market is different, in that it affords firms an ability to internalise their operations more efficiently by use of such means as global e-mail, e-mail attachments, CAD, and intranets (IBM, 1999). However, many of these communication tools also increase the firm's ability to outsource business functions and better control them (Kotabe et al., 1998), resulting in immediate enhanced bottom line financial performance (Hunt, 1997).

- *What are electronic market failures?*

The reasons why traditional markets fail are well identified in the literature, and we have already suggested above that electronic markets may reduce some of these failures. At the same time, electronic markets generate their own set of imperfections, namely: (1) market failures incurred by consumers when shopping on the Internet; and (2) market failures incurred by firms when selling or purchasing skills and resources.

Margherion (1998) has identified six of these consumer failures as they relate respectively to issues of security, privacy, indecency, intellectual property, contracts and consumer protection. The first three failures deal with the medium itself and the last three with its potential results. Security, e.g. with respect to piracy, hacking, etc., is often quoted as the number one impediment limiting E-commerce (Pitt et al., 1999). To mitigate this problem, credit card companies have created industry standards that use sophisticated algorithms to encrypt and decrypt credit card numbers. The privacy and indecency issues are already present in communication technologies. However, these are dramatically escalated, since, with a keystroke, the Internet permits the access of indecent material (Henry, 1999). Intellectual property rights, contracts and consumer protection directly relate to the global dimension of the Internet media and open up new challenges with respect to the boundaries and content of both national and international law. These uncertainties create impediments to what is purported to be a frictionless process. The last item also pertains to the application of law to firms attempting to extract monopolistic profits in global marketspace (Kobrin, 1999). Many of the above actions relate to firms working with institutions to circumvent market imperfections so that they may more fully recover returns from their ownership advantages/capabilities.

The market for the purchase of skills and resources by firms has greater imperfections in an electronic market than in a physical one. As stated previously, the key value-adding resources in an electronic world are intangible resources that, by their very nature, are hard to define and thus make informed assessments of value difficult. The technology explosion associated with the Internet has precluded firms from internally pursuing many good opportunities. In many instances, firms have used alliances as knowledge extensions to keep their options open in new emerging areas. Alliances are also being used as a means to get first-hand information and make better decisions on acquisitions. However, the increased acquisition of start-up firms by established players, in particular new foreign markets entering the e-commerce area, e.g. AOL's acquisitions of access providers in Europe, could lead to further market failures mainly related to limited competition. Even the sharing of information by alliance partners could lead to collusive behaviour, e.g. government agencies in the USA are currently evaluating the airlines' planned response to Priceline.com and the auto parts alliance.

- *Can we distinguish between static and dynamic electronic and other kinds of market failures?*

Traditional endemic market failures relate mainly to the presence of static transaction costs, such as those relating to opportunism, bounded rationality, asymmetry of information, externalities and the vertical integration of markets (Buckley and Casson, 1976, 1985; Hennart, 1982, 1989; Williamson, 1985; Peterson, 1986). Clearly, the Internet, through its ability to access information, can substantially reduce some of these imperfections. However, in a dynamic, rapidly changing environment this increases the complexity of management choices and leads to a series of innovation-related market failures (OECD, 1999). Information on the Internet also exhibits the characteristics of a public good, in the sense that one person's consumption of a particular product does not limit that of another. As stated previously, the increasing returns component of the Internet leads to significant economies of scale for the first mover (Arthur, 1996). The Internet also allows firms to better coordinate related asset-creating activities and exploit dynamic internalisation advantages.

(iii) Market power/efficiency/knowledge acquisition theories

The acquisition or access to all kinds of information (Wesson, 1993; Kogut and Zander, 1993) is appearing as a major rationale for engaging in cross-border E-commerce (Margherion, 1998): e-Bay's purchase of the Butterfield & Butterfield's high-end auction operations in Germany and Cisco Systems, the largest Internet switch manufacturer, using acquisitions as its main R&D vehicle are two such instances (Wymbs, 2000b; Rabinovitz et al., 2000). Examples of acquisitions, the sole purpose of which is to reduce competition and increase market power, include Proflowers.com acquiring Flowerfarm.com, and luxury-good retailer Ashford.com snapping up Jasmin.com, a perfume site (Rabinovitz et al., 2000). Amazon and e-Bay expressed acquisition strategy targets investment in companies that will spread their operating efficiency and franchise in new horizontal categories and in multiple regions throughout the world (Rabinovitz et al., 2000). Invariably, acquisitions increase firm revenues, a key financial metric in the evaluation of dot com companies, and also provide a way of acquiring unique resource bundles (Capron and Hulland, 1999; Rabinovitz et al., 2000).

(iv) Real options theory

As firms create innovative strategies and new information-centric business models in an increasingly uncertain world, they are, in effect, developing a portfolio of real options (Kogut and Kulatilaka, 1994). These learning options are similar to financial options and, as such, increase in value with rising uncertainty (Copeland and Keenan, 1998). This partially explains the high market capitalisation of Web-based service firms, and the vast number of start-up service firms. It also explicates why established service firms are creating Web-based spin-offs, outsourcing service functions and engaging in alliances among service firms. Consistent with real options theories, Web-based alliances are different from traditional ones in four main ways. First, they involve a much larger and varied group of companies, e.g. e-Bays value web includes over six different companies that vary from credit card processing to a competitive auction site referring customers to e-Bay; second, they rely on more informal business relationships, e.g. each part of the value web provides a unique, coordinated service integrated through information rather than ownership; third, they require leadership by one or two companies to define standards for all Web members and create incentives that attract more companies to it (OECD, 1998); and fourth, their market value is based on creating new marketspace rather than on models predicting NPV returns (Kim and Mauborgne, 1999). However, fundamental to these alliances and real options is a desire to move from a marketspace of diminishing returns to one of increasing returns.

To summarise the points made in the previous paragraphs, Table 15.1 identifies some of the modifications to the OLI configuration depicting IB activity that E-commerce requires to be made.

We now turn to examine how some of the context-specific ingredients of IB theories may need to be modified to incorporate the characteristics of E-commerce.

3. E-COMMERCE AND CONTEXT-SPECIFIC VARIABLES

The eclectic paradigm identifies three sets of contextual variables likely to affect the extent, pattern and form of MNE activity. These are: (a) the types of activities engaged in by the firms; (b) the countries or regions of origin of investing firms; and (c) certain characteristics specific to individual firms – other than their nationality of ownership – e.g. their size, products and innovative strategies. Let us consider each of these in turn in so far as they may help us explain the extent to which the emergence of E-commerce requires modification to existing theories.

3.1 Activity-Specific Factors

Before we address the effect of E-commerce on business activity, it is instructive to set the context of analysis by providing the overall size of the emerging Internet economy. In June 1999, a University of Texas project made a first attempt to quantify the Internet-related sector of the US economy (Thompson, 1999a). The results of the study suggest that the US Internet economy generated $301 billion in revenues and employed 1.2 million people in 1998. Working with the International Data Corporation, the University of Texas forecasted the worldwide Internet economy to be $1.8 trillion in 2003 (Thompson, 1999b). A Commerce Department study put the Internet economy at 8 percent of the US 1999 gross domestic product (GDP) for 1999, while a more conservative estimate by Goldman Sachs, which, *inter alia*, takes the view that a $30 book sold on Amazon.com should not count as an Internet economy transaction, put the Internet economy at 5 percent of GDP (Ledbetter, 1999). A Boston Consulting group study found 1998 B2B E-commerce transactions amounting to $671 billion, and predicts it will grow to over $2 trillion in 2003 (Paperfree, 2000). The above numbers provide a range of estimates; however, it is clear that E-commerce spending is large today (3–8 percent of the US GDP) and will likely double in percentage terms by 2003.

Let us now turn to examine some of the likely effects of the Internet on the activities of MNEs, on potential MNEs; within traditional industries and on E-commerce providers.

(i) Traditional – and likely minor impact

Traditional goods and services industries that have a relatively simple customer interface and little information and/or cultural asymmetry between buyers and sellers are likely to be the least affected by E-commerce. At McDonald's, for example, although much of the ordering function can be automated, the customer is still getting a homogeneous product (a hamburger) with a standard customer interface (a salesperson). Of course, McDonald's back office processes associated with physical commodity procedures and the supply function will use intranets and extranets (OECD, 1998). A similar minor impact is likely to be observed initially at the customer–store interface for purchasing building supplies at a store like Home Depot; however, even here, E-commerce models associated with grocery purchases are likely to be implemented.

E-commerce is likely to remain excluded from the actual manufacturing, assembling and delivery of most goods, e.g. autos ($350 bn), energy ($230 bn), but will play a key support role (Thompson, 1999b). However, if these vertically integrated industries choose to outsource key business segments, e.g. manufacturing, then the Internet could play an increased coordinating function. There will likely be slower Internet penetration of efficiency-enhancing measures in the public sector, e.g. primary and secondary education, government agencies, etc. than in the private sector. With regard to horizontally integrated activities, the more culture prone or idiosyncratic an activity is, i.e. language or contact dependent, the less likely that an international E-commerce solution will be provided (Knight, 1999).

(ii) Traditional – and likely major impact

The information content, context and preferred delivery modality of traditional products and services determine, in a large part, how the Internet affects them. This is discussed first, followed by an assessment of the effect Internet will have on the overall category.

Those industries most likely to be affected by information content are those which supply products requiring extensive buyer–seller information exchange, e.g. the sound of a CD that is trailed on Amazon.com; those which require a large number of separate transactions, e.g. Detroit's Big Three auto makers creating an auction supplier network to process $240 billion in annual purchases and cut ordering processing fees by 90 percent (Dalton, 2000); and those that require the production and consumption of the product simultaneously, e.g. reading the online version of the *Wall Street Journal* (OECD, 1999). One unique feature of E-commerce information gathering is that it may occur temporally and/or be geographically separate from the actual business transaction. Separately, consumers may research an automobile cost and features on AutoByTel.com, but purchase it from a dealer a week later.

The industries where the information context is sufficient for the customer to make a purchase decision, e.g. the size, colour and price of a dress from an online vendor like Lands End, are most affected. When one source of information must be combined with other information, e.g. a doctor's signature for ordering from Drugstore.com, the impact is dramatically reduced (Hof and McWilliams, 1998).

The last part of the information variable is the infrastructure that affects the modality of information delivery, i.e. electronically, print, in person. Goods and services industries that involve timely, stand-alone, electronic information are most likely to be replaced by Internet services (Hamel and Sampler, 1998), e.g. stock quotations (E-Trade), speciality chemical catalogues (Chemdex.com), parts ordering on the CommerceOne site being constructed for the auto industry. Dell and Cisco Systems are taking their ordering systems and most of their customer service functions online while FedEx focuses only on the customer service tracking component online.

It is estimated by Thompson (1999) that these traditional goods and services industries which made up approximately 95 percent of the US economy in the late 1990s are likely to account for 86–90 percent of the economy in 2003. The vast majority of the $1.5 trillion Internet spending in 2003 will remain between businesses for traditional cost saving (supply chain management) and revenue targeting applications (Lawrence, 2000). In fact, the International Data Corporation predicts that the percentage of B2B will increase from 72 percent in 1999 to over 86 percent in 2003 of total Internet spending (Lawrence, 2000).

(iii) E-commerce providers

More than 200 Internet firms went public in 1999 and in so doing raised about $20 billion (Ledbetter, 2000). The former number was more than double that which went public in the previous four years. Clearly, any product, or function of a product that can be delivered digitally (newspapers, books, CDs, software) or whose major processes can be linked digitally is a candidate to become an E-commerce industry. Some such deliveries will have to wait for infrastructural improvements, such as video on demand and expanded wireless, but it is expected that advances in high-speed infrastructure technology will make them viable in the very near future. For example, an exciting new range of products about to emerge is that of Internet home appliances, e.g. refrigerators electronically monitoring the use of milk and reordering its bar code when supplies are low via a wireless link to the store.

Access companies are branching out into content, such as the AOL merger with Time-Warner, and portal companies are increasing their customer base, such as Yahoo possibly merging with e-Bay (Lewis, 2000). E-commerce-related industries will be created that redefine customer information collection and use. As more transactions occur on the Internet, companies such as BroadVision and DoubleClick are assembling increasingly sophisticated customer profiles, and using artificial intelligence algorithms to target customers for advertising. To mitigate public concern and to preclude government solutions to privacy market failure, many data collection companies are supporting industry standards with respect to the information they will collect on Internet customers (Gork, 2000).

Another area where E-commerce is likely to excel is the creation of online auctions. Indeed, as *The Economist* (London) has recently observed, the Internet provides a perfect medium for aggregating buyers and sellers from all around the world (*The Economist*, 2000c). This application can be both consumer-to-consumer (e-Bay) and business-to-business (the Big Three auto parts network). Its basic property is that it creates an efficient market by congregating informed buyers and sellers in cyberspace rather than at a specific physical location. The increased number of participants makes the auctions more efficient, while the auction companies attempt to establish rules of conduct.

(iv) Cross-industry effect

More generally, the advent of E-commerce is causing us to question the appropriability of the industry as a unit of analysis. A reconfigured specialisation of Internet firms is creating a whole new set of strategic business groups (SBGs), e.g. security on the net, customer Internet tracking, shopping agents (services that electronically compare prices for consumers), routers (fast packet switches), etc. The boundaries of existing industries are being reconfigured. The US automobile industry, for example, which was previously vertically integrated, has now evolved an active auction market for parts procurement, while auto consumers are accessing information about product, prices and dealers cost on the Internet (and are gaining an advantage in price negotiations). Priceline.com is de-branding the hotel and airline sectors by allowing customers to bid for lodging and air transport, but not permitting them to question or specify a provider. Amazon.com and Chemdex.com are disintermediating the retail book distribution and chemical catalogue businesses, etc. (OECD, 1999). Customer interface processes – Web portals – have the potential to replace product groupings as a more meaningful way of segmenting businesses (Malone and Laubacher, 1998). Amazon.com's business model is based on competing for customers across a broad set of unrelated products rather than on the traditional industry model which started with a particular product class and becomes more focused until a specific product is identified for purchase (*The Economist*, 2000b).

3.2 Country- or Region-Specific Factors

There is little doubt that the Internet reduces spatially related transaction costs and makes international market transactions more efficient. Increased trade is likely to bring new pressures on hierarchical and alliance modalities, particularly by forcing them to innovate and become more efficient. However, in support of increases in alliances and FDI, Hart (1996) found that the Internet has become an effective medium for bringing together people around the world as business partners – people who probably would otherwise never meet. It is likely that in most industries all three (trade, FDI, alliances) will coexist;

however, one will probably dominate, based on the unique characteristics of the industry in question, and of its locational needs.

The assessment of trade, FDI, and alliance trade-offs using a market failure lens provides additional insights. As product markets become more imperfect, market failure due to poor information is increased. Production will be increasingly outsourced and driven to areas of low factor costs, thereby increasing trade. However, because of the increased time pressure associated with the Internet economy, existing long-distance trade patterns, for example, between the USA and Southeast Asia for computer parts, may be shortened to between the USA and Mexico. FDI either through acquisition or greenfield will both stimulate and mitigate market failures. E-commerce ventures by US firms in foreign countries associated with vertical integration will either expand their supply chain or retailing will be likely to have positive externalities on local firm E-commerce activities owing to spillover effects.

On a country-specific basis, the dominant home country for E-commerce has been, and will probably remain in the near future, the USA. In 1999, it accounted for two-thirds of the world market (Lawrence, 2000). *Inter alia*, the USA's entrepreneurial climate, *laissez-faire* government policy, low and flat-rated telecommunication access structure, high-quality tech chip and communication research, extensive PC penetration and extensive venture-capital market have all facilitated the E-commerce explosion (OECD, 1999). The spectacular advances in telecommunication technology have been a major factor leading to increases in US productivity and stock prices which have fuelled further growth in E-commerce (Henry, 1999). However, by 2003 the US E-commerce share is projected by International Data Corporation to decrease to 54 percent, with Western Europe increasing 16 percentage points to 33 percent and Asia accounting for the remaining 14 per cent (Lawrence, 2000). The major reasons for the projected percentage decline include: (i) European venture capitalists are finally realising that they need to get up to speed on the Web; (ii) the Finns, who pioneered the mobile phone revolution, are now way ahead in the next trend, namely, wireless Web; (iii) the European Union is telling US companies not to collect personal data via the Internet on its people; (iv) E-commerce and online advertising are ripe to bloom in China and Japan; (v) Spain's largest Internet provider has introduced a free service in Brazil, and this will dramatically change the country's E-commerce landscape (Standard, 2000b).

3.3 Firm-Specific Factors

We shall discuss two main groups of factors specific to influencing individual firms. The first are those identified by most theories embodied in the eclectic paradigm which treat the firm as a stand-alone entity. The second are those which view a firm's OLI configuration as being affected by the network functions and complexities of the networks in which it is involved; then it harnesses and consolidates network advantages with its own core competences.

(i) The firm as a stand-alone entity

Received economic and managerial theories of IB activity[2] view the firm as a seeker after natural resources, markets, efficiency and strategic assets.

Resource-seeking investment relates to Internet activities that are, for the most part, created rather than natural and intangible rather than tangible. With the exception of low-wage programmers in India, resource-seeking investment from Internet specialist firms will focus on acquiring marketing expertise in culturally diverse countries, through alliances and joint ventures, e.g. Lycos and AOL in India (Manzar, 1999; Rabinovitz et al., 2000). For firms wishing to save operating costs, the Internet permits a much tighter linking of manufacturers' supply chains, thereby facilitating foreign subcontracting FDI, e.g. US clothing manufacturers in Vietnam (Baxter et al., 1998). One can make a case for the reduction of Internet-related resource-seeking FDI by assuming that firms can more easily affect customer-buying behaviour in foreign nations from their home servers. If so, this may eliminate the need for a local partner who is familiar with the local market. Moreover, the Internet is likely to have a homogenising effect across countries that also would reduce the need for a local partner (Wymbs, 1997).

Market-seeking FDI by Internet companies is likely to favour a location that offers agglomerative economies, e.g. US information centres, like Silicon Valley, New York and Boston. These areas have entrepreneurs who have built billion-dollar businesses and are seeking to recycle themselves. In fact, Jim Clark of Silicon Valley has already built three billion-dollar businesses, namely, Silicon Graphic, Netscape and Healtheon (Lewis, 1999). Also, the US capital market is well schooled in funding E-commerce start-ups, which is not the case around the world. With regard to firms using E-commerce, the move online by Asian suppliers has profound implications for the way business is conducted worldwide: developing Asia is already the home to a high percentage of the world's manufacturing capacity and increased virtual links with the West will benefit Asian exporters, e.g. the Web allows the obscure computer peripherals manufacturer in Taipei to catch the eye of a large computer manufacturer in Texas (Jacob, 2000).

Efficiency-seeking investment, driven by Smithian effects, has gravitated to Silicon Valley, London, Finland, New York and Boston (Florida, 1995, 1998). However, the distributed properties of the Internet will result in other development centres springing up in possibly Singapore and Hong Kong that are both rapidly becoming knowledge-intensive coordination and management centres for Southeast Asian business (Enright, 2000). Cultures' and governments' telecommunication policies may stimulate or retard efficient production centres forming in continental Europe and Japan. For example, historically, American regulators have viewed the telephone as a basic necessity and developed pricing structures to encourage its maximum penetration. In most other countries, the telephone was been provided by a state enterprise which viewed it more as a luxury good, and priced access on a high, usage-sensitive (per minute) basis. However, in March 2000, AltaVista and NTL began flat-rate access in the UK and this is likely to encourage E-commerce usage there. Interestingly, the exact opposite is true for the cellular telephone service, where American regulators treated it as a luxury, and, until recently, permitted a duopoly market structure that resulted in relatively high prices (Aufderheide, 1999). By contrast, cellular service, particular in Europe and Japan, has been looked at as a cost-effective alternative to high-priced traditional service. Not surprisingly, because most computers today are connected via traditional telephone and cable service, the USA has developed a tremendous lead in Internet usage and applications. However, the Europeans, particularly the Scandinavian countries, and Japan are viewed as the leaders in wireless applications connecting to the Internet.

Strategic asset-seeking investment designed to protect or augment firm-specific advantages is currently being undertaken by foreign E-commerce firms investing in the USA to tap into its established information knowledge nodes like Silicon Valley and centres of funding like New York City. For example in March 1999, the Singapore AMO, a competitor of CommerceOne, moved its headquarters to Silicon Valley. AMO's chairman, T.K. Wong, said, 'This (Silicon Valley) is where the action is' (Hamilton, 2000). If you're not in Silicon Valley, you are playing a defensive strategy – waiting in Asia for some American company to come and acquire you. In the short term, the majority of the strategic asset-augmenting investment will take place primarily in two areas. The first one is leading edge technology firms, e.g. Cisco Systems, who due to their high market capitalisations, are able to buy high-quality R&D in the market through acquisition rather than develop it themselves. The second area involves E-commerce businesses that are looking to expand into new markets. As European and Asian E-commerce start-ups emerge, US cash-rich firms will actively seek to acquire them. Clearly, the increasing returns nature of the network-centric business encourages acquisitions, reducing the number of competitors and increasing first mover advantage (Rayport and Sviokla, 1998).

(ii) The firm as part of a network of interrelated activities

E-commerce, along with globalisation and the emergence of knowledge-based and alliance capitalism, is requiring scholars to reappraise their concept of the firm as a stand-alone entity. In particular the Internet, as its very name implies, is not only associated with more and deeper networking activities – both of a horizontal and vertical kind – but is upgrading the firm-specific advantages arising from such extra-firm linkages.[3] E-commerce affords the participating firms greater, more efficient, speedier and more cost-effective access to resources and customers and a different set of ownership, location and organisational capabilities than non-members. Hamel (1999) views networks to be driving the new techno-economic business paradigm and believes that a firm's strategy, i.e. response to E-commerce, is its key to survival. Strategy is particularly important because the network-centric Internet world is transforming many previous business strengths, such as broad market coverage and significant bricks-and-mortar assets into liabilities. It is forcing traditional firms to evaluate how new kinds of information and new modes of delivery will affect their businesses and whether they need to create Internet-specific responses. If they do, then they have to manage the very difficult problems of cannibalisation and channel conflict between two worlds (*The Economist*, 2000d).

This emerging paradigm for certain electronic products, e.g. news, information, CDs, software, is likely to substantially remove distance and geographic barriers from the equation. From a strategic perspective, electronic products take on the characteristics of a global product because they can be produced in one location and distributed around the world. However, from a marketing perspective, these products can be tailored to the needs of a particular country or a particular region and, as a result, have the look and feel of a multi-domestic product. In effect, the Internet permits a company to exploit previously untapped opportunities of wide reach (size of audience), great richness (customised products) and strong affiliation (personalised responses to customers' interests) (Evans and Wurster, 1998).

A second strategic implication of the network-centric Internet world is that it separates the information value chain from the production value chain. The electronic linking of supply chain production processes electronically has been going on for a while (KPMG, 1999). What appears to be new is the emergence of information businesses that collect, package and sell information on consumers' buying behaviour and habits and the emergence of agents acting on behalf of consumer groups. The former allow firms to better target customers and to create a one-to-one marketing experience, while the latter offer consumers value-added services (*The Economist*, 2000a).

More specifically, the application of the core competence of firms has to be segmented by the following four applications (*The Economist*, 2000c): business-to-business (B2B); business-to-consumer (B2C); consumer-to-consumer (C2C); and consumer-to-business (C2B). For B2B, large firms that can dictate terms to suppliers are likely to experience the greatest benefits of price reductions associated with E-commerce. For example, GE via their transaction-processing network (TPN), GM, and Ford have extracted billions of dollars of cost savings from their suppliers (Margherion, 1998).

With regard to B2C, the most impressive innovations are coming *from smaller firms* that do not have existing customer interface baggage. They are using information technology to attack separate pieces of the value chain. Each new approach to serving customers better or to making a distribution process more cost effective is brought to the well-established venture-capital market for review. Each time one of these companies obtains funding, it represents an attack on an inefficient dimension of an existing company's value chain. Few established firms have created procedures to beat back or even neutralise these aggressive start-ups.

C2C activity is associated with the proliferation of auctions such as e-Bay, while the C2B is related to the power of the Internet to drive transactions the other way around, i.e. would-be passengers bidding for airline tickets on Priceline.com (*The Economist*, 2000c).

4. CONCLUSIONS AND FUTURE RESEARCH

This chapter has attempted to reorient the received theories and the eclectic paradigm of IB activity to take account of the growth of E-commerce. Though all the dimensions are not fully fleshed out, we believe that the chapter provides a foundation to begin debate and assessment of defensible trajectories for the IB field in an information-centric world.

International business theories that seek to address the competitive advantages of MNEs appear to be applicable. The criteria of 'what a core competence is' will change, e.g. maintaining buying profiles and preferences on 22.5 million customers like Amazon.com, but the necessity of core competences to achieve and advance sustainable competitive advantages is still applicable. Internalisation to increase efficiency and reduce related transaction cost appears valid in a network-centric world, e.g. Nike, WalMart and the auto companies are using the Internet to seek out and work with suppliers (inter alia the Internet aids the exchange of data regarding design, development, specification). Even in a virtual world, location still matters. In fact, the Internet makes it all the more important for governments – local and national – to ensure their countries have (or can provide) all the necessary Internet infrastructure (robust telecommunication networks and commerce-friendly legal, financial and tax environments) to attract and retain 'E-commerce firms' and 'firms using E-commerce'. Though the Internet is labelled as a distance-insensitive medium and can efficiently create links among firms around the world, it is somewhat ironic that E-commerce firms are concentrated in relatively small areas, e.g. Silicon Alley and Silicon Valley, that can clearly be traced to computer, communication and media knowledge centres of the mid-1990s.

We believe that the Internet has, and will continue to provide, greater access to information and to opportunities to build relational assets both within and between firms. Exploring the many dimensions of how relational networks associated with OLI advantages will change the competitive dynamics among firms appears to be fertile ground for future research.

NOTES

1. For example, see Dunning (1988, 1995, 1998). For a recent exposition of the contents of the paradigm, and how it relates to a number of mainstream theories of international business, see Dunning (2000, 2001).
2. As reviewed by Dunning (2000).
3. Some of these are described in recent papers by Chen (2000) and Chen and Chen (1998).
4. Table adapted from Table 1 (Dunning, 1995) 'Reappraising the Eclectic Paradigm in an Age of Alliance Capitalism'.

REFERENCES

Anderson, E. and Gatignon, H. (1986), 'Modes of Foreign Entry: Transaction Costs and Propositions', *Journal of International Business Studies*, **17**, 1–26.

Applegate, L. (1995), 'Electronic Commerce: Trends and Opportunity', *Harvard Business School*, Case No. 9–196–006, October 6.

Arrow, K. (1999), 'Amici Curiae Brief', *DOJ vs. Microsoft Case*.

Arthur, W. (1996), 'Increasing returns in the new world of business', *Harvard Business Review*, available online at: <http://www.hbsp.harvard.edu/products/hbr/julang96/96401.html>.

Aufderheide, P. (1999), *Communication Policy and the Public Interest*, New York: The Guilford Press.

Bain, J.S. (1956), *Barriers to New Competition*, Cambridge, MA: Harvard University Press.

Barney, J.B. (1991), 'Firm Resources and Sustained Competitive Advantage', *Journal of Management*, **17**, 99–120.

Bartlett, C.A. and Ghoshal, S. (1989), *Managing Across Borders: the Transnational Solution*, Boston, MA: Harvard Business School Press.

Bartlett, C.A. and Ghoshal, S. (1993), 'Beyond the M-Form: Towards a Managerial Theory of the Firm', *Strategic Management Journal*, **14**(1).

Baxter, A., Koudal, P. and Mathur, S. (1998), *Global Report: 1998 Vision in Manufacturing*, Survey by Deloitte & Touche and Deloitte Consulting, New York.

Beck, J., Morrison, A. and Bouquet, C. (2000), *Netchising: The Next Global Wave. eCommerce and Global Business Forum*, Santa Cruz, (mimeo).

Beinhocker, Eric (1997), 'Strategy in Chaos', *McKinsey Quarterly*, **1**, 24–39.

Bernstein, P. (1998), 'Are Networks Driving the New Economy?', *Harvard Business Review*, November–December, Reprint 98602.

Boddewyn, J.J. and Iyer, G. (1999), 'International Business Research: Beyond Déjà Vu', *International Management Review*, **39**, 161–84.

Bond, James (1998), 'The divers of the information revolution – cost, computing power and convergence', *Private Sector*, Washington, DC: World Bank, pp. 27–30.
Buckley, P.J. and Casson, M.C. (1976), *The Future of the Multinational Enterprise*, London: Macmillan.
Buckley, P.J. and Casson, M.C. (1985), *The Economic Theory of the Multinational Enterprise*, London: Macmillan.
Buckley, P.J. and Casson, M.C. (1998), 'Models of Multinational Enterprises', *Journal of International Business Studies*, **29**(1), 25–44.
Cantwell, J.A. (1989), *Technological Innovation and Multinational Corporations*. Oxford: Basil Blackwell.
Cantwell, J.A. (ed.) (1994), *Transnational Corporations and Innovatory Activities, United Nations Library on Transnational Corporations*, Vol. 17, London: Routledge.
Capron, L. and Hulland, J. (1999), 'Redeployment of Brands, Sales Forces and General Market Management Expense Following Horizontal Acquisitions: A Resource-Based View', *Journal of Marketing*, **63**(2) 41–54.
Cartwright, S. and Oliver, R. (2000), 'Untangling the Value Web', *Journal of Business Strategy*, 22–27.
Caves, R.E. (1971), 'Industrial Corporations: The Industrial Economics of Foreign Investment', *Economica*, **38**, 1–27.
Caves, R.E. (1974), 'Causes of Direct Investment: Foreign Firms' Shares in Canadian and United Kingdom Manufacturing Industries', *Review of Economics and Statistics*, August, **56**, 272–93.
Caves, R.E. (1982, 1996), *Multinational Firms and Economic Analysis* (1st and 2nd edns), Cambridge: Cambridge University Press.
Chen, T.J. (2000), *Network Resources for Internalization. The Case of Taiwan's Electronics Firms*, Taipai: National Taiwan University.
Chen, H. and Chen, T.J. (1998), 'Network linkages and location choice in foreign direct investment', *Journal of International Business Studies*, **29**, 445–69.
Coase, R. and Petzinger,T, Jr (1999), 'Talking about Tomorrow', *Wall Street Journal*, 31 December, 36.
Cohen, B. (2000), 'Marketing Money: Currency Policy in the Globalized World', in A. Prakash and J. Hart (eds), *Coping with Globalization*, London and New York: Routledge, pp. 173–98.
Conner, K. (1991), 'A Historical Comparison of Resource-Based Theory and Five Schools of Thought Within Industrial Organization Economies. Do We Have a New Theory of the Firm?', *Journal of Management*, **17**, 121–54.
Conner, K.R. and Prahalad, C.K. (1996), 'A Resource Based Theory of the Firm Knowledge Versus Opportunism', *Organizational Science*, **5**, 477–501.
Copeland, T.E. and Keenan, P.T. (1998), 'Making Real Options', *The McKinsey Quarterly*, **3**, 128–41.
Dalton, G. (2000), 'The Suppliers' Demand', *The Standard*, March, 6.
Denton, N. (1997), 'Drive to plug the gap', *Financial Times*, February 3, 19.
Desmet, D., Francis, T, Hu, A. and Koller, T. (2000), 'Valuing Dot-coms', *McKinsey Quarterly*, **1**.
Dicken, P. (1998), *Global Shift*, London: Guilford Press.
Doz, Y.L., Asakawa, K., Santos, J.F.P. and Williamson, P.J. (1997), 'The Metanational Corporation, Fontainebleau, France', *INSEAD Working Paper*, **60**, 32.
DoubleClick (2000), <www.DoubleClick.net.> October 25.

Dunning, J.H. (1977), 'Trade, Location of Economic Activity and the MNE: a Search for an Eclectic Approach', in B. Ohlin, P. Hesselborn and P. Wijkman (eds), *The International Allocation of Economic Activity*, London: Macmillan, pp. 395–415.
Dunning, J.H. (1988), *Explaining International Production*, London: Unwin Hyman.
Dunning, J.H. (1993), *Multinational Enterprises and the Global Economy*, Wokingham, Berkshire: Addison Wesley.
Dunning, J.H. (1995), 'Reappraising the Eclectic Paradigm in the Age of Alliance Capitalism', *Journal of International Business Studies*, **26**, 461–91.
Dunning, J.H. (1998), 'Location and the Multinational Enterprise: a Neglected Factor', *Journal of International Business Studies*, **29**(1), 45–66.
Dunning, J.H. (2000), 'The Eclectic Paradigm as an Envelope for Economic and Business Theories of International Business Activity', *International Business Review*, **9**, 163–90.
Dunning, J.H. (2001), 'The Eclectic, or OLI, Paradigm of International Production – Past, Present and Future', *International Journal of the Economics of Business*, **8**(2), 173–90.
Dunning, J.H. and Wymbs, C. (1999), 'The Geographical Sourcing of Technology-Based Assets By Multinational Enterprises', in D. Archibugi, J. Howells and J. Michie (eds), *Innovation Policy in a Global Economy*, Cambridge: Cambridge University Press, pp. 185–224.
The Economist (2000a), 'In the Great Web Bazaar', *The Economist*, 26 February, 40–4.
The Economist (2000b), 'Amazon's Amazing Ambition', *The Economist*, 26 February, 24.
The Economist (2000c), 'First America, then the World', *The Economist*, 26 February, 49–53.
The Economist (2000d), 'Something Old, Something New', *The Economist*, 26 February, 15–16
The Economist (2000e), 'Define and Sell', *The Economist*, 26 February, 6–12.
Eika, K. and Reistadbakk, T. (1998), 'The Competitive Environment in the Banking Industry – Driving Forces and Trends', *Norges Bank, Economic Bulletin*. Oslo, Norway, December.
Eisenhardt, K.M. (1989), 'Agency Theory: An Assessment and Review', *Academy of Management Review*, **14**(1), 57–73.
Enright, M. (2000), 'Globalization, Regionalization and the Knowledge-based Economy in Hong Kong', in John H. Dunning (ed.), *Globalization, Regionalization and The Knowledge-Based Economy*, New York: Oxford University Press, pp. 381–407.
Evans, P. and Wurster, T. (1997), 'Strategy and the New Economics of Information', *Harvard Business Review*, September/October, 70–82.
Florida, R. (1995), 'Toward the Learning Region', *Futures*, **27**(5), 527–36.
Florida, R. (1998), 'Calibrating the Learning Region', in J. DelaMothe and G. Paquest (eds), *Local and Regional Systems of Innovation*, MA: Kluwer Academic Publishers.
Florida, R. (1995), 'Towards the Learning Region', *Futures*, **27**(5), 527–36.
Freeman, C. and Perez, C. (1988), 'Structural Crisis of Adjustment, Business Cycles and Investment Behavior', in G. Dosi, C. Freeman, R. Nelson, G. Silverberg, and L. Soete (eds), *Technical Change and Economic Theory*, London: Pinter, ch. 3.
Gates, W. (1999), *Business @ The Speed of Thought*, New York: Warner Books.
General Electric (GE) (1999), *Building virtual global trading communities through electronic commerce outsourcing*, White Paper.
Gimein, M. and Lash, A. (1998), 'Amazon Moves to Build E-Commerce Empire', *The Standard*, 7 August.
Gork (2000), 'DoubleClick Cries Uncle', *The Standard*, 3 March.

Graham, E.M. (1990), 'Exchange of Threats Between Multinational Firms as an Infinitely Repeated Non-Cooperative Game', *International Trade Journal*, **4**(3), 259–77.

Hagel, J. and Singer, M. (1999), 'Unbundling the Corporation', *Harvard Business Review*, March–April.

Hamel, Gary (1999), *The Strategos Manifesto*, available online at: <http://www.strategosnet.com/about/manifesto.html>.

Hamel, Gary and Sampler, Jeff (1998), 'The E-Corporation', *Fortune*, 7 December.

Hamill, J. (1997), 'The Internet and international markets', *International Marketing Review*, **14**(5), 300–23.

Hamilton, A. (2000), 'Asia: from East to West', *The Standard*, 7 February.

Hanson, W. (2000), *Internet Marketing*, United States: South-Western College Publishing.

Hart, A. (1996), 'Howdy Partner', *Internet World*, **7**(11). Available online at: <http://www.iworld.com>.

Helft, M. (2000), 'Amazon.com: More Than a Merchant', *The Standard*, 17 January.

Hennart, J.F. (1982), *A Theory of Multinational Enterprise*, Ann Arbor, MI: University of Michigan Press, pp. 81–116.

Hennart, J.F. (1989), 'The Transaction Cost Theory of the Multinational Enterprise', in C.N. Pitelis and R. Sugden (eds), *The Nature of the Transnational Firm*, London: Routledge, pp. 81–116.

Henry, D. (1999), *The Emerging Digital Economy II*. US Department of Commerce, Available online at: <http://www.ecommerce.gov>.

Henson, C. (2000), 'David.com vs. Goliath', *Best's Review*, **101**(1), 57–60.

Hill, C. (1997), 'Establishing a Standard: Competitive Strategy and Technological Standards in Winner-Take-All Industries', *The Academy of Management Executive*, **11**, 7–25.

Hof, R. and McWilliams, G. (1998), 'The 'Click Here' Economy', *BusinessWeek*, 22 June. Available online at: < http://www.businessweek.com(1998/25itspec98).htm>.

Hunt, S. (1997), 'Resource-Advantage Theory: An Evolutionary Theory of Competitive Firm Behaviors?', *Journal of Economic Issues*, **31**(1), 59–77.

Hymer, S.H., *The International Operation of National Firms: A Study of Direct Investment*, Ph.D. dissertation, M.I.T., 1960. (Published by M.I.T. Press in 1976.)

Iansiti, M and MacCormack, A. (1997), 'Developing Products on Internet Time', *Harvard Business Review*, September–October, 108–17.

IBM (1999), 'IBM Targets US10-US$15bn E-business Sales in 1999', *New Straits Times Press*, 6 April, 18.

IDA (1999), *New York City Industrial Development Agency*, New York: IDA.

Industry Standard (2000), 'Rare European Win in E-commerce', *Industry Standard*, 29 February.

Industry Standard (2000), 'The Internet Economy Goes Global', *Industry Standard*, 7 February.

Industry Standard (1999), 'March on the marts', *Industry Standard*, 16 December.

Jacob, R. (2000), 'Buyers and Sellers Flock to Online Asian Bazaar', *Financial Times*, 29 March, 10.

Kim, E.C. and Mauborgne, R. (1999), 'Importance of an Alternative Path', *Financial Times*, 10 June, 24.

Knickerbocker, F.T. (1973), *Oligopolistic Reaction and the Multinational Enterprise*, Cambridge, MA: Harvard University Press.

Knight, G. (1999), 'International Services Marketing: Review Of Research, 1980–98', *Journal of Services Marketing*, **13**(4/5), 346–60.

Kobrin, S. (1999), 'You Can't Declare Cyberspace National Territory', in D. Tapscott, (ed.), *BluePrint to the Digital Economy*, Harvard University Press, pp. 355–70.

Kobrin, S. (2000), 'Development After Industrialization: Poor Countries in an Electronically Integrated Global Economy', in N. Hood and S. Young, (eds), *The Globalization of Multinational Enterprise Activity and Economic Development*, Basingstoke: Macmillan, pp. 106–32.

Kogut, B. (1985), 'Designing Global Strategies: Profiting from Operational Flexibility', *Sloan Management Review*, Fall, **26**, 27–38.

Kogut, B. and Kulatilaka, N. (1994), 'Operational Flexibility, Global Manufacturing and the Option Value of a Multinational Network', *Management Science*, **40**(1), 123–39.

Kogut, B. and Zander, U. (1993), 'Knowledge of the Firm and the Evolutionary Theory of the Multinational Corporation', *Journal of International Business Studies*, **24**(4), 625–46.

Kotabe, M., Murray, J. and Javalgi, R. (1998), 'Global Sourcing of Services and Market Performance: an Empirical Investigation', *Journal of International Marketing*, December, 10–31.

KPMG (1999), *Supply Chain Solutions*, New York: KPMG.

Kuemmerle, W. (1999), 'The Drivers of Foreign Direct Investment into Research and Development: an Empirical Investigation', *Journal of International Business Studies*, **30**(1), 1–24.

Larson, P. (2000), 'Operators Get Worked Up Over Mobility: The Failure of All But the Biggest Internet Portals Has Not Stopped WAP Phone Companies Taking the Same Route', *FinancialTimes*, 21 June. Available online: www.ft.com.

Larson, P. (2000), Yahoo! Looks to expand abroad, *Financial Times*, 6 April, 20.

Larson, P. and Newman, C. (2000), 'NTL Internet Free-For-All is Welcome By Premier', *Financial Times*, 7 March, 9.

Laseter, T., Houston, P., Wright, J. and Park, J. (2000), 'Amazon Your Industry: Extracting Value From the Value Chain', *Strategy & Business*, 2000, 94–105.

Lawrence, S. (2000), 'The Net World in Numbers', *The Standard*, 8 February.

Ledbetter, J. (1999), 'The Internet Economy Gets Real', *The Standard*, 20 December.

Lessig, L. (1999), *Code and Other Laws of Cyberspace*, New York: Basic Books.

Lewis, M. (1999), *The New New Thing: A Silicon Valley Story*, W.W. Norton & Co.

Lewis, W. (2000), 'Yahoo! And e-Bay Restart Merger Talks', *Financial Times*, 24 March, 1.

Lipsey, R.E. (1997), 'Globalization and National Government Policies: an Economist's View', in J.H. Dunning, ed., *Governments, Globalization and International Business*, Oxford: Oxford University Press, pp. 73–113.

Lipsey, R.E. and Bekar, C. (1995), 'A Structuralist View of Technical Change and Economic Growth', in P.J. Courchene, ed., *Technology, Information & Public Policy*, Kingston, Ontario: John Deutsch Institute.

Malone, T. and Laubacher, (1998), 'The Dawn of the E-lance Economy', *Harvard Business Review*, September/October, Reprint 98508.

Manzar, O. (1999), 'Yahoo, Lycos to Launch India Portal', *The Standard*, 18 November.

Margherion, L. (1998), *The Emerging Digital Economy*, US Department of Commerce, pp. 1–50.

Maruca, R. (1999), 'Retailing: Confronting the Challenges That Face Bricks-and-Mortar Stores', *Harvard Business Review*, July/August, Reprint 99412.

Muehlbauer, J. (2000), 'Does Chemdex Need a Mom?', *Forbes*, 10 February.
Mullich J. (1997), 'Winning Through Partnering', *Web Week*, 3 March, 315. Available online at: <http://www.iworld.com>.
Nayyar, P. (1993), 'Performance Effects of Information Asymmetry', *Academy of Management Journal*, **36**(1) 28–57.
Nelson, R.R. and Winter, S. (1982), *An Evolutionary Theory of Economic Change*, Cambridge: Belknap Press.
Nelson, R.R. (1991), 'The Role of Firm Differences in an Evolutionary Theory of Technical Advance', *Science and Public Policy*, **18**(6), 347–52.
Novak, J. (2000), 'E-confusion, How Come You Pay Sales Taxes on Some Internet Purchases and Not Others?', *Forbes.com Special Internet Issue*, Spring, 26.
OECD (1999), *E-commerce*. Available online at: <http://www.oecd.org/subject/e_commerce/summary.htm>.
OECD (1998), *The Economic and Social Impact of Electronic Commerce*. Available online at: <http://www.oecd.org/subject/e_commerce/ebooks/009–026.pdf>.
Paperfree (2000), 'Multiple Messaging Standards', *Electronic Commerce World*, 12.
Peterson, H. (1986), *Business and Governments*, New York: Harper & Row.
Pitt, L., Berthon, P. and Watson, R. (1999), 'Cyberservices: Taming Service Marketing Problems With the WWW', *Business Horizons*, **42**(1), 11–18.
Porter, M.E. (1994), 'The Role of Location in Competition', *Journal of Economics of Business*, **1**(1), 35–9.
Porter, M.E. (1998), 'Location, Clusters and the 'New' Micro-Economics of Competition', *Journal of Business Economics*, Jan, **33**, 7–13.
Prahalad, C.K. and Doz, Y.L. (1987), *The Multinational Mission: Balancing Local Demands and Global Vision*, New York: The Free Press.
Priceline (2000), 'Now you can Name Your Own Price for Groceries!', *Priceline WebHouse Club*, 29 February.
Rabinovitz, J., Dalton, G. and Helft, M. (2000), 'The Urge to Merge', *The Standard*, 17 January.
Rayport, J. and Sviokla, J. (1998), *Winning in Electronic Commerce* (Tape), New York: Harvard Business School Publishing.
Reedy, J., Schullo, S. and Zimmerman, K. (2000), *Electronic Marketing*, New York: Harcourt College Publishing.
Rifkin, J. (2000), *The Age of Access: How the Shift from Ownership to Access is Transforming Capitalism*, Harmondsworth: Penguin.
Rugman, A.M. (1979), *International Diversification and the Multinational Enterprise*, Lexington, MA: Lexington Books.
Rugman, A.M. (1981), *Inside the Multinationals and The Economics of Internal Markets*, London: Croom Helm.
Sahlman, W.A. (1996), 'Some Thoughts on Business Plans', *The Entrepreneurial Venture*. Cambridge, MA: Harvard Business School Press.
Spar, D. and Bussgang, J. (1999), *Ruling Commerce in the Networld*. Available online at: <http://www.ascusc.org/jcmc/vol2/issue1/commerce.html#6>.
Sprenger, P. (2000), 'U.K. Government Backhands Dot-coms', *Industry Standard*, 24 March.
Standard (1999), 'March on the march', *Industry Standard*, December 16.
Standard (2000a), 'Rare European win in e-commerce', *Industry Standard*, February 29.
Standard (2000b), 'The Internet economy goes global', *Industry Standard*, February 7.
Strange, S. (1997), 'An International Political Economy Perspective', in J.H. Dunning, (ed.), *Governments, Globalization and International Business*, Oxford: Oxford University Press, pp. 132–45.

Tapscott, D. (1999), *Creating Value in the Networked Economy*, Cambridge, MA: Harvard Business School Press.
Taylor, P. (2000), 'How the Internet Will Reshape Worldwide Business Activity', *Financial Times*, 4 July, 1–2.
Teece, D.J., Pisano, G. and Shuen, A. (1997), 'Dynamic Capabilities and Strategic Management', *Strategic Management Journal*, **18**(7), 509–33.
Thompson. M.J. (1999a), 'Net Economy Pegged at 8301 Billion', *The Standard*, 10 June.
Thompson, M.J. (1999b), 'Forecasters are Bullish on the Internet Economy', *The Standard*, 15 November.
Timmons, J. (1990), *New Venture Creation*, Boston, MA: Irwin.
Tomkins, R. (1999), 'Reinventing the Dinosaur', *Financial Times*, 8 June, 13.
Turban, E., Lee, J., King, D. and Chung, H. (2000), *E-Commerce*, Upper Saddle River, NJ: Prentice Hall.
UNCTC (1998), *Transnational Corporations and World Development*, New York: UN.
UN (1996), *World Investment Report 1996: Investment, Trade and International Policy Arrangements*, Geneva and New York: UN.
Vernon, R. (1973), *Sovereignty at Bay*, Harmondsworth: Penguin.
Vernon, R. (1974), 'The Location of Economic Activity', in J.H. Dunning, (ed.), *In Economic Analysis and The Multinational Enterprise*, London: Allen and Unwin, pp. 89–114.
Vernon, R. (1983), 'Organizational and Institutional Responses to International Risk', in R.J. Herring, (ed.), *Managing International Risk*, Cambridge, MA: Cambridge University Press, pp. 191–222.
Vernon, R. (1994), 'Research on Transnational Corporations', *Transnational Corporations*, **3**, 137–58.
Watson, R., Akelsen, S. and Pitt, L. (1998), 'Attractors: Building Mountains in the Flat Landscape of the World Wide Web', *California Management Review*, **40**(2), 36–56.
Wernerfelt, B. (1984), 'A Resource-Based View of the Firm', *Strategic Management Journal*, **5**(2), 1–80.
Wernerfelt, B. (1995), 'The Resource Based View of the Firm: Ten Years After', *Strategic Management Journal*, **16**, 171–4.
Wesson, T.J. (1993), 'An Alternative Motivation for Foreign Direct Investment', Ph.D. dissertation, Cambridge, MA: Harvard University.
Wesson, T.J. (2001), *Foreign Direct Investment and Competitive Advantage*, Cheltenham: Edward Elgar.
Wheelwright, G. (1997), 'Experiments in Retailing', *Financial Times*, 5 March, 8.
Williamson, O.E. (1995), *The Economic Institutions of Capitalism*, New York: The Free Press.
Wymbs, C. (1997), 'Internet: its Effect on International Trade, Foreign Direct Investment and Strategic Alliance Formation', *International Telecommunications Society and International Council for Computer Communications Conference*, Calgary, Canada, June (mimeo).
Wymbs, C. (2000a), 'How Electronic Commerce is Fundamentally Changing the Service Industries', *Journal of Services Marketing*, **14**(6).
Wymbs, C. (2000b), 'The Impact of the Information Revolution of the Global Corporation', in J. DeLaMoth and G. Paquet, (eds), *Information, Innovation, and Impacts*. Boston, MA: Kluwer Academic Publishers.
Yoffie, D. and Cusumano, M. (1999), 'Building a Company on Internet Time: Lessons from Netscape', *California Management Review*, **41**(3), 8–28.

16. Relational assets, networks and international business activity*

1. INTRODUCTION

Most paradigms and theories of the determinants of international business activities – and particularly those designed to explain the extent, pattern and composition of MNE systems – are essentially asset based.

Three kinds of income generating assets are usually considered:

1. Those specific and unique to particular firms, notably MNEs or potential MNEs: these may be located in the home country of the MNEs, or in the countries which are host to their affiliates.
2. Those which are external to MNEs, but are accessed and then deployed by them: these assets may also be located in the home country of the MNEs or in foreign countries.
3. Those which relate to the ways in which these two kinds of assets are created, harnessed and coordinated by the management of MNEs – be they that of the parent companies or their foreign affiliates.

Over the years the nature, relative significance and governance of these different types of assets has changed (Table 16.1). Until the Industrial Revolution, and today in some developing countries, the critical wealth-creating assets were (and are) land and property owned by households, and the way in which these assets were (are) husbanded. For much of the nineteenth and twentieth centuries, they were the physical and financial assets owned by firms, but supplemented by those of other institutions, and accessed primarily through the market. Today, the critical assets consist of a kaleidoscope of intangible assets, especially knowledge and information embodied in human capital, both owned and accessed – from a variety of sources – and by firms.[1] Though physical and financial assets remain important, they are increasingly playing a supportive rather than a dominant role in the wealth-creation process.

The 1990s have seen an explosion of the literature on the nature and significance of knowledge capital and its competitiveness-enhancing qualities for

* First published as a chapter in F. Contractor and P. Lorange (eds) (2002), *Cooperative Strategies and Alliances*, Amsterdam and Oxford: Elsevier Science, pp. 569–93.

Table 16.1 Changing characteristics of assets

	1. Specific to ownership	2. Accessed by firms	3. Organized by firms
(a) Pre industrial revolution	• Land, property	• Labour, materials	• Internal to households • Elementary markets
	(Mainly domestically created sourced and utilized)		
(b) Nineteenth and twentieth centuries	• Machines, buildings • Financial assets • Property rights	• Labour, intermediate products	• Largely hierarchical within firms • Growth of joint ventures • More sophisticated markets
	(Mainly domestically, but increasingly foreign sourced)		
(c) Twentieth century	• Property rights • Intellectual assets • 'Connectivity' advantages (including R assets)	• Leasing of property • Intermediate products • Knowledge and information • Collective (social) assets	• Heterarchical within firms • Coalitions between firms • Networks • Markets
	(Accelerated movement towards the global or regional creation, accessing and utilization of assets)		

both firms and countries; and of the appropriate organizational modalities for its creation, sustenance, exploitation and diffusion. Indeed, one might be led to believe that the intellectual component of human capital was now the 'be all and end all' of a firm's or nation's competitive prowess.

This, in my opinion, would be misguided. Certainly when one widens the unit of analysis from that of the firm to the country, a good deal of evidence is emerging on the critical role of *social* capital (later to be defined) as a prerequisite for, and facilitator of, the productive creation and deployment of both tangible and intangible assets. Yet, in the business literature, only scant attention has been paid to (what we shall term) relational assets (R assets) – as they affect the success or failure of intra- or extra-firm associations, the latter encompassing linkages both between private and public organizations, and between organizations and persons. This domain has largely been occupied by sociologists and, latterly, by organizational scholars. Economists and business strategists have tended to approach the subject of R assets hesitantly and obliquely by their analysis of market failures and hierarchical modes of governance; and by analysing the essential conditions for successful inter-firm alliances, in terms of such ingredients as trust, reciprocity and forbearance. In recent years, however, three important articles have appeared – one by Kale, Singh and Perlmutter (2000) in *Strategic Management Journal*; one by Dyer and Singh (1998), and the other by Holm, Eriksson and Johanson (1996) in *Journal of International Business Studies* – which explicitly deal with the role of R assets as a competitiveness-enhancing advantage of firms. And it is the purpose of this chapter to offer some exploratory observations on the nature, significance, and governance of R assets, and, in particular, to examine their relevance in explaining the recent growth, structure and form of MNE-*related* activity. I use the adjective *related* advisedly, for I shall concern myself with not just MNE-*owned* activity, i.e. activity financed by FDI, but also with the totality of activities under the *effective control* of MNEs. Such activity is based not only on resources and capabilities which MNEs actually *own*, but also those to which they have *access* by one means or another, and then internalize for their own use. (I shall take up the significance of an access regime rather than an ownership regime to the international activities of firms later in this chapter.)

2. THE CHARACTERISTICS OF FIRM-SPECIFIC R ASSETS

2.1 A Definition

First a working definition. I shall define firm-specific R assets as the stock of a firm's willingness and capability to access, shape and engage in economically beneficial relationships; and to sustain and upgrade these relationships.

Such relationships, though always conducted by and between individuals, may take place both within the confines of a particular firm, and between that firm and other organizations and individuals.

The relationships between R assets and other kinds of corporate assets – be they owned or accessed by firms – are set out in Figure 16.1. As can be seen,

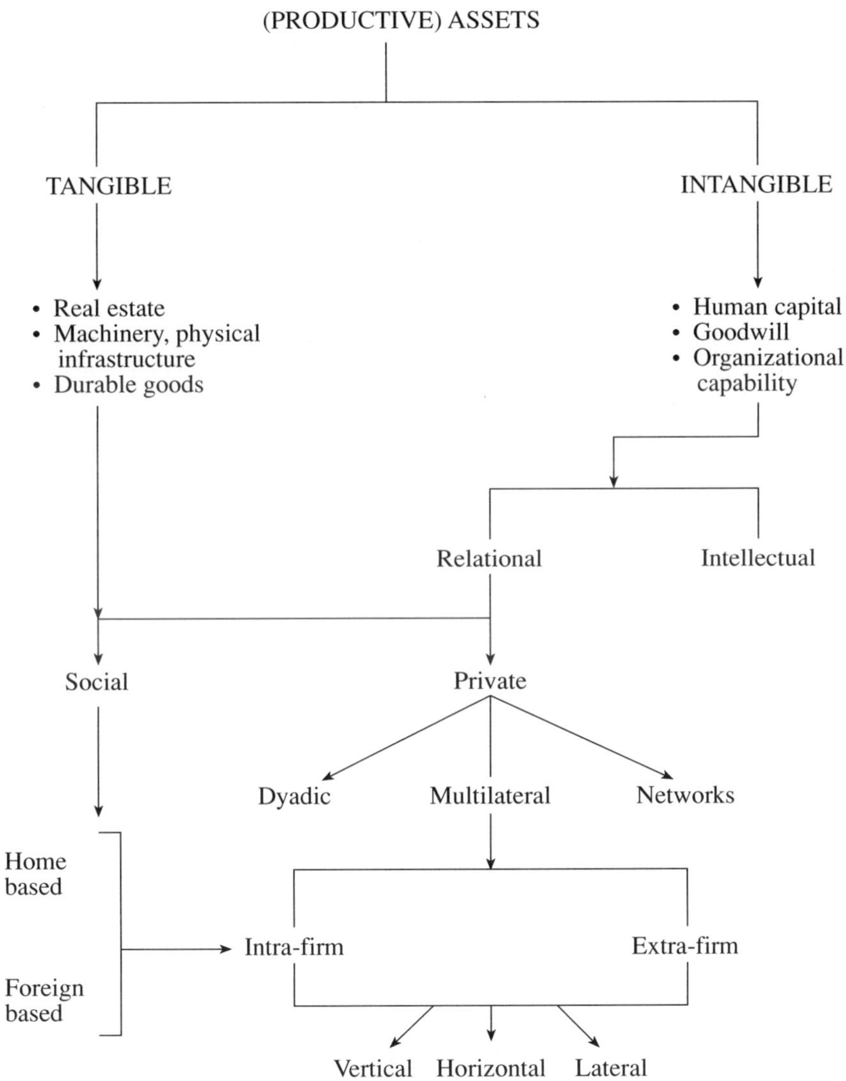

Figure 16.1 The pyramid of corporate assets

they run alongside human embodied intellectual capital, but are more empathetic and emotionally based. (This may be why economists are uneasy in dealing with them!) They are different from other assets in a number of ways, but their essential uniqueness lies in the fact that they can only be *productively employed if they are used jointly with the R assets of another economic actor*. The sociologist Amitai Etzioni believes that, to be successful, partnerships, be they between persons, corporations or governments, need to share a set of core values and objectives (Etzioni, 1996). R assets are essentially facilitating assets. When properly deployed, they affect – one way or another – virtually all functional activities of the possessing firm. These include R&D, production, sourcing, financial management marketing, as well as the exchange-specific activities of firms.

R assets are then entirely human intensive, although such assets may be embedded in, and articulated by, individuals or organizations. In their usage, R assets can give rise to a plethora of relationships, ranging from the simple, shallow and one off to the complex dense and ongoing.

Some other characteristics of R assets are set out in Table 16.2. Note, for example, they may be used in the pursuance of dyadic, multilateral or network relationships. As with other resources and capabilities, R assets need to be scarce, unique and imperfectly imitable, if they are to confer a sustainable com-

Table 16.2 Some unique characteristics of R assets

- A bundle of attributes/values
- Multifaceted in origin: internally generated, externally accessed
- Shallow and simple ⇔ deep and complex
- Dyadic ⇔ network relationships
- Like other assets, R assets need to be unique and imperfectly imitable if they are to confer a sustainable competitive advantage
- Vary according to function and activity: they range from standardized to highly idiosyncratic relationships
- Likely to be strongly contextual (reflecting cultures and ideologies which may be both country- and firm-specific)
- Unlike most other assets, R assets are only of value when combined with those of other firms: the concept of shared core values
- Unlike other assets, they do not deplete when used
- Difficult to measure as their values are not independent of other assets with which they are combined
- Value of R assets is likely to be cumulative and path dependent
- Cannot be owned; only controlled or influenced
- Are only partially mobile across national boundaries

petitive advantage on the firm(s) deploying them. Unlike some other, e.g. tangible, assets, R assets may be of negative value (i.e. a liability) to the firm; on the other hand, they do not deplete when used. They cannot be *owned*; only accessed and then controlled or influenced in the way in which they are used and combined with other assets. They are likely to be tacit and idiosyncratic, and more context specific, yet more pervasive, than most other assets. In particular, their content and effectiveness are likely to vary according to the culture, values and ideologies of each of the countries in which they are employed, and those of the firms creating or utilizing them. Lastly, although the focus of our current interest is the R assets of corporations, the concept of social R assets (or social capital) is no less gaining the attention of researchers. We shall give this latter concept more attention a little later in the chapter.

2.2 The Ingredients of R Assets

What then are the ingredients – as opposed to the characteristics – of R assets? How fungible are they? R assets are a composite or mixture – a salad bowl – of a complex set of values, attitudes and virtues, the relevance of which is likely to be highly context specific. Unlike that of tangible assets, or even knowledge capital, the value of R assets rests in the structure of the relations between and among the economic actors involved.

The list of ingredients making for successful R assets is an extremely lengthy one – see Table 16.3. Moreover, the content and configuration of these ingredients rest critically on the *raison d'être* for, and the goals of the respective partners to, the relationship, and of their particular characteristics. Thus, such values as enthusiasm, entrepreneurship, and a spirit of curiosity, risk taking, and learning intent are especially important for innovating activities. Those such as diligence, team orientation, flexibility, reliability and quality enhancement are more important for production and subcontracting-related relationships, while trust, integrity and reciprocity are the key components of successful adversarial (zero-sum game) exchange relationships.

2.3 The Governance of R Assets

Relationships between economic actors stretch along a continuum ranging from arm's-length markets to those embedded in hierarchies. In between, there is a labyrinth of non-equity bilateral and pluralistic associations – including networks. The literature is replete with explanations as to why one relationship mode is preferred to another, though most are couched in terms of the comparative transaction costs (TC) of a discrete exchange of intermediate products, rather than on the wider benefits of cooperation in non-exchange functions to the participating firms. Moreover, most explanations tend to assume there are

Table 16.3 Some ingredients of R assets:

- R assets consist of a bundle of values and virtues which need to be nurtured. The optimum bundle will vary according to the type of relationship being concluded, and the R assets of the partner organization, and are likely to be country and firm specific.

Virtues/values	Activities/Functions*
Trust	All activities
Loyalty	Innovation, production, subcontracting
Reciprocity	Innovation, production, subcontracting
Dependability	All
Willingness to learn	Innovation
Forbearance	Subcontracting, exchange
Adaptability	Innovation, production, subcontracting
Work ethic	Production
Spirit of community	All except exchange
Commitment	Innovation, production, subcontracting
Radius of virtues	All
Part of society with fund of social capital	All
Ideologies and beliefs	Innovation, production, marketing
Empathy	To some extent, in all
Curiosity	Innovation
Honesty	All, but especially in exchange and/or where there is information asymmetry, and opportunities for opportunism
Integrity	All, but especially subcontracting and production
(Avoidance of) negative virtues/values	
Opportunism	Subcontracting, exchange
Moral hazard	All
Corruption	Production, exchange
Free riding	All
Volatility	Subcontracting, marketing, exchange
Instability	Exchange

* We consider five main functions, viz. innovation, subcontracting, production, marketing and exchange.

alternative modes of undertaking a particular activity or task, when, in fact, this may not always be the case.

While, since its inception, the TC literature has always explicitly considered a number of relational specific costs and benefits – both in respect of FDI and alliances – it is less forthcoming in explaining the appropriate vehicle for identifying the contribution of R assets to the learning or even the productive activities of firms – nor, indeed, of the contribution as part of a network of firms to the upgrading of firm-specific R assets. Because they are often project based and intended to promote time-limited and very specific objectives, many contemporary cross-border strategic alliances cannot be regarded as substitutes to an FDI; nor may a purely market solution be viable.

Nevertheless, some generalizations are possible, which I think can be usefully taken up by TC scholars. In the case of shallow and simple economic relationships, and where the value of R assets is likely to be insignificant relative to that of other resources and capabilities which are neither tacit nor proprietary, then the market route or a straightforward contractual agreement may be the most cost-effective mode of usage. At the opposite extreme, in the case of thick, complex and highly idiosyncratic relationships, the success of which is vital to the competitive advantage of the firm, then, depending on the *relative* costs and benefits, and the extent to which control over the non-R assets can be exercised without ownership, the activity, or the products being traded, will either be internalized, or an alliance, with or without an equity interest, will be concluded. Since, however, by their nature, R assets are tacit and function or project specific, and they are being increasingly directed to learning-related activities, it follows that the alliance route is likely to be the one more generally favoured.

2.4 Form of R Assets

As just indicated, any relationship or association forged by a firm (or individuals within the firm) may either be among its constituent units of decision taking (over which, through ownership, it has *de jure* control) or between itself (or parts of itself) and an external economic actor or actors. These actors may be other private firms, a group or network of firms, non-governmental organizations, public corporations or international agencies.

The choice between an intra- or inter-firm creation, protection and use of R assets (the make or buy decision) is one critical decision a firm has to make. Another concerns the kind of associations to which R assets are applied. Here the extant literature on linkages, spillovers and integration is useful. Figure 16.2 identifies the main kinds of relationships. These may be between individuals, teams, special interest groups, and corporations. They may be intra- or extra-firm. We shall focus on extra-firm (and especially *inter*-firm) relationships. These, in turn, may be grouped according to the nature of the relationship. (Is it, for example, supplier or customer oriented or is it an alliance between competitors? Or is it by the type of activity, process, function or markets served?)

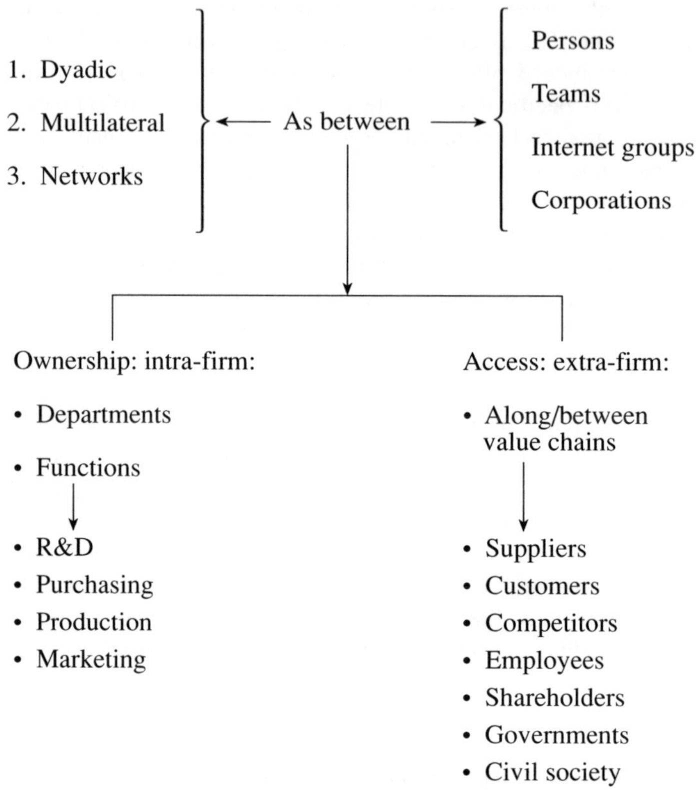

Figure 16.2 Types of R assets

To be successful, each and every association – whatever its kind – requires some R assets to be possessed by each of the economic actors involved. But how much, what kind and the appropriate governance form of these assets are likely to be highly context specific. The more intensive, pervasive and complex relationships (and hence the need for more or better-quality R assets) are likely to arise in coalitions between firms from different cultures and with different competences and experiences, which engage in innovatory and learning activities. The less demanding relationships (and hence the need for less R assets) relate to the exchange of fairly standardized products among firms from similar economic and cultural backgrounds. It is the contention of this chapter that the

R-asset-intensive activities of firms have been increasing relative to those of other activities in recent years, and that an increasing proportion of the former have been taking the form of cross-border extra-firm associations intended to access new knowledge-related and learning capabilities.

Where do networks fit into this analysis? Consider Figure 16.2. Unlike firms, most networks do not create wealth for themselves. Their value is demonstrated as and when the participants in the network internalize and efficiently utilize the benefits they offer. Frequently the gains of networks take the form of augmented R assets. If nothing else, networks help foster intra-network and inter-firm relational capital. From the work of Putman, Porter and Enright – to cite just three contemporary exponents of the benefits of the spatial clustering of related activities – we are seeing a great deal of casual evidence that such networks not only offer the constituent firms knowledge and information-related externalities, but also strengthen many of the ingredients of R assets – notably a sense of empathy, bond building, adaptability, open communication, and the promotion of shared core values and learning capabilities.

2.5 How Does one Value R Assets?

How are R assets measured? How does one quantify their output – or indeed their constituent inputs? The answer is with very great difficulty! To a certain extent, similar problems beset scholars trying to put a monetary value on other forms of intangible assets – and of knowledge capital in particular. But they arise in acute form in the case of R assets for two reasons. The first is there is no market, either for the inputs or the output of R assets, separately from that of the other assets in which they are embedded. The second is that the main ingredients of R assets (as set out in Table 16.2) are not themselves directly measurable, let alone marketable.

Table 16.4 summarizes some of the scholarly attempts to measure the R assets of firms and of countries (or societies). By and large, the proxies for social R assets, and/or their output, can more readily be obtained and are more meaningful than those of corporate R assets. Such indices as the extent of civil litigation, crime – particularly violent crime – drugs, terrorism, truancy, divorce rates, bribery, tax evasion and corruption, all testify to a degree of social dysfunction, and a breakdown of interpersonal relationships; just as others, e.g. membership or participation in churches, clubs, charitable institutions, voluntary associations etc., point to the robustness of social bonding and the moral health of the community. Some measures, e.g. size of police force, the number of social or behavioural counsellors and property rights protection may also be regarded as positive indices in so far as their presence and action are designed to protect or improve the existing stock of social relational capital.

Table 16.4 Some possible measures of R assets (or liabilities!)

At a firm level (Corporate R assets)	At a country level (Social R assets)
• Number of repeated inter-firm ties • Number, frequency and density of inter-firm linkages • Types of alliances • Survey material on significance of R assets • Codes of conduct • Absence of industrial unrest: low labour turnover • Social responsibility • Transparency and openness	• [No one measure – but package of same] • Number/quality of community groups • (Negative) Extent of crime/corruption • (Negative) Breakdown of personal relations/divorce • (Negative) Civil litigation • Radius of trust • Prison population • Surveys on quality of social capital/justice systems • Extent and depth of tax evasion

The suggested proxies for the R assets of firms are generally much less satisfactory. There are a few exceptions. One is firm-level data on labour turnover, industrial disputes, strikes, etc. but, even here, economic or regulatory rather than social reasons may be the main explanation for such incidences, or changes in same.[2] Other proxies include the extent of social responsibility – or its absence – in the form of corporate corruption, lack of safety standards and of undesirable business practices. Recent research on inter-firm coalitions has suggested measures such as the number of past alliances concluded between any two firms, the number of cliques to which a firm belongs, the type of alliance, and the level of mutual trust and commitment that arises out of the close interaction between the partners to the coalition. While some of these data make use of secondary and relatively objective measures, more recent work, especially by Dyer and Chu (2000), Holm, Eriksson and Johanson (1996), and Kale, Singh and Perlmutter (2000) and Ariño, de la Torre and Ring (2002), has relied upon the perception of corporate executives as obtained by survey data. I feel bound to say, that, notwithstanding all the problems and deficiencies of these data, I believe, for at least the next stage for advancing our understanding about the significance of R assets for corporate success, the field study is likely to offer the most productive way of proceeding.

Already, as documented by Daniel Coleman in his book *Working with Emotional Intelligence* (Coleman, 1999), there is a good deal of casual evidence that successful corporations are identifying their possession of (different kinds of) R assets as the critical distinguishing feature between themselves and their less successful competitors. Similarly, in an analysis of the distinctive qualities of star performers among 286 US and other firms by Lyle Spencer Jr, it was found that an overwhelming proportion – 80 percent – that set apart these performers from their average counterparts – depended on the emotional intelligence of their senior executive and professional staff rather than on their cognitive ability (Coleman, 1999, p. 379).

2.6 R assets and Social Capital

What now of the relationship between R assets and social capital (see Table 16.5). The term social capital has a variety of meanings (a recently published book edited by Partha Dasgupta and Ismail Serageldin (2000) for the World Bank catalogues these in some detail). For our purposes, we may start by taking a very broad interpretation of the term to include 'that part of a country's stock of tangible and intangible assets which is socially owned or controlled'. Under this umbrella, social capital includes much of the physical, legal and commercial infrastructure critical to the competitiveness of firms. A definition more directly related to R assets is 'the accumulated societal fund of economic relationships, which are embodied or reposited in both individuals, organizations, and networks of organizations, engaging in economic activity'.

Francis Fukuyama puts it a little differently. He perceives social capital as 'a country's stock of informal values or norms shared among members of a group that permits cooperation between them' (Fukuyama, 1999, p. 16). The value of this stock is likely to be more than the sum of its constituent parts, as a collection of connected R assets is likely to generate its own externalities. The balance of social capital – taking the broader definition – is then made up of an infrastructure (including tangible assets and institutional structures which 'house' social R assets, or the absence of same) such as prisons, courts of justice, religious and educational establishments, and also of societal rules, procedures, customs and routines.

Like corporate R assets, social relational capital is not a single entity, but a variety of different entities. It is identified by its function, and inheres in the macro-structure of relations between actors and among actors. The extent and content of a community's social relational capital both affects the capacity of particular firms to generate and deploy their own R assets, and, as we shall see later, can be a major influence on the kind and purpose of relationships, their form and their location – both between and across national borders.

3. THE CHANGING SIGNIFICANCE OF R ASSETS

Why is more attention now being given to R assets? The implication is that the extent, form and depth of economic relations between individuals and organizations has increased over the last 30 years or so. (Stretching back much further in time to the Industrial Revolution, R assets, particularly in primitive, e.g. tribal, societies (and some still exist in the least developed countries) were a critical component of the wealth-creating processes.) We believe this in fact has occurred, and that it has been the direct results of five interlinked developments which have occurred in the world economy. These are, first, a series of dramatic, and for the most part, systemic technological advances – particularly in all forms of informatics including E-commerce; second, the widespread liberalization of markets, both domestic and cross-border; third, the growing significance of most service sectors, which tend to be more R asset intensive than their primary or secondary sector counterparts; fourth, the emergence of several important new players on the world economic stage, e.g. China and Russia; and fifth, the emergence and maturation of the global economy, which is essentially both a facilitator and an outcome of the first four factors.

Exactly how have these changes increased both the significance of firm-specific R assets and particularly (as we shall tackle in the next section) their role in determining the extent, pattern and form of the cross-border activity of firms? Space permits me to highlight just seven of these. These are set out in Table 16.5.

1. The cutting edges of economic activity have become more idiosyncratic and innovation driven. This has increased the depth and complexity of intra- and inter-corporate economic relationships.
2. The scope and depth of *cross-border* economic relationships has noticeably increased, and in doing so, has embraced a new and wider range of values, ideologies and social customs. In successfully dealing with such associations, a fund of R assets, which acknowledges these country- or region-specific differences, and promotes the well-being of each of the participants, is critical.
3. Societal, and to some extent business, goals have changed. Rather than concentrating on efficiency-related issues, increasingly the focus is directed to transforming societies and upgrading the role of cultural values and experiences and the quality of life, e.g. with respect to leisure and the environment (Stiglitz, 1998; Rifkin, 2000). These changes are spawning many new coalitions, both among themselves and between themselves and other organizations, including NGOs and governments.
4. Competitive pressures following market liberalization have led to shedding or more disinternalization of activities of firms, and, with it, an increased reliance on external suppliers for intermediate products.
5. At the same time, the interdependence between the technologies required at different stages of the value chain, or indeed to produce any particular product, is increasing. This means that intra-firm transactions are not being replaced by arm's-length transactions but by inter-firm coalitions.

6. The rate of technological obsolescence is accelerating, and this places a premium on speeding up the learning process and the innovation process. In order to achieve their objectives, and as R&D is becoming increasingly expensive, firms are being forced to engage in the kind of strategic innovatory alliances which demand considerable R assets on the part of the constituent partners if they are to be successful.
7. Partly as a result of the above factors, firms have reconfigured their organizational profiles, and are increasingly substituting or augmenting their hierarchical (pyramidal) command structures by more heterarchical structures. These latter structures encourage more co-operative and deeper horizontal, and vertical interpersonal relationships, and, in the case of MNEs, allow foreign subsidiaries greater responsibility and autonomy in their decision taking. As a result, these affiliates are forming more and closer relationships with their local suppliers, customers and competitors, and also with their own work force.

Table 16.5 Why R assets have become more important over the last two decades

- More idiosyncratic economic activities – especially those which are knowledge intensive
- Scope and depth of cross-border relationships have increased and, with them, access to new and distinctive values, ideologies and customs
- Change in societal goals:
  - transformation vs efficiency
  - social vs economic
  - access vs ownership of products
- Competitive pressures leading to disinternalization/shedding of non-core activities of firms
- Growing interdependence of technologies, organizational capabilities
- Increased rate of obsolescence and rising cost of innovatory activities leading to more alliances
- Move towards heterarchies and a greater decision-making role by management of MNE affiliates

4. R ASSETS AND THEORIES AND PARADIGMS OF MNE ACTIVITY

What then are the implications of the growing importance of both corporate relational assets and social relational capital for our theorizing about the cross-border activities of firms – and, in particular, FDI and the formation of non-equity alliances? Let me, if you will, tackle this question through the lens of the eclectic paradigm, and also from that of a selection (and it is only a selection) of the contextually specific theories it embraces.

4.1 The O-specific Competitive Advantages of Firms

Let us first consider the ownership(O) specific, i.e. the sustainable and unique competitive, advantages of firms. These are usually considered under two headings. The first set of advantages (Oa) embraces the specific assets or proprietary rights which are under the jurisdiction of the firm, whether this is by dint of ownership, or by controlling the use of resources and capabilities which it accesses, from the market, from other firms, or from the community at large. To reiterate an earlier point, firms do not own human capital or the assets of other firms, but, by a variety of means, they are able to exercise governance over their use. Though intangible, these assets usually enable the tangible assets owned or accessed by the firm to be created or deployed more effectively.

The second type of advantage (Ot) is that which is derived from the efficient co-ordination of the first kind of assets. *Inter alia*, this includes the capability of the firm to optimize its locational portfolio of these assets, and to choose the optimum modality of governance. It is this kind of capability which is made up of an amalgam of human and organizational intellectual and R assets. Such a capability may be exercised at various strata within and between firms, according to the purpose of the association and the nature of the assets, including the R assets of the other actors participating in the activity. Such capabilities include those arising from being part of a network of related firms, and from the cumulative experience of past relationships. MNEs, in particular, may be expected to augment their R assets as a result of their value-adding activities in different economic regimes and cultures. (This has been shown to be the case in a recent research project on the internationalization of professional service firms conducted by a PhD student and myself at Rutgers University.)[3]

It is the accumulated stock of R assets and the learning and experiences attached to them, and how these are combined with externally accessed resources and capabilities, which I am suggesting should be more explicitly acknowledged by the two main contextual theories seeking to explain the content and character of the O-specific advantages of firms, viz. the industrial organization and resource-based theories. Neither theory explicitly incorporates R assets into its thinking, though, as I have already mentioned, recent efforts by Dyer and Singh, Kale, Singh and Perlmutter (2000) and Chang, Singh and Lee (2000) on the protection and building of relational capital attempt to do just this.

R assets may be internally or externally generated. Indeed, this ability, including the willingness and ability of firms to gain new R assets from both dyadic and network relationships, is itself becoming an important core competence. Since the pioneering work of Johanson and Mattson (1988) and Walter Powell (1990) a decade or more ago, various attempts have been made to explore how, and in what conditions, networks may enhance the intellectual and relational capabilities of their participants.[4] A recent paper by Tai Jy Chen (2000), for example, has identified the benefits to Taiwanese electronics firms from their membership of domestic and foreign networks. These include access to more efficient production and innovatory activities, and the opening up of new cultural horizons as a direct result of relational subcontracting. Work by Michael Enright (2000) on clusters of both foreign and domestic firms in the Hong Kong financial district mirrors and extends earlier work by Ray Vernon (1960) and Dunning and Morgan (1971), which focused on the building of trust, group loyalty, and openness, among a dense concentration of financial and other office activities in the New York Metropolitan Region, and in the 'Square Mile' of the City of London.

For reasons already stated, technological advances and globalization are underlying both the rationale for, and the benefits flowing from, dyadic alliance and network relationships. We have further suggested that, as these relationships deepen and become more complex, so the choice of partner(s) and the networks in which they participate is influenced not only by the knowledge capital offered, but also by the ability and willingness of the partners to be empathetic towards each other. While it 'takes two to tango' (as the expression goes), the likelihood of forming and sustaining such an association very much depends on the amount and quality of R assets each organization is able to bring to any co-operative or exchange venture.

Three related propositions which arise from this analysis are, then:

1. R assets are becoming a more important component of the resources and capabilities of firms engaging in cross-border activity.
2. MNEs are likely to possess a greater stock of R assets relative to non-MNEs (*inter alia* because of the number, kind and geography of linkages with which the former are associated).
3. MNEs are increasingly likely to protect or augment their core competences as a direct result of their ownership of and/or access to foreign-based R assets.

A final point about corporate R assets is that they are likely to be context specific. Thus research has suggested that Japanese MNEs, relative to US and European MNEs, in the 1980s possessed the kind of R assets most likely to promote efficient production and subcontracting arrangements in the auto and consumer electronics sectors (Dunning, 1994), while US MNEs in the 1990s recorded a comparative advantage in the kind of R assets which helped encourage team entrepreneurship and R&D-type alliances. The virtues of openness, loyalty, leveraging diversity, curiosity, reliability, empathy, prudence, bond building, and commercial integrity also vary considerably between national and/or corporate cultures. Some firms, such as the Quaker-originated UK firms of the nineteenth century, also paid especial attention to building R assets – particularly of an intra-firm character. Corporate culture can, and does, instead play a pivotal role in promoting R assets (or inhibiting their promotion).

To what extent are R assets – which reflect the ideologies and values of a particular country – transferable across national borders? For unlike most other types of assets, e.g. a particular kind of technology, R assets are not viewed as the same product by different institutions or people. Again, the experience of Japanese investors in the European and US auto industries in the 1980s and 1990s suggests that this is so. On the other hand, the literature is full of examples of the lack of sensitivity by many MNEs in seeking to impose (rather than adapt) their own R assets to those valued by their foreign associates or customers. The question of blending R assets from different cultures and social mores is likely to be one of the most taxing challenges open to MNEs over the next decade or more; and it is the firms which are successful in creating, sustaining and sympathetically melding such capabilities which are likely to be the future winners in the global marketplace.

4.2 The Location Advantages of Countries

The 'where' to locate decision of MNEs or potential MNEs has been extensively surveyed in the literature (Dunning, 1998; Siebert, 2000; Rugman and Verbeke, 2001). Scholarly research has revealed that the critical variables are likely to be both time and context specific; and are especially sensitive to the *raison d'être* for MNE activity. For example, is it natural resource or market seeking? Is it intended to be (existing) asset exploiting or asset augmenting? Is it directed to mainstream manufacturing or to services, and, if the latter, to what kind of services? Is it part of a multi-domestic strategy or a globally integrated strategy by MNEs?

One thing seems certain. In most developed countries, at least, over the last three decades or so, the most important location-bound attractions of countries have shifted from the availability, cost and quality of natural factor endowments (including unskilled labour) to that of created assets, notably intellectual capital, innovatory systems, and the institutional and communications infrastructure. As global competitive pressures and the increasing mobility of knowledge and information have brought about at least some convergence in such attractions, so attention (both by firms and governments) is being focused on 'soft' locational variables, of which social capital – and more particularly social R assets – is perhaps the most decisive. Such 'quality of life' variables, including the minimization of crime, pollution, corruption, congestion and unacceptable social behaviour, are now taking pride of place as investment determinants. And while I would not wish to press this point too far, research by Herbert Giersch (1996) and others (Brittan and Hamlin, 1995) is emphasizing the increasing role played by economic morality as a location-specific competitiveness-enhancing asset.

Turning now to developing and transition economies, while there is no doubt that the availability and quality of natural resources and low (real) labour costs remain important locational attractions (particularly in the less developed and resource-rich countries), there is increasing evidence – particularly from erstwhile Communist countries like Russia and Cambodia – that deficiencies in both institutional infrastructure and social relational capital are among the greatest obstacles to inward FDI. Business surveys on the attractiveness of both developing and developed countries to potential investors (such as those reported by the Economist Intelligence Unit, the World Competitiveness Forum and the European Round Table of Industrialists) are consistently putting the quality of social capital, and the R assets of organizations with which they have (or wish to have) associations, at, or near, the top of their locational preferences. It may be further inferred that MNEs which can optimize their global portfolio of location-specific R assets while at the same time judiciously adapting their own and their affiliates' R assets to local requirements are likely to be among the winners in an increasingly integrated, yet multicultural, world.

From this brief analysis and the points set out in Table 16.6, I would offer two further propositions:

4. Location-specific R assets are becoming a more important influence on the location choices of MNEs, both between and within countries.
5. The global locational portfolio of assets by MNEs, chosen on the above criteria, and the interaction between their own R assets and those of the institutions and the countries in which they operate, is becoming a more significant determinant of their overall competitiveness.

4.3 The Organisation of R Assets

As I have already observed, a good deal of both internalization and network theory in explaining the organizational mode (or modes) of IB activity can be used to explain that specifically relating to the creation and use of R assets. This is because each approach focuses on the motives for, and the content of, human relationships, at both an individual and organizational level. Indeed, in their attempts to identify the reasons for market failure, TC scholars have pinpointed not only knowledge-related deficiencies of arm's-length exchanges, e.g. information symmetry and bounded rationality, but also relational deficiencies, notably those arising from a lack of trust between the participants,

Table 16.6 The OLI paradigm and R assets: summary of propositions

1. O-specific:
   - R assets are becoming a more important component of the resources and capabilities of firms engaging in cross-border activity
   - MNEs are likely to possess a greater stock of R assets relative to non-MNEs (*inter alia* because of the number, kind and geography of relations with which the former are associated)
   - MNEs are increasingly likely to protect or augment their competitive advantages as a direct result of their ownership of, or access to, foreign-based R assets
2. L-specific
   - Location-specific R assets are becoming a more important influence on the location choices of MNEs, both between and within countries
   - The global locational portfolio of assets by MNEs, chosen on the above criteria, and the interaction between their own R assets and those of the institutions and the countries in which they operate, is becoming a more significant determinant of their overall competitiveness
3. I-specific
   - Access to resources and rights rather than ownership of resources and rights is likely to increase the value of R assets of firms used in conjunction with those of other organizations. Thus, one might expect cross-border activity via A&Ms and cooperative ventures to play a more important role in the future portfolio of such activity
   - Because of learning and relational-enhancing benefits generated by networks, it may be predicted that the participation by MNEs and/or their affiliates in cross-border networks will increase, relative to those of purely dyadic associations with foreign firms
   - The contribution of the R assets of the foreign affiliates to those of the MNEs of which they are part is likely to increase. Partly this is the result of flatter intra-organizational structures; and partly that of closer and deeper linkages between the affiliates and indigenous firms. The quality of such linkages is itself enhanced by the improved relational space generated by networks
4. General
   - The ability to create and sustain firm-specific R assets, and to efficiently coordinate these across national boundaries, both within their own organizations and between these and other organizations, will increasingly influence the extent, pattern and form of MNE activity
   - The presence or absence of networks of related activities is likely to be a more important determinant of the geography of MNE activity in the next decade or more
   - The increasing significance of cross-border R assets as generating and sustaining competitive advantage of firms is likely to lead to an increase in MNE activity relative to that which otherwise would have occurred
   - Though FDI seems likely to continue to be the main modality of the territorial expansion of firms, the rising importance and need to tap into extra-firm R assets is likely to lead to a higher proportion of the global sales of MNEs being accounted for, or sold to, foreign organizations with whom they have non-equity economic linkages, and over whose resources and capabilities they have some continuing control or influence

opportunism and moral hazard. Much, too, of the literature on alliances – both domestic and cross-border – explicitly acknowledges the importance of many of the ingredients of R assets (as set out earlier) as being critical to their success.

I think, however, that what is relatively new in the last decade or so, and is increasingly engaging the attention of scholars researching into networks and alliances, is first the emphasis now being given to the character and contents to intra- and inter-firm relationships as assets in their own right, and second to the ways in which their creation, access and use are organized.

Let me exemplify these last two points by offering three examples.

1. The flattening of decision trees and the movement towards heterarchical organizational structures has (a) reduced the role of the 'command' route of generating intra-firm R assets, and replaced that by a visionary, strategic guidance and decision-sharing route and (b) fostered a new appreciation that the management of subsidiaries is often more cognizant of the needs and strategies of indigenous suppliers, customers and governments, and better able to relate to them, than are their counterparts in head offices. Both these developments have led to a re-examination of the governance and geographical locus of intra-firm activities (ranging from R&D through to marketing), and have done so precisely because of the recognition of the importance of R assets as a created competitive advantage.
2. The choice between cross-border intra-firm and alliance-relational activities is being fundamentally affected by the reduced role of *ownership* (via FDI), and the increasing importance of *access* in obtaining and controlling the use of competitiveness-enhancing resources and capabilities. I have already alluded to the fragmentation and disinternalization of the value chain of many firms – which is occurring despite, or in conjunction with, the current A&M boom (UNCTAD, 2000). There are many reasons for favouring a more market-oriented route of subcontracting, which has been aided and abetted by e-commerce (Dunning and Wymbs, 2001). But knowing *where* and *how* to harness resources and capabilities you do not own (or wish to own), and how best to coordinate these with your own core competences, requires a series of inter-institutional relationships, which, to be successful, needs a fund not only of intellectual capital, but of R assets as well.

   I will not labour this point further, save to point out that since R assets are often directed to achieving very specific objectives – and that these objectives are frequently geared to optimally transforming the activities of firms rather than increasing their efficiency – received internalization theory needs revisiting.
3. It is here, too, that I believe the network approach comes into its own. As is general acknowledged, firms participate in networks because of the externalities they are perceived to confer. Inasmuch as these benefits have to be

internalized by the participating firms if they are to be realized, there is no conflict between the network approach and internalization theory. But internalization in this case is based not on the *ownership* of assets, but on control over those which are externally *accessed*. Moreover, since the intra-network connections are usually non-contractual and frequently idiosyncratic and value laden, the ability of firms to gain from any exchange of knowledge, ideas or contacts is likely to be strongly dependent on the R assets they possess, and how these interact with those of other participants in the network.

These thoughts can be reiterated in the form of three related propositions.

(a) Access to resources and rights rather than ownership of resources and rights is likely to increase the value of R assets of firms used in conjunction with those of other organizations. Thus, one might expect cross-border A&Ms and cooperative ventures to play a more important role in the future portfolio of MNE activity.
(b) Because of learning and other relational-enhancing benefits generated by networks, it may be predicted that the participation by MNEs and/or their affiliates in cross-border networks will increase, relative to purely dyadic associations with foreign firms.
(c) The contribution of the R assets of the foreign affiliates to those of the MNEs of which they are part is likely to increase. Partly this is the result of flatter intra MNE organizational structures; and partly that of the closer and deeper linkages between the affiliates and indigenous firms. Such linkages are themselves fostered by the improved relational space generated by networks.

4.4 Reconfiguring the OLI Paradigm

Putting these thoughts together, what are the implications of explicitly incorporating R assets into the theories and paradigms of MNE activity? At this stage of thinking I would offer just four further general propositions.

6. The ability to create and sustain firm-specific R assets, and to efficiently coordinate these across national boundaries, both within their own organizations and between their and other organizations, and networks of organizations, will increasingly influence the extent and pattern of MNE activity.
7. The presence or absence of networks of related activities is likely to be a more important determinant of the geography of MNE activity in the next decade or more.

8. The increasing significance of cross-border R assets as generating and sustaining the competitive advantages of firms is likely to lead to an increase in MNE-related activity, relative to that which otherwise would have occurred.
9. Though FDI seems likely to continue to be the main modality of the territorial expansion of firms, the rising importance and need to tap into extra-firm R assets is likely to lead to a higher proportion of the global sales of MNEs being accounted for, or sold to, foreign organizations with whom they have a non-equity economic linkage, and over whose resources and capabilities they have some continuing control or influence.

5. IMPLICATIONS OF THE RISING IMPORTANCE OF R ASSETS

Table 16.7 offers some points for (a) IB theory, (b) policy makers, (c) business and (d) supranational agencies. These are presented without further comment.

6. CONCLUSIONS

In this chapter I have sought to do the following:

1. I have attempted to give a sense of the importance of a hidden asset available to corporations but not often explicitly identified – much less rigorously analysed – in the literature, viz. that of the R assets which they have the power to access, internally create, sustain and utilize.
2. I have suggested that R assets have become, and are becoming, a more important part of the portfolio of competitiveness-enhancing assets of MNEs, and why the characteristics of the twenty-first century innovation-driven global economy are demanding more attention be paid to them.
3. I have identified some of the ways in which extant IB theories and paradigms may need to be modified to better incorporate both firm- and country-specific R assets. In particular, I have suggested that the growth of networks has provided additional insights into (i) the way which industrial and other clusters might augment the competitive advantages (and especially the R assets) of the participating firms; (ii) the content and value of their locational portfolios; and (iii) the ways in which they may best relate their own R assets to those of other firms, and to the contours and space of the networks, to advance their own efficiency and learning capabilities.

Table 16.7 Implications of R assets

1. For IB theory
   - *Access* to competitiveness-enhancing assets, including R assets, is becoming more important than *ownership*
   - More explicit acknowledgement of R assets – both in themselves and as enhancing non-R assets – as determinants of IB activity
   - In embracing R assets, more attention needs to be paid to cooperative modes of business relationships, and particularly to networks as aids to upgrading and sustaining firm-specific R assets and the social capital of inter-organizational associations
   - The presence and use of R assets need to be more explicitly identified in explaining the performance of MNEs
   - There is an added need for a more systemic, holistic approach to understanding IB activity – while *inter alia* specifically acknowledging the role of networks in affecting the OLI configuration facing firms

2. For policy makers (at a national or regional level)
   - Acknowledge role of intangible social capital (e.g. total macro R assets) as a location-specific competitive asset
   - Seek ways of improving social (relational) capital and encouraging virtues making up R assets (through example, the media, exhortation, legislative policies towards crime/social dysfunction). Possible increased role of NGOs in this respect

3. For businesses
   - To recognize the need to create, gain access to and sustain unique R assets through appropriate search and training methods
   - To re-examine the role and content of ethical conduct and social responsibility; and to foster relational enhancing skills and attitudes among employees
   - To upgrade and encourage codes of behaviour focusing on, and recognizing the principles of, beneficial intra- and inter-organizational relationships

4. For supranational agencies
   - To foster international acceptance of respect for virtues making up R assets
   - To promote open and harmonious relationships among individuals and organizations
   - To fight against drugs, terrorism, pornography, social dysfunction, etc.

This chapter has been a very exploratory one. I accept it has raised more questions than it has answered. In fully acknowledging all the difficulties inherent in measuring R assets it has sometimes tried 'to square the circle'! Neither (to the disappointment of some of you, I know) has it offered a single explanatory statistical equation! But while I would be the first to point out these lacunae in the work of one of my PhD students, I would like to think that age and experience offer me some privileges, including the luxury of getting away with a less than rigorous analysis while still making a useful contribution to a relatively unexplored area of research.

NOTES

1. One writer (MacPherson, 1973) regards 'the right not to be excluded' from the access to the productive resources of society as one of the key emerging competitive advantages of firms.
2. As, for example, in the case of the dramatic reduction of strikes in the UK in the 1980s.
3. In this survey, access to R assets was ranked the seventh most important of some 26 competitive advantages identified by professional service firms. They were also ranked the sixth most likely to be derived from the foreign operations. Among the most multinational and largest of these firms, this advantage was ranked first or second. Network-related benefits – particularly with clients, customers and suppliers – were generally ranked between third and fifth in order of significance (Dunning and McKaig-Berliner, 2002).
4. See especially the writings of Gulati (1998, 1999), Holm, Eriksson and Johanson (1996), Uzzi (1997) and Chen and Chen (1998).

REFERENCES

Adler, P.S. and Kwon Seok-Woo (2002), 'Social capital and prospects for a new concept', *Academy of Management Review*, forthcoming.

Ariño, A., de la Torre, J. and Ring, P.S. (2002), 'Relational quality-managing trust in corporate alliances', *California Management Review* (forthcoming).

Brittan, S. and Hamlin, A. (eds) (1995), *Market Capitalism and Moral Values*, Cheltenham, Edward Elgar.

Chang, S., Singh, H. and Lee, K. (2000), 'Complementarity, status, similarity and social capital as drivers of alliance formation', *Strategic Management Journal*, **21**, 1–22.

Chen, T.J. (2000), *Network Resources for Internationalization. The Case of Taiwan's Electronics Firms*, Taipai, National Taiwan University.

Chen, H. and Chen, T. J. (1998), 'Network linkages and location choice in foreign direct investment', *Journal of International Business Studies*, **29**, 445–69.

Coleman, D. (1999), *Working with Emotional Intelligence*, New York, Bantam Books.

Coleman, J. (1988), 'Social capital in the creation of human capital', *American Journal of Sociology*, **94**, 5095–110.

Dasgupta, P. and Serageldin, I. (2000), *Social Capital: A Multifaceted Perspective*, Washington, DC, The World Bank.

Dunning, J.H. (1994), 'The strategy of Japanese and US manufacturing investment in Europe', in Mason, M. and Encarnation, D. (eds), *Does Ownership Matter?* Oxford, The Clarendon Press, 59–86.

Dunning, J.H. (1998), 'Location and the multinational enterprise. A neglected factor?', *Journal of International Business Studies*, **29**, 67–83.

Dunning, J.H. and McKaig-Berliner, A. (2002), 'The geographical sources of competitiveness of professional business firms', *Transnational Corporations*, **11** (forthcoming).

Dunning, J.H. and Morgan, E.V. (1971), *An Economic Study of the City of London*, London, Allen and Unwin.

Dunning, J.H. and Wymbs, C. (2001), 'The Challenge of Electronic Commerce for IB Theory', *International Journal of the Economics of Business*, **8**(2), 273–302.

Dyer, J.H. and Chu, W. (2000), 'The determinants of trust in supplier-automaker relationships in the US, Japan and Korea', *Journal of International Business Studies*, **31**(2), 259–85.

Dyer, J.H. and Singh, H. (1998), 'The relational view, co-operative strategy and the sources of interorganizational competitive advantage, *Academy of Management Reviews*, **23**(4), 660–79.

Enright, M.J. (2000), 'Globalization, regionalization and the knowledge based economy in Hong Kong', in Dunning, J.H. (ed.) *Regions, Globalization, and the Knowledge Based Economy*, Oxford: Oxford University Press, pp. 131–69.

Etzioni, A. (1996), *The New Golden Rule*, New York, Basic Books.

European Round Table of Industrialists (2000), *Improved Investment Conditions*, Brussels, ERT.

Fukuyama, F. (1996), *Trust*, London, Penguin Books.

Fukuyama, F. (1999), *The Great Disruption*, New York, The Free Press.

Giersch, H. (1996), 'Economic Morality as a Competitive Asset', in Hamlin, A., Giersch, H. and Norton, A. (eds), *Markets, Morality and the Community*, Melbourne, Australia, Centre for Independent Studies, Occasional Paper, No. 65.

Gulati, R. (1998), 'Alliances and Networks', *Strategic Management Journal*, **19**, 293–317.

Gulati, R. (1999), 'Network location and learning; the influence of network resources and firm capabilities on alliance formation', *Strategic Management Journal*, **20**, 397–420.

Holm, D.B., Eriksson K. and Johanson, J. (1996), 'Business networks and cooperation in international business relationships', *Journal of International Business Studies*, **27**(5), 1033–53.

Johanson, J. and Mattson, L.-G. (1988), 'Internationalization in industrial systems – a network approach', in Hood, N. and Vahlne, J-E. (eds), *Strategies in Global Competition*, London, Croom Helm, 287–314.

Kale, P., Singh, H. and Perlmutter, H. (2000), 'Learning and Protection of Proprietary Assets in Strategic Alliances: Building Relational Capital', *Strategic Management Journal*, **21**, 217–37.

MacPherson, C. (1973), *Democratic Theory: Essays in Retrieval*, Oxford, Clarendon Press.

Powell, W. (1990), 'Neither markets nor hierarchy: network forms of organization', in Gumming, L.L. and Straw, B.M. (eds), *Research in Organizational Behavior*, Vol. 12, Greenwich, JAI Press, 295–336.

Putman, R.D. (1993), *Making Democracy Work: Civic Traditions in Modern Italy*, Princeton, NJ: Princeton University Press.

Rifkin, J. (2000), *The Age of Access*, London, Penguin Books.

Rugman, A. and Verbeke, A. (2001), 'Location and the Multinational Enterprise', in Rugman, A. and Brewer, T. (eds), *Handbook of International Business*, Oxford, Oxford University Press, pp. 150–80.
Stiglitz, J. (1998), *Towards a New Paradigm of Development*, Geneva, UNCTAD, The Prebisch Lecture for 1998.
UNCTAD (2000), *World Investment Report, Cross-Border Mergers and Acquisitions and Development*, New York and Geneva: UN.
Uzzi, B. (1997), 'Social structure and competition in inter-firm networks: the paradox of embeddedness', *Administrative Science Quarterly*, **42**, 35–67.
Vernon, R. (1960), *Metropolis 1985*, Cambridge, MA, Harvard University Press.

Subject index

access to resources 476, 477, 495–6
accounting 194
acquisitions 150–1, 287–8, 424, 458–9
activities *see* industry-specific factors
advertising expenditure 28, 29–31, 36
affiliates' competitiveness, foreign 23–43
agency theory 274–5, 427
agglomeration 420–1, 423
  see also clustering
aggressive motives for investment 25
alliance capitalism 287–94, 382, 425–8, 430–1, 446, 447
  and IDP 151–3
  implications for eclectic paradigm 294–304
  and trade theory 316, 318, 319, 322–4
alliances 151, 157, 224, 315, 344–5, 398, 458, 483
  see also alliance capitalism
AltaVista 466
Amazon.com 445, 449, 451, 452, 457, 459, 463
AMO 466
ancillary services 80
anti-trade investments 69
AOL 448, 462
Ashford.com 459
Asia 399
  East Asia 282, 365–70, 374
  financial crisis 369–70
asset-augmenting FDI *see* strategic asset-seeking FDI
asset-seeking alliance response 289–90
assets
  changing characteristics 476, 477
  complementary 297, 300, 329, 421, 453
  created *see* created assets
  intangible *see* intangible assets
  mobility of firm-specific 324–7
  natural *see* natural assets
  pyramid of corporate assets 479–80
Australia 113–14, 360
autonomous strategic change 179, 184–6, 186–7, 190
average earnings 119
average hourly compensation (AHC) 87, 91, 92, 93, 94, 95, 96
average ratio of net income to sales (AVNIS) 87, 91, 92, 94, 95, 96

banks 352–6
Barnes and Noble 455
barriers to entry 17, 32–6, 38–9, 41, 383
batch production 316
Belgium-Luxembourg 82, 90–7
BERI Environment Risk Index 119
Better Business Bureau 454
Boeing 290
boundary of the firm 284
Brazil 82, 90–2, 93, 96, 113, 128
BroadVision 462
business-to-business (B2B) 457, 467
business-to-consumer (B2C) 468
business districts 296, 297, 300–1
business history 267–8, 271, 275–6
business theories of MNE activity 408–40

Canada 82, 90–7, 360
capital expenditure per employee 28, 29–31, 36
capital imperfections theory 384, 395–6, 415
capital movements theory 10–15, 236–7, 244–5
cartels 248
catching-up process 144–6, 155, 156–7, 162–5, 168–9, 217–18
Central and Eastern Europe 152, 282
centralization 207
  locus of decision-taking 220–2

Chemdex.com 445, 463
Chile 399–400
China 152, 282, 366, 368, 399, 454
Cisco Systems 458–9, 462, 466
client-following/client-seeking behaviour 355–6
clustering 283, 293, 297, 300–1, 392–3, 420–1, 423
cognitive imperfections 60
Colombia 128
colonialism 241, 242, 243–4
common governance 200, 201, 235, 296, 298, 445, 448
comparative advantage 317, 326–7, 332
comparative market growth (CMC) 87, 95
competition 41–2
complementary assets 297, 300, 329, 421, 453
concentration coefficient 28, 29–31, 32, 33–5, 37, 38–9, 41
concentration ratio 28, 33–5, 36
consensus 291
consumer-to-business (C2B) 468
consumer-to-consumer (C2C) 468
contextual variables *see* structual (contextual) variables
continuing flow effect 11
contractual resource transfers 104–5
control 2–3
convergence 144–6, 155, 156–7, 162–5, 168–9, 217–18
coordination 320–4
correspondence analysis 124
costs 20–1, 252
  determinant of FDI 8–9
  reduction 426
  transaction costs *see* transaction costs
country-specific factors 7, 42, 106, 107, 204–5, 409–10
  and e-commerce 463–4
  and firms' global strategy 186–8, 189
  and IDP 147–9, 158–61
    character of resource endowments 158–60
    economic system 160
    governments 160–1
    non-market differences 153–4
  interdisciplinary approach 260–3
  trade and location 65–7
covariance 356
craft production 316
created assets 329–30, 423
  IDP 148–9, 161–2, 165, 166–8, 169
  mobility of firm-specific assets 324–7
  US 358–9
critical competency response 289
culture 262, 269–72, 332
currency area approach 26–7

data banks 5
debt crisis 364–5
  Mexico 368–9
decentralization 220–2
decision-taking, locus of 220–2
defensive motives for investment 25–6
Dell 462
dependent development 244
determinants of international production 1–51, 79, 80
  capital theory 10–15
  issues 2–5
  industrial organization and market structure 23–43
    recent empirical work 27–40
  location theory 18–22
  survey approach 5–10
  trade approach 15–18
developed countries 397–400, 492–3
  FDI among 398
  FDI from developing countries 398–9
  FDI in developing countries 397–8
  inward investment 339, 340, 341, 372
developing countries 397–400
  deficiencies in relational assets 493
  'falling-behind' effect 157–8, 162–5, 168–9
  FDI among 399–400
  FDI from developed countries 397–8
  FDI in developed countries 398–9
  FDI and FPI in emerging economies 364–70, 370–1, 374
  inward investment 339, 340, 341, 372
development
  aspects of international production 213–18
  IDP *see* investment development path
  and direct investment position 124–8, 129–31
  trade and 243–4

digital content 451–2
discriminant analysis 124–5
distribution 80, 193
divergence 157–8, 162–5, 168–9
diversification 105–6, 353–4, 355, 356
divestment 222–4
DoubleClick 445, 462
dynamic 'add-on' variable 179–90, 192–4
dynamic internalization theory 426
dynamic ownership advantages 413–17
dynamics of international production 213–18

East Asia 282, 365–70, 374
Eastern and Central Europe 152, 282
e-Bay 448, 454, 458, 459
eclectic paradigm 103–6, 199–233, 286–7
  alliance capitalism and 294–304
  compared with strategic management theory 176–8
  criticisms of 200–10
  e-commerce and 441–3, 444–59
  as envelope for economic and business theories of MNE activity 408–40
  extended version 191–4
  and general paradigm of foreign investment 347–57, 370
  IDP 110–13, 127, 147–8
  incorporating strategy into 178–90
  interdisciplinary approach 268–77
  and investment flows 118–25, 126
  and MNE activity 385–7, 395–7, 401
  possible extensions 211–25
  relational assets 490–7
  restatement of 210–11, 212
  and sequential relationship between FDI and FPI 363–4, 369–70, 370
  structural variables and 106, 107
  trade and location 63–71
e-commerce 441–75
  impact on international business theory 444–59
  size of Internet economy 460
  and structural variables 443–4, 460–8
e-commerce firms 452
economic history 267–8, 271, 275–6
economic orientation 160
economic structure 114–27
economic theories
  international production 174–5
  MNE activity 408–40
economies of scale 28, 29–31, 36
education/urbanisation infrastructure ratio 119
efficiency 427, 458–9
efficiency-seeking FDI 80, 253–4, 409, 410
  e-commerce 465–6
  factor-endowment/market-failure paradigm 212
  IDP 145, 146, 149
  internalization advantages 426–7
  location advantages 420–2
  ownership advantages 414–16, 417
Electronic Data Interchange (EDI) 455
emerging economies 342, 364–70, 374
endemic market failure 283–4, 321–3
entrepreneurship 174, 214, 247
entry, barriers to 17, 32–6, 38–9, 41, 383
Europe 217–18, 223, 342
European Union/Community (EU/EC) 68, 185–6, 454
evolutionary theory of the firm 386–7, 396–7, 416, 417, 449–50
exchange rate 422
'exchange of threats' theory 384, 395, 411, 415, 451
exit 285, 321
exports 36, 104–5
  export/import ratio 28, 33–5, 36, 87, 92, 96–7
  export/local production ratios 83, 84, 92, 95
  export penetration participation ratio 83–4, 85, 90–2, 93–7
  exports/affiliate sales ratio 83, 84
external environment 260–3
externalization advantages 353–7, 368, 369–70

factor endowments 52–3, 56, 204–5, 216, 223
  factor-endowment/market-failure paradigm 210–11, 212
factor immobility 244–5
factor price equalisation theorem 53
'falling-behind' effect 157–8, 162–5, 168–9

FedEx 462
finance 194, 267, 270, 431
finance capital 351–2
  see also foreign portfolio investment
firm, theory of 236–7, 238–9, 251–2, 385–7, 396–7
  evolutionary theory 386–7, 396–7, 416, 417, 449–50
  resource-based theory 386–7, 396–7, 415, 417, 449
firm-specific factors 7, 106, 107, 204–5, 410
  asset mobility 324–7
  and e-commerce 464–8
    firm as part of a network 466–8
    firm as stand-alone entity 465–6
  and global strategy 186–8, 189
  interdisciplinary approach 263–8
  strategy behaviour 205–7
flexible accelerator 12
flexible production 152, 316
Flowerfarm.com 459
'follow my leader' theory 384, 395, 411, 415, 419, 451
Ford 467
Fordism 283, 284, 316
foreign affiliates' competitiveness 23–43
foreign direct investment (FDI) 3–4, 10–15, 239, 240–55, 339–80
  Aliber theory of 207–8
  before 1914 240–2
    explanations 242–6
  difference from FPI 340–1, 346–7
  eclectic paradigm and theories of MNE activity 408–40
  emerging economies 364–70, 374
  explaining direct investment position of countries 103–37
  general paradigm of foreign investment 347–57
  geography of 397–400
  globalization and theory of MNE activity 381–407
    implications of revised paradigm of international production 395–400
  IDP *see* investment development path
  intrafirm trade 323–4
  inward 339, 340, 371, 372
  Kojima hypothesis 208–10
  landmarks in theorizing 383–95
    1960s 383–4
    1970s 384–7, 390
    1990s 387–9, 390
  motives for 25–6, 348, 409
    shifts in rationale 149–51
    and strategy 181–4, 189
    see also under individual motives
  1914–60 240, 241, 248–9
    explanations 249–52
  1960–80 240, 241, 252–4
  sequential relationship with FPI 342, 357–70
foreign portfolio investment (FPI) 10–15, 339–80
  difference from FDI 340–1, 346–7
  emerging economies 364–70, 374
  general paradigm of foreign investment 347–57
  inward 339, 341, 371, 372
  sequential relationship with FDI 342, 357–70
foreign production participation ratio 81–3, 83–4, 85, 90–2, 93–7
France 82, 90–7
Fujitsu 290

G7 331
GDP 157, 162–8
General Agreement on Tariffs and Trade (GATT) 317, 331
General Electric (GE) 445, 449, 450, 467
General Motors (GM) 467
general versus specific theories 203–5
geocentrically-oriented MNEs 207
geographic theory 262–3, 271, 273
Germany 42–3
  West Germany 82, 90–7, 128, 252
global business strategy 186–8
globalization 288–9, 334
  governments' responses to 329–30
  paradoxes of 301
  and theory of MNE activity 381–407
globally-oriented MNEs 207
GNP 108–18, 139–47
Gork, 462
governance
  alliance and hierarchical capitalism 291
  relational assets 481–3

governance advantages 200, 201, 235, 296, 298, 448, 448
government-induced incentives 421, 453–4
government policy 43, 225, 371, 393, 452–3
  IDP 140, 141, 142, 143, 145, 146, 153–4
    statistical evaluation 160–1
  macro-organization of economic activity 328–33
  trade and location 60–2
growth in sales per man (GRSPM) 87, 92, 95, 96

Healtheon 465
Heckscher-Ohlin (H-O) trade theory 52–3, 314, 325
Heckscher-Ohlin-Samuelson (HOS) model 53–4, 199, 249
hierarchies/hierarchical capitalism 283–7, 291, 315, 323–4
  eclectic paradigm 296–7, 299–300, 446, 447
Hong Kong 113, 215, 330, 399, 465
horizontal alliances 296
horizontal integration 224
human resource management 193

IBM 290, 449, 457
IDA 454
ideological environment 262, 269–72
idiosyncratic economic activities 488, 489
import-substituting manufacturing FDI *see* market-seeking FDI
income-creating activities 3
income levels 108–18, 139–47, 157, 162–8
India 215, 399
Indonesia 113
industrial integration 36–40
industrial networks 293–4, 297, 300–1
industrial organization theory 236–7, 385, 411, 414
  market structure and determinants of international production 23–43
industrialised/industrialising countries 114–18
industry-specific factors 7, 106, 107, 204–5, 409
  e-commerce 460–3
    cross-industry effect 463
    e-commerce providers 462–3
    major impact on traditional activities 461–2
    minor impact on traditional activities 460–1
  global strategy of firms 186–8, 189
  trade and location 65–7
infant industry protection 328
innovation 152, 192, 264–5, 302
  IDP 141–2, 149
innovation theory 236–7, 246–7
institutional investors 352–6
intangible assets 200, 202, 235, 323, 325, 327, 351
  alliance capitalism 295–8
  pyramid of corporate assets 479
  theories explaining ownership advantages 445–8
interdisciplinary approach 254, 259–81
  appropriate interdisciplinary paradigms 268–76
    internalization advantages 270–1, 274–6
    location advantages 270–1, 273–4
    ownership advantages 269–73
  external environment 260–3
  factors internal to the firm 263–8
interest rates 10–11
intermediate products 323
internalization advantages 103–6, 135, 176, 191–2, 408–9
  alliance capitalism 294, 297, 298–300
  development of theory of international production 235–8
    before 1914 247–8
    1914–60 252
    1960–80 253–4
  e-commerce 447, 455–9
  eclectic paradigm and theories of MNE activity 424–9
  general paradigm of foreign investment 347–8
  globalization and 393–5, 396–7
  and IDP 118–22
  incorporating strategy into eclectic paradigm 180, 184

interdisciplinary approach 270–1, 274–6
and ownership advantages 201–2
and relational assets 493–6
and structural variables 106, 107
trade and location 59–63, 66–7
types of FDI 79, 80, 116
see also eclectic paradigm
internalization theory 175–6, 385, 396–7, 415
dynamic 426
e-commerce 456–8
FDI and FPI 349, 351–7, 364
orthodox 426, 456–8
international competitive hypothesis 81, 83–4, 84–5, 90–2, 93–7
international economics 312–13
trade theory and 314–19
International Monetary Fund (IMF) 331
Balance of Payments Yearbook 106, 128, 339, 362, 371, 372
international production
determinants *see* determinants of international production
development of theory and history 234–58
before 1914 240–8
emergence of theory 238–9
1914–60 240, 241, 248–52
1960–80 240, 241, 252–4
differences between economic and business theories explaining 173, 174–8
dynamics of 213–18
specific versus general theories 203–5
international trusts 251
internationalization process 420
Internet *see* e-commerce
intrafirm trade 219–20, 315, 316, 322, 323–4
intra-industry trade 218–19, 315, 316
investment development path (IDP) 110–13, 127, 129–31, 138–72, 174, 358, 400
country-specific factors and 147–9, 158–61
nature of 138–47
possible extensions of eclectic paradigm 214–18
statistical evaluation 156–68
structural changes and 149–55, 156
structural changes in world economy 156–8, 168–9
inward investment 241, 339, 340, 341, 371, 372
IDP 110–13, 138–47, 214–18
evaluation 164, 165–8
impact on host countries 224–5
international direct investment position108–22
inward looking, import substituting systems 160

Jamaica 114
Japan 42–3, 148, 151, 223, 282, 327
alliance capitalism 292, 298, 299
FDI flows 128
government intervention 330
IDP 113, 216–18
investment by Japanese MNEs 209–10, 252–3, 299
MNEs and relational assets 491
Jasmin.com 459
J-curve 162, 163, 164–5, 169

keiretsu 292, 294, 299
Kenya 113
K-Mart 448
knowledge 382, 387
see also intangible assets
knowledge acquisition theories 427, 458–9
knowledge enhancing (dynamic) theories of location 422, 454
Kondratieff cycle 382
Korea, South 113, 128, 151, 215, 223, 330
KPMG 467

Latin America 365–70, 374
legal theory 260–1, 269–72, 273, 276
location advantages 104–6, 135–6, 176, 192, 408
alliance capitalism 294, 297, 300–2
criticisms of eclectic paradigm 202–3
development of theory of international production 235–8, 249–50
eclectic paradigm and theories of MNE activity 418–24
e-commerce 447, 451–5

general paradigm of foreign investment 347–8, 350–1, 353, 354–5
globalization and 392–3
and IDP 118–22
incorporating strategy into eclectic paradigm 180, 183
interdisciplinary approach 270–1, 273–4
and relational assets 492–3, 494
sequential relationship between FDI and FPI 363–4, 368–70
structural variables and 106, 107
trade and 56–7, 66
statistical analysis 81–97
types of FDI 78, 80, 116
see also eclectic paradigm
location theory 386, 420
determinants of international production 18–22
development of international production 236–7, 249–50
locus of decision-taking 220–2
Lycos 451

macro-economic policy 160–1
macro-organizational policy 160–1, 328–33
Malaysia 128, 400
management theory 430
interdisciplinary approach 263–4, 270, 272, 273
ownership advantages 413, 416, 418, 450
strategic 173–8
market area 250
market failure/imperfections 283–4
criticisms of eclectic paradigm 200–5
endemic 283–4, 321–3
electronic market failures 457–8
factor-endowment/market-failure paradigm 210–11, 212
responses to 321–3
and strategy 178–9
structural *see* structural market failure
trade and location 60, 63, 67–71
transactional 200–3, 211, 212
market forces, trade and 316–19
market growth 87, 95, 96
market-positioning alliance response 290
market power theories 427, 458–9
market-seeking FDI 80, 110, 145, 409, 410
before 1914 241–2
e-commerce 465
factor-endowment/market-failure paradigm 212
internalization advantages 426–7
location advantages 420–2
ownership advantages 414–16, 417
market size 20–1, 159–60
relative market size 87, 91, 92, 93, 94
market structure 20–1
industrial organization and determinants of international production 23–43
marketing 8, 193, 430
characteristics of US affiliates in UK 28–32, 33–5, 36, 37
theory and interdisciplinary approach 265–7, 270, 275
McGraw Hill Economics Department 6
mercantilism 242
mergers and aquisitions (M&A) 150–1, 287–8, 424, 458–9
Merrill Lynch 455
metanational corporation 389
Mexico 82, 90–2, 93, 96, 97, 113
debt crisis 368–9
modelling 213
monopolies 248, 412
multi-domestic firms 207
multilateral mechanisms 331–3
multinationality 188, 296, 298, 414
mutual funds 352–6
Myanmar 400

National Industrial Conference Board 6
natural assets 139, 148–9, 158–9, 324
evaluation of IDP 161–2, 165, 166–8, 169
neo-classical trade theory 316, 318
neofactor theories 54, 57
neotechnology theories 54, 57
net outward investment (NOI) 108–27, 139–47
evaluation of IDP 162–5
Netscape 465
networks 296, 315

firm as part of a network of interrelated activities 466–8
industrial 293–4, 297, 300–1
marketing theory 265–6
relational assets *see* relational assets
see also alliance capitalism
New Zealand 113
newly industrializing countries (NICs) 164–5, 166
NICE 21
Nigeria 113
non-equity collaborative ventures 220, 344–5
see also alliances
non-financial investors 352–6
non-operatives/total workers 28, 29–31
NTL 466

OECD 458, 459, 461, 463, 464
oligopolistic behaviour 421
oligopolistic-strategy model 205
optimal timing of switch 174
organization
macro-organizational policy 160–1, 328–33
micro-organizational costs and benefits 320–4
relational assets and organization structure 489, 495
strategy-related variables 193–4
of transactions 314–16
organizational theory 430
and e-commerce 450
interdisciplinary approach 254, 264–5, 270, 273–4, 274–5
and ownership advantages 414, 416, 418
see also management theory
orthodox internalization theory 426, 456–8
output
output growth/GNP growth 28, 33–5, 36
share supplied by foreign affiliates 81, 83–4, 85, 90–2, 93–7
outward investment 240
IDP 110–13, 138–47
evaluation 164, 165–8
international direct investment position 108–22
outward looking, export oriented systems 160
ownership 194
changing ownership of assets 223–4
FDI, FPI and 340, 344
ownership advantages 78–9, 103–6, 134–5, 176, 191, 408
alliance capitalism 294, 295–8
criticisms of eclectic paradigm 200–2
development of theory of international production 235–8
before 1914 246–7
1914–60 250–2
1960–80 253
eclectic paradigm and theories of MNE activity 412–18
e-commerce 445–51
general paradigm of foreign investment 347–8, 349–50, 353, 354–5
globalization and 389–92
and IDP 118–22
incorporating strategy into eclectic paradigm 179, 183–4
interdisciplinary approach 269–73
and relational assets 490–2, 494
and structural variables 106, 107
systemic theory of 63–5, 66
trade and location 54, 57–9, 63–5
statistical analysis 81–97
types of FDI 79, 80, 116
see also eclectic paradigm

participation ratios 84, 85, 90–2, 93, 94
performance indicators 87, 97
Philippines 215
Philips 290
PlanetAll 449
Political and Economic Planning 86
political science 260–1, 269–72, 273, 276
population size 119, 122
post-Fordism 152, 316
Priceline.com 448, 457, 463
principal-agent model 274–5, 427
product 193
product cycle theory 78, 174, 205, 244, 253, 383, 411
determinants of international production 16–18, 22

location advantages 419, 421
ownership advantages 414
production methods/processes 193, 316
productivity 426
US affiliates in UK 32, 38–9, 41
profitability 11–12, 14–15
Proflowers.com 459
public goods 61, 329

quasi-integration 224

rationalized FDI *see* efficiency-seeking FDI
real options theory 459
regional integration 36–40
regional science 262–3, 271, 273
relational assets 476–501
changing significance 487–9
form 483–5
governance 481–3
implications of 496, 497
ingredients 481, 482
location advantages 492–3
measuring 485–7
organization of 493–6
ownership advantages 490–2
and theories and paradigms of MNE activity 489–97
unique characteristics 480–1
relative export shares (RES) 87, 91, 93, 94, 95, 96
relative market size (RMS) 87, 91, 92, 93, 94
relative sales per man (RSM) 87, 92, 95
relative wages (RW) 87, 91, 92, 93, 94, 95, 96
research and development (R&D)
centralization in MNE home countries 68–9
expenditure by US affiliates in UK 28, 29–31, 36
resource-based theory of the firm 386–7, 396–7, 415, 417, 449
resource endowments *see* factor endowments
resource-rich countries 114–18
resource-seeking FDI 80, 241, 356, 409, 410
e-commerce 465
factor-endowment/market-failure paradigm 212
IDP 110
internalization advantages 426–7
location advantages 420–2
ownership advantages 414–16, 417
resources 412–13, 426
access to 476, 477, 495–6
distribution and MNEs 67–71
resource structure 158–9
risk 190
reduction 426
risk-diversification theory 205, 384, 395–6, 414, 419, 422
e-commerce 454–5
risk-minimization hypothesis 205–6
Russia 246

security 457
Siemens 290
signalling theory 395
Silicon Graphic 465
similarity, degree of 314–16
Singapore 113, 148, 215, 223, 327, 330, 399, 400
e-commerce 465
investment flows 128
skilled employment ratio (SER) 87, 91, 92, 93, 94
small and medium-sized firms 292–3
social capital 478, 487
see also relational assets
social environment 262
societal goals 488, 489
sourcing 193
spatial concentration 283, 293, 297, 300–1, 392–3, 420–1, 423
spatial interdependence 19, 22
spatially specific transaction costs 421
spatial specialisation 68–9
specific vs general theories 203–5
spot markets 315
stages of development paradigm 399
stages of internationalization approach 386
static ownership advantages 413–17
stock-shift effect 10–11
strategic alliances 151, 157, 224, 315, 344–5, 398, 458, 483
see also alliance capitalism

strategic asset-seeking FDI 344, 388–9, 409, 430–1
e-commerce 466
IDP 145, 149–51
internalization advantages 426–7
location advantages 420–2
ownership advantages 414–16, 417
revised paradigm of international production 395–400
strategic centres 292–3
strategic management theory 173–8
strategy 213–14
criticisms of eclectic paradigm 205–7
explaining differences in global strategy 186–8
incorporating into eclectic paradigm 178–90, 192–4
strategy induced change 179, 181–4, 187
strategy initiating change 179, 184–6, 186–7, 190
structural changes
and IDP 149–55, 156
in the world economy 156–8, 168–9
structural market failure 60, 283, 321, 322
criticisms of eclectic paradigm 200–1, 202–3
factor-endowment/market-failure paradigm 211, 212
structural (contextual) variables 106, 107, 187
criticisms of eclectic paradigm 204–7
and e-commerce 443–4, 460–8
and IDP 113–25
see also under individual variables
subcontracting relationships 151
supply characteristics of US affiliates 28, 29–31, 32, 36, 37
supply-oriented FDI *see* resource-seeking FDI
supranational institutions 331–3
surveys 5–10
systemic theory of ownership advantages 63–5, 66

Taiwan 215, 223, 330, 399
tangible assets 479
tariffs 90, 93, 94, 95
US affiliates in UK 32, 38–9, 41
taxation 119
techno-economic paradigm 443
technology 430
alliance capitalism and technological advance 288–9
co-ordination of technology transfer 70
eclectic paradigm and 63–5, 192, 214
e-commerce *see* e-commerce
globalization and technological change 382
increased rate of obsolescence 489
internalization theory 351
public good 61
rationale for FDI and 410
tertiary (service) sector 157
Time-Warner 462
'tit for tat' theory 384, 395, 411, 415, 451
Toyota 290, 452
trade
barriers to 8
determinants of international production 15–18
extending the eclectic paradigm 218–20
IDP 144
intrafirm 219–20, 315, 316, 322, 323–4
intra-industry 218–19, 315, 316
and location of economic activity 52–102
empirical tests 77–102
rationale for FDI and 69, 398
trade theory 199–200, 312–38, 430
development of theory of international production 236–7, 242–6, 248, 249
international economics and 314–19
micro-organizational costs and benefits 320–4
mobility of firm-specific assets 324–7
role of national governments 328–33
transaction costs 252
alliance capitalism 317, 318, 319
e-commerce 455–6
interdisciplinary approach 274–6
internalization advantages 393–5
spatial specific 421
transactional market failure 200–3
factor-endowment/market-failure paradigm 211, 212
transactional ownership advantages 200, 201, 235, 296, 298, 445, 448

Triad countries 144
Turkey 215

UNCTAD 147, 161, 329, 393, 398, 399, 423, 495
UNCTC 186
United Kingdom (UK) 113, 239
  capital flows between US and 358–64
  outward/inward investment ratio 130
  US manufacturing affiliates in 28–40, 41, 82, 90–7
United Nations (UN) 42, 186, 410
United States (US) 113, 130, 209–10, 233, 252
  capital flows between UK and 358–64
  Department of Commerce 4, 239, 361, 363
  e-commerce 460, 464
  FDI and FPI 342
  firms and EC 185–6
  Japanese investment in 217–18
    alliance capitalism 299
  manufacturing affiliates in UK 28–40, 41, 82, 90–7
  manufacturing firms' activities in seven countries 81–97
  relational assets in US MNEs 491
  Tariff Commission 81, 82, 86
urbanisation 119, 125

vertical alliances 296
vertical integration 224
vicious cycle of poverty (VCP) 160
voice 285, 297, 299, 302–3, 321–2, 323

wages
  average earnings 119
  average hourly compensation 87, 91, 92, 93, 94, 95, 96
  relative 87, 91, 92, 93, 94, 95, 96
WalMart 448
World Bank 161, 285, 340, 341, 357, 365, 367, 368, 373, 374
world economy: structural changes in 156–8, 168–9
World Trade Organization (WTO) 317

Yahoo 448, 451, 452

Name index

Abramovitz, M. 144
Adler, M. 36
Agmon, T. 267, 422
Aharoni, Y. 2, 14
Ahmed, A.A. 111, 118
Alam, M.S. 144
Alchian, A. 59, 254, 265
Aliber, R.Z. 26–7, 67, 78, 207–8, 267, 384, 395–6, 415, 422
Almeida, P. 388
Amin, A. 301
Anderson, E. 266, 275, 420, 426, 430, 456
Andrews, M. 6, 8–9
Antonelli, C. 423, 427
Aoki, M. 426
Applegate, L. 453
Archer, H.J. 239
Arrow, K.J. 59, 70, 453
Arthur, W. 451, 458
Asakawa, K. 389, 398, 413, 416, 418
Audretsch, D.B. 301, 418, 420
Aufderheide, P. 466

Baden Fuller, C. 290, 292
Bagehot, W. 245–6
Bain, J.S. 58, 251, 383, 412
Balassa, B. 21
Baldwin, R. 16, 17, 55
Bandera, V.N. 14
Banjerji, K. 299
Barlow, E.R. 6, 273
Barnet, R.J. 71
Barney, J.B. 425, 449
Bartlett, C. 185, 188, 264–5, 413, 416, 418, 428, 441, 450
Basi, R.S. 6, 8–9
Baumann, H. 59
Baumol, W. 144
Baxter, A. 465
Beamish, P.W. 344
Beck, J. 441
Behrman, J. 2, 4, 6, 8–9, 66, 69, 273
Bekaert, G. 368
Bekar, C. 443
Bergsten, E.F. 71
Bernstein, P. 442
Bertin, G. 5
Bieri, J. 14
Blonigen, B.A. 422
Bloomfield, A.I. 243
Boddewyn, J.J. 222, 272, 441
Bond, J. 452
Borts, G.H. 11
Bower, D.J. 303
Bradley, J. 21
Branson, W.H. 10, 11, 21
Brash, D. 6, 8–9, 21
Brittan, S. 493
Brooke, M.Z. 2, 6
Brooks, M.R. 303
Brown, W.B. 59
Bruck, N.A. 2
Bruno, M. 18
Buckley, P.J. 55, 59, 63, 110, 174, 202, 252, 303, 351, 384–5, 396, 415, 420, 426, 430, 455, 456, 458
Bye, M. 252, 286

Cairncross, A.K. 13, 42
Calvet, A.L. 234–5
Calvo, G.A. 368
Cantwell, J.A. 144, 145–6, 155, 174, 186, 201, 214, 247, 253, 302, 416, 421, 430, 449
Capron, L. 449, 459
Cartwright, S. 448, 449
Casson, M.C. 59, 63, 110, 174, 201, 202, 213, 214, 218, 222, 224, 252, 351, 384–5, 396, 415, 426, 455, 456, 458

Caves, R.E. 21, 24, 25, 54, 177, 234, 253, 313, 342, 411, 412, 414, 418, 426, 427, 456
Cavusgil, S.T. 420
Chandler, A.D. 239, 242, 248, 267, 284
Chamberlin, E.H. 251
Chang, S. 490
Chen, H. 415, 421, 422
Chen, T.J. 415, 421, 422, 491
Chilas, J.G. 68
Ching-Sung Wu 264
Chu, W. 486
Chudnovsky, D. 368
Chuhan, P. 368
Claessens, S. 368
Clark, C. 21
Clark, J. 465
Coase, R.H. 25, 59, 62, 248, 252, 254, 317, 444, 450
Cohen, B. 12, 27, 455
Coleman, D. 486–7
Commons, J.R. 248
Conner, K. 415, 449
Contractor, F. 186, 220, 224, 226
Cooper, M. 42
Copeland, T.E. 459
Cournot, A.A. 246, 252, 283
Cowling, K. 427
Creamer, D. 66
Culyer, A. 42
Cushman, D.O. 418–19, 422
Cusumano, M. 442

Dalton, G. 461
Daniels, J.D. 6, 21, 420
d' Arge, R. 14
Dasgupta, P. 487
Davidson, W.H. 204, 207
D'Cruz, J.R. 292
Deane, R.S. 6, 8–9, 21
Demsetz, H. 59, 254, 265
Desmet, D. 451
Dicken, P. 274, 420, 443
Doremus, P.N. 423
Dosi, G. 313, 416
Dowrick, S. 144, 157
Doz, Y. 176, 185, 188, 201, 263, 272, 389, 398, 413, 414, 416, 418, 428, 450
Dunning, J.H. 2, 15, 17, 21, 28, 41, 54, 55, 78, 85, 104, 138, 142, 145, 146, 147, 148, 149, 153, 155, 156, 158, 160, 162, 166, 174, 188, 200, 203, 204, 205, 209, 214, 218, 219, 222, 234, 239, 240, 241, 252, 253, 312, 314–16, 342, 347, 358, 360, 363, 382, 383, 385, 387, 388, 389, 392, 394, 400, 411, 413, 414, 415, 417, 418, 419, 422, 423, 426, 428, 430, 441–2, 445, 452, 454, 491, 492, 495
Durkheim, E. 161
Duysters, G. 344
Dyer, J.H. 486
Eisenhardt, K.M. 427
Eitman, 267
Enright, M.J. 293, 301, 304, 419, 420, 423, 465, 485, 491
Ergas, H. 204
Eriksson, K. 478, 486
Ethier, W.J. 213
Etzioni, A. 480
Evans, P. 450, 467

Falise, M. 21
Fayerweather, 263
Feldman, M.P. 301
Fernandes-Arias, E. 368
Fieldhouse, D. 251, 253
Fischer, W.A. 66, 69
Florida, R. 393, 421, 423, 454, 465
Flowers, E.B. 67, 206, 415
Floyd, J.E. 10
Forsgren, M. 265, 420
Forsyth, D.J.C. 6, 8–9, 21
Foss, N.J. 417, 428, 429, 431
Franko, L.G. 42, 204
Freeman, C. 157, 282, 289–90, 416, 443
Friar, J. 264
Frischtak, C.R.L. 368
Froot, K.A. 312, 419, 422
Fukuyama, F. 487
Furubotn, E.G. 59

Gates, W. 442
Gatignon, H. 266, 275, 420, 426, 430, 456
Gemmell, N. 144, 157
Gerlach, M.L. 291, 300

Ghoshal, S. 176, 177, 185, 188, 264–5, 413, 416, 418, 426, 428, 441, 450
Giersch, H. 19, 186, 493
Gimein, M. 449, 451
Glaismeier, A. 304
Gomes-Casseres, B. 290, 303
Graham, E.M. 67, 174, 205, 206, 273, 384, 395, 411, 415, 421, 451
Gray, H.P. 24, 25, 168, 325, 430
Greenhut, M. 19
Grosse, R. 213
Grubel, H.G. 11, 219, 267
Gruber, W. 16, 27
Guisinger, S.E. 203, 421
Gustafson, B. 426

Hagedoorn, J. 157, 288, 289–90, 344
Hahn, M. 426
Hakam, A.N. 6
Håkansson, L. 265
Hall, P. 274
Hämäläinen, T. 161
Hamel, G. 176, 263, 462, 467
Hamilton, A. 466
Hamilton, W. 303
Hamlin, A. 493
Harman, A.J. 21
Harrison, B. 292, 301
Hart, A. 463
Harvey, C.R. 368
Hayes, R.H. 224
Heckerman, D.G. 13
Heckscher, E.F. 249
Hedlund, G. 185
Helft, M. 445
Helleloid, D. 415
Helper, S. 303–4
Helpman, E. 213, 312, 317, 326
Henderson, V. 304
Hennart, J.F. 351, 385, 415, 426, 455, 456, 458
Henry, D. 455, 457, 464
Henson, C. 452
Herrigel, G.B. 301
Herring, R. 13, 43
Hilferding, R. 248
Hill, C. 450
Hill, R.D. 11
Hilmer, F.G. 300
Hirsch, S. 16, 21, 55, 57, 77, 253, 420
Hirschman, A.O. 285, 321, 332
Hof, R. 461
Hogan, W. 6
Holm, D.B. 478, 486
Hoover, E.M. 420
Horst, T. 13, 21, 26, 27, 32, 40, 55, 65, 71, 206–7
Horstman, I. 213
Horwitch, M. 264
Hotelling, H. 250, 420
Hufbauer, G.C. 16, 17, 21, 36, 54, 68
Hulland, J. 449, 459
Hunt, S. 457
Hymer, S. 22, 26, 54, 68–9, 201, 244, 252, 253, 322, 383–4, 411, 412, 414, 427

Iansiti, M. 442
Imai, K. 266
Isard, W. 420
Itami, H. 266
Iversen, C. 53
Iyer, G. 441

Jacob, R. 465
Jensen, M. 254, 427
Johanson, J. 226, 265–6, 420, 430, 478, 486, 491
Johnson, H.G. 11, 16, 18, 25, 56, 61, 70, 264
Jorgenson, D.U. 12
Jud, C.D. 13, 21

Kale, P. 478, 486, 490
Katz, J. 28
Keenan, P.T. 459
Keesing, D. 16
Keller, W.W. 423
Kenen, P.B. 10
Kennecott 290
Kim, E.C. 459
Kindleberger, C. 16, 20, 24, 213
Klein, R.W. 18
Knickerbocker, F.T. 26, 54, 67, 81, 174, 205, 206, 250, 273, 384, 395, 411, 415, 419, 421, 451
Knight, G. 461
Knudsen, C. 417
Kobrin, S. 411, 443, 444, 451, 453, 454, 457

Kogut, B. 176, 177, 201, 203, 206, 263, 273, 414, 422, 425, 427, 430, 448, 454, 458, 459
Kojima, K. 69, 78, 208–10, 244, 384
Kolde, E. 6, 8–9, 26
Koolman, G. 247
Kopecky, K.J. 11
Kopits, G. 12, 13
Kotabe, M. 457
Krause, L.R. 21
Kreinin, M.E. 6, 21
Krugman, P. 218, 312, 313, 316, 317, 326, 327, 393, 398, 418, 420
Kuemmerle, W. 388, 411, 415, 422, 454
Kuhn, T.S. 429
Kulatilaka, N. 414, 459
Kwack, S.Y. 12, 13

Lake, A. 69, 205
Lall, S. 62, 66, 79, 103, 399
Larsen, P. 452
Laseter, T. 449
Lash, A. 449, 451
Laubacher, 463
Lawrence, S. 462, 464
Lazerson, M. 301, 304
Learner, E.E. 11
Lecraw, D. 110
Ledbetter, J. 460, 462
Lee, K. 490
Lees, F.A. 2
Leiderman, L. 368
Leonard-Barton, D. 290, 303
Leontief, W. 53
Lepas, A. 21
Lessard, D.G. 174
Lessard, D.R. 267, 422
Lessig, L. 454
Levy, H. 12, 248
Lewis, M. 465
Lewis, W. 462
Liefmann, R. 248
Lilienthal, D. 253
Lim, L.Y.C. 368
Lincoln, J. 304
Lipsey, R.E. 69, 335
Lipsey, R.G. 332, 382, 443
Liu, S.X. 395
Lloyd, P. 274, 420
Lloyd, P.J. 219
Loasby, B.J. 429, 430
Lodge, G.C. 262
Lorange, P. 220, 224, 226
Loree, D.W. 421
Lorenzoni, G. 290, 292
Lösch, A. 19, 250, 420
Luostarinen, R. 420, 430

MacCormack, A. 442
MacDougall, G.D.A. 53
Madhok, A. 425
Magee, S.P. 59, 112
Makino, S. 388, 411, 415, 427
Malmberg, A. 420, 423
Malone, T. 463
Mamingi, N. 368
Manser, W. 27
Mansfield, E. 27
Manzar, O. 451, 465
Margherion, L. 445, 457, 458, 467
Markowitz, H. 12, 356
Markusen, A. 301, 393
Markusen, J.R. 213, 312, 313, 317, 326, 401, 430
Marshall, A. 239, 245–6, 247, 283, 293, 393, 419
Marx, K. 246, 247
Mason, R.H. 209–10
Matthysenns, P. 418
Mattson, L.G. 226, 265–6, 491
Mauborgne, R. 459
Mauer, L.J. 14, 21
McAleese, D. 21
McDonald's 460–1
McFeteridge, D.G. 207
McKay, J.P. 246
McManus, J.C. 54, 59, 252, 384
McWilliams, G. 461
Meckling, W. 254, 427
Mehta, D. 16, 27
Mellors, J. 12, 13
Metcalfe, J.S. 416
Meyer, K. 385
Michalet, C. 66
Mill, J.S. 245
Miller, M. 13
Miller, N.C. 11–12
Miller, R.R. 14
Mitchell, W.C. 247
Modigliani, F. 13
Mody, A. 301

Moe, T.M. 254
Montgomery, C.A. 415, 417
Montiel, P.J. 368
Moran, P. 426
Moran, T.E. 71
Morgan, E.V. 491
Morley, S. 21
Moose, J. 12
Mowery, D.C. 303
Muehlbauer, J. 445
Muller, P.E. 71
Mun, T. 242
Mundell, R.A. 10, 16, 53, 248, 325
Murray, R. 22
Musgrave, P. 71

Naisbitt, J. 292
Narula, R. 138, 147, 148, 153, 155, 156, 157, 158, 358, 400
Negandhi, A.R. 263, 273
Nelson, R.R. 302, 416, 417, 449
Nicholas, S. 214, 275–6
Nonaka, I. 264
Norman, G. 314–16
North, D. 275
Nurkse, R. 53

O'Brien, D.P. 245
Ohlin, B. 19, 52, 53, 248
Ohmae, K. 149, 217, 218, 293
Oliver, C. 423
Oliver, R. 448, 449
Oman, C. 224, 285
Ouchi, W.G. 264
Ozawa, T. 148, 155, 160, 244, 399

Pack, H. 28
Paish, G. 360
Parry, T. 26, 27, 55
Pauly, L.W. 423
Pauwells, P. 418
Pavitt, K. 201, 204
Pearce, R.D. 41, 219, 363
Peck, F.W. 423
Pejovich, S. 59
Peng, M.W. 303
Penrose, E.T. 25, 26, 40, 251–2, 286
Perez, C. 282, 382, 443
Perlmutter, H. 2, 478, 486, 490
Peterson, H. 453, 458
Petzinger, T. 444
Pigou, A.C. 282
Plummer, A. 251
Piore, M.J. 304
Piper, J.R. 7
Pisano, G. 185, 188, 416, 417, 421, 427
Piscitello, L. 421
Pitt, L. 457
Polk, J. 4
Popkin, J. 12, 13
Porter, M.E. 148, 176, 177, 185, 186, 188, 207, 263, 264, 273, 293, 313, 326, 332, 412, 416, 419, 421, 422, 423, 453, 454, 485
Posner, M.V. 16
Potter, S.T. 387
Powell, W. 491
Prachowny, M.J. 12
Prahalad, C.K. 176, 201, 263, 264, 272, 413, 415, 416, 418, 428, 449, 450
Putman, R.D. 485

Quinn, D. 16
Quinn, J.B. 300

Rabinovitz, J. 459, 465
Randaccio, F. 144
Rangan, S. 414, 419, 422
Rayport, J. 448, 466
Reddaway, N.B. 14, 15, 36, 63, 387
Reedy, J. 443
Reich, S. 423
Reinhart, C.M. 368
Remmers, H.L. 2, 6
Reuber, G.L. 21
Ricardo, D. 244–5
Richardson, J.D. 12, 13, 15
Rifkin, J. 448, 488
Robbins, J.A. 274
Robertson, D. 18
Robinson, H.J. 6, 8–9, 263, 273
Robinson, J. 251
Rolfe, S. 4
Ronstadt, R. 66
Root, F. 111, 118
Rosenberg, N. 243
Ross, S.A. 254
Rowthorn, R. 41
Rugman, A.M. 62, 174, 200, 203, 205, 267, 292, 384, 385, 395–6, 414, 415, 417, 419, 422, 426, 454, 455, 492

Ruigrok, W. 282, 285

Sabel, C. 304
Safarian, A.E. 6, 21
Sagafi-nejad, T. 266
Sagari, S. 355
Sahlman, W.A. 450
Sambharya, R.B. 299
Sampler, J. 462
Samuelson, P.A. 53, 248
Santos, J.F.P. 389, 398, 413, 416, 418
Sarnat, M. 12
Saviotti, P.P. 416
Saxenian, A.L. 304
Say, J.B. 247
Scaperlanda, A.E. 14, 21
Schmitz, A. 14
Schöllhammer, H. 7, 21
Schreiber, J. 21
Schreiner, J.C. 12
Schumpeter, J. 246, 247
Scott, A.J. 301, 304, 393, 394, 418, 419, 421
Serageldin, I. 487
Severn, A.K. 12
Shan, W. 303, 388–9
Shaver, J.M. 364
Shuen, A. 185, 188, 416, 417, 421, 427
Siddall, N.S. 368
Silverberg, G. 416
Simon, H.A. 252, 254
Singh, H. 478, 486, 490
Smith, A. 235, 242, 243–4, 246, 247, 287
Smith, K.V. 12
Soete, L. 313, 416
Sölvell, O. 420, 423
Song, J. 388–9
Southard, F.A. 54, 249, 273
Spencer, L. 487
Spitaller, E. 11
Sprenger, P. 453
Standard, 448, 453, 464
Stein, J.C. 419, 422
Stern, R.M. 11
Stevas, N.S. 246
Stevens, G.V.G. 11, 12, 13
Stiglitz, J. 488
Stobaugh, R.B. 7, 16, 20, 21, 263
Stolper, W.F. 248
Stonehill, A.I. 21, 267
Stopford, J.M. 42, 64, 205, 242, 252, 263, 264
Storper, M. 301, 393, 394, 418, 419, 421
Strange, S. 443
Strassman, W.P. 28
Strong, N. 427
Stubenitsky, F. 11
Sugden, R. 427
Svedberg, P. 239
Sviokla, J. 448, 466
Swedenborg, B. 55, 78, 79, 385

Takeuchi, H. 266
Taylor, C.T. 387
Taylor, P. 457
Teece, D.J. 70, 185, 188, 201, 263, 265, 300, 329, 388, 414, 416, 417, 421, 427, 449
Tharakan, P.K.M. 219
Thompson, M.J. 460, 461, 462
Thrift, N. 301
Tilton, J.E. 21, 69
Timmons, J. 450
Tobin, J. 12
Tolentino, P. 155
Tomkins, R. 443
Turban, E. 455

Ulgado, F. 364

Vahlne, J.E. 265, 420, 430
Vaitsos, C. 14
Van Tulder, R. 282, 285
Vaupel, J. 27
Veblen, T.B. 247
Venables, A. 312, 418
Verbeke, A. 417, 492
Vernon, B. 16, 27
Vernon, R. 2, 5, 16, 17, 21, 22, 54, 55, 66, 67, 78, 79, 84, 174, 201, 205, 213, 244, 263, 313, 327, 383–4, 411, 414, 419, 420, 421, 426, 441, 454, 491
Verspagen, B. 157
Vogel, E.F. 262
Von Thunen, J.H. 248–9

Wakefield, E.G. 247
Wallis, K.F. 14

Waterson, M. 427
Watson, R. 457
Weber, A. 19, 250, 420
Weigel, D.R. 14
Weiss, M.Y. 69
Welch, L.S. 420, 430
Wells, L.T. 16, 17, 28, 110, 264
Wender, I.T. 6
Wernerfelt, B. 415, 449
Wesson, T.J. 388, 411, 415, 427, 454, 458
Wheeler, K. 301
Wheelwright, S.C. 224
Whitaker, J.K. 246
White, J.J. 14
Whitman, M.V.N. 12
Whittaker, E. 303
Wilkins, A. 264
Wilkins, M. 242, 267, 342, 358, 359
Wilkinson, B. 16
Willett, T.D. 13, 43
Williams, J.H. 52, 250–1
Williamson, O.E. 59, 248, 252, 254, 265, 284, 411, 426, 428–9, 455, 458
Williamson, P.J. 389, 398, 413, 416, 418
Wilson, F. 21
Winter, S. 302, 416, 417, 449
Wolf, B.M. 54
Wolfe, B. 26
Wong, T.K. 466
Wortzel, W.H. 21
Wright, G. 359
Wurster, T. 450, 467
Wymbs, C. 442, 444, 454, 459, 465, 495

Yeh Rhy-song 266
Yoffie, D. 442

Zander, I. 421, 423
Zander, U. 422, 425, 427, 430, 454, 458